Sports Law for Sport Management

Sports Law for Sport Management

Ray Yasser

PROFESSOR OF LAW EMERITUS
UNIVERSITY OF TULSA COLLEGE OF LAW

James R. McCurdy

PROFESSOR OF LAW EMERITUS
GONZAGA UNIVERSITY SCHOOL OF LAW

C. Peter Goplerud III

PRESIDENT AND PROFESSOR OF LAW
FLORIDA COASTAL SCHOOL OF LAW

Maureen A. Weston

ASSOCIATE DEAN FOR RESEARCH AND PROFESSOR OF LAW
PEPPERDINE UNIVERSITY SCHOOL OF LAW

Richard Karcher

PROFESSOR
COLLEGE OF HEALTH PROMOTION AND HUMAN PERFORMANCE
EASTERN MICHIGAN UNIVERSITY

CAROLINA ACADEMIC PRESS
Durham, North Carolina

LIBRARY OF CONGRESS CATALOGING-IN-PUBLICATION DATA

Names: Yasser, Raymond L., author. | McCurdy, James R., author. |
Goplerud, C. Peter, author. | Weston, Maureen A., author. |
Karcher, Richard T., author.
Title: Sports law for sport management / Ray Yasser, James R. McCurdy,
C. Peter Goplerud III, Maureen A. Weston, Richard Karcher.
Description: Durham, North Carolina : Carolina Academic Press, LLC, [2023] |
Includes bibliographical references and index.
Identifiers: LCCN 2023013854 | ISBN 9781531025144 (paperback) |
ISBN 9781531025151 (ebook)
Subjects: LCSH: Sports—Law and legislation—United States.
Classification: LCC KF3989 .Y374 2023 | DDC 344.73/099—dc23/eng/20230509
LC record available at https://lccn.loc.gov/2023013854

Carolina Academic Press
700 Kent Street
Durham, North Carolina 27701
(919) 489-7486
www.cap-press.com

Printed in the United States of America

Contents

Sports Law for Sport Management

One

High School Athletics, Part I

State Associations and Constitutional Issues

Learning Outcomes

- Understand the source of the power and authority of high school athletics regulation.
- Understand the effect of state actor status as well as the Supreme Court's analysis for determining whether state high school athletic associations (and the NCAA) are state actors.
- Know when a state actor must afford a person the requirements of procedural due process and what those requirements entail.
- Understand the variables to consider when applying the First Amendment to athlete speech.
- Understand the Supreme Court's Fourth Amendment analysis of random drug testing of high school athletes.
- Be able to apply the Establishment Clause to a state actor's rules and policies as well as the Free Exercise Clause to restrictions on religious activity at public schools.

Key Terms

- State actor
- Entwinement
- Private association law
- Procedural due process
- Property interest
- Free speech
- Privacy
- Establishment Clause
- Free Exercise Clause
- *in loco parentis*

A. Structure, Governance, and Regulatory Authority

A wide range of regulations affects the lives of amateur athletes. The regulators are the individuals, organizations, and institutions responsible for the conduct of the athletic competition. High school athletics are typically regulated at the state level by the state high school athletic association, which is a voluntary, non-profit, and private (non-public) association consisting of the public and private high schools within the state. The association members are high schools (not individuals) and they vote on the rules, which regulate eligibility for competition as well as the rules of competition. The state association is responsible for implementing and enforcing regulations governing sport participation and possesses the power and authority to revoke eligibility of individual students and disqualify schools from participating in athletic events.

The state association's authority to govern high school athletics within the state is granted by the state legislature or by judicial decision. As an example, the Michigan state legislature designated the Michigan High School Athletic Association, incorporated in 1972, as the "official association of the state for the purpose of organizing and conducting athletic events, contests, and tournaments among schools and [decreed that it] shall be responsible for the adoption and enforcement of rules relating to eligibility of athletes in schools for participation in interschool athletic events, contests and tournaments." Mich. Comp. Laws §380.1292(2).

At the national level, the National Federation of State High School Associations (NFHS) was formed in 1923. The NFHS is a non-profit national service organization. Its mission is to serve its members and students by "providing leadership for the administration of education-based high school athletics and activities through the writing of playing rules that emphasize health and safety, educational programs that develop leaders, and administrative support to increase opportunities and promote sportsmanship." *NFHS Handbook 2020–2021.* The NFHS publishes playing rules for sixteen sports for boys and girls and provides programs and services to its members, which are state high school athletics associations. The NFHS, unlike state high school athletics associations and the NCAA, does not have sanctioning power and authority over its members.

At the regional and local levels, rules governing participation may be adopted by conferences, school boards, and school district officials, such as principals, athletic directors, and coaches. At individual schools, the athletic director responsibilities include (1) hiring, supervising, and evaluating coaches, (2) coordinating all facets of contest management, (3) determining and verifying game scheduling and athlete eligibility, and (4) transmitting relevant publicity and handling public relations. Generally, those who administer amateur athletics highly value regimentation and discipline. The result is a regulatory scheme touching upon aspects of the athlete's personal life which perhaps would be viewed as inappropriate if applied to a non-athlete. Regulations dealing with speech, drug use, off-campus behavior, and grooming, for example, can be found in the sports setting. Many high school athletic associations impose grade and enrollment requirements as well as age and transfer limitations.

Courts sometimes intervene to resolve disputes. How courts review the rules that are adopted by those responsible for the conduct of athletic competition depends largely upon whether the regulatory entity is categorized as governmental or private. The government is, of course, constrained by the U.S. Constitution. The private actor is not. When the actions of a private entity are challenged, the basic principles that apply emanate not from the U.S. Constitution but from the rather amorphous body of private association law. Traditionally, the courts have only intervened in the affairs of private associations where the organization's actions violate its own rules or where its acts constitute fraud or illegality or are arbitrary and capricious. In situations other than these, the courts historically have been hesitant to interfere.

When government's rules are challenged on constitutional grounds, the issues typically involve rights of due process, free speech, privacy, free exercise of religion, and equal protection. The Fourteenth Amendment to the U.S. Constitution limits enforcement of these rights to apply only against state officials or those acting in a state or local governmental capacity, in other words, a "state actor." If a private entity is deemed to be a state actor, it is constrained by the U.S. Constitution. The issue of whether a state high school athletic association, a private entity, is a state actor was addressed by the Supreme Court in a seminal sports law case, which you will read in the next section.

B. Threshold Constitutional Issues

1. State Action Requirement

Brentwood Academy v. Tennessee Secondary School Athletic Association (Brentwood I)

531 U.S. 288 (2001)

Justice Souter delivered the opinion of the Court.

Respondent Tennessee Secondary School Athletic Association (Association) is a not-for-profit membership corporation organized to regulate interscholastic sport among the public and private high schools in Tennessee that belong to it. No school is forced to join, but without any other authority actually regulating interscholastic athletics, it enjoys the memberships of almost all the State's public high schools (some 290 of them or 84% of the Association's voting membership), far outnumbering the 55 private schools that belong. A member school's team may play or scrimmage only against the team of another member, absent a dispensation.

The Association's rulemaking arm is its legislative council, while its board of control tends to administration. The voting membership of each of these nine-person committees is limited under the Association's bylaws to high school principals, assistant principals, and superintendents elected by the member schools, and the public school administrators who so serve typically attend meetings during regular school hours. Although the Association's staff members are not paid by the State, they are eligible to join the State's public retirement system for its employees. Member schools pay dues to the Association, though the bulk of its revenue is gate receipts at member teams' football and basketball tournaments, many of them held in public arenas rented by the Association....

The action before us responds to a 1997 regulatory enforcement proceeding brought against petitioner, Brentwood Academy, a private parochial high school member of the Association. The Association's board of control found that Brentwood violated a rule prohibiting "undue influence" in recruiting athletes, when it wrote to incoming students and their parents about spring football practice. The Association accordingly placed Brentwood's athletic program on probation for four years, declared its football and boys' basketball teams ineligible to compete in playoffs for two years, and imposed a $3,000 fine. When these penalties were imposed, all the voting members of the board of control and legislative council were public school administrators.

[Brentwood sued the Association and its executive director in federal court claiming that enforcement of the "undue influence" rule was state action and a violation of the First and Fourteenth Amendments.]

We have held that a challenged activity may be state action when it results from the State's exercise of "coercive power," when the State provides "significant encouragement, either overt or covert," or when a private actor operates as a "willful participant in joint activity with the State or its agents[.]"... We have treated a nominally private entity as a state actor when it is controlled by an "agency of the State,"... when it has been delegated a public function by the State, when it is "entwined with governmental policies" or when government is "entwined in [its] management or control[.]"...

Amidst such variety, examples may be the best teachers, and examples from our cases are unequivocal in showing that the character of a legal entity is determined neither by its expressly private characterization in statutory law, nor by the failure of the law to acknowledge the entity's inseparability from recognized government officials or agencies. *Lebron v. National Railroad Passenger Corporation*, 513 U.S. 374 (1995), held that Amtrak was the Government for constitutional purposes, regardless of its congressional designation as private; it was organized under federal law to attain governmental objectives and was directed and controlled by federal appointees. *Pennsylvania v. Board of Directors of City Trusts of Philadelphia* held the privately endowed Gerard College to be a state actor and enforcement of its private founder's limitation of admission to whites attributable to the State, because, consistent with the terms of the settlor's gift, the college's board of directors was a state agency established by state law. Ostensibly the converse situation occurred in *Evans v. Newton*, which held that private trustees to whom a city had transferred a park were nonetheless state actors barred from enforcing racial segregation, since the park served the public purpose of providing community recreation, and "the municipality remained entwined in [its] management [and] control[.]"

These examples of public entwinement in the management and control of ostensibly separate trusts or corporations foreshadow this case, as this Court itself anticipated in [*National Collegiate Athletic Association v.*] *Tarkanian, supra.*

To be sure, it is not the strict holding in *Tarkanian* that points to our view of this case, for we found no state action on the part of the NCAA.

But dictum in *Tarkanian* pointed to a contrary result on facts like ours, with an organization whose member public schools are all within a single State.

"The situation would, of course, be different if the [Association's] membership consisted entirely of institutions located within the same State, many of them public institutions created by the same sovereign."

Just as we foresaw in *Tarkanian*, the "necessarily fact-bound inquiry," leads to the conclusion of state action here. The nominally private character of the Association is overborne by the pervasive entwinement of public institutions and public officials in its composition and workings, and there is no substantial reason to claim unfairness in applying constitutional standards to it.

The Association is not an organization of natural persons acting on their own, but of schools, and of public schools to the extent of 84% of the total. Under the Association's bylaws, each member school is represented by its principal or a faculty member, who has a vote in selecting members of the governing legislative council and board of control from eligible principals, assistant principals and superintendents.

Interscholastic athletics obviously play an integral part in the public education of Tennessee, where nearly every public high school spends money on competitions among schools. Since a pickup system of interscholastic games would not do, these public teams need some mechanism to produce rules and regulate competition. The mechanism is an organization overwhelmingly composed of public school officials who select representatives (all of them public officials at the time in question here), who in turn adopt and enforce the rules that make the system work. Thus, by giving these jobs to the Association, the 290 public schools of Tennessee belonging to it can sensibly be seen as exercising their own authority to meet their own responsibilities. Unsurprisingly, then, the record indicates that half the council or board meetings documented here were held during official school hours, and that public schools have largely provided for the Association's financial support. The Association thus exercises the authority of the predominantly public schools to charge for admission to their games; the Association does not receive this money from the schools, but enjoys the schools' moneymaking capacity [gate receipts from tournament contests] as its own.

In sum, to the extent of 84% of its membership, the Association is an organization of public schools represented by their officials acting in their official capacity to provide an integral element of secondary public schooling. There would be no recognizable Association, legal or tangible, without the public school officials, who do not merely control but overwhelmingly perform all but the purely ministerial acts by which the Association exists and functions in practical terms. Only the 16% minority of private school memberships prevents this entwinement of the Association and the public school system from being total and their identities totally indistinguishable.

To complement the entwinement of public school officials with the Association from the bottom up, the State of Tennessee has provided for entwinement from top down. State Board members are assigned ex officio to serve as members of the board of control and legislative council, and the Association's ministerial employees are treated as state employees to the extent of being eligible for membership in the state retirement system.

Today the State Board's member-designees continue to sit on the Association's committees as nonvoting members, and the State continues to welcome Association employees in its retirement scheme....

The entwinement down from the State Board is therefore unmistakable, just as the entwinement up from the member public schools is overwhelming. Entwinement will support a conclusion that an ostensibly private organization ought to be charged with a public character and judged by constitutional standards; entwinement to the degree shown here requires it....

Notes and Questions

1. Does the Supreme Court's "entwinement" analysis in *Brentwood Academy* sufficiently distinguish a state high school athletic association from the NCAA and lead to the conclusion that the NCAA should not be deemed a state actor? In *NCAA v. Tarkanian*, 488 U.S. 179 (1988), the Supreme Court examined the relationship between the University of Nevada, Las Vegas (UNLV) and the NCAA regarding the NCAA's rule-making:

> UNLV is among the NCAA's members and participated in promulgating the Association's rules; it must be assumed, therefore, that Nevada had some impact on the NCAA's policy determinations. Yet the NCAA's several hundred other public and private member institutions each similarly affected those policies. Those institutions, the vast majority of which were located in States other than Nevada, did not act under color of Nevada law. It necessarily follows

that the source of the legislation adopted by the NCAA is not Nevada but the collective membership, speaking through an organization that is independent of any particular State.

2. Prior to the Supreme Court's decision in *Tarkanian*, the lower courts had viewed the NCAA as a "state" actor for a number of years, almost without exception. *See, e.g., Howard University v. National Collegiate Athletic Association*, 510 F.2d 213 (D.C. Cir. 1975); *Parish v. National Collegiate Athletic Association*, 506 F.2d 1028 (5th Cir. 1975). This trend ended with the decision in *Arlosoroff v. National Collegiate Athletic Association*, 746 F.2d 1019 (4th Cir. 1984), which followed the Supreme Court's reasoning in non-sports association cases, holding that the actions of the NCAA were not equivalent of state action (*Blum v. Yaretsky*, 457 U.S. 991 (1982) and *Rendell-Baker v. Kohn*, 457 U.S. 830 (1982)).

3. With the exception of state high school athletic associations, courts have consistently ruled that private, amateur sport organizations and governing bodies are not state actors for constitutional purposes. For example, the court in *Lafler v. Athletic Board of Control*, 536 F. Supp. 104 (W.D. Mich. 1982), ruled that no state action was involved in denying the plaintiff, a woman, the opportunity to compete in the Golden Gloves boxing competition:

> The plaintiff admits that her application to compete was submitted to the Golden Gloves competition, which is a private, not a state, organization. All parties appear to agree that the rule which prohibits the plaintiff from participating in the competition was promulgated by the United States of America Amateur Boxing Federation (USA/ABF) and adopted by the Michigan Amateur Boxing Federation.

Similarly, the Tenth Circuit Court of Appeals ruled that the governing organization of amateur basketball in the United States, ABA/USA, is not a governmental actor. *See Behagen v. Amateur Basketball Association of the United States of America*, 884 F.2d 524 (10th Cir. 1989).

2. Procedural Due Process: Deprivation of Liberty or Property

The due process clause of the Fourteenth Amendment to the U.S. Constitution provides that no state shall "deprive any person of life, liberty, or property without due process of law." If a state actor's decision or action deprives a person or entity of a property interest, that person or entity must first be afforded certain procedures consisting of (1) notice of all of the charges against the person or entity and (2) a fair hearing prior to the deprivation in order to contest the charges. Thus, in order for a state actor to be subject to the requirements of procedural due process, the person or entity claiming they were denied due process of law must first establish that the decision or action deprives them of a liberty or property interest.

Tiffany v. Arizona Interscholastic Association, Inc.

726 P.2d 231 (Ariz. Ct. App. 1986)

MEYERSON, JUDGE.

Does a high school student have a constitutional right to participate in interscholastic athletic competition during his senior year in high school? This is the primary question raised in this appeal. As explained more fully herein, we hold that defendant-appellant Arizona Interscholastic Association, Inc. (AIA) did not violate the due process clause of the fourteenth amendment when it refused to grant plaintiff-appellee John Tiffany a hardship waiver from its nineteen-year-old eligibility rule. We concur with the trial court, however, that AIA acted unlawfully by failing to follow its own bylaws in considering the request for the waiver.

Tiffany began his senior year at St. Mary's High School in Phoenix during the 1983–84 school term. He had been held back in kindergarten and first grade because of a learning disability.

Thus, he turned nineteen years of age on August 5, 1983, the month before his senior year would begin. Tiffany had participated in athletics throughout grade school and during high school. He wanted to participate in athletic competition during his senior year....

Under AIA's bylaws, if a student turns nineteen before September 1 of the school year, he is not eligible to participate in interscholastic athletics. AIA bylaws provide, however, that:

> The Executive Board in individual cases may, at its discretion and upon such terms and conditions as it may impose, waive or modify any eligibility rule when in its opinion there are circumstances beyond the control of the student or parent whereby enforcement of the rule would work an undue hardship on the student....

The parties have stipulated that the decision to hold Tiffany back in the early grades was made by his teachers and school administrators with his parents' approval. AIA does not contest that these circumstances were beyond the control of Tiffany and his parents.

At a hearing before the Executive Board of AIA, Tiffany presented evidence that he very much enjoyed his participation in interscholastic athletics, the friendship of those with whom he would compete, and the benefits from the discipline and regulation involved in playing varsity athletics. Tiffany indicated to the Executive Board that his motivation in studying came from the fact that in order to be eligible for interscholastic athletics a certain grade point average must be maintained. The Executive Board denied the request for the waiver. It is agreed by the parties that AIA has a policy of not making any exceptions to the nineteen-year-old eligibility rule....

To succeed in an action under 42 U.S.C. § 1983, a plaintiff must establish that the defendant acted under color of law to deprive the plaintiff of a right, privilege or immunity secured by the constitution or laws of the United States. It is uncontested that AIA's actions are under color of law within the meaning of 42 U.S.C. § 1983.... AIA disputes, however, that its conduct in this case deprived Tiffany of any interest cognizable under this statute.

In order to decide whether Tiffany's exclusion from interscholastic athletics during his senior year in high school violated due process (and therefore 42 U.S.C. § 1983), it first must be determined whether Tiffany had any property or liberty interest in participating in high school sports during the 1983–84 school year. The beginning point in analyzing this constitutional issue is the decision of the United States Supreme Court in *Goss v. Lopez*, 419 U.S. 565 (1975). In *Goss*, the Supreme Court held that a school could not suspend a student for ten days without insuring due process safeguards. The Court reasoned that a "State is constrained to recognize a student's legitimate entitlement to a public education as a property interest which is protected by the Due Process Clause and which may not be taken away for misconduct without adherence to the minimum procedures required by that Clause."

"[E]ducation is perhaps the most important function of state and local governments," and the total exclusion from the educational process for more than a trivial period, and certainly if the suspension is for ten days, is a serious event in the life of the suspended child. Neither the property interest in educational benefits temporarily denied nor the liberty interest in reputation, which is also implicated, is so insubstantial that suspensions may constitutionally be imposed by any procedure the school chooses, no matter how arbitrary...." We now proceed to apply the ruling of *Goss* to the case before us.

Most courts which have considered this issue have declined to hold that participation in a single year of high school athletic competition rises to the level of a constitutionally protectable property interest. For example, in *Albach v. Odle*, 531 F.2d 983 (10th Cir. 1976), the plaintiff challenged a rule automatically barring from interscholastic high school athletic competition for one year any student who transferred from his home district to a boarding school or from a boarding school to his home district. The court found that the ruling in *Goss v. Lopez* was limited to the "educational process." In language which has been cited repeatedly by other courts, the court declared:

> The educational process is a broad and comprehensive concept with a variable and indefinite meaning. It is not limited to classroom attendance but includes innumerable separate components, such as participation in athletic activity and participation in school clubs and social groups, which combine to provide an atmosphere of intellectual and moral advancement. We do not read *Goss* to establish a property interest subject to constitutional protection in each of these separate components.

Under certain limited circumstances, however, courts have found that participation in interscholastic sports rises to the level of a constitutionally protected property interest. For example, in *Boyd v. Board of Directors*, 612 F. Supp. 86 (E.D. Ark. 1985), the court held that a student could not be suspended from the high school football team without procedural due process of law protections. The court found that the plaintiff-student was an outstanding athlete and that the 1983 season was his last opportunity to participate in football at the high school level. The testimony indicated that participation in high school sports was "vital and indispensable to a college scholarship and, in essence, a college education." The court found that his participation in interscholastic athletics must be deemed a property interest protected by the due process clause of the fourteenth amendment....

In *Florida High School Activities Ass'n, Inc. v. Bryant*, 313 So. 2d 57 (Fla. Dist. Ct. App. 1975), the court affirmed the trial court which ordered the defendant to allow the plaintiff to participate in athletics during the 1974–75 school year. Although the court did not express its ruling in due process terms, it accepted the trial court's finding that basketball was an important and vital part of the plaintiff's life "'providing an impetus to his general scholastic and social development and rehabilitation from his prior problems as a juvenile delinquent.'"

As the above cases demonstrate, in the realm of constitutional law, there are very few absolutes. We are persuaded that under certain circumstances a high school student can properly establish an entitlement to due process protection in connection with a suspension or exclusion from high school athletics. We believe that an appropriate extension of the holding in *Goss v. Lopez* was expressed by the court in *Pegram v. Nelson*, 469 F. Supp. 1134 (M.D.N.C. 1979). In that case, a high school student was suspended from school for ten days and was also excluded from after-school activities for a period of four months. The court acknowledged that the "opportunity to participate in extracurricular activities is not, by and in itself, a property interest." The court recognized, however, that:

> Total exclusion from participation in that part of the educational process designated as extracurricular activities for a lengthy period of time could, depending upon the particular circumstances, be a sufficient deprivation to implicate due process.

It is not necessary in this case to define the precise parameters of the circumstances under which due process must be afforded to a student excluded from high school athletics. This is so because Tiffany has not asserted any cognizable interest beyond his claim to mere participation in one year of interscholastic sports. Tiffany argues that he very much enjoys his participation in athletics, the friendship of those that he competes with and the benefit he derives from the discipline and regulation involved in playing varsity sports. Such interests, albeit important to him, simply do not rise to the level of constitutional magnitude necessary to invoke the protection of the due process clause. We likewise conclude that the scholastic benefit derived from the incentive to maintain a certain grade point average to remain eligible for athletic competition is also an interest which is outside the scope of constitutional protection. Unlike the "deprivation of a previously granted scholarship [which] would invoke the protections of procedural due process," ... the educational stimulus Tiffany claims to derive from athletic participation is, in constitutional terms, a "mere subjective 'expectation,'" ... and not protected by procedural due process. In short, Tiffany has failed to demonstrate the type of serious damage to his "later opportunities for high education and employment," ... which would raise his interest in interscholastic athletics to a level warranting the safeguards of the due process clause.

[The court did, however, determine that the AIA had failed to exercise its discretion at the eligibility hearing.]

Notes and Questions

1. In regards to a procedural due process claim brought by a student-athlete, upon what grounds is a property right in athletic participation established? Courts have routinely held that athletics participation is a privilege, not a right such as the right to attend school until a certain age; thus, a student-athlete who is declared ineligible or prevented from competing in athletics is not being deprived of a property interest for purposes of due process. *See, e.g., Goss v. Lopez*, 419 U.S. 565 (1975) (holding that a student's legitimate entitlement to a public education is a protected property interest). *See also Indiana High School Athletic Ass'n v. Carlberg*, 694 N.E.2d 222 (Ind. 1997) (no protected interest in athletic participation at the high school level under either federal or state constitution); *Jordan v. O'Fallon Township High School District*, 706 N.E.2d 137 (Ill. App. Ct. 1999) (no protected interest in athletic participation, despite an interest in obtaining a college scholarship); *Fusato v. Washington Interscholastic Activities Ass'n*, 970 P.2d 774 (Wash. Ct. App. 1999) (no fundamental right to participate in athletics for equal protection purposes) and *Mattison v. E. Stroudsburg Univ.*, 2013 U.S. Dist. LEXIS 52579 (M.D. Pa. Apr. 10, 2013).

2. An existing college athletic scholarship, as opposed to an interest in obtaining one (a "subjective expectation"), is generally considered to be a property interest. *See, e.g., Brands v. Sheldon Community School*, 671 F. Supp. 627, 631 (N.D. Iowa 1987) ("Once awarded, a college scholarship may give rise to a property interest in its continuation....When scholarships are awarded at the discretion of a college coach, and such discretion has not yet been exercised, no property interest in the receipt of a scholarship can exist, and the plaintiff cannot invoke his expectation that he would earn a scholarship at the state tournament in order to claim a property interest in wrestling there") (citations omitted). *See also Heike v. Guevara*, 2013 U.S. App. LEXIS 5420 (6th Cir. Mar. 18, 2013) (court assumed student athlete had a constitutionally protected property interest in her scholarship). Thus, procedural due process generally requires that a student-athlete be afforded notice and an opportunity to be heard if a scholarship is being taken away or reduced.

3. When a state actor such as a state high school athletic association or school district fails to follow its own rules and regulations, some courts have recognized a property interest for purposes of procedural due process. *See, e.g., Brands*, 671 F. Supp. at 631 ("[w]hen a government must follow mandatory laws or regulations which limit its discretion to make a decision in any way or for any reason, those laws or regulations can create a property right which is deprived if those regulations are not followed").

4. Should recognition of a property interest depend on the skill level of a particular plaintiff? *See NCAA v. Yeo*, 171 S.W.3d 863 (Tex. 2005) (no property or liberty interest based on claim that student athlete had unique reputation as a world class athlete in her home country).

5. In *Brentwood II*, the Supreme Court held that Brentwood Academy failed to establish a procedural due process claim against the state athletic association because it had been afforded notice and a fair hearing:

> The decision to sanction Brentwood for engaging in prohibited recruiting was preceded by an investigation, several meetings, exchanges of correspondence, an adverse written determination from TSSAA's executive director, [and] a hearing before the director and an advisory panel composed of three members of TSSAA's Board of Control, and finally de novo review by the entire TSSAA Board of Directors. During the investigation, Brentwood was notified of all the charges against it. At each of the two hearings, Brentwood was represented by counsel and given the opportunity to adduce evidence. No evidence offered by Brentwood was excluded.

C. Constitutional Rights

Within the context of high school athletics, the United States Supreme Court has issued some important decisions involving constitutional rights in the areas of free speech (First Amendment), the right against unreasonable searches and seizures (Fourth Amendment), and freedom of religion (First Amendment).

1. Freedom of Speech

The First Amendment of the U.S. Constitution protects against government restrictions or limitations on the freedom of speech and expression. As you read in *Brentwood Academy* (*Brentwood I*), the Supreme Court held that the Tennessee Secondary School Athletic Association was a state actor. Six years later, the Supreme Court in *Tennessee Secondary School Athletic Association v. Brentwood Academy*, 127 S. Ct. 2489 (2007) (*Brentwood II*), considered the merits of Brentwood Academy's claim that the association's enforcement of a rule prohibiting "undue influence" in recruiting athletes violated its right to free speech under the First Amendment when it wrote to incoming students and their parents about spring football practice. In rejecting this claim, the majority wrote:

> The First Amendment protects Brentwood's right to publish truthful information about the school and its athletic programs. It likewise protects the school's right to try to persuade prospective student and their parents that its excellence in sports is a reason for enrolling. But Brentwood's speech rights are not absolute.... We need no empirical data to credit TSSAA's common-sense conclusion that hard-sell tactics [in a letter] directed at middle school students could lead to exploitation, distort competition between high school teams, and foster an environment in which athletics are prized more highly than academics.

Do you agree with the Court that it is a "common-sense conclusion" recruiting letters lead to exploitation, a distortion of competition, and an environment in which athletics are viewed more important than academics? Should students and their parents be denied access to information contained in a recruiting letter that will assist them in making an informed decision about which school to attend?

Most high school athletic associations have adopted an anti-recruiting rule similar to the "undue influence" recruiting rule at issue in *Brentwood I*. As an example, the Michigan High School Athletic Association's (MHSAA) "undue influence" rule provides, in pertinent part:

> The use of undue influence for athletic purposes by any person or persons directly or indirectly associated with a student, a student's parents, the school or its athletic program to secure or encourage the attendance of a student or the student's parents or guardians as residents of the school district, shall cause the student to become ineligible for interscholastic scrimmages or contests a minimum of 90 scheduled school days and a maximum of four years.

If a recruiting letter was found to be a violation of the MHSAA's "undue influence" rule, does the penalty range of 90 days to four years of ineligibility give the MHSAA too much discretion? In your view, would a four-year suspension ever be appropriate?

Problem. Review the anti-recruiting rule adopted by the high school athletic association that regulates high school athletics in your jurisdiction. Does the rule (and any rule "interpretations" provided) prohibit the type of letter that was sent to middle school students by Brentwood Academy?

When a state actor such as a public school, school district, or state high school athletic association disciplines an athlete for speech-related conduct, it raises First Amendment issues. A difficult question for athletics administrators is when is it acceptable for a high school athlete to voice his or her opposition to the way a team is being run and when does it constitute an unacceptable act of insubordination (i.e., defiance or disobedience)? In addition, high school coaches and athletics administrators need to consider how to craft and enforce rules and policies regarding inappropriate speech. Some of the key variables to consider are where the speech occurs (on or off campus), whether the speech is political or religious based, and whether the speech is a disruption of a school activity.

In 2021, the Supreme Court provided fresh guidance on assessing First Amendment protected speech of high school athletes. The issue in *Mahanoy* is whether a high school student's suspension from the junior varsity cheerleading squad based on her use of profanity in a social media post, made off campus and on a Saturday, violated the First Amendment.

Mahanoy Area School District v. B.L.

141 S. Ct. 2038 (2021)

JUSTICE BREYER delivered the opinion of the Court.

A public high school student used, and transmitted to her Snapchat friends, vulgar language and gestures criticizing both the school and the school's cheerleading team. The student's speech took place outside of school hours and away from the school's campus. In response, the school suspended the student for a year from the cheerleading team. We must decide whether the Court of Appeals for the Third Circuit correctly held that the school's decision violated the First Amendment....

I

B. L. (who, together with her parents, is a respondent in this case) was a student at Mahanoy Area High School, a public school in Mahanoy City, Pennsylvania. At the end of her freshman year, B. L. tried out for a position on the school's varsity cheerleading squad and for right fielder on a private softball team. She did not make the varsity cheerleading team or get her preferred softball position, but she was offered a spot on the cheerleading squad's junior varsity team. B. L. did not accept the coach's decision with good grace, particularly because the squad coaches had placed an entering freshman on the varsity team.

That weekend, B. L. and a friend visited the Cocoa Hut, a local convenience store. There, B. L. used her smartphone to post two photos on Snapchat, a social media application that allows users to post photos and videos that disappear after a set period of time. B. L. posted the images to her Snapchat "story," a feature of the application that allows any person in the user's "friend" group (B. L. had about 250 "friends") to view the images for a 24 hour period.

The first image B. L. posted showed B. L. and a friend with middle fingers raised; it bore the caption: "Fuck school fuck softball fuck cheer fuck everything." The second image was blank but for a caption, which read: "Love how me and [another student] get told we need a year of jv before we make varsity but tha[t] doesn't matter to anyone else?" The caption also contained an upside-down smiley-face emoji.

B. L.'s Snapchat "friends" included other Mahanoy Area High School students, some of whom also belonged to the cheerleading squad. At least one of them, using a separate cellphone, took pictures of B. L.'s posts and shared them with other members of the cheerleading squad. One of the students who received these photos showed them to her mother (who was a cheerleading squad coach), and the images spread. That week, several cheerleaders and other students approached the cheerleading coaches "visibly upset" about B. L.'s posts. Questions about the posts persisted during an Algebra class taught by one of the two coaches.

After discussing the matter with the school principal, the coaches decided that because the posts used profanity in connection with a school extracurricular activity, they violated team and school rules. As a result, the coaches suspended B. L. from the junior varsity cheerleading squad for the upcoming year. B. L.'s subsequent apologies did not move school officials. The school's athletic director, principal, superintendent, and school board, all affirmed B. L.'s suspension from the team. In response, B. L., together with her parents, filed this lawsuit in Federal District Court....

The school district filed a petition for certiorari in this Court, asking us to decide "[w]hether [*Tinker*], which holds that public school officials may regulate speech that would materially and substantially disrupt the work and discipline of the school, applies to student speech that occurs off campus." We granted the petition.

II

We have made clear that students do not "shed their constitutional rights to freedom of speech or expression," even "at the school house gate." *Tinker*, 393 U.S., at 506, 89 S.Ct. 733.... But we have also made clear that courts must apply the First Amendment "in light of the special characteristics of the school environment." One such characteristic, which we have stressed, is the fact that schools at times stand *in loco parentis*, *i.e.*, in the place of parents.

This Court has previously outlined three specific categories of student speech that schools may regulate in certain circumstances: (1) "indecent," "lewd," or "vulgar" speech uttered during a school assembly on school grounds; (2) speech, uttered during a class trip, that promotes "illegal drug use"; and (3) speech that others may reasonably perceive as "bear[ing] the imprimatur of the school," such as that appearing in a school-sponsored newspaper.

Finally, in *Tinker*, we said schools have a special interest in regulating speech that "materially disrupts classwork or involves substantial disorder or invasion of the rights of others." These special characteristics call for special leeway when schools regulate speech that occurs under its supervision.

Unlike the Third Circuit, we do not believe the special characteristics that give schools additional license to regulate student speech always disappear when a school regulates speech that takes place off campus. The school's regulatory interests remain significant in some off-campus circumstances. The parties' briefs, and those of *amici*, list several types of off-campus behavior that may call for school regulation. These include serious or severe bullying or harassment targeting particular individuals; threats aimed at teachers or other students; the failure to follow rules concerning lessons, the writing of papers, the use of computers, or participation in other online school activities; and breaches of school security devices, including material maintained within school computers.

Even B. L. herself and the *amici* supporting her would redefine the Third Circuit's off-campus/on-campus distinction, treating as on campus: all times when the school is responsible for the student; the school's immediate surroundings; travel en route to and from the school; all speech taking place over school laptops or on a school's website; speech taking place during remote learning; activities taken for school credit; and communications to school e-mail accounts or phones. And it may be that speech related to extracurricular activities, such as team sports, would also receive special treatment under B. L.'s proposed rule.

We are uncertain as to the length or content of any such list of appropriate exceptions or carveouts to the Third Circuit majority's rule. That rule, basically, if not entirely, would deny the off-campus applicability of *Tinker's* highly general statement about the nature of a school's special interests. Particularly given the advent of computer-based learning, we hesitate to determine precisely which of many school-related off-campus activities belong on such a list. Neither do we now know how such a list might vary, depending upon a student's age, the nature of the school's off-campus activity, or the impact upon the school itself. Thus, we do not now set forth a broad, highly general First Amendment rule stating just what counts as "off campus" speech and whether or how ordinary First Amendment standards must give way off campus to a school's special need to prevent, *e.g.*, substantial disruption of learning-related activities or the protection of those who make up a school community.

We can, however, mention three features of off-campus speech that often, even if not always, distinguish schools' efforts to regulate that speech from their efforts to regulate on-campus speech. Those features diminish the strength of the unique educational characteristics that might call for special First Amendment leeway.

First, a school, in relation to off-campus speech, will rarely stand *in loco parentis*. The doctrine of *in loco parentis* treats school administrators as standing in the place of students' parents under circumstances where the children's actual parents cannot protect, guide, and discipline them. Geographically speaking, off-campus speech will normally fall within the zone of parental, rather than school-related, responsibility.

Second, from the student speaker's perspective, regulations of off-campus speech, when coupled with regulations of on-campus speech, include all the speech a student utters during the full 24-hour day. That means courts must be more skeptical of a school's efforts to regulate off-campus speech, for doing so may mean the student cannot engage in that kind of speech at all. When it comes to political or religious speech that occurs outside school or a school program or activity, the school will have a heavy burden to justify intervention.

Third, the school itself has an interest in protecting a student's unpopular expression, especially when the expression takes place off campus. America's public schools are the nurseries of democracy. Our representative democracy only works if we protect the "marketplace of ideas." This free exchange facilitates an informed public opinion, which, when transmitted to lawmakers, helps produce laws that reflect the People's will. That protection must include the protection of unpopular ideas, for popular ideas have less need for protection. Thus, schools have a strong interest in ensuring that future generations understand the workings in practice of the well-known aphorism, "I disapprove of what you say, but I will defend to the death your right to say it." (Although this quote is often attributed to Voltaire, it was likely coined by an English writer, Evelyn Beatrice Hall.)

Given the many different kinds of off-campus speech, the different potential school-related and circumstance-specific justifications, and the differing extent to which those justifications may call for First Amendment leeway, we can, as a general matter, say little more than this: Taken together, these three features of much off-campus speech mean that the leeway the First Amendment grants to schools in light of their special characteristics is diminished. We leave for future cases to decide where, when, and how these features mean the speaker's off-campus location will make the critical difference. This case can, however, provide one example.

III

Consider B. L.'s speech. Putting aside the vulgar language, the listener would hear criticism, of the team, the team's coaches, and the school—in a word or two, criticism of the rules of a community of which B. L. forms a part. This criticism did not involve features that would place it outside the First Amendment's ordinary protection. B. L.'s posts, while crude, did not amount to fighting words. And while B. L. used vulgarity, her speech was not obscene as this Court has understood that term. To the contrary, B. L. uttered the kind of pure speech to which, were she an adult, the First Amendment would provide strong protection.

Consider too when, where, and how B. L. spoke. Her posts appeared outside of school hours from a location outside the school. She did not identify the school in her posts or target any member of the school community with vulgar or abusive language. B. L. also transmitted her speech through a personal cellphone, to an audience consisting of her private circle of Snapchat friends. These features of her speech, while risking transmission to the school itself, nonetheless (for reasons we have just explained, *supra*) diminish the school's interest in punishing B. L.'s utterance.

But what about the school's interest, here primarily an interest in prohibiting students from using vulgar language to criticize a school team or its coaches—at least when that criticism might well be transmitted to other students, team members, coaches, and faculty? We can break that general interest into three parts.

First, we consider the school's interest in teaching good manners and consequently in punishing the use of vulgar language aimed at part of the school community. See App. 35 (indicating that coaches removed B. L. from the cheer team because "there was profanity in [her] Snap and it was directed towards cheerleading"). The strength of this anti-vulgarity interest is weakened considerably by the fact that B. L. spoke outside the school on her own time.

B. L. spoke under circumstances where the school did not stand *in loco parentis*. And there is no reason to believe B. L.'s parents had delegated to school officials their own control of B. L.'s behavior at the Cocoa Hut. Moreover, the vulgarity in B. L.'s posts encompassed a message, an expression of B. L.'s irritation with, and criticism of, the school and cheerleading communities. Further, the school has presented no evidence of any general effort to prevent students from using vulgarity outside the classroom. Together, these facts convince us that the school's interest in teaching good manners is not sufficient, in this case, to overcome B. L.'s interest in free expression.

Second, the school argues that it was trying to prevent disruption, if not within the classroom, then within the bounds of a school-sponsored extracurricular activity. But we can find no evidence in the record of the sort of "substantial disruption" of a school activity or a threatened harm to the rights of others that might justify the school's action. Rather, the record shows that discussion of the matter took, at most, 5 to 10 minutes of an Algebra class "for just a couple of days" and that some members of the cheerleading team were "upset" about the content of B. L.'s Snapchats. But when one of B. L.'s coaches was asked directly if she had "any reason to think that this particular incident would disrupt class or school activities other than the fact that kids kept asking... about it," she responded simply, "No." As we said in *Tinker*, "for the State in the person of school officials to justify prohibition of a particular expression of opinion, it must be able to show that its action was caused by something more than a mere desire to avoid the discomfort and unpleasantness that always accompany an unpopular viewpoint." The alleged disturbance here does not meet *Tinker's* demanding standard.

Third, the school presented some evidence that expresses (at least indirectly) a concern for team morale. One of the coaches testified that the school decided to suspend B. L., not because of any specific negative impact upon a particular member of the school community, but "based on the fact that there was negativity put out there that could impact students in the school." There is little else, however, that suggests any serious decline in team morale—to the point where it could create a substantial interference in, or disruption of, the school's efforts to maintain team cohesion. As we have previously said, simple "undifferentiated fear or apprehension... is not enough to overcome the right to freedom of expression."

It might be tempting to dismiss B. L.'s words as unworthy of the robust First Amendment protections discussed herein. But sometimes it is necessary to protect the superfluous in order to preserve the necessary. "We cannot lose sight of the fact that, in what otherwise might seem a trifling and annoying instance of individual distasteful abuse of a privilege, these fundamental societal values are truly implicated."

Although we do not agree with the reasoning of the Third Circuit's panel majority, for the reasons expressed above, resembling those of the panel's concurring opinion, we nonetheless agree that the school violated B. L.'s First Amendment rights. The judgment of the Third Circuit is therefore affirmed.

It is so ordered.

[Concurring and dissenting opinions omitted.]

Notes and Comments

1. If a few "f-bombs" and a photo with raised middle fingers directed at the school's athletics programs on social media fails to meet *Tinker's* demanding standard of "substantial disruption" of a school activity, what would meet it? Would it make a difference if B. L. had made the post on social media while in the school hallways during school hours? Does the holding in *Mahanoy* seem to protect most forms of insubordination-type speech on social media that was previously unprotected before the advent of social media? For example, in *Wildman v. Marshalltown Sch. Dist.*, 249 F.3d 768 (8th Cir. 2001), the court of appeals held that the First Amendment did not protect an insubordination letter written by a sophomore student in high school and distributed to her basketball teammates. The letter stated, in pertinent part:

> I want to say something to Coach Rowles. I will not say anything to him without the whole teams [sic] support. He needs us next year and the year after and what if we aren't there for him? It is time to give him back some of the bullshit that he has given us. We are a really great team and by the time we are seniors and we ALL have worked hard we are going to have an AWESOME season. We deserve better then [sic] what we have gotten. We now need to stand up for what we believe in!

See also Marcum v. Dahl, 658 F.2d 731 (10th Cir. 1981) (permissible to dismiss two members of the women's basketball team at the University of Oklahoma for making disparaging remarks about the coach).

2. In *Mahanoy,* it is particularly noteworthy that there was no suspension from school; the sole discipline imposed was suspension from the team. The Court did not reject B. L.'s constitutional claim on the grounds that athletics participation is a privilege, not a right.

3. Most courts would view whistleblower-type speech to be deserving of First Amendment protection. Thus, an athlete cannot be disciplined for speaking about

illegal or inappropriate behavior or conduct. *See, e.g., Hysaw v. Washburn University*, 690 F. Supp. 940 (D. Kan. 1987) (football players who boycotted team claiming racial discrimination and were removed from team raise free speech and other issues under Section 1983).

4. Should a coach at a public high school or university ban social media posts during the playing season? Would it violate the First Amendment? Is it possible to craft a policy that provides notice of acceptable and unacceptable speech on social media and provides a reasonable enforcement mechanism?

Problem. A high school basketball player at a public high school knelt during the National Anthem. The local school board immediately suspended her from all extracurricular activities. Discuss what action, if any, is available to her.

2. The Right Against Unreasonable Searches and Seizures: Drug Testing

A persistent and recurring sports law topic concerns the drug testing of athletes. From a legal standpoint the problem is of recent vintage. Defining rules with some degree of specificity and predictability is a challenge. To evaluate the legality of any drug testing scheme, it is important to consider who the tester is, why the test is to be conducted, upon whom the test is to be conducted, how the test is to be administered, for what drugs will tests be conducted, and what procedures are to be triggered if someone "fails" the test, just to name a few of the variables.

The Fourth Amendment to the U. S. Constitution protects "the right of the people to be secure in their persons, houses, papers, and effects, against unreasonable searches and seizures." The collection of fluids from a person's body by public school officials constitutes a search. The pertinent issue is whether drug testing in the context of interscholastic athletics constitutes an "unreasonable" search and seizure. The Supreme Court has provided a degree of certainty. In *Earls*, reprinted below, the Court deals with drug testing of middle school and high school students involved in competitive extracurricular activities. While *Earls* answers some questions, it leaves many others open. So, as you read the Court's opinion, jot down each question that pops into your head.

Board of Education v. Earls

536 U.S. 822 (2002)

Justice Thomas delivered the opinion of the Court.

The Student Activities Drug Testing Policy implemented by the Board of Education of Independent School District No. 92 of Pottawatomie County (School District) requires all students who participate in competitive extracurricular activities to submit to drug testing....

The city of Tecumseh, Oklahoma, is a rural community located approximately 40 miles southeast of Oklahoma City. The School District administers all Tecumseh public schools. In the fall of 1998, the School District adopted the Student Activities Drug Testing Policy (Policy), which requires all middle and high school students to consent to drug testing in order to participate in any extracurricular activity. In practice, the Policy has been applied only to competitive extracurricular activities sanctioned by the Oklahoma Secondary Schools Activities Association, such as the Academic Team, Future Farmers of America, Future Homemakers of America, band, choir, pom pon, cheerleading, and athletics. Under the Policy, students are required to take a drug test before participating in an extracurricular activity, must submit to random drug testing while participating in that activity, and must agree to be tested at any time upon reasonable suspicion. The urinalysis tests are designed to detect only the use of illegal drugs, including amphetamines, marijuana, cocaine, opiates, and barbiturates, not medical conditions or the presence of authorized prescription medications.

At the time of their suit, both respondents attended Tecumseh High School. Respondent Lindsay Earls was a member of the show choir, the marching band, the Academic Team, and the National Honor Society. Respondent Daniel James sought to participate in the Academic Team. Together with their parents, Earls and James brought a 42 U.S.C. § 1983 action against the School District, challenging the Policy both on its face and as applied to their participation in extracurricular activities. They alleged that the Policy violates the Fourth Amendment as incorporated by the Fourteenth Amendment and requested injunctive and declarative relief. They also argued that the School District failed to identify a special need for testing students who participate in extracurricular activities, and that the "Drug Testing Policy neither addresses a proven problem nor promises to bring any benefit to students or the school."

Applying the principles articulated in *Vernonia School Dist. 47J v. Acton*, 515 U.S. 646 (1995), in which we upheld the suspicionless drug testing of school athletes, the United States District Court for the Western District of Oklahoma rejected respondents' claim that the Policy was unconstitutional and granted summary judgment to the School District. The court noted that "special needs" exist in the public school context and that, although the School District did "not show a drug problem of epidemic proportions," there was a history of drug abuse starting in 1970 that presented "legitimate cause for concern." The District Court also held that the Policy was effective because "it can scarcely be disputed that the drug problem among the student body is effectively addressed by making sure that the large number of students participating in competitive, extracurricular activities do not use drugs." *Id.*

The United States Court of Appeals for the Tenth Circuit reversed, holding that the Policy violated the Fourth Amendment. The Court of Appeals agreed with the District Court that the Policy must be evaluated in the "unique environment of the school setting," but reached a different conclusion as to the Policy's constitutionality. Before imposing a suspicionless drug testing program, the Court of Appeals concluded that a school "must demonstrate that there is some identifiable drug abuse problem among a sufficient number of those subject to the testing, such that testing that group of students will actually redress its drug problem." The Court of Appeals then held that because the School District failed to demonstrate such a problem existed among Tecumseh students participating in competitive extracurricular activities, the Policy was unconstitutional. We granted certiorari, and now reverse.

The Fourth Amendment to the United States Constitution protects "the right of the people to be secure in their persons, houses, papers, and effects, against unreasonable searches and seizures." Searches by public school officials, such as the collection of urine samples, implicate Fourth Amendment interests. *See Vernonia, supra,* at 652. We must therefore review the School District's Policy for "reasonableness," which is the touchstone of the constitutionality of a governmental search.

In the criminal context, reasonableness usually requires a showing of probable cause. The probable-cause standard, however, "is peculiarly related to criminal investigations" and may be unsuited to determining the reasonableness of administrative searches where the "Government seeks to *prevent* the development of hazardous conditions." The Court has also held that a warrant and finding of probable cause are unnecessary in the public school context because such requirements "'would unduly interfere with the maintenance of the swift and informal disciplinary procedures [that are] needed.'"

.... It is true that we generally determine the reasonableness of a search by balancing the nature of the intrusion on the individual's privacy against the promotion of legitimate governmental interests. But we have long held that "the Fourth Amendment imposes no irreducible requirement of [individualized] suspicion." "In certain limited circumstances, the Government's need to discover such latent or hidden conditions, or to prevent their development, is sufficiently compelling to justify the intrusion on privacy entailed by conducting such searches without any measure of individualized suspicion." Therefore, in the context of safety and administrative regulations, a search unsupported by probable cause may be reasonable "when 'special needs, beyond the normal need for law enforcement, make the warrant and probable-cause requirement impracticable.'"

Significantly, this Court has previously held that "special needs" inhere in the public school context. While schoolchildren do not shed their constitutional rights when they enter the schoolhouse, "Fourth Amendment rights... are different in public schools than elsewhere; the 'reasonableness' inquiry cannot disregard the schools' custodial and tutelary responsibility for children." *Vernonia, supra.* In particular, a finding of individualized suspicion may not be necessary when a school conducts drug testing.

In *Vernonia*, this Court held that the suspicionless drug testing of athletes was constitutional. The Court, however, did not simply authorize all school drug testing, but rather conducted a fact-specific balancing of the intrusion on the children's Fourth Amendment rights against the promotion of legitimate governmental interests. *See* 515 U.S. at 652–653. Applying the principles of *Vernonia* to the somewhat different facts of this case, we conclude that Tecumseh's Policy is also constitutional.

We first consider the nature of the privacy interest allegedly compromised by the drug testing. As in *Vernonia*, the context of the public school environment serves as the backdrop for the analysis of the privacy interest at stake and the reasonableness of the drug testing policy in general.

A student's privacy interest is limited in a public school environment where the State is responsible for maintaining discipline, health, and safety. Schoolchildren are routinely required to submit to physical examinations and vaccinations against disease. Securing order in the school environment sometimes requires that students be subjected to greater controls than those appropriate for adults. See *T. L. O., supra*, 469 U.S. at 350 (Powell, J., concurring) ("Without first establishing discipline and maintaining order, teachers cannot begin to educate their students. And apart from education, the school has the obligation to protect pupils from mistreatment by other children, and also to protect teachers themselves from violence by the few students whose conduct in recent years has prompted national concern").

Respondents argue that because children participating in nonathletic extracurricular activities are not subject to regular physicals and communal undress, they have a stronger expectation of privacy than the athletes tested in *Vernonia*. This distinction, however, was not essential to our decision in *Vernonia*, which depended primarily upon the school's custodial responsibility and authority.

In any event, students who participate in competitive extracurricular activities voluntarily subject themselves to many of the same intrusions on their privacy as do athletes. Some of these clubs and activities require occasional off-campus travel and communal undress. All of them have their own rules and requirements for participating students that do not apply to the student body as a whole. For example, each of the competitive extracurricular activities governed by the Policy must abide by the rules of the Oklahoma Secondary Schools Activities Association, and a faculty sponsor monitors the students for compliance with the various rules dictated by the clubs and activities. This regulation of extracurricular activities further diminishes the expectation of privacy among schoolchildren. *Cf. Vernonia*, 515 U.S. at 657 ("Somewhat like adults who choose to participate in a closely regulated industry, students who voluntarily participate in school athletics have reason to expect intrusions upon normal rights and privileges, including privacy.") We therefore conclude that the students affected by this Policy have a limited expectation of privacy.

Next, we consider the character of the intrusion imposed by the Policy. Urination is "an excretory function traditionally shielded by great privacy." But the "degree of intrusion" on one's privacy caused by collecting a urine sample "depends upon the manner in which production of the urine sample is monitored." *Vernonia*, 515 U.S. at 658.

Under the Policy, a faculty monitor waits outside the closed restroom stall for the student to produce a sample and must "listen for the normal sounds of urination in order to guard against tampered specimens and to insure an accurate chain of custody." The monitor then pours the sample into two bottles that are sealed and placed into a mailing pouch along with a consent form signed by the student. This procedure is virtually identical to that reviewed in *Vernonia*, except that it additionally protects privacy by allowing male students to produce their samples behind a closed stall. Given that we considered the method of collection in *Vernonia* a "negligible" intrusion, the method here is even less problematic.

In addition, the Policy clearly requires that the test results be kept in confidential files separate from a student's other educational records and released to school personnel only on a "need to know" basis....

Moreover, the test results are not turned over to any law enforcement authority. Nor do the test results here lead to the imposition of discipline or have any academic consequences. Rather, the only consequence of a failed drug test is to limit the student's privilege of participating in extracurricular activities. Indeed, a student may test positive for drugs twice and still be allowed to participate in extracurricular activities. After the first positive test, the school contacts the student's parent or guardian for a meeting. The student may continue to participate in the activity if within five days of the meeting the student shows proof of receiving drug counseling and submits to a second drug test in two weeks. For the second positive test, the student is suspended from participation in all extracurricular activities for 14 days, must complete four hours of substance abuse counseling, and must submit to monthly drug tests. Only after a third positive test will the student be suspended from participating in any extracurricular activity for the remainder of the school year, or 88 school days, whichever is longer. Given the minimally intrusive nature of the sample collection and the limited uses to which the test results are put, we conclude that the invasion of students' privacy is not significant.

Finally, this Court must consider the nature and immediacy of the government's concerns and the efficacy of the Policy in meeting them. This Court has already articulated in detail the importance of the governmental concern in preventing drug use by schoolchildren. The drug abuse problem among our Nation's youth has hardly abated since *Vernonia* was decided in 1995. In fact, evidence suggests that it has only grown worse. As in *Vernonia*, "the necessity for the State to act is magnified by the fact that this evil is being visited not just upon individuals at large, but upon children for whom it has undertaken a special responsibility of care and direction." The health and safety risks identified in *Vernonia* apply with equal force to Tecumseh's children. Indeed, the nationwide drug epidemic makes the war against drugs a pressing concern in every school.

Additionally, the School District in this case has presented specific evidence of drug use at Tecumseh schools. Teachers testified that they had seen students who appeared to be under the influence of drugs and that they had heard students speaking openly about using drugs. A drug dog found marijuana cigarettes near the school parking lot. Police officers once found drugs or drug paraphernalia in a car driven by a Future Farmers of America member. And the school board president reported that people in the community were calling the board to discuss the "drug situation." We decline to second-guess the finding of the District Court that "viewing the evidence as a whole, it cannot be reasonably disputed that the [School District] was faced with a 'drug problem' when it adopted the Policy."

Respondents consider the proffered evidence insufficient and argue that there is no "real and immediate interest" to justify a policy of drug testing nonathletes. We have recognized, however, that "[a] demonstrated problem of drug abuse... [is] not in all cases necessary to the validity of a testing regime," but that some showing does "shore up an assertion of special need for a suspicionless general search program." The School District has provided sufficient evidence to shore up the need for its drug testing program.

Furthermore, this Court has not required a particularized or pervasive drug problem before allowing the government to conduct suspicionless drug testing.... [T]he need to prevent and deter the substantial harm of childhood drug use provides the necessary immediacy for a school testing policy. Indeed, it would make little sense to require a school district to wait for a substantial portion of its students to begin using drugs before it was allowed to institute a drug testing program designed to deter drug use.

Given the nationwide epidemic of drug use, and the evidence of increased drug use in Tecumseh schools, it was entirely reasonable for the School District to enact this particular drug testing policy. We reject the Court of Appeals' novel test that "any district seeking to impose a random suspicionless drug testing policy as a condition to participation in a school activity must demonstrate that there is some identifiable drug abuse problem among a sufficient number of those subject to the testing, such that testing that group of students will actually redress its drug problem." Among other problems, it would be difficult to administer such a test. As we cannot articulate a threshold level of drug use that would suffice to justify a drug testing program for schoolchildren, we refuse to fashion what would in effect be a constitutional quantum of drug use necessary to show a "drug problem."...

We also reject respondents' argument that drug testing must presumptively be based upon an individualized reasonable suspicion of wrongdoing because such a testing regime would be less intrusive. In this context, the Fourth Amendment does not require a finding of individualized suspicion, and we decline to impose such a requirement on schools attempting to prevent and detect drug use by students. Moreover, we question whether testing based on individualized suspicion in fact would be less intrusive. Such a regime would place an additional burden on public school teachers who are already tasked with the difficult job of maintaining order and discipline. A program of individualized suspicion might unfairly target members of unpopular groups. The fear of lawsuits resulting from such targeted searches may chill enforcement of the program, rendering it ineffective in combating drug use. *See Vernonia,* 515 U.S. at 663–664 (offering similar reasons for why "testing based on 'suspicion' of drug use would not be better, but worse"). In any case, this Court has repeatedly stated that reasonableness under the Fourth Amendment does not require employing the least intrusive means, because "the logic of such elaborate less-restrictive-alternative arguments could raise insuperable barriers to the exercise of virtually all search-and-seizure powers."

Finally, we find that testing students who participate in extracurricular activities is a reasonably effective means of addressing the School District's legitimate concerns in preventing, deterring, and detecting drug use. While in *Vernonia* there might have been a closer fit between the testing of athletes and the trial court's finding that the drug problem was "fueled by the 'role model' effect of athletes' drug use," such a finding was not essential to the holding. *Vernonia* did not require the school to test the group of students most likely to use drugs, but rather considered the constitutionality of the program in the context of the public school's custodial responsibilities. Evaluating the Policy in this context, we conclude that the drug testing of Tecumseh students who participate in extracurricular activities effectively serves the School District's interest in protecting the safety and health of its students.

Within the limits of the Fourth Amendment, local school boards must assess the desirability of drug testing schoolchildren. In upholding the constitutionality of the Policy, we express no opinion as to its wisdom. Rather, we hold only that Tecumseh's Policy is a reasonable means of furthering the School District's important interest in preventing and deterring drug use among its schoolchildren. Accordingly, we reverse the judgment of the Court of Appeals.

It is so ordered.

[Concurring and dissenting opinions omitted.]

Notes and Comments

1. It seems that just about every entity with control over athletics and athletes has decided to test athletes for drugs. (It wouldn't be totally surprising to learn that the Little League has adopted a drug testing program.) Universities, conferences, amateur athletic associations, the United States Olympic & Paralympic Committee, the NCAA, the NAIA, and professional leagues, as well as some school districts and state high school athletic associations, all have adopted drug testing procedures. The result is a crazy quilt.

In sorting through the various schemes, it is important to classify the organization doing the testing as either a state actor or a private entity. At least in so far as state actors are concerned, the law is settled around the guidelines established by the Supreme Court in *Earls*. However, the Supreme Court has not spoken on the issue of how private drug testing is to be evaluated. And given the Supreme Court's now somewhat cramped view of state action, this is an extremely important area. Private high schools, private colleges, the NCAA (according to *Tarkanian*), and even the USOPC are all probably private actors. According to fairly well-established principles, these schemes would not be subjected to Fourth Amendment scrutiny but would be evaluated under the more permissive rubric of private associational law. In the world of professional sports, drug testing schemes imposed upon union members by management would be evaluated according to labor law principles.

2. According to the majority in *Earls*, students who voluntarily participate in school athletics have reason to expect intrusions upon normal rights and privileges, including privacy, and therefore students affected by the drug testing policy have a limited expectation of privacy. The Court then considered the character of the intrusion imposed by the drug testing policy and concluded that the intrusion was "negligible." Do you agree with the Court that students give up privacy in return for participation in athletics? Do you agree with the Court that the privacy intrusion is negligible? Would it matter if an overwhelming majority of student-athletes feel their privacy is invaded when some person other than their doctor demands their bodily fluids and watches them urinate in a cup?

3. The Supreme Court in *Earls* considered "the nature and immediacy of the government's concerns and the efficacy of the Policy in meeting them." Would the Court's articulation of the governmental concerns of the Pottawatomie County School District in adopting suspicionless (or random) drug testing apply to a state high school athletic association that implements a similar policy?

4. Reliability questions plague many drug testing schemes. The obvious danger of false positive readings necessitates safeguards that include a second phase of testing. Nonetheless, errors will be made. Part of the problem is that legal substances sometimes produce false readings. Another part of the problem is that labs competing for business sometimes make cost-cutting decisions that undermine reliability. And still another problem is raised by false negatives. For a more complete look at the very perplexing problem of reliability, see Lawrence Miike & Maria Hewitt, *Accuracy and Reliability of Urine Drug Tests*, 36 U. Kan. L. Rev. 641 (1988).

5. A major dilemma occurs when the substances being tested for are undetectable. This is a growing problem in sports. Two solutions exist. One method is to rely on non-analytical positive evidence, such as documents revealing the purchase of banned substances. The United States Anti-Doping Agency utilizes this method. The other option is athletic profiling. Here, a physical profile of an athlete would be created. A major departure from that profile would serve as evidence that the athlete is using banned substances. *See* James A.R. Nafziger, *Circumstantial Evidence of Doping: BALCO and Beyond*, 16 Marq. Sports L. Rev. 45 (2005).

3. Freedom of Religion

Santa Fe Independent School Dist. v. Doe

530 U.S. 290 (2000)

Justice Stevens delivered the opinion of the Court.

Prior to 1995, the Santa Fe High School student who occupied the school's elective office of student council chaplain delivered a prayer over the public address system before each varsity football game for the entire season. This practice, along with others, was challenged in District Court as a violation of the Establishment Clause of the First Amendment. While these proceedings were pending in the District Court, the school district adopted a different policy that permits, but does not require, prayer initiated and led by a student at all home games....

The Santa Fe Independent School District (District) is a political subdivision of the State of Texas, responsible for the education of more than 4,000 students in a small community in the southern part of the State. The District includes the Santa Fe High School, two primary schools, an intermediate school and the junior high school. Respondents are two sets of current or former students and their respective mothers. One family is Mormon and the other is Catholic. The District Court permitted respondents (Does) to litigate anonymously to protect them from intimidation or harassment....

The August policy, which was titled "Prayer at Football Games," was similar to the July policy for graduations. It also authorized two student elections, the first to determine whether "invocations" should be delivered, and the second to select the spokesperson to deliver them. Like the July policy, it contained two parts, an initial statement that omitted any requirement that the content of the invocation be "nonsectarian and nonproselytising," and a fallback provision that automatically added that limitation if the preferred policy should be enjoined. On August 31, 1995, according to the parties' stipulation: "[T]he district's high school students voted to determine whether a student would deliver prayer at varsity football games.... The students chose to allow a student to say a prayer at football games." A week later, in a separate election, they selected a student "to deliver the prayer at varsity football games."...

We granted the District's petition for certiorari, limited to the following question: "Whether petitioner's policy permitting student-led, student-initiated prayer at football games violates the Establishment Clause." We conclude, as did the Court of Appeals, that it does.

The first Clause in the First Amendment to the Federal Constitution provides that "Congress shall make no law respecting an establishment of religion, or prohibiting the free exercise thereof." The Fourteenth Amendment imposes those substantive limitations on the legislative power of the States and their political subdivisions.

In *Lee v. Weisman*, 505 U.S. 577 (1992), we held that a prayer delivered by a rabbi at a middle school graduation ceremony violated that Clause. Although this case involves student prayer at a different type of school function, our analysis is properly guided by the principles that we endorsed in *Lee*.

As we held in that case: "The principle that government may accommodate the free exercise of religion does not supersede the fundamental limitations imposed by the Establishment Clause. It is beyond dispute that, at a minimum, the Constitution guarantees that government may not coerce anyone to support or participate in religion or its exercise, or otherwise act in a way which 'establishes a [state] religion or religious faith, or tends to do so.'" *Id.*, at 587 (citations omitted).

In this case the District first argues that this principle is inapplicable to its October policy because the messages are private student speech, not public speech. It reminds us that "there is a crucial difference between *government* speech endorsing religion, which the Establishment Clause forbids, and *private* speech endorsing religion, which the Free Speech and Free Exercise Clauses protect." *Board of Ed. of Westside Community Schools (Dist.66) v. Mergens*, 496 U.S. 226, 250 (1990). We certainly agree with that distinction, but we are not persuaded that the pregame invocations should be regarded as "private speech."

These invocations are authorized by a government policy and take place on government property at government-sponsored school-related events. Of course, not every message delivered under such circumstances is the government's own. We have held, for example, that an individual's contribution to a government-created forum was not government speech. Although the District relies heavily on *Rosenberger* and similar cases involving such forums, it is clear that the pregame ceremony is not the type of forum discussed in those cases. The Santa Fe school officials simply do not "evince either 'by policy or by practice,' any intent to open the [pregame ceremony] to 'indiscriminate use,'... by the student body generally." Rather, the school allows only one student, the same student for the entire season, to give the invocation. The statement or invocation, moreover, is subject to particular regulations that confine the content and topic of the student's message....

In *Lee*, the school district made the related argument that its policy of endorsing only "civic or nonsectarian" prayer was acceptable because it minimized the intrusion on the audience as a whole. We rejected that claim by explaining that such a majoritarian policy "does not lessen the offense or isolation to the objectors. At best it narrows their number, at worst increases their sense of isolation and affront." Similarly, while Santa Fe's majoritarian election might ensure that *most* of the students are represented, it does nothing to protect the minority; indeed, it likely serves to intensify their offense.

Moreover, the District has failed to divorce itself from the religious content in the invocations. It has not succeeded in doing so, either by claiming that its policy is "'one of neutrality rather than endorsement'" or by characterizing the individual student as the "circuit-breaker" in the process. Contrary to the District's repeated assertions that it has adopted a "hands-off" approach to the pregame invocation, the realities of the situation plainly reveal that its policy involves both perceived and actual endorsement of religion. In this case, as we found in *Lee,* the "degree of school involvement" makes it clear that the pregame prayers bear "the imprint of the State and thus put school-age children who objected in an untenable position." *Id.*, at 590....

In addition to involving the school in the selection of the speaker, the policy, by its terms, invites and encourages religious messages. The policy itself states that the purpose of the message is "to solemnize the event." A religious message is the most obvious method of solemnizing an event. Moreover, the requirements that the message "promote good sportsmanship" and "establish the appropriate environment for competition" further narrow the types of message deemed appropriate, suggesting that a solemn, yet nonreligious, message, such as commentary on United States foreign policy, would be prohibited. Indeed, the only type of message that is expressly endorsed in the text is an "invocation"—a term that primarily describes an appeal for divine assistance. In fact, as used in the past at Santa Fe High School, an "invocation" has always entailed a focused religious message. Thus, the expressed purposes of the policy encourage the selection of a religious message, and that is precisely how the students understand the policy. The results of the elections described in the parties' stipulation make it clear that the students understood that the central question before them was whether prayer should be a part of the pregame ceremony. We recognize the important role that public worship plays in many communities, as well as the sincere desire to include public prayer as a part of various occasions so as to mark those occasions' significance. But such religious activity in public schools, as elsewhere, must comport with the First Amendment.

The actual or perceived endorsement of the message, moreover, is established by factors beyond just the text of the policy. Once the student speaker is selected and the message composed, the invocation is then delivered to a large audience assembled as part of a regularly scheduled, school-sponsored function conducted on school property. The message is broadcast over the school's public address system, which remains subject to the control of school officials. It is fair to assume that the pregame ceremony is clothed in the traditional indicia of school sporting events, which generally include not just the team, but also cheerleaders and band members dressed in uniforms sporting the school name and mascot. The school's name is likely written in large print across the field and on banners and flags. The crowd will certainly include many who display the school colors and insignia on their school T-shirts, jackets, or hats and who may also be waving signs displaying the school name. It is in a setting such as this that "[t]he board has chosen to permit" the elected student to rise and give the "statement or invocation."

In this context the members of the listening audience must perceive the pregame message as a public expression of the views of the majority of the student body delivered with the approval of the school administration. In cases involving state participation in a religious activity, one of the relevant questions is "whether an objective observer, acquainted with the text, legislative history, and implementation of the statute, would perceive it as a state endorsement of prayer in public schools." Regardless of the listener's support for, or objection to, the message, an objective Santa Fe High School student will unquestionably perceive the inevitable pregame prayer as stamped with her school's seal of approval....

The delivery of such a message—over the school's public address system, by a speaker representing the student body, under the supervision of school faculty, and pursuant to a school policy that explicitly and implicitly encourages public prayer—is not properly characterized as "private" speech....

High school home football games are traditional gatherings of a school community; they bring together students and faculty as well as friends and family from years present and past to root for a common cause. Undoubtedly, the games are not important to some students, and they voluntarily choose not to attend. For many others, however, the choice between attending these games and avoiding personally offensive religious rituals is in no practical sense an easy one. The Constitution, moreover, demands that the school may not force this difficult choice upon these students for "[i]t is a tenet of the First Amendment that the State cannot require one of its citizens to forfeit his or her rights and benefits as the price of resisting conformance to state-sponsored religious practice."...

The Religion Clauses of the First Amendment prevent the government from making any law respecting the establishment of religion or prohibiting the free exercise thereof. By no means do these commands impose a prohibition on all religious activity in our public schools. Indeed, the common purpose of the Religion Clauses "is to secure religious liberty." Thus, nothing in the Constitution as interpreted by this Court prohibits any public school student from voluntarily praying at any time before, during, or after the school day. But the religious liberty protected by the Constitution is abridged when the State affirmatively sponsors the particular religious practice of prayer.

Notes and Comments

1. In *Santa Fe*, the Supreme Court clarifies that the Establishment Clause is violated when a state actor "sponsors" a religious practice or prayer but nothing in the U.S. Constitution prohibits a public school student from "voluntarily praying" during a school-sponsored activity. The Free Exercise clause of the First Amendment, which mandates that state actors "make no laws...prohibiting the free exercise [of religion]," protects individuals to act upon their religious beliefs. In *Menora v. Illinois High School Ass'n*, 683 F.2d 1030 (7th Cir. 1982), the court rejected a claim that a state high school athletic association's rule prohibiting student-athletes from wearing hats and other headwear (except for headbands) in basketball games violated the religious freedom of Orthodox Jews to wear yarmulkes while playing. The association's justification for upholding the headwear rule was for safety reasons. In *Walsh v.*

Louisiana High School Athletic Association, 616 F.2d 152 (5th Cir. 1980), the court rejected a claim that a state high school athletic association's transfer rule infringed the religious freedom of students to participate in athletics for a period of time after transferring to a Lutheran school. According to the court, the transfer rule on its face did not make a distinction between public and private (religious-based) schools and, therefore, the rule was religiously neutral and generally applicable.

2. In *Kennedy v. Bremerton School Dist.*, 597 U.S. ___ (2022), the Supreme Court found that a public high school football coach's rights under the Free Exercise and Free Speech Clauses of the First Amendment were violated when he was terminated by the Bremerton School District for kneeling at the 50-yard line and praying, often with players, for about 15 to 30 seconds after games. During the prayer, the coach would highlight his Christian faith, express gratitude for God protecting players' health and offer words of inspiration. A key question for the Court in addressing the coach's free speech claim was whether the coach offered his prayers in his capacity as a private citizen, or whether they amounted to government speech attributable to the District:

> [I]t seems clear to us that Mr. Kennedy has demonstrated that his speech was private speech, not government speech. When Mr. Kennedy uttered the three prayers that resulted in his suspension, he was not engaged in speech "ordinarily within the scope" of his duties as a coach. He did not speak pursuant to government policy. He was not seeking to convey a government-created message. He was not instructing players, discussing strategy, encouraging better on-field performance, or engaged in any other speech the District paid him to produce as a coach. Simply put: Mr. Kennedy's prayers did not "ow[e their] existence" to Mr. Kennedy's responsibilities as a public employee.
>
> The timing and circumstances of Mr. Kennedy's prayers confirm the point. During the postgame period when these prayers occurred, coaches were free to attend briefly to personal matters—everything from checking sports scores on their phones to greeting friends and family in the stands. We find it unlikely that Mr. Kennedy was fulfilling a responsibility imposed by his employment by praying during a period in which the District has acknowledged that its coaching staff was free to engage in all manner of private speech. That Mr. Kennedy offered his prayers when students were engaged in other activities like singing the school fight song further suggests that those prayers were not delivered as an address to the team, but instead in his capacity as a private citizen. Nor is it dispositive that Mr. Kennedy's prayers took place "within the office" environment—here, on the field of play. Instead, what matters is whether Mr. Kennedy offered his prayers while acting within the scope of his duties as a coach. And taken together, both the substance of Mr. Kennedy's speech and the circumstances surrounding it point to the conclusion that he did not. *Id.* at 17–18.

The Court distinguished *Santa Fe*:

> In *Santa Fe Independent School Dist. v. Doe*, the Court held that a school district violated the Establishment Clause by broadcasting a prayer "over the public address system" before each football game. 530 U. S. 290, 294 (2000). The Court observed that, while students generally were not required to attend games, attendance was required for "cheerleaders, members of the band, and, of course, the team members themselves." *Id.*, at 311. None of that is true here. The prayers for which Mr. Kennedy was disciplined were not publicly broadcast or recited to a captive audience. Students were not required or expected to participate. And, in fact, none of Mr. Kennedy's students did participate in any of the three October 2015 prayers that resulted in Mr. Kennedy's discipline.

3. Do student-athletes have a Free Exercise claim against a public school's mandate that they be vaccinated for COVID-19 in order to be eligible to participate in athletics? In a 2021 case involving college athletes at Western Michigan University, the university's vaccination mandate permitted medical or religious exemptions and accommodations on a discretionary basis. Sixteen student-athletes applied for religious exemptions, and the university ignored or denied their requests and barred them from participating in any team activities. The student-athletes sued the university. The district court preliminarily enjoined university officials from enforcing the vaccine mandate and the university appealed. Because the policy provides a mechanism for individualized religious exemptions and the university "retains discretion to extend exemption in whole or in part," the court of appeals determined the policy was not neutral and generally applicable and, therefore, likely violated the Free Exercise Clause. *See Dahl et al. v. Bd. of Trs. of W. Mich. Univ. et al.*, 15 F.4th 728 (6th Cir. 2021) (denying university's emergency motion to stay district court's order granting injunction in favor of student-athletes). The court's holding in this particular case would most likely be binding on similar actions taken by Michigan public high schools or the Michigan High School Athletic Association, as well as public high schools or athletic associations located in other states within the Sixth Circuit.

Capstone Problem

You are employed as an assistant director for compliance at the Oklanois State High School Athletic Association (OSHSAA). The OSHSAA is headquartered in the state capital and chartered under state law. An Oklanois statute provides, in pertinent part: "The OSHSAA is the official association of the state for the purpose of organizing and conducting athletic events, contests, and tournaments among schools and shall be responsible for the adoption and enforcement of rules relating to eligibility of athletes in schools for participation in interschool athletic events, contests and tournaments."

The Governor of Oklanois has publicly commented that she would like to see OSHSAA implement drug testing regulations for all high school student-athletes in the state: "As with many other states, we've seen an uptick in drug use, particularly in vapes. Vaping has just kind of taken over school districts. The point of a drug testing program would not be to punish but to connect parents with resources and to help students cope. A student athlete would have the ability to say I can't do that because I'm going be tested and that gives them another tool to deal with peer pressure."

The Governor's proposed plan is to make each district in the state responsible to randomly test 10% of the students who participate in athletics. The test would be a five-panel test that costs about $5. It tests for nicotine, THC, opioids, cocaine and methamphetamine. The test would be overseen by the districts' athletic trainer, who is hospital certified. If a student randomly tested positive, a school administrator would meet with the family and provide the student the option to take a drug information course. The student would also lose 25% of playing time for the season, but they could still be on the team and practice.

The executive director of OSHSAA has asked you to draft a memorandum addressing the following questions:

1. As a policy matter, do you support adoption of random drug testing regulations by OSHSAA and, if so, what should those regulations consist of?
2. If the OSHSAA adopted drug testing regulations, is OSHSAA constrained by the U.S. Constitution?
3. What issues does OSHSAA need to consider in order to avoid a claim that a student-athlete was denied procedural due process?
4. What issues does OSHSAA need to consider in order to avoid a claim that drug testing violates student-athletes' privacy rights under the Fourth Amendment?

Two

High School Athletics, Part II

Eligibility Rules

Learning Outcomes

- Understand the primary objectives for each of the high school eligibility rules.
- Understand situations that justify a waiver of enforcement of an eligibility rule based on the specific facts and circumstances or "hardship."
- Consider the circumstances under which a court should overrule a decision made by an athletic association.
- Identify the applicable constitutional claims brought by student-athletes to challenge eligibility rules and decisions.

Key Terms

- Equal Protection Clause
- Rational basis test
- Strict scrutiny
- Intermediate scrutiny
- Private association law
- Arbitrary and capricious

The social and scholastic benefit derived from participation in youth and high school sports is undeniable. Studies have shown a correlation between participation in high school athletics through the 12th grade and positive academic performance in the form of an increased 12th grade GPA and probability of being enrolled in college full time at age 21. As a result, the stated mission of state high school athletic associations is to promote the academic and social development of students, to make athletics an "integral part" of the overall educational program, and to provide the "opportunity" for boys and girls to represent their school and community. Schools and high school athletic associations have adopted numerous rules intended to promote these values.

When an association's rule impacts the eligibility of an athlete to compete, the athlete or the school's athletic director may request a "waiver" of enforcement of the rule based on the specific facts and circumstances. An athlete can also seek a waiver of a rule based on "hardship" if the athlete can make a sufficient showing that he or she meets any of the specified criteria for the granting of a hardship waiver. When waivers are denied by the association, sometimes athletes legally challenge the association's enforcement of the rules against them. As you read the various rules and the principal cases addressing the enforceability of those rules, consider two important questions. First, what are the primary objectives of the rule? In other words, what are the reasons typically cited in support of the rule? Second, how much deference should the courts and legislative bodies give to schools and associations to adopt and enforce whatever rules they want in order to accomplish those objectives? In other words, under what circumstances should a court intervene?

A. Age Rules

High school athletic associations have adopted "age rules" that prohibit athletes from participation in athletics once they reach a prescribed age. The typical limitation is 19 years old with a prescribed cutoff birthdate. *See Tiffany*, supra. In *Cruz v. Pennsylvania Interscholastic Athletic Association, Inc.*, 157 F. Supp. 2d 485 (E.D. Pa. 2001), the age rule provided, "[a] pupil shall be ineligible for interscholastic athletic competition upon attaining the age of nineteen years, with the following exception: If the age of 19 is attained on or after July 1, the pupil shall be eligible, age-wise, to compete through that school year."

The *Cruz* court articulated four purposes of the age rule: (1) to protect high school athletes of customary age from the dangers and unfairness of participation with those who are older and thus perhaps physically larger, stronger, and more mature and experienced; (2) to limit the possibility that the team with the overage student will gain an unfair competitive advantage over opponents; (3) to have available the maximum number of team positions for high school athletes who are of customary age for students in high school; and (4) to maintain uniformity of standards with regard to the age of participants.

According to the National Federation of State High School Associations (NFHS), an age limitation requirement "provides commonality between student-athletes and schools in interscholastic competition; inhibits 'redshirting'; allows the participation of younger and less experienced players; enhances the opportunity for more students to participate; promotes equality of competition; avoids over-emphasis on athletics; and helps to diminish the inherent risk of injury associated with participation in interscholastic athletics." NFHS 2021–22 Handbook, p. 21.

Do you find all of these purposes stated by the *Cruz* court and the NFHS compelling? Will all students who exceed the age limitation pose a safety risk to other students and have a competitive advantage over opponents? In all sports? Should there be a waiver provision for an age rule and, if so, what facts and circumstances would warrant a high school athletic association granting a waiver request?

B. Transfer Rules

Transfer rules generally provide that a student who transfers from one school to another school without a corresponding change of residence by the student's parents results in ineligibility for athletics at the new school for a prescribed number of days following the transfer. The enforcement of transfer rules has been legally challenged by athletes on grounds that the rule is being applied arbitrarily and capriciously or on constitutional grounds.

Indiana High School Athletic Association, Inc. v. Avant

650 N.E.2d 1164 (Ind. Ct. App. 1995)

The Indiana High School Athletic Association, Inc. (IHSAA) ruled that Bilal Avant (Avant) was ineligible to participate in varsity athletics at Roosevelt High School his senior year under the IHSAA's Transfer Rule. The trial court disagreed with the IHSAA's determination and issued a preliminary injunction enjoining the IHSAA from rendering Avant ineligible for any varsity team during the 1993/1994 basketball season. IHSAA appeals.

During the summer following his junior year in high school, Avant transferred from Andrean High School (Andrean), a private high school located in Merrillville, to Roosevelt High School (Roosevelt), a public high school in Gary. Avant's parents did not change their residence; rather, Avant moved from a private school to a public school located in the same school district. Avant played basketball and baseball at Andrean during 9th grade, 10th grade, and 11th grade. In fact, he played on the varsity teams in these sports his junior year, and he was characterized as an "outstanding" athlete and player. After transferring to Roosevelt, Avant hoped to continue participating in sports.

Both Andrean and Roosevelt are members of the IHSAA and are subject to the association's athletic eligibility rules. The primary purpose of the IHSAA Transfer Rule is to eliminate school jumping and recruitment. This rule provides, in substance, that a student who transfers to a member school with a change of residence by the student's parents will have immediate full (varsity) eligibility at the new school. However, a transfer without an accompanied move by parents will result in ineligibility during the first 365 days following transfer, unless the student qualifies under a listed exception. The rules also provide for limited (junior-varsity) eligibility when a student transfers without a corresponding change of residence by the parents. On the contrary, a student who transfers for "primarily athletic reasons" will be ineligible for all athletics for the first 365 days after enrollment at the new school. The IHSAA Hardship Rule mediates the harsh effects of the eligibility rules in limited situations.

Avant completed a Transfer Report as required by the IHSAA Rules. The IHSAA Executive Committee then held a hearing on November 12, 1993 to determine Avant's eligibility for interscholastic sports. The committee's written decision found that Avant was ineligible for varsity athletics during the 1993/1994 school year. Not only did he fail to qualify for full eligibility under the IHSAA rules, Avant also failed to establish that application of the Transfer Rule to him constituted an undue hardship. The committee granted Avant limited eligibility to participate in junior-varsity athletics at Roosevelt....

We find disposition of this issue, however, to be governed by *Haas v. South Bend Community School Corporation* (1972), 259 Ind. 515, 289 N.E.2d 495. In *Haas*, our supreme court... indicated that a student cannot be arbitrarily denied the opportunity to qualify to participate in inter-scholastic athletic competition. *Haas*, 289 N.E.2d at 497. Thus, the IHSAA's decisions are reviewable under the arbitrary and capricious standard.

The IHSAA next contends that it did not act arbitrarily and capriciously when it denied Avant full eligibility for interscholastic athletics after he transferred from Andrean to Roosevelt. Avant does not contest the finding that his actions violated the Transfer Rule, thus rendering him ineligible for varsity athletics. Instead, he argues that using his technical violation of the rule to disqualify him is arbitrary and capricious since he was not recruited by Roosevelt and the basis for his decision to transfer was financial and personal hardship rather than athletics.

The motivation behind Avant's transfer to Roosevelt was a factual issue before the IHSAA. The Court of Appeals will not judge the credibility of witnesses or weigh evidence that was before the IHSAA on factual issues. Therefore, we will affirm the IHSAA's factual determinations if supported by substantial evidence of probative value.

The IHSAA determined that while the evidence was inconclusive to prove Avant's transfer was primarily for athletic purposes, the evidence sufficiently established athletics as a factor.

The IHSAA noted that Avant did not mention financial hardship when leaving Andrean or on his Transfer Report. Moreover, Avant did not follow up on the Andrean athletic director's offer to help Avant secure employment or available financial aid. Evidence indicated that Avant had disagreements with the Andrean basketball coach, as he did with all his coaches, and that he "had to put up with" the coaches' philosophy for three years. Before learning he could not play on the junior-varsity team, Avant's decision to transfer was attributed to his being unhappy at Andrean.

The IHSAA concluded that Avant did not qualify for relief under the IHSAA Hardship Rule. This rule gives the IHSAA authority to set aside the effect of any rule when:

a. Strict enforcement of the Rule in the particular case will not serve to accomplish the purpose of the Rule;
b. The spirit of the Rule has not been violated; and
c. There exists in the particular case circumstances showing an undue hardship which would result from enforcement of the Rule.

The general consideration section of the hardship rule contains the following language:

> Likewise, a change in financial condition of the student or a student's family may be considered a hardship, however, such conditions or changes in conditions must be permanent, substantial and significantly beyond the control of the student or the student's family.

While the IHSAA noted that attending Andrean did create a hardship on Avant's family, this financial hardship had existed since Avant's freshman year. Furthermore, the IHSAA found no change in the family's circumstances which would cause an undue hardship. Substantial evidence of probative value supported the IHSAA's factual determination that Avant was ineligible for varsity athletics due to his transfer. The IHSAA's decision was not arbitrary or capricious.

[After concluding that the IHSAA engages in state action subject to judicial review in making and enforcing its rules, the court of appeals addressed whether the application of the Transfer Rule to Avant constituted a violation of privileges or immunities under Art. I § 23 of the Indiana Constitution.]

On November 28, 1994, the Indiana Supreme Court affirmed the decision of the full Workers' Compensation Board of Indiana that the statutory agricultural exemption to the Indiana Workers' Compensation Act did not violate Art. I § 23. *Collins v. Day*, 644 N.E.2d 72, 82 (Ind. 1994). In doing so, the court held that claims under Art. I § 23 should be interpreted and applied independently from federal equal protection analysis. *Id.* at 75. The court articulated two requirements which must be met by legislation granting unequal privileges or immunities in order to withstand constitutional scrutiny: (1) the classification must be based upon distinctive, inherent characteristics which rationally distinguish the unequally treated class, and the disparate treatment accorded by the legislation must be reasonably related to such distinguishing characteristics; and (2) the classification must be open to any and all persons who share the inherent characteristics which distinguish and justify the classification, with the special treatment accorded to any particular classification extended equally to all such persons. *Id.* at 79. In applying this two-part standard, courts must accord considerable deference to the manner in which the legislature has balanced the competing interests involved. *Id.* at 79–80.

We first address whether the treatment of transfer students without a corresponding change of residence by their parents separately from students transferring with a change of residence by their parents is a classification based upon distinctive, inherent characteristics and, if so, whether the unequal treatment is reasonably related to such distinguishing characteristics. The Transfer Rule is designed to eliminate school jumping and recruitment of student athletes. Transfers not accompanied by a change in residence (or falling outside the thirteen exceptions) are suspect in that they are subject to substantial manipulation. The Transfer Rule deters unscrupulous students and parents from manufacturing all sorts of reasons for a transfer, thereby thinly disguising athletically motivated transfers. The distinctions between these classifications are reasonably related to achieving the IHSAA's purpose in deterring school jumping and recruitment.

Furthermore, we find that the Transfer Rule applies equally to all persons similarly situated. If a student transferring without a change in residence by his/her parents does not fit one of the thirteen listed exceptions or qualify as an "undue hardship," then the student is ineligible for varsity athletics.

We conclude that application of the two-part standard reveals no violation of Art. I § 23 in the present case.

Conclusion

We conclude that the trial court erred by enjoining the IHSAA from rendering Avant ineligible to participate in varsity athletics at Roosevelt. Although the court had jurisdiction to review the IHSAA's decision concerning Avant's eligibility, the IHSAA did not act arbitrarily or capriciously in granting Avant only limited eligibility. Moreover, the IHSAA's actions did not constitute a violation of privileges or immunities under the Indiana Constitution.

HOFFMAN, J. and DARDEN, J. concur.

Notes and Comments

1. The holding in *Avant* is consistent with other courts that have considered challenges to high school transfer rules. *See, e.g., Robbins v. Indiana High School Athletic Ass'n*, 941 F. Supp. 786 (S.D. Ind. 1996) (transfer rule does not violate constitution even where transfer motivated by religious conversion); *Jordan v. O'Fallon Township High School Dist.*, 706 N.E.2d 137 (Ill. App. Ct. 1999); *Fusato v. Washington Interscholastic Activities Ass'n*, 970 P.2d 774 (Wash. Ct. App. 1999) (narrow construction against foreign exchange student of hardship exception on transfer eligibility violates equal protection); and *Indiana High School Athletic Ass'n v. Carlberg*, 694 N.E.2d 222 (Ind. 1997) (transfer rule advances legitimate association interest).

2. According to the *Avant* court, the purpose of the transfer rule is to eliminate school jumping and recruitment of student athletes. Why is "school jumping" and recruitment a problem or concern? Do transfer rules serve any other purpose? *See Indiana High School Athletic Ass'n v. Carlberg*, 694 N.E.2d 222 (Ind. 1997) (court found that transfer rule's objectives of preserving the integrity of interscholastic athletics as

well as preventing recruiting and school transfers for athletics reasons are legitimate). *See also* NFHS 2021–22 Handbook, p. 22 (a transfer rule "assists in the prevention of students switching schools in conjunction with the change of athletic season for athletic purposes, impairs recruitment, and reduces the opportunity for undue influence to be exerted by persons seeking to benefit from a student-athlete's prowess").

3. As the *Tiffany* case in Chapter 1 demonstrates, an association must follow its own rules and a court will intervene when the association fails or refuses to do so. For a similar holding in a case involving a challenge to a transfer rule, see *Mississippi High Sch. Activities Ass'n v. R.T.*, 163 So. 3d 274, 2015 Miss. LEXIS 229 (Miss. 2015) ("[w]hile it generally is true that high school students have no legally protected right to participate in high school athletics, once a school decides to create a sports program and establish eligibility rules, the school—or as in this case, MHSAA—has a duty to follow those rules; and it may be held accountable when it does not do so").

4. In *Carlberg*, the athlete claimed that application of the transfer rule violated his constitutional rights under the Equal Protection Clause of the Fourteenth Amendment of the U.S. Constitution. In rejecting this claim, the court held that "[a]bsent a burden upon the exercise of a constitutionally protected right (none is at stake here) or creation of a suspect class (none is alleged here), the general standard of review of state action challenged under the equal protection clause is the rational basis test." The court concluded that the transfer rule is rationally related to achieving its goals and objectives. *See* Note 2, *supra*.

5. State constitutions may provide the athlete more protection in terms of rights (*e.g.*, equal protection, free speech, privacy, etc.) than that offered under the federal constitution. In *Avant*, the Indiana state constitution was interpreted as providing greater protection to the athlete than what is afforded under the Equal Protection Clause of the Fourteenth Amendment of the U.S. Constitution.

C. "No-Pass, No-Play" Rules

All state high school athletic associations have an eligibility rule that conditions athletic participation on students achieving passing grades. Their intended goals are to further academic objectives and strike an appropriate balance between athletics and academics. Academic eligibility requirements, often referred to as "no-pass, no-play" rules, may impose a requirement that athletes maintain a minimum grade point average, *e.g.*, a 2.0 GPA, or that athletes maintain passing grades in most of their classes.

It is debatable whether no-pass, no-play rules actually achieve their intended goals of furthering academic objectives, in particular that students participating in athletics will achieve better academic performance. Proponents of these rules argue that maintaining athletics eligibility provides a valuable incentive for students to satisfy minimum academic standards and that athletics participation is a privilege.

Opponents assert that these rules discriminate against students who struggle academically and the rules can cause more students to pursue academic courses that are easier to pass. For some students, athletics participation provides an added incentive to stay in school and graduate and taking athletics away from them for failing to maintain a minimum grade point average could lead them to drop out of school. *See* NFHS 2021–22 Handbook, p. 22 (academic standards "encourage appropriate academic performance and allow the use of interscholastic participation as a motivator for improved classroom performance").

Courts have consistently denied legal challenges to no-pass, no-play rules. Thus, state high school athletic associations are free to adopt these rules and determine the precise terms. An institution or school district may create more, but not less, stringent standards. For example, a school district could increase the required GPA but not decrease it.

Review the academic eligibility requirement in your state. As a high school coach, discuss whether you would be in favor of the state high school athletic association revising the rule to create more or less stringent standards.

D. Homeschool Rules

All 50 states permit homeschooling as a K-12 instructional option. According to the U.S. Census Bureau, national rates of homeschooled students grew rapidly from 1999 to 2012 and had since remained steady at about 3.3 percent. Homeschooling rates then significantly increased during the COVID-19 pandemic. In the fall of 2020, 11.1 percent of households with school-age children reported homeschooling, representing a doubling of U.S. households that were homeschooling at the start of the 20202021 school year compared to the prior year.

Given the growth of the homeschool movement in the United States, an important policy question is whether homeschooled students should be permitted by state high school athletic associations to participate in athletics. According to the National Federation of State High School Associations, approximately 30 state high school athletic associations allow homeschooled students to play sports at their local public school and about one-third of these states either require students to be enrolled at the public school part-time and taking some classes, or each school district must approve its own policy. Some of these states require homeschooled students to meet the equivalent academic standards as enrolled students. The 20 high school athletic associations that bar homeschooled students from participating in athletics require students to "attend" the school, be enrolled "full time," or be "bona fide" students of the school. For example, the Michigan High School Athletic Association (MHSAA) provides that a student may only play for the school they are enrolled in; enrolled means the student is (a) on the school records receiving active credit for at least 66% of full credit load potential for a full time student and (b) in attendance for one or more classes.

The decision whether to allow homeschooled students to participate in athletics at their local public school raises an ethical dilemma. Is it fair to deny them participation when their families pay taxes that fund the public schools just like families of public school students? Is it fair for them to take team positions away from regularly enrolled students? What educational message is sent when it is acceptable for them to play sports with, but not go to school with, other students? In states that require homeschooled students to meet the equivalent academic standards of regular students, how does a state high school athletic association ensure or verify that each homeschooled student has actually met those standards?

Courts for the most part have upheld state high school athletic association rules that bar homeschooled students from athletics participation. In *Jones v. West Virginia State Board of Education*, 622 S.E.2d 289 (W. Va. 2005), the West Virginia Supreme Court held that the West Virginia Secondary School Activities Commission's (WVSSAC) total ban on allowing homeschooled children to participate in interscholastic athletics did not violate their equal protection. According to the court, participation is neither a fundamental nor a constitutional right under the West Virginia constitution and the exclusion of homeschooled students is rationally related to a legitimate state interest because the rule (1) promotes academics over athletics and (2) protects the economic interests of the county school systems. With respect to the first justification, the court found that homeschooled students and enrolled students are graded on different standards, which would impose a burden on the school district to convert the grades and impede the ability of school officials to maintain the academic standards required for participation in athletics. With respect to the second justification, money is apportioned to counties based on class attendance and, therefore, it would create a financial burden on the county school system to support homeschooled students for whom no funds are allocated. The court also held that the rule is not arbitrary and capricious because it is rationally related to these two legitimate state purposes.

Similarly, in *Reid v. Kenowa Hills Public Schools*, 680 N.W.2d 62 (Mich. App. 2004), the Michigan Court of Appeals held that children who are not enrolled in high school have no fundamental right to participate in athletic activities, which is a privilege, not a right. Accordingly, the MHSAA's enrollment requirement did not violate the rights of non-enrolled students, who were homeschooled by their parents, to freely practice their religion and did not violate their equal protection rights.

E. Outside Competition Rules

Most state high school athletic associations have adopted some variation of a rule that limits or prohibits competition in a sport operated by teams other than the high school team (*i.e.*, club teams). According to the NFHS, a restriction on non-school athletic participation:

- protects students who choose to participate on their schools' athletic teams from exploitation by those who seek to capitalize on their skill and/or reputation;
- avoids risks incident to participation in non-school athletic programs that may have inadequate administrative oversight;
- discourages outside entities from pressuring student-athletes to miss classes while competing on non-school teams or in non-school events;
- equalizes competition by reducing any unfair advantage of students who participate in non-school athletics may have over those who do not participate in outside events;
- reduces distractions from academic preparation and other school responsibilities;
- provides some control over the trend towards year-round competitive sports seasons; and
- reduces, or even eliminates, conflicts which may arise due to: (1) time conflicts of practices, games, and playoffs, (2) differing coaching philosophies of the school coaching staff and the non-school coaching staff, and (3) team loyalty.

NFHS 2021–22 Handbook, p. 22.

In the next case, a high school swimmer sought to prevent the state high school athletic association from enforcing an outside competition rule that prohibited students from competing on both a school and non-school team *in the same sport* during the *school team's season.*

Letendre v. Missouri State High School Activities Assn.

86 S.W.3d 63 (Mo. App. 2002)

Claire Letendre seeks to enjoin the Missouri State High School Activities Association (MSHSAA) from enforcing by-law 235, which prohibits students from competing on both a school and a non-school team in the same sport during the school team's season. The trial court denied Claire's request for injunctive relief and dismissed her suit with prejudice. She appeals, claiming that the association's rule violates the Equal Protection clause of the Fourteenth Amendment and her rights of free association under the First Amendment. We affirm.

The MSHSAA is a voluntary association of 750 secondary public, private and parochial schools in Missouri. It is charged with developing uniform and equitable standards of eligibility for students and schools to participate in interscholastic activities. The rules ostensibly work to avoid interference with the educational program of the school by outside activities; to prevent exploitation of high school youth and the programs of member schools by special interest groups; and to provide a means of evaluating and controlling local, state, and national contests affecting secondary schools. The association is governed by a Constitution and by-laws adopted by its members. Claire's high school, St. Joseph's Academy, is a member of the MSHSAA.

At the time of trial, Claire was a 15 year-old sophomore earning good grades. She did not participate in any school-sponsored sports, clubs, student government, or organized activities, other than a prayer group, because she "loves to swim." Claire has been a member of the private Parkway Swim Club since the age of three, swimming in competitive meets since the age of five. She practices and competes with the private swim club team all year long, participating in regional and national meets that require out-of-state travel. Her swim club's practice schedule is Monday through Friday from 4:30 to 7:30 p.m. and on Saturdays from 6:15 to 9:30 a.m., swimming from 5,000 to 9,000 yards daily. Claire testified that her coach at the Parkway Swim Club enters her in every single event offered during her swim club seasons. Claire claimed her short-term goal is to qualify for the Senior Nationals and, ultimately, the Olympics.

On January 31, 2001, Claire attended a meeting for students interested in joining the school swim team. They discussed health forms, practice times, the season schedule and MSHSAA eligibility rules. On February 12, 2001, Claire attended another school swim team meeting held immediately prior to the first practice. Claire testified that after this meeting she knew she would become ineligible for school swimming if she chose to swim with the club team.

By-law 235(1)(a) provides that "during the sport season a student... shall neither practice nor compete as a member of a non-school team nor as an individual participant in organized non-school competition in that same sport."

The by-laws state that a school sports season begins with the "first practice." Unlike other St. Joseph Academy students who also swam for Parkway Swim Club, Claire chose to practice with her swim club team rather than her school team.

Claire filed suit for injunctive relief to bar the MSHSAA from enforcing by-law 235, claiming it violated her rights under the First and Fourteenth Amendments. After a trial on the merits, the court entered judgment, denying Claire injunctive relief and dismissing her suit with prejudice. Claire now appeals....

The power of a court to review the quasi-judicial actions of a voluntary association is limited to determining: (1) whether there are inconsistencies between the association's charter and by-laws and any action taken in respect to them; (2) whether the member has been treated unfairly, i.e., denied notice, hearing, or an opportunity to defend; (3) whether the association undertakings were prompted by malice, fraud or collusion; and (4) whether the charter or by-laws contravene public policy or law.

Courts have no power to usurp the function of the tribunals of [voluntary] associations, [like the MSHSAA] and can interfere only when those tribunals proceed without evidence or in bad faith or violate a valid part of the constitution and rules in dealing with a member, or attempt to enforce against him, to his injury, invalid provisions thereof. It is only upon the clearest showing that the rules have been violated by a decision of the association's tribunal that courts should intercede. *Id.*

Claire agrees that the Association has acted consistently with its rules, given her due process and did not act out of malice. But instead argues that by-law 235 is against public policy because it is arbitrary, capricious and violates her Constitutional rights to equal protection and free association as guaranteed by the Fourteenth Amendment of the United States Constitution.

The specific inequity she claims is that by-law 235 is internally inconsistent in that it does not affect those who wish to participate in non-athletic activities both in and outside of school; it does not affect those who participate in one sport in school and another sport outside of school; and it does not apply to athletes who participate in national or Olympic development competitions during a sport season. She maintains that the prohibition of simultaneous same-sport competition is irrational and unrelated to any legitimate goal of the association and asks us to declare by-law 235 unconstitutional as applied to her.

The Fourteenth Amendment guarantees that no person shall be denied equal protection of the law. It assures all individuals fair treatment if fundamental rights are at stake. It also eliminates distinctions based on impermissible criteria such as race, age, religion, or gender. Where there is no suspect classification or impingement on a fundamental right explicitly or implicitly protected by the U.S. Constitution, Equal Protection claims are reviewed by this Court under the "rational relationship" standard....

Claire's claim is not based upon a suspect classification, such as race, religion, national origin, or gender. Nor is it based upon a claim that her fundamental rights were violated, because she recognizes there is no fundamental right to play high school athletics. Accordingly, our inquiry is confined to whether there is a "rational relationship" between by-law 235 and any legitimate interest of the MSHSAA.

The Eighth Circuit has addressed a similar argument to the one Claire raises here. In *In re United States ex rel. Missouri State High School Activities Assn.*, three students alleged the MSHSAA transfer rule violated the Equal Protection Clause because it did not apply to "non-athletic activities." The transfer rule prohibited students who transferred from participating in interscholastic athletics for 365 days, but imposed no restriction on non-athletic activities. The court held that the transfer rule was a reasonable and neutral regulation that did not burden the choice of private education, but merely attached a restriction to all transfers, except those falling into a specific exception. The court found no violations of the federal Constitution, concluding that:

> A rational basis clearly exists for believing that the danger of incurring the harms involved in [the rule's subject matter] is greater than the danger of parallel harms in other areas. Once a rational relationship exists and it exists here,

> judicial scrutiny must cease. Whether the rule is wise or creates undue individual hardship are policy decisions better left to legislative and administrative bodies and schools themselves are by far the better agencies to devise rules and restrictions governing their extracurricular activities.

We have reviewed the history of the MSHSAA non-school competition standard. Since 1959 the rule has been reconsidered and modified fifteen times. The express purpose of these reconsiderations and modifications is to create standards that purport to serve the largest number of students. At trial the Executive Director of the MSHSAA identified several reasons for the adoption of by-law 235, including: (1) preventing or reducing interference with a school's academic program; (2) preventing interference with athletic programs by organized non-school athletics; (3) promoting and protecting competitive equity; (4) avoiding conflicts in coaching philosophy and scheduling; and (5) encouraging students not to overemphasize athletic competition.

The director of the MSHSAA testified that the association's 76 years of experience allowed them to conclude that the potential for harm is not as great in activities such as music, speech, debate and academics as in extracurricular sports. The Association has made, however, an exception for Olympic competitors because it is required by federal law. The Amateur Sports Act of 1978 allows Olympic competitors to participate in interscholastic competitions, but gives organizations such as MSHSAA exclusive jurisdiction over such competitions. The Amateur Sports Act also requires that national sports organizations minimize conflicts in scheduling of all practices and competitions through coordination with organizations such as the MSHSAA. The National Federation of State High School Associations, including the MSHSAA, pledged to enact limited exceptions to their non-school participation restrictions to accommodate the national objectives reflected in The Amateur Sports Act. All state associations have an exception similar to this.

The issue for us, then, is not whether we agree with the Association, but whether the challenged rule bears a rational relationship to a reasonable goal of the MSHSAA. A rule of a quasi-judicial voluntary association "will not be set aside if any state of facts reasonably may be conceived to justify it." If the classification has some "reasonable basis" it does not offend the Constitution simply because "in practice it results in some inequality." We conclude that there are reasonable grounds for by-law 235 because a reasonable person could believe that a legitimate goal of the Association is furthered by the rule....

Since its inception 75 years ago, the MSHSAA has received a mandate to value the best interests of all student athletes. In 1975, the Association identified outside competition during the school year as one of the "principal areas of problems facing high schools and state associations." A reasonable person could conclude that it is not in the best interest of the majority of high school students to compete in the same sport at the same time on two different teams, with different coaches, different rules, different practice schedules, and different competition schedules. The Executive Director of MSHSAA explained that one purpose of the Association is to have standards that will be in the best interest of the larger number of high school students. Here there is substantial evidence to conclude that by-law 235 is rationally related to the legitimate goal of protecting that interest. Claire's Equal Protection argument must fail.

[The Court rejected Claire's Free Association argument.]

While we might personally believe that a better rule could be drafted, one that would allow a student athlete who is getting good grades, such as Claire, to compete simultaneously on both her school and non-school swim teams, the law does not permit us to interject our personal beliefs in the name of the Constitution. Claire's constitutional challenges must fail because by-law 235 is rationally related to the MSHSAA's purpose of drafting rules that protect the welfare of the greatest number of high school athletes possible. The judgment of the trial court is, therefore, affirmed.

Notes and Comments

1. *Letendre* shows how relatively easy it is for a state high school athletic association to satisfy a rational basis test. The court accepted the MSHSAA's multiple reasons for adopting its outside competition rule and did not require the MSHSAA to provide any evidence whatsoever to support any of them. The court ruled that Claire Letendre's constitutional challenges must fail because the MSHSAA's outside competition rule "is rationally related to the MSHSAA's purpose of drafting rules that protect the welfare of the greatest number of high school athletes possible." Do you agree with the court that the rule protects the welfare of the greatest number of high school athletes possible? If the court had ruled in favor of Claire Letendre and enjoined the enforcement of MSHSAA's outside competition rule, do you think the high school athletic teams in the state of Missouri would suffer as a result? If so, in what way specifically?

2. Claire Letendre argued that MSHSAA's outside competition rule is "internally inconsistent in that it does not affect those who wish to participate in non-athletic activities both in and outside of school; it does not affect those who participate in one sport in school and another sport outside of school; and it does not apply to athletes who participate in national or Olympic development competitions during a sport season." Go back and read the five reasons that the Executive Director of the MSHSAA identified for the adoption of the outside competition rule. Does Claire have a good point?

3. Some states have adopted an outside competition rule that applies only to certain sports. Look up the outside competition rule of the high school athletic association in your state. What is the scope of the rule? Would you recommend any revisions?

F. Amateurism Rules

Maori Davenport, one of the nation's top basketball prospects at Charles Henderson High School in Alabama, was ruled ineligible by the Alabama High School Athletic Association (AHSAA) for her senior season over an $867.20 stipend check she received from USA Basketball when she played at a summer youth tournament in Mexico City in 2018. USA Basketball made the payment without first verifying whether it violated the amateurism rules of the AHSAA. Maori's family deposited the check. Three months later, after learning the payment violated AHSAA rules, they self-reported the violation and repaid the money to USA Basketball. Nevertheless, the AHSAA said any violation of its amateurism rules carried an automatic one-year suspension, which would have ended Maori's high school career. In addition, Charles Henderson High School, the defending Class 5A champion, was ordered by the AHSAA to forfeit its first four games. After Maori's appeal was rejected by the AHSAA, her parents filed a lawsuit against the AHSAA to get her eligibility restored. While drawing support from around the nation, including ESPN basketball analyst Jay Bilas, an Alabama judge granted an emergency motion that allowed her to play while the court considered her lawsuit against the AHSAA.

All state high school athletic associations have adopted rules pertaining to amateur status and awards. Generally, anything done for an athlete that is not done in the same fashion for non-athletes in the school is likely going to result in a violation of amateur status. According to the NFHS, an amateur/awards limitation "promotes amateurism, stimulates participation for the sake of the game itself, prevents exploitation of students, and encourages students to engage in athletic competition for physical, mental and social benefits." NFHS 2021–22 Handbook, p. 23. The Michigan High School Athletic Association 2021–22 Handbook (Summary) states:

> **Amateur Status and Awards**— Participation in school sports is limited to students who are amateurs—to those who have not received money or valuable consideration for involvement with one of the sports that the MHSAA sponsors a tournament in. Amateurs can't sign a pro hockey contract and then play high school baseball. Amateurs can't receive cash, gift certificates, scholarships to camp, or discounts (including those from sporting goods companies). Amateurs can't receive uniforms or equipment for participation in high school sports, nor keep school issued items (they can purchase at season's end for fair/current market value). The amateur's family can't accept these prohibited items in their place. Amateurs can't pose in school uniform to endorse a commercial product. The rule allows for meals, travel, and lodging to be accepted if in kind, not cash to buy food, but the actual meal is OK. The awards provision has a $40 cap for **symbolic** awards not including engraving which is often confused with a **cash** limit of $40. Never can a student-athlete receive cash, merchandise or gift certificates for participation in an MHSAA sponsored sport.

A large number of extreme sports athletes are teenagers and they have lucrative sponsorship deals with skateboard and snowboard companies, which raises the question whether high school athletic associations should prohibit athletes participating in high school athletics from seeking the same opportunities. After the passage of state laws governing the rights of college athletes to receive payments from third parties for the commercial use of their names, images, and likenesses in product and service endorsements and sponsorships, some states adopted similar laws pertaining to high school athletes. In your view, is there a compelling reason to treat college and high school athletes differently with respect to name, image, and likeness rights?

G. Grooming Rules and Good Conduct Rules

Schools, districts, and coaches have broad disciplinary authority when students engage in inappropriate behavior or conduct in violation of school or team rules. Rules that govern personal appearance and grooming, for example a clean-shaven rule or a hair-length policy or a dress code, often raise First Amendment claims based on the right of free expression. Most of the lawsuits challenging personal appearance and grooming rules were brought during the late 1960s and early 1970s. The seminal case on the topic is *Tinker v. Des Moines Independent Community Sch. Dist.*, 393 U.S. 503 (1969), referenced in the cheerleader speech case, *Mahanoy Area Sch. Dist. v. B.L.* (discussed in Chapter 1). In *Tinker*, the Supreme Court ruled that a public school's dress code prohibiting students from wearing black armbands violated the students' First Amendment rights. The Supreme Court said schools have a special interest in regulating speech only when it "materially disrupts classwork or involves substantial disorder or invasion of the rights of others."

Appearance and grooming rules have been upheld in court, for the most part, on the ground that such rules are a reasonable means of furthering the school's "undeniable interest in teaching hygiene, instilling discipline, asserting authority, and compelling uniformity." *Davenport v. Randolph County Bd. of Educ.*, 730 F.2d 1395, 1397 (11th Cir. 1984). In *Davenport*, students sought an injunction to prevent a school board from refusing to allow the students to participate in athletics unless they complied with a coach's "clean shaven" policy for football and basketball team members. The plaintiffs objections to the grooming code were based on a concern that shaving would cause them skin problems, however, no evidence was presented to the court or the school board that the plaintiffs themselves would be likely to suffer from such problems, and the coach of the football and basketball teams testified that he would not enforce the policy if it would have injurious results. However, hair length policies have been successfully challenged on the basis of free expression and gender discrimination. *See, e.g.*, *Holsapple v. Woods*, 500 F.2d 49, 52 (7th Cir. 1974)("Defendants have fallen far short of showing that poor discipline and lower grades are caused by hair length in violation of the school standard and are 'so aggravated, so frequent, so general, and so persistent that this invasion of student's individual freedom by the state is warranted.'"). In *Hayden v. Greensburg Community School Corp.*, 743 F.3d 569 (7th Cir. 2014), a case involving a challenge to a hair length policy on the basis of gender discrimination, the court stated:

> The Haydens plainly have made out a prima facie case of discrimination. The hair-length policy applies only to male athletes, and there is no facially apparent reason why that should be so. Girls playing interscholastic basketball have the same need as boys do to keep their hair out of their eyes, to subordinate individuality to team unity, and to project a positive image. Why, then, must only members of the boys team wear their hair short? Given the obvious disparity, the policy itself gives rise to an inference of discrimination. *Id.* at 580.

But see Long v. Zopp, 476 F.2d 180 (4th Cir. 1973) (limitation on hair length reasonable, but only during the playing season and only for health and safety reasons).

Good conduct rules prohibit certain behavior deemed inappropriate or illegal for high school age students, such as use of alcohol, drugs, and tobacco or behavior that violates community norms. The *in loco parentis* doctrine generally gives schools and coaches wide discretion to impose discipline on student-athletes for inappropriate conduct that takes place on school grounds or off-campus during team travel because the school has a legitimate interest in regulating such behavior. In the following case, a high school principal declared a wrestler ineligible to participate in the sectional, district, and state wrestling tournaments after hearing about the wrestler's alleged behavior at a party in his home.

Brands v. Sheldon Community School

671 F. Supp. 627 (N.D. Iowa 1987)

The plaintiff is a student at Sheldon Community High School. As a member of his school's wrestling team, he has amassed a nearly perfect record in four years of competition, and is a defending state champion. His performance and the equally outstanding performance of his twin brother have attracted the attention of the state media and college coaches, and each brother hopes to attend college on a wrestling scholarship.

The events leading to this decision began on January 25, 1987. The plaintiff has been understandably reluctant to give his account of what took place at his home that day, but the Sheldon Community School Board ultimately concluded that the plaintiff "as well as three other male youths engaged in multiple acts of sexual intercourse with a sixteen-year-old female student of the Sheldon Community School District...." The Court makes no judgment as to whether a preponderance of the evidence, clear and convincing evidence, or evidence beyond a reasonable doubt supports this finding.

As rumors about this incident spread throughout Sheldon Community High School, Principal David Kapfer began an investigation and interviewed the plaintiff and other parties rumored to have been involved. On February 4, the plaintiff and his mother were sent letters from Kapfer declaring the plaintiff ineligible for the remainder of the wrestling season. These letters stated that he "committed a breach of discipline by engaging in conduct which interfered with the maintenance of school discipline and by engaging in behavior which was antagonistic to the rights of (name redacted) to attain her education." The letters further stated that he violated Section III of the Discipline Policy because his conduct on January 25 was "detrimental to the best interests of the Sheldon Community School District." In a section of the letter to the plaintiff, Kapfer stated that the plaintiff's conduct "was a breach of discipline in that you: 1) engaged in bullying behavior; 2) committed an assault on (same name) in that you took acts against her resulting in physical contact which was insulting and offensive and which caused her emotional injury; 3) willfully injured (same name) by doing an unjustified act causing her serious emotional and mental injury; and 4) participated in multiple acts of sexual intercourse involving (same name) which took place on January 25, 1987." The Court makes no judgment as to whether a preponderance of the evidence, clear and convincing evidence, or evidence beyond a reasonable doubt supports these charges.

The period of ineligibility declared by the principal included the dates of the sectional, district and state wrestling tournaments. Thus, any reinstatement which would preserve the plaintiff's chance to again become a state champion would have to occur before 8:30 a.m. on February 14, when weigh-ins would take place for the sectional tournament.

Following an appeal to Superintendent Jerry Peterson on February 5, Peterson sent letters to the plaintiff and his mother affirming the principal's decision which were nearly identical to the February 4 letters. These letters were dated February 9. On February 10, the plaintiff and his mother requested a closed hearing before the School Board which began Thursday morning, February 12, and ended late that night. The Board deliberated for several hours on February 12 and 13 before reaching a decision which affirmed the administration's decision. Extensive findings of fact were made by the Board. The complaint and motions presently before this Court were filed within three hours of the Board's decision.

It became clear at this Court's February 13 hearing that the Court could not fairly consider all of the evidence admitted in time to fully resolve this matter prior to weigh-ins. This dilemma significantly increased the risk of irreparable harm, and for this reason, the Court entered a temporary restraining order which permitted the plaintiff to compete and advance in the sectional tournament. The TRO expired at the beginning of the February 16 hearing....

The plaintiff asserts that he has been deprived of five constitutional rights—his Fourteenth Amendment rights to equal protection, substantive due process and procedural due process, his Eighth Amendment right to be free from cruel and unusual punishment, and his Sixth Amendment right to counsel. The equal protection claim must be rejected because the plaintiff has not alleged that he was treated differently because of his race, ethnicity, gender, or any other suspect classification, and his interests in wrestling or receiving a college scholarship are not among the small set of rights fundamental enough to warrant separate protection under the equal protection clause. Likewise, the Eighth Amendment claim must be rejected because school discipline does not implicate Eighth Amendment concerns.... Because the Constitution limits the scope of Sixth Amendment rights to "all criminal prosecutions," U.S. Const. Amend. VI, that argument must be rejected. If any rights were violated, they can only be substantive or procedural due process rights.

Procedural Due Process

[The Court first found that the plaintiff was not deprived of a protected liberty or property interest under the Constitution.]

Even if this Court were to recognize a protected interest in participation, the Court is satisfied that the plaintiff received all process due to him. The plaintiff and his mother were notified of the charges against him and were told of opportunities for appeal. The plaintiff was given an opportunity to explain his side of the story to the principal prior to the suspension. He was given a five- to six-hour evidentiary hearing within ten days of the initial suspension, which was also early enough to permit the Board to reverse the administration's decision before the plaintiff would be precluded from participating in the state tournament. Evidence was presented on the administration's behalf by an independent attorney. The plaintiff was represented by legal counsel, who called several witnesses and rigorously cross-examined the administration's witnesses. All witnesses were sworn prior to their testimony....

Substantive Due Process

The plaintiff can show that his right to substantive due process was denied if the Board's decision was arbitrary or capricious; or if it violated one of the substantive due process rights such as the right to privacy, which cannot be deprived no matter how much procedural protection is used.

The Court is persuaded that the Board's decision was not arbitrary or capricious. The Board's objectives were legitimate. The Iowa Supreme Court has described the set of permissible school board objectives in this area in broad, sweeping terms. *Bunger v. Iowa High School Athletic Association*, 197 N.W.2d 555, 564–65 (Iowa 1972). "To some extent at least, school authorities may base disciplinary measures on immoral acts or acts definitely contrary to current mores." *Id.* at 565. The *Bunger* court also held that:

> The present case involves the advantages and enjoyment of an extracurricular activity provided by the school, a consideration which we believe extends the

> authority of a school board somewhat as to participation in that activity. The influence of the students involved is an additional consideration. Standout students, whether in athletics, forensics, dramatics, or other interscholastic activities, play a somewhat different role from the rank and file. Leadership brings additional responsibility. These student leaders are looked up to and emulated. They represent the school and depict its character. We cannot fault a school board for expecting somewhat more of them as to eligibility for their particular extracurricular activities.

Id. at 564.

The means chosen to achieve their objectives were not arbitrary or capricious. As the Nebraska Supreme Court found in a similar case involving alcohol use by athletes who were then suspended from a team:

> The rule involved in this case, even though the penalty of expulsion for the season might be deemed severe by some persons, clearly serves a legitimate rational interest and directly affects the discipline of student athletes. It cannot be said that the prescribed penalty was an arbitrary and unreasonable means to attain the legitimate end of deterrence of the use of alcoholic liquor by student athletes.

Braesch v. DePasquale, 200 Neb. 726, 265 N.W.2d 842, 846 (1978).

The plaintiff argues that he should not have been given a penalty more severe than penalties allegedly given in the past to other students for conduct the plaintiff considers to be more serious than his own. The record adequately demonstrates that the school's treatment of those students involved to the same degree in this incident could hardly have been more consistent; even the female involved was suspended from extracurricular activities. To go further and evaluate the Board's "consistency" across different times and different factual settings would require the Court to substitute its judgment concerning the relative seriousness of different acts for that of the School Board; the "arbitrary or capricious" standard of review is too narrow to authorize this kind of analysis....

In his testimony before the School Board, the plaintiff would not admit or deny that the incident took place because he believed it was a private matter. A limited right to privacy is protected by the Due Process Clause. However, that right does not keep the state and its instrumentalities from regulating private sexual conduct. The Board's findings indicate that it was not merely trying to impose its moral standard upon the plaintiff; the Board found that his acts injured another student and disrupted the school. These are legitimate school board concerns. *Tinker v. Des Moines Independent School District*, 393 U.S. 503, 513 (1969). Moreover, the school has not regulated the plaintiff as a student; by revoking his eligibility without suspending or expelling him, it has regulated him as a representative of the school, and has chosen a sanction which limits his ability to represent the school without limiting his basic rights as a student. For these reasons, the Court finds that whatever right the plaintiff has to sexual privacy after *Bowers* was not violated in this case, and the last possible ground for finding a likelihood that his substantive due process rights were violated is rejected.

Notes and Comments

1. Tom Brands went on to wrestle at the University of Iowa and compiled a record of 158–7–2 with an undefeated season in 1991 where he was 45–0. He was a four-time All-American, three-time NCAA Champion, three-time Big Ten Conference Champion, and Outstanding Wrestler at the 1992 NCAA Tournament. He was also successful on the international stage, winning a gold medal in the 1996 Summer Olympics. Brands is currently the head coach of the University of Iowa men's wrestling team.

2. Why was the *Brands* court persuaded that the school board's decision was not arbitrary or capricious?

3. In your view, what is the appropriate scope of authority for a school or school district to discipline student-athletes for off-campus behavior? Do you agree with the Brands court that "the school has not regulated the plaintiff as a student; by revoking his eligibility without suspending or expelling him, it has regulated him as a representative of the school, and has chosen a sanction which limits his ability to represent the school without limiting his basic rights as a student"?

4. Should state high school athletic associations adopt good conduct rules? In the *Bunger* case discussed in *Brands*, the Iowa Supreme Court distinguished discipline for inappropriate conduct imposed by state high school athletic associations and held that an association rule prohibiting use of alcohol outside the school year for athletes is beyond the scope of its authority.

Capstone Problem

The plaintiff, John East, has filed a motion for injunctive relief against the defendant, the State High School Activities Association (SHSAA), seeking an order which would declare Mr. East immediately eligible to participate in interscholastic varsity basketball for Memorial High School. Review the deposition testimony of John East and Drew Self and the applicable rules of the State High School Activities Association. Discuss the merits of Mr. East's case.

John East's Testimony

My name is John East. I am 19 years old, as of last month. I currently live with my father, Richard East, in Madison, State. We reside in the Memorial High School District. At the beginning of this school year, I was living with my Mom, Celia East, in Brewster, New York. I had lived with my Mom in Brewster ever since my parents divorced 15 years ago. I have visited my father regularly and for the past 4 summers I have stayed with him in Madison. We all decided that it would be best for me to move in with my Dad to finish my senior year of high school at Memorial after what happened in Brewster. I moved in with my Dad the day after Christmas.

At Brewster, I played varsity football and basketball. As a junior, I was first team All-State in football and Honorable Mention All-State in basketball. After my junior year, I ran into a few problems. First, I was arrested for shoplifting in June. We were able to work out a plea agreement and I was placed on probation. At our first football game in my senior year, I got into a fight after the game with a player from the other team. We were both suspended for 4 games. I think that is why I didn't receive any post-season awards—no All-State or even All-Conference. My grades were slipping and I was barely eligible for basketball. My parents thought I was becoming a juvenile delinquent. I guess I just wasn't listening to my Mom. The situation was what you might call unstable. My parents talked about how I might be better off living with my Dad in Madison. But I really wanted to finish my senior year at Brewster with my friends and to play basketball at Brewster.

Then an incident occurred at the beginning of the basketball season in Brewster which resulted in my being kicked off the team for the year. On November 15 following a four-team scrimmage, another player on our team took a wallet from a bag belonging to one of the game officials and brought it on the team bus. He showed the wallet to several of us. Later that day, a group of players, including me, went to the mall with the credit card. One of the guys tried to use the card. We all fled when the clerk became suspicious. The credit card was identified and traced to the referee, at which time Coach Will learned of the event and figured that members of his team were involved. Coach Will is the Brewster varsity coach. Coach Will gave all the players a chance to come forward and explain what happened. He instructed us that a player who was not involved but knew what happened would be considered equally as guilty as those who were involved. No one came forward. When the actual thief was identified, Coach suspended everyone involved, including the player who took the credit card, and four players who knew what happened (including me). The suspension was for the entire year. I just didn't want to "rat" on a friend and I didn't think it was fair that I was kicked off the team.

Mom, Dad and I then decided it would be best for me to move to Madison to live with my Dad. We didn't do anything in Brewster to appeal from Coach Will's decision. The Brewster Principal, Mr. Dean, told me and my Mom that he supported Coach Will "120%."

As I already said, I moved in with my Dad the day after Christmas and began playing basketball in the gym with the Memorial players. I knew most of them from having stayed with my Dad in previous summers. They were excited about me playing on the team because I'm 6'7" and I weigh about 240 and they all thought that I was just what they needed to compete for a state championship. Even without me, they were good; their record as of today is 13 wins and 1 loss and they are ranked 2nd in the state. Coach O'Malley knew me and when I told him I had moved in with my Dad he let me practice with the team because in State, a player is immediately eligible to play if he attends the school where one of his parents lives. (That's what Coach O'Malley told me.)

School started on January 3, and I enrolled at Memorial. At practice that day, Coach O'Malley asked me about what had happened in Brewster and I told him. Coach then talked to the principal, Mr. Bond, and I began to worry because later that day, Coach O'Malley told me that while I could practice with the team, I couldn't play in any games until they cleared everything with SHSAA. Coach told me he didn't want to forfeit games because he played an ineligible player and that I might be ineligible.

Then I sent in a hardship waiver, and it was denied by Mr. Self. I appealed to the SHSAA Board and went to a hearing before the SHSAA Board. They denied me, too. The hearing was a joke. Nobody asked a single question. They all had their minds made up before we ever got there. I heard that the vote against me was unanimous. The SHSAA secretary told me that when we called to find out if I had won my appeal. She told me the Board had decided my case 10 minutes after I left.

Drew Self's Testimony

My name is Drew Self and I am the Executive Director of the State High Schools Activities Association. I have been working in athletics all my adult life, first as a coach and then as an administrator with SHSAA.

I thought that East's case was rather straightforward. Under Rule 8(4) East was ineligible at Memorial because he was ineligible at Brewster. The purpose of the rule is clear—youngsters shouldn't be able to flee from their problems. In my investigation, I spoke privately with the principal at Brewster, Mr. Dean, and Coach Will. I even told them that if they would say they would reinstate East to the team, I could declare East eligible at Memorial. They refused to do so, and voiced strong concern that East should pay the price and not "flee" from his responsibilities. I also spoke to a newspaper reporter whose name I do not recall. The reporter called me first. He had been following the East situation because East was a local star. He told me that East was the only African-American football player at Brewster and that East's mother is white. He also went on about what he thought about East and about East moving to State. None of this mattered to me at all and nothing the reporter said figured in my decision. It was just a matter of returning a call and talking to a reporter.

I make the initial determination on a hardship request. I carefully follow the SHSAA rules. I'd say we receive about 35 to 40 hardship requests each year. Some are granted. For example, last year I granted 5 waivers for kids who were, by rule, too old to play. We have a rule which prohibits someone who turns 19 prior to August 1 from participating. I granted these waivers for a number of disabled youngsters. A student denied a waiver can appeal to the Board, as Mr. East did. In all my years here, the Board has never reversed me on a hardship—they trust my judgment. This case should never be in court. In fact, the Board unanimously supported my decision in this case.

APPLICABLE SHSAA RULES

Rule 8 Residence and Migration

(1) A student is eligible to participate at the school in the district where he or she resides.

****

(4) A student who is ineligible at his or her current school at the time of a transfer is ineligible at the school to which he or she transfers under the same terms and conditions of ineligibility.

****

(10) The Board of Directors is authorized to grant exceptions to the provisions of these rules and may reinstate a student to eligibility when it determines that the rule fails to accomplish the purpose for which it is intended, or when the rule works an undue hardship on the student.

****

ELIGIBILITY HARDSHIP CRITERIA

The following criteria will be used in considering the granting of hardship eligibility cases:

1. Children of divorced parents.
2. Attending school in the district where the parents are employed if transportation or convenience is involved.
3. Changing residence to care for members of the immediate family.
4. Changing residence due to unstable home environment.
5. Changing schools due to change in parents' financial condition.
6. Remaining in a school district where student is established.
7. Placement in a new residence by order of the State Department of Human Services, a similar organizational placement, or a court order.
8. Change in school attendance when recommended by professional staff for a student who is undergoing chemical abuse rehabilitation.

9. Penalties may not be assessed to a student when he/she participated illegally due to errors made by school personnel in the enrollment process if the student did not contribute the team.
10. Transportation and/or safety.
11. Student desires to immediately continue a program, but cannot do so at the previous school.
12. When annexations occur, student(s) may be approved with schools other than the two schools involved with the annexation if the superintendents and the majority of both boards agree to such.
13. An exception may be made to any rule in the SHSAA Handbook. However, exceptions to many rules, such as the age, semester, seasons of opportunity, attendance, scholarship, and end of season, etc., will be a rarity.

The following criteria will *not* be used when considering the granting of hardship eligibility cases:

1. Simple change in guardianship.
2. Discontentment with the school in which the student's eligibility has been established.
3. Changing schools to participate in a curriculum or an activity that is not offered (unless a student is denied the opportunity to immediately continue a program at the previous school).

Three

Intercollegiate Athletics

Learning Outcomes

- Understand the history of NCAA governance, the contemporary issues pertaining to NCAA governance, the NCAA enforcement process, and the NCAA's principle of "amateurism."
- Understand why a student-athlete has legal standing to sue the NCAA.
- Know what types of sports wagering activities are prohibited under NCAA bylaws and who is prohibited from engaging in that activity.
- Know the NCAA rules and procedures pertaining to drug use and drug testing.
- Understand what forms the contractual relationship between the student-athlete and university and the contractual rights and obligations of the parties.
- Understand the employment status of student-athletes and the key provisions in college coaches' contracts and how they function.

Key Terms

- Voluntary association
- Institutional control
- Notice of Inquiry
- Notice of Allegations
- Committee on Infractions (COI)
- Infractions Appeals Committee (IAC)
- Third-party beneficiary
- Arbitrary and capricious
- Restitution Rule
- National Letter of Intent (NLI)
- Grant-in-Aid
- The "right to control" test
- Liquidated damages

A. NCAA Governance, Core Principles, and Procedures

The National Collegiate Athletic Association (NCAA) is a voluntary association of more than 1,200 colleges and universities, athletic conferences, and sports organizations devoted to the sound administration of intercollegiate athletics. It is headquartered in Indianapolis, Indiana, and is operated on a daily basis by a large professional staff. The NCAA regulates athletic competition among its members, sets rules for eligibility to participate, defines the parameters of the amateurism foundation of the association, establishes restrictions and guidelines for recruitment of prospective student-athletes, conducts several dozen championship events in the sports sanctioned by the association, enters into television and promotional contracts relating to these championship events, and enters into agreements to license the NCAA name and logos.

The NCAA has for several decades been divided essentially into three divisions: Division I, Division II, and Division III. Division I is composed of the major athletic powers in the country, as well as many other institutions that choose to compete at the major college level. Division I is divided into Football Bowl Series (FBS) and Football Championship Series (FCS) for purposes of regulating football. And, as a result of changes initiated in 2014 that are discussed below, there is a further delineation, with some members of Division I designated as the "Power Five" conferences. This group includes members of the Big Ten Conference, the Big 12 Conference, the Atlantic Coast Conference, the Pac 12 Conference, the Southeastern Conference, and the University of Notre Dame.

The NCAA evolved out of a crisis in collegiate athletics in the early part of the 20th century following a conference convened by President Theodore Roosevelt in 1905 to respond to numerous deaths in football games. During its early years the organization was largely a discussion group and then gradually became focused on conducting championships in various sports. It did not become a strong regulatory body until the 1950s. The current three division structure was created in the 1970s. During the 1980s women's programs were integrated in the association, following a decade or so under a separate organization.

The legislative process of the NCAA has been very cumbersome, due largely to the size of the organization. The true leadership of the NCAA has toggled between the presidents of the member institutions and the athletic leadership of the schools. Only recently have the student-athletes had any sort of meaningful input into the process.

The NCAA has several sources of funding. Approximately 90% of the revenue for the association comes from its media rights. Initially, and for several decades thereafter, television contracts for the broadcast of the Division I Basketball Championship supplied the bulk of funding for the NCAA. Today, the media rights to the tournament and other sports championships include new media as well as television. The contract with CBS and Turner Broadcasting provided revenues of $10.8 billion from 2010–2024. An extension of the contract now takes it through 2032 and provides an additional $8.8 billion. The members also pay dues annually.

In 2011 the NCAA convened a retreat of 54 university presidents to discuss the many challenges facing intercollegiate athletics at that time. Among those challenges were rising costs of Division I athletics, high profile cases involving rules violations, and frustration over the handling of these matters by the NCAA system. The key topics for the retreat were academics, integrity, and financial sustainability. Following the retreat five working groups were formed, including one charged with review of the governance of Division I. In 2013 the Division I Board of Directors launched a comprehensive review of the governance structure, with the stated purpose of coming up with changes that purportedly would better serve the student-athletes. That process produced a new structure for Division I that was approved by the membership in late 2014.

The new system was intended to streamline the governance process and structure through continued transparency, responsiveness, and inclusion. It provides to the so-called Power Five conferences and Notre Dame a level of legislative autonomy never before seen in collegiate athletics. The new model grants flexibility to schools in the Atlantic Coast, Big 12, Big Ten, Pac 12, and Southeastern conferences to change rules for themselves in a list of specific areas within Division I. Most of the topic areas are related to the potential for enhanced benefits for student-athletes. The new model expands the Division I Board of Directors and creates a new body known as the Division I Council that will be responsible for day-to-day operations of the division. Student-athletes have greater representation on boards and committees than under earlier models.

The new governance structure had an immediate impact on the Division I landscape as the Power Five schools moved quickly to adopt new rules for their group. In January 2015 the group passed legislation allowing for schools to provide student athletes scholarships that cover the full cost of attendance. This produced an increase in the value of a scholarship of $2,000–$4,500 per year, depending upon the particular institution involved. It also left to the schools the determination of which sports to include and how to deal with the option with sports where scholarships are split. Legislation was also enacted that allows student-athletes to borrow money based upon future earning power, mandates the development of concussion management protocols, and prohibits schools from terminating scholarships for athletic performance reasons. Finally, the Power Five Autonomy legislation gives the opportunity to other Division I members to adopt legislation similar to that enacted under this structure by the Power Five.

In recent years a number of challenges and controversies have confronted the NCAA. In the fall of 2017, following a lengthy investigation by the FBI, the Department of Justice announced indictments against ten coaches, financial advisors, and agents in conjunction with alleged improper payments to college basketball players. Several of those indicted have either been convicted of felonies or pled guilty. The investigation implicated at least a dozen schools. Several have already been sanctioned by the NCAA, but others await their fates nearly five years later. The delay in resolving the cases has been largely due to the slow work of the Independent Accountability Review Process (IARP), which was created in response to the fallout from the FBI investigation.

In response to the investigation and indictments, the NCAA established the Independent Commission on College Basketball (Rice Commission) "to assess the state of the enterprise and to recommend transformational changes to address multiple issues and challenges." The Commission Report was issued in April 2018 and set forth numerous recommendations for improving the landscape of college basketball. The Report called on the NBA to end the so-called one and done policy. It recommended that the NCAA amend its rules regarding agents, draft eligibility, and penalties for infractions. It advocated for public membership on the NCAA Committee on Infractions (COI) and for provision of greater financial support for degree completion by players who leave school after completing at least two years of academics. Finally, it recommended that the NCAA reconsider its policies regarding athletes benefiting from the use of their name, image, and likeness (NIL).

Some of these recommendations have implemented and others are still in discussion. As this book goes to press, the NCAA and collegiate athletics are facing a myriad of issues, resolution of which may radically change the terrain. Included are the rights for athletes to benefit from the use of their NIL, the introduction of and continued operation of the transfer portal, the question of whether Power Five football and men's basketball players should continue to be denied compensation from their schools, and the question of whether federal courts will begin to apply the rule of reason under antitrust law differently in light of the Supreme Court's 2021 ruling in the *Alston* case. (See Chapter 4.)

In early 2022, the NCAA membership approved a new constitution. The new constitution reduces the size of the Board of Governors to nine members and includes a student voting member. It also shifts much of the decision making to the three divisions and the conferences. Simultaneous with this development, the NCAA Division I Transformation Committee began preparing recommendations for changes to recruiting rules, scholarship limitations, and enforcement rules. As this book goes to press, the Division I Board of Directors (in conjunction with the Transformation Committee) is adopting new rules by revising a variety of NCAA bylaws, including rules related to the infractions process and transfer restrictions. It is fairly apparent that the Division I Board of Directors is asserting much greater authority over changes to the NCAA bylaws, which historically has been within the purview of the membership pursuant to the procedures of the legislative process set forth in the Division I Manual.

The NCAA's duties and responsibilities cover a wide range of activities, including athlete eligibility, recruiting, championships, rules of competition, and enforcement. The professional staff administers the rules and regulations of the association. Membership services oversees the bulk of the administration, while the enforcement department handles investigation and prosecution of violations of the rules.

It is important to remember that the two concepts at the core of the NCAA are those relating to amateurism and the importance of education. Historically, all NCAA student-athletes were to be amateurs and the association's regulations set out explicit definitions of amateurism and specific prohibitions on the acceptance of extra benefits by student-athletes. They further define "pay" to include many items beyond the obvious salary or stipend. It has historically been a violation of the rules on amateurism for benefits to be provided to the parents or close relatives of student-athletes. Amateur status is forfeited in most situations where an athlete retains an agent or declares himself eligible for a professional sports draft. The association has established the NCAA Eligibility Center to analyze questions raised regarding participation in junior sports, particularly outside the United States, by prospective student-athletes.

Academics are the cornerstone of the NCAA and have also been an ongoing challenge for the organization. Over the last 50 years the association has grappled with issues related to academic preparedness of student athletes, graduation rates of student athletes, and academic fraud. Today, all of these issues are on the front burner, presenting the NCAA with challenges on campuses, in courtrooms, and in the public eye.

The NCAA's focus on education is best exemplified by the following from the newly adopted NCAA Constitution:

> Intercollegiate student-athletes are matriculated, degree-seeking students in good standing with their institutions who choose voluntarily to participate in NCAA sports. It is the responsibility of each member institution to establish and maintain an environment in which a student-athlete's activities are conducted with the appropriate emphasis on the student-athlete's academic experience. Intercollegiate athletics programs shall be maintained as a vital component of each institution's broader educational program. The admission, academic standing and academic progress of student-athletes shall be consistent with the policies and standards adopted by the institution. NCAA Constitution, Article 1.A.

The association establishes standards for initial eligibility of athletes entering member institutions. The bylaws set specific thresholds for scores on standardized tests and the satisfactory completion of a minimum number of core courses in high school. The origin of these policies coincides with the first time that the NCAA allowed freshman to compete in intercollegiate sports in 1971. A variety of different standards were adopted between then and 1986 when the NCAA implemented Proposition 48. This set a minimum SAT/ACT score *and* a minimum high school G.P.A. for initial eligibility to compete. The policy also required the completion of 11 core courses in high school. This rule did not adversely impact admission or the receipt of a scholarship, but it did impact eligibility to compete. It was extremely controversial, with critics and litigants contending it adversely impacted African American student-athletes and those student-athletes with learning disabilities and other environmental disadvantages. *See, e.g., Pryor v. NCAA, 288 F.3d 548 (3d Cir. 2002); Cureton v. NCAA*, 252 F.3d 267 (3d Cir. 2001). In 1996 the initial eligibility requirements were adjusted through the implementation of Proposition 16, which introduced for the first time a sliding scale for test scores and high school grades. It also increased the number of core courses required to be completed. This approach has continued to be periodically revised and beginning in 2016 a new stringent policy took effect. The new standards require completion of 16 core courses, 10 of which must be completed by the beginning of the student-athlete's senior year in high school. A minimum 2.3 G.P.A. is required in these core courses. The sliding scale for grades and ACT/SAT scores continues to be a part of the policy. A student-athlete in compliance with these requirements is eligible as a freshman for a scholarship and competition. A student-athlete attaining a G.P.A. between 2.0 and 2.3 in the core courses and meeting the sliding scale test score would be designated an academic redshirt and be eligible for a scholarship and to practice with her team, but not eligible for competition. There is a strong possibility that in the near future these requirements will be adjusted to eliminate factoring in the test scores as numerous colleges and universities are either removing the test requirement or making it optional.

The NCAA also sets forth specific requirements for "satisfactory progress towards a degree." These standards set specific grade point averages and credit hours completed for each year of matriculation. Student-athletes have typically four years of eligibility and must complete those four years within a five-year period. (There are limited exceptions to both requirements.) There are, of course, procedures in place for student-athletes ruled ineligible under any of these provisions to appeal those determinations.

The NCAA has also established an institutional academic standard that must be met by all Division I schools. The Academic Performance Program sets forth a combination of rewards and penalties designed to encourage high levels of academic performance within athletic programs. This Program has two key components: the Academic Progress Rate (APR) and the Graduation Success Rate (GSR). The APR is calculated using a formula that takes into account each semester that a student-athlete is in school and each semester that she is academically eligible to compete. The program sets a level of success that must be met by each sport within an institution's athletic program, using a four-year average. Sports attaining the success mark are eligible to participate in NCAA championship competition and those with extremely high scores receive special recognition. Those missing the mark are subject to a graduated penalty structure, with the ultimate sanction being a bar on participating in postseason competition. The APR rules have recently been challenged by athletes and former athletes who attended HBCU institutions. The plaintiffs alleged that the program discriminates on the basis of race and asked for injunctive relief and damages. *Manassa v. NCAA*, Case 1:20-cv-3172 (S.D. Ind. 2020). The NCAA's motion to dismiss was denied in September of 2021.

Finally, in recent years academic integrity has become a very visible issue for the NCAA and its member institutions. Two schools, the University of North Carolina-Chapel Hill and the University of Missouri, have had front-page academic fraud issues in recent years. The NCAA conducted a lengthy investigation of academic misconduct that occurred between 2002 and 2011 at North Carolina. The specific focus was on independent study courses that were created and graded in many cases by a departmental secretary. There was also evidence of grade changes, forged faculty signatures, and transcript alterations. Student athletes were "guided" to these courses to assure continuing eligibility. North Carolina argued that the NCAA did not have jurisdiction over this type of case and, more importantly, that there was not an impermissible benefit to the student athletes as the courses were open to all students. The Committee on Infractions (COI) ultimately agreed and did not impose penalties on the school.

In response to the North Carolina case and other cases, and the vagueness of the association's authority to discipline schools for academic integrity flaws, the NCAA adopted new policies covering academic misconduct in 2016. The new policy punishes impermissible academic assistance and provides for sanctions against institutions, as well as coaches and staff members. Impermissible assistance is defined as substantial academic assistance to athletes not generally available to all students. Schools are required to have and to enforce written academic integrity standards for all students. And no special academic exceptions can be granted to athletes. *See* NCAA Division I Manual, Section 14.9.

Shortly after the new rules became effective in 2016, Missouri self-reported misconduct committed by a tutor at the institution. The tutor admitted completing academic work for 12 student-athletes during 2015 and 2016. While the tutor indicated she felt pressure to ensure the student-athletes were passing courses, there was no indication that athletic officials had directed her to do the work for them. The school cooperated fully with the NCAA. In contrast with the UNC case, the COI imposed significant sanctions on three sports, including post-season bans, scholarship limitations, and restrictions on recruiting. The Infractions Appeals Committee upheld all of the findings and sanctions in November 2019.

In most sports at the Division I level there is intense recruitment of the student-athletes prior to their enrollment in a member institution, as well as while they are enrolled, due to the changes in the transfer rules. The NCAA bylaws set out a very explicit framework for the recruitment process. The regulations limit, among other things, the number of visits made by coaches to athletes, the number of visits to campuses made by the athletes, the number and types of contacts made by coaches, and the times of year that contacts may be made. The rules also severely restrict the participation of alumni and boosters in the recruitment process.

Once the athlete has enrolled at a member institution and is part of one of the athletic teams, there are restrictions on the number of hours set for practice, the times of year for competition, and the number of contests. In addition, the NCAA conducts and regulates post-season competition in more than 20 sports for men and women.

A critical aspect of NCAA governance and regulation is the concept of "institutional control." The NCAA bylaws require that each institution control its program in a manner consistent with the rules and regulations of the association. The President/CEO of the institution is ultimately responsible for maintaining this control. This includes the responsibility for watching over the conduct of athletic administrators, coaches, faculty, and supporters of the program. The most serious violation that the university can commit is "failure to maintain institutional control." The primary responsibility for an institution in the operation of its athletic program is to maintain control of it. Factors indicating sufficient control include:

- Promotion of a culture of compliance
- Oversight of all operations
- Policies and procedures to ensure control
- Education and training
- Due diligence in delegating authority
- Enforcement response and prevention of reoccurrence
- Risk assessment and modification

Division I Enforcement Charging Guidelines—NCAA.org.

When an institution fails to exercise institutional control, enforcement steps in. The association's enforcement staff will commence an investigation when an institution is alleged to have violated a provision of NCAA rules. There are a number of ways in which alleged violations come to the attention of the NCAA. Frequently they are a result of self-reporting by the institutions. There are also instances of investigations being initiated as a result of information provided by opposing schools, recruits, and reporters. All investigations are treated as confidential until announcements are made according to the prescribed procedures. Ultimate adjudication of violations typically occurs in front of the Committee on Infractions (COI).

The enforcement process has evolved over the years. The most recent changes in the process occurred following the release of the Rice Commission Report. The most significant change was the creation of the Independent Accountability Resolution Process, a 15-member committee that serves as an alternative to the COI. The intent was to have an independent forum that would streamline the process. As will be discussed, it has actually created a logjam.

The Working Group ultimately recommended, and the membership approved, a new enforcement policy which provided for multi-level new structure of violations, a more efficient process, and a new set of penalties. If the enforcement staff receives information indicating an institution has possibly acted in violation of the association's governing legislation, it will evaluate the information and determine what level of violation may be involved. If it concludes a potential Level III (lesser of the three levels) violation is presented, the staff will proceed to work with the school and the conference where possible to resolve the matter and impose appropriate penalties at the staff level. There is an opportunity for appeal to the COI from this determination.

If the staff determines there is relevant and reliable information involving a Level I or II violation (the most serious violations), the staff will serve a Notice of Inquiry on the CEO of the institution. This notice will detail the potential violations, the sport, and the individuals involved. At this point the school should begin to conduct its own investigation. The school will also be informed of its obligation to cooperate with the NCAA staff. Bylaw 19.2.3. Failure to cooperate will itself be a Level I violation. Following the preliminary investigation, the process can go one of three directions: the case may be closed for lack of evidence; Level III violations may be found and summary disposition discussions begin with the school; and a Level I or II violation may be found and a Notice of Allegations issued to the school. The structure includes the two most serious institutional and individual violations from the old system: lack of institutional control and unethical conduct. For individual members of the athletic program and those members of the institution responsible for the program, the highest level of responsibility is to conduct themselves in an honest and ethical manner. There is also a requirement that head coaches bear ultimate responsibility for the conduct of their staff and must steadfastly monitor the actions of the staff. Bylaw 11.1.1.1.

Following an investigation, the COI will conduct a hearing to determine findings and any penalties deemed appropriate. This hearing will involve the institution's representatives, involved parties, the enforcement staff, and, where appropriate, the report of an independent hearing officer. Following the hearing, the COI will issue its report, which will include penalties. The COI will consider both mitigating and aggravating factors in assessing penalties. Potential penalties range from public censure and reprimand to the "death penalty," the total shut-down of a program or particular sport for a set time. Other potential penalties include reduction in scholarships allowed, forfeiture of tournament money, and ineligibility for appearances on television. The school has the opportunity to appeal the ruling to the Infractions Appeals Committee (IAC). The IAC will receive written "briefs" from the institution and from the COI. It will also hold a hearing involving all interested parties. This process has on occasion produced modified findings and penalties.

Further details concerning the process and reports of decisions by the COI may be found at www.ncaa.org. *See also* Division I Manual, art. 19.

Notes and Comments

1. As of the 2021–22 academic year, there are 357 schools in Division I, with eight additional schools transitioning to Division I from Division II or III. Four other schools announced in 2022 that they intend to transition. Since 1986, numerous schools have made the transition to Division I from Divisions II and III. The motivation for movement to Division I is generally thought to be prestige and enhanced revenues. All Division I institutions have the potential to share in the NCAA Basketball Tournament revenue and can benefit from some of the special funding that has been established to support student athletes and academic programs.

2. A school desiring to move from Division II or III to Division I must go through a lengthy process. It begins with the filing of an application by the school and its sponsoring conference with the Strategic Vision and Planning Committee. Once the application is accepted the school is on provisional status and must annually file a strategic plan, compliance reports, and conform to all Division I rules. During this four-year reclassification process, schools are not eligible to receive distributions from the various NCAA funding programs or participate in championships. Typically, reclassifying schools are forced to schedule many more games and events away from home than is the case for active members. Recruiting can also be a challenge during the process because of the length of time required and the lack of any guarantees active membership will be achieved.

At one time it was a seven-year process, unless a school was returning to Division I, in which case it took three-years. In 2007, Houston Baptist University (HBU), then a NAIA school, filed an application with the NCAA to return to Division I of which it had formerly been a member. Following notice that the NCAA had accepted its application, HBU moved forward with significant investment in new sports, facilities and operational budgets believing the three-year provisional period would apply. But, early in the process, the NCAA notified HBU that it would be subject to the seven-year period since its "staff" had, just weeks before HBU's application was filed, editorially revised the Manual to require returning members to complete a seven-year provisional period. The NCAA contended that this change was editorial only, not substantive, and therefore not subject to the normal process for amendment which would require action by the full membership at the Annual Convention. HBU disagreed and proceeded to file actions in state court contending the NCAA had violated its own rules (*Houston Baptist Univ. v. NCAA*, No. 2008–14492 (Harris Cty. Tex. 2008)) and in federal court alleging violations of the antitrust laws (*Houston Baptist Univ. v. NCAA*, No. 4:08-cv-01112 (S.D. Tex. 2008)). The state case was settled prior to trial and the federal lawsuit was withdrawn. The state settlement provided for HBU to proceed on a three-year path to active membership. The federal case was dropped by the plaintiffs.

B. Amateurism and the "Student-Athlete"

1. Extra Benefits and NIL

The NCAA has a general prohibition on student-athletes receiving "extra benefits," defined in the Division I Manual as follows:

> An extra benefit is any special arrangement by an institutional employee or representative of the institution's athletics interests to provide a student-athlete or the student-athlete family member or friend a benefit not expressly authorized by NCAA legislation. Receipt of a benefit by student-athletes or their family members or friends is not a violation of NCAA legislation if it is demonstrated that the same benefit is generally available to the institution's students or their family members or friends or to a particular segment of the student body (e.g., international students, minority students) determined on a basis unrelated to athletics ability. Bylaw 16.02.3.

Bylaw 13.02.15 defines a "representative of the institution's athletics interests" as "an individual, independent agency, corporate entity (e.g., apparel or equipment manufacturer) or other organization who is known (or who should have been known) by a member of the institution's executive or athletics administration to: (a) Have participated in or to be a member of an agency or organization promoting the institution's intercollegiate athletics program; (b) Have made financial contributions to the athletics department or to an athletics booster organization of that institution; (c) Be assisting or to have been requested (by the athletics department staff) to assist in the recruitment of prospective student-athletes; (d) Be assisting or to have assisted in providing benefits to enrolled student-athletes or their family members; or (e) Have been involved otherwise in promoting the institution's athletics program." Over time, the NCAA has promulgated numerous interpretations of, and exceptions to, the extra benefits prohibition, including who constitutes a representative of the institution's athletics interests, which fuels arguments that "amateurism" simply means whatever the NCAA says it means.

There have historically been restrictions on the ability of student-athletes to be paid for promotional and endorsement activities that benefited them solely because of their athletic skills. For a number of years advocates for college athletes had been promoting the notion that they should be able to be paid for the use of their NILs in the sale of products and services. In 2019, California enacted legislation, effective January 1, 2023, that recognized NIL rights for student-athletes. During the first half of 2021, nearly two dozen other states passed similar legislation with July 1, 2021 or soon thereafter effective dates. In late 2020, the NCAA membership considered new rules allowing for the use of NIL that would be voted on by the membership at the Convention in January 2021, but the NCAA President ultimately decided that it would not be submitted to such vote. The Division I Board of Directors instead issued an "interim policy," effective July 1, 2021, that revised the existing NCAA bylaws related to promotional and endorsement activities. The key limitations in the NCAA policy are that the NIL agreements cannot be "pay for play," an inducement to be enrolled at a particular school, and there must be a quid pro quo in the agreement. Athletes may enter into NIL agreements with boosters and they are allowed to use agents and/or attorneys.

Nearly 30 states have NIL laws in effect, although not one of them has been enforced nor even an attempt made to enforce one. There are strong similarities among the various statutes, but there are also subtle differences requiring close consideration by those entering into contractual arrangements. Most give the athletes a significant amount of latitude in striking deals, although some list specific types of endorsements that are prohibited, including tobacco products, marijuana, gambling, and pornography. Most allow the athletes to have legal representation and/or agents, with some requiring those representatives to be licensed in the particular state. Many require the athletes to disclose the details of contracts, with some requiring the athletes to secure the approval of their schools for each contract. Several of the laws require schools to provide financial literacy education for their athletes. Most have provisions speaking to conflicts between an athlete's contract and an existing school contract such as an apparel or shoe contract. Several of the statutes have provisions relating to the use of the school's logo or colors by the athletes in the context of an NIL deal. However, all of these statutes lack clarity as to who can bring an action, and what the remedy or penalty is, for a violation.

In the initial two years of the NIL era, hundreds of college athletes have struck deals ranging from compensation worth less than a hundred dollars to, apparently, six- or seven-figure deals. Collectives have been launched at dozens of schools to serve as facilitators of NIL deals for athletes. And, in a few cases, wealthy supporters of schools have done large deals directly with athletes. It is suspected that many of the deals have not been disclosed to the schools, contrary to expectations or requirements. Individual schools have established NIL policies for their athletes that provide the schools with ability to review the deals and ensure compliance with NCAA rules. Despite these efforts, a number of highly publicized deals have raised questions and led to NCAA scrutiny. Many of the deals appear to provide recruiting advantages for the schools.

Although the 2004 *Bloom* case that follows predates the NIL "interim policy" adopted by the Division I Board of Directors in 2021, the case is still good law with respect to the legal standards that apply to claims brought by student-athletes against the NCAA under private association law principles. Despite the arrival of NIL opportunities for all college athletes, there is a pending antitrust case brought by current and former athletes seeking damages for lost NIL opportunities. *House v. NCAA*, 4:20-cv-03919 (N.D. Cal. 2020) (See Chapter 4).

Bloom v. National Collegiate Athletic Association

93 P.3d 621 (Colo. App. 2004)

In this dispute concerning eligibility to play college football, plaintiff, Jeremy Bloom, appeals the trial court's order denying his request for a preliminary injunction against defendants, the National Collegiate Athletic Association (NCAA) and the University of Colorado (CU). We affirm.

I. Background

Bloom, a high school football and track star, was recruited to play football at CU. Before enrolling there, however, he competed in Olympic and professional World Cup skiing events, becoming the World Cup champion in freestyle moguls. During the Olympics, Bloom appeared on MTV, and thereafter was offered various paid entertainment opportunities, including a chance to host a show on Nickelodeon. Bloom also agreed to endorse commercially certain ski equipment, and he contracted to model clothing for Tommy Hilfiger.

Bloom became concerned that his endorsements and entertainment activities might interfere with his eligibility to compete in intercollegiate football. On Bloom's behalf, CU first requested waivers of NCAA rules restricting student-athlete endorsement and media activities...

The NCAA denied CU's requests, and Bloom discontinued his endorsement, modeling, and media activities to play football for CU during the 2002 fall season. However, Bloom instituted this action against the NCAA for declaratory and injunctive relief, asserting that his endorsement, modeling, and media activities were necessary to support his professional skiing career, something which the NCAA rules permitted.

In his complaint, Bloom alleged: (1) as a third-party beneficiary of the contract between the NCAA and its members, he was entitled to enforce NCAA bylaws permitting him to engage in and receive remuneration from a professional sport different from his amateur sport; (2) as applied to the facts of this case, the NCAA's restrictions on endorsements and media appearances were arbitrary and capricious; and (3) those restrictions constituted improper and unconscionable restraints of trade.

II. Standard of Review

[The court discussed the standard of review for injunctive relief.]

III. Claims on Appeal

Initially, we limit our consideration on appeal to Bloom's claims of breach of contract and arbitrary and capricious action by the NCAA.

IV. Standing

...the trial court found, and we agree, that the NCAA's constitution, bylaws, and regulations evidence a clear intent to benefit student athletes. And because each student athlete's eligibility to compete is determined by the NCAA, we conclude that Bloom had standing in a preliminary injunction hearing to contest the meaning or applicability of NCAA eligibility restrictions...

V. Probability of Success

Bloom contends that the trial court erred in assessing the probability of success on his contract claims. We disagree.

Initially, we note that, as a third-party beneficiary, Bloom has rights no greater than those of the parties to the contract itself, here, the NCAA and its member institutions.

A. Interpretation of NCAA Bylaws

Bloom relies on NCAA Bylaw 12.1.2, which states that "[a] professional athlete in one sport may represent a member institution in a different sport." He asserts that, because a professional is one who "gets paid" for a sport, a student-athlete is entitled to earn whatever income is customary for his or her professional sport, which, in the case of professional skiers, primarily comes from endorsements and paid media opportunities.

We recognize that, like many others involved in individual professional sports such as golf, tennis, and boxing, professional skiers obtain much of their income from sponsors. We note, however, that none of the NCAA's bylaws mentions, much less explicitly establishes, a right to receive "customary income" for a sport.

To the contrary, the NCAA bylaws prohibit every student-athlete from receiving money for advertisements and endorsements. Bylaw 12.5.2.1.

Additionally, while NCAA Bylaw 12.5.1.3 permits a student-athlete to continue to receive remuneration for activity initiated prior to enrollment in which his or her name or picture is used, this remuneration is only allowed, if, as pertinent here, "the individual became involved in such activities for reasons independent of athletics ability;... no reference is made in these activities to the individual's name or involvement in intercollegiate athletics; [and]... the individual does not endorse the commercial product."

Further, NCAA Bylaw 12.4.1.1 prohibits a student-athlete from receiving "any remuneration for value or utility that the student-athlete may have for the employer because of the publicity, reputation, fame or personal following that he or she has obtained because of athletics ability." Unlike other NCAA bylaws, the endorsements and media appearance bylaws do not contain any sport-specific qualifiers. See, e.g., NCAA Bylaw 12.3.1 (ineligibility of student-athlete to compete in intercollegiate sport based on agreement with agent to market athlete's athletic ability or reputation "in that sport").

In our view, when read together, the NCAA bylaws express a clear and unambiguous intent to prohibit student-athletes from engaging in endorsements and paid media appearances, without regard to: (1) when the opportunity for such activities originated; (2) whether the opportunity arose or exists for reasons unrelated to participation in an amateur sport; and (3) whether income derived from the opportunity is customary for any particular professional sport.

An NCAA official testified that both the endorsement and media appearance provisions have been consistently applied and interpreted in a nonsport-specific manner. Indeed, another NCAA official related that association members had resisted efforts to change the endorsement rule to be sport-specific. Although the evidence is conflicting, the record supports the trial court's conclusion that, from the beginning, CU understood that the endorsement and media activity rules were nonsport-specific in scope.

Thus, even if the bylaws were viewed as ambiguous, the record supports the trial court's conclusion that the bylaws would ultimately be interpreted in accordance with the NCAA's and its member institutions' construction of those bylaws.

B. Application of Bylaws to Bloom

The NCAA's "Principle of Amateurism" states:

> Student-athletes shall be amateurs in an intercollegiate sport, and their participation should be motivated primarily by education and by the physical, mental and social benefits to be derived. Student participation in intercollegiate athletics is an avocation, and student-athletes should be protected from exploitation by professional and commercial enterprises.

NCAA Const. art. 2.9.

The NCAA's purpose, in this regard, is not only "to maintain intercollegiate athletics as an integral part of the educational program," but also to "retain a clear line of demarcation between intercollegiate athletics and professional sports." NCAA Const. art. 1, § 1.3.1.

Here, the trial court found that application of the endorsement and media appearance rules in Bloom's case was rationally related to the legitimate purpose of retaining the "clear line of demarcation between intercollegiate athletics and professional sports."

The trial court noted that salaries and bonuses are an acceptable means for attaining income from professional sports, but endorsement income is not acceptable if a student-athlete wishes to preserve amateur eligibility. According to NCAA officials: (1) endorsements invoke concerns about "the commercial exploitation of student-athletes and the promotion of commercial products"; and (2) it is not possible to distinguish the precise capacity in which endorsements are made. A CU official related that generally, the endorsement rule prevents students from becoming billboards for commercialism, and in Bloom's case, there would "be no way to tell whether he is receiving pay commensurate with his... football ability or skiing ability."

Similar concerns underlie the NCAA's prohibition on paid entertainment activity. Paid entertainment activity may impinge upon the amateur ideal if the opportunity were obtained or advanced because of the student's athletic ability or prestige, even though that activity may further the education of student-athletes such as Bloom, a communications major. As the trial court noted, there are "various shades of gray within which such events could fall." And, as should be evident, the NCAA does not prohibit unpaid internships, externships, or other educational opportunities in the entertainment field.

In this case, Bloom presented evidence that some of his acting opportunities arose not as a result of his athletic ability but because of his good looks and on-camera presence. However, the record contains evidence that Bloom's agent and the Tommy Hilfiger company marketed Bloom as a talented multi-sport athlete, and a representative from a talent agency intimated that Bloom's reputation as an athlete would be advantageous in obtaining auditions for various entertainment opportunities. Further, the NCAA indicated, when asked to interpret its rules, that it was unable, due to insufficient information, to determine which of Bloom's requested media activities were, in fact, unrelated to his athletic ability or prestige.

Bloom also asserts that the NCAA is arbitrary in its application of the endorsement and media bylaws. He notes that, while the NCAA would bar him from accepting commercial endorsements, it will allow colleges to commercially endorse athletic equipment by having students wear the equipment, with identifying logos and insignias, while engaged in intercollegiate competition. But the trial court determined, and we agree, that this application of the bylaws has a rational basis in economic necessity: financial benefits inure not to any single student-athlete but to member schools and thus to all student-athletes, including those who participate in programs that generate no revenue.

Bloom further argues that the NCAA is arbitrary in the way it applies its bylaws among individual students. Bloom presented evidence that, in one instance, a student-athlete was permitted to make an unpaid, minor appearance in a single film. But the NCAA could rationally conclude that this situation was different: Bloom did not seek permission to make an unpaid appearance in one specific instance; he wanted to take advantage of any number of television and film opportunities, and he wanted to be paid. Bloom also presented evidence that a second student-athlete was permitted to appear on television while he participated in his professional sport. But Bloom did not show that the NCAA would prohibit him from appearing on television while participating in his professional sport.

Bloom has thus failed to demonstrate any inconsistency in application which would lead us to conclude that the NCAA was arbitrarily applying its rules.

For these reasons, we agree with the trial court that Bloom failed to demonstrate a reasonable probability of success on the merits.

Accordingly, the trial court's order is affirmed.

2. Use of Agents

NCAA Bylaw 12.3 generally prohibits the use of agents by collegiate athletes. Even agreements for future representation are prohibited. As is the case with much of the Division I Manual, there are exceptions to this prohibition. As noted earlier, under the NIL interim policy, athletes are allowed to use the services of agents for the purpose of obtaining and negotiating NIL deals. In addition, athletes who are professional in a sport, but have collegiate eligibility in another, may have an agent for the professional sport so long as the written agreement with the agent is limited to the sport in which the athlete is a professional. There are also exceptions for athletes in baseball and ice hockey that allow the use of an agent prior to initial enrollment in college. Finally, the NCAA recently enacted an agent certification program for agents who represent basketball players. The following case takes a close look at Bylaw 12.3.

Oliver v. National Collegiate Athletic Association

920 N.E.2d 203 (Ct. Common Pleas, Ohio 2009)

Tone, Judge.

Facts

[The plaintiff, Andrew Oliver, is in his junior year of college at Oklahoma State University and is a pitcher on their baseball team. He is an Ohio resident.] The plaintiff, in February 2006, retained the services of Robert M. Baratta, Tim Baratta, and Icon Sports Group, d.b.a. Icon Law Group, as his sports advisors and attorneys. In June of the same year, the Minnesota Twins of Major League Baseball drafted the plaintiff in the 17th round of the draft. At the end of the summer, the Minnesota Twins met with the plaintiff and his father at the Oliver family home in Vermilion before the plaintiff left for his freshman year of college. Tim Baratta also attended the meeting, at his own request, at the Oliver home. During the meeting the Minnesota Twins offered the plaintiff $390,000 to join their organization. After heeding the advice of his father, the plaintiff rejected the offer and chose to attend OSU in the fall on a full scholarship for which he had already signed a letter of intent in the fall of 2005.

The plaintiff played his freshman and sophomore years for OSU, and during that period he never received any invoices requesting payment for any services rendered by his advisors. In fact, the plaintiff avers that the advisors provided nothing of value to him.

In March 2008, plaintiff decided to terminate the Barattas and Icon Sports and retain the Boras Corporation. The plaintiff communicated his intentions of termination to Robert Baratta. In April 2008, the plaintiff received a letter and an invoice from the Barattas for $113,750 for legal services.

On May 19, 2008, the previous attorneys mailed, faxed, and e-mailed a letter to the [NCAA]complaining about the plaintiff and reporting alleged violations by the plaintiff, i.e. the meeting at the Olivers' home that Tim Baratta had attended. As a result of the allegations, OSU and the defendant investigated the alleged violations in relationship to the plaintiff's amateur status. In May 2008, the plaintiff was indefinitely suspended from playing baseball and was informed by OSU staff that he had violated NCAA Bylaw 12.3.1 by (1) allowing his previous attorneys to contact the Minnesota Twins by telephone and (2) by allowing Tim Baratta to be present in his home when a representative from the Minnesota Twins tendered an offer to him. On August 18, 2008, the plaintiff was reinstated as a result of a temporary restraining order issued by this court. However, in October 2008, OSU filed for reinstatement of the plaintiff with the NCAA even though the temporary restraining order had reinstated the plaintiff. Subsequently, in December 2008, the plaintiff was suspended for one year and charged a year of eligibility by the defendant. The penalty was subsequently reduced to 70 percent of the original suspension and no loss of eligibility for the plaintiff.

Arguments

The plaintiff requests that this court enter a declaratory judgment and injunctive relief enjoining the NCAA Bylaw 12.3.2.1 as unenforceable because the plaintiff retained legal counsel (the Barattas) to represent him and that legal counsel is subject to the exclusive regulation of the Ohio Supreme Court. Therefore, the defendant has no authority to promulgate a rule that would prevent a lawyer from competently representing his client. As such, the plaintiff maintains that, NCAA Bylaw 12.3.2.1 is void because it is against the public policy of the state of Ohio.

Furthermore, the plaintiff argues that NCAA Bylaw 12.3.2.1 is arbitrary and capricious because, it does not impact a player's amateur status but instead limits the player's ability to effectively negotiate a contract that the player or a player's parent could negotiate.

Finally, the plaintiff requests that this court also enter a declaratory judgment and permanent injunction enjoining the defendant from enforcing NCAA Bylaw 19.7. [This Bylaw, which is now 19.13, allows the NCAA to sanction a school for an NCAA "amateurism" violation involving an athlete in a situation where an appeals court overturns a court order issued in favor of the athlete that allows the athlete to compete and the school complies with the order (*i.e.* does not withhold the athlete from competition).] The plaintiff argues that the bylaw interferes with the Ohio Constitution's delegation of all judicial power to the courts of this state and, consistent with that premise, exists solely to coerce or direct its agents and members to ignore court orders that are binding upon member institutions of the defendant.

Breach of Contract

Since the inception of this case, the defendant has argued that it has no contractual relationship with the plaintiff. What is obvious is that there is a contractual relationship between the defendant and its member institution, OSU. The defendant, as an unincorporated association consisting of public and private universities and colleges, adopts rules governing member institutions' recruiting, admissions, academic eligibility, and financial-aid standards for student athletes. The basic purpose of the NCAA is stated in Bylaw 1.3.1: The competitive athletics programs of member institutions are designed to be a vital part of the educational system. A basic purpose of this Association is to maintain intercollegiate athletics as an integral part of the educational program and the athlete as an integral part of the student body and, by so doing, retain a clear line of demarcation between intercollegiate athletics and professional sports.

The defendant has argued and this court agrees that there is no contract between the defendant and the plaintiff by way of a national letter of intent or the plaintiff's financial aid package. However, an action for breach of contract by a third party can be brought when the parties to a contract intended to benefit the third party....

It is unquestionable that the defendant and OSU's contractual agreement is created to confer a benefit on the student-athletes. The purpose of the NCAA, and the obligation of member institutions, forms a contract in which the defendant promises, among many things, to initiate, stimulate and improve intercollegiate athletic programs for student athletes. OSU promises to enforce the defendant's legislation as it relates to its members and "protect and enhance the physical and educational well-being of student athletes." The constitution of the NCAA, the operating and the administrative bylaws (the NCAA Divisional Manual) represents the contract between the association and its member institutions whereby student-athletes remain amateurs in an intercollegiate sport, where they are "motivated primarily by education and by the physical, mental and social benefits to be derived." According to the principles of the agreement, "student participation in intercollegiate athletics is an avocation, and student-athletes should be protected from exploitation by professional and commercial enterprises." Each entity binds itself to follow the directives of the contractual manual in order to promote an intercollegiate amateur athletic program for student-athletes.

To the extent that the plaintiff's claim of arbitrary and capricious action asserts a violation of the duty of good faith and fair dealing that is implied in the contractual relationship between the NCAA and its members, his position as a third-party beneficiary of that contractual relationship affords him standing to pursue his claims.

Good Faith and Fair Dealing

[S]ince this court has determined that the agreement between the defendants has an implied covenant of good faith and fair dealing as it relates to the plaintiff, there must be in fact honesty and reasonableness in the enforcement of the contract. Therefore, the defendant, and for that matter OSU, was required to deal honestly and reasonably with the plaintiff as a third-party beneficiary regarding their contractual relationship. Surely each party is entitled to the benefit of its bargain. With that stated, if this court determines that Bylaw 12.3.2.1 is void because it is against the public policy of Ohio or because it is arbitrary and capricious, and Bylaw 19.7 interferes with the delegation of judicial power to the courts of this state, then the defendant has not dealt with the plaintiff honestly or reasonably and the defendant has breached the contract.

The plaintiff asserts that the bylaw promulgated by the defendant prevented his lawyers from competently representing him. Therefore the plaintiff argues, the bylaw is void because it is against public policy. Bylaw 12.3.2.1 states: "A lawyer may not be present during discussions of a contract offer with a professional organization or have any direct contact (in person, by telephone or by mail) with a professional sports organization on behalf of the individual. A lawyer's presence during such discussions is considered representation by an agent."

In contrast, the defendant argues that Bylaw 12.3.2.1 helps to retain a clear line of demarcation between collegiate and professional sports that is a fundamental goal of the member institutions. Furthermore, according to the defendant, it preserves an amateur model of collegiate athletics, and the defendant contends that this court should not intervene since the bylaw is the will of the NCAA membership.

It is important to fully understand the fact pattern of what transpired and what caused the plaintiff to be pronounced ineligible. At the end of the summer of 2006, representatives from the Minnesota Twins met with the plaintiff and his father at the Oliver home. According to the plaintiff's testimony, the plaintiff's father contacted the Barattas to inform them of the meeting. Tim Baratta told the plaintiff's father that he thought he should be there. While all the parties were at the Oliver home, the Twins offered the plaintiff a $390,000 contract, which he rejected after seeking the advice of his father. However, Tim Baratta's presence at the Oliver home, even though no testimony ever portrayed that Mr. Baratta was involved in any of the conversations between the plaintiff and the Twin's representative, just Baratta's presence (the presence of an attorney/advisor who advised the plaintiff that he would keep his amateurism status safe) in that room, violated Bylaw 12.3.2.1 and stripped the plaintiff of his eligibility to play baseball through the entire season.

Bylaw 12.3, entitled "Use of Agents," states the general principle that a student-athlete is ineligible to participate in intercollegiate sports if he or she agrees to be represented by an agent.

However, the crux of this case falls under Bylaw 12.3.2, which carves out an exception to the no agent rule by allowing a student-athlete to retain a lawyer (not even the defendant can circumvent an individual's right to counsel). Yet, the exception to the rule, i.e., NCAA Bylaw 12.3.2 which allows legal counsel for student-athletes attempts to limit an attorney's role as to that representation and, in effect, such as in the case here, puts the onus on the student-athlete. See NCAA Bylaw 12.3.2.1.

The status of the no-agent rule, as firmly pointed out in the direct testimony of Kevin Lennon, vice president of membership services, is a prohibition against agents, not lawyers. Therein lies the problem. It is impossible to allow student-athletes to hire lawyers and attempt to control what that lawyer does for his client by Bylaws 12.3.2 or 12.3.2.1. These rules attempt to say to the student-athlete that he or she can consult with an attorney but that the attorney cannot negotiate a contract with a professional sport's team. This surely does not retain a clear line of demarcation between amateurism and professionalism. The student-athlete will never know what his attorney is doing for him or her, and quite frankly neither will the defendant. The evidence is very clear that this rule is impossible to enforce and as a result is being enforced selectively. Further, as in this case, it allows for exploitation of the student-athlete "by professional and commercial enterprises," in contravention of the positive intentions of the defendant.

Was Barratta's presence in that room a clear indication that the plaintiff, a teenager who had admitted at trial that he was in no position to negotiate a professional contract and whose father testified to the same, was a professional? According to Bylaw 12.3.2.1, the no-agent rule, he was. As such the following issues must be resolved: Is the no-agent rule against the public policy of Ohio? Is it arbitrary? Is it capricious?

The plaintiff testified that he hired the Barattas in part because they were attorneys and they promised that they would protect his amateur status. From the testimony given at trial, the court is aware that the defendant permits student-athletes and their parents to negotiate contracts while in the presence of a sports representative but to have an attorney present in the room would in some way smear the line of demarcation between what is amateurism and what is professionalism. An attorney's duty, in Ohio, in Oklahoma, in all 50 states, is to represent his client competently. Perhaps another term is used, other than that of "competently" within each state's professional code of conduct, but it all boils down to the attorney being skilled and proficient and simply having the know-how to represent the best interests of his client.

For a student-athlete to be permitted to have an attorney and then to tell that student-athlete that his attorney cannot be present during the discussion of an offer from a professional organization is akin to a patient hiring a doctor, but the doctor is told by the hospital board and the insurance company that he cannot be present when the patient meets with a surgeon because the conference may improve his patient's decision-making power. Bylaw 12.3.2.1 is unreliable (capricious) and illogical (arbitrary) and indeed stifles what attorneys are trained and retained to do.

This court appreciates that a fundamental goal of the member institutions and the defendant is to preserve the clear line of demarcation between amateurism and professionalism. However, to suggest that Bylaw 12.3.2.1 accomplishes that purpose by instructing a student-athlete that his attorney cannot do what he or she was hired to do is simply illogical. An example of a clear line of demarcation between amateurism and professionalism is indeed drawn within the bylaws and is done so in Bylaw 12.02.3: "A professional athlete is one who receives any kind of payment, directly or indirectly, for athletics participation except as permitted by the governing legislation of the Association."

If the membership and the NCAA decide that Bylaw 12.02.3 does not accomplish that purpose, so be it. But no entity, other than that one designated by the state, can dictate to an attorney where, what, how, or when he should represent his client. With all due respect, surely that decision should not be determined by the NCAA and its member institutions, no matter what the defendant claims is the purpose of the rule. If the defendant intends to deal with this athlete or any athlete in good faith, the student-athlete should have the opportunity to have the tools present (in this case an attorney) that would allow him to make a wise decision without automatically being deemed a professional, especially when such contractual negotiations can be overwhelming even to those who are skilled in their implementation.

Arbitrary and Capricious

[The court held that Bylaw 19.7, the so-called restitution rule, is arbitrary and capricious and therefore invalid.]

The court determines by clear and convincing evidence that the plaintiff would suffer immediate and irreparable injury, loss, or damage if injunctive relief is not granted. If an injunction is not granted, the plaintiff would suffer loss of his college baseball experience, impairment or loss of his future baseball professional career, loss in being available for the upcoming draft because he is less likely to be seen, and ongoing damage to the plaintiff's reputation and baseball career. In comparison, the defendant's witnesses stated that if relief were granted, it would be confusing as to which institutions would have to follow this court's ruling. Would it be Ohio members, Oklahoma members, all institutions? However, since this court has personam jurisdiction, this argument is not as persuasive as the plaintiff's and the scales of justice have tilted in the plaintiff's favor.

Judgment accordingly.

Notes and Comments

1. Both *Bloom* and *Oliver* demonstrate that a college athlete has standing to challenge an NCAA "amateurism" rule as a third-party beneficiary to the NCAA's bylaws by claiming that the rule is arbitrary and capricious on its face or as it is being ap-

plied. An amateurism rule is arbitrary and capricious on its face if the rule is not rationally related to "retain[ing] a clear line of demarcation between intercollegiate athletics and professional sports." In *Oliver*, Judge Tone noted: "These rules attempt to say to the student-athlete that he or she can consult with an attorney but that the attorney cannot negotiate a contract with a professional sport's team. This surely does not retain a clear line of demarcation between amateurism and professionalism. The student-athlete will never know what his attorney is doing for him or her, and quite frankly neither will the defendant. The evidence is very clear that this rule is impossible to enforce and as a result is being enforced selectively. Further, as in this case, it allows for exploitation of the student-athlete 'by professional and commercial enterprises,' in contravention of the positive intentions of the defendant." How did the court of appeals in *Bloom* conclude that the "no endorsement" rule is rationally related to preserving amateurism? Did the *Bloom* court merely defer to the NCAA on this question?

2. In the closing paragraph of the opinion in *Oliver*, Judge Tone wrote: "If an injunction is not granted, the plaintiff would suffer loss of his college baseball experience, impairment or loss of his future baseball professional career, loss in being available for the upcoming draft because he is less likely to be seen, and ongoing damage to the plaintiff's reputation and baseball career." Professor Karcher testified as an expert witness on behalf of Oliver and provided a damages report regarding his lost earning capacity. The NCAA had appealed Judge Tone's ruling but rather than risk losing again on appeal, the NCAA entered a settlement with Oliver. Under the terms of the settlement, the NCAA agreed to pay Oliver $750,000 conditioned upon Judge Tone vacating his ruling that struck down the NCAA's "no agent" rule and "restitution rule." Judge Tone approved the settlement and vacated the ruling, which effectively kept both rules on the NCAA's books. For a theoretical and practical perspective on damages for lost earning capacity in a professional sports career, *see* Richard T. Karcher, *Rethinking Damages for Lost Earning Capacity in a Professional Sports Career: How to Translate Today's Athletic Potential into Tomorrow's Dollars*, 14 Chapman L. Rev. 75 (2010).

3. The NCAA's Restitution Rule, currently Bylaw 19.13, provides that "if a student-athlete who is ineligible under the terms of the constitution, bylaws or other legislation of the Association is permitted to participate in intercollegiate competition contrary to such NCAA legislation but in accordance with the terms of a court restraining order or injunction operative against the institution attended by such student-athlete or against the Association, or both, and said injunction is voluntarily vacated, stayed or reversed or it is finally determined by the courts that injunctive relief is not or was not justified, the Board of Directors may take any one or more..." of several actions against the school or the athlete. Most onerous would be vacating team records during the participation of the athlete, including victories. It also allows for the institution to be required to return television receipts and to potentially be subject to sanctions for infractions.

4. In *Banks v. NCAA*, 977 F.2d 1081 (7th Cir. 1992), the plaintiff had contended that the association's rules precluding athletes from declaring for professional drafts and retaining agents without losing eligibility violated the antitrust laws. The Seventh Circuit held that the plaintiff failed to allege an identifiable effect on an identifiable market. Nor had he alleged that the rules diminished competition. *See also Williams v. Univ. of Cincinnati*, 752 N.E.2d 367 (Ohio Ct. Cl. 2001), in which the court found no breach of contract where student athlete had lost his eligibility and scholarship for, among other things, receipt of extra benefits. The court found that these actions were strictly his and the loss of the scholarship was in no part due to inappropriate actions by the university.

5. In 2018, Orike Ogunbowale made the game winning shot in each of Notre Dame's Women's Final Four games. Shortly thereafter she was invited to appear as a participant in the TV show, *Dancing with the Stars*. The show awards prize money to competitors. She was granted a waiver by the NCAA from the rules noted in *Bloom* and became eligible to receive prize money. The waiver, however, prohibited her from participating or appearing in any promotional materials or videos for the show which relies in part on viewer voting. Ultimately, she exited the show during Week 2, which according to some commentators was a direct result of the NCAA's restriction on making promotional appearances. Was the NCAA's action here consistent with *Bloom*?

6. Does the NCAA have the authority to regulate agents and impose a certification process for agents who represent college basketball players? *See* Edelman & Karcher, *The NCAA's Agent Certification Program: A Critical and Legal Analysis*, 11 Harvard J. Sports & Ent. L. 155 (2020) (providing a critical analysis of the policies and procedures of the NCAA agent certification program and concluding that the NCAA lacks the legal authority to regulate and certify basketball player agents under its agent certification program and that the agent certification program likely constitutes an illegal group boycott that violates federal antitrust law, specifically §1 of the Sherman Act).

Problem

You work in the athletic department at Midwestern State University and have been contacted by the president and the athletic director regarding a problem that has just come to their attention. Two of the school's former football players may have been ineligible during their just completed senior seasons as a result of signing contracts with an agent. The president is reasonably convinced that the two players both signed with the agent just prior to the start of their senior year and may have received money from the agent as well. The two players were high draft choices and are just now beginning their rookie years in the NFL.

The agent involved has been successful for many years, although there have always been rumors concerning his practices. However, he has never actually encountered legal difficulties, and is in good standing with the NFLPA, which regulates player agents. It is well known that he is very friendly with the offensive coordinator of the Midwestern State football team and has represented him in various dealings over the years. The president is concerned about the ramifications for the school's sports programs and would also like to take some action against the agent. Discuss the problems that may face the school regarding NCAA rules and the possible courses of action regarding the agent.

C. NCAA Rules Related to the "Integrity of the Game": Sports Wagering Activity and Drug Testing

1. Sports Wagering

The two key questions regarding the NCAA bylaws that prohibit sports wagering are: (1) What types of sports wagering activities are prohibited? and (2) Who is prohibited from engaging in that activity?

Regarding the first question, prohibited sports wagering activity involves placing, accepting or soliciting a wager (i.e., giving up an item of value via a bookmaker or parlay card, the internet, and pools or fantasy leagues in which an entry fee is required) on "any institutional practice or any competition (intercollegiate, amateur or professional) in a sport in which the [NCAA] conducts championship competition, in bowl subdivision football and in emerging sports for women." Thus, a college football player cannot bet on professional football or even men's or women's basketball but he can bet and gamble on horse racing, blackjack, slot machines, race car driving, and boxing/mixed martial arts.

The answer to the second question:

a. Staff members of an institution's athletics department;
b. Non-athletics department staff members who have responsibilities within or over the athletics department (e.g., chancellor or president, faculty athletics representative, individual to whom athletics reports);
c. Staff members of a conference office; and
d. Student-athletes.

In addition, all of the foregoing individuals shall not knowingly provide information to anyone involved in or associated with any type of sports wagering activities concerning intercollegiate, amateur, or professional athletics competition.

2. Drug Use and Testing

Under NCAA bylaws, student-athletes are required to provide written consent to random, year-round drug testing by the NCAA. NCAA member institutions may also implement their own drug testing programs. The NCAA maintains a list of banned drug classes on its website and provides examples of banned substances under each class; however, the banned drug classes list makes it clear, "There is no complete list of banned substances." NCAA bylaws require schools to provide drug education to its student-athletes.

A positive test for performance-enhancing drugs results in a loss of one full year of eligibility for the first offense. A second positive test results in the loss of all remaining eligibility. A student-athlete who tests positive for narcotics shall be ineligible for competition during 50% of a season, and a second positive test results in loss of a year of eligibility.

There are penalties if a student-athlete breaches the NCAA drug-testing program protocol. A student-athlete who fails to show up for testing is treated as having tested positive for a performance-enhancing drug. Also, a student-athlete who is "involved in a case of clearly observed tampering with an NCAA drug-test sample," as documented per NCAA drug-testing protocol by a drug-testing crew member, shall be ineligible for participation in postseason and regular-season competition for two calendar years (*i.e.*, 730 days).

Athletics department staff members who have knowledge of a student-athlete's use at any time of a substance within the banned drug classes are subject to disciplinary action under NCAA bylaws if they fail to follow institutional procedures dealing with drug abuse. They commit unethical conduct violations for knowing involvement in providing a banned substance or impermissible supplement to student-athletes, or knowingly providing medications to student-athletes contrary to medical licensure, commonly accepted standards of care in sports medicine practice, or state and federal law.

An institution may appeal a drug-testing penalty to the Committee on Competitive Safeguards and Medical Aspects of Sports, and the committee's determination is final, binding, and conclusive. The most common challenges are procedural-based, related to the collection or testing of the samples, and "knowledge" challenges. For a knowledge challenge, the student-athlete must show either (1) that he/she did not know and could not reasonably have known or suspected (even with the exercise of utmost caution) that he/she had been administered a banned substance by a third party, *or* (2) that he/she asked questions about a particular substance and the athletics administrator erroneously assured him/her that the substance does not list a banned ingredient.

Notes and Comments

1. The California Supreme Court has held that the NCAA's drug testing program is consistent with the privacy provisions of the California Constitution. *Hill v. NCAA*, 865 P.2d 633 (Cal. 1994). Although a lower California appellate court had ruled that drug testing by the NCAA violated the California Constitution, the court reversed and reasoned that, although the athletes had significant privacy interests,

the interest of the NCAA in protecting the safety and health of athletes and in maintaining the reputation of its programs outweighed the students' interests. *See* Anthony Cruz Jr., *After Ten Years of Litigation, NCAA Drug Testing Is Upheld by California Supreme Court*, SPORTS LAW., July/Aug. 1994, at 1; Karen E. Crummy, Note, *Urine or You're Out: Student-Athletes' Right of Privacy Stripped in* Hill v. NCAA, 29 U.S.F. L. REV. 197 (1994); Stephen M. Kennedy, Note, *Emasculating a State's Constitutional Right to Privacy: The California Supreme Court's Decision in* Hill v. NCAA, 68 TEMP. L. REV. 1497 (1995). *See also* Ted O'Neal, *The Constitutionality of NCAA Drug Testing: A Fine Specimen for Examination*, 46 SMU L. REV. 513 (1992). In *Brennan v. Board of Trustees for University of Louisiana Systems*, 691 So. 2d 324 (La. App. 1997), the court rejected a student-athlete's indirect challenge (suing the university) to the NCAA's drug-testing program. The *Brennan* court found that health and competitive balance outweighed the student-athlete's diminished privacy interest.

2. The Colorado Supreme Court struck down the drug testing scheme of the University of Colorado, finding that the testing violated both the United States and Colorado Constitutions. *University of Colorado v. Derdeyn*, 863 P.2d 929 (Colo. 1993). The extent to which the principles announced in *Board of Education v. Earls*, 536 U.S. 822 (2002), covered in Chapter 1, would change the holding in *Derdeyn* is unclear since: (1) *Derdeyn* was based in part upon state constitutional principles and (2) *Derdeyn* was a college situation while *Earls* involved a high school. One pertinent distinction between *Derdeyn* and *Hill* is the University of Colorado is clearly a state actor while the *Hill* Court found that the NCAA was not a state actor.

D. The Contractual Relationship Between the Athlete and University

Contract law principles apply to the university-athlete relationship. The contractual relationship between the two parties arises from two key documents: the National Letter of Intent (NLI) and the Statement of Financial Assistance (*i.e.*, the Grant-in-Aid). Litigation can result when there is a dispute between the parties over the scope of the rights and obligations that arise from this contractual relationship. College athletics administrators must have a general understanding of the applicable legal principles and NCAA regulations.

1. The National Letter of Intent (NLI) and the Grant-in-Aid

The NLI is "a binding agreement between a prospective student-athlete and an NLI member institution." National Letter of Intent, *About the National Letter of Intent (NLI)*, http://www.nationalletter.org/aboutTheNli/index.html. An enforceable contract is created between the two parties to the NLI by the following exchange of promises:

1. A prospective student-athlete agrees to attend the institution full-time for one academic year.
2. The institution agrees to provide athletics financial aid for one academic year. *Id.*

The NLI serves as a recruiting prohibition, applied after a prospective student-athlete signs the NLI, that requires all other NCAA member institutions to cease recruitment of the prospective student-athlete. *Id.* At the time the NLI is signed, the prospective student-athlete must receive a written offer of athletics financial aid for the entire academic year from the institution named in this document, and the offer must list the terms, conditions, and amount of the athletics aid award. National Letter of Intent, *NLI Provisions*, http://www.nationalletter.org/nliProvisions/index.html. Thus, a student-athlete who attends an institution as a "walk-on" does not sign an NLI.

Problem

Review the following excerpt of the NLI and identify three circumstances under which a student-athlete would no longer be bound to the institution.

This NLI shall be declared null and void if any of the following occur:

a. **Admissions Requirement.** This NLI shall be declared null and void if the institution named in this document notifies me in writing that I have been denied admission or, by the opening day of classes in the fall, has failed to provide me with written notice of admission, provided I have submitted a complete admission application. It is my obligation to provide, by request, my academic records and an application for admission to the signing institution. If I fail to submit the necessary academic credentials and/or application to determine an admission decision prior to September 1, the NLI office per its review with the institution will determine the status of the NLI.

If I am eligible for admission, but the institution named in this document defers my admission to a subsequent term, the NLI will be declared null and void; however, this NLI remains binding if I defer my admission.

b. **Eligibility Requirements.** This NLI shall be declared null and void if, by the opening day of classes in the fall, I have not met NCAA initial eligibility requirements; NCAA, conference or institution's requirements for athletics financial aid; or two-year college transfer requirements, provided I have submitted all necessary documents for eligibility determination.

(1) This NLI shall be rendered null and void if I become a nonqualifier per the NCAA Eligibility Center. This NLI remains valid if I am a partial qualifier per NCAA Division II rules unless I do not meet the institution's policies for receipt of athletics aid.

(2) It is my obligation to register with and provide information to the NCAA Eligibility Center. If I fail to submit the necessary documentation for an initial-eligibility decision and have not attended classes at the signing institution, the NLI office per its review with the institution will determine the status of the NLI.

....

e. **Recruiting Rules Violation.** If eligibility reinstatement by the NCAA student-athlete reinstatement staff is necessary due to NCAA and/or conference recruiting rules violations, the institution must notify me that I have an option to have the NLI declared null and void due to the rules violation. It is my decision to have the NLI remain valid or to have the NLI declared null and void, permitting me to be recruited and not be subject to NLI penalties.

***

Athletics financial aid is called a "grant-in-aid" in NCAA terminology. Under NCAA bylaws, "[a] full grant-in-aid is financial aid that consists of tuition and fees, room and board, books and other expenses related to attendance at the institution up to the cost of attendance." Bylaw 15.02.6. The Statement of Financial Assistance is the document that contains the terms and conditions of a student-athlete's grant-in-aid. Beginning in 2012, a university may give a student-athlete a grant-in-aid for a multi-year term (from one to a maximum of five years) that cannot be terminated by the university before the end of the term due to injury or unsatisfactory athletic performance. There are numerous NCAA bylaws that regulate the grant-in-aid, including the circumstances under which a grant-in-aid can be canceled, reduced, or not renewed.

2. Consequences Arising from a Breach of Contract

Taylor v. Wake Forest University

191 S.E.2d 379 (N.C. Ct. App. 1972)

This action was instituted for the recovery of educational expenses incurred by George J. Taylor, father, and Gregg F. Taylor, son, after alleged wrongful termination of an athletic scholarship issued to Gregg F. Taylor by Wake Forest University.

As early as December 1965, football coaches at Wake Forest were in communication with Gregg Taylor soliciting his enrollment at Wake Forest. This interest was engendered by the football playing ability of Gregg Taylor. Not only was Wake Forest interested in him, but other colleges and universities were likewise showing an interest. As a result of this interest and negotiations, Gregg Taylor and his father, George Taylor, on 27 February 1967, submitted an application entitled, "Atlantic Coast Conference Application For A Football Grant-In-Aid Or A Scholarship."

This application was accepted by Wake Forest on 24 May 1967. It provided in part:

> "This Grant, if awarded, will be for 4 years provided I conduct myself in accordance with the rules of the Conference, the NCAA, and the Institution. I agree to maintain eligibility for intercollegiate athletics under both Conference and Institutional rules. Training rules for intercollegiate athletics are considered rules of the Institution, and I agree to abide by them.
>
> If injured while participating in athletics supervised by a member of the coaching staff, the Grant or Scholarship will be honored; and the medical expenses will be paid by the Athletic Department.
>
> This grant, when approved, is awarded for academic and athletic achievement and is not to be interpreted as employment in any manner whatsoever."

At the time of the execution of the agreement between the Taylors and Wake Forest, some of the rules of the NCAA prohibited:

> (a) Gradation or cancellation of institutional aid during the period of its award on the basis of a student-athlete's prowess or his contribution to a team's success.
>
> (b) Gradation or cancellation of institutional aid during the period of its award because of an injury which prevents the recipient from participating in athletics.
>
> (c) Gradation or cancellation of institutional aid during the period of its award for any other athletic reason, except that such aid may be gradated or canceled if the recipient (1) voluntarily renders himself ineligible for intercollegiate competition, or (2) fraudulently misrepresents any information on his application, letter of intent or tender, or (3) engages in serious misconduct warranting substantial disciplinary penalty.
>
> Any such gradation or cancellation of aid is permissible only if (1) such action is taken by the regular disciplinary and/or scholarship awards authorities of the institution, (2) the student has had an opportunity for a hearing, and (3) the action is based on institutional policy applicable to the general student body.

At the time the contract was entered into Wake Forest did not have a written Grant-In-Aid policy. This policy was not put in writing until January 1969. One of the written policy provisions was to the effect that financial aid could be terminated for "[r]efusal to attend practice sessions or scheduled work-outs that are a part of the athletic program or to act in such a manner as to disrupt these sessions." The Wake Forest Athletic Director set out in an affidavit:

> "[T]he policy of requiring student athletes to regularly attend practice sessions was in effect at the defendant university when the first scholarship was granted more than 30 years ago."

In compliance with the contract entered into, Gregg Taylor enrolled and became a student at Wake Forest at the beginning of the Fall Session 1967. He participated in the football program during the Fall of 1967.

At the end of that semester, his grade average was 1.0 out of a possible 4.0. Wake Forest required a 1.35 grade average after freshman year, a 1.65 grade average after sophomore year, and a 1.85 grade average after junior year. The 1.0 grade average received by Gregg Taylor for the first semester of his freshman year in the Fall of 1967 was thus below the grade average required by Wake Forest. Gregg Taylor notified the football coach on 6 February 1968 that he would not participate in regular practice sessions of the football team during the Spring of 1968 until his grades had improved. For the second semester of his freshman year, which was the Spring of 1968, Gregg Taylor obtained a 1.9 grade average. This brought his grade average above what Wake Forest required even after junior year. Despite this improvement in his grade average, Gregg Taylor decided that he would not further participate in the football program, and in the fall of his sophomore year, which was the Fall of 1968, Gregg Taylor attained a 2.4 grade average. Gregg Taylor continued in his refusal to participate in the football program.

Wake Forest notified Gregg Taylor on or about 1 May 1969 that a hearing would be held on 14 May 1969 before the Faculty Athletic Committee as to whether his scholarship should be terminated. At this hearing Gregg Taylor was notified that the Faculty Athletic Committee would recommend to the Scholarship Committee that his scholarship be terminated because of his failure to participate in the football program at Wake Forest. Thereafter, the Scholarship Committee of Wake Forest accepted the recommendation of the Faculty Athletic Committee, and on 10 July 1969, the Scholarship Committee notified Gregg Taylor that his scholarship had been terminated as of the end of the 1968–1969 academic year, which was the end of Gregg Taylor's sophomore year.

Gregg Taylor continued to attend Wake Forest during the 1969–1970 academic year, which was his junior year, and likewise, the academic year of 1970–1971, which was his senior year; and he received an undergraduate degree from Wake Forest in June 1971.

As a result of the termination of the scholarship, expenses in the amount of $5500 were incurred during those two academic years. It is for this sum of $5500 that his action was instituted.

The defendant Wake Forest moved for summary judgment pursuant to Rule 56 of the Rules of Civil Procedure on the ground that there was no genuine issue as to any material fact and that the defendant was entitled to judgment as a matter of law. This motion was allowed, and the plaintiffs appealed.

Plaintiffs contend that there was a genuine issue as to a material fact and that a jury should determine whether Gregg Taylor acted reasonably and in good faith in refusing to participate in the football program at Wake Forest when such participation interfered with reasonable academic progress.

The plaintiff's position depends upon a construction of the contractual agreement between plaintiffs and Wake Forest. As stated in the affidavit of George J. Taylor, the position of the plaintiffs is that it was orally agreed between plaintiffs and the representative of Wake Forest that:

> "[I]n the event of any conflict between educational achievement and athletic involvement, participation in athletic activities could be limited or eliminated to the extent necessary to assure reasonable academic progress."

And plaintiffs were to be the judge as to what "reasonable academic progress" constituted.

We do not agree with the position taken by plaintiffs. The scholarship application filed by Gregg Taylor provided:

> "... I agree to maintain eligibility for intercollegiate athletics under both Conference and Institutional rules. Training rules for intercollegiate athletics are considered rules of the Institution, and I agree to abide by them."

Both Gregg Taylor and his father knew that the application was for "Football Grant-In-Aid Or A Scholarship," and that the scholarship was "awarded for academic and athletic achievement." It would be a strained construction of the contract that would enable the plaintiffs to determine the "reasonable academic progress" of Gregg Taylor. Gregg Taylor, in consideration of the scholarship award, agreed to maintain his athletic eligibility and this meant both physically and scholastically. As long as his grade average equaled or exceeded the requirements of Wake Forest, he was maintaining his scholastic eligibility for athletics. Participation in and attendance at practice were required to maintain his physical eligibility. When he refused to do so in the absence of any injury or excuse other than to devote more time to studies, he was not complying with his contractual obligations.

The record disclosed that Wake Forest fully complied with its agreement and that Gregg Taylor failed to do so. There was no "genuine issue as to any material fact" and summary judgment was proper.

Ross v. Creighton University

957 F.2d 410 (7th Cir. 1992)

RIPPLE, CIRCUIT JUDGE.

Kevin Ross filed suit against Creighton University (Creighton or the University) for negligence and breach of contract arising from Creighton's alleged failure to educate him. The district court dismissed Mr. Ross' complaint for failure to state a claim.

In the spring of 1978, Mr. Ross was a promising senior basketball player at Wyandotte High School in Kansas City, Kansas. Sometime during his senior year in high school, he accepted an athletic scholarship to attend Creighton and to play on its varsity basketball team.

Creighton is an academically superior university. Mr. Ross comes from an academically disadvantaged background. At the time of his enrollment at Creighton, Mr. Ross was at an academic level far below that of the average Creighton student. For example, he scored in the bottom fifth percentile of college-bound seniors taking the American College Test, while the average freshman admitted to Creighton with him scored in the upper twenty-seven percent. According to the complaint, Creighton realized Mr. Ross' academic limitations when it admitted him, and, to induce him to attend and play basketball, Creighton assured Mr. Ross that he would receive sufficient tutoring so that he "would receive a meaningful education while at Creighton." ...

Mr. Ross attended Creighton from 1978 until 1982. During that time he maintained a D average and acquired 96 of the 128 credits needed to graduate. However, many of these credits were in courses such as Marksmanship and Theory of Basketball, and did not count towards a university degree. Mr. Ross alleges that he took these courses on the advice of Creighton's Athletic Department, and that the department also employed a secretary to read his assignments and prepare and type his papers. Mr. Ross also asserts that Creighton failed to provide him with sufficient and competent tutoring that it had promised.

When he left Creighton, Mr. Ross had the overall language skills of a fourth grader and the reading skills of a seventh grader....

Mr. Ross filed suit against Creighton in Cook County (Illinois) Circuit Court for negligence and breach of contract. [Creighton removed the matter to federal district court on diversity grounds.]

Mr. Ross' complaint advances three separate theories of how Creighton was negligent towards him. First, he contends that Creighton committed "educational malpractice" by not providing him with a meaningful education and preparing him for employment after college. Second, Mr. Ross claims that Creighton negligently inflicted emotional distress upon him by enrolling him in a stressful university environment for which he was not prepared, and then by failing to provide remedial programs that would have helped him survive there. Third, Mr. Ross urges the court to adopt a new cause of action for the tort of "negligent admission," which would allow recovery when an institution admits, and then does not adequately assist, a woefully unprepared student. The complaint also sets forth a contract claim, alleging that Creighton contracted to provide Mr. Ross "an opportunity... to obtain a meaningful college education and degree, and to do what was reasonably necessary... to enable [Mr. Ross] to obtain a meaningful college education and degree." ... It goes on to assert that Creighton breached this contract by failing to provide Mr. Ross adequate tutoring; by not requiring Mr. Ross to attend tutoring sessions; by not allowing him to "red-shirt," that is, to forego a year of basketball, in order to work on academics;

and by failing to afford Mr. Ross a reasonable opportunity to take advantage of tutoring services. Mr. Ross also alleges that Creighton breached a promise it had made to him to pay for a college education.

The Negligence Claims

[The court rejected the negligence claims of the plaintiff, based essentially on the principle that there are no adequate standards against which to measure such a claim.]

The Contract Claims

In counts two and three of his complaint, Mr. Ross alleges that Creighton breached an oral or a written contract that it had with him. When read as a totality, these allegations fairly allege that Creighton agreed, in exchange for Mr. Ross' promise to play on its basketball team, to allow him an opportunity to participate, in a meaningful way, in the academic program of the University despite his deficient academic background. The complaint further alleges, when read as a totality, that Creighton breached this contract and denied Mr. Ross any real opportunity to participate in and benefit from the University's academic program when it failed to perform five commitments made to Ross: (1) "to provide adequate and competent tutoring services," (2) "to require [Mr. Ross] to attend tutoring sessions," (3) to afford Mr. Ross "a reasonable opportunity to take full advantage of tutoring services," (4) to allow Mr. Ross to red-shirt, and (5) to provide funds to allow Mr. Ross to complete his college education.

It is held generally in the United States that the "basic legal relation between a student and a private university or college is contractual in nature. The catalogues, bulletins, circulars, and regulations of the institution made available to the matriculant become a part of the contract."

There is no question, we believe, that Illinois would adhere to the great weight of authority and bar any attempt to repackage an educational malpractice claim as a contract claim. As several courts have noted, the policy concerns that preclude a cause of action for educational malpractice apply with equal force to bar a breach of contract claim attacking the general quality of an education....

To state a claim for breach of contract, the plaintiff must do more than simply allege that the education was not good enough. Instead, he must point to an identifiable contractual promise that the defendant failed to honor. Thus, as was suggested in *Paladino*, if the defendant took tuition money and then provided no education, or alternately, promised a set number of hours of instruction and then failed to deliver, a breach of contract action may be available....

We read Mr. Ross' complaint to allege more than a failure of the University to provide him with an education of a certain quality. Rather, he alleges that the University knew that he was not qualified academically to participate in its curriculum. Nevertheless, it made a specific promise that he would be able to participate in a meaningful way in that program because it would provide certain specific services to him. Finally, he alleges that the University breached its promise by reneging on its commitment to provide those services and, consequently, effectively cutting him off from any participation in and benefit from the University's academic program. To adjudicate such a claim, the court would not be required to determine whether Creighton had breached its contract with Mr. Ross by providing deficient academic services. Rather, its inquiry would be limited to whether the University had provided any real access to its academic curriculum at all.

Accordingly, we must disagree respectfully with our colleague in the district court as to whether the contract counts of the complaint can be dismissed at the pleadings stage. In our view, the allegations of the complaint are sufficient to warrant further proceedings. We emphasize, however, the narrow ground of our disagreement. We agree—indeed we emphasize—that courts should not "take on the job of supervising the relationship between colleges and student athletes or creating in effect a new relationship between them." We also recognize a formal university student contract is rarely employed and, consequently, "the general nature and terms of the agreement are usually implied, with specific terms to be found in the university bulletin and other publications; custom and usages can also become specific terms by implication."

Nevertheless, we believe that the district court can adjudicate Mr. Ross' specific and narrow claim that he was barred from any participation in and benefit from the University's academic program without second-guessing the professional judgment of the University faculty on academic matters.

Notes and Comments

1. What are the two requirements, identified by the court in *Taylor*, must be met for student-athletes to satisfy the contractual obligation of maintaining their *athletic* eligibility?

2. The court in *Ross* provided numerous reasons for refusing to recognize a student-athlete's "educational malpractice" claim against a university. Do you agree with the court's reasoning?

3. What does *Ross* say that a student-athlete needs to prove in order to state a claim for breach of an oral agreement? *See also Fortay v. Univ. of Miami*, 1994 U.S. Dist. Lexis 1865 (alleged promises that included representations that Miami would provide guidance enabling the plaintiff to develop his football skills, that Miami would not recruit other quarterbacks, and that the plaintiff would be Miami's starting quarterback by his third year were sufficient to support a breach of oral contract claim);

Hairston v. Southern Methodist University, 441 S.W.3d 327 (Tex. App. 2013) (rejecting plaintiff's claim premised on a coach's alleged oral promise of a scholarship).

Problem

Barney Moore is a freshman student-athlete on the basketball team at Southern State University (SSU). In high school, Moore was highly recruited, with over a dozen of the prominent basketball schools offering him a scholarship. The schools were impressed with his abilities as a point guard and his general leadership qualities. All made extensive promises to him concerning his role at their school. SSU was no different. The assistant coaches who visited with Moore and his parents consistently stated that if he came to SSU he not only would play for four years, but he would start for four years at point guard. The coaches further assured that he would be groomed for stardom in the National Basketball Association. They noted several other SSU players, point guards to be exact, who had gone on to fame and fortune in the NBA. They also promised extensive tutoring and other assistance with his educational experience.

Barney Moore was convinced by the SSU coaches and was truly excited about attending SSU. He was, therefore, quite shocked when the head coach abruptly resigned in order to take a position at another school one week after Moore had signed his letter of intent to go to SSU. The new coaching staff came on board near the end of the spring and all during the summer prior to the beginning of Moore's freshman year continued to phone and visit him at home to assure him that everything the prior coaching staff had promised would happen. Moore, however, asked for release from the letter of intent so he could go to another school. The coaches refused to release him and his only options were to stay or transfer and lose a year of eligibility. Reluctantly, Moore decided to honor his end of the agreement and arrived on time for the beginning of classes.

Once informal workouts and regular practice had begun, Moore realized that another point guard, a junior college transfer who arrived in late summer, was catching the eyes of the coaching staff. Once the season began, the other player was the starter, and during the season Moore averaged eight minutes of playing time per game and only scored two points per game. He was extremely disappointed and depressed about the situation. He was also having difficulties in the classroom, which he attributed to the fact that the tutoring promised during his recruitment had never materialized. Overwhelmed by the time commitment involved with basketball, Moore began to think very seriously about continuing to play at SSU. Upon discussing this with the coaches he was told that they really wanted to "redshirt" him the following year and groom him for the starting role the year after, when the current starter would be gone. Moore did not want to sit out and lose more ground.

Moore wonders if he has a possible legal action against SSU in the event his scholarship is terminated. What would you tell him and why?

E. The College Athlete as "Employee"

1. College Athletes' Rights under Workers' Compensation Laws

This section explores the question as to whether college athletes are employees for workers' compensation purposes. In order to understand how injured athletes fit into various workers' compensation schemes, it is first necessary to understand how such schemes typically operate.

Every state has its own workers' compensation statute. These statutes all reflect a type of bargain struck between employers and employees. The gist of the bargain is that injured employees give up their rights to pursue common-law tort claims (with the promise of full recovery but with the concomitant danger of no recovery) in exchange for a more certain, albeit limited, recovery under the workers' compensation statute. The employer, in turn, relinquishes common-law defenses to tort actions (like contributory negligence and assumption of risk) but enjoys the assurance that damage awards will be limited. Typically, the scheme is funded by insurance paid by the employer into a fund administered by a specialized agency empowered to process claims. In deference to this common-sense political bargain, most courts tend to liberally construe workers' compensation schemes to bring as many workers as reasonably possible under the law's umbrella, and to defer to the judgment of the specialized agency.

Generally, a workers' compensation law makes the employer strictly liable for an injury to an employee that occurs in the course of employment. Eligibility for benefits is conditioned upon the existence of an employer-employee relationship. An employee is generally defined as a person in the service of another under a contract of hire, written or implied. The threshold inquiry is whether the injured worker fits the state's definition of an employee. A recurring question that arises is whether a particular worker is an employee (and thus covered) or an independent contractor (who would fall outside the coverage of the act).

Each state has developed its own tests for making this determination in cases where the worker-employer relationship is not entirely clear. The tests adopted appear to fall into two basic categories—the "nature of the work" test and the "right to control" test. Under the nature of the work test, the court focuses upon whether the worker's efforts are inextricably linked to a significant aspect of the employer's business. Under the "right to control" test, the focus is upon the employer's ability to manipulate the efforts of the worker. A greater understanding of the tests used can be better achieved in the context of a particular case arising in a specific jurisdiction.

Assuming that the injured worker is regarded as an employee, the next question is whether the injury "arose out of" or was "in the course of" the employment. These phrases have been the focus of more than a considerable amount of litigation. As a general rule, the courts tend to look for a causal connection between the injury and the employment. The test of causation is met if it is the employment that brings the worker into the orbit of the risk that in fact resulted in the injury.

The basic elements of recovery under most acts include medical expenses and lost earnings. Medical expenses are compensable if reasonably incurred. In regard to lost earnings (and impaired earning capacity), the basis for the amount of available benefits turns on the employee's average weekly wage just prior to the injury. Incapacity to work is classified as temporarily total, temporarily partial, permanently partial, or permanently total. Benefits are paid as a percentage of the average weekly wage. The percentage varies from state to state, and is often accompanied by a statewide cap on both periodic payments and the overall amount payable. The acts also provide for additional benefits for injuries that result in specific consequences, like the loss of the use of a limb or the loss of sight. Benefits are payable to dependents in cases of worker death. While workers' compensation laws are generally premised on some common grounds, it must be kept in mind that each state's scheme has its own nuances.

The college athlete's acceptance of the grant-in-aid, as previously addressed in the previous section, creates a contractual relationship between the athlete and the educational institution that grants the award. In a series of cases, college athletes have sought to recover for their injuries under workers' compensation laws. The important issue in such litigation is whether they are employees of the educational institution that provides them with a grant-in-aid. *Waldrep* is one of the more recent cases.

Waldrep v. Texas Employers Insurance Association

21 S.W.3d 692 (Tex. App. 2000)

Lee Yeakel.

Appellant Alvis Kent Waldrep, Jr. was awarded workers' compensation benefits by the Texas Workers' Compensation Commission (the "Commission") for an injury he sustained while playing football for Texas Christian University ("TCU"). Appellee Texas Employers Insurance Association (TEIA), in receivership, Texas Property and Casualty Insurance Guaranty Association appealed the award to the district court.

Background

Waldrep graduated from high school in Alvin, Texas in 1972. During his junior and senior years, TCU was among many schools interested in recruiting Waldrep, a young man known for his athletic ability as well as his good academic record. Tommy Runnels, a TCU assistant football coach, visited Waldrep frequently at his home and school, attempting to interest Waldrep in TCU's football and academic programs. During one home visit, Waldrep's mother asked Runnels what would happen if Waldrep were injured during his football career at TCU. Runnels assured Waldrep and his family that TCU would "take care of them" and emphasized that Waldrep would keep his scholarship even if he were injured and could not play football.

Waldrep was very impressed with the facilities at TCU and believed that his abilities would fit in well with TCU's football program. He was also aware that recruitment and his future involvement in athletics at TCU were governed by the rules of the Southwest Athletic Conference ("Southwest Conference") and the National Collegiate Athletic Association ("NCAA"). To affirm his intent to attend school at TCU and participate in TCU's football program, Waldrep signed two documents. First, Waldrep signed a pre-enrollment form ("Letter of Intent"), which demonstrated his formal desire to play football for TCU and penalized him if he decided to enter a different school within the Southwest Conference. Waldrep later signed a financial aid agreement ("Financial Aid Agreement"), ensuring that Waldrep's room, board, and tuition would be paid while attending TCU and that Waldrep would receive ten dollars per month for incidentals. This cash payment was generally referred to as "laundry money." Both documents were contingent on Waldrep's meeting TCU's admission and scholastic requirements for athletic awards.

In August 1972, Waldrep enrolled at TCU. In October 1974, while playing football for TCU against the University of Alabama, Waldrep was critically injured. He sustained a severe injury to his spinal cord and was paralyzed below the neck. Today, Waldrep has no sensation below his upper chest. In 1991, Waldrep filed a workers' compensation claim for his injury. The Commission entered an award in his favor. TEIA appealed this decision to the district court. In a trial *de novo*, a jury found that Waldrep was not an employee of TCU at the time of his injury. The district court rendered judgment in favor of TEIA. On appeal, Waldrep presents five issues. The first addresses whether, as a matter of law, Waldrep was an employee of TCU. The final four challenge various evidentiary rulings made by the district court.

Discussion

Status as an Employee for Workers' Compensation Purposes

By his first issue, Waldrep asserts that at the time of his injury he was an employee of TCU *as a matter of law*. We begin by noting that Waldrep is attacking the legal sufficiency of an adverse answer to a jury question on which he had the burden of proof. After hearing all of the evidence, the jury declined to find that Waldrep was an employee of TCU at the time of his injury....

We are confronted with a situation novel to Texas jurisprudence: whether, for workers' compensation law purposes, a recipient of a scholarship or financial aid from a university becomes that university's employee by agreeing in return to participate in a university-sponsored program. Cases decided under the various workers' compensation statutes in effect from time to time have almost uniformly determined the existence of an employer-employee relationship by an analysis of whether the claimant of workers' compensation benefits was an *employee* as distinguished from an *independent contractor*.... These authorities do not conveniently overlay the facts presented here, as there is no allegation that Waldrep was an independent contractor. Yet they are instructive in one significant aspect: one may receive a benefit from another in return for services and not become an employee.

The jury charge defined "employee" as "a person in the service of another under a contract of hire, express or implied, oral or written, whereby the employer has the right to direct the means or details of the work and not merely the result to be accomplished." Thus, in failing to find that Waldrep was TCU's employee, the jury may have believed that there was no contract of hire between Waldrep and TCU or, if there was, it did not give TCU the right to direct the means or details of Waldrep's "work." We will examine both possibilities.

Existence of Contract of Hire

For the purpose of workers' compensation law, the employer-employee relationship may be created *only* by a contract. Waldrep strongly urges that the Letter of Intent and Financial Aid Agreement are express contracts of hire that set forth the terms of Waldrep's "employment." However, we do not find these documents to be so clear. At best, they only partially set forth the relationship between Waldrep and TCU. By their terms, they generally bound Waldrep to TCU to the exclusion of other Southwest Conference schools, if he intended to participate in athletics, and extended him financial aid so long as he complied with the admission and scholastic requirements of TCU and the rules and regulations of both TCU and the Southwest Conference. These requirements, rules, and regulations are not specifically described in either of the agreements. Nor does the record in this case set them forth in any detail. The Letter of Intent and Financial Aid Agreement are also silent with regard to whether any rules or regulations of the NCAA would apply to Waldrep or affect his relationship with TCU. Yet it is undisputed that before Waldrep signed the Letter of Intent and Financial Aid Agreement, both he and TCU understood that his recruitment and future football career at TCU would be governed by and subject to the rules of the NCAA.

TEIA, on the other hand, posits that Waldrep clearly and simply did not have a contract of hire....

Mindful of the district court's definition of employee, the jury was left to determine if there was a "contract of hire" between Waldrep and TCU. We observe that "the most basic policy of contract law... is the protection of the justified expectations of the parties."... Was it the expectation of Waldrep and TCU that Waldrep would become TCU's employee? To form a contract, the parties must mutually assent to its terms. Whether there is such assent is determined "based on objective standards of what the parties said and did and not on their alleged subjective states of mind."... Because the Letter of Intent and Financial Aid Agreement do not evidence the entire agreement between Waldrep and TCU, we consider them against "the background of circumstances surrounding [their] execution."... We may also look to the parties' conduct after execution of the documents, and such conduct "may be a strong factor in determining just what the real agreement contemplated." [Citation omitted.]

On the facts of this record, any contract of hire must have been a contract whereby TCU hired Waldrep to attend the university, remain in good standing academically, and play football. However, if Waldrep played football for pay, he would have been a professional, not an amateur.

The evidence reflects that the actions of both Waldrep and TCU were consistent with a joint intention that Waldrep be considered an amateur and not a professional. It is undisputed that before Waldrep signed the Letter of Intent and Financial Aid Agreement, both he and TCU understood that his recruitment and future football career at TCU would be governed by and subject to the rules of the NCAA. The record indicates that the NCAA's policies and rules in effect at that time exhibited a concerted effort to ensure that each school governed by these rules made certain that student-athletes were not employees. Indeed, the rules declared that the fundamental policy of the NCAA was "to maintain intercollegiate athletics as an integral part of the educational program and the athlete as an integral part of the student body, and, by so doing, retain a clear line of demarcation between college athletics and professional sports." *NCAA Manual* at 5. Following its policy, the evidence reflects that the NCAA rules made the principle of amateurism foremost and established several requirements to ensure that the student-athlete would not be considered a professional. For example, the NCAA had strict rules against student-athletes taking pay for participation in sports, and student-athletes were ineligible to participate if they were receiving or had received a salary from a professional sports organization.

Additionally, the record reflects that Waldrep and TCU did not treat the financial aid Waldrep received as "pay" or "income." First, as previously noted, the NCAA rules provided that student-athletes would be ineligible if they used their skill for pay in any form; however, that same rule goes on to state that "a student-athlete may accept scholarships or educational grants-in-aid from his institution" as these benefits do not conflict with the NCAA rules. As the NCAA rules were based upon a principle of amateurism and strictly prohibited payment for play, these two provisions together indicate that the NCAA and its participating institutions did not consider the acceptance of financial aid from the institution to be "taking pay." Moreover, the rules provided that any financial aid that exceeded tuition and fees, room and board, required course-related supplies and books, and incidental expenses of fifteen dollars per month would be considered "pay" for participation in intercollegiate athletics. TCU gave Waldrep financial aid for these items but nothing more, indicating that TCU did not intend to pay Waldrep for his participation. Of equal significance, TCU never placed Waldrep on its payroll, never paid him a salary, and never told him that he would be paid a salary. There is no evidence that Waldrep expected a salary. No social security or income tax was withheld from Waldrep's grant-in-aid. Waldrep never filed a tax return reporting his financial aid.

The evidence further reflects that Waldrep and TCU intended that Waldrep participate at TCU as a *student*, not as an *employee*. During the recruitment process, TCU never told Waldrep that he would be an employee, and Waldrep never told TCU that he considered himself to be employed. Moreover, a basic purpose of the NCAA, which governed Waldrep's intercollegiate football career, was to make the student-athlete an integral part of the student body. According to the NCAA rules, "an amateur student-athlete is one who engages in athletics for the education, physical, mental and social benefits he derives therefrom, and to whom athletics is an avocation." *NCAA Manual* at 6. Of importance is the evidence that Waldrep was aware when he signed the Letter of Intent and Financial Aid Agreement that he would still receive financial aid even if hurt or unable to play football, as long as he complied with the rules of the Southwest Conference. Thus, TCU could not "fire" Waldrep as it could an employee. In addition, when Waldrep signed the agreements, he still had to meet the scholastic requirements for athletic awards and qualify for admission to TCU in order to enroll and participate in the football program. Waldrep testified that he knew when he signed the agreements that in order to play football at TCU he would have to maintain certain academic requirements as a student. Thus, his academic responsibilities dictated whether he could continue to play football.

Financial-aid awards are given to many college and university students based on their abilities in various areas, including music, academics, art, and athletics. Sometimes these students are required to participate in certain programs or activities in return for this aid. But, as the Supreme Court of Indiana observed, "scholarship recipients are considered to be students seeking advanced educational opportunities and are not considered to be professional athletes, musicians or artists employed by the university for their skill in their respective areas." *Rensing v. Indiana State Univ. Bd. of Trustees*, 444 N.E.2d 1170 (Ind. 1983).

Although the record in this case contains facts from which the jury could have found that Waldrep and TCU were parties to a contract of hire, there is also probative evidence to the contrary. Viewing the evidence in the light most favorable to the jury's verdict, we hold that the record before us reflects more than a mere scintilla of evidence that Waldrep was not in the service of TCU under a contract of hire.

Right to Direct the Means or Details of Waldrep's Work

If, however, we assume the jury found that a contract existed between Waldrep and TCU, we must determine whether there is some evidence concerning TCU's right to direct the means or details of Waldrep's "work." The definition of "employee" submitted to the jury correctly states the recognized test to determine whether an employer-employee relationship exists: the *right* of the employer to direct or control the means or details of the employee's work. To determine whether there is a right of control, "we first must look to the terms of the employment contract." Where there is no express contract or where the terms of the contract are indefinite, the *exercise* of control "may be the best evidence available to show the actual terms of the contract." However, "'the *right* to control' remains the supreme test and the 'exercise of control' necessarily presupposes a right to control which must be related to some agreement expressed or implied." (citation omitted)

The record reflects that TCU *exercised* direction and control over all of the athletes in its football program, including non-scholarship players, while they were participating in the *football program*. Waldrep admitted that his high school coaches exercised the same type of control over his participation in sports as the coaches at TCU. Waldrep further testified that he did everything that the coaches told him to do because he wanted to, because he loved the game, and because he wanted to be the best, not because he had to. The evidence is clear that TCU did not have the right to direct or control all of Waldrep's activities during his tenure at the school. The NCAA rules protected Waldrep's financial-aid award even if his physical condition prevented him from playing football for any reason. Moreover, TCU could not simply cancel Waldrep's grant-in-aid based on his "athletic ability or his contribution to [the] team's success," or even, in certain circumstances, if he quit.

The fact that the athletic department at TCU established practice and meeting times to be observed by those playing football does not establish that TCU had the *right* to direct and control all aspects of the players' activities while enrolled in the university. Waldrep's acceptance of financial aid from TCU did not subject him to any extraordinary degree of control over his academic activities.

Waldrep clearly presented evidence that TCU *exercised* direction or control over some of his activities while a student at the university. Perhaps the jury might have found this sufficient to prove that TCU had the *right* to direct the means or details of Waldrep's activities, but the jury declined to do so. Viewing the evidence in the light most favorable to the jury's verdict, we hold that the record before us reflects more than a mere scintilla of evidence disputing TCU's right of control.

On appeal, Waldrep bears a heavy burden in seeking reversal and rendition based on an adverse finding to a jury issue on which he had the burden of proof. The record before us reflects evidence both for and against the jury's finding. The district court properly left the jury to determine the issue of employment. The circumstances presented in the record before us do not establish an employer-employee relationship as a matter of law. We hold that there is some evidence to support the jury's verdict declining to find that Waldrep was an employee of TCU at the time of his injury.

[The court then ruled adverse to Waldrep on several evidentiary issues.]

Conclusion

In conclusion, we note that we are aware college athletics has changed dramatically over the years since Waldrep's injury. Our decision today is based on facts and circumstances as they existed almost twenty-six years ago. We express no opinion as to whether our decision would be the same in an analogous situation arising today;

therefore, our opinion should not be read too broadly. Having disposed of all of the issues before us, we affirm the district court's judgment.

Notes and Comments

1. Have we allowed for an injured student-athlete to "fall through the cracks" by not providing some type of assured compensation for the injury? Should universities be required to carry long-term medical and disability insurance for injured athletes?

2. The litmus test of whether a college athlete should be considered an employee for workers' compensation purposes is the existence of a quid pro quo arrangement. When competent evidence shows that the student's performance of athletic services is given as consideration for financial aid, the courts should recognize the student's status as a student-employee. An objective appraisal of the relevant cases reveals the better reasoned approach: the ordinary athletic scholarship does indeed create an employer-employee relationship. For a variety of unarticulated reasons—foremost among them the fear of uncharted waters—it is not surprising that the courts have tended to refuse to hold that the amateur athletes are employees. It is an uncomfortable and unsettling realization that scholarship athletes are really employees, but it is a conclusion that an honest appraisal compels. And it is a conclusion from which a number of beneficial consequences will undoubtedly flow, contributing to the reform of a system much in need of constructive change.

3. The *Waldrep* court found that TCU exercised control and direction over all football players but, nevertheless, Waldrep's acceptance of a grant-in-aid "did not subject him to any extraordinary degree of control over his academic activities." Is it accurate to say that college athletes are not subject to any extraordinary degree of control over their academic activities? *See* Richard T. Karcher, *Big-Time College Athletes' Status as Employees*, 33 J. Lab. & Emp. L. 31, 49 (2018) ("It is unclear why the [*Waldrep*] court concluded that universities do not exercise control over an athlete's academic activities, because athletic departments provide academic counseling programs, tutoring programs, class monitors, and study halls, not all of which are voluntary. The court also failed to acknowledge the myriad NCAA academic standards and requirements to which athletes must adhere to retain eligibility and GIAs.").

4. With regard to whether the grant-in-aid was a contract of hire, the *Waldrep* court focused on the parties' expectations, concluding that no such contract existed. The court relied on the fact that the NCAA has strict rules against "taking pay for participation in sports" and that TCU did not treat the financial aid as "pay," or "income," as he was never placed on TCU's payroll or paid a salary, no social security or income tax was withheld, and Waldrep never filed a tax return. *But see Coleman v. W. Mich. Univ.*, 336 N.W.2d 224, 226 (Mich. Ct. App. 1983) ("In return for his services as a football player, [Coleman] received certain items of compensation which are measurable in money, including room and board, tuition and books."); *Van Horn v. Indus. Accident Comm'n*, 219 Cal. App. 2d 457, 464 (1963) (form of re-

muneration is immaterial in assessing whether consideration was paid for college athlete's services; "direct compensation in the form of wages is not necessary to establish the [employment] relationship so long as the service is not gratuitous").

5. Disability or sports accident insurance? Educational institutions typically are insured for claims against the university. The NCAA Catastrophic Injury Insurance Program also covers student-athletes who are catastrophically injured while participating in a covered intercollegiate athletic activity, or whose qualifying medical expenses exceed $90,000. The NCAA pays the entire premium for the policy, which has a $25,000 death benefit and a maximum benefit of $20 million with a $90,000 deductible. This program, however, typically covers players with very serious injuries and not the many other types of less serious injuries that frequently occur as a result of competitive play.

2. College Athletes' Rights under the Labor Laws

Northwestern University and College Athletes Players Association (CAPA), Petitioner

Case 13-RC-121359 August 17, 2015

Decision on Review and Order

By Chairman Pearce and Members Miscimarra, Hirozawa, Johnson, and McFerran

Introduction

In this representation case, the Petitioner asks the Board to find that Northwestern University's football players who receive grant-in-aid scholarships are employees within the meaning of Section 2(3) of the National Labor Relations Act and direct an election in a unit of these grant-in-aid players. The Regional Director agreed with the Petitioner, found that the grant-in-aid scholarship players are employees within the meaning of Section 2(3), and directed an election. Because this case raises important issues concerning the scope and application of Section 2(3), as well as whether the Board should assert jurisdiction in the circumstances of this case even if the players in the petitioned-for unit are statutory employees, we granted Northwestern University's request for review and invited the parties and interested amici to file briefs addressing the issues.

After carefully considering the arguments of the parties and interested amici, we find that it would not effectuate the policies of the Act to assert jurisdiction in this case, even if we assume, without deciding, that the grant-in-aid scholarship players are employees within the meaning of Section 2(3). As explained below, we address this case in the absence of explicit congressional direction regarding whether the Board should exercise jurisdiction. We conclude that asserting jurisdiction in this case would not serve to promote stability in labor relations. Our decision today is limited to the grant-in-aid scholarship football players covered by the petition in this particular case; whether we might assert jurisdiction in another case involving grant-in-aid scholarship football players (or other types of scholarship athletes) is a question we need not and do not address at this time.

Background

On March 26, 2014, the Regional Director for Region 13 issued a Decision and Direction of Election in which he found that a petitioned-for unit of all football players receiving grant-in-aid athletic scholarships (scholarship players) from Northwestern University are employees within the meaning of Section 2(3) of the Act and that the petitioned-for unit is appropriate. Thereafter, in accordance with Section 102.67 of the Board's Rules and Regulations, Northwestern filed a timely request for review, contending that the scholarship players are not statutory employees. The Petitioner filed an opposition. On April 24, 2014, the Board granted the Employer's request for review.

....

Summary of Facts

The facts—which are largely undisputed—are set forth in the Regional Director's decision... Northwestern is a university with its main campus in Evanston, Illinois. During the 2013–2014 academic year, about 112 athletes were on the football team, of whom 85 received a grant-in-aid scholarship. The scholarship is worth about $61,000 per year (or more, if the recipient enrolls in summer classes). The scholarship amount is calculated based on tuition, fees, room, board, and books, and the scholarship funds are directly applied to those expenses. As a result, none of the money is directly disbursed to the players, except that upperclassmen living off-campus receive a monthly stipend earmarked for their room and board (and disbursed to them in the form of a personal check).

The football team—along with Northwestern's 18 other varsity sports—is part of the Department of Athletics and Recreation. Head Coach Pat Fitzgerald oversees a staff of 13 assistant coaches; in addition, the team is supported by various other personnel, including strength and conditioning coaches, athletic trainers, video office personnel, and football operations staff. Fitzgerald reports to Athletic Director James J. Phillips, who in turn reports to Northwestern's president, Morton Schapiro.

Northwestern is a member of both the National Collegiate Athletic Association (the NCAA) and The Big Ten Conference (Big Ten). Its athletes compete under the auspices of these organizations, and the school's athletics program operates within certain constraints by which members of these associations agree to be bound. For example, the NCAA dictates the maximum number of grant-in-aid scholarships a school can award, caps the number of players who can participate in preseason football practices, sets the minimum academic requirements that football players must meet to remain eligible to play (including the requirements that players be enrolled as students, carry a full class load, and maintain a certain minimum grade point average (GPA)), controls the terms and content of the scholarship, defines amateur status that players must maintain (including prohibiting players football team's away games and also appears to dictate the wording in the scholarship "tender" that a player receives. This "tender" specifies that the scholarship award is subject to the player's compliance with the school's policies and NCAA's and Big Ten's regulations. Northwestern's football team competes in the NCAA Division I Football Bowl Subdivision (FBS), college football's highest level of play. At present, about 125 schools compete at that level. Only 17 of those schools—including Northwestern—are private colleges or universities, and Northwestern is the only private school in the 14-member Big Ten.

Scholarship players are required to devote substantial hours to football activities, but they are also full-time students. They receive no academic credit for their football endeavors. Although some players testified that they learned valuable skills and life lessons from playing football and consider Coach Fitzgerald to be a "teacher," playing football does not fulfill any sort of degree requirement, and no coaches teach courses or are part of the academic faculty.

Northwestern's football program generated some $30 million in revenue during the 2012–2013 academic year, although the program also incurred close to $22 million in expenses. Over a 10-year period ending in 2012–2013, the football program generated about $235 million in revenue and incurred roughly $159 million in expenses. That revenue was derived from ticket sales, Big Ten broadcast contracts, stadium rights, and merchandise sales. According to Department of Athletics Chief Financial Officer Steve Green, although the football program generates net revenue, the Department of Athletics' overall annual expenses exceed revenues, and Northwestern must subsidize the department to balance its budget.

Analysis

The parties and amici have largely focused on whether the scholarship players in the petitioned-for unit are statutory employees. If the players are not statutory employees, then the Board lacks authority to direct an election or certify a representative.... But as the Supreme Court has stated—and as Northwestern and several amici at least implicitly argue—even when the Board has the statutory authority to act (which it would in this case, were we to find that the scholarship players were statutory employees), "the Board sometimes properly declines to do so, stating that the policies of the Act would not be effectuated by its assertion of jurisdiction in that case." *NLRB v. Denver Building Trades Council*, 341 U.S. 675, 684 (1951). As noted previously, we address this case without explicit congressional direction, but "[t]he absence of explicit congressional direction... does not preclude the Board from reaching any particular type of employment."

After careful consideration of the record and arguments of the parties and amici, we have determined that, even if the scholarship players were statutory employees (which, again, is an issue we do not decide), it would not effectuate the policies of the Act to assert jurisdiction. Our decision is primarily premised on a finding that, because of the nature of sports leagues (namely the control exercised by the leagues over the individual teams) and the composition and structure of FBS football (in which the overwhelming majority of competitors are public colleges and universities over which the Board cannot assert jurisdiction), it would not promote stability in labor relations to assert jurisdiction in this case.

We emphasize that this case involves novel and unique circumstances. The Board has never before been asked to assert jurisdiction in a case involving college football players, or college athletes of any kind. There has never been a petition for representation before the Board in a unit of a single college team or, for that matter, a group of college teams. And the scholarship players do not fit into any analytical framework that the Board has used in cases involving other types of students or athletes. In this regard, the scholarship players bear little resemblance to the graduate student assistants or student janitors and cafeteria workers whose employee status the Board has considered in other cases. The fact that the scholarship players are students who are also athletes receiving a scholarship to participate in what has traditionally been regarded as an extracurricular activity (albeit a nationally prominent and extraordinarily lucrative one for many universities, conferences, and the NCAA) materially sets them apart from the Board's student precedent. Yet at the same time, the scholarship players are unlike athletes in undisputedly professional leagues, given that the scholarship players are required, inter alia, to be enrolled full time as students and meet various academic requirements, and they are prohibited by NCAA regulations from engaging in many of the types of activities that professional athletes are free to engage in, such as profiting from the use of their names or likenesses. Moreover, as explained below, even if scholarship players were regarded as analogous to players for professional sports teams who are considered employees for purposes of collective bargaining, such bargaining has never involved a bargaining unit consisting of a single team's players, where the players for competing teams were unrepresented or entirely outside the Board's jurisdiction. As a result, nothing in our precedent requires us to assert jurisdiction in this case. Given the absence of any controlling precedent, we find it appropriate to consider whether the Board should exercise its discretion to decline to assert jurisdiction in this case, even assuming the Board is otherwise authorized to act.

Notwithstanding the dissimilarities, discussed above, FBS football does resemble a professional sport in a number of relevant ways. In particular, institutions that have FBS teams are engaged in the business of staging football contests from which they receive substantial revenues (via gate receipts, concessions and merchandise sales, and broadcasting contracts). As in professional sports, the activity of staging athletic contests must be carried out jointly by the teams in the league or association involved. See *NCAA v. Board of Regents of University of Oklahoma*, 468 U.S. 85, 101 (1984) ("Some activities can only be carried out jointly. Perhaps the leading example is league sports.") (quotations omitted); *North American Soccer League*, 236 NLRB 1317, 1321 (1978) ("Each club operates on an independent basis, although, of course, each team is dependent upon every other team for its financial success, as is true in other organized team sports."). Put differently, unlike other industries, in professional sports, as in FBS football, there is no "product" without direct interaction among the players and cooperation among the various teams.

For this reason, as in other sports leagues, academic institutions that sponsor intercollegiate athletics have banded together and formed the NCAA to, among other things, set common rules and standards governing their competitions, including those applicable to FBS football. The NCAA's members have also given the NCAA the authority to police and enforce the rules and regulations that govern eligibility, practice, and competition. The record demonstrates that the NCAA now exercises a substantial degree of control over the operations of individual member teams, including many of the terms and conditions under which the scholarship players (as well as walk-on players) practice and play the game. As in professional sports, such an arrangement is necessary because uniform rules of competition and compliance with them ensure the uniformity and integrity of individual games, and thus league competition as a whole. There is thus a symbiotic relationship among the various teams, the conferences, and the NCAA. As a result, labor issues directly involving only an individual team and its players would also affect the NCAA, the Big Ten, and the other member institutions. Many terms applied to one team therefore would likely have ramifications for other teams. Consequently, "it would be difficult to imagine any degree of stability in labor relations" if we were to assert jurisdiction in this single-team case. Indeed, such an arrangement is seemingly unprecedented; all previous Board cases concerning professional sports involve leaguewide bargaining units. See, e.g., *National Football League*, 309 NLRB 78 (1992); *Blast Soccer Associates*, 289 NLRB 84 (1988) (leaguewide representation for Major Indoor Soccer League players); *Major League Rodeo*, 246 NLRB 743 (1979); *North American Soccer League*, 245 NLRB 1301 (1979); *American Basketball Assn.*, 215 NLRB at 281; *National Football League Management Council*, 203 NLRB 958, 961 (1973) (indicating that before the National Football League (NFL) merged with the rival American Football League, the latter league's players had leaguewide representation).

Just as the nature of league sports and the NCAA's oversight renders individual team bargaining problematic, the way that FBS football itself is structured and the nature of the colleges and universities involved strongly suggest that asserting jurisdiction in this case would not promote stability in labor relations. Despite the similarities between FBS football and professional sports leagues, FBS is also a markedly different type of enterprise. In particular, of the roughly 125 colleges and universities that participate in FBS football, all but 17 are state-run institutions. As a result, the Board cannot assert jurisdiction over the vast majority of FBS teams because they are not operated by "employers" within the meaning of Section 2(2) of the Act. More starkly, Northwestern is the only private school in the Big 10, and thus the Board cannot assert jurisdiction over any of Northwestern's primary competitors. This too is a situation without precedent because in all of our past cases involving professional sports, the Board was able to regulate all, or at least most, of the teams in the relevant league or association.

In such a situation, asserting jurisdiction in this case would not promote stability in labor relations. Because most FBS teams are created by state institutions, they may be subject to state labor laws governing public employees. Some states, of course, permit collective bargaining by public employees, but others limit or prohibit such bargaining. At least two states—which, between them, operate three universities that are members of the Big Ten—specify by statute that scholarship athletes at state schools are not employees. Under these circumstances, there is an inherent asymmetry of the labor relations regulatory regimes applicable to individual teams. In other contexts, the Board's assertion of jurisdiction helps promote uniformity and stability, but in this case, asserting jurisdiction would not have that effect because the Board cannot regulate most FBS teams. Accordingly, asserting jurisdiction would not promote stability in labor relations.

As an additional consideration, we observe that the terms and conditions of Northwestern's players have changed markedly in recent years and that there have been calls for the NCAA to undertake further reforms that may result in additional changes to the circumstances of scholarship players. For example, the NCAA's decision to allow FBS teams to award guaranteed 4-year scholarships, as opposed to 1-year renewable scholarships, has reduced the likelihood that scholarship players who become unable to play will lose their educational funding, and possibly their educational opportunity. We note that our decision to decline jurisdiction in this case is based on the facts in the record before us, and that subsequent changes in the treatment of scholarship players could outweigh the considerations that motivate our decision today.

For these reasons, we conclude, without deciding whether the scholarship players are employees under Section 2(3), that it would not effectuate the policies of the Act to assert jurisdiction in this case.

We emphasize that our decision today does not concern other individuals associated with FBS football, but is limited to Northwestern's scholarship football players. In this regard, we observe that the Board has exercised jurisdiction in other contexts involving college athletics. The Board has, for example, adjudicated cases involving athletic coaches, college physical plant employees who performed functions in support of athletic events, and referees. Our decision today should not be understood to extend to university personnel associated with athletic programs.

Further, we are declining jurisdiction only in this case involving the football players at Northwestern University; we therefore do not address what the Board's approach might be to a petition for all FBS scholarship football players (or at least those at private colleges and universities). The record before us deals solely with Northwestern's football team and, in the absence of any evidence concerning the players and athletes at other schools, we do not decide any issues about them today.

As a final note, the Board's decision not to assert jurisdiction does not preclude a reconsideration of this issue in the future. For example, if the circumstances of Northwestern's players or FBS football change such that the underpinnings of our conclusions regarding jurisdiction warrant reassessment, the Board may revisit its policy in this area.

Conclusion

The Board has never asserted jurisdiction, or even been asked to assert jurisdiction, in a case involving scholarship football players or similarly situated individuals, and for the reasons stated above, we decline to do so in this case. Processing a petition for the scholarship players at this single institution under the circumstances presented here would not promote stability in labor relations. Moreover, recent changes, as well as calls for additional reforms, suggest that the situation of scholarship players may well change in the near future. For these reasons and the others set forth above, even if the scholarship players were statutory employees (which the Board does not here decide), we have concluded that it will not effectuate the policies of the Act to assert jurisdiction in this case.

Order

The petition is dismissed.

Notes and Comments

1. The NLRB recognized that FBS football "resemble[s] a professional sport" in that "institutions that have FBS teams are engaged in the business of staging football contests from which they receive substantial revenues" and, like professional sports, the "product" of FBS football requires "direct interaction among the players and cooperation among the various teams." As a result, the structure of college sports suggests that unionization would, as in professional sports, require league-wide (*i.e.*, conference-wide) bargaining units, which is why the NLRB decided not to assert jurisdiction over one school in the Big Ten conference.

2. College athletes in revenue-generating sports also have much in common with unionized professional athletes, which might support viewing these "student-athletes" as employees. FBS and NFL players share the following commonalities: (1) average careers of three to four years with corresponding job security concerns; (2) identical job duties and substantially similar game and practice schedules; (3) susceptibility to the same varieties of potentially career-ending injuries; (4) similar safety concerns regarding play and equipment; (5) teams dispersed both regionally

and nationally; (6) league rules restricting player transfers between teams; (7) disciplinary actions (suspension or termination) for violating team or league rules; (8) disparate levels of skill and talent; (9) competition among teams to secure players' services; (10) disparate team revenues and profits; and (11) licensing value in athletes' names and likenesses. Karcher, *Big-Time College Athletes' Status as Employees,* 33 J. Lab. & Emp. L. 31, 36 (2018).

3. The Regional Director in *Northwestern University*, applying the common law "control" test, provided a detailed explanation as to why the Northwestern football players meet the statutory definition of employees under the NLRA. *See* Decision and Direction of Election, Northwestern Univ., Case 13-RC-121359, at 14–18 (NLRB Mar. 26, 2014). On review, the NLRB implicitly acknowledged that they are employees under the NLRA. Can a "student-athlete" be both a student *and* an employee? Can a university be both the athlete's educator *and* employer? *See* Trs. of Columbia Univ. in the City of N.Y., 364 N.L.R.B. No. 90, at 7 (Aug. 23, 2016) ("a graduate student may be both a student *and* an employee; a university may be both the student's educator *and* employer").

4. In *Berger v. NCAA*, 843 F.3d 285 (7th Cir. 2016), the court held that a track and field athlete at the University of Pennsylvania, a member of the Ivy League, did not establish that she was an employee for purposes of the Fair Labor Standards Act and thus was not entitled to minimum wage compensation for her participation. (Ivy League members do not award athletic scholarships.) The court relied on the "economic reality" of the "working relationship" to make a determination regarding potential employee status. It relied quite heavily on the NCAA's amateurism rules and other courts' interpretation of the concept. It also found that most courts have declined to find employee status in workers' compensation cases. Can a distinguishing argument be made by an athlete in a revenue sport who is on scholarship? In a concurring opinion, Judge David Hamilton added "a note of caution" that "the plaintiffs in this case did not receive athletic scholarships and participated in a non-revenue sport." *Berger*, 843 F.3d at 294 (Hamilton, J., concurring).

F. Coaching and Institutional Contracts

1. Coaching Contracts

Rodgers v. Georgia Tech Athletic Association

303 S.E.2d 467 (Ga. Ct. App. 1983)

Pope, Judge.

Franklin C. "Pepper" Rodgers brought this breach of contract action against the Georgia Tech Athletic Association to recover the value of certain perquisites which had been made available to him as the head coach of football at the Georgia Institute of Technology.... The issue presented for resolution by this appeal is whether Rodgers is entitled to recover the value of certain perquisites or "fringe benefits" of his position as head coach of football under the terms of his contract of employment with the Association.

Rodgers was removed from his coaching position by vote of the Association's Board of Trustees on December 18, 1979, notwithstanding a written contract of employment through December 31, 1981. In addition to an annual salary, the contract provided that Rodgers, as an employee of the Association, would be entitled "to various insurance and pension benefits and perquisites" as he became eligible therefor. Rodgers makes no claim for base salary, health insurance and pension plan benefits, all of which were provided voluntarily by the Association through December 31, 1981, the expiration date of the contract. Rather, his claim is solely for the value of the aforesaid "perquisites," to which he claims entitlement under this employment contract.

Rodgers lists some 29 separate items as such perquisites. In support of his motion for summary judgment, Rodgers categorized these items into two groups: A. Items provided directly to him by the Association but discontinued when Rodgers was relieved of his duties, and B. Items provided by sources other than the Association by virtue of his position as head coach of football. These items are listed in the Appendix to this opinion.

The subject contract was in the form of a letter from the Association dated April 20, 1977 offering Rodgers the position of head coach of football for three years at an annual salary plus certain benefits and perquisites. This contract provided that Rodgers could be terminated for illness or other incapacity continuing for three months, death, or "any conduct or activity involving moral turpitude or which in the opinion of [the Board of Trustees] would constitute an embarrassment to the school." Rodgers accepted this contract on April 25, 1977. This contract was extended until January 1, 1982 by a subsequent letter agreement between the parties. At its December 18, 1979 meeting, the Association's Board of Trustees determined that a change should be made in the position of head coach of football.

Rodgers asserts essentially two theories of recovery: (a) breach of contract, and (b) appropriation of a "property right."

[The court summarily disposed of the second theory and proceeded to resolve the breach of contract issue.]....

Rodgers contends that he was terminated or fired from his employment by the Association.

However, the evidence of record supports the Association's view that Rodgers was merely relieved of his duties as the head coach of football yet remained an employee of the Association, albeit without any function or duties, for the duration of his contract.

In addition to a salary, health insurance and pension benefits, the contract provided that Rodgers, as an employee of the Association, was entitled to "perquisites" as he became eligible therefor. Thus, Rodgers was entitled to the perquisites (or their value) for which he was eligible during the duration of his contract. The problem presented here for resolution is to determine whether any of the items listed in the Appendix were indeed perquisites to which Rodgers was entitled pursuant to his contract.

First, we must determine the intention of the parties as to the scope of the perquisites to which Rodgers was entitled under the contract.... The pertinent language of the contract provides: "You, as Head Coach of Football, will devote your time, attention, skill, and efforts to the performance of your duties as Head Coach under the policies established by the Athletic Board and the Athletic Director, and you will receive compensation at [an] annual rate of $35,175.00 payable in equal monthly installments. In addition, as an employee of the Association, you will be entitled to various... perquisites as you become eligible therefor." The Association contends that the language "as an employee of the Association" limited Rodgers' eligibility for perquisites to those items common to all Association employees. Rodgers argues that he was not only entitled to those perquisites common to all Association employees, but that he was also entitled to additional perquisites for which he became eligible as the head coach of football....

[T]he record discloses that Rodgers, during his tenure as head coach of football, did receive perquisites in addition to those received by other Association employees. Accordingly, we conclude that the parties intended that Rodgers would receive perquisites, as he became eligible therefor, based upon his position as head coach of football and not merely as an employee of the Association.

We must next determine the nature of the items for which Rodgers seeks damages, *i.e.*, whether the items listed in the Appendix are perquisites vel non. We will first address ourselves to those items listed in Section A of the Appendix and address separately those items listed in Section B.

(a) The Association asserts that Rodgers was not entitled to any of the items listed in Section A because they were expense account items—"tools" to enable him to more effectively execute his duties as head coach of football. Rodgers counters that those items were an integral part of the total compensation package that he received as head coach of football and constituted consideration for his contract of employment. We certainly agree with the Association that Rodgers would be entitled to recover only "compensatory damages that he suffered by reason of the breach of his contract; in other words, that the proper measure of damages arising from the breach of the contract of employment was actual loss sustained by the breach, and not the gross amount of [his] wages and expenses [under the contract]." [Citations omitted.] However, the evidence offered as to the nature of the items in Section A was in considerable dispute.. Thus, with three exceptions, we cannot say as a matter of law either that Rodgers was entitled to the items listed in Section A as perquisites of his employment, or that he was not.

The three exceptions to this finding are the services of a secretary, the services of an administrative assistant, and the cost of trips to football conventions, clinics, etc. The undisputed purpose of the services of the secretary and administrative assistant was to assist Rodgers in fulfilling his duties under the contract. Since Rodgers had been relieved of his duties as head coach of football, and, thus, had no responsibilities under the contract, he had no need for these support services. Also, since Rodgers had been relieved of his coaching duties, the Association was not obligated to pay his expenses for trips to various football related activities, these costs clearly being business-related and not in the nature of compensation.

(b) We turn our attention finally to those items in Section B of the Appendix—items which Rodgers asserts were perquisites he received from sources other than the Association by virtue of his position as head coach of football at Georgia Tech. The Association argues that Rodgers' claim for recovery of these items was in the nature of a tort claim for humiliation and injury to feelings. Rodgers counters that these items were perquisites within the contemplation of the parties which constituted part of the consideration for the contract even though they were provided by sources other than the Association.

... [W]e must now determine whether Rodgers may recover the items in Section B under his breach of contract theory.

Can Rodgers' loss of the items in Section B be traced solely to the Association's breach of the contract? Rodgers testified that he received these perquisites as a result of his being head coach of football at Georgia Tech. The record discloses, however, that the items relating to housing and the cost of premiums on a life insurance policy were discontinued several years prior to the Association's breach of contract and were, in fact, not related to the breach. Thus, these items were properly excluded by the trial court. The remaining items were discontinued as the direct result of Rodgers being relieved of his duties as head coach of football.

Did these remaining items arise naturally and according to the usual course of things, and were they such as the parties contemplated as a probable result of a breach? There is no evidence of record showing that the Association had any knowledge of Rodgers' free lodging at certain Holiday Inns or of his membership in Terminus International Tennis Club. Thus, the loss of these items could not be such as was contemplated as a probable result of a breach of the contract. The evidence was in dispute as to the remaining items—profits from his television and radio shows and from his summer football camp plus the loss of use of a new automobile and tickets to professional sporting events—*i.e.*, whether such items were contemplated by the parties at the time the contract was executed as perquisites or fringe benefits to which Rodgers would be entitled as the result of his position as head coach of football at Georgia Tech. These items are of the type commonly provided to head coaches at major colleges and universities. There was some evidence that the Association knew that Rodgers would receive (and, in fact, did receive) these benefits as the result of his head coaching position and that his removal from that position would result in the loss of these benefits. In fact, some members of the Association assisted Rodgers in obtaining many of these items. Also, there was at least some evidence by which the amount of these items could be fixed. Therefore, summary judgment in favor of the Association as to these items was inappropriate.... For these same reasons, summary judgment in favor of Rodgers was properly denied.

In summary, a question of fact remains as to whether Rodgers is entitled to recover those items listed in Section A of the Appendix not excluded in this opinion and also those items in Section B not heretofore excluded, any recovery being subject to proof of the amount of his damages as set forth in this opinion. All items which have been excluded are denoted by asterisks in the Appendix.

Judgment affirmed in part; reversed in part.

DEEN, P.J., and SOGNIER, J., concur.

Appendix

A. Benefits and Perquisites Received by Rodgers Directly from the Georgia Tech Athletic Association.

1. gas, oil, maintenance, repairs, other auto mobile expenses;
2. automobile liability and collision insurance;
3. general expense money;
4. meals available at the Georgia Tech training table;
5. eight season tickets to Georgia Tech home football games during all of 1980 and 1981;
6. two reserved booths, consisting of approximately 40 seats at Georgia Tech home football games during fall of 1980 and 1981;
7. six season tickets to Georgia Tech home basketball games for 1980 and 1981;
8. four season tickets to Atlanta Falcon home football games for 1980 and 1981;
9. four game tickets to each out-of-town Georgia Tech football game during fall of 1980 and 1981;
10. pocket money at each home football game during fall of 1980 and 1981;
11. pocket money at each out-of-town Georgia Tech football game during fall of 1980 and 1981;
12. parking privileges at all Georgia Tech home sporting events;

13. the services of a secretary;
14. the services of an administrative assistant;
15. the cost of admission to Georgia Tech home baseball games during spring of 1980 and 1981;
16. the cost of trips to football coaches' conventions, clinics, and meetings and to observe football practice sessions of professional and college football teams;
17. initiation fee, dues, monthly bills, and cost of membership at the Capital City Club;
18. initiation fee, dues, monthly bills, and cost of membership at the Cherokee Country Club;
19. initiation fee and dues at the East Lake Country Club.

B. Benefits and Perquisites Received by Rodgers from Sources Other Than the Georgia Tech Athletic Association by Virtue of Being Head Coach of Football.

1. profits from Rodgers' television football show, "The Pepper Rodgers Show," on Station WSB-TV in Atlanta for the fall of 1980 and 1981;
2. profits from Rodgers' radio football show on Station WGST in Atlanta for the fall of 1980 and 1981;
3. use of a new Cadillac automobile during 1980 and 1981;
4. profits from Rodgers' summer football camp, known as the "Pepper Rodgers Football School," for June, 1980 and June, 1981;
5. financial gifts from alumni and supporters of Georgia Tech for 1980 and 1981;
6. lodging at any of the Holiday Inns owned by Topeka Inn Management, Inc. of Topeka, Kansas, for the time period from December 18, 1979 through December 31, 1981;
7. the cost of membership in Terminus International Tennis Club in Atlanta for 1980 and 1981;
8. individual game tickets to Hawk basketball and Braves baseball games during 1980 and 1981 seasons;
9. housing for Rodgers and his family in Atlanta for the period from December 18, 1979 through December 31, 1981;
10. the cost of premiums of a $400,000.00 policy on the life of Rodgers for the time period from December 18, 1979 through December 31, 1981.

O'Brien v. The Ohio State University

2006 Ohio Misc. LEXIS 52 (Ct. of Claims Feb. 15, 2006)

Opinion By: Joseph T. Clark

Facts

On April 12, 1997, plaintiff was hired by defendant as the head coach of the men's basketball team. Plaintiff had worked as a basketball coach for more than 20 years prior to his taking the position.

On May 14, 1998, Alex Radojevic, a 21-year-old basketball player from Yugoslavia, arrived on the campus of The Ohio State University for an unofficial visit.... By all accounts, Radojevic was a prized recruit, a "difference maker."

In early September... Radojevic received word that his father had passed away. According to plaintiff, Radojevic was distraught by the news of his father's death and he had expressed concern for his mother who was living in a war-torn region of Yugoslavia. Radojevic was unable to offer her any financial assistance and he could not return home for fear of being forced into military service.

In late September or early October plaintiff learned that in 1996 Radojevic had signed a contract to play professional basketball for a Yugoslavian team and had received some of the compensation due him under the contract. Although Radojevic played only sparingly with the team, plaintiff learned that the team had tendered additional payments which Radojevic reportedly refused to accept. Plaintiff testified that based upon this information he concluded that Radojevic was a professional basketball player and that he was not eligible to play college basketball.

Although plaintiff and his staff were aware of the professional contract, they continued to recruit Radojevic. On November 11, 1998, Radojevic signed a document known as a National Letter of Intent (NLI) which is utilized by NCAA member institutions to establish the commitment of a prospect to attend a particular institution.

At some time in mid-to-late December 1998, plaintiff was asked to provide financial assistance to the Radojevic family. While the details surrounding the request are sketchy, it appears that the request originated from a man by the name of Spomenko Patrovic, a Yugoslavian national who worked as a waiter in New York City and who claimed to be either Radojevic's relative or his legal guardian. Plaintiff testified that in late December 1998 or early January 1999 he removed $6,000 in cash from a drawer in his office desk and placed it in an unmarked envelope. He gave the envelope to then assistant coach, Paul Biancardi, with instructions to deliver the envelope to Patrovic in New York City. Patrovic was to have the money delivered to the Radojevic family in Yugoslavia.

Plaintiff has characterized the transaction as a loan. He has acknowledged, however, that there was no written loan agreement and that the terms for repayment were not discussed. Plaintiff maintains that it was Radojevic's dire family circumstances and not his interest in Radojevic as a potential college player that prompted him to provide the loan. He testified that he was certain that the loan did not violate NCAA rules because Radojevic had surrendered his amateur status in 1996. Plaintiff was also certain that there was no NCAA prohibition against lending money to the family of a professional basketball player.

In February 1999, an NCAA student-athlete reinstatement representative notified defendant that Radojevic had signed a professional basketball contract in 1996. When Ferdinand "Andy" Geiger, defendant's athletic director, approached plaintiff and the coaching staff with this information he was assured that the circumstances surrounding the 1996 contract were such that Radojevic could regain his amateur status by applying to the NCAA for reinstatement. Defendant immediately declared Radojevic ineligible for competition in accordance with an NCAA directive and on March 24, 1999, defendant filed an application for his reinstatement. The application was denied and on May 24, 1999, the NCAA subcommittee denied the appeal from that decision.

Radojevic never enrolled as a student-athlete at defendant's institution and he never played basketball for defendant's team. He entered the 1999 NBA draft and was selected by the Toronto Raptors as the 12th pick in the first round.

Approximately three months later, on September 15, 1999, plaintiff signed an NCAA Certificate of Compliance certifying that during the 1998–1999 academic year he had "reported through the appropriate individuals * * * any knowledge of violations of NCAA legislation involving [the] institution."

In March 1999, defendant's men's basketball team completed one of its most successful seasons in recent memory. The team had won 27 games, a Big Ten conference title, and had advanced to the Final Four in the NCAA tournament. Plaintiff won several post-season awards for his coaching, including national coach-of-the-year honors.

On the heels of this great success, Andy Geiger felt so enthusiastic about the basketball program and its head coach that he initiated discussions with plaintiff regarding a new contract.... The new agreement took effect September 12, 1999. Everyone involved in the negotiation process agreed that the terms of plaintiff's new contract were much more favorable to plaintiff than those contained in his prior agreement.... The new agreement also placed significant limitations upon defendant's right to terminate plaintiff's employment.

On April 24, 2004, defendant held its annual spring football game at Ohio Stadium. Geiger had asked plaintiff to attend the game so that he could address a gathering of alumni. Just prior to the time that Geiger was to make his remarks, plaintiff pulled him aside and informed him about the financial assistance he had provided to the Radojevic family in 1998. He told Geiger that he had provided the assistance because of the serious financial hardships facing Radojevic's family and that his motives were purely humanitarian. Plaintiff explained that the transaction would likely be revealed to the public in a lawsuit that had been filed by a woman named Kathy Salyers. Plaintiff wanted Geiger to hear about the loan from him personally rather than from the press.

On cross-examination at trial, Geiger acknowledged that during this conversation he told plaintiff "we will try to work through this together." Geiger also testified that he believed that plaintiff's motivation for making the loan was purely humanitarian and that he had referred to the loan as a "noble act." Geiger claimed that plaintiff admitted that the loan was made in violation of NCAA rules. Both plaintiff and Geiger have testified that the conversation was brief, lasting no more than five minutes. However, plaintiff strongly disagreed with Geiger's assertion that he had admitted violating NCAA rules.

Sometime in May 2004,... Geiger learned of Saylers' allegation that she had provided improper benefits to Slobodan Savovic throughout his playing career. After returning to Columbus, Ohio, Geiger summoned plaintiff to meet with him... on May 26, 2004. During a five or ten minute meeting, Geiger told plaintiff that the loan had been reported to the NCAA and that there was going to be an investigation. Geiger also suggested that plaintiff hire an attorney. Plaintiff contacted Geiger on the following day and asked him if he was going to be fired. According to plaintiff, Geiger told him he was not going to be fired. Plaintiff testified that he apologized to Geiger for putting him in an "awkward position" and offered to talk about resigning his coaching position if the university felt that public knowledge of the loan would harm the basketball program. Plaintiff, however, refused to discuss the allegations regarding Slobodan Savovic.

At approximately 7:30 a.m. on June 8, 2004, plaintiff was summoned to Geiger's office for a meeting. At 8:30 a.m., Geiger handed plaintiff a letter notifying him of defendant's intention to terminate his employment as head coach of the men's basketball team and informing him that his dismissal would be announced at a news conference that afternoon. Plaintiff was given an option to resign his employment in lieu of termination.

...At an afternoon press conference Geiger announced plaintiff's dismissal, effective immediately.

On May 13, 2005, more than 11 months after plaintiff's dismissal, defendant received a "Notice of Allegations" from the NCAA. The notice contained enumerated allegations against the men's basketball program, the women's basketball program, and the men's football program. Six of the violations involved Slobodan Savovic and three concerned the loan to the Radojevic family.

Breach of Contract

[Defendant notified plaintiff of its intention to terminate his contract for cause, but gave him the option of resigning. However, the defendant indicated that there would be no further compensation under either option. Several specific contract provisions related to compliance with NCAA rules were cited in the letter. Plaintiff refused to resign.]

The letter clearly identifies the contractual provisions upon which defendant relies in exercising its right of termination. Specifically, defendant claims that plaintiff breached Section 4.1 which provides in relevant part:

> "4.1 In consideration of the compensation specified in this agreement, Coach shall:
>
> "(d) Know, recognize and comply with all applicable laws, policies, rules and regulations of Ohio State, the Big 10 Conference and the NCAA; supervise and take appropriate steps to ensure that Coach's assistant coaches, any other employees for whom Coach is administratively responsible and the members of the Team know, recognize and comply with all such laws, policies, rules and regulations; and *immediately report to the Director and to the Department of Athletics Compliance Office if Coach has reasonable cause to believe that any person or entity, including without limitation, representatives of Ohio State's athletic interests, has violated or is likely to violate any such laws, policies, rules or regulations.* Coach shall cooperate fully with the Department's Compliance Office at all times." (Emphasis added.)

Upon review of the language used by the parties in Section 4.1(d), the court finds that plaintiff could breach his duties thereunder if either he fails to comply with NCAA rules *or* he has reasonable cause to believe that an NCAA violation has occurred and that he fails to immediately report it to the director. As written, Section 4.1(d) could be breached by plaintiff without the actual commission of an infraction so long as plaintiff had reasonable grounds to believe that an infraction had or was likely to occur.

NCAA Rules

There is no question in this case that plaintiff failed to immediately report the loan to either defendant's director or its Department of Athletics Compliance. In fact, plaintiff told no one about the loan for almost five years. Thus, at the outset the court must determine whether plaintiff had reasonable cause to believe that he had violated an NCAA rule when he loaned money to the Radojevic family.

In the June 8, 2004, letter, defendant identified NCAA Bylaw 13.2.1 as the primary violation. That Bylaw provides in pertinent part:

> "13.2.1 General Regulation. An institution's staff member or any representative of its athletics interests shall not be involved, directly or indirectly, in making arrangements for or giving, or offering to give any financial aid or other benefits to the prospect or the prospect's relatives or friends, other than expressly permitted by NCAA regulations."

Plaintiff's position is that the loan to the Radojevic family did not violate Bylaw 13.2.1 because Alex Radojevic was a professional athlete at the time the loan was made.

Ultimately, the determination whether plaintiff committed a major infraction of NCAA rules and what sanctions, if any, may be imposed upon defendant will be made by the NCAA Committee on Infractions and not this court. As of the date of publication of this decision, the NCAA has yet to decide the issue. In this case, in order to determine that plaintiff breached Section 4.1(d) of the employment agreement, the court need only find that plaintiff had reasonable cause to believe that he committed an infraction when he made the loan to the Radojevic family. The circumstances surrounding plaintiff's decision to make the loan combined with plaintiff's subsequent words and conduct convince the court that plaintiff had reasonable cause to believe that he had committed an infraction.

Plaintiff testified that he found out about the professional contract in September 1998 and that he was certain at that time that Radojevic was not eligible to play college basketball. Yet Radojevic signed an NLI and he was brought in for an official visit. Professor Swank [the plaintiff's expert] was unable to think of any reason why Radojevic would be offered an NLI and invited to make an official visit to the school if plaintiff were convinced that Radojevic was ineligible to play.

....

In consideration of all of the evidence presented, the court finds that in December 1998 plaintiff had reasonable grounds to believe that he had violated NCAA Recruiting Bylaw 13.02.1 by making a loan to the family of Alex Radojevic. Plaintiff's conduct in making the loan and then failing to report it to the director was a breach of Section 4.1(d) of the contract.

Materiality and Termination for Cause

As stated above, plaintiff's 1999 employment contract placed significant limitations upon defendant's right to terminate plaintiff's employment. For example, defendant was obligated to pay plaintiff a substantial portion of his remaining salary if plaintiff were terminated other than for cause. Conversely, if plaintiff were terminated for cause, defendant would be under no obligation to pay plaintiff any further compensation. Furthermore, it is clear from the plain language of the agreement that not every failure of performance by plaintiff provides cause for termination. The specific language of the contract at issue is Section 5.1 which states:

"5.1 Terminations for Cause—Ohio State may terminate this agreement at any time for *cause*, which, for the purpose of this agreement, shall be limited to the occurrence of one or more of the following:

"(a) a material breach of this agreement by Coach, which Coach fails to remedy to OSU's reasonable satisfaction, within a reasonable time period, not to

> exceed thirty (30) days, after receipt of a written notice from Ohio State specifying the act(s), conduct or omission(s) constituting such breach;
>
> "(b) a violation by Coach (or a violation by a men's basketball program staff member about which Coach knew or should have known and did not report to appropriate Ohio State personnel) of applicable law, policy, rule or regulation of the NCAA or the Big Ten Conference which leads to a 'major' infraction investigation by the NCAA or the Big Ten Conference and which results in a finding by the NCAA or the Big Ten Conference of lack of institutional control over the men's basketball program or which results in Ohio State being sanctioned by the NCAA or the Big Ten Conference...
>
> "(c) any criminal conduct by Coach that constitutes moral turpitude or other improper conduct that, in Ohio State's reasonable judgment, reflects adversely on Ohio State or its athletic programs."

Defendant does not contend that plaintiff's termination for cause can be justified either by Section 5.1(b) or 5.1(c). The notice of termination references only Section 5.1(a). Thus, in deciding whether plaintiff's employment was terminated for cause, the court need only consider whether plaintiff's breach was "material".

Under common law, "a 'material breach' is a failure to do something that is so fundamental to a contract that the failure to perform that obligation defeats the essential purpose of the contract or makes it impossible for the other party to perform under the contract." ... Defendant contends that plaintiff's conduct in violating NCAA rules and thereafter failing to immediately report the violation constitutes a "material breach" of the employment agreement and provides defendant with sufficient cause to terminate plaintiff's employment pursuant to paragraph 5.1(a).

Section 4.1(d)

... [I]n view of the language used in Section 4.1(d) of the contract it is clear that defendant reasonably expected plaintiff to refrain from violating NCAA rules, to monitor assistant coaches and players to assure their compliance with those rules, to exercise a reasonable degree of vigilance to uncover any violations, and to immediately report any suspected violations.

The specific conduct allegedly constituting plaintiff's breach of contract was described by Julie Vanatta as follows:

> "A. And it's the University's belief that everything in conjunction with the payment to Alex Radojevic and the reinstatement appeal of Alex Radojevic is a violation of 4.1(d)."

Defendant argues that plaintiff's breach of Section 4.1(d) deprived it of the benefit it reasonably expected from the employment agreement in three ways: subjecting defendant to NCAA sanctions; adversely affecting defendant's reputation in the community; and breaching the trust between plaintiff and defendant's athletic director.

Compliance

With respect to Section 4.1(d) of the instant agreement, it is clear to the court that NCAA compliance is important to defendant; it is one of the specified duties of the coach. However, Section 5.1(b) of the contract contemplates a chain of events whereby plaintiff could retain his employment in the face of an ongoing major infractions investigation by the NCAA and that he could remain so employed absent the imposition of certain serious sanctions. From this language the court concludes that the parties did not consider plaintiff's performance under Section 4.1(d) of the contract to be so critical that a failure of any kind would justify immediate termination for cause. If defendant reasonably expected perfect compliance, Section 5.1(b) would not have been made part of the agreement.

Similarly, Section 5.5 of the agreement provides the court with insight into the relative importance of absolute NCAA compliance. Section 5.5 provides:

> "5.5 Suspension of Other Disciplinary Action. If Coach is found to have violated any law, policy, rule or regulation of the NCAA, the Big Ten Conference or Ohio State, Coach may be subject to suspension or other disciplinary or corrective action as set forth in the applicable enforcement procedures (subject to the provisions of Section 5.6 hereof)."

Reading such provision in conjunction with Section 5.1(b) it is clear that a violation of NCAA rules, even a major infraction, will not justify termination for cause under Section 5.1(a) unless that violation has some independent significance which prevents future performance.

Geiger testified that, in his opinion, defendant had no choice but to immediately terminate plaintiff's employment. Suspension, Geiger explained, was not a viable option. "A. We're now in the 19th month of the NCAA process. Having a coach in limbo or having a coach suspended would be grossly unfair to the young people that play basketball at Ohio State, would have arrested any development of our program, and that is—that was an untenable solution." (Trial Transcript, Page 783, Line 21 through Page 784, Line 1.)

It is difficult to square Geiger's testimony with the language of the parties' agreement. Although Geiger testified that suspending plaintiff for the pendency of the NCAA investigation was an "untenable solution," the agreement entered into by the parties clearly contemplates such action. Moreover, at the time the parties entered into the 1999 employment agreement Geiger was aware that NCAA investigations proceed very slowly. When asked if he had told plaintiff that the NCAA investigation would move at a snail's pace he answered: "I probably did because they always do." Based upon the language of the agreement, and the evidence admitted in this case, the court finds that defendant bargained away its right to immediately dismiss plaintiff simply because of the inconvenience occasioned by a protracted NCAA investigation.

Conclusion

In summary, Geiger's June 8, 2004, letter speaks to a single, isolated recruiting infraction by plaintiff and plaintiff's failure to timely disclose that violation. The evidence shows that the violation consists of a loan made to the family of a prospect for humanitarian reasons. The evidence also demonstrates that such prospect was ineligible to participate in intercollegiate athletics at the time that the loan was made. Although plaintiff breached his contract by making the loan under these circumstances, the court is persuaded, given the contract language, that this single, isolated failure of performance was not so egregious as to frustrate the essential purpose of that contract and thus render future performance by defendant impossible. Because the breach by plaintiff was not a material breach, defendant did not have cause to terminate plaintiff's employment. Defendant's decision to do so without any compensation to plaintiff was a breach of the parties' agreement.

For the foregoing reasons, the court finds that plaintiff has proven his claim of breach of contract by a preponderance of the evidence and accordingly, judgment shall be rendered in favor of plaintiff. [The court subsequently ruled that O'Brien was entitled to $2.4 million in damages. The ruling was upheld on appeal and the university ultimately paid O'Brien nearly $3 million in damages and interest on the judgment.].

Buyout Clauses

Most coaching contracts contain liquidated damages (buyout) clauses that provide for payment by the university to the coach of a set amount if their contract is terminated without cause and, conversely, for payment by the coach to the university of a set amount if they choose to leave for another job. Only recently have institutions chosen to enforce the clauses against the coaches.

Kent State filed a breach of contract action against Geno Ford, its former basketball coach, for terminating his employment with Kent State and taking a similar job at Bradley University even though there were four years remaining on his contract with Kent State. The school was successful in enforcing the liquidated damages clause in the contract and was awarded damages of $1.2 million. The court held the clause to be a reasonable assessment of actual damages and that it was not a penalty. The court noted that both parties clearly agreed to the clause and contemplated such damages to be available for either side should there be an early termination. *Kent State Univ. v. Ford*, 26 N.E. 3d 868 (Ohio Ct. App. 2015).

Kent State might have served as a precedent for a case brought by Oklahoma State University against Joe Wickline, a former assistant football coach who took a position as an assistant at Texas. His contract provided for a $600,000 buyout for early termination unless he took a position in the NFL or a college job where he had play-calling responsibilities. His new job was as offensive line coach and co-offensive coordinator. Depositions indicated conflicting testimony as to his play-calling responsibilities. Ultimately the case was settled, with Texas paying a smaller amount to buy out Wickline's contract.

Notes and Comments

1. Coaching contracts are far different today than those utilized at the time Pepper Rodgers was the coach at Georgia Tech. There was a time when coaches were hired with a handshake agreement or, in the more complicated situations, a brief letter agreement. The university administrator and the coach today, particularly in the revenue producing sports, typically start with a Term Sheet developed within a few days of the hiring. Then the two sides embark on sometimes complex negotiations resulting in multi-page contracts. Concern over early termination and details of outside income agreements has caused both coaches and university officials to desire intricate written contracts. In drafting such contracts there should be a number of key considerations, important to both sides of the agreement. These include such items as:

a. the term of the agreement;
b. the compensation and the source of compensation;
c. the duties and responsibilities of the coach (specific details are desirable);
d. an indication that the coach may be reassigned to other duties if his or her coaching duties are terminated;
e. a liquidated damages clause covering early termination by the coach or early termination *without cause* by the university;
f. a description of the ground for termination *for cause* by the university, including intentional or major violations of NCAA rules (some schools include in this clause an option to terminate if the coach is found to have violated rules while at a previous school);
g. the provisions relating to outside income, including limitations and reporting requirements (outside income generally would be from summer camps, endorsements, radio and television shows, and shoe contracts);
h. the clauses relating to the hiring of assistant coaches and scheduling (the head coach's role in both tasks should be spelled out in the contract); and
i. fringe benefits, including expense accounts, retirement, insurance, season tickets, and any other standard university benefits.

For a detailed description of collegiate coaching contracts see Richard T. Karcher, *The Coaching Carousel in Big-Time Intercollegiate Athletics: Economic Implications and Legal Considerations*, 20 Fordham Intell. Prop. Media & Ent. L.J. 1 (2009); Martin J. Greenberg, *Symposium: National Sports Law Institute Board of Advisors: Termination of College Coaching Contracts: When Does Adequate Cause to Terminate Exist and Who Determines Its Existence?*, 17 Marq. Sports L. Rev. 197 (2006); Robert W. Ferguson, *Slam Dunk: Negotiating Coaching Contracts for Women's College Basketball Programs*, 19 Ent. & Sports Law 8 (2001); Edward N. Stoner II & Arlie R. Nogay, *The Model University Coaching Contract ("MCC"): A Better Starting Point for Your Next Negotiation*, 16 J.C. & U.L. 43 (1989).

2. In recent years, both coaches and universities have shown an increased interest in challenging dismissals and decisions of coaches to depart an institution. Following the conclusion of the 2009 college football season, both Texas Tech and the University of South Florida fired head football coaches for allegedly abusing players in various ways. Both Mike Leach (Texas Tech) and Jim Leavitt (USF) sued their former employers over the terminations. The lawsuits were both motivated by the fact that the schools had terminated both for cause, thus leaving them with no compensation following the dismissals. Leach's case was dismissed on sovereign immunity grounds. The dismissal was upheld on appeal. *Leach v. Texas Tech Univ.*, 335 S.W.3d 386 (Tex. App. 2011) (*Leach v. Tex. Tech Univ.*, 2012 Tex. LEXIS 140 (Tex. S. Ct. 2012). USF and Leavitt reached a settlement in early 2011. Leavitt received $2.75 million.

Conversely, the University of West Virginia and Marist University both instituted litigation against coaches who left both schools for "greener pastures." West Virginia sought to enforce a $4 million buyout clause in Rich Rodriguez's contract when he left to take the head coach position at Michigan in 2007. Rodriguez, unlike other coaches, apparently did not negotiate either with West Virginia or Michigan regarding payment of the buyout. Instead he chose not to pay it, claiming the university had failed to comply with various terms of his contract. Ultimately, he settled, agreeing to pay the entire amount. Marist brought an action against both its former basketball coach Matt Brady and his new employer James Madison University, following his acceptance of the new position. Marist contended that Brady breached his contract, which did not contain a buyout clause, and that James Madison intentionally interfered with the contract. Marist obtained a default judgment in 2010 against James Madison, which paid Marist $100,000 to settle the lawsuit. Marist obtained a jury verdict against the coach but no damages were awarded.

All of these cases suggest a greater willingness to actually attempt to enforce contractual provisions in coaching relationships. This is in contrast to years of custom and practice in which coaches have been free to move at any point in time, and schools have been free to remove them at any point in time. It also appears that schools are much more willing to take action against coaches who are being abusive to players, or even engaging in personal misconduct of other types. Careful drafting now is paramount.

3. Coaches, as with any employees, enjoy the various protections provided by federal and state law against discrimination, slander, and other injurious actions taken by an employer. For example, universities must be cautious when terminating the contract of an older coach. A jury found against the University of Notre Dame in an action filed by Joseph Moore, a former football coach who was fired from his job as an assistant at the age of 64. The official reason given was that he "did not measure up to the standards of Notre Dame." There was evidence introduced at trial, including comments made by the head coach who fired Moore, that age was a strong factor in the termination. *Moore v. The University of Notre Dame*, 22 F. Supp. 2d 896 (N.D. Ind. 1998); *Moore v. The University of Notre Dame*, 968 F. Supp. 1330 (N.D. Ind. 1997).

4. University administrators have a variety of avenues open to them in dealing with coaches and their employment relationships in times of difficulty. For example, the University of Alabama fined its head football coach $360,000 and reduced the length of his contract from five years to three years following his admission of certain actions amounting to an improper relationship with a university employee. The university took this action simultaneous with the settlement of a sexual harassment action filed by the employee. *Alabama Upholds DuBose Penalties*, ATLANTA CONSTITUTION, Aug. 13, 1999, p.5D.

Termination of contracts will often be preceded by varying degrees of due process, depending upon whether the school involved is a public institution and depending upon institutional or state governmental requirements. *See, e.g.*, *Weaver v. Nebo School Dist.*, 29 F. Supp. 2d 1279 (D. Utah 1998) (decision not to assign a teacher as volleyball coach because of her candor concerning her sexual orientation constituted retaliation for exercise of First Amendment rights); *Lancaster v. Independent School Dist. No. 5*, 149 F.3d 1228 (10th Cir. 1998) (teacher's coaching responsibilities not part of his teaching duties and therefore not protected by due process).

2. Institutional and Conference Contracts and Licensing Agreements

Another area where university administrators and legal counsel must be concerned with contractual matters is in connection with radio, television, and streaming rights to athletic events involving the school's teams. The school's rights and obligations, as well as those of the media organization, must be clearly spelled out in the contract. Such items as the description and location of the production facilities, promotional responsibilities, distribution rights, advertising rights, and compensation must be articulated.

Schools must also be careful in drafting agreements simply to engage in an athletic contest with another school. Items such as provision of officials, the site of the game, share of gate receipts, fixed guarantees for playing the game, broadcast rights, and ticket allocation must be clearly spelled out in any agreement.

The specific provisions of a contract for a game have occasionally come into conflict. An example is in a matter involving two television networks, two colleges, and two Major League Baseball teams. On Saturday, September 21, 1996, San Diego State University and the University of Oklahoma were scheduled to play a football game in Jack Murphy Stadium in San Diego at 1:00 p.m., with the game carried as a regional telecast by ABC Sports. Later that day, the San Diego Padres were to play the Los Angeles Dodgers at 8:00 p.m. In late August, the Fox Broadcasting Network announced that it would show the Padres-Dodgers game as its Saturday Game of the Week in a national broadcast pursuant to its contract with Major League Baseball. Game time was set to be 12:30 p.m. setting up a serious conflict with the football game. Major League Baseball and the Padres claimed to have priority at Jack Murphy Stadium, but the City of San Diego, owner of the stadium, initially sided with the university. Ultimately ABC decided, in the course of discussions with all of the parties, to drop the game from its scheduled telecasts. The football game was then re-scheduled for 8:05 p.m. and the baseball game was carried as per FOX's plans as the Game of the Week.

More recently, COVID-19 has created an opportunity for institutions to tweak their force majeure clauses to include pandemics. Some clauses utilized limiting language that could be problematic when dealing with a cancelation due to COVID.

In the era of conference realignment, with institutions jumping from long-established relationships with other schools, conference agreements must be carefully drafted. Typically, leagues will have a constitution and bylaws that govern the operation and administration of the conference.

From the end of the 1990s until the writing of this book, there has been considerable instability among the Division I athletic conferences. The Big Ten expanded to 16 members, while the Big 12 shrank to 10 for a number of years and then added four new members when two members left in 2022. The Pac 10 became the Pac 12 and the Southeastern Conference grew to include 16 members. Other conferences outside of the Power 5 have seen considerable movement in recent years. Some of the moves have been amicable, but some moves have led to litigation, including several cases involving Conference USA in 2022. The most prevalent reason for this shift was economics, largely driven by the opportunity for lucrative television contracts for football and men's basketball. Today, most conferences include in their constitution and bylaws steep fees, typically several million dollars, for exiting the conference. In 2022, for example, the schools leaving the American Athletic Conference for the Big 12 are required to give at least 27 months' notice and pay $10 million each. The conference has indicated it will let them leave early, but it will cost more than $10 million.

A final area where contractual language is critical for collegiate athletic programs is licensing. It has become critical because, like so many other aspects of intercollegiate athletics, it has become big business. In 2013, revenue from officially licensed collegiate products exceeded $4.6 billion. In that year, the University of Texas received nearly $10 million in royalties. In order to enter into the necessary contracts for exploitation and protection purposes, a thorough understanding of the Lanham Act (15 U.S.C. § 1051 *et seq.*) is necessary, including an understanding of trademarks, the function of trademarks, and the registration of trademarks. Then it will be important to have a thorough comprehension of the law and business of licensing trademarks and logos. *See* Chapter 13, below. *See also* GREENBERG & GRAY, SPORTS LAW PRACTICE ch. 8 (2d ed. 1998).

Problem

You work in the athletic department at Western Iowa University, a Division I member of the NCAA. You have just received a call from the president of the university informing you of complaints he has received from four members of the men's basketball team concerning their coach. They contend that he has been abusive, both physically and mentally, for the last year. They also charge that he has made racist and homophobic slurs repeatedly in practices and during games. The president asks you to look into this matter.

What steps would you take to respond to the president's request?

In the course of conducting the investigation, you discover that there is a video that covers several practices over a three-month period and substantially supports the allegations of the players. As you are preparing your final report to the president you discover additional evidence indicating the coach has engaged in abusive behavior similar to that alleged by the players at his sons' junior sports events and has been forcibly removed from venues on at least two occasions. Somehow this never turned up in the media.

What course of action do you advise the president to take? What legal issues are raised? What concerns would you have? Are there any potential actions the NCAA could take in this matter?

Four

Amateur Sports and Antitrust Law

Learning Outcomes

- Understand the policy objectives of the Sherman Antitrust Act and how Section 1 applies to the NCAA.
- Learn about the history of antitrust lawsuits involving the NCAA and understand the holdings in the key cases.
- Consider the legality of a variety of limitations and restrictions imposed on NCAA member institutions and student-athletes.
- Consider the scope of the Supreme Court's ruling in *Alston*.

Key Terms

- Sherman Act
- Restraint on trade
- Input restriction
- Output restriction
- Rule of reason
- Anticompetitive effects
- Procompetitive purposes

A. Introduction to the Federal Antitrust Laws

The antitrust laws have played a very significant role in shaping sports in this country. Chapter 6 of the book explores the relationship between professional sports and antitrust laws. This chapter focuses upon the antitrust status of the organizations, particularly the NCAA, which regulate amateur sports activities.

Beginning with the passage of the Sherman Antitrust Act in 1890, Congress has enacted legislation designed to protect and foster the competitive process in the American marketplace. The body of antitrust law consists of this legislation, along with cases interpreting the legislation. The law applies to activity that involves or affects interstate commerce. According to the 1955 Report of the Attorney General's National Committee to Study the Antitrust Laws:

> The general objective of the antitrust laws is promotion of competition in open markets. This policy is a primary feature of private enterprise. Most Americans have long recognized that opportunity for market access and fostering of market rivalry are basic tenets of our faith in competition as a form of economic organization.

At the risk of gross oversimplification, the general objective of the antitrust law—the promotion of competition in open markets—can be thwarted in two fundamental ways. First, economic rivals can act collusively to reduce competition. Second, the market structure itself can be such that competition is restricted. Thus, antitrust law aims at: (a) eliminating anti-competitive collusion and (b) preventing monopolistic and oligopolistic market structures.

The language of the Sherman Act reflects these twin aims. Under Section 1 of the Act, "every contract, combination... or conspiracy" that restrains trade is prohibited. 15 U.S.C. §1 (1989). A violation of this section requires action by more than one person. In theory, a firm acting on its own will not violate Section 1. The gist of a Section 1 offense is an agreement among business entities or persons which seeks to limit or destroy competition. This would be labeled an unreasonable restraint of trade. Section 2 declares that "every person who shall monopolize, or attempt to monopolize, or combine or conspire... to monopolize" is guilty of an offense. 15 U.S.C. §2 (1989). Historically, the antitrust litigation in amateur sport revolves around Section 1 claims; thus this Chapter focuses on the significant Section 1 cases involving the NCAA and its member institutions.

Even though the NCAA is a non-profit organization whose members are educational institutions and its participants in athletics may be amateurs, intercollegiate athletics are clearly big business. As the Fifth Circuit noted nearly 50 years ago, "While organized as a non-profit organization, the NCAA and its member institutions are, when presenting amateur athletics to a ticket-paying, television-buying public, engaged in a business venture of far greater magnitude than the vast majority of 'profit-making' enterprises." *Hennessey v. NCAA*, 564 F.2d 1136, 1149 n. 14 (5th Cir. 1977). The NCAA bylaws include all of the regulations that govern the operation of NCAA intercollegiate athletics, including rules pertaining to "amateurism," recruiting, extra benefits, and academic standards. The collective adoption and enforcement of NCAA bylaws by the member institutions satisfies the "contract, combination... or conspiracy" element for purposes of Section 1. However, a Section 1 violation only occurs if a court concludes that concerted action restricting competition constitutes an "unreasonable" restraint on trade. As you read the cases in this chapter, focus your attention on how the plaintiff is alleging that the rule or policy at issue restricts competition and how the court assesses the "reasonableness" of that restraint on trade.

There are two basic analytical approaches that courts use in the antitrust context, the per se rule and the rule of reason (including a so-called quick look version).

Certain actions are so obviously contrary to the law that they have no competitive rationale. If a court finds an action is illegal per se, it will not examine the conduct's impact on the market or any procompetitive qualities argued by the defendant. It will simply declare it to be a violation of the Sherman Act. Rule of reason analysis, on the other hand, requires an analysis of the restraint's effect on competition and involves what is characterized by the courts as a burden shifting process. The plaintiff must first satisfy the burden of showing that the agreement in question had a substantially adverse effect on competition. If the plaintiff establishes there has been a substantially adverse impact on competition, the defendant must then present evidence of the procompetitive benefits of the conduct involved. If the defendant succeeds in showing procompetitive effects, it is then up to the plaintiff to "prove that the challenged conduct is not reasonably necessary to achieve the legitimate objectives or that those objectives can be achieved in a substantially less restrictive manner. Ultimately, if these steps are met, the harms and benefits must be weighed against each other in order to judge whether the challenged behavior is, on balance, reasonable." *Law v. NCAA*, 134 F.3d 1010, 1019 (10th Cir. 1998). In *Law* the court used the "quick look" rule of reason analysis. This approach is used in settings where a practice is horizontal price fixing and would normally trigger use of the per se approach, but where other reasons counsel against the per se rule. Thus, the court will go directly to an analysis of whether there are procompetitive justifications for the practice that outweigh the adverse effects.

B. Collegiate Sports Antitrust Issues

Problem

Members of the NCAA, as noted in Chapter 3, voted several years ago to significantly overhaul the governance structure of the organization. The changes provide members of the so-called Power 5 conferences and Notre Dame the autonomy to establish their own governance rules regarding recruitment of athletes, compensation for student-athletes, and other aspects of collegiate athletics. Under the structure, the other conferences theoretically can adopt similar rules, but most have expressed concern over the cost and feasibility of doing so for their member institutions. Shortly after the new legislation passed, the Power 5 approved numerous changes. Included among the provisions is the authority for the Power Five schools to provide grants-in-aid that cover the full cost of attendance. The Power 5 conferences have continued to pass and implement changes in the rules, including support for travel for families of student-athletes participating in the NCAA basketball championship and the College Football Playoff and allowance of financial support for student-athletes' mental health issues. The gap between the "haves" and the "have-nots" in Division I has grown significantly.

You work in the athletic department at Southern Christian University (SCU), a mid-tier member of Division I, and are hearing numerous complaints about the governance structure from people within your school and your conference as well. They are concerned about the impact of this system on SCU and the other schools in the conference, all of which have invested a significant amount in new facilities, coaches, and recruitment in order to be competitive. They fear competitive opportunities are going to be diminished as the Power 5 circle the wagons and only compete against one another. And, as the Power 5 schools are all paying full cost of attendance, the annual cash "*Alston* payments," and perhaps even more, they will not be able to compete for student-athletes. SCU also insists that all the "NIL" money that is being funneled by boosters of Power 5 schools is fueling the competition disparities between the Power 5 and the rest of Division I. SCU believes this will only increase the commercialism rampant in Division I. How would Section 1 of the Sherman Act apply to a potential lawsuit brought by SCU and the other schools in its conference? What additional information or data would you want in order to evaluate a potential claim? In explaining your answers, apply the principles learned from the cases in this chapter (and reference specific cases).

National Collegiate Athletic Association v. Board of Regents of the University of Oklahoma

468 U.S. 85 (1983)

Justice Stevens delivered the opinion of the Court.

The University of Oklahoma and the University of Georgia contend that the National Collegiate Athletic Association has unreasonably restrained trade in the televising of college football games. After an extended trial, the District Court found that the NCAA had violated § 1 of the Sherman Act and granted injunctive relief. 546 F. Supp. 1276 (W.D. Okla. 1982). The Court of Appeals agreed that the statute had been violated but modified the remedy in some respects. 707 F.2d 1147 (10th Cir. 1983). We granted certiorari, 464 U.S. 913 (1983), and now affirm.

I. The NCAA

Since its inception in 1905, the NCAA has played an important role in the regulation of amateur collegiate sports.... With the exception of football, the NCAA has not undertaken any regulation of the televising of athletic events.

Some years ago, five major conferences together with major football-playing independent institutions organized the College Football Association (CFA). The original purpose of the CFA was to promote the interests of major football playing schools within the NCAA structure. The Universities of Oklahoma and Georgia, respondents in this Court, are members of the CFA.

History of the NCAA Television Plan

On January 11, 1951, a three-person "Television Committee," appointed during the preceding year, delivered a report to the NCAA's annual convention in Dallas. Based on preliminary surveys, the committee had concluded that "television does have an adverse effect on college football attendance and unless brought under some control threatens to seriously harm the nation's overall athletic and physical system." A television committee was appointed to implement the decision and to develop an NCAA television plan for 1951.

The committee's 1951 plan provided that only one game a week could be telecast in each area, with a total blackout on 3 of the 10 Saturdays during the season. A team could appear on television only twice during a season. The plan also provided that the NORC would conduct a systematic study of the effects of the program on attendance. The plan received the virtually unanimous support of the NCAA membership....

During each of the succeeding five seasons, studies were made which tended to indicate that television had an adverse effect on attendance at college football games. During those years the NCAA continued to exercise complete control over the number of games that could be televised.

From 1952 through 1977 the NCAA television committee followed essentially the same procedure for developing its television plans. It would first circulate a questionnaire to the membership and then use the responses as a basis for formulating a plan for the ensuing season. The plan was then submitted to a vote by means of a mail referendum. Once approved, the plan formed the basis for NCAA's negotiations with the networks. Throughout this period the plans retained the essential purposes of the original plan. Until 1977 the contracts were all for either 1- or 2-year terms. In 1977 the NCAA adopted "principles of negotiation" for the future and discontinued the practice of submitting each plan for membership approval. Then the NCAA also entered into its first 4-year contract granting exclusive rights to the American Broadcasting Co. (ABC) for the 1978–1981 seasons. ABC had held the exclusive rights to network telecasts of NCAA football games since 1965.

The Current Plan

The plan adopted in 1981 for the 1982–1985 seasons is at issue in this case. This plan, like each of its predecessors, recites that it is intended to reduce, insofar as possible, the adverse effects of live television upon football game attendance. It provides that "all forms of television of the football games of NCAA member institutions during the Plan control periods shall be in accordance with this Plan."

In separate agreements with each of the carrying networks, ABC and the Columbia Broadcasting System (CBS), the NCAA granted each the right to telecast the 14 live "exposures" described in the plan, in accordance with the "ground rules" set forth therein. Each of the networks agreed to pay a specified "minimum aggregate compensation to the participating NCAA member institutions" during the 4-year period in an amount that totaled $131,750,000. In essence the agreement authorized each network to negotiate directly with member schools for the right to televise their games.

Except for differences in payment between national and regional telecasts,... the amount that any team receives does not change with the size of the viewing audience, the number of markets in which the game is telecast, or the particular characteristic of the game or the participating teams. Instead, the "ground rules" provide that the carrying networks make alternate selections of those games they wish to televise, and thereby obtain the exclusive right to submit a bid at an essentially fixed price to the institutions involved.

The plan also contains "appearance requirements" and "appearance limitations" which pertain to each of the 2-year periods that the plan is in effect. The basic requirement imposed on each of the two networks is that it must schedule appearances for at least 82 different member institutions during each 2-year period. Under the appearance limitations no member institution is eligible to appear on television more than a total of six times and more than four times nationally, with the appearances to be divided equally between the two carrying networks.

Thus, although the current plan is more elaborate than any of its predecessors, it retains the essential features of each of them. It limits the total amount of televised intercollegiate football and the number of games that any one team may televise. No member is permitted to make any sale of television rights except in accordance with the basic plan.

Background of this Controversy

Beginning in 1979 CFA members began to advocate that colleges with major football programs should have a greater voice in the formulation of football television policy than they had in the NCAA. CFA therefore investigated the possibility of negotiating a television agreement of its own, developed an independent plan, and obtained a contract offer from the National Broadcasting Co. (NBC). This contract, which it signed in August 1981, would have allowed a more liberal number of appearances for each institution, and would have increased the overall revenues realized by CFA members.

In response the NCAA publicly announced that it would take disciplinary action against any CFA member that complied with the CFA-NBC contract. On September 8, 1981, respondents commenced this action in the United States District Court for the Western District of Oklahoma and obtained a preliminary injunction preventing the NCAA from initiating disciplinary proceedings or otherwise interfering with CFA's efforts to perform its agreement with NBC. Notwithstanding the entry of the injunction, most CFA members were unwilling to commit themselves to the new contractual arrangement with NBC in the face of the threatened sanctions and therefore the agreement was never consummated.

II

There can be no doubt that the challenged practices of the NCAA constitute a "restraint of trade" in the sense that they limit members' freedom to negotiate and enter into their own television contracts. In that sense, however, every contract is a restraint of trade, and as we have repeatedly recognized, the Sherman Act was intended to prohibit only unreasonable restraints of trade.

It is also undeniable that these practices share characteristics of restraints we have previously held unreasonable. The NCAA is an association of schools which compete against each other to attract television revenues, not to mention fans and athletes. As the District Court found, the policies of the NCAA with respect to television rights are ultimately controlled by the vote of member institutions. By participating in an association which prevents member institutions from competing against each other on the basis of price or kind of television rights that can be offered to broadcasters, the NCAA member institutions have created a horizontal restraint—an agreement among competitors on the way in which they will compete with one another. A restraint of this type has often been held to be unreasonable as a matter of law. Because it places a ceiling on the number of games member institutions may televise, the horizontal agreement places an artificial limit on the quantity of televised football that is available to broadcasters and consumers. By restraining the quantity of television rights available for sale, the challenged practices create a limitation output; our cases have held that such limitations are unreasonable restraints of trade.

Horizontal price fixing and output limitation are ordinarily condemned as a matter of law under an "illegal *per se*" approach because the probability that these practices are anticompetitive is so high;... Nevertheless, we have decided that it would be inappropriate to apply a *per se* rule to this case.... what is critical is that this case involves an industry in which horizontal restraints on competition are essential if the product is to be available at all.

What the NCAA and its member institutions market in this case is competition itself—contests between competing institutions. Of course, this would be completely ineffective if there were no rules on which the competitors agreed to create and define the competition to be marketed. A myriad of rules affecting such matters as the size of the field, the number of players on a team, and the extent to which physical violence is to be encouraged or proscribed, all must be agreed upon, and all restrain the manner in which institutions compete. Moreover, the NCAA seeks to market a particular brand of football—college football. The identification of this "product" with an academic tradition differentiates college football from and makes it more popular than professional sports to which it might otherwise be comparable, such as, for example, minor league baseball. In order to preserve the character and quality of the "product," athletes must not be paid, must be required to attend class, and the like. And the integrity of the "product" cannot be preserved except by mutual agreement; if an institution adopted such restrictions unilaterally, its effectiveness as a competitor on the playing field might soon be destroyed. Thus, the NCAA plays a vital role in enabling college football to preserve its character, and as a result enables a product to be marketed which might otherwise be unavailable. In performing this role, its actions widen consumer choice—not only the choices available to sports fans but also those available to athletes—and hence can be viewed as procompetitive.

. . . .

III

The anticompetitive consequences of this arrangement are apparent. Individual competitors lose their freedom to compete. Price is higher and output lower than they would otherwise be, and both are unresponsive to consumer preference. This latter point is perhaps the most significant, since "Congress designed the Sherman Act as a 'consumer welfare prescription.'" . . . A restraint that has the effect of reducing the importance of consumer preference in setting price and output is not consistent with this fundamental goal of antitrust law. Restrictions on price and output are the paradigmatic examples of restraints of trade that the Sherman Act was intended to prohibit. . . . At the same time, the television plan eliminates competitors from the market, since only those broadcasters able to bid on television rights covering the entire NCAA can compete. Thus, as the District Court found, many telecasts that would occur in a competitive market are foreclosed by the NCAA's plan.

Petitioner argues, however, that its television plan can have no significant anticompetitive effect since the record indicates that it has no market power—no ability to alter the interaction of supply and demand in the market. We must reject this argument for two reasons, one legal, one factual.

. We have never required proof of market power in such a case. This naked restraint on price and output requires some competitive justification even in the absence of a detailed market analysis.

As a factual matter, it is evident that petitioner does possess market power. The District Court employed the correct test for determining whether college football broadcasts constitute a separate market—whether there are other products that are reasonably substitutable for televised NCAA football games. Petitioner's argument that it cannot obtain supracompetitive prices from broadcasters since advertisers, and hence broadcasters, can switch from college football to other types of programming simply ignores the findings of the District Court. It found that intercollegiate football telecasts generate an audience uniquely attractive to advertisers and that competitors are unable to offer programming that can attract a similar audience. These findings amply support its conclusion that the NCAA possesses market power. Indeed, the District Court's subsidiary finding that advertisers will pay a premium price per viewer to reach audiences watching college football because of their demographic characteristics is vivid evidence of the uniqueness of this product.

Thus, the NCAA television plan on its face constitutes a restraint upon the operation of a free market, and the findings of the District Court establish that it has operated to raise prices and reduce output. Under the Rule of Reason, these hallmarks of anticompetitive behavior place upon petitioner a heavy burden of establishing an affirmative defense which competitively justifies this apparent deviation from the operations of a free market.... We turn now to the NCAA's proffered justifications.

IV

The District Court did not find that the NCAA's television plan produced any procompetitive efficiencies which enhanced the competitiveness of college football television rights; to the contrary it concluded that NCAA football could be marketed just as effectively without the television plan.

V

Throughout the history of its regulation of intercollegiate football telecasts, the NCAA has indicated its concern with protecting live attendance. This concern, it should be noted, is not with protecting live attendance at games which are shown on television; that type of interest is not at issue in this case. Rather, the concern is that fan interest in a televised game may adversely affect ticket sales for games that will not appear on television.

... [T]he District Court found that there was no evidence to support that theory in today's market.

By seeking to insulate live ticket sales from the full spectrum of competition because of its assumption that the product itself is insufficiently attractive to consumers, petitioner forwards a justification that is inconsistent with the basic policy of the Sherman Act....

VI

Petitioner argues that the interest in maintaining a competitive balance among amateur athletic teams is legitimate and important and that it justifies the regulations challenged in this case. We agree with the first part of the argument but not the second.

It is reasonable to assume that most of the regulatory controls of the NCAA are justifiable means of fostering competition among amateur athletic teams and therefore procompetitive because they enhance public interest in intercollegiate athletics. The specific restraints on football telecasts that are challenged in this case do not, however, fit into the same mold as do rules defining the conditions of the contest, the eligibility of participants, or the manner in which members of a joint enterprise shall share the responsibilities and the benefits of the total venture.

The television plan is not even arguably tailored to serve such an interest. It does not regulate the amount of money that any college may spend on its football program, nor the way in which the colleges may use the revenues that are generated by their football programs, whether derived from the sale of television rights, the sale of tickets, or the sale of concessions or program advertising. There is no evidence that this restriction produces any greater measure of equality throughout the NCAA than would a restriction on alumni donations, tuition rates, or any other revenue-producing activity.

Perhaps the most important reason for rejecting the argument that the interest in competitive balance is served by the television plan is the District Court's unambiguous and well supported finding that many more games would be televised in a free market than under the NCAA plan.

VII

The NCAA plays a critical role in the maintenance of a revered tradition of amateurism in college sports. There can be no question but that it needs ample latitude to play that role, or that the preservation of the student-athlete in higher education adds richness and diversity to intercollegiate athletics and is entirely consistent with the goals of the Sherman Act. But consistent with the Sherman Act, the role of the NCAA must be to preserve a tradition that might otherwise die; rules that restrict output are hardly consistent with this role. Today we hold only that the record supports the District Court's conclusion that by curtailing output and blunting the ability of member institutions to respond to consumer preference, the NCAA has restricted rather than enhanced the place of intercollegiate athletics in the Nation's life. Accordingly, the judgment of the Court of Appeals is Affirmed.

[Justice White, with whom Justice Rehnquist joined, filed a lengthy dissent that took a very conservative, almost idyllic, view of intercollegiate athletics.]

Law v. NCAA

134 F.3d 1010 (10th Cir. 1998)

Ebel, Circuit Judge.

Defendant-Appellant the National Collegiate Athletic Association ("NCAA") promulgated a rule limiting annual compensation of certain Division I entry-level coaches to $16,000. Basketball coaches affected by the rule filed a class action challenging the restriction under Section 1 of the Sherman Antitrust Act. The district court granted summary judgment on the issue of liability to the coaches and issued a permanent injunction restraining the NCAA from promulgating this or any other rules embodying similar compensation restrictions. The NCAA now appeals, and we affirm.

I. Background

....

During the 1980s, the NCAA became concerned over the steadily rising costs of maintaining competitive athletic programs, especially in light of the requirements imposed by Title IX of the 1972 Education Amendments Act to increase support for women's athletic programs. The NCAA observed that some college presidents had to close academic departments, fire tenured faculty, and reduce the number of sports offered to students due to economic constraints. At the same time, many institutions felt pressure to "keep up with the Joneses" by increasing spending on recruiting talented players and coaches and on other aspects of their sports programs in order to remain competitive with rival schools. In addition, a report commissioned by the NCAA known as the "Raiborn Report" found that in 1985 42% of NCAA Division I schools reported deficits in their overall athletic program budgets, with the deficit averaging $824,000 per school. The Raiborn Report noted that athletic expenses at all Division I institutions rose more than 100% over the eight-year period from 1978 to 1985. Finally, the Report stated that 51% of Division I schools responding to NCAA inquiries on the subject suffered a net loss in their basketball programs alone that averaged $145,000 per school.

Part of the problem identified by the NCAA involved the costs associated with part-time assistant coaches. The NCAA allowed Division I basketball teams to employ three full-time coaches, including one head coach and two assistant coaches, and two part-time coaches. The part-time positions could be filled by part-time assistants, graduate assistants, or volunteer coaches. The NCAA imposed salary restrictions on all of the part-time positions. A volunteer coach could not receive any compensation from a member institution's athletic department. A graduate assistant coach was required to be enrolled in a graduate studies program of a member institution and could only receive compensation equal to the value of the cost of the educational experience (grant-in-aid)....The NCAA limited compensation to part-time assistants to the value of full grant-in-aid compensation based on the value of out-of-state graduate studies.

Despite the salary caps, many of these part-time coaches earned $60,000 or $70,000 per year. Athletic departments circumvented the compensation limits by employing these part-time coaches in lucrative summer jobs at profitable sports camps run by the school or by hiring them for part-time jobs in the physical education department in addition to the coaching position. Further, many of these positions were filled with seasoned and experienced coaches, not the type of student assistant envisioned by the rule.

In January of 1989, the NCAA established a Cost Reduction Committee (the "Committee") to consider means and strategies for reducing the costs of inter-collegiate athletics "without disturbing the competitive balance" among NCAA member institutions. In his initial letter to Committee members, the Chairman of the Committee thanked participants for joining "this gigantic attempt to save intercollegiate athletics from itself." It was felt that only a collaborative effort could reduce costs effectively while maintaining a level playing field because individual schools could not afford to make unilateral spending cuts in sports programs for fear that doing so would unduly hamstring that school's ability to compete against other institutions that spent more money on athletics. In January of 1990, the Chairman told NCAA members that the goal of the Committee was to "cut costs and save money." It became the consensus of the Committee that reducing the total number of coaching positions would reduce the cost of intercollegiate athletic programs.

The Committee proposed an array of recommendations to amend the NCAA's bylaws, including proposed Bylaw 11.6.4 that would limit Division I basketball coaching staffs to four members—one head coach, two assistant coaches, and one entry-level coach called a "restricted-earnings coach." The restricted-earnings coach category was created to replace the positions of part-time assistant, graduate assistant, and volunteer coach. The Committee believed that doing so would resolve the inequity that existed between those schools with graduate programs that could hire graduate assistant coaches and those who could not while reducing the overall amount spent on coaching salaries.

A second proposed rule, Bylaw 11.02.3, restricted compensation of restricted-earnings coaches in all Division I sports other than football to a total of $12,000 for the academic year and $4,000 for the summer months (the "REC Rule" for restricted-earnings coaches). The Committee determined that the $16,000 per year total figure approximated the cost of out-of-state tuition for graduate schools at public institutions and the average graduate school tuition at private institutions, and was thus roughly equivalent to the salaries previously paid to part-time graduate assistant coaches. The REC Rule did not prevent member institutions from using savings gained by reducing the number and salary of basketball coaches to increase expenditures on other aspects of their athletic programs.

The NCAA adopted the proposed rules, including the REC Rule, by majority vote in January of 1991, and the rules became effective on August 1, 1992. The rules bind all Division I members of the NCAA that employ basketball coaches. The schools normally compete with each other in the labor market for coaching services.

In this case, plaintiffs-appellees were restricted-earnings men's basketball coaches at NCAA Division I institutions in the academic year 1992–93. They challenged the REC Rule's limitation on compensation under section 1 of the Sherman Antitrust Act, 15 U.S.C. § 1 (1990), as an unlawful "contract, combination... or conspiracy, in restraint of trade."

... [T]he district court permanently enjoined the NCAA from enforcing or attempting to enforce any restricted earnings coach salary limitations against the named plaintiffs, and it further enjoined the NCAA from "reenacting the compensation limitations embodied in [the REC Rule]." The NCAA appeals the permanent injunction.

Rule of Reason Analysis

We apply the rule of reason approach in this case.

Courts have imposed a consistent structure on rule of reason analysis by casting it in terms of shifting burdens of proof. Under this approach, the plaintiff bears the initial burden of showing that an agreement had a substantially adverse effect on competition. If the plaintiff meets this burden, the burden shifts to the defendant to come forward with evidence of the procompetitive virtues of the alleged wrongful conduct. If the defendant is able to demonstrate procompetitive effects, the plaintiff then must prove that the challenged conduct is not reasonably necessary to achieve the legitimate objectives or that those objectives can be achieved in a substantially less restrictive manner. Ultimately, if these steps are met, the harms and benefits must be weighed against each other in order to judge whether the challenged behavior is, on balance, reasonable.

A. Anticompetitive Effect

The NCAA argues that the district court erred by failing to define the relevant market and by failing to find that the NCAA possesses power in that market.

The NCAA misapprehends the purpose in antitrust law of market definition, which is not an end unto itself but rather exists to illuminate a practice's effect on competition.... where a practice has obvious anticompetitive effects—as does price-fixing—there is no need to prove that the defendant possesses market power. Rather, the court is justified in proceeding directly to the question of whether the procompetitive justifications advanced for the restraint outweigh the anti-competitive effects under a "quick look" rule of reason.

We find it appropriate to adopt such a quick look rule of reason in this case. Under a quick look rule of reason analysis, anticompetitive effect is established, even without a determination of the relevant market, where the plaintiff shows that a horizontal agreement to fix prices exists, that the agreement is effective, and that the price set by such an agreement is more favorable to the defendant than otherwise would have resulted from the operation of market forces. Under this standard, the undisputed evidence supports a finding of anticompetitive effect. Because the REC Rule was successful in artificially lowering the price of coaching services, no further evidence or analysis is required to find market power to set prices.

Finally, the NCAA cites *Hennessey v. NCAA*, 564 F.2d 1136 (5th Cir. 1977). In *Hennessey*, assistant football and basketball coaches challenged a NCAA bylaw limiting the number of assistant coaches member institutions could employ at any one time. The Fifth Circuit upheld the rule, concluding that the plaintiff failed to show that the rule was an unreasonable restraint of trade after weighing the anticompetitive effects with the procompetitive benefits of the restriction.

Hennessey is not controlling for a variety of reasons. First, the REC Rule is distinguishable from the agreement at issue in *Hennessey*. *Hennessey* addresses a restriction on the number of assistant coaches that a Division I school could employ whereas the REC Rule limits salary of a certain category of coaches. Therefore, the analysis of the reasonableness of the restraint in *Hennessey*, which did not involve a naked restriction on price, will not control the analysis of the reasonableness of the REC Rule.

Second, the *Hennessey* court placed the burden of showing the unreasonableness of the coaching restriction in that case on the plaintiff and then found that the plaintiff could not make such a showing because the rule had only recently been implemented. In our analysis, the plaintiff only has the burden of establishing the anticompetitive effect of the restraint at issue. Once the plaintiff meets that burden, which the coaches have done in this case by showing the naked and effective price-fixing character of the agreement, the burden shifts to the defendant to justify the restraint as a "reasonable" one. It is on this step that the defendant NCAA stumbles.

Third, *Hennessey* predates the Supreme Court's opinion in *Board of Regents*. The Fifth Circuit very well may have reached a different result in *Hennessey* if it had the benefit of that precedent, because *Board of Regents* suggests a less deferential approach to the NCAA than the approach taken in *Hennessey*. Finally, of course, *Hennessey* is not Tenth Circuit precedent, and accordingly is not binding authority on us.

B. Procompetitive Rationales

In *Board of Regents* the Supreme Court recognized that certain horizontal restraints, such as the conditions of the contest and the eligibility of participants, are justifiable under the antitrust laws because they are necessary to create the product of competitive college sports. Thus, the only legitimate rationales that we will recognize in support of the REC Rule are those necessary to produce competitive intercollegiate sports. The NCAA advanced three justifications for the salary limits: retaining entry-level coaching positions; reducing costs; and maintaining competitive equity. We address each of them in turn.

1. Retention of Entry-Level Positions

The NCAA argues that the plan serves the procompetitive goal of retaining an entry-level coaching position. The NCAA asserts that the plan will allow younger, less experienced coaches entry into Division I coaching positions. While opening up coaching positions for younger people may have social value apart from its affect [sic] on competition, we may not consider such values unless they impact upon competition....

The NCAA also contends that limiting one of the four available coaching positions on a Division I basketball team to an entry level position will create more balanced competition by barring some teams from hiring four experienced coaches instead of three. However, the REC Rule contained no restrictions other than salary designed to insure that the position would be filled by entry-level applicants; it could be filled with experienced applicants. In addition, under the REC Rule, schools can still pay restricted-earnings coaches more than $16,000 per year by hiring them for physical education or other teaching positions. In fact, the evidence in the record tends to demonstrate that at least some schools designated persons with many years of experience as the restricted-earnings coach Nothing in the record suggests that the salary limits for restricted-earnings coaches will be effective at creating entry-level positions. Thus, the NCAA failed to present a tri-able issue of fact as to whether preserving entry-level positions served a legitimate procompetitive end of balancing competition.

2. Cost Reduction

The NCAA next advances the justification that the plan will cut costs. How-ever, cost-cutting by itself is not a valid procompetitive justification. If it were, any group of competing buyers could agree on maximum prices.

We are dubious that the goal of cost reductions can serve as a legally sufficient justification for a buyers' agreement to fix prices even if such cost reductions are necessary to save inefficient or unsuccessful competitors from failure. Nevertheless, we need not consider whether cost reductions may have been required to "save" intercollegiate athletics and whether such an objective served as a legitimate procompetitive end because the NCAA presents no evidence that limits on restricted-earning coaches' salaries would be successful in reducing deficits, let alone that such reductions were necessary to save college basketball. Moreover, the REC Rule does not equalize the overall amount of money Division I schools are permitted to spend on their basketball programs. There is no reason to think that the money saved by a school on the salary of a restricted-earnings coach will not be put into another aspect of the school's basketball program, such as equipment or even another coach's salary, thereby increasing inequity in that area.

3. Maintaining Competitiveness

We note that the NCAA must be able to ensure some competitive equity between member institutions in order to produce a marketable product: a "team must try to establish itself as a winner, but it must not win so often and so convincingly that the outcome will never be in doubt, or else there will be no marketable 'competition.'" The NCAA asserts that the REC Rule will help to maintain competitive equity by preventing wealthier schools from placing a more experienced, higher-priced coach in the position of restricted-earnings coach.

While the REC Rule will equalize the salaries paid to entry-level coaches in Division I schools, it is not clear that the REC Rule will equalize the experience level of such coaches. Nowhere does the NCAA prove that the salary restrictions enhance competition, level an uneven playing field, or reduce coaching inequities. Thus, on its face, the REC Rule is not directed towards competitive balance nor is the nexus between the rule and a compelling need to maintain competitive balance sufficiently clear on this record to withstand a motion for summary judgment.

For the reasons discussed above, we AFFIRM the district court's order granting a permanent injunction barring the NCAA from reenacting compensation limits such as those contained in the REC Rule based on its order granting summary judgment to the plaintiffs on the issue of antitrust liability.

O'Bannon v. National Collegiate Athletic Association

802 F.3d 1049 (9th Cir. 2015), *cert. denied* 137 S. Ct. 277 (2016)

Opinion

BYBEE, CIRCUIT JUDGE:

... For more than a century, the National Collegiate Athletic Association (NCAA) has prescribed rules governing the eligibility of athletes at its more than 1,000 member colleges and universities. Those rules prohibit student-athletes from being paid for the use of their names, images, and likenesses (NILs). The question presented in this momentous case is whether the NCAA's rules are subject to the antitrust laws and, if so, whether they are an unlawful restraint of trade.

After a bench trial and in a thorough opinion, the district court concluded that the NCAA's compensation rules were an unlawful restraint of trade. It then enjoined the NCAA from prohibiting its member schools from giving student-athletes scholarships up to the full cost of attendance at their respective schools and up to $5,000 per year in deferred compensation, to be held in trust for student-athletes until after they leave college.

I

A. The NCAA

[The court set forth a detailed history and description of the NCAA.]

B. The Amateurism Rules

One of the NCAA's earliest reforms of intercollegiate sports was a requirement that the participants be amateurs.... But the NCAA, still a voluntary organization, lacked the ability to enforce this requirement effectively, and schools continued to pay their athletes under the table in a variety of creative ways; a 1929 study found that 81 out of 112 schools surveyed provided some sort of improper inducement to their athletes.

The NCAA began to strengthen its enforcement capabilities in 1948, when it adopted what became known as the "Sanity Code"—a set of rules that prohibited schools from giving athletes financial aid that was based on athletic ability and not available to ordinary students....

In 1956, the NCAA departed from the Sanity Code's approach to financial aid by changing its rules to permit its members, for the first time, to give student-athletes scholarships based on athletic ability. These scholarships were capped at the amount of a full "grant in aid," defined as the total cost of "tuition and fees, room and board, and required course-related books." Student-athletes were prohibited from receiving any "financial aid based on athletics ability" in excess of the value of a grant-in-aid, on pain of losing their eligibility for collegiate athletics.

In August 2014, the NCAA announced it would allow athletic conferences to authorize their member schools to increase scholarships up to the full cost of attendance. The 80 member schools of the five largest athletic conferences in the country voted in January 2015 to take that step, and the scholarship cap at those schools is now at the full cost of attendance.

In addition to its financial aid rules, the NCAA has adopted numerous other amateurism rules that limit student-athletes' compensation and their interactions with professional sports leagues. An athlete can lose his amateur status, for example, if he signs a contract with a professional team, enters a professional league's player draft, or hires an agent. And, most importantly, an athlete is prohibited—with few exceptions—from receiving *any* "pay" based on his athletic ability, whether from boosters, companies seeking endorsements, or would-be licensors of the athlete's name, image, and likeness (NIL).

C. The *O'Bannon* and *Keller* Litigation

In 2008, Ed O'Bannon, a former All-American basketball player at UCLA, visited a friend's house, where his friend's son told O'Bannon that he was depicted in a college basketball video game produced by Electronic Arts (EA), a software company that produced video games based on college football and men's basketball from the late 1990s until around 2013. The friend's son turned on the video game, and O'Bannon saw an avatar of himself—a virtual player who visually resembled O'Bannon, played for UCLA, and wore O'Bannon's jersey number, 31. O'Bannon had never consented to the use of his likeness in the video game, and he had not been compensated for it.

In 2009, O'Bannon sued the NCAA and the Collegiate Licensing Company (CLC), the entity which licenses the trademarks of the NCAA and a number of its member schools for commercial use, in federal court. The gravamen of O'Bannon's complaint was that the NCAA's amateurism rules, insofar as they prevented student-athletes from being compensated for the use of their NILs, were an illegal restraint of trade under Section 1 of the Sherman Act, 15 U.S.C. § 1.

D. The District Court's Decision

[The court presented a detailed description of the district court's ruling. The court restates the relevant arguments and theories in the analysis and ruling below.]

II

[The court then states that it will review the district court's fact findings for clear error and its conclusions of law *de novo*.]

III

On appeal, the NCAA contends that the plaintiffs' Sherman Act claim fails on the merits, but it also argues that we are precluded altogether from reaching the merits, for three independent reasons: (1) The Supreme Court held in *NCAA v. Board of Regents of the University of Oklahoma*, 468 U.S. 85 (1984), that the NCAA's amateurism rules are "valid as a matter of law"; (2) the compensation rules at issue here are not covered by the Sherman Act at all because they do not regulate commercial activity; and (3) the plaintiffs have no standing to sue under the Sherman Act because they have not suffered "antitrust injury." We find none of these three arguments persuasive.

A. *Board of Regents* Did Not Declare the NCAA's Amateurism Rules "Valid as a Matter of Law"

We consider, first, the NCAA's claim that, under *Board of Regents*, all NCAA amateurism rules are "valid as a matter of law."

The *Board of Regents* Court certainly discussed the NCAA's amateurism rules at great length, but it did not do so in order to pass upon the rules' merits, given that they were not before the Court. Rather, the Court discussed the amateurism rules for a different and particular purpose: to explain why NCAA rules should be analyzed under the Rule of Reason, rather than held to be illegal per se. The *Board of Regents* Court decided, however, that because college sports could not exist without certain horizontal agreements, NCAA rules should not be held per se unlawful even when—like the television rules in Board of Regents—they appear to be pure "restraints on the ability of member institutions to compete in terms of price and output." *Bd. of Regents*, 468 U.S. at 103.

Board of Regents, in other words, did not approve the NCAA's amateurism rules as categorically consistent with the Sherman Act. Rather, it held that, because many NCAA rules (among them, the amateurism rules) are part of the "character and quality of the [NCAA's] 'product,'" *id.* at 102, no NCAA rule should be invalidated without a Rule of Reason analysis. The Court's long encomium to amateurism, though impressive-sounding, was therefore dicta.

B. The Compensation Rules Regulate "Commercial Activity"

The NCAA next argues that we cannot reach the merits of the plaintiffs' Sherman Act claim because the compensation rules are not subject to the Sherman Act at all.

This argument is not credible. Although restraints that have no effect on commerce are indeed exempt from Section 1, the modern legal understanding of "commerce" is broad, "including almost every activity from which the actor anticipates economic gain."

It is no answer to these observations to say, as the NCAA does in its briefs, that the compensation rules are "eligibility rules" rather than direct restraints on the terms of agreements between schools and recruits.... The mere fact that a rule can be characterized as an "eligibility rule," however, does not mean the rule is not a restraint of trade; were the law otherwise, the NCAA could insulate its member schools' relationships with student-athletes from antitrust scrutiny by renaming every rule governing student-athletes an "eligibility rule."

In other words, the substance of the compensation rules matters far more than how they are styled. And in substance, the rules clearly regulate the terms of commercial transactions between athletic recruits and their chosen schools: a school may not give a recruit compensation beyond a grant-in-aid, and the recruit may not accept compensation beyond that limit, lest the recruit be disqualified and the transaction vitiated. The NCAA's argument that its compensation rules are "eligibility" restrictions, rather than substantive restrictions on the price terms of recruiting agreements, is but a sleight of hand. There is real money at issue here.

We therefore conclude that the NCAA's compensation rules are within the ambit of the Sherman Act.

C. The Plaintiffs Demonstrated that the Compensation Rules Cause Them Injury in Fact

We conclude that the plaintiffs have shown that they are injured in fact as a result of the NCAA's rules having foreclosed the market for their NILs in video games. We therefore do not reach the thornier questions of whether participants in live TV broadcasts of college sporting events have enforceable rights of publicity or whether the plaintiffs are injured by the NCAA's current licensing arrangement for archival footage.

IV

Having rejected all of the NCAA's preliminary legal arguments, we proceed to review the plaintiffs' Section 1 claim on the merits....

A. Significant Anticompetitive Effects Within a Relevant Market

As we have recounted, the district court made the following factual findings: (1) that a cognizable "college education market" exists, wherein colleges compete for the services of athletic recruits by offering them scholarships and various amenities, such as coaching and facilities; (2) that if the NCAA's compensation rules did not exist, member schools would compete to offer recruits compensation for their NILs; and (3) that the compensation rules therefore have a significant anticompetitive effect on the college education market, in that they fix an aspect of the "price" that recruits pay to attend college (or, alternatively, an aspect of the price that schools pay to secure recruits' services). These findings have substantial support in the record.

...[T]he NCAA makes three modest arguments about why the compensation rules do not have a significant anticompetitive effect. First, it argues that because the plaintiffs never showed that the rules reduce output in the college education market, the plaintiffs did not meet their burden of showing a significant anticompetitive effect. Second, it argues that the rules have no anticompetitive effect because schools would not pay student- athletes anything for their NIL rights in any event, given that those rights are worth nothing. And finally, the NCAA argues that even if the district court was right that schools would pay student-athletes for their NIL rights, any such payments would be small, which means that the compensation rules' anticompetitive effects cannot be considered significant.

We can dispose of the first two arguments quickly. First, the NCAA's contention that the plaintiffs' claim fails because they did not show a decrease in output in the college education market is simply incorrect. Here, the NCAA argues that output in the college education market "consists of opportunities for student-athletes to participate in FBS football or Division I men's basketball," and it quotes the district court's finding that these opportunities have "increased steadily over time." *See O'Bannon*, 7 F. Supp. 3d at 981. But this argument misses the mark. Although output reductions are one common kind of anticompetitive effect in antitrust cases, a "reduction in output is not the *only* measure of anticompetitive effect."

The "combination[s] condemned by the [Sherman] Act" also include "price-fixing... by purchasers" even though "the persons specially injured... are sellers, not customers or consumers." *Mandeville Island Farms, Inc. v. Am. Crystal Sugar Co.*, 334 U.S. 219, 235 (1948). At trial, the plaintiffs demonstrated that the NCAA's compensation rules have just this kind of anticompetitive effect: they fix the price of one component of the exchange between school and recruit, thereby precluding competition among schools with respect to that component. The district court found that although consumers of NCAA football and basketball may not be harmed directly by this price-fixing, the "student-athletes themselves are harmed by the price-fixing agreement among FBS football and Division I basketball schools." *O'Bannon*, 7 F. Supp. 3d at 972–73. The athletes accept grants-in-aid, and no more, in exchange for their athletic performance, because the NCAA schools have agreed to value the athletes' NILs at zero, "an anticompetitive effect." *Id.* at 973. This anticompetitive effect satisfied the plaintiffs' initial burden under the Rule of Reason....

Second, the NCAA's argument that student-athletes' NILs are, in fact, worth nothing is simply a repackaged version of its arguments about injury in fact, which we have rejected.

Finally, we reject the NCAA's contention that any NIL compensation that student-athletes might receive in the absence of its compensation rules would be de minimis and that the rules therefore do not significantly affect competition in the college education market. This "too small to matter" argument is incompatible with the Supreme Court's holding in *Catalano, Inc. v. Target Sales, Inc.*, 446 U.S. 643 (1980) (per curiam). In *Catalano*, a group of beer retailers sued a group of beer wholesalers, alleging that the wholesalers had secretly agreed to end their customary practice of extending the retailers interest-free credit for roughly a month after the delivery of beer. *Id.* at 644. The Court unanimously held that this agreement was unlawful per se. It reasoned that the agreement was clearly a means of "extinguishing one form of [price] competition among the sellers," given that credit terms were part of the price of the beer, and that the agreement was therefore tantamount to price-fixing. *Id.* at 649. The Court was not concerned with whether the agreement affected the market adversely: "It is no excuse that the prices fixed are themselves reasonable." *Id.* at 647.

The NCAA's compensation rules function in much the same way as the agreement at issue in *Catalano*: they "extinguish[] one form of competition" among schools seeking to land recruits. Because we agree with the district court that the compensation rules have a significant anticompetitive effect on the college education market, we proceed to consider the procompetitive justifications the NCAA proffers for those rules.

B. Procompetitive Effects

As discussed above, the NCAA offered the district court four procompetitive justifications for the compensation rules: (1) promoting amateurism, (2) promoting competitive balance among NCAA schools, (3) integrating student-athletes with their schools' academic community, and (4) increasing output in the college education market. The district court accepted the first and third and rejected the other two.

... [T]he NCAA focuses its arguments to this court entirely on the first proffered justification—the promotion of amateurism.

... [W]e fail to see how the restraint at issue in this particular case—*i.e.*, the NCAA's limits on student-athlete compensation—makes college sports more attractive to recruits, or widens recruits' spectrum of choices in the sense that Board of Regents suggested. As the district court found, it is primarily "the opportunity to earn a higher education" that attracts athletes to college sports rather than professional sports, O'Bannon, 7 F. Supp. 3d at 986, and that opportunity would still be available to student-athletes if they were paid some compensation in addition to their athletic scholarships.

Indeed, if anything, loosening or abandoning the compensation rules might be the best way to "widen" recruits' range of choices; athletes might well be more likely to attend college, and stay there longer, if they knew that they were earning some amount of NIL income while they were in school.... We therefore reject the NCAA's claim that, by denying student-athletes compensation apart from scholarships, the NCAA increases the "choices" available to them.

The NCAA's second point has more force—the district court probably underestimated the NCAA's commitment to amateurism.... But the point is ultimately irrelevant. Even if the NCAA's concept of amateurism had been perfectly coherent and consistent, the NCAA would still need to show that amateurism brings about some procompetitive *effect* in order to justify it under the antitrust laws. *See id.* at 101–02 & n.23. The NCAA cannot fully answer the district court's finding that the compensation rules have significant anticompetitive effects simply by pointing out that it has adhered to those rules for a long time. Nevertheless, the district court found, and the record supports that there is a concrete procompetitive effect in the NCAA's commitment to amateurism: namely, that the amateur nature of collegiate sports increases their appeal to consumers. We therefore conclude that the NCAA's compensation rules serve the two procompetitive purposes identified by the district court: integrating academics with athletics, and "preserving the popularity of the NCAA's product by promoting its current understanding of amateurism."

C. Substantially Less Restrictive Alternatives

The third step in the Rule of Reason analysis is whether there are substantially less restrictive alternatives to the NCAA's current rules.

The district court identified two substantially less restrictive alternatives: (1) allowing NCAA member schools to give student-athletes grants-in-aid that cover the full cost of attendance; and (2) allowing member schools to pay student-athletes small amounts of deferred cash compensation for use of their NILs. *O'Bannon*, 7 F. Supp. 3d at 1005–07. We hold that the district court did not clearly err in finding that raising the grant-in-aid cap would be a substantially less restrictive alternative, but that it clearly erred when it found that allowing students to be paid compensation for their NILs is virtually as effective as the NCAA's current amateur-status rule.

1. Capping the permissible amount of scholarships at the cost of attendance

All of the evidence before the district court indicated that raising the grant-in-aid cap to the cost of attendance would have virtually no impact on amateurism: Dr. Mark Emmert, the president of the NCAA, testified at trial that giving student-athletes scholarships up to their full costs of attendance would not violate the NCAA's principles of amateurism because all the money given to students would be going to cover their "legitimate costs" to attend school. Other NCAA witnesses agreed with that assessment. *Id.* at 983. Nothing in the record, moreover, suggested that consumers of college sports would become less interested in those sports if athletes' scholarships covered their full cost of attendance, or that an increase in the grant-in-aid cap would impede the integration of student-athletes into their academic communities. *Id.*

The NCAA, along with fifteen scholars of antitrust law appearing as *amici curiae*, warns us that if we affirm even this more modest of the two less restrictive alternative restraints identified by the district court, we will open the floodgates to new lawsuits demanding all manner of incremental changes in the NCAA's and other organizations' rules. The NCAA and these *amici* admonish us that as long as a restraint (such as a price cap) is "reasonably necessary to a valid business purpose," it should be upheld; it is not an antitrust court's function to tweak every market restraint that the court believes could be improved.

We agree with the NCAA and the *amici* that, as a general matter, courts should not use antitrust law to make marginal adjustments to broadly reasonable market restraints. The particular restraint at issue here, however—the grant-in-aid cap that the NCAA set below the cost of attendance—is not such a restraint. To the contrary, the evidence at trial showed that the grant-in-aid cap has no relation whatsoever to the procompetitive purposes of the NCAA: by the NCAA's own standards, student-athletes remain amateurs as long as any money paid to them goes to cover legitimate educational expenses.

Thus, in holding that setting the grant-in-aid cap at student-athletes' full cost of attendance is a substantially less restrictive alternative under the Rule of Reason, we are not declaring that courts are free to micromanage organizational rules or to strike down largely beneficial market restraints with impunity. Rather, our affirmance of this aspect of the district court's decision should be taken to establish only that where, as here, a restraint is *patently and inexplicably* stricter than is necessary to accomplish all of its procompetitive objectives, an antitrust court can and should invalidate it and order it replaced with a less restrictive alternative.

A compensation cap set at student-athletes' full cost of attendance is a substantially less restrictive alternative means of accomplishing the NCAA's legitimate procompetitive purposes. And there is no evidence that this cap will significantly increase costs; indeed, the NCAA already permits schools to fund student-athletes' full cost of attendance. The district court's determination that the existing compensation rules violate Section 1 of the Sherman Act was correct and its injunction requiring the NCAA to permit schools to provide compensation up to the full cost of attendance was proper.

2. Allowing students to receive cash compensation for their NILs

In our judgment, however, the district court clearly erred in finding it a viable alternative to allow students to receive NIL cash payments untethered to their education expenses. The question is whether the alternative of allowing students to be paid NIL compensation unrelated to their education expenses, is "virtually as effective" in preserving amateurism as *not* allowing compensation.

We cannot agree that a rule permitting schools to pay students pure cash compensation and a rule forbidding them from paying NIL compensation are both *equally* effective in promoting amateurism and preserving consumer demand. Both we and the district court agree that the NCAA's amateurism rule has procompetitive benefits. But in finding that paying students cash compensation would promote amateurism as effectively as not paying them, the district court ignored that not paying student-athletes is *precisely what makes them amateurs.*

Having found that amateurism is integral to the NCAA's market, the district court cannot plausibly conclude that being a poorly-paid professional collegiate athlete is "virtually as effective" for that market as being as amateur. Or, to borrow the Supreme Court's analogy, the market for college football is distinct from other sports markets and must be "differentiate[d]" from professional sports lest it become "minor league [football]." *Bd. of Regents*, 468 U.S. at 102.

Aside from the self-evident fact that paying students for their NIL rights will vitiate their amateur status as collegiate athletes, the court relied on threadbare evidence in finding that small payments of cash compensation will preserve amateurism as well the NCAA's rule forbidding such payments. Most of the evidence elicited merely indicates that paying students large compensation payments would harm consumer demand more than smaller payments would—not that small cash payments will preserve amateurism. Thus, the evidence was addressed to the wrong question. Instead of asking whether making small payments to student-athletes served the same procompetitive purposes as making no payments, the evidence before the district court went to a different question: Would the collegiate sports market be better off if the NCAA made small payments or big payments? For example, the district court noted that a witness called by the NCAA, Bernard Muir, the athletic director at Stanford University, testified that paying student-athletes modest sums raises less concern than paying them large sums. The district court also relied on Dr. Dennis's opinion survey, which the court read to indicate that in the absence of the NCAA's compensation rules, "the popularity of college sports would likely depend on the size of payments awarded to student-athletes." *O'Bannon*, 7 F. Supp. 3d at 983. Dr. Dennis had found that payments of $200,000 per year to each athlete would alienate the public more than would payments of $20,000 per year. *Id.* at 975–76, 983. At best, these pieces of evidence indicate that small payments to players will impact consumer demand less than larger payments. But there is a stark difference between finding that small payments are less harmful to the market than large payments—and finding that paying students small sums is virtually as effective in promoting amateurism as not paying them.

Finally, the district court, and the dissent, place particular weight on a brief interchange during plaintiffs' cross-examination of one of the NCAA's witnesses, Neal Pilson, a television sports consultant formerly employed at CBS. Pilson testified that "if you're paid for your performance, you're not an amateur," and explained at length why paying students would harm the student-athlete market. Plaintiffs then asked Pilson whether his opinions about amateurism "depend on the level of the money" paid to players, and he acknowledged that his opinion was "impacted by the level." When asked whether there was a line that "should not be crossed" in paying players, Pilson responded "that's a difficult question. I haven't thought about the line. And

I haven't been asked to render an opinion on that." When pressed to come up with a figure, Pilson repeated that he was "not sure." He eventually commented that "I tell you that a million dollars would trouble me and $5,000 wouldn't, but that's a pretty good range." When asked whether deferred compensation to students would concern him, Pilson said that while he would not be as concerned by deferred payments, he would still be "troubled by it."

So far as we can determine, Pilson's offhand comment under cross-examination is the sole support for the district court's $5,000 figure. But even taking Pilson's comments at face value, as the dissent urges, his testimony cannot support the finding that paying student-athletes small sums will be virtually as effective in preserving amateurism as not paying them. Pilson made clear that he was not prepared to opine on whether pure cash compensation, of any amount, would affect amateurism. Indeed, he was never asked about the impact of giving student-athletes small cash payments; instead, like other witnesses, he was asked only whether big payments would be worse than small payments. Pilson's casual comment—"[I] haven't been asked to render an opinion on that. It's not in my report"—that he would not be troubled by $5,000 payments is simply not enough to support the district court's far-reaching conclusion that paying students $5,000 per year will be as effective in preserving amateurism as the NCAA's current policy.

The difference between offering student-athletes education-related compensation and offering them cash sums untethered to educational expenses is not minor; it is a quantum leap.[1] Once that line is crossed, we see no basis for returning to a rule of amateurism and no defined stopping point; we have little doubt that plaintiffs will continue to challenge the arbitrary limit imposed by the district court until they have captured the full value of their NIL. At that point the NCAA will have surrendered its amateurism principles entirely and transitioned from its "particular brand of football" to minor league status. *Bd. of Regents*, 468 U.S. at 101–02. In light of that, the meager evidence in the record, and the Supreme Court's admonition that we must afford the NCAA "ample latitude" to superintend college athletics, *Bd. of Regents*, 468 U.S. at 120, we think it is clear the district court erred in concluding that small payments in deferred compensation are a substantially less restrictive alternative restraint. We thus vacate that portion of the district court's decision and the portion of its injunction requiring the NCAA to allow its member schools to pay this deferred compensation.

1. The district court suggested that compensating athletes beyond the full cost of attendance would not be problematic because student-athletes are already permitted to accept Pell grants that raise their total aid package above the cost of attendance. *O'Bannon*, 7 F. Supp. 3d at 1000; Dissent at 65. This reasoning was faulty because it improperly equates compensation intended for education-related expenses *(i.e.*, Pell grants) with pure cash compensation. The fact that Pell grants (which are available to athletes and nonathletes alike) have not eroded the NCAA's culture of amateurism says little about whether cash payments into trust funds to compensate student-athletes for their prowess on the gridiron or the court would do so.

NCAA v. Alston, et al.

141 S. Ct. 2141 (2021)

Justice Gorsuch delivered the opinion of the Court.

In the Sherman Act, Congress tasked courts with enforcing a policy of competition on the belief that market forces "yield the best allocation" of the Nation's resources. *National Collegiate Athletic Assn. v. Board of Regents of Univ. of Okla.*, 468 U. S. 85, 104, n. 27 (1984). The plaintiffs before us brought this lawsuit alleging that the National Collegiate Athletic Association (NCAA) and certain of its member institutions violated this policy by agreeing to restrict the compensation colleges and universities may offer the student-athletes who play for their teams. After amassing a vast record and conducting an exhaustive trial, the district court issued a 50-page opinion that cut both ways. The court refused to disturb the NCAA's rules limiting under graduate athletic scholarships and other compensation related to athletic performance. At the same time, the court struck down NCAA rules limiting the education-related benefits schools may offer student-athletes—such as rules that prohibit schools from offering graduate or vocational school scholarships. Before us, the student-athletes do not challenge the district court's judgment. But the NCAA does.

I

A

[The Court set forth a detailed history of the NCAA, including discussion of its amateurism policy.]

In recent years, changes have continued. The NCAA has created the "Student Assistance Fund" and the "Academic Enhancement Fund" to "assist student-athletes in meeting financial needs," "improve their welfare or academic support," or "recognize academic achievement." These funds have supplied money to student-athletes for "postgraduate scholarships" and "school supplies," as well as "benefits that are not related to education," such as "loss of-value insurance premiums," "travel expenses," "clothing," and "magazine subscriptions." In 2018, the NCAA made more than $84 million available through the Student Activities Fund and more than $48 million available through the Academic Enhancement Fund. Assistance may be provided in cash or in kind, and there is no limit to the amount any particular student-athlete may receive. Since 2015, disbursements to individual students have sometimes been tens of thousands of dollars above the full cost of attendance.

The NCAA has also allowed payments "'incidental to athletics participation,'" including awards for "participation or achievement in athletics" (like "qualifying for a bowl game") and certain "payments from outside entities" (such as for "performance in the Olympics"). The NCAA permits its member schools to award up to (but no more than) two annual "Senior Scholar Awards" of $10,000 for students to attend graduate school after their athletic eligibility expires. Finally, the NCAA allows schools to fund travel for student-athletes' family members to attend "certain events."

At the center of this thicket of associations and rules sits a massive business. The NCAA's current broadcast contract for the March Madness basketball tournament is worth $1.1 billion annually. Its television deal for the FBS conference's College Football Playoff is worth approximately $470 million per year. Beyond these sums, the Division I conferences earn substantial revenue from regular-season games. For example, the Southeastern Conference (SEC) "made more than $409 million in revenues from television contracts alone in 2017, with its total conference revenues exceeding $650 million that year." All these amounts have "increased consistently over the years."

Those who run this enterprise profit in a different way than the student-athletes whose activities they oversee. The president of the NCAA earns nearly $4 million per year. Commissioners of the top conferences take home between $2 to $5 million. College athletic directors average more than $1 million annually. And annual salaries for top Division I college football coaches approach $11 million, with some of their assistants making more than $2.5 million.

B

The plaintiffs are current and former student-athletes in men's Division I FBS football and men's and women's Division I basketball. They filed a class action against the NCAA and 11 Division I conferences (for simplicity's sake, we refer to the defendants collectively as the NCAA). The student-athletes challenged the "current, interconnected set of NCAA rules that limit the compensation they may receive in exchange for their athletic services." Specifically, they alleged that the NCAA's rules violate §1 of the Sherman Act, which prohibits "contract[s], combination[s], or conspirac[ies] in restraint of trade or commerce." 15 U. S. C. §1.

After pretrial proceedings stretching years, the district court conducted a 10-day bench trial.

In applying the rule of reason, the district court began by observing that the NCAA enjoys "near complete dominance of, and exercise[s] monopsony power in, the relevant market"—which it defined as the market for "athletic services in men's and women's Division I basketball and FBS football, wherein each class member participates in his or her sport-specific market." The "most talented athletes are concentrated" in the "markets for Division I basketball and FBS football." There are no "viable substitutes," as the "NCAA's Division I essentially *is* the relevant market for elite college football and basketball." In short, the NCAA and its member schools have the "power to restrain student-athlete compensation in any way and at any time they wish, without any meaningful risk of diminishing their market dominance."

The district court then proceeded to find that the NCAA's compensation limits "produce significant anticompetitive effects in the relevant market." Though member schools compete fiercely in recruiting student-athletes, the NCAA uses its monopsony power to "cap artificially the compensation offered to recruits." In a market without the challenged restraints, the district court found, "competition among schools would increase in terms of the compensation they would offer to recruits, and student athlete compensation would be higher as a result." "Student-athletes would receive offers that would more closely match the value of their athletic services." And notably, the court observed, the NCAA "did not meaningfully dispute" any of this evidence. ("[T]here's no dispute that the—the no-pay-for-play rule imposes a significant restraint on a relevant antitrust market").

The district court next considered the NCAA's procompetitive justifications for its restraints. The NCAA's only remaining defense was that its rules preserve amateurism, which in turn widens consumer choice by providing a unique product—amateur college sports as distinct from professional sports. Admittedly, this asserted benefit accrues to consumers in the NCAA's seller-side consumer market rather than to student-athletes whose compensation the NCAA fixes in its buyer-side labor market. But, the NCAA argued, the district court needed to assess its restraints in the labor market in light of their procompetitive benefits in the consumer market—and the district court agreed to do so.

Turning to that task, the court observed that the NCAA's conception of amateurism has changed steadily over the years. The court noted that the NCAA "nowhere define[s] the nature of the amateurism they claim consumers insist upon." And, given all this, the court struggled to ascertain for itself "any coherent definition" of the term, noting the testimony of a former SEC commissioner that he's "'never been clear on... what is really meant by amateurism.'" Nor did the district court find much evidence to support the NCAA's contention that its compensation restrictions play a role in consumer demand. The plaintiffs presented economic and other evidence suggesting as well that further increases in student-athlete compensation would "not negatively affect consumer demand." At the same time, however, the district court did find that one particular aspect of the NCAA's compensation limits "may have some effect in preserving consumer demand." Specifically, the court found that rules aimed at ensuring "student-athletes do not receive unlimited payments unrelated to education" could play some role in product differentiation with professional sports and thus help sustain consumer demand for college athletics. The court next required the student-athletes to show that "substantially less restrictive alternative rules" existed that "would achieve the same procompetitive effect as the challenged set of rules." In light of these standards, the court found the student-athletes had met their burden in some respects but not others. The court rejected the student-athletes' challenge to NCAA rules that limit athletic scholarships to the full cost of attendance and that restrict compensation and benefits unrelated to education. These may be price-fixing agreements, but the court found them to be reasonable in light of the possibility that "professional-level cash payments... could blur the distinction between college sports and professional sports and thereby negatively affect consumer demand."

The court reached a different conclusion for caps on education-related benefits—such as rules that limit scholarships for graduate or vocational school, payments for academic tutoring, or paid posteligibility internships. On no account, the court found, could such education related benefits be "confused with a professional athlete's salary." If anything, they "emphasize that the recipients are students." Enjoining the NCAA's restrictions on these forms of compensation alone, the court concluded, would be substantially less restrictive than the NCAA's current rules and yet fully capable of preserving consumer demand for college sports.

The court then entered an injunction reflecting its findings and conclusions. Nothing in the order precluded the NCAA from continuing to fix compensation and benefits unrelated to education; limits on athletic scholarships, for example, remained untouched. The court enjoined the NCAA only from limiting education-related compensation or benefits that conferences and schools may provide to student athletes playing Division I football and basketball. The court's injunction further specified that the NCAA could continue to limit cash awards for academic achievement—but only so long as those limits are no lower than the cash awards allowed for athletic achievement (currently $5,980 annually). The court added that the NCAA and its members were free to propose a definition of compensation or benefits "'related to education.'" And the court explained that the NCAA was free to regulate how conferences and schools provide education-related compensation and benefits. The court further emphasized that its injunction applied only to the NCAA and multi-conference agreements—thus allowing individual conferences (and the schools that constitute them) to impose tighter restrictions if they wish. The district court's injunction issued in March 2019, and took effect in August 2020. Both sides appealed. In the end, the court of appeals affirmed in full, explaining its view that "the district court struck the right balance in crafting a remedy that both prevents anticompetitive harm to Student-Athletes while serving the procompetitive purpose of preserving the popularity of college sports."

C

Unsatisfied with this result, the NCAA asks us to reverse to the extent the lower courts sided with the student athletes.

II

A

. . . [W]e focus only on the objections the NCAA *does* raise. Principally, it suggests that the lower courts erred by subjecting its compensation restrictions to a rule of reason analysis. In the NCAA's view, the courts should have given its restrictions at most an "abbreviated deferential review," before approving them. The NCAA offers a few reasons why. Perhaps dominantly, it argues that it is a joint venture and that collaboration among its members is necessary if they are to offer consumers the benefit of intercollegiate athletic competition. [The Court rejected this argument, finding that the dispute is complex and requires more than a quick review.]

B

Even if background antitrust principles counsel in favor of the rule of reason, the NCAA replies that a particular precedent ties our hands. The NCAA directs our attention to *Board of Regents*, where this Court considered the league's rules restricting the ability of its member schools to televise football games. On the NCAA's reading, that decision expressly approved its limits on student-athlete compensation—and this approval forecloses any meaningful review of those limits today.

We see things differently. *Board of Regents* explained that the league's television rules amounted to "[h]orizontal price fixing and output limitation[s]" of the sort that are "ordinarily condemned" as "'illegal *per se*.'" The Court declined to declare the NCAA's restraints *per se* unlawful only because they arose in "an industry" in which some "horizontal restraints on competition are essential if the product is to be available at all." Our analysis today is fully consistent with all of this. Indeed, if any daylight exists it is only in the NCAA's favor. While *Board of Regents* did not condemn the NCAA's broadcasting restraints as *per se* unlawful, it invoked abbreviated antitrust review as a path to condemnation, not salvation.

Board of Regents may suggest that courts should take care when assessing the NCAA's restraints on student-athlete compensation, sensitive to their procompetitive possibilities. But these remarks do not suggest that courts must reflexively reject *all* challenges to the NCAA's compensation restrictions. Student-athlete compensation rules were not even at issue in *Board of Regents*. And the Court made clear it was only assuming the reasonableness of the NCAA's restrictions: "It is reasonable to *assume* that most of the regulatory controls of the NCAA are justifiable means of fostering competition among amateur athletic teams and are therefore procompetitive...." Accordingly, the Court simply did not have occasion to declare— nor did it declare—the NCAA's compensation restrictions procompetitive both in 1984 and forevermore.

Whether an antitrust violation exists necessarily depends on a careful analysis of market realities. If those market realities change, so may the legal analysis. When it comes to college sports, there can be little doubt that the market realities have changed significantly since 1984. Since then, the NCAA has dramatically increased the amounts and kinds of benefits schools may provide to student-athletes. For example, it has allowed the conferences flexibility to set new and higher limits on athletic scholar ships. It has increased the size of permissible benefits "incidental to athletics participation." And it has developed the Student Assistance Fund and the Academic Enhancement Fund, which in 2018 alone provided over $100 million to student-athletes. Nor is that all that has changed. In 1985, Division I football and basketball raised approximately $922 million and $41 million respectively. By 2016,

NCAA Division I schools raised more than $13.5 billion. From 1982 to 1984, CBS paid $16 million per year to televise the March Madness Division I men's basketball tournament. In 2016, those annual television rights brought in closer to $1.1 billion.

Given the sensitivity of antitrust analysis to market realities—and how much has changed in this market—we think it would be particularly unwise to treat an aside in *Board of Regents* as more than that. This Court may be "infallible only because we are final," but those sorts of stray comments are neither.

C

[The Court rejected the NCAA's argument that a rule of reason analysis was inappropriate because it is not a commercial enterprise.]

III

A

While the NCAA devotes most of its energy to resisting the rule of reason in its usual form, the league lodges some objections to the district court's application of it as well.

[The three steps in the process] do not represent a rote checklist, nor may they be employed as an inflexible substitute for careful analysis. As we have seen, what is required to assess whether a challenged restraint harms competition can vary depending on the circumstances. The whole point of the rule of reason is to furnish "an enquiry meant for the case, looking to the circumstances, details, and logic of a restraint" to ensure that it unduly harms competition before a court declares it unlawful.

As its first step, the district court required the student-athletes to show that "the challenged restraints produce significant anticompetitive effects in the relevant market." This was no slight burden. As we have seen, based on a voluminous record, the district court held that the student-athletes had shown the NCAA enjoys the power to set wages in the market for student-athletes' labor—and that the NCAA has exercised that power in ways that have produced significant anticompetitive effects. Perhaps even more notably, the NCAA "did not meaningfully dispute" this conclusion.

Unlike so many cases, then, the district court proceeded to the second step, asking whether the NCAA could muster a procompetitive rationale for its restraints. This is where the NCAA claims error first crept in. At the first step of its inquiry, the court asked whether the NCAA's entire package of compensation restrictions has substantial anticompetitive effects *collectively*. Yet, at the second step, the NCAA says the district court required it to show that each of its distinct rules limiting student-athlete compensation has procompetitive benefits *individually*. The NCAA says this mismatch had the result of effectively—and erroneously—requiring it to prove that each rule is the least restrictive means of achieving the procompetitive purpose of differentiating college sports and preserving demand for them.

We agree with the NCAA's premise that antitrust law does not require businesses to use anything like the least restrictive means of achieving legitimate business purposes. To the contrary, courts should not second-guess "degrees of reasonable necessity" so that "the lawfulness of conduct turn[s] upon judgments of degrees of efficiency." That would be a recipe for disaster, for a "skilled lawyer" will "have little difficulty imagining possible less restrictive alternatives to most joint arrangements." And judicial acceptance of such imaginings would risk interfering "with the legitimate objectives at issue" without "adding that much to competition." …

While we agree with the NCAA's legal premise, we cannot say the same for its factual one. Yes, at the first step of its inquiry, the district court held that the student-athletes had met their burden of showing the NCAA's restraints collectively bear an anticompetitive effect. And, given that, yes, at step two the NCAA had to show only that those same rules collectively yield a procompetitive benefit. The trouble for the NCAA, though, is not the level of generality. It is the fact that the district court found unpersuasive much of its proffered evidence. Recall that the court found the NCAA failed "to establish that the challenged compensation rules … have any direct connection to consumer demand." To be sure, there is a wrinkle here. While finding the NCAA had failed to establish that its rules collectively sustain consumer demand, the court did find that "some" of those rules "may" have procompetitive effects "to the extent" they prohibit compensation "unrelated to education, akin to salaries seen in professional sports leagues." The court then proceeded to what corresponds to the third step…, where it required the student-athletes "to show that there are substantially less restrictive alternative rules that would achieve the same procompetitive effect as the challenged set of rules." And there, of course, the district court held that the student-athletes partially succeeded—they were able to show that the NCAA could achieve the procompetitive benefits it had established with substantially less restrictive restraints on education-related benefits.

Even acknowledging this wrinkle, we see nothing about the district court's analysis that offends the legal principles the NCAA invokes. The court's judgment ultimately turned on the key question at the third step: whether the student athletes could prove that "substantially less restrictive alternative rules" existed to achieve the same procompetitive benefits the NCAA had proven at the second step. Of course, deficiencies in the NCAA's proof of procompetitive benefits at the second step influenced the analysis at the third. But that is only because, however framed and at whichever step, anticompetitive restraints of trade may wind up flunking the rule of reason to the extent the evidence shows that substantially less restrictive means exist to achieve any proven procompetitive benefits.

Simply put, the district court nowhere—expressly or effectively—required the NCAA to show that its rules constituted the *least* restrictive means of preserving consumer demand. Rather, it was only after finding the NCAA's restraints "'patently and inexplicably stricter than is necessary'" to achieve the procompetitive benefits the league had demonstrated that the district court proceeded to declare a violation of the Sherman Act. That demanding standard hardly presages a future filled with judicial micromanagement of legitimate business decisions.

B

In a related critique, the NCAA contends the district court "impermissibly redefined" its "product" by rejecting its views about what amateurism requires and replacing them with its preferred conception.

This argument, however, misapprehends the way a defendant's procompetitive business justification relates to the antitrust laws. Firms deserve substantial latitude to fashion agreements that serve legitimate business interests—agreements that may include efforts aimed at introducing a new product into the marketplace. But none of that means a party can relabel a restraint as a product feature and declare it "immune from §1 scrutiny." In this suit, as in any, the district court had to determine whether the defendants' agreements harmed competition and whether any procompetitive benefits associated with their restraints could be achieved by "substantially less restrictive alternative" means.

The NCAA's argument not only misapprehends the inquiry, it would require us to overturn the district court's factual findings. While the NCAA asks us to defer to its conception of amateurism, the district court found that the NCAA had not adopted any consistent definition. Instead, the court found, the NCAA's rules and restrictions on compensation have shifted markedly over time. The court found, too, that the NCAA adopted these restrictions without any reference to "considerations of consumer demand," and that some were "not necessary to preserve consumer demand." None of this is product redesign; it is a straightforward application of the rule of reason.

C

The NCAA claims, too, that the district court's injunction threatens to "micromanage" its business.

Once more, we broadly agree with the legal principles the NCAA invokes. [The court described the role of district courts regarding structure of analysis and remedies in the context of antitrust litigation.]

Once again, though, we think the district court honored these principles. The court enjoined only restraints on education-related benefits—such as those limiting scholarships for graduate school, payments for tutoring, and the like. The court did so, moreover, only after finding that relaxing these restrictions would not blur the distinction between college and professional sports and thus impair demand—and only after finding that this course represented a significantly (not marginally) less restrictive means of achieving the same procompetitive benefits as the NCAA's current rules.

Even with respect to education-related benefits, the district court extended the NCAA considerable leeway. As we have seen, the court provided that the NCAA could develop its own definition of benefits that relate to education and seek modification of the court's injunction to reflect that definition.

The court explained that the NCAA and its members could agree on rules regulating how conferences and schools go about providing these education-related benefits. The court said that the NCAA and its members could fix education-related cash awards, too—so long as those "limits are never lower than the limit" on awards for athletic performance. And the court emphasized that its injunction applies only to the NCAA and multi-conference agreements; individual conferences remain free to reimpose every single enjoined restraint tomorrow—or more restrictive ones still.

In the end, it turns out that the NCAA's complaints really boil down to three principal objections.

First, the NCAA worries about the district court's inclusion of paid post-eligibility internships among the education-related benefits it approved. The NCAA fears that schools will use internships as a way of circumventing limits on payments that student-athletes may receive for athletic performance. The NCAA even imagines that boosters might promise post-eligibility internships "at a sneaker company or auto dealership" with extravagant salaries as a "thinly disguised vehicle" for paying professional-level salaries. This argument rests on an overly broad reading of the injunction. The district court enjoined only restrictions on education-related compensation or benefits "that may be made available *from conferences or schools*." Accordingly, as the student-athletes concede, the injunction "does not stop the NCAA from continuing to prohibit compensation from" sneaker companies, auto dealerships, boosters, "or anyone else." The NCAA itself seems to understand this much. Following the district court's injunction, the organization adopted new regulations specifying that only "a conference or institution" may fund post-eligibility internships. (NCAA Bylaw 16.3.4(d)). Even when it comes to internships offered by conferences and schools, the district court left the NCAA considerable flexibility. The court refused to enjoin NCAA rules prohibiting its members from providing compensation or benefits unrelated to legitimate educational activities—thus leaving the league room to police phony internships. As we've observed, the district court also allowed the NCAA to propose (and enforce) rules defining what benefits do and do not relate to education. Accordingly, the NCAA may seek whatever limits on paid internships it thinks appropriate. And, again, the court stressed that individual conferences may restrict internships however they wish. All these features underscore the modesty of the current decree.

Second, the NCAA attacks the district court's ruling that it may fix the aggregate limit on awards schools may give for "academic or graduation" achievement no lower than its aggregate limit on parallel athletic awards (currently $5,980 per year). This, the NCAA asserts, "is the very definition of a professional salary." Meanwhile, the NCAA says, the district court's decree would allow a school to pay players thousands of dollars each year for minimal achievements like maintaining a passing GPA. The basis for this critique is unclear. The NCAA does not believe that the athletic awards it presently allows are tantamount to a professional salary. And this portion of the injunction sprang directly from the district court's finding that the cap on athletic participation awards "is an amount that has been shown not to decrease consumer demand." Indeed, there was no evidence before the district court suggesting that corresponding academic awards would impair consumer interest in any way. Again, too, the district court's injunction affords the NCAA leeway. It leaves the NCAA free to reduce its athletic awards. And it does not ordain what criteria schools must use for their academic and graduation awards. So, once more, if the NCAA believes certain criteria are needed to ensure that academic awards are legitimately related to education, it is presently free to propose such rules—and individual conferences may adopt even stricter ones.

Third, the NCAA contends that allowing schools to provide in-kind educational benefits will pose a problem. This relief focuses on allowing schools to offer scholarships for "graduate degrees" or "vocational school" and to pay for things like "computers" and "tutoring." But the NCAA fears schools might exploit this authority to give student-athletes "'luxury cars'" "to get to class" and "other unnecessary or inordinately valuable items" only "nominally" related to education.

Again, however, this over-reads the injunction in ways we have seen and need not belabor. Under the current decree, the NCAA is free to forbid in-kind benefits unrelated to a student's actual education; nothing stops it from enforcing a "no Lamborghini" rule. And, again, the district court invited the NCAA to specify and later enforce rules delineating which benefits it considers legitimately related to education. To the extent the NCAA believes meaningful ambiguity really exists about the scope of its authority— regarding internships, academic awards, in-kind benefits, or anything else—it has been free to seek clarification from the district court since the court issued its injunction three years ago. The NCAA remains free to do so today. To date, the NCAA has sought clarification only once—about the precise amount at which it can cap academic awards—and the question was quickly resolved. Before conjuring hypothetical concerns in this Court, we believe it best for the NCAA to present any practically important question it has in district court first.

The judgment is *Affirmed.*

JUSTICE KAVANAUGH, concurring.

. . . [T]his case involves only a narrow subset of the NCAA's compensation rules—namely, the rules restricting the *education-related* benefits that student athletes may receive, such as post-eligibility scholarships at graduate or vocational schools. The rest of the NCAA's compensation rules are not at issue here and therefore remain on the books. Those remaining compensation rules generally restrict student athletes from receiving compensation or benefits from their colleges for playing sports. And those rules have also historically restricted student athletes from receiving money from endorsement deals and the like. I add this concurring opinion to underscore that the NCAA's remaining compensation rules also raise serious questions under the antitrust laws. Three points warrant emphasis.

First, the Court does not address the legality of the NCAA's remaining compensation rules. As the Court says, "the student-athletes do not renew their across-the-board challenge to the NCAA's compensation restrictions. Accordingly, we do not pass on the rules that remain in place or the district court's judgment upholding them. Our review is confined to those restrictions now enjoined."

Second, although the Court does not weigh in on the ultimate legality of the NCAA's remaining compensation rules, the Court's decision establishes how any such rules should be analyzed going forward. After today's decision, the NCAA's remaining compensation rules should receive ordinary "rule of reason" scrutiny under the antitrust laws. The Court makes clear that the decades-old "stray comments" about college sports and amateurism made in *Board of Regents of Univ. of Okla.* 1984), were dicta and have no bearing on whether the NCAA's current compensation rules are lawful. And the Court stresses that the NCAA is not otherwise entitled to an exemption from the antitrust laws. As a result, absent legislation or a negotiated agreement between the NCAA and the student athletes, the NCAA's remaining compensation rules should be subject to ordinary rule of reason scrutiny.

Third, there are serious questions whether the NCAA's remaining compensation rules can pass muster under ordinary rule of reason scrutiny. Under the rule of reason, the NCAA must supply a legally valid procompetitive justification for its remaining compensation rules. As I see it, however, the NCAA may lack such a justification. The NCAA acknowledges that it controls the market for college athletes. The NCAA concedes that its compensation rules set the price of student athlete labor at a below-market rate. And the NCAA recognizes that student athletes currently have no meaningful ability to negotiate with the NCAA over the compensation rules.

The NCAA nonetheless asserts that its compensation rules are procompetitive because those rules help define the product of college sports. Specifically, the NCAA says that colleges may decline to pay student athletes because the defining feature of college sports, according to the NCAA, is that the student athletes are not paid.

In my view, that argument is circular and unpersuasive. The NCAA couches its arguments for not paying student athletes in innocuous labels. But the labels cannot disguise the reality: The NCAA's business model would be flatly illegal in almost any other industry in America.

The bottom line is that the NCAA and its member colleges are suppressing the pay of student athletes who collectively generate *billions* of dollars in revenues for colleges every year. Those enormous sums of money flow to seemingly everyone except the student athletes. College presidents, athletic directors, coaches, conference commissioners, and NCAA executives take in six- and seven-figure salaries. Colleges build lavish new facilities. But the student athletes who generate the revenues, many of whom are African American and from lower-income backgrounds, end up with little or nothing.

Everyone agrees that the NCAA can require student athletes to be enrolled students in good standing. But the NCAA's business model of using unpaid student athletes to generate billions of dollars in revenue for the colleges raises serious questions under the antitrust laws. In particular, it is highly questionable whether the NCAA and its member colleges can justify not paying student athletes a fair share of the revenues on the circular theory that the defining characteristic of college sports is that the colleges do not pay student athletes. And if that asserted justification is unavailing, it is not clear how the NCAA can legally defend its remaining compensation rules.

If it turns out that some or all of the NCAA's remaining compensation rules violate the antitrust laws, some difficult policy and practical questions would undoubtedly ensue. Among them: How would paying greater compensation to student athletes affect non-revenue-raising sports? Could student athletes in some sports but not others receive compensation? How would any compensation regime comply with Title IX? If paying student athletes requires something like a salary cap in some sports in order to preserve competitive balance, how would that cap be administered?

And given that there are now about 180,000 Division I student athletes, what is a financially sustainable way of fairly compensating some or all of those student athletes? Of course, those difficult questions could be resolved in ways other than litigation. Legislation would be one option. Or colleges and student athletes could potentially engage in collective bargaining (or seek some other negotiated agreement) to provide student athletes a fairer share of the revenues that they generate for their colleges, akin to how professional football and basketball players have negotiated for a share of league revenues. Regardless of how those issues ultimately would be resolved, however, the NCAA's current compensation regime raises serious questions under the antitrust laws. To be sure, the NCAA and its member colleges maintain important traditions that have become part of the fabric of America—game days in Tuscaloosa and South Bend; the packed gyms in Storrs and Durham; the women's and men's lacrosse championships on Memorial Day weekend; track and field meets in Eugene; the spring softball and baseball World Series in Oklahoma City and Omaha; the list goes on. But those traditions alone cannot justify the NCAA's decision to build a massive money-raising enterprise on the backs of student athletes who are not fairly compensated. Nowhere else in America can businesses get away with agreeing not to pay their workers a fair market rate on the theory that their product is defined by not paying their workers a fair market rate. And under ordinary principles of antitrust law, it is not evident why college sports should be any different. The NCAA is not above the law.

Notes and Comments

1. There is a case pending in U. S. District Court in California contending the NCAA's rules, prior to the adoption of the NIL Interim Policy by the D-I Board of Directors on July 1, 2021, prohibiting athletes from receiving money for their NIL violates the antitrust laws. The court denied the NCAA's motion to dismiss in June 2021. The case raises a variety of NIL issues, including a claim that the athletes are entitled to benefit from the television revenue generated by their athletic participation. *See House v. NCAA*, 545 F.Supp.3d 804, (N.D. Calif. 2021). Similar claims were made, pre-*Alston*, in *Marshall v. ESPN*, 111 F. Supp. 3d 815 (M.D. Tenn. 2015), where the court dismissed plaintiff student athletes' claims that the broadcast of their competition without compensation to them for their right to publicity was a violation of state law and the Sherman Act. The court found that under Tennessee law there was no violation of their right to publicity by virtue of broadcasting collegiate sports. And, since there are no rights established, there could be no antitrust injury either.

2. Following the decision of the Tenth Circuit in *Law*, the NCAA entered into a $54.5 million settlement with approximately 2,000 Division I assistant coaches who filed suit against the NCAA alleging the restricted earnings rule violated federal antitrust laws.

Two cases that never made it to trial raised claims over limitations placed on the number of grants-in-aid a school may award in football and the total value of the grant-in-aid. The case involving the limit on the number of grants-in-aid was filed by a group of walk-on players. The plaintiffs survived an initial motion to dismiss, but the court denied their motion to certify a class for the case. *In re NCAA 1-A Walk-On Football Player Litigation*, 2006 U.S. Dist. LEXIS 28824 (W.D. Wash. May 3, 2006). Ultimately, following the court's rejection of a motion to file an amended complaint, this case was dropped.

The other case, brought by former Division I football and basketball players, focuses on the limitations of the grant-in-aid itself. *White v. NCAA*, 2006 U.S. Dist. LEXIS 101366 (C.D. Cal. Sept. 20, 2006). This case was ultimately settled. The $10 million settlement covered athletes competing during a six-year window and provided each with approximately $2,500 in supplemental funds per year for up to three years. The funds were apparently intended to cover the gap between the value of a typical grant-in-aid and the true cost of attendance.

3. There have been several recent challenges to the NCAA's rules regarding transferring from one institution to another. The rules formerly required a student-athlete to sit out from competition for one year after transferring. *Deppe v. NCAA*,

893 F.3d 498 (7th Cir. 2018), is the most recent challenge, raising allegations that the rules violate Section 1 of the Sherman Act. The court rejected the arguments, holding there is a presumption that an NCAA rule is pro-competitive if it helps maintain amateurism or is directly tied to education. Here, since it is a rule tied to eligibility for competition, the court held it to be pro-competitive. *See also Pugh v. NCAA,* 2016 U.S. Dist. LEXIS 132122 (S.D. Ind. 2016). As discussed in Chapter 3, the NCAA has relaxed its transfer restrictions and athletes now may transfer one time without having to sit out of competition for a year.

4. A group of Southern Methodist University alumni, football players, and cheerleaders brought an antitrust action following the imposition of the death penalty by the NCAA in 1987. The gist of the claim was that the action of the NCAA violated the antitrust and civil rights laws by restricting the benefits that may be awarded athletes. The action was dismissed because several of the plaintiffs lacked standing and the others had failed to state a claim upon which relief could be granted. *McCormack v. NCAA*, 845 F.2d 1338 (5th Cir. 1988). Is there anything in *O'Bannon* or *Alston* that might cause a different result if this case were to arise today?

5. The majority in *Alston* affirmed the district court's ruling that the NCAA could continue to limit cash awards for academic achievement—but only so long as those limits are no lower than the cash awards allowed for athletic achievement (currently $5,980 annually). In other words, each NCAA member institution is free to decide if it wants to make annual cash payments up to $5,980 to its athletes. In late 2021 and early 2022, Power 5 schools began announcing plans to fund these cash payments. In the aftermath of the *Alston* decision, the sports media has focused most of its attention on Justice Kavanaugh's "blistering" criticism of the NCAA's business model. However, concurring opinions are not binding on lower courts, which, as a result of the majority opinion, will be called upon to determine the proper scope of antitrust law's application (*i.e.*, the rule of reason) to NCAA rules that restrict compensation. Although the majority opinion does not address NCAA rules that restrict student-athletes from licensing their name, image, and likeness for use in the advertisement and sale of products and services, many media commentators have speculated that the D-I Board of Directors adopted the NIL interim policy out of fear of the *Alston* ruling. What is the scope of the *Alston* ruling? In other words, how should lower courts apply the Supreme Court's holding to other "amateurism" issues such as the "no draft" rule (athletes lose eligibility if they enter or declare for a professional draft or do not withdraw from the draft by a certain date) or the "no agent" rule (athletes lose eligibility if they agree to be represented by an agent)? *See Banks v. NCAA*, 977 F.2d 1081 (7th Cir.), *cert. denied*, 508 U.S. 908 (1992) (holding that the NCAA's no draft rule and no agent rule do not violate the antitrust laws).

6. NCAA standards for non-wood baseball bats have also spawned antitrust litigation. One bat manufacturer brought an action against the NCAA and several other manufacturers, alleging manipulation of the market by changing standards.

The federal district court dismissed the matter, finding no antitrust injury had been proved. *Baum Research & Development Co. v. Hillerich & Bradsby*, 31 F. Supp. 2d 1016 (E.D. Mich. 1998). One of the defendants in that case, Easton Sports, itself filed suit against the NCAA alleging unlawful restraint of trade in its amendment of design and performance standards for baseball bats. *Easton Sports, Inc. v. NCAA*, Case No. 98–2351-KHV (D. Kan. 1998). The matter was settled in October 1999, following the NCAA's establishment of revised standards and criteria for approval of bats.

Capstone Problem

You are the associate athletic director at Coronado State University. One of your athletes has sued the NCAA and the court recently held a hearing on the plaintiff's motion for preliminary injunction. Preliminary injunctions are court orders entered prior to trial for the purpose of protecting the rights of the plaintiff from irreparable injury during the pendency of the action. The plaintiff must demonstrate a reasonable likelihood of success on the merits, and that without the injunction, s/he will suffer some immediate and irreparable harm.

Read the deposition testimony below. Having reviewed the case file and the testimony, be prepared to discuss the merits of your athlete's case against the NCAA at the next athletic department staff meeting.

In the United States District Court,

Southern District of Coronado

Archie Williams,

Plaintiff

v.

National Collegiate Athletic Association (NCAA),

Defendant

Statement of the Case

The plaintiff, Archie Williams, has filed a motion for injunctive relief against the defendant, National Collegiate Athletic Association (NCAA), seeking an order that would declare Mr. Williams immediately eligible to participate in intercollegiate varsity basketball for Coronado State University.

Depositions of Archie Williams and Mark Emmert, Executive Director of the NCAA, are included in this file.

The motion for injunctive relief is based on a theory that the NCAA violated the antitrust laws.

Archie Williams Deposition Testimony

My name is Archie Williams. I am 20 years old and a freshman at Coronado State University. I am here on a basketball scholarship. I attended high school at Hollywood High School in Hollywood, Coronado, and I was a very successful basketball player there, but I guess you could say I wasn't a very successful student. After I graduated from Hollywood High, I did not qualify academically for an athletic scholarship. That's when Dr. Bryant talked to me about going to Santa Monica Institute (SanMo) for a year before going to college, so I could better prepare myself academically and basketball-wise.

Dr. Bryant is an eye surgeon in Hollywood, he does that laser surgery. He is also a big basketball fan and he sponsors a bunch of AAU teams. I have played AAU summer ball on one of his teams ever since I was in seventh grade. Dr. B., as we all call him Dr. B., told me he thought I could get D-I [Division I] offers if I spent an additional year at a prep school like SanMo Institute. He said he would arrange for it and pay for it. I guess he always liked me a lot because he picked up on the fact that I really like him. He is this really short, pudgy white guy who just loves hoops. He's funny. Anyway, he told me he just wanted to help me and that I could repay him by doing my best and by promising to help someone else down the road—kind of like that bad movie, *Pay It Forward*. I'll never forget that, though. Dr. B also helped me find a job working a few hours at his doctor's office.

I had a great year at SanMo. I guess you could say I blossomed. It was a little bit like military school but it really helped me academically. And our basketball team was awesome. We had 8 guys on the team who received D-I scholarships. And I retook some classes and retook the SAT three times. SanMo provided us with tutors who helped a lot. I qualified for a scholarship and Coronado State offered me one and I took it. Dr. B didn't influence me about where to go to college. I had lots of offers and he just said to go to the place that "felt right." I chose Coronado State on my own.

When I arrived on campus at Coronado State, I found out that the athletic director wanted to see me right away. I went to see him the next day. His name is Bill Cox. He asked me all about AAU ball in the summer and SanMo and Dr. B., and I told him everything. About a month later, he told me that the NCAA had determined I was ineligible and that I had to agree to repay Dr. B. in order to get my eligibility back and that in any case I was suspended for one year and would lose one year of eligibility. I spoke to Dr. Bryant about all this, and he told me that he had spoken with a lawyer who thought I would have a good case. So that's when I contacted my lawyer, who's here today.

Dr. B. Told me he spent $30,000 for all the SanMo-related stuff. He also told me he didn't want me to pay him back. He said that he helped me because he knew I was a person who had a good heart who would help someone else down the road. I remember that he said to me, all I want in return from you is a promise that if you ever get a chance to help somebody else the way you were helped, that you would do it. I promised him I would.

I just want to play basketball at CSU and don't think it's fair that the NCAA is saying I am ineligible for a year and can only get my eligibility back if I agree to repay Dr. B. the $30,000. Right know, I don't have $30, let alone $30,000. And Dr. B. doesn't even want the money back.

Emmett Marks, NCAA President, Deposition Testimony

My name is Emmett Marks. I am the President of the National Collegiate Athletic Association. I have been working in athletics all my adult life, first as a football coach, then as an athletic director, and more recently, as an administrator with the NCAA. I have been President for the past 3 years.

Last April, we initiated an investigation into so-called prep schools like Santa Monica Institute. We had been receiving reports that some of these schools were using basketball players who were being provided financial support from outsiders. This would mean that these youngsters are running afoul of our amateurism rules if they subsequently attend and play basketball at one of our member schools. We viewed this problem as very serious because it undermines our guiding principle that our student-athletes are amateurs. It also creates a condition where unsavory types could unduly influence youngsters to attend one school or another by providing illegal financial support. In other words, these so-called sponsors could steer kids to a particular program. We are simply trying to protect amateurism and avoid undue influence by modern-day flesh peddlers.

In the course of our investigation, we asked all athletic directors to determine if any of their incoming scholarship athletes had attended Santa Monica Institute or about 10 other preparatory schools we had identified as problem schools. We learned about Archie Williams' situation as a result of a report we received from Mr. Cox, the athletic director at Coronado State.

As far as we are concerned, the facts are not in dispute and the application of our rules makes clear that Archie Williams is ineligible. We tried to fashion a humane response to the problem. We requested that Coronado State University declare Mr. Williams ineligible for this year, with the understanding that Mr. Williams would have his eligibility restored if he would agree to repay the sponsor $30,000. That was the amount that we found to be illegal. We also advised Coronado State that it would be permissible to keep Mr. Williams on scholarship and that he could practice but not travel with the team. Finally, we advised Coronado State that Mr. Williams would lose one year of eligibility and would thus have three years of competition available if he were eventually reinstated. Coronado State agreed with what we advised, and notified Mr. Williams accordingly. We are acting in the best interest of all our member schools, who subscribe to the amateurism principle and want very much to keep unsavory elements away from our young student athletes.

Archie Williams v. NCAA

(Stipulated Chronology)

May 20 (18 Months Ago)	Williams graduates from Hollywood High School
September 6	Williams enrolls in Santa Monica Institute
April 15	Williams signs letter of intent to attend CSU
June 10	Williams graduates from SanMo Institute
August 25–26	Williams arrives at CSU and meets with A.D. Cox
September 3	Williams learns of NCAA decision
September 8	Williams files this action against NCAA
September 17	Depositions taken
September 25 (Today)	Hearing on Motion for Injunctive Relief

Five

Sex-Based Discrimination in Amateur Athletics

Learning Outcomes

- Gain an understanding of the meaning of "gender equity" and how such equity is measured and attained.
- Consider the various contexts in which gender equity issues have arisen in athletics.
- Know how the Equal Protection Clause and Title IX apply to gender equity issues in high school and intercollegiate athletics.
- Learn how Title IX is regulated and enforced.
- Understand the Title IX regulations addressing sexual misconduct on campus.
- Consider the application of Title IX to transgender athlete participation.
- Learn how anti-discrimination laws apply to gender equity issues in an employment context involving coaches.

Key Terms

- Equal protection clause
- Protected class
- Intermediate scrutiny
- Title IX
- Equal treatment
- "Laundry list"
- Effective accommodation
- Three-part test
- Title VII
- Equal Pay Act

A. Introduction

This chapter examines the important and often controversial questions: What is the meaning of "gender equity" in amateur athletics and how is such equity to be measured and attained? Does gender equity consist of treating both sexes in exactly the same manner when it comes to participation in athletes?

In the sports context, difficult questions arise as one endeavors to create a sports structure that does not unfairly discriminate on the basis of sex. Must a female be afforded an opportunity to try out for the "men's team"? Does it matter that a "women's team" already exists in that sport? Does it matter that although no "women's team" exists, the sport is a violent, contact sport? Must a male be afforded an opportunity to try out for the "women's team" in a sport for which there is no "men's team"? What about transgender athletes and the right to participate? Is simple "open participation" in sport nonetheless discriminatory in impact?

Prior to 1970, few lawsuits challenged sexual discrimination in athletics. Social conscience and the women's movement changed matters dramatically. Beginning in the 1970s, suits by women alleging sexual discrimination violative of the Fourteenth Amendment began to emerge. The passage of Title IX of the Educational Amendments Act of 1972 provided a statutory remedy to complement the constitutional theories. In relevant part, Title IX provides:

> No person in the United States shall, on the basis of sex, be excluded from participation in, be denied the benefits of, or be subjected to discrimination under any education program or activity receiving federal financial assistance.

20 U.S.C. § 1681(a). Title IX has resulted in substantial increases in programs for women, but also litigation resulting from the elimination of certain men's programs.

The following cases and materials examine gender equity issues in sports both from a constitutional perspective as well as within the meaning and application of Title IX. The materials also consider other remedies that might be available in the gender equity context. Finally, the chapter considers requirements stemming from expansion of the application of Title IX to cases involving sexual harassment and sexual abuse and violence.

Sidebar: Equity on the Playing Field

Problem 1

Shirley Wynn is a 16-year-old high school junior. She is an extremely talented tennis player, enjoying a very high national junior ranking. Her high school has a girls' tennis team on which she played last year, but she wants to play on the boys' team this year. Her argument is that she will have better competition if she plays against boys and thus will better prepare herself for collegiate and professional competition that appears likely to be in her future. The state high school athletic association prohibits girls from competing on boys' teams and vice versa. Shirley wants to take whatever action may be necessary to be allowed to play against the male competition. What advice would you give her and what action would you suggest she take?

Problem 2

Liz Zimmer, an athletically talented 16-year-old high school sophomore, wants to try out for her high school football team. The Washahoma State High School Athletic Association regulations prohibit female participation on boys' teams in all contact sports. The regulations specify that football, basketball, hockey, and wrestling are contact sports. By all accounts, Liz is physically capable of playing high school football. She is bigger and stronger, and a better athlete, than many of the boys on the team. The coach, citing the regulation, has refused to allow her to try out.

Liz has petitioned the State High School Athletic Association for a waiver to allow her to participate. You are counsel to the association. How would you advise your client?

B. Constitutional Issues

Hoover v. Meiklejohn

430 F. Supp. 164 (D. Colo. 1977)

MATSCH, JUDGE.

[Plaintiff filed a class action suit alleging that the Colorado High School Activities Association's rule limiting participation in interscholastic soccer competition to male students violated the Constitution's Equal Protection Clause.]

The plaintiff is 16 years old and a student in the eleventh grade at Golden High School, one of twelve senior high schools operated by Jefferson County School District R-1.

The plaintiff is 5'4" tall, weighs 120 pounds, and is in excellent physical condition. In the fall of 1976, Golden High School had a varsity soccer team which engaged in interscholastic competition with other public high schools in Colorado. The teacher-coach, Tracy Fifer, permitted participation by Donna Hoover as the only female on the team. She engaged in the conditioning and skills drills at the team's practice sessions and she played in junior varsity games, which were unofficial contests played between the same schools whose varsity teams met in sanctioned competition. Although she was stunned on one occasion as a result of a collision with a much larger player, she did not suffer any disabling injury in the games or in any practice sessions.

On or about September 28, 1976, the principal of Golden High School directed that the plaintiff be removed from the soccer team because her participation was in violation of Rule XXI, § 3 of the Colorado High School Activities Association....

The Association sanctions interscholastic competition in many sports, including soccer.

While the Association has no sex classification for cross-country and baseball, the sport of soccer is limited by Rule XXI, § 3, as follows:

> Participation in this activity shall be limited to members of the male sex.
>
> NOTE: Because inordinate injury risk jeopardizes the health and safety of the female athlete, participation in this activity is limited to members of the male sex.

Soccer is a relatively new sport in Colorado high schools. It was first sanctioned five years ago and the state championship program was developed only two years ago. The decision to limit soccer to males resulted from consultation with a committee of the Colorado Medical Society designated as "Medical Aspects of Sports Committee." That group consists of seven physicians, from different geographical areas, whose practice involves pediatrics and orthopedics. Members of that committee testified at the trial of this case that the recommendation to classify soccer as a contact sport and to prohibit mixed sex play was the result of a perception of physiological differences which would subject the female players to an inordinate risk of injury.

Primarily, the committee was concerned with risks attendant upon collisions in the course of play. While the rules of soccer prohibit body contact (except for a brush-type shoulder block when moving toward the ball), there are frequent instances when players collide in their endeavors to "head" the ball. In those instances, contact is generally in the upper body area.

There is agreement that after puberty the female body has a higher ratio of adipose tissue to lean body weight as compared with the male, and females have less bone density than males. It is also true that, when matured, the male skeletal construct provides a natural advantage over females in the mechanics of running. Accordingly, applying the formula of force equals mass times acceleration, a collision between a male and a female of equal weights, running at full speed, would tend to be to the disadvantage of the female. It is also true that while males as a class tend to have an advantage in strength and speed over females as a class, the range of differences among individuals in both sexes is greater than the average differences between the sexes. The association has not established any eligibility criteria for participation in interscholastic soccer, excepting for sex. Accordingly, any male of any size and weight has the opportunity to be on an interscholastic team and no female is allowed to play, regardless of her size, weight, condition or skill.

Interscholastic athletic competition is an integral part of the educational program of public high schools in Colorado. The prevalent view is set forth in Section 1 of the association's by-laws:

> The program of the interscholastic athletics in high schools shall be so organized and administered as to contribute to the health, worthy use of leisure time, citizenship and character objectives of secondary education.

The defendants on the board of education and the professional educators in control of the activities association have concluded that the game of soccer is among those which serve an educational purpose and governmental funds have been provided for it. It is a matter of common knowledge that athletics are a recognized aspect of the educational program offered at American colleges and universities and that many of them offer scholarships to males and females for their agreement to participate in intercollegiate sports competition. Such offers result from organized recruiting programs directed toward those who have demonstrated their abilities on high school teams. Accordingly, the chance to play in athletic games may have an importance to the individual far greater than the obvious momentary pleasure of the game.

This case has been presented and argued by both counsel within the framework of the two-tiered analysis familiar to equal protection decisions. If a "fundamental" right or interest is denied or impaired or if a classification is made on a "suspect" basis, the court must look with "strict scrutiny" to determine whether there is justification by a "compelling" state interest. Where there is neither a "fundamental" interest nor a "suspect" classification, a difference in the effects of state action is constitutionally permitted if it is "rationally related" to a "legitimate" state objective.

The defendants have argued and the plaintiff concedes that the Supreme Court has excluded education from "fundamental" rights by reserving that category to those which are explicitly or implicitly recognized in the language of the Constitution....

The Supreme Court has exhibited an obvious reluctance to label sex as a "suspect" classification because the consequences of the application of the many "invidious" discrimination precedents to all separations by sex could lead to some absurd results. For example, would the Constitution preclude separate public toilets?

In a very recent Supreme Court opinion, *Craig v. Boren*, 429 U.S. 190 (1976), Mr. Justice Brennan, writing for the Court, attempted to define a new standard of review, saying:

> To withstand constitutional challenge, previous cases establish that classifications by gender must serve important governmental objectives and must be substantially related to achievement of those objectives....

That language may be considered a "middle-tier approach" requiring something between "legitimate" and "compelling," viz, "important," and something more than a "rational" relationship but less perhaps than "strict scrutiny," viz, "substantially" related.

1. The importance of the opportunity being unequally burdened or denied.

The opportunity not merely burdened but completely denied to the plaintiff and the class she represents is the chance to compete in soccer as a part of a high school educational experience. Whether such games should be made available at public expense is not an issue. The content of an educational program is completely within the majoritarian control through the representatives on the school board. But, whether it is algebra or athletics, that which is provided must be open to all. The Court in *Brown* expressed a constitutional concern for equality in educational opportunity and this controversy is squarely within that area of concern. Accordingly, without reference to any label that would place this opportunity on one of two or more "tiers," it must be given a great importance to Donna Hoover and every other individual within her class. Surely it is of greater significance than the buying of beer, considered in *Craig*, supra.

2. The strength of the state interest served in denying it.

The failure to establish any physical criteria to protect small or weak males from the injurious effects of competition with larger or stronger males destroys the credibility of the reasoning urged in support of the sex classification.

3. The character of the group whose opportunities are denied.

Women and girls constitute a majority of the people in this country. To be effective citizens, they must be permitted full participation in the educational programs designed for that purpose. To deny females equal access to athletics supported by public funds is to permit manipulation of governmental power for a masculine advantage.

Any notion that young women are so inherently weak, delicate or physically inadequate that the state must protect them from the folly of participation in vigorous athletics is a cultural anachronism unrelated to reality. The Constitution does not permit the use of governmental power to control or limit cultural changes or to prescribe masculine and feminine roles.

It is an inescapable conclusion that the complete denial of any opportunity to play interscholastic soccer is a violation of the plaintiffs right to equal protection of the law under the Fourteenth Amendment. This same conclusion would be required under even the minimal "rational relationship" standard of review applied to classifications which are not suspect and do not involve fundamental rights. The governmental purpose in fielding a soccer team is to enhance the secondary school educational experience. The exclusion of girls to protect them from injury cannot be considered to be in furtherance of that education objective.

While Rule XXI is invalid under either method of analysis, there is a difference between them which is revealed in considering both the remedy required here and the possible ramifications of this case for future controversies.

The parties here agree that the effective equalization of athletic opportunities for members of both sexes would be better served by comparable teams for members of each sex and that under current circumstances mixed-sex teams would probably be dominated by males. Accordingly, it is conceded that "separate but equal" teams would satisfy the equality of opportunity required by the Constitution.

Given the lack of athletic opportunity for females in past years, the encouragement of female involvement in sports is a legitimate objective and separation of teams may promote that purpose.... It may also justify the sanction of some sports only for females, of which volleyball may be an example.

Separate soccer teams for males and females would meet the constitutional requirement of equal opportunity if the teams were given substantially equal support and if they had substantially comparable programs. There may be differences depending upon the effects of such neutral factors as the level of student interest and geographic locations. Accordingly, the standard should be one of comparability, not absolute equality.

In arriving at the conclusion that the defendants are in violation of the Fourteenth Amendment by providing interscholastic soccer only for male high school students, I am aware that there will be many concerned about the ramifications of this ruling. Football, ice hockey and wrestling are also made available only for males in Colorado, and volleyball is provided only for females. While there is now no reason to rule beyond the specific controversy presented by the evidence, it would seem appropriate to make some general observations about constitutional concerns in athletic programs supported by public funds.

The applicability of so fundamental a constitutional principle as equal educational opportunity should not depend upon anything so mutable as customs, usages, protective equipment and rules of play. The courts do not have competence to determine what games are appropriate for the schools or which, if any, teams should be separated by sex. What the courts can and must do is to insure that those who do make those decisions act with an awareness of what the Constitution does and does not require of them. Accordingly, it must be made clear that there is no constitutional requirement for the schools to provide any athletic program, as it is clear that there is no constitutional requirement to provide any public education. What is required is that whatever opportunity is made available be open to all on equal terms.

It must also be made clear that the mandate of equality of opportunity does not dictate a disregard of differences in talents and abilities among individuals. There is no right to a position on an athletic team. There is a right to compete for it on equal terms.

Adherence to the traditional equal protection analysis in these school sports cases can cause an unwelcome intrusion into issues which should be beyond the court's concern. It may here be observed that the flexibility which is suggested by common sense would be precluded by strict adherence to the two-tiered analysis if sex classifications are considered "suspect" or if some level of justification higher than "rational relationship" is required. In *Cape v. Tennessee Secondary School Athletic Association*, 424 F. Supp. 792 (E.D. Tenn. 1976), the holding was that the United States Constitution was violated because Tennessee high school girls could not play the same game of full court basketball permitted by the rules governing boys' teams. Is the full court dribble a matter of constitutional importance? In *Brenden v. Independent School District*, 477 F.2d 1292 (8th Cir. 1973), the court emphasized that "non-contact" sports were involved. Should equality of opportunity be measured according to style of play? Must there be "measure for measure" in each sport? Will girls be hurt by playing soccer with boys? The courtroom is not the place and the adversary process is not the method by which these questions should be answered. Fundamental principles of participatory democracy must not be trivialized by elevating every public controversy to a constitutional level.

This case has been kept within the confines of a particular sport because that is the way the parties chose to present it. The importance of an opportunity for both sexes to participate in a total athletic program presenting a variety of choices for those with differing interests and abilities is far different from the importance of an opportunity for a boy to play volleyball or a girl to play football. The strength of the state interest and the character of the groups affected will also differ according to the scope of the total program.

The plaintiff has asked for an order requiring the school board to permit her to play on the Golden High School soccer team and to enjoin the other defendants from imposing any penalty or other sanction upon that high school or any competing team because of that permission. Because there is no obligation to provide any soccer program and because equal opportunity can be given to the plaintiff class either by mixed-sex or comparable separate-sex teams, the defendants have a choice of actions to be taken. They may decide to discontinue soccer as an interscholastic athletic activity; they may decide to field separate teams for males and females, with substantial equality in funding, coaching, officiating and opportunity to play; or they may decide to permit both sexes to compete on the same team. Any of these actions would satisfy the equal protection requirements of the Constitution. What the defendants may not do is to continue to make interscholastic soccer available only to male students.

Notes and Comments

1. The United States Supreme Court has analyzed the standards for determining an equal protection violation where the questioned classification was gender-based. In *United States v. Virginia*, 518 U.S. 515 (1996), the Court found that the establishment of a single-sex public military school in Virginia denied equal protection of the laws to women. The Court reiterated that gender classifications are subject to height-

ened scrutiny and that parties seeking to defend gender-based governmental action must demonstrate an "exceedingly persuasive justification." Any challenged classification must serve an important governmental objective and the means developed must be substantially related to achieving that objective. Under this intermediate scrutiny standard, justifications must be real, not concocted for purposes of responding to litigation.

2. The gender equity issue has arisen in a wide variety of contexts. The cases have involved situations in which there was a men's team and no women's team, a women's team and no men's team, separate but allegedly unequal teams for men and women, teams in the same sport but playing under different rules, and teams in the same sport but playing in different seasons. *See Libby v. Illinois High School Association*, 921 F.2d 96 (7th Cir. 1990); *Habetz by Habetz v. Louisiana High School Athletic Association*, 915 F.2d 164 (5th Cir. 1990).

3. Is there a valid claim of sex discrimination when a state high school athletic association authorizes separate seasons of play for high school athletic teams separated or substantially separated according to gender? For example, what is the result if boys play tennis in the spring and girls play tennis in the fall? *See Striebel v. Minnesota State High School League*, 321 N.W.2d 400 (Minn. 1982) (holding that league's policy of separate seasons for boys' and girls' athletic teams was constitutional).

4. What is the appropriate approach for a court to take when a boy wants to play on a girls' team in a noncontact sport in which there is no boys' team? *See Clark v. Arizona Interscholastic Association*, 695 F.2d 1126 (9th Cir. 1982) (a girls-only volleyball team promotes a strong government interest in supporting equal opportunities for females in athletics and redressing past inequities); and *Gomes v. Rhode Island Interscholastic League*, 469 F. Supp. 659 (D.R.I. 1979) (boy allowed to play on girls' volleyball team where previously no opportunity for boys to play the sport).

5. To what extent do you think that the decisions of the courts are motivated by the type of relief sought? Female athletes as plaintiffs could request (1) the opportunity to participate on an exclusively male team; (2) the creation of an exclusively female team; or (3) the opportunity to participate on an exclusively male team despite the existence of a female team.

Would Donna Hoover have been afforded an opportunity to play on the boys' soccer team if the school had fielded a girls' team? Male plaintiffs could request similar relief. Would a male plaintiff be successful if he sought the creation of, for example, a boys' volleyball team where there was only a girls' team?

It is also important to remember that the defendant, a school district or a university, can shape the ultimate relief given to the plaintiff. In *Hoover*, the court points out that the school district has the option to either allow the female plaintiff to participate on the boys' team, create an exclusively girls' team, or not offer the particular sport at all. However, as we will see in the second part of this chapter, the school may not have all of these options if Title IX issues are raised by a plaintiff.

6. The opportunity to participate on a particular athletic team has not been the only relief sought by female athletes. Consider the claim, as noted in *Hoover*, that rule variations in the same sport violate the Equal Protection Clause.

In *Cape v. Tennessee Secondary Sch. Athletic Association*, 563 F.2d 793 (6th Cir. 1977), the court reversed the trial court's finding that the difference between rules for high school girls' and boys' basketball did violate equal protection. The rules for the girls' teams mandated six players per team, and three of the six players (forwards) were required to stay on the offensive end of the court and the other three players (guards) stayed on the defensive end. Only forwards were allowed to shoot. Since her coach made her play guard, the plaintiff claimed that she was at a disadvantage in obtaining a college scholarship in basketball because she could not develop her skills (e.g., shooting) to play the full court game. The court reasoned that since no challenge was made to the separation of boys and girls in basketball teams, there must be, for purposes of this case, some difference in physical abilities between boys and girls. Therefore, according to the court, there was no reason why the rules could not "be tailored to accommodate [the physical differences]."

Compare Cape and *Jones with Dodson v. Arkansas Activities Association*, 468 F. Supp. 394, 395 (E.D. Ark. 1979). In *Dodson*, the court noted the decisions in *Cape* and *Jones*, but declined to follow them. In doing so, the court said: "To the extent that the reasoning of those cases is contrary to this opinion, the Court respectfully disagrees. They are not binding authority here, and their reasoning seems, with deference, unpersuasive." *Dodson*, 468 F. Supp. at 398–99.

C. Title IX

1. History of Title IX

Title IX is a federal civil rights law that is part of the Education Act Amendments of 1972. The Act prohibits sex-based discrimination in public or private education programs or activities operated by recipients of federal funds. Title IX applies to all aspects of an educational institution's activities, including athletics. The Act has received notable attention, particularly in intercollegiate and interscholastic athletics. It provides a cause of action separate and apart from constitutional challenges.

As noted above, Title IX of the Education Amendments of 1972 to the Civil Rights Act of 1964 provides that:

> No person in the United States shall, on the basis of sex, be excluded from participation in, be denied the benefits of, or be subjected to discrimination under any education program or activity receiving federal financial assistance.

20 U.S.C. §1681(a). The U.S. Department of Health, Education, and Welfare (HEW), initially charged with implementing the Act, issued regulations nearly three

years following passage of the law, 45 C.F.R. pt. 86 (1975). With respect to athletics, the regulations defined equal opportunity as consisting of two parts: (1) *equal accommodation*, which measures whether the institution's or school district's athletics participation opportunities reflect the interests and abilities of both sexes, and (2) *equal treatment*, which measures whether male and female students have similar access to a "laundry list" of various athletic program components and resources. The regulations required schools to be in compliance by July 1978. Confusion abounded as to the appropriate interpretation of the regulations and coverage of the Act to intercollegiate athletics.

In response, HEW issued its *1979 Policy Interpretation: Title IX and Intercollegiate Athletics* to clarify the meaning of and test for compliance with Title IX, particularly in intercollegiate athletics. This test for 'equal opportunity' provided for a comparison of:

> Availability, quality and kinds of benefits, opportunities and treatment of the members of both sexes. Institutions will be in compliance if the compared program components are equivalent, that is, equal or equal in effect. Under this standard, identical benefits, opportunities or treatment are not required, provided the overall effect of any differences is negligible.

44 Fed. Reg. 71,413–15 (1979). Consider how the court in *Cohen v. Brown, infra,* analyzes application of the 1979 Policy Interpretation.

A brief history of key judicial decisions interpreting Title IX helps illuminate the factors and policies of gender equity in the sports context. In *Cannon v. University of Chicago*, 441 U.S. 677 (1979), the Supreme Court held that even though no express provision in the Act authorizes private individuals to bring actions, there is an implied right of action. Yet, five years later, *Grove City College v. Bell*, 465 U.S. 555 (1984), held that Title IX was "program-specific" and thus applied only to particular programs within a university or public school. Under this interpretation, Title IX applied only to athletic programs that received federal funding. Since most athletic programs do not receive direct federal funding, the net result of *Grove City* was that Title IX became neglected and ineffective. Several years later, Congress legislatively overruled *Grove City* when it passed the Civil Rights Restoration Act of 1987 (20 U.S.C. §§1687–88). In this legislation, Congress extended the full reach of Title IX to any program of any institution or public school that accepts federal funding.

The next significant development in Title IX history came in the decision in *Franklin v. Gwinnett County Public Schools*, 503 U.S. 60 (1992) which ruled that monetary damages are available in Title IX actions, at least for those involving intentional violations of the Act.

As a result of the above cases and the 1987 legislation, nearly all colleges, universities, community colleges, and public elementary and secondary school districts are covered by the Act. Federal funding of any sort received by the institution or school district, even if unrelated to athletics, will cause the athletic program to come under the coverage of the Act. Thus, private colleges are subject to Title IX because they directly receive federal financial assistance when they enroll students who receive federal loan money earmarked for educational expenses. By contrast, the Supreme Court has ruled that the NCAA is not subject to Title IX. In *NCAA v. Smith*, 525 U.S. 459 (1999), the Court held that the receipt of dues by the association from its members who receive federal funds does not make the NCAA subject to Title IX because, unlike student federal loans, member dues are not paid to the NCAA with federal funds earmarked for that purpose. The Court, however, left open two questions regarding the impact of the Act on the NCAA. First, it refused to rule on whether the NCAA directly or indirectly receives federal funding through the National Youth Sports Program (NYSP) the association administers. Second, the Court declined an opportunity to rule on the effect of a federal funds recipient ceding controlling authority over a federally funded program. Specifically, the athlete had argued that the action of member institutions, virtually all of which are recipients of federal funds, in turning over governing authority to the NCAA makes the association subject to the act. On remand, the district court ruled against the plaintiff on both issues. The Third Circuit, however, found that the allegations regarding the relationship between the NYSP and the NCAA, coupled with the receipt of federal funds by the NYSP, if proven, would subject the NCAA to the Act. *Smith v. NCAA*, 266 F.3d 152 (3d Cir. 2001).

As of 1979, the U.S. Department of Education (formerly HEW) and its Office of Civil Rights (OCR) is responsible for Title IX enforcement. The original regulations and 1979 Policy Interpretation are still the law of the land. 34 C.F.R. pt. 106. The 1979 Policy Interpretation and 1996 and 1998 clarifications of the policy interpretation have been critical to the enforcement of the Act. The 1998 Policy Interpretation called for the investigators to evaluate the following areas: (1) athletic financial assistance; (2) equivalency in other athletic benefits and opportunities ("equal treatment"); and (3) effective accommodation of student interests and abilities ("equal accommodation"). The interpretation also directs investigators to evaluate the following factors (the "laundry list") within athletic programs when attempting to determine compliance with the equal treatment part of Title IX:

1. Whether the selection of sports and levels of competition effectively accommodate the interests and abilities of members of both sexes;
2. The provision of equipment and supplies;
3. Scheduling of games and practice time;
4. Travel and per diem allowance;
5. Opportunity to receive coaching and academic tutoring;
6. Assignment and compensation of coaches and tutors;
7. Provision of locker rooms, practice, and competitive facilities;

8. Provision of medical and training facilities and services;
9. Provision of housing and dining facilities and services; and
10. Publicity.

34 C.F.R. § 106.41(c) (1998).

In 2020, the Department of Education, for the first time, promulgated regulations pursuant to Title IX setting forth requirements for processing matters involving sexual harassment or sexual assault. These regulations, the issues surrounding the promulgation, and several highly publicized cases of sexual assault in collegiate athletic environments are detailed below in Section 3.

2. Effective Accommodation

As noted in the cases that follow, several courts have focused their analyses on the so-called three-part test set out in the policy interpretation to determine, at least threshold, compliance. This test provides, in essence, three ways in which a school may be found to be in compliance. The court will look to one of these benchmarks: (1) whether intercollegiate level participation opportunities for male and female students are provided in numbers substantially proportionate to their respective enrollments; (2) where the members of one sex have been and are underrepresented among intercollegiate athletes, whether the institution can show a history and continuing practice of program expansion that is demonstrably responsive to the developing interest and abilities of the members of that sex; or (3) where the members of one sex are underrepresented among intercollegiate athletes and the institution cannot show a continuing practice of program expansion such as cited above, whether it can be demonstrated that the interests and abilities of the members of that sex have been fully and effectively accommodated by the present program.

Cohen v. Brown University

101 F.3d 155 (1st Cir. 1996)

BOWNES, SENIOR CIRCUIT JUDGE.

This is a class action lawsuit charging Brown University, its president, and its athletics director (collectively "Brown") with discrimination against women in the operation of its intercollegiate athletics program, in violation of Title IX of the Education Amendments of 1972, 20 U.S.C. §§ 1681–1688 ("Title IX"), and its implementing regulations, 34 C.F.R. §§ 106.1–106.71. The plaintiff class comprises all present, future, and potential Brown University women students who participate, seek to participate, and/or are deterred from participating in intercollegiate athletics funded by Brown.

This suit was initiated in response to the demotion in May 1991 of Brown's women's gymnastics and volleyball teams from university-funded varsity status to donor-funded varsity status. Contemporaneously, Brown demoted two men's teams, water polo and golf, from university-funded to donor-funded varsity status. As a consequence of these demotions, all four teams lost, not only their university funding, but most of the support and privileges that accompany university-funded varsity status at Brown.

[The court described the various stages of the litigation which included two different rulings by the district court and one prior ruling by the First Circuit. This matter is an appeal from a judgment entered following a lengthy bench trial in which Brown was found to have violated Title IX.]

I.

Brown operates a two-tiered intercollegiate athletics program with respect to funding: although Brown provides the financial resources required to maintain its university-funded varsity teams, donor-funded varsity athletes must themselves raise the funds necessary to support their teams through private donations. The district court noted that the four demoted teams were eligible for NCAA competition, provided that they were able to raise the funds necessary to maintain a sufficient level of competitiveness, and provided that they continued to comply with NCAA requirements. The court found, however, that it is difficult for donor-funded varsity athletes to maintain a level of competitiveness commensurate with their abilities and that these athletes operate at a competitive disadvantage in comparison to university-funded varsity athletes. For example, the district court found that some schools are reluctant to include donor-funded teams in their varsity schedules and that donor-funded teams are unable to obtain varsity-level coaching, recruits, and funds for travel, equipment, and post-season competition.

Brown's decision to demote the women's volleyball and gymnastics teams and the men's water polo and golf teams from university-funded varsity status was apparently made in response to a university-wide cost-cutting directive. The district court found that Brown saved $62,028 by demoting the women's teams and $15,795 by demoting the men's teams, but that the demotions "did not appreciably affect the athletic participation gender ratio."

Plaintiffs alleged that, at the time of the demotions, the men students at Brown already enjoyed the benefits of a disproportionately large share of both the university resources allocated to athletics and the intercollegiate participation opportunities afforded to student athletes. Thus, plaintiffs contended, what appeared to be the even-handed demotions of two men's and two women's teams, in fact, perpetuated Brown's discriminatory treatment of women in the administration of its intercollegiate athletics program. In the course of the preliminary injunction hearing, the district court found that, in the academic year 1990–91, Brown funded 31 intercollegiate varsity teams, 16 men's teams and 15 women's teams, and that, of the 894 undergraduate students competing on these teams, 63.3% (566) were men and 36.7% (328) were women. During the same academic year, Brown's undergraduate enrollment comprised 52.4% (2,951) men and 47.6% (2,683) women. The district court also summarized the history of athletics at Brown, finding, inter alia, that, while nearly all of the men's varsity teams were established before 1927, virtually all of the women's varsity teams were created between 1971 and 1977, after Brown's merger with Pembroke College. The only women's varsity team created after this period was winter track, in 1982.

In the course of the trial on the merits, the district court found that, in 1993–94, there were 897 students participating in intercollegiate varsity athletics, of which 61.87% (555) were men and 38.13% (342) were women. During the same period, Brown's undergraduate enrollment comprised 5,722 students, of which 48.86% (2,796) were men and 51.14% (2,926) were women. The district court found that, in 1993–94, Brown's intercollegiate athletics program consisted of 32 teams, 16 men's teams and 16 women's teams. Of the university-funded teams, 12 were men's teams and 13 were women's teams; of the donor-funded teams, three were women's teams and four were men's teams. At the time of trial, Brown offered 479 university-funded varsity positions for men, as compared to 312 for women; and 76 donor-funded varsity positions for men, as compared to 30 for women. In 1993–94, then, Brown's varsity program—including both university—and donor-funded sports—afforded over 200 more positions for men than for women. Accordingly, the district court found that Brown maintained a 13.01% disparity between female participation in intercollegiate athletics and female student enrollment, and that "although the number of varsity sports offered to men and women are equal, the selection of sports offered to each gender generates far more individual positions for male athletes than for female athletes."

In computing these figures, the district court counted as participants in intercollegiate athletics for purposes of Title IX analysis those athletes who were members of varsity teams for the majority of the last complete season....

The district court found from extensive testimony that the donor-funded women's gymnastics, women's fencing and women's ski teams, as well as at least one women's club team, the water polo team, had demonstrated the interest and ability to compete at the top varsity level and would benefit from university funding.

The district court did not find that full and effective accommodation of the athletics interests and abilities of Brown's female students would disadvantage Brown's male students.

II.

Title IX provides that "no person in the United States shall, on the basis of sex, be excluded from participation in, be denied the benefits of, or be subjected to discrimination under any education program or activity receiving Federal financial assistance." 20 U.S.C.A. § 1681(a) (West 1990). As a private institution that receives federal financial assistance, Brown is required to comply with Title IX.

Title IX also specifies that its prohibition against gender discrimination shall not "be interpreted to require any educational institution to grant preferential or disparate treatment to the members of one sex on account of an imbalance which may exist" between the total number or percentage of persons of that sex participating in any federally supported program or activity, and "the total number or percentage of persons of that sex in any community, State, section, or other area." 20 U.S.C.A. § 1681(b) (West 1990). Subsection (b) also provides, however, that it "shall not be construed to prevent the consideration in any… proceeding under this chapter of statistical evidence tending to show that such an imbalance exists with respect to the participation in, or receipt of the benefits of, any such program or activity by the members of one sex." *Id.*

Applying § 1681(b), the prior panel held that Title IX "does not mandate strict numerical equality between the gender balance of a college's athletic program and the gender balance of its student body." The panel explained that, while evidence of a gender-based disparity in an institution's athletics program is relevant to a determination of noncompliance, "a court assessing Title IX compliance may not find a violation solely because there is a disparity between the gender composition of an educational institution's student constituency, on the one hand, and its athletic programs, on the other hand."

The Policy Interpretation establishes a three-part test, a two-part test, and factors to be considered in determining compliance under 34 C.F.R. § 106.41(c)(1). At issue in this appeal is the proper interpretation of the first of these, the so-called three-part test, which inquires as follows:

1. Whether intercollegiate level participation opportunities for male and female students are provided in numbers substantially proportionate to their respective enrollments; or
2. Where the members of one sex have been and are underrepresented among intercollegiate athletes, whether the institution can show a history and continuing practice of program expansion which is demonstrably responsive to the developing interest and abilities of the members of that sex; or
3. Where the members of one sex are underrepresented among intercollegiate athletes, and the institution cannot show a continuing practice of program expansion such as that cited above, whether it can be demonstrated that the interests and abilities of the members of that sex have been fully and effectively accommodated by the present program.

44 Fed. Reg. at 71,418.

The district court held that, "because Brown maintains a 13.01% disparity between female participation in intercollegiate athletics and female student enrollment, it cannot gain the protection of prong one." Nor did Brown satisfy prong two.

While acknowledging that Brown "has an impressive history of program expansion," the district court found that Brown failed to demonstrate that it has "maintained a continuing practice of intercollegiate program expansion for women, the underrepresented sex." The court noted further that, because merely reducing program offerings to the overrepresented gender does not constitute program expansion for the underrepresented gender, the fact that Brown has eliminated or demoted several men's teams does not amount to a continuing practice of program expansion for women. As to prong three, the district court found that Brown had not "fully and effectively accommodated the interest and ability of the underrepresented sex 'to the extent necessary to provide equal opportunity in the selection of sports and levels of competition available to members of both sexes.'"...

IV.

Brown contends that the district court misconstrued and misapplied the three-part test. Specifically, Brown argues that the district court's interpretation and application of the test is irreconcilable with the statute, the regulation, and the agency's interpretation of the law, and effectively renders Title IX an "affirmative action statute" that mandates preferential treatment for women by imposing quotas in excess of women's relative interests and abilities in athletics.

[The court addressed Brown's contention that the district court was requiring affirmative action in violation of the constitution and dismissed this argument.]

Brown maintains that the district court's decision imposes upon universities the obligation to engage in preferential treatment by requiring quotas in excess of women's relative interests and abilities. With respect to prong three, Brown asserts that the district court's interpretation of the word "fully" "requires universities to favor women's teams and treat them better than men's [teams]... forces them to eliminate or cap men's teams... [and] forces universities to impose athletic quotas in excess of relative interests and abilities."...

Brown argues that the district court's interpretation of the three-part test requires numerical proportionality, thus imposing a gender-based quota scheme in contravention of the statute. This argument rests, in part, upon Brown's reading of 20 U.S.C. § 1681(b) as a categorical proscription against consideration of gender parity. Section 1681(b) provides:

> Nothing contained in subsection (a) of this section shall be interpreted to require any educational institution to grant preferential or disparate treatment to the members of one sex on account of an imbalance which may exist with respect to the total number or percentage of persons of that sex participating in or receiving the benefits of any federally supported program or activity, in comparison with the total number or percentage of persons of that sex in any community, State, section or other area....

20 U.S.C.A. § 1681(b)....

In any event, the three-part test is, on its face, entirely consistent with § 1681(b) because the test does not require preferential or disparate treatment for either gender. Neither the Policy Interpretation's three-part test, nor the district court's interpretation of it, mandates statistical balancing; "rather, the policy interpretation merely creates a presumption that a school is in compliance with Title IX and the applicable regulation when it achieves such a statistical balance."

The test is also entirely consistent with § 1681(b) as applied by the prior panel and by the district court. As previously noted, *Cohen II* expressly held that "a court assessing Title IX compliance may not find a violation solely because there is a disparity between the gender composition of an educational institution's student constituency, on the one hand, and its athletic programs, on the other hand." The panel then carefully delineated the burden of proof, which requires a Title IX plaintiff to show, not only "disparity between the gender composition of the institution's student body and its athletic program, thereby proving that there is an underrepresented gender," but also "that a second element—unmet interest—is present," meaning that the underrepresented gender has not been fully and effectively accommodated by the institution's present athletic program. Only where the plaintiff meets the burden of proof on these elements and the institution fails to show as an affirmative defense a history and continuing practice of program expansion responsive to the interests and abilities of the underrepresented gender will liability be established. Surely this is a far cry from a one-step imposition of a gender-based quota.

The prior panel held that "the fact that the overrepresented gender is less than fully accommodated will not, in and of itself, excuse a shortfall in the provision of opportunities for the underrepresented gender." Instead, the law requires that, absent a demonstration of continuing program expansion for the underrepresented gender under prong two of the three-part test, an institution must either provide opportunities in proportion to the gender composition of the student body so as to satisfy prong one, or fully accommodate the interests and abilities of athletes of the underrepresented gender under prong three.

Brown has contended throughout this litigation that the significant disparity in athletics opportunities for men and women at Brown is the result of a gender-based differential in the level of interest in sports and that the district court's application of the three-part test requires universities to provide athletics opportunities for women to an extent that exceeds their relative interests and abilities in sports.

We view Brown's argument that women are less interested than men in participating in intercollegiate athletics, as well as its conclusion that institutions should be required to accommodate the interests and abilities of its female students only to the extent that it accommodates the interests and abilities of its male students, with great suspicion. To assert that Title IX permits institutions to provide fewer athletics participation opportunities for women than for men, based upon the premise that women are less interested in sports than are men, is (among other things) to ignore the fact that Title IX was enacted in order to remedy discrimination that results from stereotyped notions of women's interests and abilities.

Interest and ability rarely develop in a vacuum; they evolve as a function of opportunity and experience. The Policy Interpretation recognizes that women's lower rate of participation in athletics reflects women's historical lack of opportunities to participate in sports.

Thus, there exists the danger that, rather than providing a true measure of women's interest in sports, statistical evidence purporting to reflect women's interest instead provides only a measure of the very discrimination that is and has been the basis for women's lack of opportunity to participate in sports. Prong three requires some kind of evidence of interest in athletics, and the Title IX framework permits the use of statistical evidence in assessing the level of interest in sports.[1] Nevertheless, to allow a numbers-based lack-of-interest defense to become the instrument of further discrimination against the underrepresented gender would pervert the remedial purpose of Title IX. We conclude that, even if it can be empirically demonstrated that, at a particular time, women have less interest in sports than do men, such evidence, standing alone, cannot justify providing fewer athletics opportunities for women than for men. Furthermore, such evidence is completely irrelevant

---

1. Under the Policy Interpretation,

Institutions may determine the athletic interests and abilities of students by nondiscriminatory methods of their choosing provided:

a. The processes take into account the nationally increasing levels of women's interests and abilities;
b. The methods of determining interest and ability do not disadvantage the members of an underrepresented sex;
c. The methods of determining ability take into account team performance records; and
d. The methods are responsive to the expressed interests of students capable of intercollegiate competition who are members of an underrepresented sex.

44 Fed. Reg. at 71,417.

The 1990 version of the Title IX Athletics Investigator's Manual, an internal agency document, instructs investigating officials to consider, inter alia, the following: (i) any institutional surveys or assessments of students' athletics interests and abilities; (ii) the "expressed interests" of the underrepresented gender; (iii) other programs indicative of interests and abilities, such as club and intramural sports, sports programs at "feeder" schools, community and regional sports programs, and physical education classes. As the district court noted, however, the agency characterizes surveys as a "simple way to identify which additional sports might appropriately be created to achieve compliance.... Thus, a survey of interests would follow a determination that an institution does not satisfy prong three; it would not be utilized to make that determination in the first instance." *Cohen III*, 897 F. Supp. at 210; *see* Valerie M. Bonnette & Lamar Daniel, Department of Education, Title IX Athletics Investigator's Manual 22, 27 (1990) (explaining that a survey or assessment of interests and abilities is not required by the Title IX regulation or the Policy Interpretation but may be required as part of a remedy when OCR has concluded that an institution's current program does not equally effectively accommodate the interests and abilities of students).

where, as here, viable and successful women's varsity teams have been demoted or eliminated....

VII.

Brown may achieve compliance with Title IX in a number of ways: It may eliminate its athletic program altogether, it may elevate or create the requisite number of women's positions, it may demote or eliminate the requisite number of men's positions, or it may implement a combination of these remedies. I leave it entirely to Brown's discretion to decide how it will balance its program to provide equal opportunities for its men and women athletes. I recognize the financial constraints Brown faces; however, its own priorities will necessarily determine the path to compliance it elects to take....

[The court analyzed Brown's submitted plan and generally agreed with the district court that it did not represent a good faith effort to comply with the dictates of Title IX. However, the court held that the district court erroneously substituted its own plan rather than accepting Brown's alternative plan of reducing men's sports until proportionality was achieved.]

VIII.

Affirmed in part, reversed in part, and remanded for further proceedings. No costs on appeal to either party.

Biediger v. Quinnipiac University

667 F.3d 910 (2d Cir. 2012)

Reena Raggi, Circuit Judge.

[Quinnipiac University appeals the issuance of a permanent injunction after a bench trial at which Quinnipiac was found to have violated Title IX by failing to afford equal participation opportunities in varsity sports to female students. *See Biediger v. Quinnipiac Univ.*, 728 F. Supp. 2d 62 (D. Conn. 2010).] Quinnipiac faults the district court for excluding from its count of the total athletic participation opportunities afforded female students: (1) 11 roster positions on the women's indoor and outdoor track and field teams, held by members of Quinnipiac's women's cross-country team who were required to join the track teams even though they were unable to compete in 2009–10 because they were injured or "red-shirted"; and (2) all 30 roster positions on Quinnipiac's nascent women's competitive cheerleading team, based on a finding that the team did not afford the athletic participation opportunities of a varsity sport. Quinnipiac further contends that, even if these 41 roster positions should not count as varsity athletic participation opportunities for women, the district court erred in concluding that (3) the resulting 3.62% disparity between the percentage of all participation opportunities in varsity sports afforded female students (58.25%) and the percentage of enrolled female undergraduates (61.87%) established a Title IX violation warranting the challenged injunctive relief.

This lawsuit has its origins in Quinnipiac's March 2009 announcement that in the 2009–10 academic year, it would eliminate its varsity sports teams for women's volleyball, men's golf, and men's outdoor track and field, while simultaneously creating a new varsity sports team for women's competitive cheerleading. Plaintiffs, five Quinnipiac women's volleyball players and their coach, Robin Sparks, filed this action in April 2009, charging the university with violating Title IX by denying women equal varsity athletic participation opportunities, and seeking an injunction that, among other things, prevented Quinnipiac from eliminating its women's volleyball team.... In June 2010, the district court conducted a bench trial on plaintiffs' claim of disproportionate allocation of athletic participation opportunities and, finding in their favor, granted permanent injunctive relief....

OCR explained that, "[a]s a general rule, all athletes who are listed on a team's squad or eligibility list and are on the team as of the team's first competitive event are counted as participants." Further, "an athlete who participates in more than one sport will be counted as a participant in each sport in which he or she participates." It is not necessary for an athlete to meet minimum criteria of playing time or athletic ability to count as a participant. As OCR explained, "athletes who practice but may not compete" nevertheless "receive numerous benefits and services, such as training and practice time, coaching, tutoring services, locker room facilities, and equipment, as well as important non-tangible benefits derived from being a member of an intercollegiate athletic team." Thus, "it is necessary to count all athletes who receive such benefits when determining the number of athletic opportunities provided to men and women." In a letter accompanying the 1996 Clarification, however, OCR sounded a note of caution: for an athlete to be counted, he or she must be afforded a participation opportunity that is "real, not illusory," in that it offers the same benefits as would be provided to other *bona fide* athletes.

In a 2008 letter, OCR explained that a genuine athletic participation opportunity must take place in the context of a "sport. If a school is a member of a recognized intercollegiate athletic organization, such as the National Collegiate Athletic Association ("NCAA"), that subjects the activity at issue to its organizational requirements, OCR will "presume" that the activity is a sport and that participation can be counted under Title IX. But if that presumption does not apply or has been rebutted, OCR will determine whether the activity qualifies as a sport by reference to several factors relating to "program structure and administration" and "team preparation and competition."

Eight years earlier, in 2000, OCR had issued two letters stating that cheerleading, whether of the sideline or competitive variety, was presumptively not a sport, and that team members could not be counted as athletes under Title IX....

OCR affords schools considerable "flexibility and choice" in deciding how to provide substantially proportionate athletic opportunities to students of both sexes, including by eliminating teams, placing caps on its rosters, or "[e]xpanding... athletic opportunities through new sports".

At trial, Quinnipiac maintained that it offered athletic participation opportunities to male and female undergraduates substantially proportionate to their respective enrollments. Quinnipiac maintained that women represented 61.87% of the total student body and 62.27% of all varsity athletes, while men represented 38.13% of the student body and 37.73% of all varsity athletes.

Plaintiffs challenged Quinnipiac's count of its varsity athletes, arguing that (1) the university manipulated its team rosters to produce artificially undersized men's teams and artificially oversize women's teams; (2) counting the same women's membership on cross- country, indoor track, and outdoor track teams as three distinct athletic participation opportunities was unwarranted because Quinnipiac's indoor and outdoor track teams did not afford cross-country athletes genuine and distinct benefits; and (3) women who participated on the competitive cheerleading team should not be counted at all because the activity had not yet achieved the status of an intercollegiate varsity sport.

After trial, the district court issued a detailed memorandum of decision in favor of plaintiffs. [The district court declined to find the defendant had manipulated rosters and did not find violations associated with the total counts for the track and cross country teams.] The district court also decided that none of the 30 roster positions assigned to women's competitive cheerleading should be counted because the activity did not yet afford genuine athletic participation opportunities in a varsity sport.... The district court counted a total of 400 varsity athletic participation opportunities. Of these 400, it found that 233—or 58.25%—were assigned to women and 167—or 41.75%—were assigned to men. See id. The district court observed that "in strictly numerical terms," a 3.62% disparity between Quinnipiac's women's 58.25% varsity athletic participation and their 61.87% representation in the undergraduate population reflected only "a borderline case of disproportionate athletic opportunities for women." Nevertheless, the district court concluded that the disparity was significant enough to support judgment in favor of plaintiffs because (1) the disparity was caused by Quinnipiac's own actions and not by natural fluctuations in enrollment; and (2) it was reasonable to expect Quinnipiac to close the gap because the 38 roster positions needed for that purpose would be enough to field a viable women's athletic team, and such a team already existed in the form of the women's volleyball team.

Accordingly, the district court entered a declaratory judgment finding Quinnipiac to have violated Title IX and its implementing regulations by discriminating against women in failing to provide equal athletic participation opportunities to female students, and it permanently enjoined Quinnipiac from continuing to discriminate in this manner....

Quinnipiac contends that the district court finding of sex discrimination is infected by three errors: (1) the exclusion of 11 positions on the women's indoor and outdoor track teams from its count of varsity athletic participation opportunities, (2) the exclusion of all 30 competitive cheerleading positions from its count of varsity athletic participation opportunities, and (3) the determination that an identified 3.62% disparity between women's representation in Quinnipiac's student body and on its varsity sports teams sufficed to show that women were not afforded substantially proportionate varsity athletic participation opportunities....

Before the district court, plaintiffs argued that Quinnipiac should not be allowed to count as 54 athletic participation opportunities the cross-country, indoor track, and outdoor track roster positions held by the same 18 women. As the district court recognized, the issue admitted no easy resolution. The 1996 Clarification plainly states that "an athlete who participates in more than one sport will be counted as a participant in each sport in which... she participates." But the trial evidence reflected circumstances not addressed in the 1996 Clarification: Quinnipiac's women cross-country runners were not afforded a choice as to whether to participate in more than one sport; they were required to do so. Specifically, their participation on the cross-country team was conditioned on their membership on the indoor and outdoor track teams. No other Quinnipiac athletes were required to join multiple sports teams. Notably, male cross-country runners were not required to join men's indoor and outdoor track teams, as Quinnipiac had no such teams in 2009–10. Indeed, male cross-country runners were prohibited from representing Quinnipiac as individual entrants in indoor and outdoor track events. As the district court recognized, these circumstances raise questions as to whether simultaneous participation on the women's cross-country, indoor track, and outdoor track teams at Quinnipiac represented three genuine athletic opportunities, or whether cross-country runners' mandated participation on the indoor and outdoor track teams was simply a form of alternative off-season training for the cross-country runners, one that allowed Quinnipiac to inflate the rosters of its women's indoor and outdoor track teams.

In this respect, the district court carefully reviewed evidence that we only summarize: Quinnipiac had a highly competitive women's cross-country team, which, by the 2009–10 school year, had won the last five New England Conference championships; cross-country runners' mandated participation on the indoor and outdoor track teams afforded these runners more training time (albeit for a different type of running) during the cross-country off-season than NCAA rules would otherwise have allowed; Quinnipiac expanded its indoor and outdoor track teams' rosters to accommodate mandated participation by cross-country runners; despite the resulting large rosters, Quinnipiac's indoor and outdoor track teams participated in only the minimum number of track and field tournaments required by the NCAA and were never competitive for team awards as no Quinnipiac athletes entered field events; and Quinnipiac offered scholarship money only to those members of the indoor and outdoor track teams who also ran cross-country. The totality of these circumstances suggested that the 60 positions on Quinnipiac's indoor and outdoor track team rosters were not reflective of genuine participation opportunities in these sports, but were inflated to afford mandated year- round training for the 18 members of the women's cross-country team.

[The court then tracked the district court's analysis of the actual performances of the women in order to reach a number who would be counted.]

Thus, the district court concluded that for injured and red-shirted cross-country runners, the athletic participation opportunities afforded by mandated membership on the indoor and outdoor track teams were "truly illusory."

What was not illusory, however, was Quinnipiac's ability to "pad[] its rosters" with female athletes who had "no hope of competing or otherwise participating meaningfully during the indoor and outdoor track seasons." As the district court aptly observed, it would be "unacceptable for Quinnipiac to pump up its women's track team rosters" by requiring every injured field hockey, soccer, and volleyball player to join these teams even though they "would never actually compete in the indoor and outdoor track seasons and, for that matter, would never want to enter a race." But, the district court found, "that is essentially what Quinnipiac is doing with its injured cross-country runners." Thus, the district court discounted Quinnipiac's claimed 30 athletic participation opportunities in indoor track by five, and its claimed 30 athletic participation opportunities in outdoor track by six. We conclude that this reduction in the total number of athletic participation opportunities for women runners in cross-country, indoor track, and outdoor track from Quinnipiac's claimed 78 to an actual 67 is fully supported by the record evidence and by the applicable law.

In challenging this action, Quinnipiac complains that it was denied due process by lack of notice that the question of whether injured and red-shirted cross-country runners were afforded genuine athletic participation opportunities in indoor and outdoor track was at issue. We are not convinced....

Quinnipiac further complains that it was not given notice that the district court would draw a negative inference about the genuineness of the indoor and outdoor track participation opportunities afforded female cross-country runners from the fact that the runners were required to join the track team. A factfinder's ability to draw reasonable inferences from the evidence is well established,... and Quinnipiac points us to no precedent holding that a factfinder must notify parties in advance of the particular inferences it is inclined to draw from record evidence. Indeed, we here reject that argument....

Competitive cheerleading, which Quinnipiac decided to create as a new women's varsity sport team for 2009–10, is a late twentieth-century outgrowth of traditional sideline cheerleading. Whereas sideline cheerleaders generally strive to entertain audiences or solicit crowd reaction at sport or school functions, a competitive cheerleading team seeks to pit its skills against other teams for the purpose of winning.

Thus, to distinguish the two activities, competitive cheerleaders do not attempt to elicit crowd response; generally do not use pom-poms, megaphones, signs, or other props associated with [sideline] cheerleading teams;... wear uniforms consisting of shorts and jerseys, much like what women's volleyball players don; and emphasize the more gymnastic elements of sideline cheerleading, such as aerial maneuvers, floor tumbling, and balancing exercises, to the exclusion of those activities intended to rally the watching audience.

The district court nevertheless concluded that the 30 roster positions that Quinnipiac assigned competitive cheerleading for 2009–10 could not be counted under Title IX because the activity did not yet afford the participation opportunities of a varsity "sport." Preliminary to reaching this conclusion, the district court observed that competitive cheerleading is not yet recognized as a "sport," or even an "emerging sport," by the NCAA, action that would have triggered a presumption in favor of counting its participants under Title IX. Nor has DOE recognized competitive cheerleading as a sport; to the contrary, in two letters in 2000, OCR indicated competitive cheerleading is presumptively not a sport, while leaving open the possibility for a different conclusion with respect to a particular cheerleading program. There is, however, no record evidence of any competitive cheerleading program being recognized by DOE as a sport.

Mindful of these circumstances, the district court proceeded carefully to review the structure, administration, team preparation, and competition of Quinnipiac's competitive cheerleading program to determine whether it nevertheless qualified as a sport whose athletic participation opportunities should be counted for purposes of Title IX. The district court found that in terms of the team's operating budget, benefits, services, and coaching staff, competitive cheerleading was generally structured and administered by Quinnipiac's athletics department in a manner consistent with the school's other varsity teams. With respect to factors relating to the team's preparation and competition, the district court found that the competitive cheerleading team's practice time, regimen, and venue were consistent with other varsity sports. Further, as with other varsity sports, the length of the competitive cheerleading season and the minimum number of competitions in which a team would participate were pre-determined by a governing athletic organization, the recently formed National Competitive Stunt and Tumbling Association, of which Quinnipiac was a founding member. Finally, the purpose of the team—to compete athletically at the intercollegiate varsity level—was akin to that of other varsity sports.

At the same time, however, the district court identified a number of circumstances that sufficiently distinguished Quinnipiac's competitive cheerleading program from traditional varsity sports as to "compel[] the decision that, for the 2009–10 season," the program could not "be counted as a varsity sport for purposes of Title IX." First, Quinnipiac did not—and, in 2009–10, could not—conduct any off-campus recruitment for its competitive cheerleading team, in marked contrast not only to the school's other varsity sports teams but also to a typical NCAA Division I sports program. The district court explained the significance of this circumstance: "Although the women on the Quinnipiac competitive cheer team were athletically able, they would have been all the more talented had [Coach] Powers been able to seek out the best competitive cheerleaders around the country, as any other varsity coach would have been able to do."

More important, no uniform set of rules applied to competitive cheerleading competition throughout the 2009–10 season. Indeed, in the ten competitions in which the Quinnipiac team participated during the regular season, it was judged according to five different scoring systems. Further, in these competitions, Quinnipiac did not face only varsity intercollegiate competitive cheerleading teams. Rather, it was challenged by "a motley assortment of competitors," including collegiate club opponents who did not receive varsity benefits, collegiate sideline cheerleading teams, and all-star opponents unaffiliated with a particular academic institution, some of whom may still have been high-school age. As the district court observed, "application of a uniform set of rules for competition and the restriction of competition to contests against other varsity opponents" are the "touchstones" of a varsity sports program. "Those features ensure that play is fair in each game, that teams' performances can be compared across a season, and that teams can be distinguished in terms of quality."

The concerns raised by these irregularities in season competition were only aggravated by aspects of post-season play. Notably, competitive cheerleading offered no progressive playoff system leading to a championship game. Rather, it provided an open invitational, which neither excluded any team on the basis of its regular season performance nor ranked or seeded participating teams on that basis. Instead, all entrants competed in a single championship round in which the team with the highest score won. That round, moreover, was subject to a new rule of competition that had not applied to Quinnipiac in any of its regular season competitions: a mandatory 45–60 second "spirit" segment in which a team was judged by the intensity of the response it elicited from the crowd and the number of the sponsoring brand's props that it employed, features that Quinnipiac's coach confirmed were more characteristic of sideline rather than competitive cheerleading. Viewing the totality of these circumstances, the district court concluded that the competitive cheerleading team's post-season competition did not conform to expectations for a varsity sport.

... Thus, it ruled that Quinnipiac's 30 roster positions for competitive cheerleading could not be counted for Title IX purposes because the activity did not yet afford women genuine participation opportunities in a varsity sport.

... [W]e conclude for the same reasons stated in detail by the district court and summarized in this opinion that, although there are facts on both sides of the argument, in the end, the balance tips decidedly against finding competitive cheerleading presently to be a "sport" whose participation opportunities should be counted for purposes of Title IX. Like the district court, we acknowledge record evidence showing that competitive cheerleading can be physically challenging, requiring competitors to possess "strength, agility, and grace." Similarly, we do not foreclose the possibility that the activity, with better organization and defined rules, might some day warrant recognition as a varsity sport. But, like the district court, we conclude that the record evidence shows that "that time has not yet arrived." ...

Having reduced Quinnipiac's claimed athletic participation opportunities for women by 41—representing 30 competitive cheerleaders and 11 cross-country runners required to join the indoor and outdoor track teams but unable to compete on those teams because of their injuries or red-shirt status—the district court correctly found that the school had a total of 400 varsity athletic participation opportunities, of which 233, or 58.25%, were assigned to women. Because enrollment data established that 61.87% of Quinnipiac's undergraduate population were women, this indicated a 3.62% disparity in the athletic opportunities that Quinnipiac afforded women. The district court concluded that this disparity was sufficient to support a finding that Quinnipiac had failed to afford female students varsity athletic participation opportunities substantially proportionate to their enrollment.

Quinnipiac argues that a 3.62% disparity is too small to support such a finding....

Quinnipiac's arguments fail to persuade. First, its emphasis on the relatively small percentage of disparity is unwarranted. The district court itself recognized that "in strictly numerical terms," a 3.62% disparity presents "a borderline case of disproportionate athletic opportunities." But as the 1996 Clarification makes clear, substantial proportionality is not determined by any bright-line statistical test. While a district court outside this circuit reports finding no case in which a disparity of two percentage points or less has been held to manifest a lack of substantial proportionality, we do not pursue the issue because the disparity in this case is greater than 2%, and we do not, in any event, understand the 1996 Clarification to create a statistical safe harbor at this or any other percentage. Instead, the Clarification instructs that substantial proportionality is properly determined on a "case-by-case basis" after a careful assessment of the school's "specific circumstances," including the causes of the disparity and the reasonableness of requiring the school to add additional athletic opportunities to eliminate the disparity. The district court's challenged ruling was based on precisely this analysis.

Specifically, the district court pointed to record evidence showing that the 3.62% identified disparity was almost entirely attributable to Quinnipiac's own careful control of its athletic rosters. Although Quinnipiac claims that, but for a 0.27% increase in female enrollment in 2009–10 beyond its control, the disparity would have been only 3.35%, the difference is not one that undermines the district court's conclusion that Quinnipiac's voluntary actions largely caused the disparity....

Finally, we do not understand the district court to have ruled, as Quinnipiac suggests, that no matter how small a disparity, if it can be closed by the creation of a new sports team, a school will be found not to have afforded substantially proportionate athletic opportunities. Rather, we understand the court to have discussed the possible creation of a new sports team only to explain why it was reasonable to expect Quinnipiac to add additional athletic opportunities for women to close the identified 3.62% disparity. In so concluding, the district court noted that, insofar as the gap reflected 38 positions, each of Quinnipiac's women's varsity teams had 30 or fewer roster spots, making it "certain that an independent sports team could be created from the shortfall of participation opportunities." Moreover, the district court observed that little effort was required for Quinnipiac to afford the additional participation opportunities of an independent sports team: "That independent sports team would be the eliminated women's volleyball squad, a team that, based on Quinnipiac's 2010–11 roster target, requires a mere 14 players to compete." Of course, the district court did not suggest that Quinnipiac's compliance with Title IX was dependent on it forever fielding a women's volleyball team. But the ease with which Quinnipiac could afford these particular additional varsity athletic opportunities was a "specific circumstance[]" that, pursuant to the 1996 Clarification, supported the conclusion that a 3.62% disparity in this case demonstrated that Quinnipiac was not affording substantially proportionate varsity athletic participation opportunities to its female students.

Accordingly, we reject Quinnipiac's challenge to the district court's finding that the school engaged in sex discrimination in violation of Title IX, and we affirm the order enjoining Quinnipiac from continuing such discrimination....

Accordingly, the district court's order enjoining Quinnipiac from continuing to discriminate against female students by failing to provide them with equal athletic participation opportunities is AFFIRMED.

Notes and Comments

1. *Cohen* went through several stages in both the district court and the circuit court prior to the opinion above. *See Cohen v. Brown University*, 991 F.2d 888 (1st Cir. 1993). Following the opinion in the principal case, the Supreme Court denied certiorari, *Brown Univ. v. Cohen*, 520 U.S. 1186 (1997). The case was remanded to the district court, and ultimately the university and the plaintiffs settled the matter, with the university agreeing to specific improvements and additions to its women's athletic program. Two decades later the university announced plans to demote a number of varsity sports to club sport status. A challenge to the plan was filed and the university ultimately agreed to a settlement that includes an end date in 2024 for the 1998 consent decree. Several athletes challenged the settlement, but it was ultimately upheld by the First Circuit in 2021 and the Supreme Court declined to take jurisdiction of the matter.

2. In *Mayerova v. Eastern Michigan University*, 346 F.Supp.3d 983 (E.D. Mich. 2018), two female student-athletes representing a class of current and future participants of the women's tennis and softball teams at Eastern Michigan University filed

a Title IX lawsuit against the university for failure to provide effective accommodation. EMU had cut those two sports (in addition to two men's sports) for cost savings. For the 2017–2018 school year, women comprised 59.5% of EMU's undergraduate enrollment and 44.3% of its athletes. Given this clear disparity, EMU did not claim to provide "substantially proportionate" athletic opportunities to its female student-athletes and the court found that EMU did not satisfy the second or third parts of the Three-Part Test. In January 2020, the parties entered a settlement in which EMU agreed to reinstate the women's tennis team and continue to support it, add a new women's lacrosse team, promise an additional $2 million for women's sports over the next three years, and pay $125,000 to the two named plaintiffs plus their attorney's fees.

3. The "contact sport exception" contained in the Title IX regulations, 34 C.F.R. § 106.41(b), provides:

> A recipient may operate or sponsor separate teams for members of each sex where selection for such teams is based upon competitive skill or the activity involved is a contact sport. However, where a recipient operates or sponsors a team in a particular sport for members of one sex but operates or sponsors no such team for members of the other sex, and athletic opportunities for members of that sex have previously been limited, members of the excluded sex must be allowed to try-out for the team offered unless the sport involved is a contact sport. For the purposes of this part, contact sports include boxing, wrestling, rugby, ice hockey, football, basketball and other sports the purpose or major activity of which involves bodily contact.

In *Mercer v. Duke University*, 19 F.3d 643 (4th Cir. 1999), the court held that, where a university permits members of the opposite sex to try out for a single-sex contact sports team, Title IX will protect the athlete against discriminatory treatment. This interpretation would, however, allow a school to deny participation opportunities in the contact sport without subjecting itself to liability. In this case, Duke University had allowed a female athlete to try out for the football team as a walk-on kicker. Following one academic year of practicing and working with the team, she was told by the kicking coach that she had made the team. During the subsequent season she claims that she was the subject of discriminatory treatment and ultimately she was told that she was dropped from the team. Her claim is that she was dropped because of her sex. The matter was remanded to the district court. The trial produced a verdict in favor of the plaintiff for one dollar in compensatory damages and two million dollars in punitive damages. The court vacated the award of punitive damages finding them not available in actions brought to enforce Title IX. However, the plaintiff was awarded approximately $350,000 in attorney's fees. *Mercer v. Duke University*, 190 F.3d 643 (4th Cir. 1999). *See also Barnett v. Texas Wrestling Ass'n*, 16 F. Supp. 2d 690 (N.D. Tex. 1998) (state association not in violation of Title IX for its exclusion of females from wrestling matches against males).

4. *McCormick v. School Dist. of Mamaroneck*, 370 F.3d 275 (2d Cir. 2004), provides an example of a treatment and benefits case in which two girls claimed that their school districts violated Title IX by scheduling girls' high school soccer in the spring and boys' high school soccer in the fall. The regional and state championships in soccer were scheduled at the end of the fall season and thus, according to the plaintiffs, the girls were deprived of the opportunity to compete in their sports championships due to conflicts with other opportunities to play soccer during the spring. The court held that when a high school athletic association holds championships for boys and girls in the same sport, but in different seasons, a violation of Title IX will be found if the girls are found to be at a significant disadvantage with regard to scheduling of games and practice time. A very important point addressed in *McCormick* is that compliance with the equal treatment part of Title IX is determined on a program-wide basis in which the components of all of the sports within the athletics program are evaluated. As explained in *McCormick*, "a school that provides better equipment to the men's basketball team than to the women's basketball team would be in compliance with Title IX if it provided comparably better equipment to the women's soccer team than to the men's soccer team." *Id.* at 293–94.

5. For an example of a finding of intentional discrimination leading to damages, see *Pederson v. Louisiana State University*, 213 F.3d 858 (5th Cir. 2000) (finding sex discrimination against female students in denying athletic opportunities based on sexism and stereotypes).

6. Men have also raised Title IX issues, particularly where sports programs are cut in an effort to accommodate women's sports teams. *See Neal v. Board of Trustees of the California State University*, 2002 U.S. App. LEXIS 24451 (9th Cir. Nov. 26, 2002), *cert. denied*, 540 U.S. 874 (2003); *Miami Univ. Wrestling Club v. Miami Univ.*, 302 F.3d 608 (6th Cir. 2002); *Chalenor v. Univ. of N.D.*, 291 F.3d 1042 (8th Cir. 2002); *Kelley v. Board of Trustees*, 35 F.3d 265 (7th Cir. 1994); and *Gonyo v. Drake University*, 879 F. Supp. 1000 (S.D. Iowa 1995). The National Wrestling Coaches Association filed suit in early 2002 against the United States Department of Education contending it is enforcing Title IX in a manner that unlawfully discriminates against men. Specifically, the association contended that the Department's Three Part Test for determining compliance with the participation opportunities portion of Title IX exceeded the authority granted by the statute. The D.C. Circuit dismissed the case, finding the association lacked standing to bring the action. *National Wrestling Coaches Ass'n v. Dept. of Education*, 366 F.3d 930 (D.C. Cir. 2004), *cert. denied*, 545 U.S. 1104 (2005). *See also Equity in Ath., Inc. v. Dept. of Educ.*, 639 F.3d 91 (4th Cir. 2011).

7. Much of the national publicity concerning Title IX cases has focused on collegiate programs; however, a significant volume of litigation involves high school and middle school programs. Indeed, in one state, Oklahoma, there were 10 separate cases filed in a three-year time period. Most of these cases have focused on equal

treatment and benefits, particularly facilities and quality of coaching. *See* Ray Yasser & Samuel J. Schiller, *Gender Equity in Interscholastic Sports: The Final Saga: The Fight for Attorneys' Fees*, 34 TULSA L.J. 85 (1998); Ray Yasser & Samuel J. Schiller, *Gender Equity in Interscholastic Sports: A Case Study*, 33 TULSA L.J. 273 (1997); Ray Yasser & Samuel J. Schiller, *Gender Equity in Athletics: The New Battleground of Interscholastic Sports*, 15 CARDOZO ARTS & ENT. L.J. 371 (1997).

8. In 1994, Congress enacted the Equity in Athletics Disclosure Act (EADA), Pub. L. No. 103–382, 108 Stat. 3969, codified at 20 U.S.C. §1092(g). The Act requires schools with intercollegiate athletic programs to prepare and disseminate a report annually containing the following information:

a. the number of male and female undergraduate students attending the institution;

b. a listing of the varsity sports teams, including the number of participants per team, total operating expenses, whether the head coach is male or female, the number of assistant coaches, and how many are male or female;

c. the total amount of money spent on athletically related student aid;

d. the ratio of athletically related student aid awarded to male athletes to that awarded to female athletes;

e. the total amount of expenditures spent on recruiting, broken down for men's and women's teams;

f. the total annual revenues generated for all men's teams and for all women's teams;

g. the average salary of head coaches for men's teams and the average salary of head coaches for women's teams; and

h. the average salary for assistant coaches of men's teams and the average salary for assistant coaches of women's teams.

The first such reports were published October 1, 1996, with the information pertaining to the 1995–96 academic year. Similar reports have been published each year. *See* 34 C.F.R. pt. 668. https://ope.ed.gov/athletics/#/

Problem

You are the associate athletic director in charge of Title IX compliance at a small private university with a total enrollment of approximately 4,500 students. More than 2,000 of the students receive federal student loans. Several of the university's buildings, including the administration building, were built with the help of federal funds. The school has a work-study program that is funded in part with federal monies. The school is a mid-level Division I member of the NCAA and participates in 17 varsity sports, including football at the FBS level.

It is summertime, and in the brief lull between the end of the basketball season and the start of the football season, you receive a series of emails from the athletic director, Joe Daniels, to wit:

June 15

As you know, we have recently become concerned about Title IX compliance and its possible impact on our programs, particularly the threat to our football and men's basketball teams. We need to find out if there are any legitimate issues to cause us concern.

June 18

Per our telephone conversation on June 16, in which you requested more information, the following is pertinent data for your consideration:

	Scholarships	Participants	Funding**
Men's Sports*			
baseball	11	35	$1,290,000
golf	4	8	378,400
tennis	4	8	349,200
track/cross-country	12	35	803,300
hockey	18	35	1,518,000
swimming	9	25	493,300
TOTAL	**58**	**146**	**$4,832,200**
Women's Sports			
golf	4	8	$363,300
tennis	4	8	359,200
basketball	15	15	2,383,600
swimming	12	20	584,400
volleyball	12	15	729,650
track	10	28	726,300
soccer	10	20	987,000
rowing	10	18	639,300
TOTAL	**75**	**132**	**$6,772,450**

* I have not included the men's football and basketball teams in these figures because they are significant revenue-producing sports. Women's basketball, hockey, and baseball also produce a minimal amount of revenue.

** The funding figures represent the total operating budget for each sport, including, but not limited to, expenditures for coaches' salaries, equipment, travel, recruitment, and overhead. It does not include scholarship expenses. Tuition, fees, and room and board for the coming year will be $51,500 per student.

June 25

Per our telephone conversation on June 22, it is my view that revenue-producing sports shouldn't be included in Title IX figures because they generate money, while the other sports do not. But here is the financial information regarding football: In football we have 85 scholarships, 115 participants, and $13,825,000 in expenditures. The football program brings in $27,500,000 per year in revenues. In basketball, we have 13 scholarships, 15 participants, $6,735,000 in expenditures, and $12,900,000 in revenues. Stadium and operational costs are not included.

The football team practices and plays home games at the University Stadium, where its training facilities and locker rooms are also located. The men's basketball and women's basketball, swimming, and volleyball teams all practice and play in the new sports center, which has one basketball court and several practice courts. The only conflict over practice times has been in scheduling basketball team practices. The men have the practice courts from 2 p.m. to 5 p.m. weekdays, the women from 7 a.m. to 10 a.m. We have received some complaints about this because a few of the women basketball players had class conflicts.

All of the men's and women's teams (except football and men's and women's basketball) travel to and from games in university vans, and occasionally spend the night at away-game locations. When they're at tournaments or have to spend the night, they stay at a Fairfield Inn, Hampton Inn, or other comparable facilities.

The football and basketball teams travel by air and generally stay overnight in the away-game locations for at least one night.

The football team keeps two orthopedists on retainer to treat injuries incurred in practice and games. Athletes on the other teams rely on the physicians from the student health clinic for onsite help during games. There is a full-time training staff of three certified trainers and two full-time weight training specialists. All are available for all athletes.

We have a tutoring program available to all athletes. Our experience has shown that members of the football and basketball teams usually need tutorial help far more often than members of the other teams.

The base salaries for our head coaches for football and men's basketball are $1,100,000 per year. The baseball coach is also full-time, and makes a salary of $225,000 per year. The women's basketball coach makes $595,000 per year. The total compensation packages for each of the above coaches is greater than listed due to additional radio and television, shoe, automobile, and miscellaneous outside perks associated with the position.

We conducted a survey of students last fall and received approximately 900 responses: 700 from men (who account for 2,000 of the total student body) and 200 from women (who account for 2,500 of the total number of students). Generally, the students appeared to be satisfied with the school's athletic program, but expressed an interest in women's soccer and lacrosse. We have recently added soccer to our program for women.

Two female athletes recently complained to me about the athletic program and threatened to file a Title IX complaint with the Department of Education. I explained to them that such an action would virtually destroy our school's football and (men's) basketball teams, and they backed down.

Last fall a female student from Argentina who had extensive soccer experience wanted to try out as a place kicker for our football team. The coach told her no women were allowed on the team.

Prepare a memorandum to your Athletic Director answering these questions:

1. What violations of Title IX, if any, do you see? What additional information do you need to have in order to provide the AD with answers to his questions?
2. If the school is not in compliance, what actions must be taken to eliminate the violations?
3. Going forward, what sort of strategy regarding Title IX compliance should the school have?

3. Title IX and Sexual Misconduct on Campus

Sexual harassment, assault, or misconduct also constitute a form of sex-based discrimination. The Supreme Court held in *Davis v. Monroe County Board of Education, 526 U.S. 629 (1999)*, that schools could be liable for monetary damages under Title IX for sexual harassment of students or its employees only where the school had "actual knowledge" and acted with "deliberate indifference." Yet for purposes of compliance with Title IX and receipt of federal funds, the Department of Education, Office of Civil Rights (OCR) has issued guidance requiring recipients to institute measures to prevent, eliminate, investigate, and remedy effects of sexual harassment and misconduct on campus. Accordingly, under Title IX, institutions are required to institute reporting, grievance, and investigation procedures in matters involving sexual harassment, assault, or violence. In a 2011 Dear Colleague Letter, the OCR directed that schools develop and circulate policies and procedures for the investigation and adjudication of sexual misconduct issues. The guidance, issued during the Obama Administration, required schools to provide training for all school officials likely to come into contact with victims of sexual violence, including training for dealing with the victim psychological needs. When a complaint was filed with campus law enforcement officials, they were required to advise the complainant of their right to file a Title IX complaint. The adjudication policies developed by schools were required to employ a preponderance of the evidence standard. These policies and procedures had to be included in the school's annual submission of campus crime statistics under the Clery Act.

In 2017, under the Trump Administration, the DOE rescinded the 2011 guidance and later engaged in its own rule-making process, finally issuing Final Regulations in May 2020. 85 Fed. Reg. 30026 (May 19, 2020). Key portion of these regulations, in 34 CFR §106.45, include

- The narrower definition of "sexual harassment"—only conduct that is so severe and pervasive and objectively offensive that it denies a person equal educational access is subject to the regulations;
- Quid pro quo harassment and Clery Act/VAWA offenses (sexual assault, dating violence, etc.) are not subject to the "severe, pervasive, offensive" evaluation;
- Schools to balance Title IX enforcement with 1st Amendment rights, respecting free speech and academic freedom;
- The "single investigator" model can no longer be used by schools; the decision maker must be separate from the investigator;
- Removing requirements that colleges and universities designate most employees as mandatory reporters, whereas formerly athletic directors, coaches, and trainers were mandatory reporters;
- All employees in K-12 settings are mandatory reporters;
- The regulations set forth specific, detailed requirements regarding training for Title IX personnel;
- Schools must investigate off-campus sexual misconduct that occurs in educational activities, such as college owned buildings or college sponsored trips, but not in off-campus apartments or study abroad programs—data indicates that a very high percentage of sexual assaults occur in off-campus housing settings;
- Schools must ensure that each party has an advisor, who may be an attorney;
- A statement of presumption that a respondent is not responsible for the alleged conduct until a determination regarding responsibility is made at the conclusion of the grievance process;
- Detailed requirements for filing a formal complaint, notice to all parties, and other aspects of required procedures related to initiation of a case and the investigation thereof;
- The requirement to provide remedies and resources to a complainant in order to ensure their equal access to education;

- Hearings in higher education cases must be live, although they can be virtual; K-12 schools do not have to provide live hearings;
- At the hearing, each party's advisor must be allowed to ask the other party and any other witnesses all relevant questions and follow-up questions, including challenges to credibility; this cross-examination must be conducted in real time, but never by a party;
- At the request of either party, the parties must be provided separate rooms for participating in the hearing through the use of technology that enables the parties to see and hear each other;
- Rape Shield protection must be provided to complainants;
- School's policies and procedures must set forth whether the standard of proof is "preponderance of the evidence" or "clear and convincing"—standard selected must be used for all formal complaints of sexual harassment including those where employees and faculty are respondents;
- Decision maker must issue a written determination regarding responsibility with findings of fact, conclusions about whether the alleged conduct occurred, rationale for the result, any disciplinary sanctions imposed on the respondent, and whether remedies will be provided to the complainant;
- School must offer an opportunity to both parties to appeal a decision regarding responsibility, including a dismissal of a formal complaint;
- Schools may offer and facilitate informal resolution options, but are not required to offer them;
- Retaliation is expressly prohibited.

The accused's right to cross-examination in the final regulations is consistent with recent rulings by the Sixth Circuit mandating such rights. *Doe v. Baum,* 903 F.3d 575 (6th Cir. 2018); *Doe v. Univ. of Cincinnati,* 872 F.3d 393 (6th Cir. 2017).

These regulations are juxtaposed with two very high-profile horrific sexual assault investigations at Michigan State University, University of Michigan, and The Ohio State University. All three of these cases involve athletic department team physicians, and all involve hundreds of victims. The Michigan State case involved a team doctor who was also a physician for dozens of Olympic gymnasts. He was convicted of multiple counts of sexual abuse in three separate cases and is serving sentences amounting to life without parole. The university settled with more than 300 victims for $500 million. The Department of Education fined the university $4.5 million for its violations of Title IX and the Clery Act. The Michigan and Ohio State cases have also been settled by the universities with regard to most of the victims.

In 2021, the DOE under the Biden Administration engaged in its own review of the regulations and has since proposed revisions entitled *Nondiscrimination on the Basis of Sex in Education Programs or Activities Receiving Federal Financial Assistance* (87 FR 41,390 (July 12, 2022). This proposal contains numerous significant changes, including:

- A broader definition of sexual harassment triggering application of the regulations
    - Defined as unwelcome sex-based conduct that is *sufficiently severe or pervasive* that based on totality of the circumstances, subjectively and objectively, denies or limits a person's ability to participate in or benefit from the educational program or activity.
    - As noted above, the current regulations are triggered only when the conduct is severe and pervasive *and* objectively offensive.
- The option to include a right for cross-examination, except for schools in the Sixth Circuit.
- Schools may opt for a single investigator model where one individual is both the investigator and the decision maker.
- The preponderance of the evidence standard would be required, unless a school uses the clear and convincing standard for all comparable processes.
- A broader group of institutional employees would be mandatory reporters of instances of inappropriate conduct.
- The current requirement for a live hearing is removed.
- Increased protection for LGBTQ students and students who are pregnant.
- Off-campus and international conduct would be covered to a greater degree than under the current regulations.
- More individuals subject to the training requirements.
- Increased opportunities for informal resolution.

Final regulations are anticipated to be issued by summer of 2023.

4. Title IX and Gender Identity

The Supreme Court has held that sex-based discrimination can also include unfavorable treatment on the basis of sexual orientation, gender identity, and intersex traits. *Bostock v. Clayton County*, 140 U.S. S. Ct. 7131, 1741, 590 U.S. ____ (2020) (analyzing discrimination under Title VII of the Civil Rights Act of 1964, 42 U.S.C. 2000e, *et. seq.*). In 2021, the OCR issued a memorandum stating that

Title IX similarly protects against discrimination on the basis of gender identity and sexual orientation. Yet the policies for the rights of transathletes to participate in sport, particularly in the female category, vary significantly by sport, level, and state. In 2021, Penn swimmer Lia Thomas, a transwoman, won at the NCAA swimming championships after having met then NCAA requirements of at least one year of testosterone suppressing treatments. Her participation was challenged in a complaint lodged by "Concerned Women for America." In 2022, the NCAA issued an updated transgender athlete policy calling for participation to be determined by the national governing body for that sport. International swimming federation (FINA) regulations, for example, require that transwomen be prohibited unless having undergone hormone suppressing treatment before puberty. Nearly twenty states have passed laws restricting transathletes from competing in female category sports. At the Olympic level, international sport federations also have varied regulations on trans participation.

D. Employment Discrimination

The materials in the prior sections have focused on the claims of participants under the Federal Constitution and Title IX. The focus in this section shifts to coaches and claims they may have under appropriate circumstances under Title IX, the Equal Pay Act of 1963 (29 U.S.C. § 206(d)), and Title VII of the Civil Rights Act of 1964 (42 U.S.C. § 2000e *et seq.*).

Problem

Bernie Johnson was hired as women's basketball coach at Eastern Oklanois University, a public institution that is a Division I member of the NCAA. After about 18 months on the job he began to have discussions with the athletic director about the manner in which his program, and women's athletics in general, was being treated. He believed the university was in violation of Title IX and said so. The Athletic Director told him to concentrate on his job as coach, citing a 4–21 record the previous season and the fact that the team was about to begin a new season that did not look promising.

During the second season Johnson continued to complain about unequal treatment for his team, even at times making such comments to the press. He also complained about the compensation differential that existed between his contract and the coach of the men's team at Eastern Oklanois. Following that season, in which the team struggled to a 9–16 record, the school informed him that his contract would not be renewed. Johnson has come to you seeking advice as to whether he has any legal recourse. What questions will you ask him? What information do you need? What will be your advice?

Stanley v. University of Southern California

178 F.3d 1069 (9th Cir. 1999), *cert. denied*, 528 U.S. 1022 (1999)

Hug, Chief Judge:

Appellant Marianne Stanley appeals from the district court's order granting summary judgment in favor of defendants University of Southern California and Michael Garrett on Stanley's claims of discrimination and breach of employment contract.

Factual and Procedural Background

Marianne Stanley was hired as head coach of the women's basketball team for the University of Southern California ("USC") in 1989. Her initial contract, signed in July of that year, was for a four-year term, expiring June 30, 1993. The contract provided that she would make a base salary of $60,000 per year. This base salary was increased to $62,000 per year in 1992. The women's basketball program at USC enjoyed much success during Stanley's tenure.

Defendant Michael Garrett is the Athletic Director at USC. On April 20, 1993, two months prior to the expiration of Stanley's contract, Stanley and Garrett had an initial meeting to negotiate a new contract. The parties disagree over what took place at this meeting. Stanley contends that on that date she entered into a contract for a salary equivalent to that of George Raveling, the USC men's basketball coach. It is undisputed that Garrett expressly stated that USC could not pay her that salary, but that he would make her a formal offer in writing shortly after that meeting.

On April 27, 1993, Garrett offered Stanley, in writing, a three-year contract providing $80,000 in year one, $90,000 in year two, and $100,000 in year three, with a $6,000 per year housing allowance for each of the three years. The parties met again on May 27, 1993, at which point Garrett claims that Stanley rejected the April 27 offer because she insisted that her compensation should be equivalent to Raveling's. Stanley argues that she never rejected this offer, but simply disagreed as to the amount of compensation, because the April 27 offer was inconsistent with the April 20 offer—for Raveling's salary level—that she already had accepted.

On June 7, 1993, Stanley proposed a three-year contract providing $96,000 per year for the first eighteen months, and a salary equivalent to that of Raveling for the remainder of the term. Garrett rejected this offer. Stanley then retained an attorney who, on June 18, 1993, proposed to Garrett a three-year contract with an automatic two-year renewal provision, and total compensation of $88,000 for year one, $97,000 for year two, and $112,000 for year three, plus additional incentives. Garrett rejected this offer and withdrew the April 27 offer.

On June 21, 1993, Garrett sent to Stanley's attorney a written offer for a one-year contract for $96,000. Stanley's existing contract expired on June 30, 1993, but Stanley continued to perform her duties. On July 13, while on a recruiting trip,

Stanley asked Garrett if he would still offer her a multi-year contract. He indicated that his June 21 one-year contract offer was USC's final offer, and that Stanley would have to accept or reject it by the end of the day. Stanley did not respond, but sent a memo to Garrett on July 14 requesting additional time to consider the offer. On July 15 Garrett revoked the offer, informed Stanley that he was seeking a new coach for the team, and requested that Stanley perform no further services for USC.

On August 30, 1993, the district court denied the motion for preliminary injunction, and Stanley appealed. This court affirmed the denial of the preliminary injunction in an opinion filed January 6, 1994. *Stanley v. University of Southern California*, 13 F.3d 1313 (9th Cir. 1994) ("*Stanley I*"). Between September 1993 and February 1994, Stanley amended her complaint several times, and defendants' motions to dismiss were granted as to several claims. Stanley's Third Amended Complaint alleges the following causes of action: (1) violation of the Equal Pay Act, 29 U.S.C. § 206(d)(1) and California Fair Employment and Housing Act ("FEHA"); (2) violation of Article I, § 8 of the California Constitution; (3) violation of Title IX of the Civil Rights Act of 1972, 20 U.S.C. § 1681; (4) retaliation; (5) wrongful discharge in violation of public policy; (6) breach of express contract; (7) breach of implied-in-fact contract; and (8) breach of implied covenant of good faith and fair dealing. Stanley sought reinstatement, declaratory relief, injunctive relief preventing USC from further discriminating against her, back pay, three million dollars in compensatory damages, and five million dollars in punitive damages.

On October 17, 1994, defendants filed a motion for summary judgment. After Stanley was allowed additional time to conduct discovery, on March 10, 1995, the district court granted summary judgment for USC and Garrett. This appeal followed.

Discussion

I. Discrimination Claims

A. Equal Pay Act Claim

The Equal Pay Act provides in relevant part:

> No employer having employees subject to any provisions of this section shall discriminate, within any establishment in which such employees are employed, between employees on the basis of sex by paying wages to employees... at a rate less than the rate at which he pays wages to employees of the opposite sex in such establishment for equal work on jobs the performance of which requires equal skill, effort, and responsibility, and which are performed under similar working conditions....

29 U.S.C. § 206(d)(1).

In an Equal Pay Act case, the plaintiff has the burden of establishing a prima facie case of discrimination by showing that employees of the opposite sex were paid different wages for equal work. The prima facie case is limited to a comparison of the jobs in question, and does not involve a comparison of the individuals who hold the jobs.... To make out a prima facie case, the plaintiff bears the burden of showing that the jobs being compared are "substantially equal." ... Significantly, under the Act, the plaintiff need not demonstrate that the jobs in question are identical; she must show only that the jobs are substantially equal.

Circuit courts employ a two-step "substantially equal" analysis in Equal Pay Act cases. In *Brobst v. Columbus Srvs. Int'l*, 761 F.2d 148 (3d Cir. 1985), the Third Circuit described this approach, writing that "the crucial finding on the equal work issue is whether the jobs to be compared have a 'common core' of tasks, i.e., whether a significant portion of the two jobs is identical." When a plaintiff establishes such a "common core of tasks," the court must then determine whether any additional tasks, incumbent on one job but not the other, make the two jobs "substantially different."

Here, we may assume that the men's and women's coaching jobs share a common core of tasks. Garrett—U.S.C.'s athletic director and a defendant in this case—has acknowledged that the women's and men's coaches "have the same basic responsibilities" with regard to recruiting athletes and administering the basketball programs. In his declaration, Garrett also stated:

> Both the women's and men's head basketball coaches have the following general duties and responsibilities: basketball program; coaching and discipline of team members; general supervision over the personal and academic lives of the student athletes; and supervision over assistant coaches, part-time coaches and other athletic department personnel involved in the women's and men's basketball programs.

The parties are in serious dispute, however, as to whether the additional responsibilities borne by the men's coach, but not by the women's coach, suffice to make the two jobs "substantially different." The defendants point out that the men's coach bears greater revenue generating responsibilities, that he is under greater media and spectator pressure to produce a winning program, and that he actually generates more revenue for the University.

Stanley claims that the differences between the two jobs are attributable to previous gender-based decisions on the part of the University. Essentially, Stanley claims that the differences between the two jobs result from the University's historically disparate treatment of male and female teams; namely, its decisions to invest in and promote the men's program more than the women's program. She then claims that because the differences between the jobs derive from previous gender-based decisions on the part of the University, the differences cannot be relied on to determine that the jobs are "substantially different."

The University, on the other hand, argues that the differences between the two jobs are not attributable to anything it has done or failed to do in the past. According to USC, the reason that women's basketball does not generate the same amount of revenue as men's basketball, and that the women's coach is not under the same pressure as the men's coach, is that there simply is not a sufficient spectator or media market for women's basketball games. Accordingly, it contends that the differences in responsibilities in the two jobs legitimately suffice to make them "substantially different."

A defendant may rebut a prima facie case by showing that the disparity in pay is a "differential based on any... factor other than sex." 29 U.S.C. § 206(d)(1). Defendants here assert an affirmative defense (that is, a nondiscriminatory reason for the pay differential) based on Stanley and Raveling's markedly disparate levels of experience and qualifications. The record convincingly supports their claim. When Raveling began coaching at U.S.C., he had thirty-one years of coaching experience. He had been the coach of the men's Olympic basketball team. He had been *twice* named national coach of the year, and *twice* named PAC-10 coach of the year. On top of his coaching experience, Raveling also had nine years of marketing and promotional experience, and was the author of several books on basketball. When Stanley started coaching at U.S.C., three years after Raveling became head coach of the men's team, she had seventeen years of experience coaching basketball, or *fourteen years less experience* than Raveling. She never coached an Olympic team. She had no marketing or promotional experience other than that she gained as a coach. She had never published a book about basketball.

Coaches with substantially more experience and significantly superior qualifications may, of course, be paid more than their less experienced and qualified counterparts, even when it is the male coach who has the greater level of experience and qualifications. By alleging that the pay differential at issue here was due to Stanley and Raveling's markedly different levels of experience and qualifications, the defendants have proffered a factor "other than sex," to explain the difference in pay.

Where the defendant demonstrates that a pay differential was based on a factor other than sex, the employee may prevail by showing that the employer's proffered nondiscriminatory reason is a "pretext for discrimination." On this appeal, Stanley bears the burden of demonstrating a material fact regarding pretext in order to survive summary judgment.

Stanley's pretext argument, however, fails to meet even this minimal burden.

In the end, therefore, we are left with these *undisputed* facts: Stanley had far less relevant experience and qualifications than Raveling. She had fourteen years less experience as a basketball coach. She, unlike Raveling, never coached the Olympic team. She had no marketing experience outside coaching. She had never written any books on basketball. Accordingly, Stanley has failed to raise a genuine issue of fact as to Raveling's markedly "superior experience," and qualifications. *EEOC Notice* at 23. In short, she has failed to raise a genuine issue of fact as to the University's non-discriminatory reason for paying Raveling a higher salary.

Accordingly, we affirm the district court's decision to grant the defendants' motion for summary judgment on the Equal Pay Act claim.

[The court then rejected Stanley's arguments based on California statutes, Title IX and retaliation. It also upheld the district court's granting of summary judgment on several contractual claims. The court further affirmed the lower court's ruling on recusal of the trial judge. The court did find the district court had abused its discretion in awarding excessive costs to the defendants and remanded the case for re-taxing of costs.]

PREGERSON, dissenting:

By focusing on the differences between Stanley's and Raveling's qualifications, the majority skips over the many ways in which gender discrimination insidiously affected the University's treatment of the women's basketball program and Stanley as its Head Coach. The University's half-hearted promotion of the women's basketball program, its intensive marketing of the men's basketball program, and the formidable obstacles Stanley faced as a woman athlete in a male-dominated profession contributed to this disparate treatment.

It is hard for me to square these realities with the majority's ruling denying Stanley relief without a trial.

Therefore, I dissent.

Bowers v. Baylor University

862 F. Supp. 142 (W.D. Tex. 1994)

WALTER S. SMITH, JR.

I. Background

Plaintiff, Pam Bowers ("Bowers"), was hired by Baylor University ("Baylor") to coach its women's basketball team in 1979. In 1989, Bowers began to complain about the disparate allocation of resources in the men's and women's basketball programs, including but not limited to the disparate terms and conditions of her employment versus the terms and conditions of employment by and between Baylor and the men's basketball coach. Her first contact with the Office of Civil Rights of the Department of Education was in March of 1989, and Baylor was aware of plaintiff's complaints at or about the same time.

Bowers' employment was initially terminated by Baylor in 1993. Bowers alleges that the termination was premised on alleged violations of NCAA and Southwest Conference rules, and that her win-loss record was not even mentioned. After her termination, Bowers filed a complaint with the Office of Civil Rights and the Equal

Employment Opportunity Commission. Immediately after filing the complaint, Bowers was notified that she would be reinstated (1) on the same terms under which she had been employed the previous 14 years, or (2) on a two year written contract. Bowers alleges that she was forced to accept the first offer because the terms of the written contract were vague and ambiguous and Baylor refused to discuss them.

Despite her reinstatement, Bowers continued to pursue her employment complaints with the federal agencies. In an employment evaluation of August 30, 1993, Bowers' win-loss record was mentioned, and she was informed that she needed to achieve a winning season. On or about March 28, 1994, Bowers was notified in writing that her employment would be terminated as of May 31, 1994 because of her unsuccessful win-loss record throughout her employment at Baylor.

Bowers' claims are asserted exclusively under Title IX of the Education Amendments of 1972. 20 U.S.C. §§ 1681–88. She contends that Baylor and various members of its administration violated Title IX by discriminating against her on the basis of sex and by retaliating against her for challenging Baylor's allegedly discriminatory conduct.

Bowers seeks a declaratory judgment that Baylor's practices were unlawful, a permanent injunction to restrain further discrimination, a mandatory injunction to reinstate her as Baylor's head women's basketball coach, back pay and benefits, compensatory damages of $1 million, and punitive damages in excess of $3 million. Bowers' claims are not based upon an express remedy found in Title IX, but rather on a theory that she has an implied cause of action under Title IX.

III. Discussion

A. Baylor's Motion

Baylor believes that Bowers' Title IX claims should be dismissed for lack of subject matter jurisdiction and for failure to state a claim for which relief can be granted. Specifically, Baylor argues that Title IX does not provide employees such as Bowers with a private cause of action for damages. Bowers disagrees, and believes that Supreme Court precedent, although not directly on point, dictates that this motion be denied.

Title IX does not expressly authorize an employee to file a private suit for damages. In fact, Title IX contains no mention of employees or employment discrimination at all. Likewise, Title IX contains no mention of damages and no mention of lawsuits to be brought by private citizens.

The Supreme Court was first confronted with the issue of whether a private cause of action was implicit in Title IX in *Cannon v. University of Chicago*, 441 U.S. 677 (1979). In that case, a university student brought suit alleging that she had been excluded from the medical education program on the basis of her gender. The district court dismissed her case, holding that the proper remedy was loss of federal funds by the institution. The Supreme Court disagreed, and after analyzing the four factors of *Cort v. Ash*, 422 U.S. 66 (1975), held that the female student could maintain her lawsuit despite the absence of any express authorization for it in Title IX.[2]

Over the dissenting voices of three justices, the Supreme Court went one step further in *Franklin v. Gwinnett County Public Schools*, 112 S. Ct. 1028, 117 L. Ed. 2d 208 (1992). In *Franklin*, a female high school student brought suit against her school district under Title IX because she had been subjected to sexual harassment by a male coach at the school. The district court dismissed the case on the ground that Title IX does not authorize an award of monetary damages. The Supreme Court reversed, and held that not only did Title IX create an implied cause of action for the plaintiff, as the Court had recognized in *Cannon*, but it also authorized monetary damages as a remedy.

Neither the Fifth Circuit Court of Appeals nor the Supreme Court has directly addressed the issue of whether an employee of a school receiving federal funds has a private cause of action for damages under Title IX.

The Supreme Court first analyzed the broad directive in Title IX that "no person" may be discriminated against on the basis of gender, and held that employees who directly participate in federal programs or who directly benefit from federal grants, loans, or contracts clearly fall within Title IX. *North Haven Board of Education* at 520. The Court stated:

> Because [Title IX] neither expressly nor impliedly excludes employees from its reach, we should interpret the provision as covering and protecting these 'persons' unless other considerations counsel to the contrary. After all, Congress easily could have substituted 'student' or 'beneficiary' for the word 'person' if it had wished to restrict the scope of [Title IX].

Id. at 521. Based upon these three Supreme Court decisions, this Court is of the opinion that a private cause of action for damages under Title IX does exist in this case, and Baylor's Motion to Dismiss should be denied. Baylor's brief is quite thorough in its discussion to the contrary, and is similar to Supreme Court dissents in the above cases. While this Court and a minority of Supreme Court justices might agree with Baylor's reasoning, current precedent dictates a ruling in favor of the plaintiff. The Supreme Court's approval of the regulations in *North Haven Board*

---

2. The four factors that a court must analyze to determine whether Congress intended a statute to create a remedy for a specific class of persons was set forth in *Cort*. These factors are:

> (a) whether the statute was enacted for the benefit of a special class of which the plaintiff is a member;
>
> (b) whether there is any indication of legislative intent to create a private remedy;
>
> (c) whether implication of such a remedy is consistent with the underlying purposes of the legislative scheme; and
>
> (d) whether implying a federal remedy is inappropriate because the subject matter involves an area basically of concern to the States.

Cort at 78.

of Education, and the Supreme Court's decisions in *Cannon* and *Franklin*, lead this Court to the conclusion that the Supreme Court would take the next logical step of recognizing Bowers' cause of action under Title IX.

B. Individual Defendant's Motion

[The court granted the individual defendants' motion to dismiss, holding that Title IX does not permit claims against individual employees of institutions.]

IV. Conclusion

Based upon the foregoing, the Court is of the opinion that the plaintiff has alleged a cause of action under Title IX against Baylor University, but has failed to state a cause of action against the individual defendants. Accordingly, it is

ORDERED that the Motion of Defendant Baylor University to Dismiss Plaintiff's Claims is DENIED.

Notes and Comments

1. The position taken by the court in *Bowers* was affirmed by the Supreme Court in *Jackson v. Birmingham Bd. of Education*, 544 U.S. 167 (2005) (coach fired because of complaints he lodged against a school regarding gender equity violations has a cause of action for retaliation pursuant to Title IX).

2. *See Bartges v. University of North Carolina, Charlotte*, 908 F. Supp. 1312 (W.D.N.C. 1995), in which the court focuses on both Title VII and Title IX claims surrounding the dismissal of a coach who had raised concerns about gender discrimination in the athletic program. *See also Clay v. Board of Trustees of Neosho Cty. Community College*, 905 F. Supp. 1488 (D. Kan. 1995).

3. *Deli v. University of Minnesota*, 863 F. Supp. 958 (D. Minn. 1994), raises equal pay issues under both Title VII and Title IX. The court determined that the plaintiff female coach of the women's gymnastics team had failed to demonstrate that her position was substantially equal to the positions of coaches of men's teams. It also held that Title VII and the Equal Pay Act do not prohibit salary discrimination based on the gender of athletes being coached. See also *Miller v. Bd. of Regents of Univ. of Minn*, 2018 WL 659851 (D. Minn. 2018) in which the court rejected a claim under the EPA by the former head coach of a Division I women's ice hockey team. The court found that the levels of responsibility for the women's coach and the men's coach were not comparable. Specifically, the court stated that the men's team "attracts vastly more attention, draws vastly higher attendance, and earns vastly more revenue than the women's hockey team" and "the men's hockey coach is under more pressure to win—and has more demands on his time—than the women's hockey coach." However, this was but one argument put forth by the plaintiff. She ultimately prevailed on Title VII discrimination allegations and Title IX retaliation claims and was awarded nearly $2 million. *See also Bedard v. Roger Williams University*, 989 F. Supp.

94 (D.R.I. 1997) (associate athletic director had no cause of action for discrimination pursuant to Title IX when she was terminated).

4. *See also* Terry W. Dodds, *Equal Pay in College Coaching: A Summary of Recent Decisions*, 24 S. Ill. U. L.J. 319 (2000); Michelle R. Weiss, Comment, *Pay Equity for Intercollegiate Coaches: Exploring the EEOC Enforcement Guidelines*, 13 Marq. Sports L. Rev. 149 (2002).

5. Additional cases include *Perdue v. City of New York*, 13 F. Supp. 2d 326 (E.D.N.Y. 1998) (ruling that former women's basketball coach provided substantial evidence to support jury determination of equal pay violation and Title VII intentional discrimination claim, awarded $85,000 in compensatory damages, $135,829 in back pay, and $134,829 in liquidated damages—based on the willfulness finding—pursuant to the EPA, plus attorney's fees and costs provided for by both the EPA and Title VII); and *Lowrey v. Texas A&M University System*, 11 F. Supp. 2d 895 (S.D. Tex. 1998) (denying defendant's motion for summary judgment on female athletic coordinator's retaliation claims under Title VII and Title IX).

Six

League Formation, Governance & Decision-Making

Learning Outcomes

- Learn about the characteristics and organizational structure of professional sport league operations, as well as the various restraints on trade that exist in professional sport leagues.
- Understand how Section 1 and Section 2 of the Sherman Act apply to intra- and inter-league competition.
- Understand the arguments related to the single entity defense and its applicable scope in light of the Supreme Court's ruling in *American Needle.*
- Learn the history of baseball's antitrust exemption.
- Understand the scope of the commissioner's authority and discretionary powers.
- Gain an understanding of how professional sport leagues' rules and decisions, including commissioner decisions, can be challenged by team owners.

Key Terms

- Sherman Act
- Single entity defense
- Curt Flood Act
- Commissioner's "best interests" authority
- Anticompetitive effects
- Procompetitive purposes
- Monopolization
- Monopoly power
- Group licensing

A. Introduction

This chapter considers governance and legal issues arising from the working relations of members of the various professional sports leagues. Essential matters include league membership and operational structure, as well as the myriad business issues arising from stadium/arena arrangements, concessions contracts, various media and broadcasting issues, websites and social media, contracts of coaches and players, merchandising of consumer goods, and marketing through season and group ticket sales, sponsorships, and public relations. A modern phenomenon includes the opportunity to brand the leagues and teams with content provided 24/7 through the use of internet websites, social media, and other digital platforms.

The legal relationships between teams in a professional sport league are conducted according to provisions of governing documents, generally referred to as the league constitution and bylaws. Those documents are joined with the collective bargaining agreement entered between the league and the players association. Professional sport leagues enact many rules and regulations that govern the operation of competition and the business of the sport, and league commissioners resolve disputes involving league members and players. Their operations are subject to three primary areas of federal law: antitrust law (this chapter), labor law (Chapter 7) and intellectual property law (Chapter 11). Sometimes conflict arises between rival leagues, thus necessitating analysis of league governance from an external perspective. The common ground for attack is found in application of the antitrust or competition laws, joined with contract and other theories.

B. Sports League Operations

1. Fundamental Characteristics

a. Market Opportunity

As indicated by the problems and cases below, sports leagues are unique business entities. The teams appear to the average fan as individual firms competing both on and off the field. Many aspects of club operations, however, are conducted jointly with other teams in the league. More importantly, it is the league, not the teams, that generates the fundamental market opportunity to produce professional sports games within each member club's territory. The league transfers to each member club derivative rights in the naked market opportunity, a property interest, to enable the member clubs to gain economic rewards by enhancing the inherent value of the business opportunity through team marketing and other operations.

It is noteworthy that no matter how many professional sports teams were organized independently historically, the clubs gained market opportunities by obtaining them from various leagues. A club could purchase an inaugural or expansion franchise in a league, or an existing franchise from a team owner with league approval. Sometimes teams would merge with a different league to gain the market opportunities. Even if teams form independently to join in creating a league, the market opportunity arises and exists as a league asset, just as does cash from operations and other property. A team cannot play a game without other teams.

The clubs of a league are joined together, and with the league, pursuant to the terms of a constitution and bylaws. Thus, the clubs and the league enjoy a contractual relationship, and, of course, are governed by decisions made by league directors. As you will observe from reading the cases below, the traditional approach of litigants and the resulting judicial scrutiny focuses on contract and tort claims, including fiduciary duties. Plaintiffs have also utilized federal statutory schemes, including the antitrust laws, for the basis of their arguments. Parties rarely discern and debate rights and duties that emanate from the property interests at stake. But the fixed treatment of professional sports entities as business organizations tied only by contract to league operations diverts focus from the basic characteristics of the market opportunity, the core property interest, shared by the league and member teams. Weistart and Lowell, in The Law of Sports 307–08 (1979) [*citing, Metropolitan Base Ball Association v. Simmons*, 1 Pa. County Ct. 134, 17 Phila. 419 (1885)], anticipate the conflict:

> [F]or the purpose of analyzing most private law issues, it can be said that the basic relationship between the clubs within a league is one of contract.... While this sort of contract analysis represents the approach most typically taken to intraleague controversies, the courts have indicated that other principles may be applied in appropriate circumstances. For example, it is often held that membership in an association such as a league gives rise to property interests which are entitled to protection.... This characterization may be particularly apt in the sports context since the league serves a basic business function, and actions of the league may have impact upon a member's access to certain "property" in the form of economic rewards.

Viewing the league-club relationships from the property law perspective generates a distinct approach to recurring legal issues. For example, a question arises whether a team owner has purchased the sticks in the bundle of property rights that enables sale or relocation of the team operations.

b. Tragedy of the Commons Phenomenon

Within the league-club contractual relationship, league constituent members possess distinct duties to protect market opportunities of the league as a whole, as well as protect individual club operations. The inherent opportunity for club owners to place their own team interests above league interests reveals a "tragedy of the commons" phenomenon whereby the pursuit of maximum benefits by individual entities results in a ruination of the whole. The phenomenon is described in the classic writing of Hardin, *Tragedy of the Commons*, 162 Science 1243 (1968). Hardin envisioned a common grazing area utilized by individual animal owners. It is to the benefit of each individual animal owner to introduce an additional animal unit to the commons. But the increased use of the common property resource leads to overgrazing and detriment to all. The tragic result occurs because the individual animal owners did not take into account the costs or benefits to others, including the community, in deciding to increase the grazing burden. The ignored costs or benefits, existing outside the decision-making formula, are referred to as "externalities."

The conflict arises in at least three contexts: the individual team pursuit of players and/or geographic locations or ownership groups that benefit the individual club, but not the long-term interests of the league as a whole. Neglect of the costs and benefits to the league generates an externality problem that leads to market failure. Costs threatening the public good, "fan interest," for example, may arise by loss of competitive balance in the player market. It may also occur by saturation of market support infrastructure, including fan interest, advertising, sponsorship capital, media contracts, and merchandising. League constraints on club relocation, transfer of ownership, and player movement are designed to internalize the external costs in order to prevent the tragedy of partial or total league failure. The tragedy can also arise as a result of inter-league warfare, as is explored at Section E., below.

The "tragedy of the commons" concept is regularly applied in many contexts other than sport leagues. Society utilizes various mechanisms that serve to internalize costs or benefits to avoid the tragedy. Hardin advocated "mutual coercion agreed upon," which suggests regulation and/or consensual arrangements. Hardin, *Tragedy of the Commons*, 162 Sci. 1243 (1968). Demsetz urges the use of property rights to deal with externalities. Demsetz, *Toward a Theory of Property Rights*, 57 J. Amer. Econ. Rev. 347, 348 (1967). Calabresi and Melamed encourage the use of property rights, rules of liability, and the power of eminent domain. Calabresi & Melamed, *Property Rules, Liability Rules and Inalienability: One View of the Cathedral*, 85 Harv. L. Rev. 1089, 1094–95 (1972). Pigou strongly favors the use of taxation as a means of internalizing externalities. Pigou, The Economics of Welfare (1920). Professional sports leagues utilize a combination of the traditional mechanisms to avoid the potential tragedy. *See* McCurdy, *The Fundamental Nature of Professional Sports Leagues, Constituent Clubs, and Mutual Duties to Protect Market Opportunities: Organized Baseball Case Study*, in Kurlantzick, Legal Issues in Professional Baseball 119, 142–166 (2005).

As you work through the problems below, attempt to identify the "common property resources" that are vulnerable to the tragedy in the particular circumstance and the manner in which the league constraints address the potential peril.

c. Uncertainty of Outcome Hypothesis/Competitive Balance

A basic premise in traditional professional sports league models is the "uncertainty of outcome" hypothesis. *See* Rottenberg, *The Baseball Player's Labor Market*, 64 J. Political Econ. 242–258 (1956); Neale, *The Peculiar Economics of Professional Sports*, 78 Q.J. Econ. 1–14 (1964). The theory posits that fan interest will wane in the face of declining competitive balance among teams in a league. Thus, professional sports leagues make great efforts to structure league operations in a manner that is designed to maintain the envisioned balance in opportunity for team success in league play. Professional sports leagues commonly use various regulatory devices in the attempt to generate fan interest:

Amateur Player Draft	Professional Player Draft
Free Agency Rules	Roster Limitations
Salary Cap	Luxury Tax
Signing Period Limitations	Waiver Rules—Priority
Schedule Manipulation	Playoff Structure
Promotion & Relegation	Revenue Sharing

Competitive balance is one of the most extensively and continually analyzed issues in sports economics. Historic analysis focused on the prospect of winning a game on fan attendance, as single-game ticket sales comprised the dominant league revenues. *See, e.g.*, El-Hodiri & Quirk, *An Economic Model of a Professional Sports League*, 79 J. POL. ECON. 1302 (1971). The single-game outcome analysis remains viable today. *See* Fort & Quirk, *Optimal Competitive Balance in Single-Game Ticket Sports*, 11 J. SPORTS ECON. 587–601 (2010). *See also* Davis, *Analyzing the Relationship Between Team Success and MLB Attendance with GARCH Effects*, 10 J. SPORTS ECON. 44–58 (2009).

Other economists offer that it is the probability of winning a championship that drives the fan base. Whitney, *Winning Games Versus Winning Championships: The Economics of Fan Interest and Team Performance*, 26 ECON. INQUIRY 703–24 (1988). Another study analyzes the potential outcome further by examining the (1) short-run uncertainty of the result of an individual game; (2) uncertainty over a season regarding the eventual winners; (3) uncertainty during a season arising from play by teams in contention for a championship; and (4) long-run uncertainty arising from competition not being dominated by a single club. Cairns, Jennett & Sloane, *The Economics of Professional Team Sports: A Survey of Theory & Evidence*, 13 J. ECON. STUDIES 3–80 (1986).

The North American restructure of postseason play to enable the maximum number of teams to compete for a playoff spot reportedly has generated positive effects regarding fan demand. *See* Longley & Lacey, *The "Second" Season: The Effects of Playoff Tournaments on Competitive Balance Outcomes in the NHL and NBA*, 13 J. SPORTS ECON. 471–493 (2012); Lee, *The Impact of Postseason Restructuring on the Competitive Balance and Fan Demand in Major League Baseball*, 10 J. SPORTS ECON. 219–235 (2009).

The development of substantial out of local market broadcast/cable/satellite and digital markets for professional sports league season play and championship series creates different sets of factors for consideration in analyzing the effect of competitive balance. Tainsky, Xu, & Zhou, *Qualifying the Game Uncertainty Effect: A Game-Level Analysis off NFL Postseason Broadcast Ratings*, 15 J. Sports Econ. 219–236 (2012).

Examination of the lack of competitive balance in the Premier League and Champions League (European football—soccer) provides interesting contrast to the North American leagues. Kuper and Szymanski argue that fans prefer unbalanced leagues. Admitting that a game must be significant to draw fans, the authors explain that most fans in the stadium are fans of the home team and desire an unbalanced outcome. Further, dominant teams may create a special interest of their own. Another identified factor arises from the joys of the "David and Goliath" match, *citing* Hirshleifer, *The Paradox of Power*, 3 Eco. & Pol. 177 (1991). The authors recognize from the work of Forrest and Simmons that TV viewers care most about competitive balance, and that most people tend to feel inequality is unfair when it is the result of money. Kuper & Szymanski, Soccernomics 200–212 (2012). The "promotion and relegation" system through which teams are transferred between upper and lower divisions based on performance during the completed season adds meaning and significance to games that are not meaningful for championship purposes. *See* Dobson & Goddard, The Economics of Football (2001).

Yet, a countering theory argues that it is an overlapping mix of motivations that stimulates fan interest, including social and cultural factors over the long-run that result in habit persistence. Downward & Dawson, The Economics of Professional Team Sports 130–56 (2000). Jozsa and Guthrie conclude: "In the business of sports, successful teams create and sustain an illusion so potent and so deeply ingrained in the minds of many fans that after a certain point the attachment of fans becomes involuntary." Jozsa & Guthrie Jr., Relocating Teams & Expanding Leagues in Professional Sports: How the Major Leagues Respond to Market Conditions 136 (1999).

By whatever theory, competitive balance is acknowledged as a public good that is vulnerable to the occurrence of the tragedy of the commons phenomenon. Daly & Moore, *Externalities, Property Rights & the Allocation of Resources in Major League Baseball*, 19 Econ. Inquiry 77 (1981). Unrestricted competition in the market for players can result in domination by strong market clubs. Consequently, fan interest may wane with the attendant reduction in the market support infrastructure for the league as a whole. Other writers make a persuasive argument that the talent that turns an average team into a contender makes a disproportionately large contribution to the team's success. Krautmann & Ciecka, *The Postseason Value of an Elite Player to a Contending Team*, 10 J. Sports Econ. 168–179 (2009). The intense market for star athletes, comprised of "have" and "have-not" clubs, generates an overbidding phenomenon that results in "destructive competition" whereby some participants abandon the market. Whitney, *Bidding Till Bankrupt: Destructive Competition in Professional Team Sports*, 31 Econ. Inquiry 100 (1993). The tragedy occurs due to failure to take into consideration what economists refer to as a "limited positive production network externality." Rascher, *A Test of the Optimal Positive Production Network Externality in Major League Baseball*, in SPORTS ECONOMICS 27 (1999).

The primary scholarly and industry efforts focus upon league devices designed to impede the movement of players from weak market clubs to strong market teams. El-Hodiri and Quirk rely on Rottenberg's pioneering work to conclude that the combination of the reserve clause and amateur draft alone does not inhibit the feared movement of players from weak market teams to strong ones. Where player talent can be bought and sold, the Coase Theorem assures that the assignment of property rights should not alter the allocation of resources. Coase, *The Problem of Social Cost*, 3 J.L. & ECON. 1 (1960). A recurring question concerns the necessary mix of additional devices needed to avoid the inevitable tragedy.

An empirical study of the effects of the draft and reserve clause on league balance in Major League Baseball from 1965 to 1976, however, concluded that the two devices together served as an effective restraint and the traditional views should be reconsidered. Daly & Moore, *id.*, at 94. Other scholars find that the improvement in competitive balance in Major League Baseball is attributable to the size of the talent pool population. Schmidt & Berri, *On the Evolution of Competitive Balance: The Impact of an Increasing Global Search*, 41 ECON. INQUIRY 692, 703 (2003). The effect of free agency on the efforts to assure competitive balance may be debated, although the Coase Theorem suggests there should be no impact. *See* Fishman, *Competitive Balance & Free Agency in Major League Baseball*, 14 DUKE J. ECON. 4 (2002). One writer questions whether the introduction of free agency into the mix has a negative sum effect on the quality of talent within a league, and that the attendant competitive balance is the result of "self-imposed mediocrity." Vrooman, *A General Theory of Professional Sports Leagues*, 61 S. ECON. J. 971, 989 (1995). Andrew Zimbalist compares Major League Baseball's post-1995 competitive imbalance to the period of New York Yankees dominance in the 1950s and early 1960s to determine that "attendance (and revenue) today is more sensitive to team performance than it was 40 and 50 years ago." ZIMBALIST, MAY THE BEST TEAM WIN: BASEBALL ECONOMICS & PUBLIC POLICY 51 (2003). Professor Anzivino uses 18 correlations to calculate that "there is no question that high-payroll teams have a competitive advantage over low-payroll teams. Further, except for the NFL, the advantage is very significant, anticompetitive and unhealthy for the fans and the leagues." Anzivino, *The Correlation Between Team Payroll & Competitive Performance in Professional Sports Leagues*, 22 ENT. & SPORTS LAW. 1 (Summer 2004). Professor Fort concludes that the sharing of gate revenue and national media revenues and the amateur draft do not work to eliminate the competitive imbalance problem, but that a combination of local revenue sharing, luxury tax on payroll, and salary cap can lead to successful results. FORT, SPORTS ECONOMICS 171–72 (2003).

Professors Berri, Schmidt, and Brook, in WAGES OF WINS (2006), conclude that the measurement of competitive balance should focus on outcome in the regular season, not the post-season; competitive balance appears to be dictated primarily by the underlying population of talent, not league policy; and it is not clear whether fans truly care about the level of balance in a league.

2. General Organizational Structure

Each professional sports league possesses a distinct organizational form established by the league's governing documents. Some leagues operate within the typical business corporation structure, and others utilize the nonprofit status for the conduct of league affairs. Other leagues exist as unincorporated associations. Regardless of form, league operations require centralized decision-making. A typical league decision-making structure includes a "board of directors" type committee of owners, joined by a league president or commissioner with varying powers. The NFL, for example, is an unincorporated association, not operated for profit. The NFL Properties, Inc. is the profit-making arm of the League. The NFL Executive Committee includes one representative from each member club and possesses general decision-making powers as provided by the NFL Constitution. The NFL Commissioner is present at meetings of the Executive Committee, and likely wields considerable influence. *See generally* HARRIS, THE LEAGUE: THE RISE AND DECLINE OF THE NFL (1986).

Both the NBA and NHL are also unincorporated associations, with respective commissioners, "Boards of Governors," and separate "Properties" entities. The National League and American League, as noted above, are independent leagues. The two major leagues are joined by the Major League Agreement. The Major League Agreement establishes the Office of the Commissioner. League-wide merchandising efforts are performed by Major League Baseball Properties, Inc.

Each of the minor baseball leagues possesses a constitution and bylaws that delegate decision-making powers to a board of directors and league president. As revealed in the *New Orleans Pelicans* case below, some decisions of minor baseball leagues require interim ratification by the President of the National Association of Professional Baseball Leagues and oversight of the Office of the Commissioner. Professional sports leagues function as private associations. Courts are reluctant to scrutinize actions of private associations, except where the league activities are deemed to lack fundamental fairness or are considered arbitrary and capricious.

Leagues, of course, must conduct the decision process according to the terms of the leagues' governing documents. The law of private associations as applied in amateur sports is discussed above. Courts regularly review league decision-making for compliance with the antitrust laws. The application of the antitrust statutes to amateur sports, including an introduction of the Sherman Act, is addressed in Chapter 4. Most league governing documents, including collective bargaining agreements, provide for arbitration of intra-league disputes.

League directors, sitting as governing board members of the league entity, possess fiduciary duties of care and loyalty. League directors must make decisions for the league as a whole and may not act in their own self-interest to the detriment of the league. League decisions, in order to protect the market opportunity, must make efforts to include all costs, including externalities, in the decision formula to avoid the tragedy of the commons phenomenon. Given that the league has delegated certain autonomous property rights in the league's market opportunity, clubs possess potential conflicts of interest in given situations. As you will observe from the cases and materials below, although the fiduciary relationship is generally recognized, the fiduciary principles are yet to play a significant role in legal challenges to league decision-making.

League governing documents vest general and specific powers in the board of directors as a whole, special committees comprised of board members, and the league president or commissioner. The board exercises delegated legislative power in amending the governing documents and otherwise promulgating or acquiescing in rules and regulations. The executive authority for implementation, administration, and enforcement of league rules established by the governing documents and league regulations may be delegated to the board sitting *en banc* or specially created committees, and/or the president/commissioner. Delegated adjudicatory power may reside in the board as a whole, special committees, and/or the president/commissioner. Any collective bargaining agreement joins with the league governing documents to govern in matters relating to players. Official league actions are traditionally challenged as *ultra vires*, contrary to the terms of governing documents or regulations, and in violation of common law principles and statutes, including the antitrust laws.

C. Legal Limits on Internal League Governance

1. Application of Antitrust Laws

A claim filed pursuant to Section 1 of the Sherman Antitrust Act alleges that two or more parties have entered into an agreement or conspiracy that unreasonably restrains trade in product and geographic markets. A longstanding question concerns whether professional sports leagues are "single entities," thus incapable of conspiracy, or a collection of individual firms that routinely enter into agreements by promulgating rules, administering the executive powers of the league, and adjudicating matters. The argument that professional sports leagues are "single entities" whose internal decisions are not subject to antitrust scrutiny is often based on the U.S. Supreme Court's holding in *Copperweld Corp. v. Independence Tube Corp.*, 467 U.S. 752 (1984), that a parent corporation and its wholly owned subsidiary constituted a single firm for Section 1 purposes.

Major League Soccer (MLS) established a limited liability company that owns all of the teams in the league, intellectual property rights, tickets, equipment, and broadcast rights. MLS establishes league schedules, enters into stadium leases, pays the salaries of referees and league personnel, and has sole responsibility for contracting with and compensating players and assigning the players to designated teams. MLS, however, relinquishes some control over team operations to certain investors who provide management services and operate with some degree of autonomy. In return for the services, MLS pays each operator a "management fee" equaling a share of local ticket receipts and concessions, local broadcast revenues, revenues from overseas tours, MLS Championship Game revenues, and revenues from exhibition games. Remaining revenues are distributed equally to all investors.

In 1997, eight named players sued MLS, the United States Soccer Federation, and the operator/investors, alleging violations of Sections 1 and 2 of the Sherman Antitrust Act (as well as claims under the Clayton Act) resulting from the agreement not to compete for player services. The United States District Court granted the MLS motion for summary judgment, holding that MLS and its investors comprised a single entity and, therefore, could not conspire in violation of Section 1. *Fraser v. Major League Soccer, L.L.C.*, 97 F. Supp. 2d 130 (D. Mass. 2000). The Court of Appeals for the First Circuit, however, rejected the "single entity" rationale, viewing the MLS structure as a "hybrid arrangement, somewhere between a single company… and a cooperative arrangement between existing competitors." It suggested an appropriate "rule of reason" analysis, reshaped toward a body of more flexible rules for interdependent multi-party enterprises. *Fraser v. Major League Soccer, L.L.C.*, 284 F.3d 47 (1st Cir. 2002).

In the next case, the Supreme Court addressed the "single entity" issue in the context of the NFL joint merchandising through NFL Properties.

American Needle, Inc. v. National Football League

560 U.S. 183 (2010)

JUSTICE STEVENS delivered the opinion of the Court.

"Every contract, combination in the form of a trust or otherwise, or, conspiracy, in restraint of trade" is made illegal by § 1 of the Sherman Act. The question whether an arrangement is a contract, combination, or conspiracy is different from and antecedent to the question whether it unreasonably restrains trade. This case raises that antecedent question about the business of the 32 teams in the National Football League (NFL) and a corporate entity that they formed to manage their intellectual property. We conclude that the NFL's licensing activities constitute concerted action that is not categorically beyond the coverage of § 1. The legality of that concerted action must be judged under the Rule of Reason.

Originally organized in 1920, the NFL is an unincorporated association that now includes 32 separately owned professional football teams. Each team has its own name, colors, and logo, and owns related intellectual property. Like each of the other teams in the league, the New Orleans Saints and the Indianapolis Colts, for example, have their own distinctive names, colors, and marks that are well known to millions of sports fans.

Prior to 1963, the teams made their own arrangements for licensing their intellectual property and marketing trademarked items such as caps and jerseys. In 1963, the teams formed National Football League Properties (NFLP) to develop, license, and market their intellectual property. Most, but not all, of the substantial revenues generated by NFLP have either been given to charity or shared equally among the teams. However, the teams are able to and have at times sought to withdraw from this arrangement.

Between 1963 and 2000, NFLP granted nonexclusive licenses to a number of vendors, permitting them to manufacture and sell apparel bearing team insignias. Petitioner, American Needle, Inc., was one of those licensees. In December 2000, the teams voted to authorize NFLP to grant exclusive licenses, and NFLP granted Reebok International Ltd. an exclusive 10-year license to manufacture and sell trademarked headwear for all 32 teams. It thereafter declined to renew American Needle's nonexclusive license.

American Needle filed this action in the Northern District of Illinois, alleging that the agreements between the NFL, its teams, NFLP, and Reebok violated §§ 1 and 2 of the Sherman Act. In their answer to the complaint, the defendants averred that the teams, NFL, and NFLP were incapable of conspiring within the meaning of § 1 "because they are a single economic enterprise, at least with respect to the conduct challenged." After limited discovery, the District Court granted summary judgment on the question "whether, with regard to the facet of their operations respecting exploitation of intellectual property rights, the NFL and its 32 teams are, in the jargon of antitrust law, acting as a single entity." The court concluded "that in that facet of their operations they have so integrated their operations that they should be deemed a single entity rather than joint ventures cooperating for a common purpose."

The Court of Appeals for the Seventh Circuit affirmed. The panel observed that "in some contexts, a league seems more aptly described as a single entity immune from antitrust scrutiny, while in others a league appears to be a joint venture between independently owned teams that is subject to review under § 1." Relying on Circuit precedent, the court limited its inquiry to the particular conduct at issue, licensing of teams' intellectual property. The panel agreed with petitioner that "when making a single-entity determination, courts must examine whether the conduct in question deprives the marketplace of the independent sources of economic control that competition assumes." The court, however, discounted the significance of potential competition among the teams regarding the use of their intellectual property because the teams "can function only as one source of economic power when collectively producing NFL football." The court noted that football itself can only be carried out jointly. ("Asserting that a single football team could produce a football game... is a Zen riddle: Who wins when a football team plays itself"). Moreover,

"NFL teams share a vital economic interest in collectively promoting NFL football… [to] compet[e] with other forms of entertainment." "It thus follows," the court found, "that only one source of economic power controls the promotion of NFL football," and "it makes little sense to assert that each individual team has the authority, if not the responsibility, to promote the jointly produced NFL football." Recognizing that NFL teams have "license[d] their intellectual property collectively" since 1963, the court held that § 1 did not apply.

As the case comes to us, we have only a narrow issue to decide: whether the NFL respondents are capable of engaging in a "contract, combination…, or conspiracy" as defined by § 1 of the Sherman Act, 15 U.S.C. § 1, or, as we have sometimes phrased it, whether the alleged activity by the NFL respondents "must be viewed as that of a single enterprise for purposes of § 1." *Copperweld Corp. v. Independence Tube Corp.*, 467 U.S. 752 (1984).

Taken literally, the applicability of § 1 to "every contract, combination… or conspiracy" could be understood to cover every conceivable agreement, whether it be a group of competing firms fixing prices or a single firm's chief executive telling her subordinate how to price their company's product. But even though, "read literally," § 1 would address "the entire body of private contract," that is not what the statute means.

The meaning of the term "contract, combination… or conspiracy" is informed by the "'basic distinction'" in the Sherman Act "'between concerted and independent action'" that distinguishes § 1 of the Sherman Act from § 2. Section 1 applies only to concerted action that restrains trade. Section 2, by contrast, covers both concerted and independent action, but only if that action "monopolize[s]," U.S.C. § 2, or "threatens actual monopolization,"… a category that is narrower than restraint of trade. Monopoly power may be equally harmful whether it is the product of joint action or individual action.

Congress used this distinction between concerted and independent action to deter anticompetitive conduct and compensate its victims, without chilling vigorous competition through ordinary business operations. The distinction also avoids judicial scrutiny of routine, internal business decisions.

We have long held that concerted action under § 1 does not turn simply on whether the parties involved are legally distinct entities. Instead, we have eschewed such formalistic distinctions in favor of a functional consideration of how the parties involved in the alleged anticompetitive conduct actually operate.

As *Copperweld* exemplifies, "substance, not form, should determine whether a[n]… entity is capable of conspiring under § 1." This inquiry is sometimes described as asking whether the alleged conspirators are a single entity. That is perhaps a misdescription, however, because the question is not whether the defendant is a legally single entity or has a single name; nor is the question whether the parties involved "seem" like one firm or multiple firms in any metaphysical sense. The key is whether the alleged "contract, combination…, or conspiracy" is concerted action—that is, whether it joins together separate decisionmakers. The relevant inquiry, therefore, is whether there is a "contract, combination ... or conspiracy" amongst "separate economic actors pursuing separate economic interests," ... such that the agreement "deprives the marketplace of independent centers of decisionmaking," ... and therefore of "diversity of entrepreneurial interests," ... and thus of actual or potential competition.

Because the inquiry is one of competitive reality, it is not determinative that two parties to an alleged § 1 violation are legally distinct entities. Nor, however, is it determinative that two legally distinct entities have organized themselves under a single umbrella or into a structured joint venture.

The NFL teams do not possess either the unitary decisionmaking quality or the single aggregation of economic power characteristic of independent action. Each of the teams is a substantial, independently owned, and independently managed business. "[T]heir general corporate actions are guided or determined" by "separate corporate consciousnesses," and "[t]heir objectives are" not "common." ... The teams compete with one another, not only on the playing field, but to attract fans, for gate receipts and for contracts with managerial and playing personnel....

Directly relevant to this case, the teams compete in the market for intellectual property. To a firm making hats, the Saints and the Colts are two potentially competing suppliers of valuable trademarks. When each NFL team licenses its intellectual property, it is not pursuing the "common interests of the whole" league but is instead pursuing interests of each "corporation itself," ... teams are acting as "separate economic actors pursuing separate economic interests," and each team therefore is a potential "independent cente[r] of decisionmaking,".... Decisions by NFL teams to license their separately owned trademarks collectively and to only one vendor are decisions that "depriv[e] the marketplace of independent centers of decisionmaking," and therefore of actual or potential competition....

In defense, respondents argue that by forming NFLP, they have formed a single entity, akin to a merger, and market their NFL brands through a single outlet. But it is not dispositive that the teams have organized and own a legally separate entity that centralizes the management of their intellectual property. An ongoing § 1 violation cannot evade § 1 scrutiny simply by giving the ongoing violation a name and label. "Perhaps every agreement and combination in restraint of trade could be so labeled." ...

The NFL respondents may be similar in some sense to a single enterprise that owns several pieces of intellectual property and licenses them jointly, but they are not similar in the relevant functional sense. Although NFL teams have common interests such as promoting the NFL brand, they are still separate, profit-maximizing entities, and their interests in licensing team trademarks are not necessarily aligned.... Common interests in the NFL brand "*partially* unit[e] the economic interests of the parent firms," ... but the teams still have distinct, potentially competing interests.

It may be, as respondents argue, that NFLP "has served as the 'single driver' of the teams" "promotional vehicle," "'pursu[ing] the common interests of the whole.'" … But illegal restraints often are in the common interests of the parties to the restraint, at the expense of those who are not parties. It is true, as respondents describe, that they have for some time marketed their trademarks jointly. But a history of concerted activity does not immunize conduct from § 1 scrutiny. "Absence of actual competition may simply be a manifestation of the anticompetitive agreement itself…."

Respondents argue that nonetheless, as the Court of Appeals held, they constitute a single entity because without their cooperation, there would be no NFL football. It is true that "the clubs that make up a professional sports league are not completely independent economic competitors, as they depend upon a degree of cooperation for economic survival." … But the Court of Appeals' reasoning is unpersuasive.

The justification for cooperation is not relevant to whether that cooperation is concerted or independent action. A "contract, combination… or conspiracy," § 1, that is necessary or useful to a joint venture is still a "contract, combination… or conspiracy" if it "deprives the marketplace of independent centers of decisionmaking," *Copperweld*, 467 U.S., at 769, 104 S. Ct. 2731. See *NCAA*, 468 U.S., at 113, 104 S. Ct. 2948 ("[J]oint ventures have no immunity from antitrust laws"). Any joint venture involves multiple sources of economic power cooperating to produce a product. And for many such ventures, the participation of others is necessary. But that does not mean that necessity of cooperation transforms concerted action into independent action; a nut and a bolt can only operate together, but an agreement between nut and bolt manufacturers is still subject to § 1 analysis. Nor does it mean that once a group of firms agree to produce a joint product, cooperation amongst those firms must be treated as independent conduct. The mere fact that the teams operate jointly in some sense does not mean that they are immune.

The question whether NFLP decisions can constitute concerted activity covered by § 1 is closer than whether decisions made directly by the 32 teams are covered by § 1. This is so both because NFLP is a separate corporation with its own management and because the record indicates that most of the revenues generated by NFLP are shared by the teams on an equal basis. Nevertheless we think it clear that for the same reasons the 32 teams' conduct is covered by § 1, NFLP's actions also are subject to § 1, at least with regards to its marketing of property owned by the separate teams. NFLP's licensing decisions are made by the 32 potential competitors, and each of them actually owns its share of the jointly managed assets…. Apart from their agreement to cooperate in exploiting those assets, including their decisions as the NFLP, there would be nothing to prevent each of the teams from making its own market decisions relating to purchases of apparel and headwear, to the sale of such items, and to the granting of licenses to use its trademarks.

We generally treat agreements within a single firm as independent action on the presumption that the components of the firm will act to maximize the firm's profits. But in rare cases, that presumption does not hold. Agreements made within a firm can constitute concerted action covered by § 1 when the parties to the agreement act on interests separate from those of the firm itself, and the intrafirm agreements may simply be a formalistic shell for ongoing concerted action....

For that reason, decisions by the NFLP regarding the teams' separately owned intellectual property constitute concerted action. Thirty-two teams operating independently through the vehicle of the NFLP are not like the components of a single firm that act to maximize the firm's profits. The teams remain separately controlled, potential competitors with economic interests that are distinct from NFLP's financial well-being.... Unlike typical decisions by corporate shareholders, NFLP licensing decisions effectively require the assent of more than a mere majority of shareholders. And each team's decision reflects not only an interest in NFLP's profits but also an interest in the team's individual profits.... The 32 teams capture individual economic benefits separate and apart from NFLP profits as a result of the decisions they make for the NFLP. NFLP's decisions thus affect each team's profits from licensing its own intellectual property. "Although the business interests of" the teams "will *often* coincide with those of the" NFLP "as an entity in itself, that commonality of interest exists in every cartel...."

Football teams that need to cooperate are not trapped by antitrust law. "[T]he special characteristics of this industry may provide a justification" for many kinds of agreements.... The fact that NFL teams share an interest in making the entire league successful and profitable, and that they must cooperate in the production and scheduling of games, provides a perfectly sensible justification for making a host of collective decisions. But the conduct at issue in this case is still concerted activity under the Sherman Act that is subject to § 1 analysis.

Other features of the NFL may also save agreements amongst the teams. We have recognized, for example, "that the interest in maintaining a competitive balance" among "athletic teams is legitimate and important," While that same interest applies to the teams in the NFL, it does not justify treating them as a single entity for § 1 purposes when it comes to the marketing of the teams' individually owned intellectual property. It is, however, unquestionably an interest that may well justify a variety of collective decisions made by the teams. What role it properly plays in applying the Rule of Reason to the allegations in this case is a matter to be considered on remand.

Accordingly, the judgment of the Court of Appeals is reversed, and the case is remanded for further proceedings consistent with this opinion.

It is so ordered.

Notes and Comments

1. The *American Needle v. NFL* case on remand was reported as settled in February 2015. The U. S. District Court had previously denied the NFL's Motion for Summary Judgment, concluding that "American Needle has presented [sufficient] evidence that shortly following the execution of the exclusive agreement between

Reebok and NFL Properties, wholesale prices of licensed hats rose by a significant degree while output of those items dropped." *American Needle, Inc. v. New Orleans Saints et al.*, No. 04-cv-7806, 2014 U.S. Dist. LEXIS 47527 N.D. Ill. Apr. 2014).

2. *Deutscher Tennis Bund v. ATP Tour, Inc.*, 610 F.3d 820 (3d Cir. 2010), was the first case decided regarding the single entity issue after the U.S. Supreme Court's opinion in *American Needle.* The ATP (7-member Board of Directors) adopted changes to its Brave New World Plan, which included a downgrade of the Hamburg, Germany, Tournament from first tier to second tier (the Hamburg Tournament had been first tier from 1990 to 2009). The Hamburg Tournament Owners and the German and Qatar Tennis Federations filed suit against ATP alleging the Brave New World Plan and resulting demotion of the Hamburg Tournament violated Sections 1 and 2 of the Sherman Antitrust Act. The ATP contended that the Hamburg Tournament was demoted due to lack of investment, decrease in attendance, unfavorable weather, and decline of interest in tennis in Germany. The ATP also argued it was a single entity under *Copperweld.* The Third Circuit affirmed the trial court jury verdict that the plaintiffs did not prove the ATP "entered into any contract(s), combination(s), or conspiracy(ies) with any separate entity or entities" and, therefore, the ATP's single entity defense was not addressed by the court. For a comprehensive review of the *Deutscher Tennis Bund* litigation, see Rodenberg & Hauptman, *American Needle's Progeny? Tennis and Antitrust*, 2 Pace Intell. Prop. Sports & Ent. L.F. 103 (2012).

3. Does the *Deutscher Tennis Bund* decision permit individual sports leagues to control tournament sanctioning, tournament scheduling, ranking points, and broadcasting and merchandising rights? *See* Gibson, *The Association of Tennis Professionals: From Player Association to Governing Body*, J. Applied Bus. Econ., *available at* http://www.na-businesspress.com/JABE/Jabe105/GibsonWeb.pdf (Answers in the affirmative). The Court in *American Needle* recognizes the legitimacy of the argument that special characteristics of leagues and the need for competitive balance are justifications for "many kinds of agreements." Thus, the Court noted when "restraints on competition are essential if the product is to be available at all," *per se* rules of illegality are inapplicable, and instead the restraint must be judged according to the flexible Rule of Reason. Similarly, as we learned in Chapter 4, courts do not apply a *per se* rule to NCAA restraints in large part out of recognition that a certain degree of cooperation is necessary if the type of competition that the NCAA and its member institutions seek to market is to be preserved.

4. For the opinion of one court recognizing a possibility that the NBA could be understood as "one firm," see *Chicago Professional Sports Limited Partnership v. National Basketball Association*, 1996 U.S. Dist. LEXIS 1525 (N.D. Ill. Feb. 13, 1996) ("single entity" issue remanded to U.S. District Court).

5. In *City of Mt. Pleasant v. Associated Elec. Coop., Inc.*, 838 F.2d 268 (8th Cir. 1988), the court affirmed a grant of summary judgment, concluding that a collective of separately owned and operated electric power utilities constituted a single economic enterprise for Section 1 purposes. The members of the Mt. Pleasant coopera-

tive, like the NFL teams, were separately owned. The NFL clubs, however, are more closely integrated in some respects than the coop members. Although the NFL clubs set individual ticket prices, as the coop members set individual power rates, the members of the league share at least 80 to 90% of their revenues and equalize many of their expenses. The NFL clubs have also jointly entered into a collective bargaining agreement with the players' union that establishes minimum salaries and salary cap. The members of the coop are linked together by supply contracts, while the NFL clubs are contractually linked pursuant to the NFL Constitution and Bylaws. Whereas the coop members generally compete among themselves for customers, only the NFL teams located in the same community compete for live fans. *See* NFL Brief at 549 PLI/Pat 665, 668 (Feb.–Mar. 1999).

6. The United States Court of Appeals for the Fourth Circuit relied on the *Copperweld* analysis to affirm a trial court determination that the PGA and member sections were "single entities," and legally incapable of conspiracy. *Seabury Management, Inc. v. Professional Golfers' Association of America, Inc.*, 52 F.3d 322 (4th Cir. 1995) (unpublished disposition), *aff'g in part and rev'g in part, Seabury Management, Inc. v. PGA*, 878 F. Supp. 771 (D. Md. 1994). The U.S. District Court stated:

> While the MAPGA is not a wholly-owned subsidiary of the PGA and these entities are separately incorporated, the evidence at trial established that as pertinent to this case the PGA and its member sections function as a single economic unit with the PGA possessing ultimate control over the actions of individual sections.
>
> The Court finds it significant that the sections are governed by the PGA Constitution, by policies adopted either at PGA annual meetings or by the PGA Board of Directors, and by other pertinent policy documents, such as trademark licensing agreements. *Id.* at 777.

7. The United States Supreme Court, in *American Needle,* distinguishes *Copperweld* and states the question as whether the agreement joins together "separate economic actors pursuing separate economic interests," not the "common interests of the whole." Can you make an argument that league membership and relocation decisions reflect the "common interest of the whole"?

8. In a case challenging the pooling arrangement of Major League Baseball Properties, the court held that plaintiff did not adequately provide evidence of an adverse impact on competition within a relevant market. *Major League Baseball Properties, Inc. v. Salvino*, 542 F.3d 290 (2d Cir. 2008).

Problem

A group of investors plans to initiate a professional rugby league that is comprised of teams in the United States and other countries. The league will invite participation from an elite group of existing clubs currently operating in the United States and other countries in various leagues and federations. Only the world-class clubs will be accepted, although the group expects many teams around the world to apply. The group desires to structure league operations as a "single entity." It also wants to maintain competitive balance among the teams in the league, utilizing the traditional mechanisms. The league will not jointly market team logo merchandise, as commonly done in other professional leagues, but will sell exclusive league-wide sponsorships. Consider the following:

1. Is it legally possible to construct a professional sports league as a "single entity" in light of the *American Needle* case?
2. Can a professional sports league exist as a single entity for some purposes and not for others?
3. Describe any test or criteria presented in *American Needle* that may be utilized to determine whether a professional sports league is properly structured as a single entity.
4. Whether envisioned competition should be structured as a series of tournaments rather than set up as a traditional sports league in order to exist as a "single entity."

2. The Baseball Antitrust Exemption

The historical baseball antitrust exemption emanates from Justice Holmes' opinion in *Federal Baseball Club v. National League*, 259 U.S. 200 (1922). The National League, formed in 1876, successfully countered economic opposition from competing leagues during the 1800s, including the American Association (1881), Union Association (1884), and the Players' League (1889). In 1901, the Western League, a minor league, moved into Cleveland, a city recently abandoned by the National League, and several east coast cities. The Western League proclaimed itself the American League and began to raid National League rosters. After fierce litigation and economic battle, the National and American Leagues joined together in the National Agreement in 1903, to protect the respective rosters and other common interests.

In 1913, the Federal League formed and attempted to sign professional players in both the American and National Leagues. After the 1915 season, the American and National Leagues agreed to pay a sizable sum of money to the Federal League owners for a dissolution of the league and enabled some Federal League members to purchase American or National League franchises. The Baltimore club of the Federal League filed a lawsuit alleging the parties to the agreement conspired to monopolize the baseball business in violation of the Sherman Act. The Supreme Court ruled that baseball was not subject to the reach of the antitrust laws but was merely the business of "giving exhibitions of baseball, which are purely state affairs," and was "not a subject of commerce."

As indicated in the 1972 *Flood* opinion below, baseball maintained its judicially recognized exemption from the antitrust laws despite judicial challenges and intense congressional scrutiny during the 1950s, 60s, and 70s. During the same period, the Supreme Court declined to extend the exemption to other sports, such as football, boxing, and basketball. In *Flood*, the Court reaffirmed the exemption, although noting that baseball is a business and is engaged in interstate commerce. As you read the opinion, try to answer why the Court reaffirmed the historical baseball antitrust exemption. Also, focus on how the Court addresses the nature and scope of the historical baseball antitrust exemption. Should the exemption be limited to the "reserve clause," or should it extend to the "business of baseball"? What are the limits of a "business of baseball" definition?

Flood v. Kuhn

407 U.S. 258 (1972)

Mr. Justice Blackmun delivered the opinion of the Court.

For the third time in 50 years the Court is asked specifically to rule that professional baseball's reserve system is within the reach of the federal antitrust laws....

The petitioner, Curtis Charles Flood, born in 1938, began his major league career in 1956 when he signed a contract with the Cincinnati Reds for a salary of $4,000 for the season. He had no attorney or agent to advise him on that occasion. He was traded to the St. Louis Cardinals before the 1958 season. Flood rose to fame as a center fielder with the Cardinals during the years 1958–1969. In those 12 seasons he compiled a batting average of .293. His best offensive season was 1967 when he achieved .335. He was .301 or better in six of the 12 St. Louis years. He participated in the 1964, 1967, and 1968 World Series. He played errorless ball in the field in 1966, and once enjoyed 223 consecutive errorless games. Flood has received seven Golden Glove Awards. He was co-captain of his team from 1965–1969. He ranks among the 10 major league out-fielders possessing the highest lifetime fielding averages.

But at the age of 31, in October 1969, Flood was traded to the Philadelphia Phillies of the National League in a multi-player transaction. He was not consulted about the trade. He was informed by telephone and received formal notice only after the deal had been consummated. In December he complained to the Commissioner of Baseball and asked that he be made a free agent and be placed at liberty to strike his own bargain with any other major league team. His request was denied.

Flood then instituted this antitrust suit in January 1970 in federal court for the Southern District of New York. The defendants (although not all were named in each cause of action) were the Commissioner of Baseball, the presidents of two major leagues, and the 24 major league clubs. In general, the complaint charged violations of the federal antitrust laws and civil rights statutes, violation of state statutes and the common law, and the imposition of a form of peonage and involuntary servitude contrary to the Thirteenth Amendment and 42 U.S.C. § 1994. Petitioner sought declaratory and injunctive relief and treble damages.

Flood declined to play for Philadelphia in 1970, despite a $100,000 salary offer, and he sat out the year. After the season was concluded, Philadelphia sold its rights to Flood to the Washington Senators. Washington and the petitioner were able to come to terms for 1971 at a salary of $110,000. Flood started the season but, apparently because he was dissatisfied with his performance, he left the Washington club on April 27, early in the campaign. He has not played baseball since then....

[The trial court judge] held that *Federal Baseball Club v. National League*, 259 U.S. 200 (1922), and *Toolson v. New York Yankees, Inc.*, 346 U.S. 356 (1953), were controlling; that it was not necessary to reach the issue whether exemption from the antitrust laws would result because aspects of baseball now are a subject of collective bargaining;.... [The trial court judge] included a statement of personal conviction to the effect that "negotiations could produce an accommodation on the reserve system which would be eminently fair and equitable to all concerned" and that "the reserve clause can be fashioned so as to find acceptance by player and club."

On appeal, the Second Circuit felt "compelled to affirm." ...

We granted certiorari in order to look once again at this troublesome and unusual situation.

... It seems appropriate now to say that:

1. Professional baseball is a business and it is engaged in interstate commerce.

2. With its reserve system enjoying exemption from the federal antitrust laws, baseball is, in a very distinct sense, an exception and an anomaly. *Federal Baseball* and *Toolson* have become an aberration confined to baseball.

3. Even though others might regard this as "unrealistic, inconsistent, or illogical," the aberration is an established one, and one that has been recognized not only in *Federal Baseball* and *Toolson*, but in *Shubert, International Boxing*, and *Radovich*, as well, a total of five consecutive cases in this Court. It is an aberration that has been with us now for half a century, one heretofore deemed fully entitled to the benefit of *stare decisis*, and one that has survived the Court's expanding concept of interstate commerce. It rests on a recognition and an acceptance of baseball's unique characteristics and needs.

4. Other professional sports operating interstate—football, boxing, basketball, and, presumably, hockey and golf—are not so exempt.

5. The advent of radio and television, with their consequent increased coverage and additional revenues, has not occasioned an overruling of *Federal Baseball* and *Toolson*.

6. The Court has emphasized that since 1922 baseball, with full and continuing congressional awareness, has been allowed to develop and to expand unhindered

by federal legislative action. Remedial legislation has been introduced repeatedly in Congress but none has ever been enacted. The Court, accordingly, has concluded that Congress as yet has had no intention to subject baseball's reserve system to the reach of the antitrust statutes. This, obviously, has been deemed to be something other than mere congressional silence and passivity.

7. The Court has expressed concern about the confusion and the retroactivity problems that inevitably would result with a judicial overturning of *Federal Baseball*. It has voiced a preference that if any change is to be made, it come by legislative action that, by its nature, is only prospective in operation.

8. The Court noted in *Radovich* that the slate with respect to baseball is not clean. Indeed, it has not been clean for half a century.

This emphasis and this concern are still with us. We continue to be loath, 50 years after *Federal Baseball* and almost two decades after *Toolson*, to overturn those cases judicially when Congress, by its positive inaction, has allowed those decisions to stand for so long and, far beyond mere inference and implication, has clearly evinced a desire not to disapprove them legislatively.

Accordingly, we adhere once again to *Federal Baseball* and *Toolson* and to their application to professional baseball. We adhere also to *International Boxing* and *Radovich* and to their respective applications to professional boxing and professional football. If there is any inconsistency or illogic in all this, it is an inconsistency and illogic of long standing that is to be remedied by the Congress and not by this Court. If we were to act otherwise, we would be withdrawing from the conclusion as to congressional intent made in *Toolson* and from the concerns as to retrospectivity therein expressed. Under these circumstances, there is merit in consistency even though some might claim that beneath that consistency is a layer of inconsistency.

The conclusion we have reached makes it unnecessary for us to consider the respondents' additional argument that the reserve system is a mandatory subject of collective bargaining and that federal labor policy therefore exempts the reserve system from the operation of federal antitrust laws.

We repeat for this case what was said in *Toolson*:

> "Without re-examination of the underlying issues, the [judgment] below [is] affirmed on the authority of *Federal Baseball Club of Baltimore v. National League of Professional Baseball Clubs, supra*, so far as that decision determines that Congress had no intention of including the business of baseball within the scope of the federal antitrust laws."

And what the Court said in *Federal Baseball* in 1922 and what it said in *Toolson* in 1953, we say again here in 1972: the remedy, if any is indicated, is for congressional, and not judicial, action.

The judgment of the Court of Appeals is AFFIRMED....

Mr. Justice Marshall, with whom Mr. Justice Brennan joins, dissenting.

This is a difficult case because we are torn between the principle of *stare decisis* and the knowledge that the decisions in *Federal Baseball* (1922), and *Toolson* (1953), are totally at odds with more recent and better reasoned cases.

The importance of the antitrust laws to every citizen must not be minimized. They are as important to baseball players as they are to football players, lawyers, doctors, or members of any other class of workers. Baseball players cannot be denied the benefits of competition merely because club owners view other economic interests as being more important, unless Congress says so.

Has Congress acquiesced in our decisions in *Federal Baseball Club* and *Toolson?* I think not. Had the Court been consistent and treated all sports in the same way baseball was treated, Congress might have become concerned enough to take action. But, the Court was inconsistent, and baseball was isolated and distinguished from all other sports. In *Toolson* the Court refused to act because Congress had been silent. But the Court may have read too much into this legislative inaction.

To the extent that there is concern over any reliance interests that club owners may assert, they can be satisfied by making our decision prospective only. Baseball should be covered by the antitrust laws beginning with this case and henceforth, unless Congress decides otherwise.

Accordingly, I would overrule *Federal Baseball Club* and *Toolson* and reverse the decision of the Court of Appeals.

The Curt Flood Act of 1998

In late 1998, both houses of Congress unanimously passed the Curt Flood Act of 1998 and forwarded the bill for presidential signature. The Act is the only congressional legislation relating to the historical baseball antitrust exemption recognized by the United States Supreme Court in 1922. Both the Major League Baseball Players Association and Major League Baseball encouraged Congress to seek removal of the exemption as it relates to major league labor matters. Removal of the exemption in this context enables major league baseball players to enjoy the same rights under antitrust laws as do other professional athletes.

The original bill, S. 53, was introduced by Senator Hatch to amend the Clayton Act (15 U.S.C. § 12 *et seq.*) to extend application of the antitrust laws to major league baseball. It specifically provided that the amendment shall not be construed to affect the applicability or nonapplicability to the amateur draft, the minor league reserve clause, the Professional Baseball Agreement between the major and minor leagues, other minor league matters, any restraint by professional baseball on franchise relocation, and the application of the Sports Broadcasting Act of 1961. The National Association of Professional Baseball Leagues (NAPBL), the minor league umbrella organization, quickly became involved in the debate. The NAPBL desired to protect its 17 leagues and 175 clubs located in the United States from ancillary impact resulting from the loosely worded bill. The Curt Flood Act of 1998 states that "the conduct, acts, practices, or agreements of persons in the business of organized professional major league baseball directly relating to or affecting employment of major league baseball players to play baseball at the major league level are subject to the antitrust laws to the same extent such conduct, acts, practices, or agreements would be subject to the antitrust laws if engaged in by persons in any other professional sports business affecting interstate commerce." 15 U.S.C. § 27(a). The Act further provides that it does not extend the reach of the antitrust laws to baseball matters not relating to major league employment. The activities include minor league employment, and both major and minor league non-labor activities.

Modern Scrutiny of the Exemption

Events of the past years generated from time to time a renewed focus upon the traditionally recognized baseball antitrust exemption. The Major League Baseball strike of 1994 compelled Congress to reexamine the validity and scope of the exemption. The recurring relocation of NFL clubs from existing cities and publicly owned facilities to competing locations further motivated Congress to consider the exemption during the 1995 and 1996 sessions. Interestingly, in the latter instance, congressional committees contemplated the creation of an express exemption similar to that of baseball enabling the NFL, NBA, and other professional sports leagues to prevent the movement of a club from one city to another. Congress returned to focus on the exemption as a result of Major League Baseball's contemplated "contraction" of the Minnesota Twins and Montreal Expos in 2001, and the concurrent labor negotiations that resulted in a collective bargaining agreement.

More recently, the City of San Jose challenged the baseball antitrust exemption in an attempt to utilize the antitrust laws to confront MLB's failure to approve a relocation of the Oakland A's to the city. Thus, the nature, scope, and appropriateness of the baseball antitrust exemption continues as a significant sports law debate after the passage of the Curt Flood Act of 1998.

City of San Jose v. Office of the Commissioner

776 F.3d 686 (9th Cir. 2015)

KOZINSKI, J.

The City of San Jose steps up to the plate to challenge the baseball industry's 92-year old exemption from the antitrust laws. It joins the long line of litigants that have sought to overturn one of federal law's most enduring anomalies.

Major League Baseball's (MLB) constitution requires that each of the league's 30 member clubs play their home games within a designated operating territory. For the Oakland Athletics, that territory is comprised of two California counties: Alameda and Contra Costa. Faced with dwindling attendance and revenue, the

Athletics want to move to San Jose, which they consider a more profitable venue. But there's a snag: San Jose falls within the exclusive operating territory of the San Francisco Giants, and relocation to another franchise's territory is prohibited unless approved by at least three-quarters of MLB's clubs.

MLB has not rushed to grant this approval. In 2009, MLB established a "Special Relocation Committee" to investigate the implications of the move for the league, but four years later the committee was "still at work," with no resolution in sight. In the meantime, the Athletics moved forward with their plan to build a stadium in San Jose by entering into an option agreement with the city that gave them the right to purchase six parcels of land the city had set aside. But, because MLB hadn't yet approved the move, the Athletics were unable to perform on the agreement, and the land sat idle.

Believing that the delay was MLB's attempt to stymie the relocation and preserve the Giant's local monopoly, San Jose filed suit. It alleged violations of state and federal antitrust laws, of California's consumer protection statute and of California tort law. Relying on the baseball industry's historic exemption from the antitrust laws, the district court granted MLB's motion to dismiss on all but the tort claims. San Jose appeals, arguing that the baseball exemption does not apply to antitrust claims relating to franchise relocation. We review *de novo*....

Our analysis is governed by three Supreme Court cases decided over the course of half a century: taken together, they set the scope of baseball's exemption from the antitrust laws. *See generally*, Stuart Banner, *The Baseball Trust: A History of Baseball's Antitrust Exemption* (2013)....

Flood and its progenitors... upheld the baseball exemption for two fundamental reasons: (1) fidelity to the principle of stare decisis and the concomitant aversion to disturbing reliance interests created by the exemption; and (2) Congress' apparent acquiescence in the holdings of *Federal Baseball* and *Toolson*.

San Jose first argues that *Flood* applies only to baseball's "reserve clause"—the particular provision at issue in that case—and not to other facets of the baseball industry, like franchise relocation. In other words, San Jose urges that we limit *Flood* to its facts. Such a drastic limitation on *Flood*'s scope is foreclosed by our precedent. Under the baseball exemption, we have rejected an antitrust claim that was wholly unrelated to the reserve clause. *See Portland Baseball Club, Inc. v. Kuhn*, 491 F.2d 1101, 1103 (9th Cir. 1974). In *Portland Baseball*, a former minor league franchise owner bought suit against MLB. The owner argued that MLB failed to comply with the terms of an agreement it struck with minor league teams to provide compensation in the event a major league franchise moved into a minor league franchise's territory.... One of the plaintiff's claims was that MLB's monopolization of the baseball industry rendered minor league teams unable to negotiate on fair terms.... Even though the antitrust claim in *Portland Baseball* had nothing to do with the reserve clause, we cited *Flood* in upholding the claim's dismissal....

San Jose next contends that if we are to hold that the baseball exemption extends beyond the reserve clause, we must remand to the district court to determine whether franchise relocation is sufficiently related to "baseball's unique characteristics and needs" to warrant exemption. This argument appears to be derived from a single sentence in *Flood*, which states that the baseball exemption "rests on a recognition and acceptance of baseball's unique characteristics and needs." ... From this line alone, San Jose argues that the *Flood* Court intended a fact-sensitive inquiry whenever the antitrust exemption is challenged. But, aside from the isolated language San Jose quotes, nothing in *Flood* suggests that the reserve clause was exempted based on some fact-sensitive analysis of the role the clause played within the baseball industry.

Rather, *Flood*'s stare decisis and congressional acquiescence rationales suggest the Court intended the exemption to have the same scope as the exemption established in *Federal Baseball* and *Toolson*. After all, it would make little sense for *Flood* to have contracted (or expanded) the exemption from the one established in the cases in which Congress acquiesced and which generated reliance interests. And, *Federal Baseball* and *Toolson* clearly extend the baseball exemption to the entire "business of providing public baseball games for profit between clubs of professional baseball players." ...

It is undisputed that restrictions on franchise relocation relate to the "business of providing public baseball games for profit between clubs of professional baseball players." ... The designation of franchises to particular geographic territories is the league's basic organizing principle. Limitations on franchise relocation are designed to ensure access to baseball games for a broad range of markets and to safeguard the profitability—and thus viability—of each ball club. Interfering with franchise relocation rules therefore indisputably interferes with the public exhibition of professional baseball....

That doesn't necessarily mean all antitrust suits that touch on the baseball industry are barred. In *Twin City Sportservice, Inc. v. Charles O. Finley & Co., Inc.*, 512 F.2d 1264 (9th Cir. 1975), for example, we assessed an antitrust claim by a baseball franchise against stadium concessionaires without any reference to the baseball exemption. Nor does it mean that MLB or its franchises are immune from antitrust suit. There might be activities that MLB and its franchises engage in that are wholly collateral to the public display of baseball games, and for which antitrust liability may therefore attach. But San Jose does not—and cannot—allege that franchise relocation is such an activity. To the contrary, few, if any, issues are as central to a sports league's proper functioning as its rules regarding the geographic designation of franchises.

Flood's congressional acquiescence rationale applies with special force to franchise relocation. In 1998, Congress passed the Curt Flood Act, which withdrew baseball's antitrust exemption with respect to the reserve clause and other labor issues, but explicitly *maintained* it for franchise relocation.... ("This section does not create, permit or imply a cause of action by which to challenge under the antitrust laws, or otherwise apply the antitrust laws to... franchise location or relocation")....

The exclusion of franchise relocation from the Curt Flood Act demonstrates that Congress (1) was aware of the possibility that the baseball exemption could apply to franchise relocation; (2) declined to alter the status quo with respect to relocation; and (3) had sufficient will to overturn the exemption in other areas. *Flood's* clear implication is that the scope of the baseball exemption is coextensive with the degree of congressional acquiescence, and the case for congressional acquiescence with respect to franchise relocation is in fact far stronger than it was for the reserve clause at issue in *Flood* itself.

In short, antitrust claims against MLB's franchise relocation policies are in the heartland of those precluded by *Flood's* rationale. San Jose's claims under the Sherman and Clayton Acts must accordingly be dismissed.

Like Casey, San Jose has struck out here....

AFFIRMED.

Notes and Comments

1. An important judicially-created exemption from the application of the antitrust laws, that applies to all league sports that have labor unions, is the "non-statutory labor exemption." The United States Supreme Court in *Brown v. Pro Football, Inc.*, 518 U.S. 231 (1996) (in Chapter 7, labor relations), holds that the "non-statutory labor exemption" compels organized labor to rely on the labor laws, not the antitrust laws, in bargaining even after expiration of a collective bargaining agreement and past impasse in negotiations. Also, the Sports Broadcasting Act of 1961 exempts joint television broadcasting agreements from the reach of the antitrust laws. 15 U.S.C. Sections 1291–1295.

2. Interestingly, economists have long recognized the peculiar workings of markets in the professional sports area that result in monopoly leagues. *See, e.g.*, Neale, *The Peculiar Economics of Professional* Sports, 78 QUARTERLY J. ECON. 1–14 (1964). A traditional professional sports league model concludes that the player contract reserve clause and amateur draft do not inhibit the feared movement of players to the highest bidders. *See* Rottenberg, *The Baseball Player's Labor Market*, 64 J. POL. ECON. 242, 255 (1956). Thus, where players can be bought and sold, league constraints will not necessarily deter movement of players from weak to strong markets.

3. The case of *Piazza v. Major League Baseball*, 831 F. Supp. 420 (E.D. Pa. 1993), holding that the baseball antitrust exemption was limited to the reserve clause as a result of the application of the English Rule of *Stare Decisis*, was followed in two Florida court decisions, *Butterworth v. National League of Prof'l Baseball Clubs*, 644 So. 2d 1021 (Fla. 1994), *aff'd*, *Major League Baseball v. Crist*, 331 F.3d 1177 (11th Cir.

2003), and *Morsani v. Major League Baseball*, 663 So. 2d 653 (Fla. Dist. Ct. App. 1995), but rejected in *Major League Baseball v. Butterworth*, 181 F. Supp. 2d 1316 (N.D. Fla. 2001) ("The Court determined that the decision whether to terminate baseball's antitrust exemption should be made by Congress, not by the Court.... The Court's rationale remains every bit as valid today as it was when *Flood* was decided."), and *Minnesota Twins Partnership v. State by Hatch*, 592 N.W.2d 847 (Minn. 1999) ("*Piazza* ignores what is clear about *Flood*—that the Supreme Court had no intention of overruling *Federal Baseball* or *Toolson*...."). *See also Major League Baseball v. Crist*, 331 F.3d 1177 (11th Cir. 2003) ("Lest there be any doubt about the matter, the district court forcefully destroyed the notion that the antitrust exemption should be narrowly cabined to the reserve system."). For a commentary describing the "flawed analysis" of *Piazza*, see Scibilia, *Baseball Franchise Stability and Consumer Welfare: An Argument for Reaffirming Baseball's Antitrust Exemption with Regard to Its Franchise Relocation Rules*, 6 SETON HALL J. SPORT L. 409 (1996).

4. The *Piazza* court's application of the English Rule of "*result stare decisis*" rather than the American system of "*rule stare decisis*" to limit the exemption to the reserve clause was seemingly made in error. *See Salerno v. American League of Professional Baseball Clubs*, 429 F.2d 1003 (2d. Cir. 1970) (overruling of Supreme Court holdings is the exclusive privilege of the Supreme Court).

5. The *Flood* Court had 50 years of antitrust and commercial law development to aid its analysis. The national perspective changed drastically during the 50-year period between *Federal Baseball Club* and *Flood*. One aspect of the inquiry that had not changed was "baseball's unique characteristics and needs, the point seized upon by the City of San Jose in its challenge to the exemption" *See generally* Abrams, *The Curt Flood Act: Before the Flood: The History of Baseball's Antitrust Exemption*, 9 MARQ. SPORTS L.J. 307 (1999).

6. The court in *City of San Jose* rejected Plaintiff's argument that MLB club relocation decisions were not included in "baseball's unique characteristics and needs" as expressed by the U.S. Supreme Court in *Flood*. Is the *San Jose* court correct in concluding that the U.S. Supreme Court in *Flood* did not limit the precedential scope of *Federal Baseball* and *Toolson* to the reserve clause? What is the rationale of the *Flood* Court's adherence to *Toolson*? Did the Supreme Court, in *Flood*, recognize the doctrine of "reliance" as an alternative rationale for the 1953 *Toolson* case? *Compare* the Court's statement in *Radovich*:

> Vast efforts had gone into the development and organization of baseball since that [Federal Baseball] decision and enormous capital had been invested in reliance on its permanence. Congress had chosen to make no change. All this, combined with the flood of litigation that would follow its repudiation, the harassment that would ensue, and the retroactive effect of such a decision, led the Court to the practical result that it should sustain the unequivocal line of authority reaching over many years.

Radovich v. National Football League, 352 U.S. 445, 450–51 (1957).

7. The existence of the minor leagues distinguishes organized baseball from other professional sports. Do the "business of baseball" or "reserve clause" definitions of the exemption encompass the minor leagues, or the hierarchy of agreements forming the structure of the minor leagues?

The long-standing contractual relationship between the minor leagues and Major League Baseball is unique to professional baseball, although professional hockey has developed a similar structure and the NBA has organized its development league. Contemporaneously with and subsequent to the *Federal Baseball* decision in 1922, the major and minor leagues constructed a more than 75-year contractual relationship to develop players of major league quality and provide baseball entertainment for fans in North America. Branch Rickey, in 1921, began to successively develop the farm system approach to player development (others, including the Cleveland Indians, had tried it before). Commissioner Landis initially opposed the farm system. Necessities over time moved the minor leagues from a position of relative independence in 1921 to a state of dependence on major league sharing of expenses in modern times. Without the antitrust exemption, the farm system of "organized baseball" is subject to attack under the Sherman and Clayton Acts. The baseball antitrust exemption enabled investment in the minor league system by major league clubs, minor leagues and clubs, and minor league communities to develop unhindered by challenges under the antitrust laws and costs of litigation.

8. Courts have consistently held that the baseball antitrust exemption is applicable to cases involving minor league baseball. *See, e.g., Miranda v. Selig*, 860 F.3d 1237 (9th Cir. 2017) (citing Curt Flood Act enumerated protection of Minor League Baseball); *Triple-A Baseball Club Assoc. v. Northeastern Baseball, Inc.*, 832 F.2d 214 (1st Cir. 1987); *Professional Baseball Schools & Clubs, Inc. v. Kuhn*, 693 F.2d 1085 (11th Cir. 1982); *Portland Baseball Club v. Kuhn*, 491 F.2d 1101 (9th Cir. 1974); *New Orleans Pelicans Baseball, Inc. v. National Association of Professional Baseball Leagues, Inc.*, 1994 U.S. Dist. LEXIS 21468 (E.D. La. Mar. 2, 1994). The congressional testimony of "Bud" Selig and Stan Brand, as well as others throughout the years, affirms that some minor league business operations will fail in the event the antitrust exemption is removed. *Testimony of Allan H. "Bud" Selig, President of the Milwaukee Brewers Baseball Club and Chair of the Major League Executive Council*, before the Economic and Commercial Law Subcommittee of the Committee on the Judiciary, U.S. House of Representatives, Sept. 22, 1994; *Testimony of Stanley M. Brand, Vice-President, National Association of Professional Baseball Leagues, Inc.*, before the Subcommittee on Labor-Management Relations of the Committee on Education and Labor, U.S. House of Representatives, Sept. 29, 1994.

9. The fact that Congress had refused to legislatively repeal the baseball antitrust exemption, although given the opportunity, had significant bearing on the *Flood* decision. Congress' passage of the Curt Flood Act of 1998, expressly removing the exemption in the limited area of major league labor relations, provided another op-

portunity to legislatively repeal the exemption in broader areas. Perhaps more importantly, the Curt Flood Act expressly provided that removal of the exemption would not apply to enumerated business and other activities, including "franchise relocation." Should the City of San Jose argument be considered frivolous?

10. Several courts have enunciated limits to the reach of the baseball antitrust exemption. For court rulings holding the exemption does not extend to baseball's contracts for TV broadcasting rights, see *Laumann v. NHL*, 56 F. Supp. 3d 280 (S.D.N.Y. 2014); *Garber v. Office of the Commissioner*, 120 F. Supp. 3d 334 (S.D.N.Y. 2014)] followed by Section H, *infra. See also Henderson Broadcasting Corp. v. Houston Sports Ass'n, Inc.*, 541 F. Supp. 263 (S.D. Tex. 1982) (radio broadcaster challenging cancellation of contract); *Postema v. National League of Professional Baseball Clubs*, 799 F. Supp. 1475 (S.D.N.Y. 1992) (umpires); *Twin City Sportservice, Inc. v. Charles O. Finley*, 365 F. Supp. 235 (N.D. Cal. 1972), *rev'd on other grounds*, 512 F.2d 1264 (9th Cir. 1975) (concessions); *Fleer v. Topps Chewing Gum & Major League Baseball Players Ass'n*, 658 F.2d 139 (3d Cir. 1981) (baseball cards).

11. The baseball antitrust exemption, existing as a matter of federal law, preempts state antitrust law to the contrary. *See Major League Baseball v. Butterworth*, 181 F. Supp. 2d 1316 (N.D. Fla. 2001), *aff'd, Major League Baseball v. Crist*, 331 F.3d 1177 (11th Cir. 2003); *State v. Milwaukee Braves, Inc.*, 144 N.W.2d 1 (Wis. 1966).

12. For arguments that the baseball antitrust exemption results in adverse effects on consumers, see Ross, *The Effect of Baseball's Status as a Legal "Anomaly and Aberration," in* LEGAL ISSUES IN PROFESSIONAL BASEBALL 215 (Kurlantizick ed., 2005). *Compare* Nathanson, *The Irrelevance of Baseball's Antitrust Exemption: A Historical Review*, 58 RUTGERS L. REV. 1 (2005) (baseball antitrust exemption is largely irrelevant to the actual workings of the business of baseball); Ostertag, *Baseball's Antitrust Exemption: Its History and Continuing Importance*, 4 VA. SPORTS & ENT. L.J. 54 (2004) (exemption plays its most important role ever in contributing to the preservation of the overall health of the sport).

3. Challenges to the Commissioner's "Best Interests of the Game" Authority

The commissioners and/or presidents of the various professional sports leagues and federations notoriously possess dominant powers in governing league matters. As the *Finley v. Kuhn* case below reveals, the perceived value of unfettered "commissioner power" arose amidst the chaos generated by the "Black Sox" scandal. The vesting of broad governing authority in a commissioner, however, is not limited to professional baseball. The commissioner of the National Football League possesses similar powers, as do the commissioners of the NBA and other leagues.

The initial source of the commissioner's powers is the league constitution and bylaws. Thus, a dispute concerning the scope of a commissioner's authority requires construction of the intent of league members in drafting and adopting the league constitution. The constitutions and bylaws of most professional sports leagues broadly authorize the commissioners to take discretionary action in the following traditional areas:

1. Approval of player contracts;
2. Resolution of disputes between player and club;
3. Resolution of disputes between clubs;
4. Resolution of disputes between player or club and the league;
5. Disciplinary matters, involving players, clubs, front office personnel, owners, and others; and
6. Rulemaking authority.

Charles O. Finley & Co., Inc. v. Kuhn

569 F.2d 527 (7th Cir. 1978)

SPRECHER, CIRCUIT JUDGE.

The two important questions raised by this appeal are whether the Commissioner of baseball is contractually authorized to disapprove player assignments which he finds to be "not in the best interests of baseball" where neither moral turpitude nor violation of a Major League Rule is involved, and whether the provision in the Major League Agreement whereby the parties agree to waive recourse to the courts is valid and enforceable.

Joe Rudi, Rollie Fingers and Vida Blue were members of the active playing roster of the Oakland A's baseball club and were contractually bound to play for Oakland through the end of the 1976 baseball season. On or about June 15, 1976, Oakland and Blue entered a contract whereby Blue would play for Oakland through the 1979 season, but Rudi and Fingers had not at that time signed contracts for the period beyond the 1976 season.

If Rudi and Fingers had not signed contracts to play with Oakland by the conclusion of the 1976 season, they would at that time have become free agents eligible thereafter to negotiate with any major league club, subject to certain limitations on their right to do so that were then being negotiated by the major league clubs with the Players Association.

On June 14 and 15, 1976, Oakland negotiated tentative agreements to sell the club's contract rights for the services of Rudi and Fingers to the Boston Red Sox for $2 million and for the services of Blue to the New York Yankees for $1.5 million....

The defendant Bowie K. Kuhn is the Commissioner of baseball (Commissioner), having held that position since 1969. On June 18, 1976, the Commissioner disapproved the assignments of the contracts of Rudi, Fingers and Blue to the Red Sox and Yankees "as inconsistent with the best interests of baseball, the integrity of the game and the maintenance of public confidence in it." The Commissioner expressed his concern for (1) the debilitation of the Oakland club, (2) the lessening of the competitive balance of professional baseball through the buying of success by the more affluent clubs, and (3) "the present unsettled circumstances of baseball's reserve system."...

Basic to the underlying suit brought by Oakland and to this appeal is whether the Commissioner of baseball is vested by contract with the authority to disapprove player assignments which he finds to be "not in the best interests of baseball." In assessing the measure and extent of the Commissioner's power and authority, consideration must be given to the circumstances attending the creation of the office of Commissioner, the language employed by the parties in drafting their contractual understanding, changes and amendments adopted from time to time, and the interpretation given by the parties to their contractual language throughout the period of its existence.

Prior to 1921, professional baseball was governed by a three-man National Commission formed in 1903.... Between 1915 and 1921, a series of events and controversies contributed to a growing dissatisfaction with the National Commission....

On September 28, 1920, an indictment issued charging that an effort had been made to "fix" the 1919 World Series by several Chicago White Sox players. Popularly known as the "Black Sox Scandal," this event rocked the game of professional baseball and proved the catalyst that brought about the establishment of a single, neutral Commissioner of baseball.

In November, 1920, the major league club owners unanimously elected federal Judge Kenesaw Mountain Landis as the sole Commissioner of baseball and appointed a committee of owners to draft a charter setting forth the Commissioner's authority. In one of the drafting sessions an attempt was made to place limitations on the Commissioner's authority. Judge Landis responded by refusing to accept the office of Commissioner.

On January 19, 1921, Landis told a meeting of club owners that he had agreed to accept the position upon the clear understanding that the owners had sought "an authority... outside of your own business, and that a part of that authority would be a control over whatever and whomever had to do with baseball." Thereupon, the owners voted unanimously to reject the proposed limitation upon the Commissioner's authority, they all signed what they called the Major League Agreement.... The agreement, a contract between the constituent clubs of the National and American Leagues, is the basic charter under which major league baseball operates.

The Major League Agreement provides that "[t]he functions of the Commissioner shall be... to investigate... any act, transaction or practice... not in the best interests of the national game of Baseball" and "to determine what preventative, remedial or punitive action is appropriate in the premises, and to take such action...." Art. l, Sec. 2(a) and (b).

The Major League Rules, which govern many aspects of the game of baseball, are promulgated by vote of major league club owners. Major League Rule 12(a) provides that "no... [assignment of players] shall be recognized as valid unless... approved by the Commissioner."

The Major Leagues and their constituent clubs severally agreed to be bound by the decisions of the Commissioner and by the discipline imposed by him. They further agreed to "waive such right of recourse to the courts as would otherwise have existed in their favor." Major League Agreement, Art. VII, Sec. 2....

The Commissioner has been given broad power in unambiguous language to investigate any act, transaction or practice not in the best interests of baseball, to determine what preventative, remedial or punitive action is appropriate in the premises, and to take that action. He has also been given the express power to approve or disapprove the assignments of players.... [I]ndicative of the nature of the Commissioner's authority is the provision whereby the parties agree to be bound by his decisions and discipline imposed and to waive recourse to the courts.

The Major League Agreement also provides that "[i]n the case of conduct by Major Leagues, Major League Clubs, officers, employees or players... action by the Commissioner for each offense *may include*" a reprimand, deprivation of a club of representation at joint meetings, suspension or removal of non-players, temporary or permanent ineligibility of players, and a fine not to exceed $5,000 in the case of a league or club and not to exceed $500 in the case of an individual. Art. 1. Sec. 3.

The court concluded that the enumeration does not purport to be exclusive and provides that the Commissioner may act in one of the listed ways without limiting him to those ways.

The court further concluded that the principles of construction that the specific controls the general, or that the expression of some kinds of authority operates to exclude unexpressed kinds, do not apply since the Commissioner is empowered to determine what preventative, remedial or punitive action is appropriate in a particular case and the listed sanctions are punitive only....

[W]e agree with the district court that Section 3 does not purport to limit that authority.

Despite the Commissioner's broad authority... Oakland has attacked the Commissioner's disapproval of the Rudi-Fingers-Blue transactions on a variety of theories which seem to express a similar thrust in differing language.

The complaint alleged that the "action of Kuhn was arbitrary, capricious, unreasonable, discriminatory, directly contrary to historical precedent, baseball tradition, and prior rulings and actions of the Commissioner."...

The plaintiff has argued that it is a fundamental rule of law that the decisions of the head of a private association must be procedurally fair. Plaintiff then argued that it was "procedurally unfair" for the Commissioner to fail to warn the plaintiff that he would "disapprove large cash assignments of star players even if they complied with the Major League Rules."

In the first place it must be recalled that prior to the assignments involved here drastic changes had commenced to occur in the reserve system and in the creation of free agents. In his opinion disapproving the Rudi, Fingers and Blue assignments, the Commissioner said that "while I am of course aware that there have been cash sales of player contracts in the past, there has been no instance in my judgment which had the potential for harm to our game as do these assignments, particularly in the present unsettled circumstances of baseball's reserve system and in the highly competitive circumstances we find in today's sports and entertainment world."

In the second place, baseball cannot be analogized to any other business or even to any other sport or entertainment. Baseball's relation to the federal antitrust laws has been characterized by the Supreme Court as an "exception," an "anomaly" and an "aberration." Baseball's management through a commissioner is equally an exception, anomaly and aberration.... Standards such as the best interests of baseball, the interests of the morale of the players and the honor of the game, or "sportsmanship which accepts the umpire's decision without complaint," are not necessarily familiar to courts and obviously require some expertise in their application. While it is true that professional baseball selected as its first Commissioner a federal judge, it intended only him and not the judiciary as a whole to be its umpire and governor.

As we have seen... the Commissioner was vested with broad authority and that authority was not to be limited in its exercise to situations where Major League Rules or moral turpitude was involved....

During his almost 25 years as Commissioner, Judge Landis found many acts, transactions and practices to be detrimental to the best interests of baseball in situations where neither moral turpitude nor a Major League Rule violation was involved, and he disapproved several player assignments.

On numerous occasions since he became Commissioner of Baseball in February 1969, Kuhn has exercised broad authority under the best interests clause of the Major League Agreement....

On several occasions Charles O. Finley, the principal owner of the plaintiff corporation and the general manager of the Oakland baseball club, has himself espoused that the Commissioner has the authority to exercise broad powers pursuant to the best interests clause, even where there is no violation of the Major League Rules and no moral turpitude is involved.

Oakland relied upon Major League Rule 21, which deals, in Oakland's characterization of it, with "(a) throwing or soliciting the throwing of ball games, (b) bribery by or of players or persons connected with clubs or (c) umpires, (d) betting on ball games, and (e) physical violence and other unsportsmanlike conduct" as indicating the limits of what is "not in the best interests of baseball." However, Rule 21(f) expressly states:

Nothing herein contained shall be construed as exclusively defining or otherwise limiting acts, transactions, practices or conduct not to be in the best interests of Baseball; and any and all other acts, transactions, practices or conduct not to be in the best interests of Baseball are prohibited, and shall be subject to such penalties including permanent ineligibility, as the facts in the particular case may warrant.

... [W]e agree with the district court's finding and conclusion that the Commissioner "acted in good faith, after investigation, consultation and deliberation, in a manner which he determined to be in the best interests of baseball" and that "[w]hether he was right or wrong is beyond the competence and the jurisdiction of this court to decide." ...

The district court granted the defendant's motion for summary judgment as to Count II of the complaint, which sought to establish a violation of the Sherman Antitrust Act. The court said that "Baseball, anomaly of the antitrust law, is not subject to the provisions of that Act." The plaintiff on appeal has argued that any exemption which professional baseball might enjoy from federal antitrust laws applies only to the reserve system.

The Supreme Court has held three times that "the business of baseball" is exempt from the federal antitrust laws.

[I]t appears clear from the entire opinions in the three baseball cases, ... that the Supreme Court intended to exempt the business of baseball, not any particular facet of that business, from the federal antitrust laws....

Although the waiver of recourse clause is generally valid..., we do not believe that it forecloses access to the courts under all circumstances. Thus, the general rule of nonreviewability which governs the actions of private associations is subject to exceptions 1) where the rules, regulations or judgments of the association are in contravention to the laws of the land or in disregard of the charter or bylaws of the association and 2) where the association has failed to follow the basic rudiments of due process of law. Similar exceptions exist for avoiding the requirements of arbitration under the United States Arbitration Act.

We affirm the district court's judgment....

Notes and Comments

1. The scope of the Commissioner's authority is defined by the league constitution and bylaws read *in pari materia* with the collective bargaining agreement. Thus, a common question is whether commissioner actions are *ultra vires*. The commissioner must also follow procedures set forth in the enabling documents. *See National Hockey League Players' Association v. Bettman*, 1994 U.S. Dist. LEXIS 1160 (S.D.N.Y. Feb. 4, 1994); *Atlanta National League Baseball Club, Inc. v. Kuhn*, 432 F. Supp. 1213 (N.D. Ga. 1977) (suspension of owner Ted Turner upheld, but Commissioner's deci-

sion to deprive club of first-round draft choice held to be *ultra* vires). The Commissioner usually possesses broad authority to take unilateral action in governing league matters, including the power to promulgate rules, unless the action involves a mandatory subject of collective bargaining under federal labor law (see Chapter 7). For a case in which imposition of a fine system by the Commissioner constituted an unfair labor practice, see *National Football League Players Association v. NLRB*, 503 F.2d 12 (8th Cir. 1974).

2. League constitutions and bylaws generally vest the Commissioner with adjudicatory authority to arbitrate disputes between clubs. Most league documents provide a procedure for the "protest" of games. Thus, a club may "protest" a game, alleging a violation of league rules. A threshold question concerns the standing of the club to protest. The party protesting the game must follow the procedures set forth in the league constitution. May a team protest a game between two other teams? The Salt Lake Trappers attempted to protest a game between the Butte Copper Kings and Great Falls Dodgers. The question of standing was not reached by the President of the Pioneer Baseball League as the Trappers failed to follow "protest" procedures set forth in the Constitution and Bylaws.

3. After the advent of player associations, the collective bargaining agreement joined with the constitution and bylaws to form the two primary documents defining the scope of commissioner authority. For a discussion of the historical use of the Commissioner's "best interests" authority to discipline players for misconduct, see Karcher, *The Commissioner's Power to Discipline Players for On- and Off-field Misconduct, in* THE OXFORD HANDBOOK OF AMERICAN SPORTS LAW (McCann ed., 2017). The collective bargaining agreement may modify, limit, or otherwise affect the power of the commissioner as established by the league constitution. What alternative dispute resolution model should the players association propose to assure fairness and efficiency in matters that historically have been submitted to the league commissioner for arbitration? The collective bargaining agreement often makes commissioner decisions in disciplinary matters subject to review through an arbitration mechanism. Most collective bargaining agreements, including those in the non-sports industry context, contain a requirement of "just cause" for worker discipline. *In the Matter of Arbitration Between National Basketball Players Association on Behalf of Player Latrell Sprewell and Warriors Basketball Club and National Basketball Association* (Feerick, Arb., Mar. 4, 1998) (arbitrator reduces punishment for workplace violence, reading together the "just cause" and "arbitrary and capricious" provisions of the collective bargaining agreement). For an examination of the power of a commissioner in disciplinary matters and the impact of review through arbitration, see Pollack, *Take My Arbitrator, Please: Commissioner "Best Interests" Disciplinary Authority in Professional Sports*, 67 FORDHAM L. REV. 1645 (1999) (argues that to properly maintain the integrity of professional baseball and basketball, the MLBPA and NBPA should recognize that commissioners need non-reviewable authority to make disciplinary decisions). *See also* Parlow, *Professional Sports League*

Commissioners' Authority and Collective Bargaining, 11 TEX. REV. ENT. & SPORTS L. 179 (2010).

4. Commissioner of Baseball Peter V. Ueberroth and then Commissioner-elect A. Bartlett Giamatti initiated an investigation regarding allegations that Cincinnati Reds Manager Pete Rose wagered on major league baseball games in violation of league rules. Giamatti retained John M. Dowd as Special Counsel for the purpose of conducting an investigation of the matter. On May 9, 1989, Dowd submitted a report to Giamatti summarizing the evidence obtained during the investigation. Commissioner Giamatti scheduled a hearing on the matter for June 26, 1989. Rose responded by filing suit in state court seeking a temporary restraining order and injunction prohibiting Giamatti from conducting the disciplinary proceedings. Rose alleged seven causes of action under state common law, as follows:

1. breach of contract;
2. breach of an implied covenant of good faith and fair dealing;
3. breach of fiduciary duty;
4. promissory estoppel;
5. tortious interference with contract;
6. negligence; and
7. common law of "due process and natural justice."

The crux of the complaint contended that Rose was denied the right to a fair hearing by an unbiased decision maker. The case opinion contains an excellent review of the history of the Commissioner's Office, and the current procedures utilized by the Commissioner. The injunction was continued pending appeal. *Rose v. Giamatti*, 721 F. Supp. 924 (S.D. Ohio 1989). The parties settled the matter without further court action. *See generally* RESTON, COLLISION AT HOMEPLATE (1991). The Dowd Report (Investigation of Pete Rose), which was filed with the Office of the Commissioner, is provided at 68 MISS. L.J. 915 (1999).

5. George Steinbrenner, owner of the New York Yankees, agreed to a lifetime ban from major league baseball as part of a settlement in a case initiated by Commissioner Vincent under Art. I, Sec. 2(a) and (b), Major League Agreement. Steinbrenner allegedly paid gambler Howard Spira $40,000 for information on then Yankee outfielder Dave Winfield. For a case describing the investigation and process utilized by the Office of the Commissioner, see *Steinbrenner v. Esquire Reporting Co.*, 1991 U.S. Dist. LEXIS 7438 (S.D.N.Y. June 3, 1991). George Steinbrenner was again suspended in May 1997, by the executive council, ruling in lieu of a Commissioner, as a result of the Yankee's deal with Adidas and the Yankee's suit filed against MLB. The council prohibited Steinbrenner and the Yankees from participation on all of baseball's governing committees. The suspension did not bar Steinbrenner from running the Yankees.

6. On July 7, 1992, the Chicago Cubs sued Commissioner Vincent, contending the Commissioner exceeded his authority under the Major League Agreement by ordering geographic realignment of the National League divisions. The National League Constitution provides that no club may be realigned without the club's consent.

On March 4, 1992, 10 National League clubs voted to approve realignment of the Chicago Cubs, St. Louis Cardinals, Cincinnati Reds, and Atlanta Braves. The New York Mets and Chicago Cubs voted in the negative, with the Cubs vetoing the change under the National League Constitution. Commissioner Vincent ordered the realignment "in the best interests of baseball," claiming authority under Art. I, Sec. 2, Major League Agreement. Are general Commissioner powers vested under the Major League Agreement paramount to express provisions of the National and American League Constitutions?

The United States District Court granted a temporary injunction prohibiting Commissioner-ordered realignment. The court ruled that Art. VIII of the Major League Agreement limits Commissioner exercise of Art. I power to disputes "other than those whose resolution is expressly provided for by another means in this Agreement, the Major League Rules, the Constitution of either Major League or the Basic Agreement." Art. VIII, Sec. 1. The Commissioner resigned office shortly thereafter, and Major League Baseball did not further challenge the ruling. *Chicago National League Baseball Club, Inc. v. Vincent*, 1992 U.S. Dist. LEXIS 11033 (N.D. Ill. July 24, 1992) (Findings of Fact, Conclusions of Law, and Order withdrawn and vacated; Preliminary Injunction dissolved, Action dismissed, Sept. 24, 1992).

7. In 1994, Major League Baseball club owners restructured the powers of the Commissioner. Article I of the Major League Agreement was modified by the addition of a new Section 5, which made clear that the Commissioner possessed no authority under the best interests of baseball power to intervene in any matter relating to a subject of collective bargaining between the clubs and the Major League Baseball Players Association. The section overturns precedent established by former Commissioners Bowie Kuhn and Peter Ueberroth. The owners, however, amended Article I, Section 2(a) to make the Commissioner the Chair of the Player Relations Committee, the negotiating arm of MLB in labor matters. Thus, the Commissioner is no longer authorized to act unilaterally and independently in labor negotiations but retains an integral position as Chair of the negotiation committee. A new Section 4 was also added to Article I to prohibit the Commissioner from utilizing the best interests of baseball power to resolve issues that are properly resolved by the member clubs pursuant to the Major League Agreement and League Constitutions. An express exception enables the Commissioner to act in cases involving the integrity of, or public confidence in, the national game of baseball. Article V, Section 2(e) was amended to state, "All League specific matters shall be decided by a vote of the Member Clubs of such League pursuant to the League Constitution." Interestingly, no mention is made of the authority of owners to remove the Commissioner from

office, although the dismissal of League Presidents is provided for in a new Article I, Section 10. For the conflicting views of commentators as to the effect of the amendments on the role of the Commissioner, see Arcella, *Major League Baseball's Disempowered Commissioner: Judicial Ramifications of the 1994 Restructuring*, 97 COLUM. L. REV. 2420, 2421 (1997) (Commissioner power curtailed); Reinsdorf, *The Powers of the Commissioner in Baseball*, 7 MARQ. SPORTS L.J. 211, 231–35 (1996) (Commissioner power enhanced).

8. Marge Schott, former owner of the Cincinnati Reds, was suspended on two occasions for making comments considered inappropriate under the "best interests" standard. Can you identify limitations on the power of the Commissioner's Office under the "best interests" standard? Does the Commissioner's authority extend to internal club operations? Should speech, even if "politically incorrect" speech, be protected from sanction? Commissioner discipline of players for speech-related conduct is generally subject to the "just cause" standard. The standard is applied according to the "common law of the workplace," regarding employee discipline for speech, both within and outside the workplace. *See generally* Kurlantzick, *John Rocker and Employee Discipline for Speech*, 16 LAB. LAW. 439 (2001); Gershenfeld, *Discipline and Discharge*, *in* COMMON LAW OF THE WORKPLACE: THE VIEWS OF ARBITRATORS ch. 6 (Antoine ed., 2005). *See also* Fielder, *Keep Your Mouth Shut and Listen: The NFL Player's Right of Free Expression*, 10 U. MIAMI BUS. L. REV. 547 (2002); Dean, *Can the NBA Punish Dennis Rodman? An Analysis of First Amendment Rights in Professional Basketball*, 23 VT. L. REV. 157 (1998).

9. In 2022, Robert Sarver, owner of the NBA Phoenix Suns and WNBA Phoenix Mercury, received a one-year suspension and $10 million fine after a 10-month NBA investigation found he violated workplace standards. According to the investigation, the misconduct included "the use of racially insensitive language, unequal treatment of female employees; sex-related statements and conduct; and harsh treatments of employees that on occasion constituted bullying." He "engaged in instances of inequitable conduct toward female employees, made many sex-related comments in the workplace, made inappropriate comments about the physical appearance of female employees and other women, and on several occasions, engaged in inappropriate physical conduct toward male employees." Eight years earlier, Los Angeles Clippers owner Donald Sterling was caught on tape making racist remarks in April 2014. That led to protests from players and other groups, leading to Sterling's lifetime banishment from the league by NBA Commissioner Adam Silver. Sterling soon after was forced to sell the franchise.

10. Numerous NFL players through the years have been disciplined by the Commissioner for a variety of different situations involving off-field misconduct. Does the "best interests" power of the Commissioner extend to off-field private matters involving players? The NFL's Personal Conduct Policy vests seemingly unfettered power in the Commissioner to issue large fines and suspensions for a broad range of off-the-field behaviors. Should the matter have been the subject of

collective bargaining? *See* Parlow, *Professional Sports League Commissioners' Authority and Collective Bargaining*, 11 TEX. REV. ENT. & SPORTS L. 179 (2010); Marks, *Personal Foul on the National Football League Players Association: How Union Director Gene Upshaw Failed the Union's Members by Not Fighting the Enactment of the Personal Conduct Policy*, 40 CONN. L. REV. 1581 (2008). In 2015, MLB and the MLBPA reached agreement on a collectively-bargained domestic violence policy, which provides that the commissioner decides the appropriate discipline, with no minimum or maximum penalty set forth under the policy, and punishment is not dependent on whether the player was convicted of a crime or pled guilty. MLB players can appeal before a 3-person arbitration panel comprised of a league representative, a players association representative, and an agreed-upon independent arbitrator.

11. WNBA President, Laurel Richie, suspended all-star players Brittney Griner and Glory Johnson seven games each for their actions in a domestic violence incident. The sanction included mandatory counseling. The WNBA regular season consists of 34 games. The suspensions were the longest in league history. Commissioner Richie consulted with various experts in exercising her authority in the matter. She made the elements included in the decision-making and process available to the public, stating that transparency was important for the league and fan support.

Problem

Rob Timmons is a billionaire owner of a club in the Rugby Football League (RFL) and known to most football/soccer fans throughout the nation. He is outspoken on many social issues and plans to run for Congress in the near future. Timmons recently gained national headlines with his interview on ESPN in which he openly criticized the President and the United States' military actions abroad. He stated that he would refuse to stand for the National Anthem until the war ended. He also referred to the majority of his co-owners as "sheep." He inferred that any players or coaches who were not of English ancestry were not mentally competent to make major decisions, on the field or off the field.

Club representatives report that the public, fan-based backlash has swamped the front office with telephone calls and letters objecting to Timmons's statements and the club's continued association with him. Club and RFL sponsors threaten to cancel advertising and other contracts. Civil and human rights organizations have joined in the chorus of protest of Timmons's association with the RFL.

Andrew Cverko, Commissioner of the League, issued a statement condemning Timmons's statements. He has ordered the immediate suspension of Timmons from any team-related executive decisions or duties. Cverko states that he plans to take league action to compel Timmons's forfeiture of the franchise.

The Constitution and Bylaws of the RFL enable the Commissioner to exercise authority, as follows:

Art. 8—The Commissioner shall have full, complete, and final jurisdiction and authority to arbitrate:

a. Any dispute involving two or more members of the League;

b. Any dispute involving players, coaches, and/or other employees and members of the League;

c. Any dispute between a player and any official of the League;

d. Any dispute involving a member of the League or any employees of the members of the League, or any combination thereof, that in the opinion of the Commissioner constitutes conduct detrimental to the best interests of the League and professional rugby.

Art. 9—The Commissioner shall interpret and from time to time establish policy and procedure in respect to the provisions of the Constitution and Bylaws and any enforcement thereof.

Art. 10—The Commissioner is authorized to hire legal counsel and take or adopt appropriate legal action or such other steps as he deems necessary and proper in the best interests of the League and professional rugby, whenever any party not a member of the League, or a member thereof, is guilty of any conduct detrimental either to the League, its member clubs or employees, or to professional rugby.

Art. 11—Whenever the Commissioner, after notice and hearing, decides that an owner, shareholder, player, coach, officer, or other person has either violated the Constitution and Bylaws of the League, or has been or is guilty of conduct detrimental to the welfare of the League or professional rugby, the Commissioner shall have complete authority to:

1. Suspend for a prescribed period of time and/or fine a person in amount not in excess of $5,000.00;
2. Cancel any contract or agreement;
3. Cancel or require forfeiture of any interest in a franchise, with the approval of a majority of owners;
4. Impose other such additional punishment as the Commissioner shall deem appropriate.

Timmons strenuously objects to the suspension, contending that the Constitution does not empower the Commissioner to deprive him of his right to manage his property interest in the club. He points out that he has had no hearing or "due process" in the matter. He loudly declares that neither the Commissioner nor owners have the power to divest him of his franchise.

The RFL Constitution & Bylaws, in Article 23, provides:

a. The owners, sitting as a Board of Directors, shall conduct a hearing concerning the forfeiture of a franchise in the RFL when called upon to do so according to the terms of the Constitution & Bylaws;

b. In the event the Board shall determine that a franchise should forfeit and return to the RFL, such forfeiture shall be immediate, and the divested owner(s) of the franchise shall receive no compensation for the value of the franchise or interests ancillary to the franchise, but may remove all personal property and retain all real property owned by the franchise;

c. In the event the owner of a franchise voluntarily transfers and returns the franchise to the RFL in lieu of forfeiture, the RFL shall sell the franchise to an approved owner pursuant to the terms of the Constitution & Bylaws and transmit the sale proceeds to the former owner(s), less any expenses associated with the transfer and sale, and/or outstanding fines or assessments due the RFL.

You are the Associate Commissioner for the RFL and Commissioner Cverko asks for your opinion regarding the process that is mandated for both the suspension sanction and the envisioned forfeiture of the franchise. He also asks whether you are aware of any legal principles that may limit his discretion in sanctioning Timmons, or in implementing the forfeiture action.

D. League Decision-Making

1. League Membership and Franchise Ownership

Professional sports leagues traditionally restrict membership by and through formal and informal rules requiring approval of franchise sales and further prohibiting certain classes of ownership. The National Football League, for example, requires approval by 3/4 of club owners of all transfers of ownership interests in an NFL club, other than transfers within a family. Although the organizational structure of an NFL member may exist as a sole proprietorship, association, partnership, or corporation, the entity must be organized for purposes of operating a professional football club. The NFL has traditionally respected an uncodified policy barring the sale of ownership interests in an NFL club to the public through offerings of publicly traded stock. *See Sullivan v. National Football League*, 34 F.3d 1091 (1st Cir. 1994).

League approval processes are designed to assure that (1) member club operations are adequately capitalized; (2) *pro forma* budgets are reasonably projected; (3) the new ownership and club are otherwise economically secure; and (4) owners are of sound moral character and otherwise compatible with league members. Approval is required for the sale of clubs by members of the league, and for sale of expansion franchises by the league. League directors must act in the best interests of the league as a whole, thereby assuring that all costs are internalized within the decision-making. As the *Levin* case, below, indicates, leagues owners sometimes utilize "subjective" criteria in scrutinizing prospective members.

As you work through the cases and the Problem below, attempt to identify the impact that a league membership decision may have on the integrity and stability of the league-generated market opportunity. Roger Noll emphasizes that a poorly managed team affects other clubs in the league, and the league as a whole. If a club is not operated efficiently, its games with other teams may be unpopular, affecting the financial status of all clubs. Because revenues are shared, the return is less than optimal. The league also has an interest in the integrity of operations. Noll, *The Economics of Sports Leagues, in* 1 LAW OF AMATEUR AND PROFESSIONAL SPORTS ch. 19 (Uberstine ed., 2008).

Morsani v. Major League Baseball

663 So. 2d 653 (Fla. Dist. Ct. App. 1995)

RYDER, ACTING CHIEF JUDGE.

Frank Morsani and the Tampa Bay Baseball Group (TBBG) seek review of the trial court's dismissal of their complaint alleging tortious interference with advantageous contractual and business relationships... in connection with their attempt to acquire a major league baseball team....

Appellants were plaintiffs in a multi-count suit against sixty defendants, nearly all of whom were associated with major league baseball in one capacity or another at the relevant times. The complaint alleged that the defendants had tortiously interfered with various contractual rights and advantageous business relationships which the plaintiffs had developed over the years in their efforts to acquire ownership of a major league baseball team in Tampa, Florida....

Counts I through III of the complaint alleging tortious interference correspond to the plaintiffs' attempts to purchase a team through negotiations with owners of Minnesota Twins, Inc. and Texas Rangers, Ltd. and to acquire an expansion team, respectively....

The complaint alleges that in 1982, Morsani attended the major league baseball winter meetings, expressed his desire to purchase a major league baseball team and sought advice from various defendants concerning the team's purchase and relocation to the Tampa Bay area. Upon the defendants' advice, TBBG was formed. Various defendants told the plaintiffs that they would support and approve the sale of the Minnesota Twins, Inc. to them if they would secure a site to build a major league baseball stadium in the Tampa Bay area. At an expense in excess of $2 million, the plaintiffs secured a long-term lease with the Tampa Sports Authority for the construction of a baseball stadium and entered into negotiations with the shareholders of Minnesota Twins, Inc. for the purchase of their stock.

In 1984, the owners of 51% of the stock of Minnesota Twins, Inc., Calvin Griffith and Thelma Griffith-Haynes, agreed to sell their controlling interest to the plaintiffs for approximately $24 million on condition that they first buy H. Gabriel Murphy's 42.14% minority interest in the corporation. The plaintiffs then negotiated and entered into a fully-executed written contract with Murphy for the purchase of his interest, at a purchase price of $11.5 million. The contract provided that its closing was conditioned upon prior approval by the owners of other American League teams, as the Constitution of the American League required, and any other approvals which might validly be required. Thereafter, with full knowledge of these agreements, various of the defendants conspired together and used improper means to prevent the plaintiffs from consummating their purchase. They caused Griffith and Griffith-Haynes to sell their 51% interest to Carl Pohlad. They also demanded that the plaintiffs assign their contract with Murphy to Pohlad, and that Murphy consent to the assignment. At the time this assignment was demanded, the value of the minority interest purchased by the plaintiffs had increased from $11.5 million to $25 million.

The plaintiffs balked at the demand and sought payment for the $13.5 million increase in value of the contract, as well as reimbursement of the $2 million previously expended, as a condition to assigning the contract to Pohlad. The relevant defendants then threatened the plaintiffs. These threats were that plaintiffs would never own an interest in a major league baseball team, and that there would never be a major league baseball team in the Tampa Bay area, unless the plaintiffs assigned the contract as demanded and accepted only $250,000.00 for the assignment, and, further, that they agree to forbear pursuing any legal remedies for the additional $15 million plus in damages in exchange for obtaining an ownership interest in another major league baseball team in time to begin the 1993 season. In exchange for the promise of another team, the plaintiffs assigned their contract to Pohlad.

The complaint also alleged that in 1988, several defendants informed the plaintiffs that they would support and approve the sale of Texas Rangers, Ltd. to the plaintiffs. The plaintiffs then reached an agreement with Eddie Gaylord for the purchase of his 33% interest in the partnership, and entered into a written contract with Eddie Chiles for the purchase of his 58% controlling interest in the partnership. Thereafter, with full knowledge of these agreements, various defendants conspired together and used improper means to prevent the plaintiffs from consummating their purchase. They caused both Gaylord and Chiles to breach their agreements with the plaintiffs in favor of a Texas investor. They then, again, threatened the plaintiffs that they would never own an interest in a major league baseball team, and that there would never be a major league baseball team in the Tampa Bay area, unless the plaintiffs agreed to forbear pursuing any legal remedies in exchange for obtaining an ownership interest in another major league baseball team in time to begin the 1993 season. In exchange for the renewed and continuing promise of another team, the plaintiffs once again withheld their claims.

Some of the defendants informed the plaintiffs in 1988 that, consistent with the prior promises made to obtain their forbearance, the plaintiffs would be awarded an expansion team in time to begin the 1993 season. Thereafter, various defendants conspired together and used improper means to prevent the plaintiffs from obtaining the promised team. In 1989, they interfered with the plaintiffs' advantageous business relationships by demanding that one of the investors in TBBG relinquish his interest as a condition of obtaining the team, and thereby reduced the corporation's financial viability. The defendants then prohibited the plaintiffs from obtaining any additional financial backing from persons or entities not located in the Tampa Bay area, including Sam Walton. These interferences reduced the financial viability of the plaintiffs well below that of a competitor group led by H. Wayne Huizenga, and effectively eliminated the plaintiffs from contention for the promised expansion team which began the 1993 season as The Florida Marlins in Miami.

To establish the tort of interference with a contractual or business relationship, the plaintiff must allege and prove (1) the existence of a business relationship under which the plaintiff has legal rights, (2) an intentional and unjustified interference with that relationship by the defendant and (3) damage to the plaintiff as a result of the breach of the business relationship....

The appellants acknowledge that a cause of action for tortious interference does not exist against one who is himself a party to the contract allegedly interfered with.... They urge, however, that none of the defendants except Calvin Griffith and Thelma Griffith-Haynes owned stock in Minnesota Twins, Inc., and only they and Gabriel Murphy could contract to sell their stock in the Twins to the plaintiffs. They further contend that the various defendants' approval rights do not make them parties to the contract.

The trial court concluded that the existence of the defendants' approval rights made them, as the leagues and teams, the source of the business opportunity allegedly interfered with, and, therefore, were incapable of interference. See *Genet Co. v. Anheuser-Busch, Inc.*, 498 So. 2d 683 (Fla. App. 1986). *Genet*, however, is distinguishable because the brewer's decision to disapprove the proposed transfer was based entirely on business considerations. No malice was shown. Here, the appellants have alleged the use of threats, intimidation and conspiratorial conduct.

[I]t is clear that the privilege to interfere in a contract because of a financial interest is not unlimited. The better view is that it is necessary for the interfering party to have a financial interest in the business of the third party which is in the nature of an investment in order to justify the interference.... Furthermore, a privilege to interfere with a third party's conduct does not include the purposeful causing of a breach of contract.

Where there is a qualified privilege to interfere with a business relationship, the privilege carries with it the obligation to employ means that are not improper. As the appellants have pleaded their cause of action, the defendants' approval rights were exercised outside the context of the proper exercise of their rights.

We conclude, therefore, that Counts I, II and III state a cause of action for tortious interference with advantageous contractual and business relationships and reverse their dismissal.

DANAHY and LAZZARA, JJ., concur.

New Orleans Pelicans Baseball Club, Inc. v. National Association of Professional Baseball Leagues, Inc.

1994 U.S. Dist. LEXIS 21468 (E.D. La. 1994)

FELDMAN, DISTRICT JUDGE.

This case involves the unsuccessful attempt of plaintiff to purchase and relocate a AA Southern League baseball club to New Orleans. The National League added two expansion teams for 1993, the Colorado Rockies, and the Florida Marlins. Likewise, the AAA International League added two clubs, in Ottawa, Canada and Charlotte, North Carolina. These changes displaced minor league clubs previously operating in those cities. Consequently, the AAA Denver Zephyrs and the AAA Charlotte Knights needed to find new homes. In search of a new home, the Zephyrs explored the possibility of relocating to New Orleans. The plaintiff claims, however, that the Zephyrs abandoned this idea due to lack of financing.

This litigation arises from the attempts by the New Orleans Pelicans, Inc. to purchase the Charlotte Knights from Charlotte Baseball Inc. and relocate the team to the New Orleans area. The plaintiff and Charlotte Baseball Inc. were brought together by the President of the Southern League, Jimmy Bragan.... In August 1992, the plaintiff signed a letter of intent to purchase the Charlotte Knights of the Southern League, and conditioned the purchase on the ability of the Pelicans to move the club to the New Orleans territory....

On November 2, 1992, President Moore gave written approval of the Control Interest Transfer. Three days later, on November 5, he issued a conditional written approval of the relocation of the Charlotte club to New Orleans "subject to the possibility of (1) a protest by another League, or [and here is the spark that fueled the dispute] (2) the submissions of notice by a club of a League of higher classification of its protection of, or request to relocate to, territory that would include any portion of your proposed relocation territory." This letter required that such a notice be in writing and received by the close of business on November 20, 1992....

On November 18, 1992, the Zephyrs, who play in the American Association, submitted a written request for the New Orleans territory; President Moore notified plaintiff of this change of events the following day.

On November 20, 1992, the American Association are said to have voted, in a conference call, 7 to 1 in favor of the Zephyr's relocation to New Orleans. The result of this vote was, defendants claim, communicated orally to Mr. Moore by a representative of the American Association, Branch Rickey, that same day. Plaintiff disputes whether this vote was taken in accordance with the American Association's by-laws, and whether the result of the vote was communicated orally to Mr. Moore before the November 20, 1992 deadline.

On November 23, 1992, Mr. Moore announced three requirements that the Zephyrs had to meet by December 1, 1992 in order to receive consideration of their desire to try to relocate to the New Orleans territory. Specifically, he required permission of the American Association for relocation and approval of the proposed playing facility; a copy of a lease on a facility in which the franchise would play; and approval of the major league team affiliate of the relocation and proposed playing facility.

On December 6, despite the Zephyr's failure to comply with the December 1, 1992 deadline, Moore granted Denver's request to relocate, and thus, thwarted the application of the plaintiff. Then Moore denied an appeal by the Southern League and the PBEC refused to review the Moore decision or the entire history of the transaction.

The Pelicans never purchased the Charlotte club. The plaintiff, of course, blames this on the defendants. The Charlotte club has since been sold to another and is playing temporarily in Nashville, Tennessee. The Zephyrs did relocate to New Orleans and played their 1993 home games at UNO.

This Court stated the following in its Order and Reasons, dated April 30, 1992, denying defendants' motion to dismiss:

> To be entitled to relief, the plaintiff must prove: (1) that the New Orleans territory was open at the time the Pelicans claimed it, but was thereafter protected and the Pelicans were entitled to protection by the defendants after it was granted to them; (2) that the defendants violated their own rules and expanded their rules to benefit the Zephyrs; (3) that the defendants' actions were intentional, arbitrary and capricious; (4) that the New Orleans territory was never properly claimed by the Zephyrs and was properly awarded to the Pelicans; (5) that the New Orleans territory was never properly claimed by the League to which the Zephyrs belong; and (6) that after the Zephyrs claimed the territory, the defendants acted improperly because they did not enforce their own rules, requirements and deadlines.

Defendants claim that the plaintiff's suit must fail because the Pelicans never had territorial rights protected by the PBA or the NAA and the defendants properly awarded those rights to the Zephyrs. In support of this argument, the defendants maintain that the November 2, 1992 letter merely approved the Pelicans' Application for Control Interest Transfer, the ownership rights, but did not approve the team's relocation to New Orleans. They further argue that the November 5, 1992 letter properly set forth the requirements of Rule 34(E) and that those requirements were satisfied when the Zephyrs submitted, on November 18, 1992, a written application for the New Orleans territory, which the League approved on November 20, 1992....

Plaintiff asserts that material facts are in dispute as to whether defendants acted arbitrarily and capriciously by allowing the Zephyrs to relocate to the New Orleans area. Specifically, plaintiff claims first, that there are material questions of fact regarding the effect of the November 2, 1992 letter.... Second, plaintiff asserts that material questions of fact abound regarding whether Moore exceeded the scope of his authority under the rules of baseball in his November 5th letter and whether the conditions of that letter were properly satisfied....

Under Louisiana law, courts will generally not interfere with the internal judgments of a private association, except in cases in which the action complained of is arbitrary, capricious or unjustly discriminatory....

The question before the Court, therefore, is whether there is a genuine issue of a material fact that the defendants acted arbitrarily and capriciously in this case. A genuine issue of material facts exists where the evidence is such that a reasonable jury could find that the defendants acted arbitrarily and capriciously. Reviewing the evidence in a light most favorable to the plaintiff, the Court finds that the defendants are not entitled to summary relief.

Two fact issues trump summary judgment. First, the meaning of the letter of November 2, 1992. That letter explicitly approved the Application for Control Interest Transfer; however, the letter may also have awarded the plaintiff territorial rights in the New Orleans territory. The text itself is inconclusive....

Next, the Court finds that the controversial letter of November 5, 1992 and the circumstances that followed present the strongest reasons for denying summary judgment. In fact, the success or failure of plaintiff's case will ride on the letter of November 5, 1992. It provides in part:

> ...I hereby approve the proposed relocation subject to the possibility of (1) a protest by another League, or (2) the submission of notice by a club of a league of higher classification of its protection of, or request to relocate to, territory that would include any portion of your proposed relocation territory. To be effective, any such protest or notice must be in writing and received by the National Association office before 5:00 p.m. on November 20, 1992.

At first blush, it seems that President Moore's second condition departs from the textual grant of Rule 34, which controls the relocation of teams. Rule 34 says:

> ...The Commissioner and the President of the Minor League Association shall have fifteen (15) days from the date of approval of the proposed expansion or relocation to grant permission for the occupation of the territory, and during that fifteen (15) day period a *League of higher classification* that applies for the rights to the same territory shall be given preference.

President Moore's letter states, however, that a club of a higher classification may also express an interest in an area; in contrast, Rule 34 states only that a league of a higher classification may express such an interest. This distinction takes on significant meaning given what ensued after the fifteen day deadline was triggered. It is this tension that animates the fight.

It is undisputed that the Zephyrs expressed interest in the New Orleans area in writing on November 18, 1992. It is further undisputed that the American Association, in a 7 to 1 vote, approved the Zephyrs' request on November 20, 1992.

The defendants' first and basic problem with these events is that the Zephyrs are most assuredly a club, not a league. Moore has admitted that his authority comes from the rules of baseball and that he cannot legislate. Thus, a material question of fact remains regarding whether the conditions set forth in the letter of November 5, 1992 were within Moore's authority as President of the National Association.

Defendants argue that all this is irrelevant because the American Association approved the Zephyrs' move on November 20, 1992, and orally notified President Moore of their vote later that day. Plaintiff correctly points out that the record is far from clear as to whether President Moore received notice of the vote on November 20. Moreover, President Moore's letter expressly required that any notice had to be in writing. Instead, it was given orally. Accordingly, even if the notice was given on November 20, 1992, it was arguably not given in accordance with the guidelines set forth by President Moore himself. These unresolved fact issues could give content to the arbitrary and capricious characterization of unwelcomed conduct and must be resolved at trial.

Consequently, the Court Denies defendants' motion for summary judgment on plaintiff's claims relating to the arbitrary and capricious conduct of defendants....

If plaintiff proves that the arbitrary and capricious decisions of defendants caused it to lose its rights to the New Orleans territory, plaintiff will be entitled to specific performance, in the form of being granted rights to the New Orleans territory. That is the only way to return plaintiff to the status quo prior to the arbitrary and capricious acts complained of, unless compensation is a provable alternative.

Ultimately, the Court agrees with plaintiff that it would be inappropriate for the Court to attempt to speculate on what might happen if plaintiff wins. Accordingly, the Court rejects defendants' argument that plaintiff is not entitled to specific performance.

Defendants argue that the rules of baseball exist for the benefit of the Leagues and the Clubs that are subject to the NAA and PBA. Defendants argument focuses on the fact that, because the Pelicans do not own a club within a NAPBL member league, they are not capable of relocating to New Orleans.

Plaintiff asserts that this argument incorrectly assumes that the Pelicans never had rights to the New Orleans territory. They claim that defendants' argument puts the cart before the horse. These arguments echo those to which the Court has already spoken.

The Court still agrees with plaintiff. Defendants' argument overlooks plaintiff's theory in this case. Plaintiff's case turns on whether the Pelicans were awarded rights to the New Orleans territory; if a jury finds that they were awarded those rights, then plaintiff is entitled to relief in some form, regardless of the present ownership status of the AA team. Whether the Pelicans own a team today is irrelevant to whether defendants deprived that team of their rights to the New Orleans territory.

Levin v. National Basketball Association

385 F. Supp. 149 (S.D.N.Y. 1974)

OWEN, DISTRICT JUDGE.

The plaintiffs, two businessmen, in 1972 had an agreement to buy the Boston Celtics basketball team, one of the 17-member National Basketball Association.

N.B.A., as its constitution recites, is a joint venture "organized to operate a league consisting of professional basketball teams each of which shall be operated by a member of the Association." It has been in existence since 1946. Each of its joint ventures holds a franchise to operate a team. While the teams compete vigorously on the basketball court, the joint venturers are dependent upon one another as partners in the league format to make it possible. N.B.A. operates through its Board of Governors which consists of one governor designated by each member. Action by the Board on a transfer of membership requires the affirmative vote of three quarters of the members of the Board.

When plaintiffs applied to the N.B.A... that motion failed to carry at the meeting of the Board of Governors on June 15, 1972, there being two votes in favor, thirteen votes opposed and one not present.

Plaintiffs immediately demanded and were granted a personal hearing before the Board. Following the presentation of their case a second vote was taken. It was, however, to identical effect.

There is a sharp dispute on the reason for the rejection. Plaintiffs contend that they were rejected because of their friendship and business associations with one Sam Schulman, owner of the Seattle SuperSonics, who was an anathema to the other members of the league. Plaintiff Levin testified in a deposition that he was told the "real" reason by Basketball Commissioner Kennedy and Richard Bloch, President of the Phoenix Suns and Chairman of the N.B.A. Finance Committee. According to Levin, Kennedy said:

> "I don't have to draw you a picture.... They are obviously worried that if you fellows are also owners, that you will side with Sam Schulman in all matters in the future and cause the league more troubles than they now have with Sam as it is."

[A]ccording to Levin, Bloch said:

> "You are with Sam Schulman.... They are obviously worried that you fellows, being close to Sam, are going to be siding with him on any matters that come up before the NBA."

On the other hand, the reason given by the N.B.A. for the rejection was that the business association between the plaintiffs and Schulman violated the "conflict of interest" provision of the N.B.A. constitution. That provision reads: A member shall not exercise control directly or indirectly, over any other member of the Association. This provision is necessary, N.B.A. claims, in order that the league may enjoy public support because there is in fact, and the public believes there is, intense competition in the league framework between the *teams* operated by the N.B.A. members.

In any event plaintiffs, rejected, sold their rights in the Celtics elsewhere and commenced this action.

In order to survive defendants' motion for summary judgment, plaintiffs must demonstrate that the conduct complained of is a violation of the antitrust laws. While it is true that the antitrust laws apply to a professional athletic league, and that joint action by members of a league can have antitrust implications this is not such a case. Here the plaintiffs wanted to *join* with those unwilling to accept them, *not to compete with them*, but to be partners in the operation of a sports league for plaintiffs' profit. Further, no matter which reason one credits for the rejection, it was not an anti-competitive reason. Finally, regardless of the financial impact of this rejection upon the plaintiffs, if any, the exclusion of the plaintiffs from membership in the league did not have an anti-competitive effect nor an effect upon the public interest. The Celtics continue as an operating club, and indeed are this year's champion.

The law is well established that it is competition, and not individual competitors, that is protected by the antitrust laws.

It is also clear that where the action the plaintiffs attack, the rejection from co-partnership, has neither anti-competitive intent nor effect, that conduct is not violative of the antitrust laws.

Since there was no exclusion of plaintiffs from competition with the alleged excluders, nor anti-competitive acts by them and no public injury occasioned thereby, the defendants' acts did not constitute a violation of the antitrust laws and defendants' motion for summary judgment is granted....

Notes and Comments

1. For discussion of the application of antitrust and other legal principles to the various leagues' decision-making processes, see GREENBERG & GRAY, 1 SPORTS LAW PRACTICE §§ 11.04, 11.06 (2d ed. 2009); Roberts, *Antitrust Issues in Professional Sports, in* 3 LAW OF PROFESSIONAL AND AMATEUR SPORTS ch. 21 (Uberstine ed., 2008). *See* Chapter 7 (labor relations), below, for treatment of antitrust law as applied to professional sports league player restraints.

2. Is the *Morsani* court's recognition of the tortious interference with a contractual relationship claim persuasive? Is the defendant accurate in arguing that Major League Baseball is a party to the contract and thus cannot interfere with the contract? Does MLB exist as a party due to its approval power status? Which party may be said to "own" the Minnesota Twins franchise? In *Hollywood Baseball Association v. Commissioner*, 42 T.C. 234 (1964), the U.S. Tax Court described the relationship of the Pacific Coast League and its members, as follows:

> The P.C.L. had the exclusive right to play monopoly baseball in certain areas of the west coast of the United States, including Los Angeles and San Francisco. This exclusive right to play establishment baseball in the relevant areas was inherent in the P.C.L.'s membership in the general system of organized professional baseball.
>
> The member teams of the P.C.L. had *derivative rights* from the league under the general entity scheme of organized baseball. A franchise membership in the P.C.L. entitled the holder to operate a P.C.L. team within the territory controlled by the league and granted the right to play P.C.L. baseball as a member of the league.... It bestowed on the member an equal share of the P.C.L. exclusive territorial rights within the baseball monopoly, including allocable rights to televise and radiocast games played against home teams in the P.C.L. area. It entitled the franchise holder to the privilege of being an equal partner in the league, including all league assets and property rights.
>
> Separate, distinct, and divisible from rights derived from the P.C.L. franchise ownership were so-called territorial rights. The league territorial right was the right to play exclusive entity baseball in several areas. A team territorial right was the right to play home games within a certain area. (Emphasis added)

Must an applicant for league membership secure a transfer of "derivative rights" (market opportunity) from the league? Does the *Morsani* court indicate that a party to a contract may nevertheless tortiously interfere where the party employs "improper means," including malice, in its process for approval? Can similar arguments be made on the basis of the implied covenant to fairly deal with applicants for league membership.

3. A question that has remained dormant in judicial scrutiny of professional sports league decisions focuses upon the exact nature of the "derivative rights" that the league assigns to the club operators. As explained above, the naked market opportunity is a property interest generated by the league. The league could choose to conduct games as a syndicate or private concern, as did the National League at the turn of the twentieth century. The league could relocate the team, expand or contract, or sell the opportunity outright. But, the syndicated approach proved unpopular with the fans. *See* SCULLY, THE BUSINESS OF MAJOR LEAGUE BASEBALL 4 (1989). Instead, the leagues assign the "derivative rights" to team operators. Definition of the nature of the assigned interests may be aided by Hohfeldian analysis. The

club owner purchases some sticks in the market opportunity "bundle of sticks," but not the stick enabling the operator to sell the franchise. The league retains the stick that provides the right to alienate the opportunity. The operator possesses, in Hohfeldian terminology, only a "privilege" to suggest sale to a new operator. The team owners have "privileges," thinking they are "rights," and the courts generally do not see the difference. The typical approach of litigants and the resulting judicial examination treats the issues as if the team operator obtains all of the sticks in the bundle, and then contracts or regrants away some rights. Viewing the league-team relationship from a property perspective generates interesting questions regarding the respective rights and duties of the parties, standing, and whether the league is a "single entity" for antitrust purposes.

For an example of a seemingly confused judicial analysis of the rights and duties of the league and teams with respect to sale of a franchise, see *Triple-A Baseball Club Associates v. Northeastern Baseball, Inc.*, 655 F. Supp. 513, *aff'd in part, rev'd in part*, 832 F.2d 214 (1st Cir. 1987). The International League Constitution required that membership in the League could only be assigned upon the approval of five League Directors. The International League argued at trial that the league transfers membership and the attendant rights at the time the League Directors approve of the suggested assignment. The trial court construed the language of the Constitution to empower the club owner with the "exclusive power to do the actual assigning." "[T]he league's only role in the process is to grant its approval and thereby confer upon the member the power to effectively assign." *Id.* at 544. Thus, the court ruled that the club owner has the "exclusive" right to alienate the market opportunity, but cannot exercise the right until the league has conferred the power to do so. Arguably, an exclusive right without the power to exercise it does not fit well within Hohfeldian property law concepts. A better approach may be found through isolation of the sticks in the bundle. For a detailed analysis utilizing the Hohfeldian construct, see McCurdy, *The Fundamental Nature of Professional Sports Leagues, Constituent Clubs, and Mutual Duties to Protect Market Opportunities: Organized Baseball Case Study*, *in* LEGAL ISSUES IN PROFESSIONAL BASEBALL 129–42 (Kurlantzick ed., 2005).

4. In *Fishman v. Estate of Wirtz*, 594 F. Supp. 853 (N.D. Ill. 1984), the plaintiff succeeded in proving that the defendant violated the antitrust laws by preventing the closing of a contract to purchase the Chicago Bulls of the NBA. Defendant actions also violated state law as a tortious interference with a contract. It is noteworthy that the alleged NBA coconspirators reached settlement with the plaintiff prior to trial. The *Fishman* case provides exhaustive treatment of damage issues in antitrust actions as applied to professional sports.

5. Do fiduciary duties limit the discretion of league owners to approve or reject the sale of member clubs? *See Professional Hockey Corporation v. World Hockey Association*, 143 Cal. App. 3d 410 (1983). League directors possess fiduciary duties to make decisions for the league as a whole, including the duty of loyalty. Thus, league

owners may not act in their own self-interest to the detriment of the league. *See also Triple-A Baseball Club Association v. Northeastern Baseball, Inc.*, 655 F. Supp. 513 (D. Me. 1987), *rev'd on other grounds*, 832 F.2d 214 (1st Cir. 1987) (directors and officers of a corporation owe a fiduciary duty to the corporation, including a duty to deal in good faith with the interests of those in a minority position with regard to any particular issue); The *Raiders II* court determined that NFL directors owed members of the league an implied contractual duty of "good faith and fair dealing" when acting on behalf of the league. *See* 791 F.2d 1356 (9th Cir. 1986). Watson, *What's "Love" Got to Do with It?: Potential Fiduciary Duties Among Professional Sports Team Owners*, 9 Sports Law. J. 152 (2002).

For discussion of plaintiffs' claim that federation directors violated fiduciary duties of loyalty, due care, and good faith, see *Deutscher Tennis Bund v. ATP Tour, Inc*, 610 F.3d 820 (3d Cir. 2010). The court stated that the "business judgment rule" is a presumption that in making business decisions the directors of a corporation acted on an informed basis, in good faith and in the honest belief that the action taken was in the best interests of the company. The burden is on the party challenging the decision to establish facts rebutting the presumption. Also, the challenging party must normally demonstrate that a "majority" of the director defendants have a financial interest in the transaction.

6. Historically, owners of franchises in a specific professional sports league have also possessed ownership interests in franchises in other leagues. An NFL rule banning "cross-ownership" was successfully challenged as a violation of Section 1 of the Sherman Antitrust Act. *North American Soccer League v. National Football League*, 670 F.2d 1249 (2d Cir. 1982). A fiduciary has a duty not to profit at the expense of the beneficiary and not to enter into competition with the beneficiary. Restatement (Second) of Trusts § 170 cmt. A (1959). The question of whether ownership of a franchise in another league constitutes competition likely depends on evidence of cross-elasticity of demand and other factors. The opportunity to operate competing sports operations within the league territory may lead to ruinous competition, depleting the common pool of resources, such as fan interest and loyalty. In the event the market possesses the ability to support an additional sports operation, the opportunity may exist for league expansion. The "cross-owner" may be seen as seizing the league's expansion opportunity for the director's own benefit, arguably a violation of the duty of loyalty. *See generally* Laby, *Resolving Conflicts of Duty in Fiduciary Relationships*, 54 Am. U.L. Rev. 75 (2004).

7. Do league owners possess duties benefiting parties who are not contractually related with them as league members, but desire to join the league? Do the league owner's duties to league members, including the prospective seller of a franchise, extend to prospective buyers through a third-party beneficiary theory? Does the filing of a non-refundable application fee create an express contract between the league and applicant for membership? In any event, does a prospective buyer of a

league franchise enjoy an implied contract with league owners? Does there exist an implied trust relationship between the league and applicant? Which party has better standing to bring suit against the league, prospective buyer or seller?

8. Can you identify legal principles serving to constrain a rejected applicant's claim that the league decision was arbitrary and capricious? Is the use of informal or non-codified rules by league owners always subject to the arbitrary and capricious argument? What should be the standard of review? In the *Pelicans* case, Mike Moore interpreted Rule 34 of the National Association Agreement. Does the court's holding indicate that construction of a formal rule made by league owners is subject to question according to principles of "contract law"? "Statutory construction"?

9. Most leagues utilize various exculpatory clauses in the applications for prospective league members. Typical clauses include:

A. Waiver of recourse statements;

B. Indemnity clauses; and

C. Liquidated damages provisions.

Applications generally recite that the decision by the league is made in the league's "sole and absolute discretion, and may be based on subjective and objective criteria." Waiver of recourse paragraphs provide that "the league and its officers and directors shall not be liable to the applicant for any claim arising out of or in any way related to the proposed transfer of the club to the applicant. Applicant further covenants to indemnify the league, its directors and officers, employees, and agents for payment of any attorney's fees, court costs, and expenses incurred in defense of any claim brought against them relating to the application, process, and approval or disapproval of the application or any individual applicants." Finally, a liquidated damages provision stipulates that "the sole and exclusive remedy against the league, its directors and officers, employees or agents shall be for the return of any application fee paid to the league."

League applications require submission of biographical and financial information regarding all individuals and entities included in the prospective ownership group. Applications regularly require applicants to agree to "indemnify and hold harmless the league, its directors and officers, employees, agents, clubs, and designees" from any and all claims, obligations, liabilities, proceedings, judgments, damages, costs, and expenses, including attorney's fees, incurred by any of the indemnified parties and arising out of or related in any way to the release of any information or credit reports.

Are the typical exculpatory clauses adequate to shield the league and its owners from litigation by rejected applicants? What arguments can be used to circumvent the insulation sought by the provisions? Should a league require indemnification by the club owner seeking to transfer membership? For a case in which plaintiff challenged the adequacy of a "release" provision, claimed the release was secured as a result of economic duress, and argued the release was a "part and parcel" of the alleged conspiracy and therefore unenforceable, see *V.K.K. Corporation v. National Football League*, 244 F.3d 114 (2d Cir. 2001).

10. Can *Levin* be explained as a result of plaintiff's failure to prove injury? Does the development of arguments in cases involving league reliance on informal rules or subjective standards differ from the effort in cases concerning formal league rules? Does the likelihood that a prospective owner may utilize the antitrust laws to force itself into a relationship with league members who have heretofore rejected it have any public policy implications for the law of private associations?

11. Does a league member who wishes to sell a club, but is not allowed to do so, possess standing to bring an antitrust claim? Is the identity of the relevant market a question of law or one of fact? In *Sullivan v. National Football League*, 34 F.3d 1091 (1st Cir. 1994), a league member successfully prosecuted an antitrust action challenging an unofficial NFL rule that restricted owners from selling shares in their teams to the public. The jury rendered a verdict in plaintiff's favor for $38 million, reduced through remittitur to $17 million, but trebled pursuant to the Sherman Act for a final judgment of $51 million.

On appeal, the NFL argued that (1) NFL clubs do not compete with each other for the sale of ownership interests, thus there can be no injury to competition and (2) plaintiff did not present sufficient evidence to create a *prima facie* case for jury consideration. The Court of Appeals for the First Circuit ruled that the NFL's policy against public ownership restricts competition between clubs for the sale of their ownership interests. The court affirmed the jury findings of a "nationwide market for the sale and purchase of ownership interests" in NFL clubs generally, and the Patriots in particular, and that the NFL policy had an "actual harmful effect" on competition within the market. The court, determining various errors at trial, reversed and remanded for a new trial. *Id.* at 1095. The second trial resulted in a hung jury. After court supervised mediation, the case was settled for a reported $11.5 million.

In a related case, Chuck Sullivan filed an antitrust action, alleging that the NFL rule against public sales of shares prevented plaintiff from securing stadium financing. The First Circuit affirmed the district court holding that plaintiff lacked standing individually and as assignee of assets of corporation, considering that the alleged injury was not an antitrust injury, injury was indirect, and any damages were highly speculative. *Sullivan v. Tagliabue*, 25 F.3d 43 (1st Cir. 1994), *aff'g*, 828 F. Supp. 114 (D. Mass. 1994).

12. **Problem**: In the fall of 2001, the Commissioner of Baseball announced that MLB contemplated the contraction of the number of clubs for play in the following year, focusing primarily on the Minnesota Twins and Montreal Expos. Although the contraction did not occur and was barred by the subsequent collective bargaining agreement between MLB and the MLBPA, what arguments could be made that contraction constitutes an illegal restraint of trade under Section 1 of the Sherman An-

titrust Act? What is the likely response of MLB? For a brief description of the competing antitrust arguments, see Alloy, *Addition by Subtraction*, *in* LEGAL ISSUES IN PROFESSIONAL BASEBALL (Kurlantzick ed., 2005); Day, *Labor Pains: Why Contraction Is Not the Solution to Major League Baseball's Competitive Balance Problems*, 12 FORDHAM INTELL. PROP. MEDIA & ENT. L.J. 521 (2002). *See also* Brand & Giorgione, *Contraction in Baseball the Effect of Baseball's Antitrust Exemption and Contraction on Its Minor League Baseball System: A Case Study of the Harrisburg Senators*, 10 VILL. SPORTS & ENT. L.J. 49 (2003).

Problem

A large media-based corporation desires to purchase an NFL club and an NBA team. The corporation contemplates securing ownership interests in either existing franchises or expansion clubs. Assume that each of the relevant leagues requires approval of the sale of a franchise by a 3/4 vote of league members. Also assume that each league has a rule prohibiting ownership of more than one professional sports franchise.

1. What general legal constraints, including contract, tort, and fiduciary principles, apply to league owners in their league decision-making roles?
2. Identify the essential elements of an antitrust claim for use in the event of league rejection of a sale of a franchise.
3. What evidentiary matters are significant in the contemplated antitrust actions? Develop a checklist of needed data.

2. Franchise Relocation

Professional sports leagues traditionally restrict the movement of a club from one location to another by and through formal and informal rules requiring approval of franchise relocation. The transfer of a league member's operations to a new locale also serves to relocate the club's "territory," within which the club is assured exclusive operations. For example, the National Association Agreement, Sec. 10.06, governing minor league baseball clubs and leagues, provides for territorial protection for each franchise, as follows:

(A) **League Control of Territories**. Each League shall have control of its clubs' territories until its membership is terminated.

(B) **Territorial Protection**. Each club shall be granted protected territorial rights covering a specific geographical area ('territory') within which only that club may operate and play its home games.... [Protected area is defined as the county in which the club operates; another National Association club may not operate within a 15-mile 'buffer' located in counties surrounding the protected county, unless written permission is granted by the protected club, or an exception is granted pursuant to Sec. 10.06(E).]

League approval processes are designed to assure that (1) potential relocation sites possess adequate demographic and other characteristics needed to maintain league stability; (2) relocation does not exacerbate travel and scheduling demands; (3) the newly created "territory" does not encroach upon existing "territorial rights"; (4) approval does not undermine geographic diversity required for league-wide marketing; and (5) contractual and moral duties to cities, including notions of loyalty, are satisfied.

The league approval process serves as a mechanism to assure that all costs are internalized within the decision-making by league directors. Inefficiencies resulting from the existence of "externalities" leads to the tragedy of the commons phenomenon. Various costs in utilizing the commons are likely to escape detection in relocation decisions made by individual clubs. The costs include fan loyalty to the existing team, stable relationships with communities, league-wide interest in protection of rivalries and the existence of geographic diversity, and the availability of media, advertising, and sponsorship money. As the cases below indicate, a league often permits club relocation conditioned on the payment of a "relocation fee." The "fee" includes the value of the league-generated naked market opportunity. It also covers the costs to the league as a whole and to other league members. Questions concerning the proper amount of the fee generate considerable conflict.

As you review the cases, consider the following questions and issues:

1. Describe the elements of an antitrust action challenging formal and informal league rules requiring league approval of franchise movement.
2. What factors are relevant according to the *Raiders and Clippers* cases? Provide a comparative analysis of the factors as applied to the relocation of the Seattle Sonics to Oklahoma City in the NBA; the move of the St. Louis Rams to Los Angeles; the relocation of the Oakland Raiders to Las Vegas; and the move of the San Diego Chargers to Los Angeles.
3. Identify available defenses for use by professional sports leagues in antitrust cases.
4. Is congressional action needed for protection of cities and taxpayers from harm resulting from franchise relocation? If so, what is the nature of the legislative solution?

Los Angeles Memorial Coliseum Commission v. National Football League

726 F.2d 1381 (9th Cir. 1984)

J. Blaine Anderson, Circuit Judge:

In 1978, the owner of the Los Angeles Rams, the late Carroll Rosenbloom, decided to locate his team in a new stadium, the "Big A," in Anaheim, California. That left the Los Angeles Coliseum without a major tenant. Officials of the Coliseum then began the search for a new National Football League occupant. They inquired of the League Commissioner, Pete Rozelle, whether an expansion franchise might be located there but were told that at the time it was not possible. They also negotiated with existing teams in the hope that one might leave its home and move to Los Angeles.

The L.A. Coliseum ran into a major obstacle in its attempts to convince a team to move. That obstacle was Rule 4.3 of Article IV of the NFL Constitution. In 1978, Rule 4.3 required unanimous approval of all the 28 teams of the League whenever a team... seeks to relocate in the home territory of another team. Home territory is defined in Rule 4.1 as

> the city in which [a] club is located and for which it holds a franchise and plays its home games, and includes the surrounding territory to the extent of 75 miles in every direction from the exterior corporate limits of such city....

In this case, the L.A. Coliseum was still in the home territory of the Rams.

The Coliseum viewed Rule 4.3 as an unlawful restraint of trade in violation of § 1 of the Sherman Act, 15 U.S.C. § 1, and brought this action in September of 1978. The district court concluded, however, that no present justiciable controversy existed because no NFL team had committed to moving to Los Angeles.

The NFL nevertheless saw the Coliseum's suit as a sufficient threat to warrant amending Rule 4.3. In late 1978, the Executive Committee of the NFL,... changed the rule to require only three-quarters approval by the members of the League for a move into another team's home territory.

Soon thereafter, Al Davis, managing general partner of the Oakland Raiders franchise, stepped into view. His lease with the Oakland Coliseum had expired in 1978. He believed the facility needed substantial improvement and he was unable to persuade the Oakland officials to agree to his terms. He instead turned to the Los Angeles Coliseum.

In January, 1980, the L.A. Coliseum believed an agreement with Davis was imminent and reactivated its lawsuit against the NFL, seeking a preliminary injunction to enjoin the League from preventing the Raiders' move. The district court granted the injunction, but this court reversed, finding that an adequate probability of irreparable injury had not been shown. On March 1, 1980, Al Davis and the Coliseum signed a "memorandum of agreement" outlining the terms of the Raiders' relocation in Los Angeles.... In response, the League brought a contract action in state court, obtaining an injunction preventing the move. In the meantime, the City of Oakland brought its much-publicized eminent domain action against the Raiders in its effort to keep the team in its original home....

Over Davis' objection that Rule 4.3 is illegal under the antitrust laws, the NFL teams voted on March 10, 1980, 22–0 against the move, with five teams abstaining....

The Los Angeles Memorial Coliseum Commission then renewed its action against the NFL and each member club. The Oakland Alameda County Coliseum, Inc. was permitted to intervene. The Oakland Raiders cross-claimed against the NFL and is currently aligned as a party plaintiff.

The action was first tried in 1981, but resulted in a hung jury and mistrial. A second trial was conducted, with strict constraints on trial time. The court was asked to determine if the NFL was a "single business entity" and as such incapable of combining or conspiring in restraint of trade.... The court concluded the League was not a "single entity."

The jury returned a verdict in favor of the Los Angeles Memorial Coliseum Commission and the Oakland Raiders on the antitrust claim and for the Raiders on their claim of breach of the implied promise of good faith and fair dealing....

On June 14, 1982, the court issued its judgment on the liability issues, permanently enjoining the NFL and its member clubs from interfering with the transfer of the Oakland Raiders' NFL franchise from the Oakland Coliseum to the Los Angeles Memorial Coliseum....

The damages trial was completed in May 1983 with the jury returning a verdict awarding the Raiders $11.55 million and the Los Angeles Coliseum $4.86 million. These awards were trebled by the district court pursuant to 15 U.S.C. § 15....

The rule of reason requires the fact-finder to decide whether under all the circumstances of the case the agreement imposes an unreasonable restraint on competition.

When judicial experience with a particular kind of restraint enables a court to predict with certainty that the rule of reason will condemn that restraint, the court will hold that the restraint is per se unlawful....

In the present case, the district judge found that the unique nature of the business of professional football made application of a per se rule inappropriate. The court therefore instructed the jury that it was to decide whether Rule 4.3 was an unreasonable restraint of trade. The parties do not contest the appropriateness of this basic reasonableness inquiry. The NFL, however, raises two arguments against the lower court's judgment finding section 1 liability. First, the NFL contends that it is a single entity incapable of conspiring to restrain trade under section 1. Second, it insists that Rule 4.3 is not an unreasonable restraint of trade under section 1.

[The court rejected the "single entity" defense argument.]

As elaborated upon by this circuit: "Rule of reason analysis calls for a 'thorough investigation of the industry at issue and a balancing of the arrangement's positive and negative effects on competition.'" This balancing process is not applied, however, until after the plaintiff has shown the challenged conduct restrains competition. To establish a cause of action, plaintiff must prove these elements: "(1) An agreement among two or more persons or distinct business entities; (2) Which is intended to harm or unreasonably restrain competition; (3) And which actually causes injury to competition."

Our rejection of the NFL's single entity defense implicitly recognized the existence of the first element... we have no doubt the plaintiffs also met their burden of proving the existence of the second element. Rule 4.3 is on its face an agreement to control, if not prevent, competition among the NFL teams through territorial divisions. The third element is more troublesome.

It is in this context that we discuss the NFL's ancillary restraint argument. Also, a showing of injury to competition requires "[p]roof that the defendant's activities had an impact upon competition in a relevant market."...

In a quite general sense, the case presents the competing considerations of whether a group of businessmen can enforce an agreement with one of their co-contractors to the detriment of that co-contractor's right to do business where he pleases. More specifically, this lawsuit requires us to engage in the difficult task of analyzing the negative and positive effects of a business practice in an industry which does not readily fit into the antitrust context. Section 1 of the Sherman Act was designed to prevent agreements among competitors which eliminate or reduce competition and thereby harm consumers. Yet, as we discussed in the context of the single entity issue, the NFL teams are not true competitors, nor can they be.

The NFL's structure has both horizontal and vertical attributes. On the one hand, it can be viewed simply as an organization of 28 competitors, an example of a simple horizontal arrangement. On the other, and to the extent the NFL can be considered an entity separate from the team owners, a vertical relationship is disclosed. In this sense the owners are distributors of the NFL product, each with its own territorial division. In this context it is clear that the owners have a legitimate interest in protecting the integrity of the League itself. Collective action in areas such as League divisions, scheduling and rules must be allowed, as should other activity that aids in producing the most marketable product attainable. Nevertheless, legitimate collective action should not be construed to allow the owners to extract excess profits. In such a situation the owners would be acting as a classic cartel. Agreements among competitors, i.e., cartels, to fix prices or divide market territories are presumed illegal under § 1 because they give competitors the ability to charge unreasonable and arbitrary prices instead of setting prices by virtue of free market forces.

On its face, Rule 4.3 divides markets among the 28 teams, a practice presumed illegal, but, as we have noted, the unique structure of the NFL precludes application of the per se rule. Instead, we must examine Rule 4.3 to determine whether it reasonably serves the legitimate collective concerns of the owners or instead permits them to reap excess profits at the expense of the consuming public.

The NFL contends it is entitled to judgment because plaintiffs failed to prove an adverse impact on competition in a relevant market....

In the antitrust context, the relevant market has two components: the product market and the geographic market.... Two related tests are used in arriving at the product market: first, reasonable interchangeability for the same or similar uses; and second, cross-elasticity of demand, an economic term describing the responsiveness of sales of one product to price changes in another. Similar considerations determine the relevant geographic market, which describes the "economically significant" area of effective competition in which the relevant products are traded.

The Raiders attempted to prove the relevant market consists of NFL football (the product market) in the Southern California area (the geographic market). The NFL argues it competes with all forms of entertainment within the United States, not just Southern California. The L.A. Coliseum claims the relevant market is stadia offering their facilities to NFL teams (the product market) in the United States (the geographic market). The NFL agrees with this geographic market, but argues the product market involves cities competing for all forms of stadium entertainment, including NFL football teams.

That NFL football has limited substitutes from a consumer standpoint is seen from evidence that the Oakland Coliseum sold out for 10 consecutive years despite having some of the highest ticket prices in the League. A similar conclusion can be drawn from the extraordinary number of television viewers—over 100 million people—that watched the 1982 Super Bowl, the ultimate NFL product. NFL football's importance to the television networks is evidenced by the approximately $2 billion they agreed to pay the League for the right to televise the games from 1982–1986....

The evidence from which the jury could have found a narrow pro football product market was balanced, however, with other evidence which tended to show the NFL competes in the first instance with other professional sports, especially those with seasons that overlap with the NFL's. On a broader level, witnesses... testified that NFL football competes with other television offerings for network business, as well as other local entertainment for attendance at the games.

In terms of the relevant geographic market, witnesses, testified,... that NFL teams compete with one another off the field for fan support in those areas where teams operate in close proximity such as New York City-New Jersey, Washington, D.C.-Baltimore, and formerly San Francisco-Oakland.... Also, the San Francisco Forty Niners and the New York Giants were paid $18 million because of the potential for harm from competing with the Oakland Raiders and the New York Jets, respectively, once those teams joined the NFL as a result of the merger with the American Football League....

Testimony also adequately described the parameters of the stadia market. On one level, stadia do compete with one another for the tenancy of NFL teams. Such competition is shown by the Rams' move to Anaheim....

It is true, as the NFL argues, that competition among stadia for the tenancy of professional football teams is presently limited. It is limited, however, because of the operation of Rule 4.3. Prior to this lawsuit, most teams were allowed to relocate only within their home territory.... There was evidence to the effect that the NFL in the past remained expressly noncommitted on the question of team movement. This was done to give owners a bargaining edge when they were renegotiating leases with their respective stadia. The owner could threaten a move if the lease terms were not made more favorable.

The NFL claims that it is places, not particular stadia, that compete for NFL teams. This is true to a point because the NFL grants franchises to locales (generally a city and a 75 mile radius extending from its boundary). It is the individual stadia, however, which are most directly impacted by the restrictions on team movement. A stadium is a distinct economic entity and a territory is not....

We conclude with one additional observation. In the context of this case in particular, we believe that market evidence, while important, should not become an end in itself. Here the exceptional nature of the industry makes precise market definition especially difficult.... The critical question is whether the jury could have determined that Rule 4.3 reasonably served the NFL's interest in producing and promoting its product, *i.e.*, competing in the entertainment market, or whether Rule 4.3 harmed competition among the 28 teams to such an extent that any benefits to the League as a whole were outweighed....

The NFL has awarded franchises exclusive territories since the 1930s... League members saw exclusive territories as a means to aid stability, ensuring the owner who was attempting to establish an NFL team in a particular city that another would not move into the same area, potentially ruining them both.

Rule 4.3 is the result of that concern. Prior to its amendment in 1978, it required unanimous League approval for a move into another team's home territory. That, of course, gave each owner an exclusive territory and he could vote against a move into his territory solely because he was afraid the competition might reduce his revenue.... Currently three-quarters approval is required for all moves.

That the purpose of Rule 4.3 was to restrain competition among the 28 teams may seem obvious and it is not surprising the NFL admitted as much at trial. It instead argues that Rule 4.3 serves a variety of legitimate League needs, including ensuring franchise stability. We must keep in mind, however, that the Supreme Court has long rejected the notion that "ruinous competition" can be a defense to a restraint of trade. Conversely, anticompetitive purpose alone is not enough to condemn Rule 4.3. The rule must actually harm competition, and that harm must be evaluated in light of the procompetitive benefits the rule might foster....

The competitive harms of Rule 4.3 are plain. Exclusive territories insulate each team from competition within the NFL market, in essence allowing them to set monopoly prices to the detriment of the consuming public. The rule also effectively foreclosed free competition among stadia such as the Los Angeles Coliseum that wish to secure NFL tenants.... If the transfer is upheld, direct competition between the Rams and Raiders would presumably ensue to the benefit of all who consume the NFL product in the Los Angeles area.

The NFL argues, however, that territorial allocations are *inherent* in an agreement among joint venturers to produce a product.... We agree that the nature of NFL football requires some territorial restrictions in order both to encourage participation in the venture and to secure each venturer the legitimate fruits of that participation.

Rule 4.3 aids the League, the NFL claims, in determining its overall geographical scope, regional balance and coverage of major and minor markets. Exclusive territories aid new franchises in achieving financial stability, which protects the large initial investment an owner must make to start up a football team. Stability arguably helps ensure no one team has an undue advantage on the field. Territories foster fan loyalty which in turn promotes traditional rivalries between teams, each contributing to attendance at games and television viewing.

Joint marketing decisions are surely legitimate because of the importance of television.... The League must be allowed to have some control over the placement of teams to ensure NFL football is popular in a diverse group of markets.

Last, there is some legitimacy to the NFL's argument that it has an interest in preventing transfers from areas before local governments, which have made a substantial investment in stadia and other facilities, can recover their expenditures....

The NFL argues that the requirement of Rule 4.3 that three-quarters of the owners approve a franchise move is reasonable because it deters unwise team transfers. While the rule does indeed protect an owner's investment in a football franchise, no standards or durational limits are incorporated into the voting requirement to make sure that concern is satisfied. Nor are factors such as fan loyalty and team rivalries necessarily considered.

The NFL claims that... [s]ince the owners are guided by the desire to increase profits, they will necessarily make reasonable decisions, the NFL asserts, on such issues of whether the new location can support two teams, whether marketing needs will be adversely affected, etc. Under the present Rule 4.3, however, an owner need muster only seven friendly votes to prevent three-quarters approval for the sole reason of preventing another team from entering its market, regardless of whether the market could sustain two franchises. A basic premise of the Sherman Act is that regulation of private profit is best left to the marketplace rather than private agreement. The present case is in fact a good example of how the market itself will deter unwise moves, since a team will not lightly give up an established base of support to confront another team in its home market.

The NFL's professed interest in ensuring that cities and other local governments secure a return on their investment in stadia is undercut in two ways. First, the local governments ought to be able to protect their investment through the leases they negotiate with the teams for the use of their stadia. Second, the NFL's interest on this point may not be as important as it would have us believe because the League has in the past allowed teams to threaten a transfer to another location in order to give the team leverage in lease negotiations.

Finally, the NFL made no showing that the transfer of the Raiders to Los Angeles would have any harmful effect on the League. Los Angeles is a market large enough for the successful operation of two teams, there would be no scheduling difficulties, facilities at the L.A. Coliseum are more than adequate, and no loss of future television revenue was foreseen. Also, the NFL offered no evidence that its interest in maintaining regional balance would be adversely affected by a move of a northern California team to southern California.

It is true, as the NFL claims, that the antitrust laws are primarily concerned with the promotion of *interbrand* competition. To the extent the NFL is a product which competes with other forms of entertainment, including other sports, its rules governing territorial division can be said to promote interbrand competition. Under this analysis, the territorial allocations most directly suppress intrabrand, that is, NFL team versus NFL team, competition. A more direct impact on intrabrand competition does not mean, however, the restraint is reasonable....

To withstand antitrust scrutiny, restrictions on team movement should be more closely tailored to serve the needs inherent in producing the NFL "product" and competing with other forms of entertainment. An express recognition and consideration of those objective factors espoused by the NFL as important, such as population, economic projections, facilities, regional balance, etc., would be well advised. Fan loyalty and location continuity could also be considered....

Some sort of procedural mechanism to ensure consideration of all the above factors may also be necessary, including an opportunity for the team proposing the move to present its case. In the present case, for example, testimony indicated that some owners, as well as Commissioner Rozelle, dislike Al Davis and consider him a maverick. Their vote against the Raiders' move could have been motivated by animosity rather than business judgment.

The NFL is a unique business organization to which it is difficult to apply antitrust rules which were developed in the context of arrangements between actual competitors....

We believe antitrust principles are sufficiently flexible to account for the NFL's structure. To the extent the NFL finds the law inadequate, it must look to Congress for relief.

The judgment finding the NFL liable to...the Raiders, and enjoining the NFL from preventing the Raiders from relocating to Los Angeles is Affirmed.

National Basketball Association v. SDC Basketball Club, Inc.

815 F.2d 562 (9th Cir.), *cert. dismissed*, 484 U.S. 960 (1987)

Ferguson, Circuit Judge:

Once again this court must consider the application of federal antitrust law to a sports league's effort to restrain the movement of a member franchise. In this case, the league, the National Basketball Association (NBA), seeks declaratory judgment that it may restrain the movement of its franchise, the Los Angeles Clippers (nee San Diego Clippers), and that it may impose a charge upon them for the Clippers' unilateral usurpation of the "franchise opportunity" available in the Los Angeles market....

The Clippers currently operate a professional basketball franchise in the Los Angeles Sports Arena. The franchise is a member of the NBA.... In the early 1980s, the then San Diego Clippers desired to move their franchise to Los Angeles. The Clippers abandoned their effort after the NBA filed suit in the Southern District of California....

In 1984, this court rendered the decision in *Raiders I*. The *Raiders I* panel found that the National Football League (NFL) was not immune from the antitrust laws as a single business entity. Possible antitrust violations within the league thus properly are tested by "rule of reason" antitrust analysis....

The NBA asserts that Article 9 was not the only limitation upon franchise movement. Article 9 provided that no team could move into a territory operated by another franchise without that franchise's approval. The Clippers complied with this requirement, as the Los Angeles Lakers agreed in writing to waive their rights under Article 9. The NBA argues, however, that the league as a body must be permitted to consider moves in order to give effect to a number of constitutional provisions for the exclusiveness of franchise territories. Article 9, it contends, limits the actions of the NBA as a league and does not prescribe the only strictures on franchise movement.

The NBA also began proceedings to adopt a new rule governing the consideration of franchise moves, later adopted as Article 9A....

[T]he Clippers argue, as they must to support summary judgment, that the "NBA three-quarters rule... is illegal under *Raiders I*"—*i.e.*, either that the NBA rule is void as a matter of law under *Raiders I*, or that the NBA has not adduced genuine issues of fact to allow the rule to stand. The Clippers assert that the rule "is illegal as applied... [but that under *Raiders I*], a professional sports league's club relocation rule must at least be 'closely tailored' and incorporate objective standards and criteria such as population, economic projections, playing facilities, regional balance, and television revenues." Putting to the side, for the moment, NBA's adamant and repeated assertions that such standards have been incorporated in the evaluation of franchise movements, the Clippers misperceive the effect of the *Raiders* cases. The Clippers' confusion, and that of a number of commentators, may derive from the *Raiders I* panel's painstaking efforts to guide sports leagues toward procedures that might, in all cases, withstand antitrust analysis. The objective factors and procedures recounted by the Clippers are "well advised," and might be sufficient to demonstrate procompetitive purposes that would save the restriction from the rule of reason. They are not, however, necessary conditions to the legality of franchise relocation rules.

The NBA asserts a number of genuine issues of fact: (1) the purpose of the restraint as demonstrated by the NBA's use of a variety of criteria in evaluating franchise movement, (2) the market created by professional basketball, which the NBA alleges is substantially different from that of professional football, and (3) the actual effect the NBA's limitations on movements might have on trade. The NBA's assertions, if further documented at trial, create an entirely different factual setting than that of the Raiders and the NFL. Further, as the NBA correctly notes, the antitrust issue here is vastly different than that in the *Raiders* cases: the issue here is "whether the mere requirement that a team seek [NBA] Board of Governor approval before it seizes a new franchise location violates the Sherman Act." The NBA here did not attempt to forbid the move. It scheduled the Clippers in the Sports Arena, and when faced with continued assertions of potential antitrust liability, brought this suit for declaratory relief. Given the *Raiders I* rejection of per se analysis for franchise movement rules of sports leagues, and the existence of genuine issues of fact regarding the reasonableness of the restraint, the judgment against the NBA must be reversed.

Notes and Comments

1. The "players" in the typical relocation case include the franchise owner desiring to relocate operations, the existing member city and facility, the relocation city and facility, and the defendants, voting league members and league entity. Which of the potential plaintiffs possesses standing to maintain an antitrust claim? Are the losses suffered by the existing host city a result of league violations of the antitrust laws? Which parties, if any, possess standing to challenge a league's granting of a relocation application that is allegedly made in violation of league policies and rules, as opposed to a league denial of an application for relocation? For a discussion of antitrust claims by cities, including issues of standing, see Mitten & Burton, *Professional Sports Franchise Relocations from Private Law and Public Law Perspectives: Balancing Marketplace Competition, League Autonomy, and the Need for a Level Playing Field*, 56 Md. L. Rev. 57 (1997).

2. The NFL, after the *Raiders* decision, established a policy that favors stable team-community relations, obligating clubs to work diligently and in good faith of obtain and maintain suitable stadium facilities in and maximize fan support in the

home community. NFL Const. & Bylaws, Article 4.3, provides that each club's primary responsibility to the NFL and member clubs is to advance the interests of the NFL in its home city; that no club has an "entitlement" to relocate simply because it perceives an opportunity for enhanced club revenues; that relocation may be available if a club's viability in its home city is threatened by circumstances that cannot be remedied by diligent efforts of the club working in conjunction with the NFL; or relocation is available if compelling NFL interests warrant a franchise relocation.

3. In *Sullivan v. National Football League*, 34 F.3d 1091 (1st Cir. 1994), the court recognized that the NFL had submitted evidence of record at trial to support the "equal involvement defense" doctrine. The defense is an absolute bar to an antitrust suit where the plaintiff bears "substantially equal responsibility for an anticompetitive restriction by creating, approving, maintaining, continually and actively supporting, relying upon, or otherwise utilizing" the restriction to the plaintiff's benefit. What evidence is available for the defendant's use in attempting to prove the defense by a preponderance in "relocation" cases? Interestingly, the owner of the Seattle Seahawks, Ken Behring, voiced, in February 1996, his intention to relocate the Seahawks to the Los Angeles area. Mr. Behring and other NFL owners, reportedly, had previously agreed to "save" the Los Angeles territory for league expansion to benefit all NFL owners.

4. The damages portion of *Los Angeles Memorial Coliseum Comm'n v. NFL* (*Raiders II*) appears at 791 F.2d 1356 (9th Cir. 1986). The court upheld the jury's treble damage award to the Coliseum Commission in the amount of $14,580,243. The Raiders' award of $34,633,146 was remanded for a determination of the amount of set-off due the NFL for the lost value of the Los Angeles area league-generated opportunity. The Court stated:

> The value of the Los Angeles opportunity arose not only from the economic potential of one of the nation's largest media markets, but also from the NFL's well-established and widely followed nationwide entertainment product.... If and when the NFL placed an expansion team in the Los Angeles area, the accumulated value of the Los Angeles opportunity would have been realized by the NFL through charging the new expansion team owner for the expansion opportunity.
>
> As indicated above, the value of the league's expansion opportunities belonged to the league as a whole, or in other words, was owned in part by each franchise owner. Unquestionably, when the Raiders moved to Los Angeles, they appropriated for themselves the expansion value.... Although by moving out of Oakland the Raiders "gave back" an expansion opportunity to the NFL, the uncontradicted testimony at trial showed the Los Angeles market to be a significantly more lucrative franchise opportunity.... Al Davis testified that the Raiders increased their value by some $25 million by moving to Los Angeles....

> As a result, the injunction permitting the Raiders to play NFL football in Los Angeles… provided them with a windfall benefit beyond the scope of the antitrust verdict.

Id.

The offset ruling remedied a potential defect in *Raiders* I identified by Weistart that the opinion requires the league to give to an insider what could be sold for a considerable amount to an outsider. *See* Weistart, *League Control of Market Opportunities: A Perspective on Competition and Cooperation in the Sports Industry*, 1984 DUKE L.J. 1013. The underlying premise of Professor Weistart's analysis and that of Professor Roberts' concern that league members have the opportunity to place team interests above league interests—a forecasting of the "tragedy of the commons." Significantly, the offset is to be applied prior to the trebling of the damages. Professor Shropshire points out that an offset of $25 million to the Raiders' actual damages of approximately $11.5 million results in Al Davis owing the NFL an amount of about $13.5 million. SHROPSHIRE, THE SPORTS FRANCHISE GAME 40 (1995). It is little surprise that the matter was resolved by an out-of-court settlement.

5. The accepted notion that the value of a relocation or an expansion site is generated by the league is fundamental to the concept of a league and its operations. A part of the indemnification payment is equal to the portion of the value of the relocation site generated by the NFL. In *St. Louis Convention & Visitors Commission v. National Football League*, 154 F.3d 851 (8th Cir. 1998), NFL club owners had approved the Rams' relocation from Los Angeles to St. Louis only after its owner agreed to pay the NFL a $29 million relocation fee. Another element of the indemnification package includes the amount of rebate owed pursuant to television and broadcast contracts resulting from the substitution of a lesser market for the existing one. What other cost elements can you identify? Draft guidelines that would serve to direct the NFL owners in constructing an indemnification payment package. *See generally* GREENBERG & GRAY, 1 SPORTS LAW PRACTICE, § 11.04(1)(b) (2009). Professor Fort constructs an expansion fee formula that combines the discounted net present values of expected team profits, expected local revenue impacts, and expected media package impacts. FORT, SPORTS ECONOMICS 135–39 (2003). The formula serves to include in the calculation external costs and benefits that would otherwise be overlooked in the decision-making process, and therefore would result in an inefficient allocation of resources.

The NBA approved the Seattle Sonics relocation to Oklahoma City, establishing a $30 million relocation fee. For an examination of the dynamics surrounding the Sonics relocation case, see McCurdy, *Thunder on the Road from Seattle to Oklahoma City: Moving from NOPA to ZOPA in the NBA, in* LEGAL ISSUES IN AMERICAN BASKETBALL ch. IV (Kurlantzick ed., 2011).

6. Reportedly, the NFL had discussed plans to charge a "flip tax" to an owner who relocates to Los Angeles and then sells the club within a specified period of time. *Kaplan, NFL Plans 'Flip Tax' if L.A. Owner Sells Club*, SPORTS BUS. J., September 28, 2015, p. 5.

7. Do league members possess fiduciary duties, similar to partners in a partnership, which prevent the relocation of existing clubs to potential expansion cities to the detriment of the league as a whole?

8. The City of Oakland attempted to retain the Raiders through a condemnation action. *See City of Oakland v. Oakland Raiders*, 646 P.2d 835 (Cal. 1982). The California Court of Appeals upheld a lower court judgment on remand that eminent domain acquisition was invalid under the Commerce Clause. *City of Oakland v. Oakland Raiders*, 174 Cal. App. 3d 414, 421 (1985). For discussion of other cities' use of eminent domain power, see Greenberg, *Professional Sports Franchises: Retention Methods, Escape Clauses, and Franchise Relocation, in* 3 Law of Amateur and Professional Sports ch. 23 (Uberstine ed., 2008).

9. Professor Zimbalist views the root of the "relocation" problem as lying in the leagues' monopoly status. He proposes a solution that creates competition between separate leagues, whereby each league attempts to occupy all viable cities before the other, expand into any markets that could support a team, and place more teams in markets that are capable of supporting multiple teams. In this manner, the "supply and demand situation would balance out." Commissioner Tagliabue, conversely, argues that cities would be protected by congressional recognition of league exemption from antitrust scrutiny. Which of the arguments is more persuasive? Given present day economic realities, can the supply-demand equation balance as proposed? Professor Zimbalist also recognizes that demographically lesser cities, as a result of new stadium economics, can now compete with larger cities. Does the continual increase in the number of viable facilities and cities assure an imbalance with a static supply of major league quality players? In this sense, is the economic demand for professional sports teams different from consumer demand for scarce resources? Is the monopoly a "natural monopoly"? Does the answer vary according to time period and factual circumstances? *See* Noll & Zimbalist, *Economic Impact of Sports Teams and Facilities in Sports, in* Jobs and Taxes: The Economic Impact of Sports Teams and Stadiums 65 (Noll & Zimbalist eds., 1997); Piraino, Jr., *The Antitrust Rationale for the Expansion of Professional Sports Leagues*, 57 Ohio St. L.J. 1677 (1996); Ross, *New Economy, New Regime Second Annual Symposium of the American Antitrust Institute: Antitrust Options to Redress Anticompetitive Restraints and Monopolistic Practices by Professional Sports Leagues*, 52 Case W. Res. L. Rev. 133 (2001); Quirk & Fort, Hard Ball ch. 6 (1999).

10. Stadium leases negotiated between clubs and governmental entities, or stadium authorities, sometimes include clauses enabling the city or stadium authority to seek a decree of specific performance of the lease where a club breaches or threatens to breach the lease by relocating to another city. The clauses as well as the general equitable principles may be judicially recognized. The legal issue becomes more important, as professional sports teams vacate traditional home territories for better financial opportunities elsewhere, or venues cannot continue to fund operations at the expected level due to recession or other causes.

3. Merchandising and Broadcasting

For more than three decades, professional sports leagues have enjoyed the emergence of broadcasting and merchandising opportunities to join with the historical gate receipts and venue-related sales as the primary stream of team and league revenues. The development of league marketing strategies generally flows with the evolution of technology and distribution networks. The advancement of the marketing opportunities generates legal questions that were not present at the advent of the league structures.

Broadcasting

Today, sports programming occupies a considerable status in national and global entertainment markets. The programming not only includes the transmission of live games but also the distribution of non-live game contests, real time scores, performance highlights, and related content. The presence of multi-channel video programming distribution mechanisms changes the professional sports paradigm. The broadcasting ventures generate revenues that rival the traditional ticket and venue-related sales dominance. The various video platforms also serve to deliver game and other content to non-live game fans (many are out-of-market) that are greater in number than the fans in live attendance.

Historical Response to Broadcasting Opportunities/Regulation

Professional sports leagues confronted the initial broadcast opportunities presented by the invention of analog TV transmission with suspicion and fear similar to the response of the NCAA chronicled in *NCAA v. Board of Regents,* Chapter 4, *supra.* The primary fear focused on the potential negative impact of televised games on home-game live attendance. Unlimited distribution of televised games was thought to give rise to the threat of a "tragedy of the commons," which would ultimately end in the undermining of the economic stability of clubs and the ultimate ruination of the league.

The choice made by an individual club to broadcast its game on a national scale may not take into account the effects on other franchises and the league as a whole. The externalities are generally recognized as the impact on home games and telecasts of other teams, including the possibility of strong teams drawing fan support, television audience, and sponsorship money from weaker clubs. The customary league sharing of national broadcast revenues is designed to enable weaker clubs to compete in the market for players and assure competitive balance among teams. National broadcasting and marketing also emphasizes and promotes the "league product" and season, thus justifying league control over the area. The necessity of some league control over the delivery of games to the national audience is commonly accepted, although questions of the proper mix of nationally delivered games generate considerable controversy. *See* Fisher, Maxwell, & Schouten, *The Economics of Sports Leagues—The Chicago Bulls Case*, 10 Marq. Sports L.J. 1 (1999).

In the attempt to avoid the workings of the potential peril, the professional sports league broadcast field has been regulated by the imposition of league rules, the application of the antitrust laws, and regulation by federal statutes and agency rules. *See generally* Boliek, *Antitrust, Regulation, and the "New" Rules of Sports Telecasts*, 65 Hastings L.J. 501 (2014). Professional sports leagues commonly restrict the broadcast of league games to protect "live" game production within the home market, and otherwise assure benefits for the league as a whole.

Leagues first gained approval from the league directors (clubs) for the pooling of broadcasts for league distribution. The program enabled the league to gain control of and limit the output of broadcasts for the purposes described above. It also had the effect of creating a scarce product, the sale of which generated substantial revenues for the league as a whole. The pooling of games was further protected by the Sports Broadcasting Act of 1961, 15 U.S.C. § 1291 (2006):

> "[Antitrust law] shall not apply to any joint agreement [involving] organized professional team sports of football, baseball, basketball or hockey... in the sponsored telecasts of the games...."

Blackout Rules

Leagues promulgated "blackout rules" that prohibited the broadcast of a team's games into another team's territory when the home team is playing a home game or broadcasting its away game in the home territory. The NFL "blackout" rule was challenged in *United States v. NFL (NFL I)*, 116 F. Supp. 319 (E.D. Pa. 1953). The court held the rule a valid restriction of broadcast rights to serve the interests of the league as a whole. The court, however, ruled the NFL overreached in restricting the sale of broadcast rights into another market when there was not a team physically playing in the market. The decision was soon superseded by the Sports Broadcasting Act of 1961, *supra*. Leagues commonly require local broadcast stations to black out a game if a team has not sold a specified percentage of tickets within a certain time frame.

The Federal Communications Commission (FCC) regulates the communications industry pursuant to authority delegated by the Communications Act of 1934. Although the multi-channel video programming platforms deliver the same content, the FCC regulates each separately according to the terms of the enabling legislation (wire/radio, §§ 151–621; satellite systems, §§ 700–69; local TV, §§ 1101–10; and broadband, §§ 1301–05).

The FCC promulgated "blackout rules" to join with league restraints, which were operative from 1975 until the fall of 2014. The FCC regulations served to insulate leagues from challenge pursuant to the antitrust laws. On September 30, 2014, the FCC repealed the "blackout rules" that prohibited cable and satellite operators from airing any sports event that had been blacked out on a local broadcast station. FCC Order, 14–141. The Commission found that the "blackout rules" were no longer justified in light of the significant changes in the sports industry since the rules were first adopted. It observed that television revenues have replaced ticket sales as the NFL's main source of revenue, and blackouts of NFL games are increasingly rare. The Commission also found that the NFL is unlikely to move its games from free, over-the-air broadcast television, to satellite and cable pay TV as a result of the elimination of the sports "blackout rules."

Regional Sports Networks

The dominant role of media in professional sports league marketing has resulted from creative efforts in programming and distribution. The regional sports networks (RSNs) secure broadcast rights from the teams and/or league, the media rights holders. The RSN markets the programming to cable and direct broadcast satellite providers, who sell to subscribers in the form of sports channels or packages.

The continually escalating traditional "rights fee" associated with the RSN model greatly impacts the economics of professional sports teams and leagues. The profitability of the RSNs motivates teams to venture into the broadcast business with equity investment in team-owned RSNs. The ownership structures of team-owned RSNs vary. Teams (content providers) often partner with network producers in the RSN ventures. The team-owned RSN enables the team or league to not only gain the valuables rights fee, but also the profits associated with the equity stake in the RSN. Importantly, the team-owned RSN provides the distribution mechanism for 24–7 team branding through non-live game programming. Vince Gennaro, in DIAMOND DOLLARS (2007), states, "The ultimate payoff for launching and operating a successful RSN is the creation of an asset that can be of equal or greater value than the team itself." *Id.*

Interestingly, if the RSN is cable-affiliated, the network must be made available to competing distributors at a reasonable price according to FCC regulations. 47 U.S.C. § 532 (c)(2006) [Cable Television Protection & Competition Act of 1992, 106 Stat. 1460, allowed to sunset in 2012, except for RSNs]. Revision of Program Access Rules, 77 Fed. Reg. 66026–65 at 66026–27, codified at 47 CFR pt. 76.

Direct broadcast satellite providers, e.g., DirecTV, are not mandated to sell rights to the programming by FCC regulation. The administrative disparity between cable and satellite systems enables a league to create an exclusive arrangement, such as NFL Sunday Ticket. Historically, exclusive distributorships have been scrutinized according to the antitrust laws to determine whether the vertical restraint and its preclusion of input for competitors reduce competition. For a detailed description of the RSN relationships and analysis of the content distribution model under the competition policies and regulations, *see* Moss, *Regional Sports Networks, Competition, and the Consumer*, 21 LOYOLA CONSUMER L. REV. 56 (2008).

Merchandising

League members also enter into contractual arrangements enabling the joint marketing of "logo bearing" merchandise. Typically, individual club rights are assigned to a "league entity" that is empowered to license the use of the league and club marks or other identifying insignia on merchandise sales, advertising, and other promotional ventures. The league entity is usually authorized to actively promote the marketing of licensed goods, thereby gaining economies of scale in the merchandising efforts. The entity frequently sells "exclusive sponsorship rights" at a premium price. Revenues generated through the program are shared by league members on a prearranged basis.

In the next case, National Football League Properties, Inc., the NFL entity administering the contractual arrangement between NFL members, filed an action against the Dallas Cowboys, Texas Stadium Corporation, and Cowboys owner, Jerry Jones, alleging that individual sponsorship contracts made through the stadium corporation violated the joint contract, the Lanham Act, and other common-law principles.

National Football League Properties, Inc. v. Dallas Cowboys Football Club, Ltd.

922 F. Supp. 849 (S.D.N.Y. 1996)

SCHEINDLIN, DISTRICT JUDGE:

Defendants Dallas Cowboys Football Club, Ltd., Texas Stadium Corporation, and Jerral W. Jones (together, "Defendants") move, pursuant to Fed.R.Civ.P. 12(b)(6), to dismiss this lawsuit for failure to state a claim upon which relief can be granted.

The National Football League ("NFL") is an unincorporated association comprised of 30 Member Clubs, including the Defendant Dallas Cowboys Football Club, Ltd. ("Cowboys Partnership"), which owns and operates the football team known as the Dallas Cowboys. Effective October 1, 1982, entities owning 26 of the then 28 Member Clubs entered into a trust agreement (the "Trust Agreement") which created the NFL Trust. The Trust Agreement provided that each Member Club would transfer to the NFL Trust the exclusive right to use its "Club Marks" for commercial purposes (with certain limited exceptions). These "Club Marks" include a team's name, helmet design, uniform design, and identifying slogans.... The Member Clubs also granted to the NFL Trust the exclusive right to use NFL Marks, such as the NFL Shield Design, and the names "NFL," "American Football Conference," "National Football Conference," and "Super Bowl."...

As soon as the NFL Trust was created, it entered into a "License Agreement" with Plaintiff NFL Properties, Inc. that provides Plaintiff with "the exclusive right to license the use of the Trust Property on all types of articles of merchandise and in connection with all types of advertising and promotional programs."... The Club Marks of the Cowboys Partnership, like the marks of other Member Clubs, are included in the Trust Property exclusively licensed to Plaintiff.

Plaintiff has been active in promoting the NFL and its Member Clubs, and has issued hundreds of licenses for the use of Club Marks.... Plaintiff has also entered into agreements with companies involved in specific product categories—such as soft drinks or charge cards—to be exclusive sponsors of the NFL and its Member Clubs. Sponsors are given the right to use the Club Marks and NFL Marks in advertising, promotion and packaging, to promote themselves as an "Official Sponsor" of the NFL and, in some cases, as an "Official Sponsor" of the Member Clubs.... The revenue generated from Plaintiff's sale of licensing and sponsorship rights is shared equally by the Member Clubs, which are the sole shareholders of Plaintiff....

Plaintiff contends that Defendants have embarked upon a wrongful plan and scheme which violates the Trust and License Agreements and infringes upon Plaintiff's rights. Specifically, the Complaint alleges that Defendants have entered into a number of highly-publicized contractual arrangements—with Dr. Pepper, Pepsi, and NIKE—that "impermissibly exploit the Club Marks and the NFL Marks, and thus wrongfully misappropriate revenue that belongs to plaintiff and should be shared among all the Member Clubs." ... The Complaint also alleges that Defendants are negotiating a similar contract with American Express.... Although all of the contractual arrangements Plaintiff mentions are nominally between the "sponsors" and Defendant Texas Stadium Corporation, Plaintiff claims that Defendants are using Texas Stadium as a "stand in" to help the Cowboys Partnership circumvent its obligations under the Trust and License Agreements....

The Complaint further alleges that Defendants misappropriated Club Marks and NFL Marks in solicitation materials they submitted to potential sponsors. In particular, Plaintiff asserts that Defendants used Club Marks—including the Cowboys "Star" logo—and NFL Marks—including the NFL's "Shield" logo—in the solicitation booklet they sent to Dr. Pepper.... Plaintiff contends that Defendants had no right to use such marks for any purpose....

Defendants deny that their actions in any way violate either the Trust Agreement or the License Agreement. In support of their argument, Defendants have submitted copies of the contracts Texas Stadium entered into with Nike, Pepsi, and Dr. Pepper, as well as the contract it eventually entered into with American Express. Defendants maintain that none of these contracts grant sponsors the right to use any Trust Property—namely, either Club Marks or NFL Marks; indeed, they note that the contracts with Pepsi, Nike and American Express explicitly state that the sponsor is not entitled to use any Club Marks.... Defendants argue that all of Plaintiff's claims are based on false assertions that are refuted by the underlying contracts, and that Plaintiff's action should therefore be dismissed. ...

Plaintiff's claim for breach of contract withstands Defendants' motion to dismiss for a number of reasons. First, although the contracts do not contain the language discussed above, they do grant other rights which may violate the Trust and License Agreements. The Pepsi contract grants Pepsi the right to use a logo which says

"Texas Stadium/Home of America's Favorite Team," which Plaintiff claims is a Club Mark. The logo licensed for use by American Express contains a star which Plaintiff claims is similar to the star that appears on the Dallas Cowboys' helmets. Accepting Plaintiff's allegation that Texas Stadium entered into these contracts as a "stand in" for the Cowboys Partnership, and drawing all inferences in favor of Plaintiff, the use of either of these logos would violate the Trust and License Agreements.

Second, the Complaint alleges that Defendants engaged in conduct which might violate the Trust and License Agreements—namely, a concerted campaign to create the impression that companies such as NIKE and Pepsi were sponsors of the Dallas Cowboys organization. During a nationally televised game, Defendant Jones, who controls both the Cowboys Partnership and Texas Stadium Corporation, allegedly escorted the CEO of NIKE to the Dallas Cowboys' sideline while both men prominently wore NIKE branded attire.... The Complaint further alleges that Jones ordered team personnel not to dress in apparel licensed by Plaintiff during this game, so that "[m]illions of television viewers observed no apparel brand other than NIKE" on the Cowboys' sideline.... Hence, despite contractual provisions to the contrary, in practice Defendants may have authorized NIKE apparel to be worn on the Dallas Cowboys' sideline, adjacent to players wearing the Club Marks.

Plaintiff also alleges that, in furtherance of their scheme to mislead the public, the Dallas Cowboys and NIKE jointly issued a press release in which the CEO of NIKE referred to the agreement as one with the "Dallas Cowboys"; and that Defendant Jones announced that the entire Cowboys organization drinks Pepsi, and posed for pictures at a press conference dressed in a "shirt emblazoned with a Cowboys Club Mark and boots emblazoned with a Pepsi logo...."... All of the above conduct may constitute an impermissible use of Club Marks (*e.g.*, the name "Dallas Cowboys" and the team's uniforms), since under the Trust and License Agreements the Cowboys Partnership gave Plaintiff the exclusive right to use these marks for commercial purposes. At a minimum, alleging such conduct is sufficient to state a claim for breach of the implied duty of good faith, which constitutes a breach of contract under New York law....

Finally, the Complaint alleges that Defendants misappropriated Club Marks and NFL Marks in solicitation materials they sent to potential sponsors. Specifically, the Complaint states that Defendants used the Club's "Star" logo and the NFL's "Shield" logo in a solicitation booklet they sent to Dr. Pepper.... Because the Trust and License Agreements give Plaintiff the exclusive right to use these Marks for commercial purposes, Defendants may have breached these agreements by using these Marks in a solicitation booklet. Defendants' counsel conceded that his clients' use of the Marks in solicitation materials was "[a]bsolutely inappropriate" and "probably violated their obligations...."

Plaintiff also alleges that Defendants violated § 43(a) of the Lanham Act, 15 U.S.C. § 1125(a), which provides in relevant part:

> (a)(1) Any person who, on or in connection with any goods or services, or any container for goods, uses in commerce any word, term, name, symbol, or device, or any combination thereof, or any false designation of origin, false or misleading description of fact, or false or misleading representation of fact, which—
>
> (A) is likely to cause confusion, or to cause mistake, or to deceive as to the affiliation, connection, or association of such person with another person, or as to the origin, *sponsorship, or approval* of his or her goods, services, or commercial activities of another person,... shall be liable in a civil action by any person who believes that he or she is or is likely to be damaged by such act (emphasis added).

Such a claim requires only a valid trademark and a likelihood of confusion on the part of the public.

Plaintiff has the exclusive right to use NFL Marks and Club Marks for commercial purposes. Plaintiff clearly alleges that Defendants have commercially exploited Club Marks and NFL Marks by using them to solicit a sponsorship agreement and by authorizing their use in agreements with Dr. Pepper, Pepsi, NIKE.... As described above, Plaintiff also alleges that Defendants, through various press conferences and public appearances, have sought to create the impression that a relationship exists between the Cowboys and various sponsor companies.... Of course, whether the marks used by Defendants were NFL Marks or Club Marks is a question of fact.

There are decisions of this Court which suggest that an exclusive licensee of the right to distribute goods bearing a certain trademark cannot bring an action under s 43(a) of the Lanham Act against the trademark owner for permitting the use of the trademark in violation of the licensing agreement. The reasoning of these cases is that where the trademark owner, who is the source of the goods, authorizes the use of the mark for "genuine" goods, there can be no likelihood of confusion as to the source of the goods and, consequently, the quality of the goods.

Plaintiff's interest in the marks, however, is in authorizing the international corporate sponsorship of goods, not in selling goods. In this context the concepts of genuine goods, quality of goods, and source of goods have little significance. The quality, source, or genuineness of Pepsi or NIKE shoes, for example, are primarily reflected by their respective marks regardless of whether they are sponsored by the Cowboys or the NFL. As neither Plaintiff nor Defendants sell or manufacture goods, it makes little sense to focus on the source of the goods.... Rather, in the sponsorship context, the focus should be on the nature of Defendants' activities regarding marks which Plaintiff has the exclusive right to commercially exploit. Plaintiff has pleaded that Defendants have used NFL Marks and Club Marks in a manner which is likely to confuse the public as to Plaintiff's "sponsorship or approval" of Dr. Pepper, Pepsi, and NIKE.... These allegations are sufficient to state a cause of action under the broad language of § 43(a) of the Lanham Act.

For the reasons set forth above, Defendants' motion is granted in part and denied in part.

So Ordered.

Notes and Comments

1. The Dallas Cowboys counter sued the NFL Trust alleging that the "Trust is a classic price-fixing cartel that has eliminated competition among NFL clubs." *Dallas Cowboys Football Club, Ltd. v. National Football League Trust*, 1996 U.S. Dist. LEXIS 1550 (S.D.N.Y. Oct. 18, 1995), at Complaint, Paragraph 1. The Dallas Cowboys identified relevant markets as follows:

> (a) the market for the rights to use the marks of major league professional football clubs and otherwise to affiliate with major league professional football for purposes of advertising and promoting goods and services ("professional football sponsorship market") and (b) the market for the rights to use the marks of major league professional football clubs on apparel and other goods ("professional football merchandise market"). [*Id.* at Complaint, Paragraph 25.]
>
> The relevant geographic market for assessing competition in the professional football sponsorship market and the professional football merchandise market is the United States. Defendants have market power and monopoly power in the professional football merchandise market. On information and belief, there are also local and regional submarkets of both the professional football sponsorship market and the professional football merchandise market. [*Id.* at Complaint, Paragraph 28.]

2. The NFL (NFL Properties) and Jerry Jones settled the matter on terms acceptable to the Cowboys. For commentaries analyzing the dispute, see Hoffman, *Dallas' Head Cowboy Emerges Victorious in a Licensing Showdown with the NFL:* National Football League Properties v. Dallas Cowboys Football Club, et al., 7 Seton Hall J. Sport L. 255 (1997); Hale, *Jerry Jones Versus the NFL: An Opportunity to Apply Logically the Single Entity Defense to the NFL*, 4 Sports Law. J. 1 (1997).

3. The Yankee Stadium-Adidas sponsorship deal (10 years; $95 million) provides a scenario similar to the Dallas Cowboys litigation. In that case, George Steinbrenner wore an Adidas pin on his lapel; members of the front office, groundskeepers, and stadium personnel wore Adidas gear; and Adidas signage appeared prominently at Yankee Stadium. MLB Properties objected to the sponsorship as a violation of MLB's policy (established by the 1995 Agency Agreement) of having merchandising arrangements exclusively authorized by Properties. The Yankees responded by filing suit challenging the joint marketing policy as a violation of the antitrust laws. (Interestingly, an attorney conflict of interest question arose as the New York law firm also represented Time Warner, owner of the Atlanta Braves, a defendant in the action.)

Like the *Cowboys* case, the matter was settled on terms favorable to the Yankees. For analysis of the legal issues and ultimate settlement, see Weinberger, *Baseball Trademark Licensing and the Antitrust Exemption: An Analysis of* New York Yankees Partnership v. Major League Baseball Enterprises, Inc., 23 COLUM.-VLA J.L. & ARTS 75 (1999).

4. The Court of Appeals for the Second Circuit affirmed the trial court's award of summary judgment for defendant, Major League Baseball Properties, in an antitrust suit brought by a merchandise manufacturer and distributor. The court held that the plaintiff presented no evidence to indicate that activities by MLB's licensing authority had an adverse effect on competition in a relevant market. The court stated that the plaintiff's burden cannot be met merely by a showing that the plaintiff is harmed as an individual competitor. *Major League Baseball Properties, Inc. v. Salvino, Inc.*, 542 F.3d 290 (2d Cir. 2008) (J. Sotomayor *concurring* on basis of ancillary restraints doctrine).

5. Are all joint commercial efforts by league members subject to attack under Section 1 of the Sherman Antitrust Act? Season ticket arrangements of professional clubs have been challenged as illegal under the antitrust laws. *See, e.g., Driskill v. Dallas Cowboys Football Club*, 498 F.2d 321 (5th Cir. 1974); *Coniglio v. Highwood Services, Inc.*, 495 F.2d 1286 (2d Cir. 1974). For an action filed for a refund of ticket prices on the basis that the club was moving, see *Stern v. Cleveland Browns Football Club, Inc.*, 1996 Ohio App. LEXIS 5802 (Dec. 20, 1996).

6. For a challenge of the NFL's "blackout rule," which prohibits live local telecasts of home games that are not sold out 72 hours before game-time, but not radio broadcasts, as a violation of the Americans with Disabilities Act of 1990, 42 U.S.C. § 12182, *see Stoutenborough v. NFL*, 59 F.3d 580 (6th Cir. 1995) ("Blackout rule" does not violate ADA). *See* Mathews, *Sports Broadcasting Blackouts: A Harbinger of Change in a Rapidly Evolving Media Landscape*, 18 HOUS. BUS. & TAX L.J. 202 (2018).

7. For a case challenging the price for satellite broadcasts under the antitrust laws, see *Shaw v. Dallas Cowboys Football Club*, 172 F.3d 299 (3d Cir. 1999) (Sports Broadcasting Act does not exempt from antitrust scrutiny the NFL's agreement to sell its teams' pooled television broadcast rights to a direct broadcast satellite distributor).

8. On March 19, 2002, the New York Yankees and New Jersey Nets, through holding companies and along with minority partner Goldman Sachs, launched YesNetwork. The venture proved highly successful both from the live-game distribution perspective and the programming of related content both from the live-game distribution perspective and the programming of related content serving to brand the teams' marketing efforts. Among other programs, YesNetwork produced New York Giants (NFL) magazine segments, various college sports games, and tape-delayed Manchester United games (English football). In November 2012, News Corporation acquired 49% equity interest in YesNetwork, which was transferred to 21st Century Fox. In early 2014, 21st Century Fox became the network's majority owner by pur-

chasing an additional 31% interest (total ownership interest of 80%). After the Disney Company (owner of ESPN) acquired 21st Century Fox, the company sold YesNetwork to the New York Yankees, Sinclair Broadcasting, and Amazon for $3.5 million, in order to receive Department of Justice antitrust approval.

9. The Minnesota Twins launched its team-owned cable and satellite RSN, Victory Sports One, in October 2003. The RSN collapsed one month into the 2004 season as a result of the failure of the RSN to negotiate deals with local area cable and direct broadcast satellite distributors. The Memphis Grizzles of the NBA also failed to successfully operate a team-owned RSN. *See generally* Dixon, *A Channel Worth Changing? The Individual Regional Sports Network: Proliferation, Profits, Parity & the Potential Administrative & Antitrust Issues That Could Follow,* 33 J. Nat'l Ass'n Admin. L. Judiciary 302 (2013).

10. In October 2012, the Houston Astros (46.5%), the Houston Rockets (31.5%), and Comcast (22%) entered into a partnership to form the RSN, Comcast Sports Net Houston (CSN Houston). Although the quality of production was high, the business expectations never developed, with hundreds of millions of dollars of lost revenue opportunities, tens of millions of dollars in legal and other costs, and squandered public relations in the greater Houston market. The projected market included portions of Texas, Oklahoma, Arkansas, and Louisiana. Reportedly, carriers were amenable to providing CSN Houston for the monthly subscriber fee of $4.00 in the Houston area, but refused to provide across the region even with much lower subscriber fees. Comcast initiated Chapter 11 involuntary bankruptcy proceedings. Finally, the court approved a reorganization plan that enables a new partnership owned by AT&T Teleholdings and DirecTV Sports Networks that is marketed as Root Sports Houston. Legal conflicts among the original partners remain for resolution. *Houston Regional Sports Network, L.P. v. Comcast Corporation Inc.,* United States Bankruptcy Court, Southern District of Texas, Houston Division, Case No. 13–35998, Demand for Jury Trial, Paragraph 24, filed June 11, 2015.

11. Various shifts in consumer behavior, such as cord-cutting, have negatively impacted RSN revenues, the values of RSNs, and the packaging and distribution of sports programming. For a comprehensive analysis of the media industry disruption and the effect upon the sports industry, see Sussman, *Are Our Pastimes Past Their Time? How Will the Media Industry Disruption & Changes to the Legal Environment Affect the Sports Industry?* 67 Syracuse L. Rev. 449 (2017).

12. For antitrust attacks on the NFL's Sunday Ticket package, *see In re NFL Sunday Ticket Antitrust Litigation,* 2017 U.S. Dist. LEXIS 121354 (C.D. Cal., June 30, 2017) (Court dismissed plaintiffs' claims for failure to prove existence of "relevant market" and antitrust injury).

13. In 2006, Time Warner and Comcast Corporation purchased cable systems from Adelphia Communications Corporation. The FCC placed restrictions on Time Warner to prevent it from unreasonably denying coverage for rival unaffiliated

RSNs. Time Warner denied MASN's request for carriage on its analog tier in North Carolina. MASN filed a complaint with the FCC alleging a violation of the 1992 Cable Act. The FCC ruled that Time Warner did not unfairly discriminate as it was willing to carry MASN on its digital cable tier. The Fourth Circuit concluded that the FCC decision was not arbitrary and capricious, given the Time Warner evidence that there was not enough consumer demand for MASN coverage. Thus, Time Warner's action regarding MASN was in pursuit of legitimate business purposes, not a result of unfair discrimination. *TCR Sports Broadcasting Holding, L.L.P. v. FCC*, 679 F.3d 269 (4th Cir. 2012).

14. Advances in technology introduce unique channels for the distribution of professional sports content and the attendant legal issues. A live streaming video application, Meerkat, enables consumers to upload video footage from smartphones to the internet for instantaneous viewing. Twitter developed an online application, Periscope, that allows consumers to watch live videos for up to 24 hours after the initial broadcast. Does the broadcast or rebroadcast of commercial sporting events infringe on leagues' and clubs' intellectual property rights in the games? *See* Edelman, *From Meerkat to Periscope: Does Intellectual Property Law Prohibit the Live Streaming of Commercial Sporting Events?*, 39 COLUM. J.L. & ARTS 469 (2016).

15. "Daily fantasy sports" has quickly grown to a multimillion-dollar industry. In 2018, the United States Supreme Court held the federal statute, Professional and Amateur Sports Protection Act (PASPA), which prohibited state-authorized sports gambling unconstitutional. *Murphy v. NCAA*, 138 S. Ct. 1461 (2018). Sports betting and gambling is expected to become a multi-billion dollar industry.

E. League versus League—Monopoly

League decision-making sometimes is challenged by parties who are not members of or otherwise associated with the league. Typical suits are filed by a newly organized league against an established league. There is little question that the underlying purpose of an established league's efforts in head-to-head competition is to dominate the market. The relevant query is whether the dominant league has unfairly prevented competition to gain the market position. The attack from parties external to league operations usually focuses on Section 2 of the Sherman Act. The Act prohibits the misuse of monopoly power. Thus, a plaintiff must show that the defendant: (1) possesses monopoly power and (2) has misused the power. The plaintiff must establish the relevant "product market" and "geographic market" to prove existence of monopoly power. Defendant actions are considered to qualify as "misuse" of monopoly power where the actions illegally exclude or prevent competition.

The elements of plaintiff's antitrust action are explained in *American Football League v. National Football League*, 205 F. Supp. 60, 63 (D. Md. 1962), as follows:

The several charges of (a) monopolization, (b) attempt to monopolize and (c) combination or conspiracy to monopolize require proof of different elements.

(a) *Monopolization.* To prove monopolization... plaintiffs must show (1) that defendants possessed monopoly power and (2) that they undertook some course of action the consequence of which was to exclude competition or prevent competition or which was undertaken with the purpose or intent to accomplish that end....

(1) 'Monopoly power is the power to control prices or exclude competition.' The test of monopoly power in this case... is whether the NFL had sufficient power to prevent the formation or successful operation of a new league....

(2) A business organization which has acquired monopoly power is guilty of monopolization if it undertakes a course of action the consequences of which would be to exclude competitors or prevent competition. Proof of specific intent is not necessary....

(b–c). *Attempt and Conspiracy.* There may be an attempt... or conspiracy to monopolize without... monopoly power.... The requisite intent to monopolize must be present and predominate.

American Football League v. National Football League

205 F. Supp. 60 (D. Md. 1962)

THOMSEN, CHIEF JUDGE.

In this action for treble damages and injunctive relief under the antitrust laws, plaintiffs, the American Football League (AFL) and its members, charge defendants, the National Football League (NFL) and most of its members, with monopolization, attempted monopolization and conspiracy to monopolize major league professional football....

The AFL was organized in the latter half of 1959, and began play in 1960. Joe Foss has been its only Commissioner. At the time this suit was filed, October 14, 1960, its member teams or franchisees and the principal owners thereof were [8 clubs]....

The NFL was organized in 1920 and since 1933 has had from 10 to 14 teams. Bert Bell served as Commissioner until his death on October 11, 1959; thereafter Austin Gunsel was Acting Commissioner until January 1960, when Pete Rozelle was elected Commissioner. As of the date of suit, its teams, their principal owners, and others who figured prominently in the evidence were [14 clubs]....

The successful operation of a major league professional football team requires (1) membership in a league in which the several clubs are reasonably well matched in playing strength and are located in areas which can and will support the teams by attendance throughout the season sufficient to provide adequate revenues for both the home and visiting clubs, (2) the acquisition of a group of capable players, and (3) the sale of television rights. Plaintiffs allege that defendants monopolized, attempted to monopolize and conspired to monopolize each of these three areas of competition.

With respect to (1), plaintiffs contend that they have shown that all defendants *monopolized* and that all defendants, except the Washington Redskins, *attempted* to monopolize and *conspired* to monopolize the metropolitan areas in which franchises can successfully be located. Plaintiffs argue that the granting of NFL franchises to Dallas and to Minneapolis-St. Paul, at the times and under the circumstances shown by the evidence, and statements made with respect to a proposed franchise for Houston, constituted an exercise of monopoly power, and that those acts were done as part of an attempt or a conspiracy to monopolize. On the other hand, defendants deny that they had monopoly power, and contend that those franchises were granted and those statements were made pursuant to a policy of expansion adopted by the NFL before the AFL was organized, and that the timing was at most an effort by the NFL and its members to compete more effectively with proposed AFL teams in particular cities.

With respect to (2) above—acquisition of players—plaintiffs conceded at the close of their case that they had not proved *any* violation of the antitrust laws entitling them to recover herein.

With respect to (3), they conceded that they had not shown the requisite intent to support their charge that defendants had *attempted* to monopolize or *conspired* to monopolize with respect to the sale of TV or radio rights; but they contend that they have shown that defendants possessed monopoly power, and that the approval by the NFL Commissioner of the TV contract made by the Baltimore Colts and Pittsburgh Steelers with the National Broadcasting Company was an exercise of that power which renders defendants liable on the charge of monopolization. Defendants contend that the Commissioner was obliged to approve the contract under the principles laid down by Judge Grim in the *United States v. National Football League*, 116 F. Supp. 319 (E.D. Pa. 1953), and it was agreed that further evidence and argument on this point should await the decision of the court on the question whether the NFL had monopoly power.

The several charges of (a) monopolization, (b) attempt to monopolize and (c) combination or conspiracy to monopolize require proof of different elements.

(a) *Monopolization*. To prove monopolization in this private antitrust suit plaintiffs must show (1) that defendants possessed monopoly power and (2) that they undertook some course of action the consequence of which was to exclude competition or prevent competition in the business of major league professional football or which was undertaken with the purpose or intent to accomplish that end.

(1) "Monopoly power is the power to control prices or exclude competition." ... [A] party has monopoly power if it has "over 'any part of the trade or commerce among the several States,' a power of controlling prices or unreasonably restricting competition."

"Monopoly is a relative word." Whether the sole business in a particular field has monopoly power depends upon the nature of the business. Those wishing to operate professional football teams must belong to a league. The test of monopoly power in this case, therefore, is whether the NFL had sufficient power to prevent the formation or successful operation of a new league. It is not sufficient that they might have had the power to exclude a new league from a particular city or group of cities, unless the power to exclude from that city or group of cities would have effectively prevented the formation or operation of a new league.

(2) A business organization which has acquired monopoly power is guilty of monopolization if it undertakes a course of action the consequence of which would be to exclude competitors or prevent competition. Proof of a specific intent is not necessary.

However, it cannot be required to forego normal competitive business methods to further legitimate business ends, as distinguished from acts which are done with the intent to create or preserve a monopoly, or which would have the consequence of excluding competitors from a relevant market.

(b)–(c). *Attempt and Conspiracy.* There may be an attempt to monopolize, or a combination or conspiracy to monopolize, without the offender or offenders actually having monopoly power. But an essential element of an attempt to monopolize, or of a combination or conspiracy to monopolize, is a specific intent to destroy competition or build monopoly. Neither rough competition nor unethical business conduct is sufficient. The requisite intent to monopolize must be present and predominant.

The intent must be to gain control over some relevant market sufficient to set prices in that market or to exclude competitors therefrom. An intent to exclude competitors from only part of the relevant market would not be sufficient to create liability for an attempt or a conspiracy, unless as plaintiffs contend in this case, defendants believed that by excluding the AFL from certain cities, *e.g.*, Dallas and Minneapolis-St. Paul, they could effectively exclude it from the entire market, and acted with that specific intent as their preponderant motive.

Relevant Market

The market which must be studied to determine whether a business organization has monopoly power will vary with the part of commerce under consideration. The "part of the trade or commerce among the several States" involved in the present action is major league professional football. Essentially, the relevant market is nationwide; but because of the nature of major league professional football, there are several areas of effective competition between plaintiffs and defendants.

The competition for players and coaches is nationwide. The competition for the sale of TV and radio rights to networks or sponsors is essentially nationwide. The competition for attendance at games, and the competition between the telecast of a game from one city and the actual playing of a game in another city, is generally confined to the area in which the game is being played. The competition between the leagues for metropolitan areas in which franchises can profitably be located is the most important aspect of the competition in this case. This area of competition is essentially nationwide, embracing all cities and metropolitan areas which may reasonably be expected to support a major league professional football team. Consideration must also be given to the fact that at least six and probably eight teams are necessary for the successful operation of a league, and that only a few cities, at most, under present conditions, can successfully support two teams.

Findings of Fact

[The facts as presented here are gleaned from the decision on appeal of this case, 323 F.2d 124 (4th Cir. 1963)].

[T]he two football leagues, American and National, are unincorporated associations. Each has a commissioner who exercises some executive and administrative authority, but, in each, ultimate control is vested in the owners of the football teams for whose benefit the league exists. In each instance, the teams are corporations, each of which was the holder of a franchise to operate a professional football team in a designated city. Most of the corporate team owners are controlled and dominated by a single individual, though in a minority of instances the role of the dominant individual is played by a small group of two or three, and in one instance of five. It is these individuals who exercise ultimate control of the leagues with which they are associated.

The National Football League was organized in 1920. For a number of years its existence was precarious. Until the last ten years, its membership was far from static, and until 1946 every major league professional football team operating in the United States was associated with it. In 1945, the All American Football Conference was organized, and it operated through the four seasons of 1946–1949 with eight teams, except that two of the teams were merged in 1949, and in the last season, there were but seven teams. Thereafter the All American Football Conference disbanded, but three of its teams were received into the National Football League, and teams franchised in those three cities, Baltimore, Cleveland and San Francisco, were operated under National League franchises when this action was commenced.

In 1959, the National Football League operated with twelve teams located in eleven cities. There were two teams in Chicago and one each in Cleveland, New York, Philadelphia, Pittsburgh, Washington, Baltimore, Detroit, Los Angeles, San Francisco, and Green Bay, Wisconsin. In 1960 two additional franchises were placed, one in Dallas and one in Minneapolis-St. Paul, the Dallas team beginning play in 1960 and the Minneapolis-St. Paul team in 1961. In 1961, one of the Chicago teams, the Cardinals, was transferred to St. Louis.

The American Football League was organized in 1959, and began with a full schedule of games in 1960. Affiliated with it were eight teams located in eight cities,

Boston, Buffalo, Houston, New York, Dallas, Denver, Los Angeles and Oakland. After the 1960 season, the Los Angeles team was moved to San Diego.

Players and TV

The NFL has avoided competition among its teams for outstanding college players by its player selection system, sometimes called a draft. Such a system is probably necessary for the successful operation of a league. The AFL adopted a similar system.

The NFL has minimized competition between attendance at its games and telecasts of other NFL games by prohibiting the telecasting of NFL games into a city where an NFL game is being played.... The AFL adopted a similar policy.

On several occasions during the late Summer and Fall of 1959, Hunt, on behalf of the AFL, sought an agreement with the NFL which (1) provided for a common player draft and (2) would have prohibited the telecasting of any game of either league into city whether either an NFL or an AFL game was being played. This would have seriously restricted if not entirely eliminated the telecasting of "away" games of the New York, Los Angeles, and Dallas teams back to those cities and would have otherwise seriously diluted the value of the TV rights. Moreover, both proposals were of doubtful validity, at best, although plaintiffs contend that a common player draft would be a reasonable restriction on commerce, for reasons which need not be elaborated here. Both proposals were promptly and repeatedly rejected by the NFL owners.

For many years most of the NFL games have been telecast over the CBS network through arrangements made by the teams or their sponsors. On or about March 30, 1960, Pittsburgh and Baltimore reached an agreement with NBC for nationwide telecasts of their regular season games. This arrangement was opposed by the other NFL teams and by Commissioner Rozelle, and was detrimental to other NFL clubs as well as to the AFL clubs. Plaintiffs concede that this action was not taken with the specific intent to injure the AFL and it members.

The TV arrangements of the AFL were handled by an organization inexperienced in dealing with sports promotion. After presenting unsatisfactory plans to ABC and NBC, the AFL made a very profitable deal with ABC, which had been negotiating with Hunt since the middle of 1959.

Monopoly Power

Plaintiffs contend that defendants had the power to prevent or exclude competition by plaintiffs in the business of major league professional football. As we have seen, the principal areas of competition are for (1) a sufficient number of cities capable of supporting teams to form a practicable league, (2) players, and (3) the sale of TV rights.

(1) *Cities.* There are many cities in the United States capable of supporting competently managed major league professional football teams. Hunt testified that in his opinion a metropolitan area of 500,000 or more with proper management and

under the right circumstances will support such a team. On all the evidence a figure of 700,000 appears more reasonable. There are 52 metropolitan areas in the United States with a population over 500,000 of which 31 have more than 700,000 and 24 more than 1,000,000.

Aside from population, the material factors in determining whether a city is a suitable location for a professional football franchise include an adequate stadium, available financial backing, weather, fan enthusiasm, and proximity to another professional football team or other competing sports.

Some problems, such as stadium inadequacies, can often be resolved once the probability of obtaining a professional football franchise has been sufficiently established. For example, Oakland and Houston are in the process of constructing new stadiums; Minneapolis and San Diego expanded the seating capacity of their existing stadiums.

It is doubtful whether under present conditions any cities except possibly New York and one or two other large metropolitan areas can support two teams. The AFL, however, had no difficulty in finding owners for the franchises Hunt wished to place in New York and Los Angeles, and had applications from several other NFL cities. There is no reason to believe that the Oakland club will not be successful, once its stadium is completed, although it is located in the San Francisco Bay area, where it must compete with the NFL 49'ers.

The owners of a franchise must be prepared to absorb a large initial loss; profit projection is speculative and eventual profits are usually small. Naturally most investors would prefer to have a franchise in an established, financially successful league rather than in a newly organized unproved league. However, the lure of owning a successful team is very attractive to many rich men, as well as to sports promoters; witness the applications received by the AFL from Vancouver, Seattle, Portland, San Francisco, San Diego, Newark, Buffalo, Kansas City, St. Louis, Louisville, New Orleans, Miami and Atlanta, as well as from the eight cities originally selected, plus Oakland.

Fan enthusiasm may be built up over the years; poor college football towns may be developed into loyal supporters of a professional team, e.g., Baltimore, where it has also been shown that established competing attractions, such as horse racing, are not fatal. Plaintiffs have failed to show any lack of sufficient qualified applicants for franchises to support a second league.

No doubt the NFL could have forced the AFL out of any particular city except New York and possibly one or two other very large cities, plus Dallas and Houston, where rich owners are determined to fight it out. But it was not financially practicable for the NFL to expand into all the cities in which the AFL might place teams. There is no evidence that the NFL has ever contemplated more than 16 teams, and it is probably not feasible to operate a larger league. Even during 1959, after the AFL was organized, the NFL owners were unwilling to weaken their own league by expanding into any area which they did not believe would prove a suitable addition to the NFL.

Plaintiffs suggest that defendants had the power to add enough new cities to the NFL to destroy the AFL, and after having destroyed it, to drop the cities the NFL did not want. But the NFL did not have the resources to add more than two new teams at once nor more than four new teams within the next five years without so weakening the existing clubs as to make such action undesirable and not practically possible.

(2) *Players*. In 1959 the NFL had most of the ablest players under contract. However, colleges graduate annually large numbers of talented players, and, because after the season starts professional football rosters are usually limited to around 35 players, many good players are released each year after the training season and are available to be signed by clubs in any league. Moreover, NFL players become free agents after a period of years.

By March 1960, the AFL clubs had submitted 365 player contracts to the AFL commissioner for approval, and an estimated 668 players had signed contracts with one of the AFL teams. Plaintiffs were able to compete successfully with the NFL and with the Canadian League for the services of many highly qualified players. AFL clubs signed six of the 12 first choices of the NFL teams in the 1959 draft, and competition from the AFL and the Canadian League deprived two NFL clubs of the services of more than half of their first 10 draft choices.

The NFL has no power to prevent the AFL from signing an adequate number of qualified players.

(3) *TV*. The evidence shows that defendants did not have the power to exclude plaintiffs from adequate television outlets.

The AFL admits that it has been notably successful in its operations, and gives promise of increasing success. Like the NFL, it has an expansion committee.

Defendants did not have the power to prevent or unreasonably to restrict competition. Therefore, they are not liable on the claim of monopolization.

Intent

Since defendants did not have monopoly power, plaintiffs must rely on their claims that defendants attempted or conspired to monopolize. To recover on either of those claims plaintiffs must show that some acts were done or some course of action undertaken with the specific intent to destroy the AFL as a competitor.

The acts relied on by plaintiffs are the offering and granting of franchises to Dallas and Minneapolis and the conditional offer of a franchise to Houston, at the times and under the circumstances those acts were done. To prove the requisite intent, plaintiffs rely particularly on (a) the August 29, 1959, announcement with respect to Dallas and Houston, (b) various proposals and suggestions made by NFL owners to AFL owners between September and November 1959, and (c) the statements and telegrams in November 1959 with respect to the Minnesota franchise.

(a) The announcement on August 29 that the committee would recommend the grant of franchises to Dallas and Houston to begin play in 1961 was in line with the general plan for the expansion of the NFL during the years 1961–1965, which had been agreed upon by most of the owners before the AFL was contemplated. As we have seen, various motives induced the several owners to go along with these plans. Some were attracted by the great enthusiasm for foot-ball in Texas, the size of the Cotton Bowl in Dallas, and the Rice Stadium and plans for a municipal stadium in Houston. The Philadelphia Eagles wanted a 16-team league with two eight-team divisions. Some felt that the good of the league, as well as the good of the sport in competition with other sports, called for expansion into areas that were clearly ready, as soon as the financial and playing strength of the NFL clubs made it feasible to stock new clubs with players, and they were being urged to do so by Hester, the attorney who was lobbying for the Sports Bill. Weather, local rivalry and scheduling convenience also made the two cities in Texas an attractive pair.

At the request of Murchison, in October 1959, the effective date of the Dallas franchise was advanced one year, from 1961 to 1960, in order to permit the NFL team to start at the same time as the AFL team. This was done for business reasons, *i.e.*, to enable the NFL team to compete more effectively with the AFL team in Dallas for season ticket sales, choice of dates in the Cotton Bowl, newspaper support and the like.

Plaintiffs note that several of the NFL owners told Hunt's attorney that they did not believe Dallas could support two teams. That does not prove that their predominant intent in granting a franchise to Dallas, or advancing the playing date to 1960, was to destroy the AFL. Their views were at least equally consistent with their claimed desire to strengthen Murchison's competitive position as against Hunt's Dallas AFL team, so that the NFL team would have a better chance to survive. Although some of the NFL owners may have felt that this competition might discourage the AFL from continuing its team in Dallas or even from continuing operations as a league, this was not a predominant or principal motive in granting the franchise or advancing the date.

(b) Pauley and Murchison were particularly anxious to avoid competing teams in their respective cities (Los Angeles and Dallas), and many of the meetings and proposals during the Fall of 1959 arose out of the desire of those NFL owners to find a solution for their special problems. Their efforts were encouraged by some of the other NFL owners and were welcomed by many of the AFL owners, who really wanted franchises in the NFL, and in most instances would have been satisfied with a share in such a franchise. All of the owners, AFL as well as NFL, were anxious to avoid costly competition in signing players. The offers and suggestions of the NFL owners were not made with any predominant intent to destroy the AFL, but as part of the effort being made by both sides to find solutions to their mutual problems.

(c) After it was clear that the Rice Stadium in Houston would not be made available to the NFL, most of the owners agreed that Minneapolis-St. Paul should replace Houston as one of the first two franchises to be granted in accordance with the expansion policy to which all but Marshall had agreed. Undoubtedly, the November telegrams were sent at the request of Johnson and Winter to persuade Winter's associates, Boyer and Skoglund, to give up the AFL franchise, so that the NFL could come into the Twin Cities without competition there. It was obvious that Minneapolis-St. Paul could not support two teams, and the NFL wanted to have a successful team there. As in the case of Dallas, that was a business reason, different from an intent to destroy the new league. The evidence does not support plaintiffs' contention that an intent to destroy the AFL was a predominant motive of defendants.

If the NFL had had monopoly power, the course of action followed by the NFL owners might have been sufficient to create liability for monopolization, which does not require proof of specific intent; but the actual motives and intent were not such as would support liability on the claim of attempt to monopolize or the claim of conspiring to monopolize....

Judgment will be entered in favor of the defendants, with costs.

United States Football League v. National Football League

634 F. Supp. 1155 (S.D.N.Y. 1986)

LEISURE, DISTRICT JUDGE:

The United States Football League and certain of its member clubs (collectively referred to as the "USFL") have sued the National Football League, its commissioner and certain of its member clubs (hereinafter collectively referred to as the "NFL") to obtain declaratory and injunctive relief and to recover damages resulting from alleged violations of Section 1 and 2 of the Sherman Anti-Trust Act, 15 U.S.C. §§ 1 & 2, and the common law.

Contentions of the Parties

"Television is at the heart of this case."... The USFL alleges that its inability to obtain a network television contract for the Fall of 1986 was a result of "coercive" pressure applied by the NFL to the three networks not to agree to a Fall 1986 contract with the USFL. In addition, the USFL alleges that the existence of the NFL's three network television contracts has the effect of precluding a new major professional football league from ever having its games televised, thereby depriving it of the television revenues and nationwide exposure a new league requires to be able to compete successfully against the NFL.

The NFL contends that none of the "factual" allegations about the other professional football leagues, the prior antitrust suits against the NFL, or the events surrounding the 1961 and 1966 legislation are probative of any factual issue relating to the USFL's alleged antitrust injury and damages....

Applicable Law

The USFL argues that all three violations of Section 2—monopolization, attempted monopolization, and conspiracy to monopolize—require proof of both anticompetitive intent and analysis of the defendants' market power, including the sources of that power....

The USFL contends that in appropriate cases, prior antitrust violations and the history of the relevant market are admissible to establish market power and intent....

The USFL also argues that evidence of conspiratorial conduct occurring before plaintiffs' damage period is admissible to establish the intent, motive and method of the defendants' conspiracies against the USFL....

AAFC and WFL Allegations

The NFL argues that there are no allegations in the complaint, nor have any facts been presented by the USFL, showing that the NFL caused the AAFC's dissolution in 1947 or the WFL's dissolution in 1975....

At oral argument, the USFL conceded that the allegations concerning the AAFC appear in the pleadings for background purposes only. Accordingly, with respect to the AAFC, the motion is granted. The USFL shall make no reference, and shall offer no evidence at trial, that implies that the NFL caused the demise of the AAFC.... This ruling does not, however, preclude the USFL from referring to the AAFC in the context of a presentation for background purposes of the history of professional football in the United States.

Two incidents have come to the Court's attention that provide a basis for allegations that the NFL harmed or attempted to harm the WFL. The first arose out of the 1973 attendance by Robert Wussler, then President of CBS Sports, at a WFL owners meeting. The USFL claims that NFL Commissioner Rozelle let it be known to the networks that he considered Wussler's attendance to be an unfriendly act. The USFL relies upon this incident both to prove that the NFL entertained anticompetitive intent toward the WFL and to prove that in 1981–82 the NFL pressured the networks not to give the fledgling USFL a television contract. In December 1981, the USFL's publicity agent invited the President of CBS Sports to attend a January 1982 Florida meeting of prospective USFL owners. One CBS executive advised the other not to attend since Wussler's attendance at the 1973 WFL meeting "was enormously embarrassing to CBS and considered an unfriendly act by Pete [Rozelle]."

When questioned about the Wussler incident during his deposition in this case, Commissioner Rozelle recalled that he told Robert Wood, President of CBS in 1973, that Rozelle had heard that Wussler, the head of CBS Sports, had attended a WFL meeting. "I was somewhat surprised because CBS had just entered into a four year contract with us for playing Sunday." ...

Rozelle's testimony concerning this incident raises a material question of fact as to whether there was an attempt to pressure CBS, if not the other networks, to avoid any involvement with the WFL. This is consistent with the USFL's theory that the same tactics have been used to discourage the networks from giving the USFL a contract to televise USFL games....

The second instance of alleged NFL misconduct directed against the WFL is set forth in § 61(a) of the amended complaint, which alleges that in 1985 the NFL "re-instituted a policy, first developed by the defendant NFL Member Clubs when the WFL came into being and abandoned by the defendant NFL Member Clubs after the WFL's demise" to permit the signing of free agent players to NFL contracts for future seasons after the completion of the sixth weekend of play in the current season. Previously, such signings were not allowed until the end of the then current season.

While there is little or no evidence that the change in the free agent signing rule harmed the WFL, the NFL's alleged parallel response to the two leagues raises a triable issue of fact as to the NFL's monopolistic intent with respect to the WFL and later the USFL. The decisions in *United States v. Grinnell Corp.*... and *Lorain Journal Co. v. United States*, support the proposition that the history of how a monopolist achieved its position is relevant. The USFL has presented specific facts demonstrating that the allegations that the NFL unlawfully caused or attempted to cause the demise of the WFL are not "fanciful." Accordingly, with respect to the WFL, the motion is denied.

AFL Allegations

The USFL's allegations concerning the AFL are also defective.... Paragraph 22 of the amended complaint quotes a statement by the owner of the Washington Redskins in 1960, Mr. Marshall, that the only reason for the expansion was to destroy the new AFL. In *American Football League v. National Football League* it was held that these allegations were false. The AFL's claims of monopolization, attempted monopolization and conspiracy to monopolize against the NFL were dismissed....

The NFL urges that in the interests of stability in the law and judicial economy that these findings should be given collateral estoppel effect and that the USFL not be permitted to resurrect stale claims that were rejected when they were fresh... unless the USFL presents new, credible, persuasive evidence which could not have been presented at the original trial, the allegations concerning the AFL should not be presented to the jury.... Accordingly the motion is granted. Plaintiffs shall make no reference nor offer any evidence at trial concerning supposed conduct by the NFL directed at the AFL....

On Motion for Partial Summary Judgment

The NFL has moved, pursuant to Fed. R. Civ. P. 56, for partial summary judgment as to:

> 1) plaintiffs' "stadium-related" claims; 2) plaintiffs' "disparagement" claims; and 3) plaintiffs' "game officials" claims....

I. Stadium-Related Conduct

In essence, the USFL alleges that the NFL and its member clubs, acting separately as well as in various alliances, engaged in numerous acts directed at preventing existing and potential USFL clubs from gaining adequate access to suitable stadium facilities.... The USFL has also asserted a separate common law claim, for intentional interference with contractual relations, based on defendants' stadium-related conduct.

The NFL has suggested, and the USFL does not seriously contest, that the allegations may be divided into four separate groups: 1) alleged denials of access to stadia during the spring; 2) alleged denials of access to stadia during the fall (following the USFL's decision to abandon its spring schedule); 3) alleged delays in obtaining stadium leases; 4) alleged harm to USFL franchises through the granting of stadium leases with disadvantageous terms.

The NFL contends that the USFL has offered no admissible evidence that establishes either: 1) direct involvement by the NFL in the stadium lease and use arrangements negotiated by individual NFL clubs; or 2) any concerted action by NFL clubs or uniformity of position by such clubs with regard to the terms of stadium leases. To the contrary, the NFL insists, the deposition testimony of key NFL figures establishes the absence of such league involvement or concerted action. Having reviewed the record with considerable care, this Court agrees that a large portion of the evidence proffered by the USFL is either inadmissible hearsay that may not be relied upon in opposing a motion for summary judgment, or is simply immaterial to the allegations plaintiffs are seeking to prove.

Nonetheless, it may be assumed, for purposes of the ensuing discussion of *Noerr-Pennington* immunity, that the USFL's stadium-related allegations are supported by admissible evidence....

A. Noerr-Pennington

It is undisputed that, in all but one instance, the USFL's allegations of denial of stadium access are directed at the failure of a state or local governmental authority to grant a lease to a potential USFL team, to grant a lease as quickly as plaintiffs would have liked, or to grant a lease on terms sufficiently favorable to the USFL lessee. Plaintiffs reject any suggestion, however, that these local governmental authorities exercised "free discretion" in considering applications by USFL clubs for stadium leases. Rather, the USFL alleges that, in numerous instances, the governmental authorities that own and operate local stadia have dealt harshly with USFL applicants as a direct result of pressure by the NFL and/or its member clubs. Such pressure, the USFL maintains, includes threats by NFL clubs to abandon certain cities and stadia; or (in cities that do not currently have NFL franchises) engaging in the practice of "franchise dangling." Not surprisingly, the USFL argues that such behavior is overtly anticompetitive.

In each of the instances in which the decision whether or not to lease to a USFL club rested with a local governmental authority, plaintiffs' allegations of misconduct invariably turn on the involvement of one or more of the NFL defendants in the lease-approval process. Usually, such involvement was manifested by the local NFL club's presentation of its viewpoint to the appropriate city body on public issues.

Such petitioning conduct, the NFL asserts, amounts to an exercise of free speech that cannot possibly give rise to liability under the federal antitrust laws. Under the *Noerr-Pennington* doctrine, "mere solicitation of governmental action through legislative processes, even though the sole purpose of the defendants is to restrain competition, is an activity which is fully protected by the First Amendment and is immune from Sherman Act liability." *Miracle Mile Associates v. City of Rochester*....

The USFL contends that the *Noerr-Pennington* doctrine cannot be invoked to immunize anticompetitive activity directed at government agencies acting in a purely commercial or proprietary capacity.... Recent decisions by federal courts of appeal, however, suggest that the *Noerr-Pennington* doctrine should not be given such a limited construction.

The Ninth Circuit, for example, has squarely held that there is no "commercial exception" to the *Noerr-Pennington* doctrine....

Having reviewed the relevant authority, this Court concludes that *Noerr-Pennington* may indeed be applied to immunize petitioning conduct directed at government agencies acting in a proprietary capacity, even if such conduct may be characterized as anticompetitive....

II. Disparagement

The USFL alleges that part of the NFL's Section 2 violation was "a deliberate and widespread campaign launched by the defendants... to disparage the USFL and its business prospects." Specifically, plaintiffs allege that the NFL's "defamatory campaign has involved, among other things, the dissemination of press reports reflecting negatively on the USFL to the press and the media; and the making of disparaging and threatening remarks in an attempt to... drive the USFL out of major league professional football in the United States."

As noted earlier, plaintiffs have not asserted a separate claim under the antitrust laws based on the NFL's "disparagement" of the USFL. Plaintiffs do maintain, however, that the jury is entitled to consider the NFL's campaign of negative publicity as an integral part of defendants' aggregate anticompetitive conduct which, taken as a whole, violates the Sherman Act....

Although disparagement by itself will not give rise to a cause of action under the federal antitrust laws,... product disparagement coupled with the power to exclude competition may be illegal under the Sherman Act. Nonetheless, the mere dissemination of unflattering opinion or information about a competitor, unaccompanied by misstatements of fact, simply does not amount to a violation of the antitrust laws....

In this case, no triable issue of fact exists concerning the truth or falsity of the opinion or information disseminated by the NFL about the USFL, since plaintiffs have identified no specific misrepresentation of fact made by any defendant. Thus, even though the NFL may have consciously denigrated the USFL in the public forum, such a pattern of behavior, unaccompanied by false statement, does not constitute predatory or anticompetitive conduct as a matter of law.

Evidence of defendants' "anti-USFL" campaign may be admissible at trial as probative of defendants' intent, or of the "purpose or character" of the NFL's anticompetitive conduct. In addition, evidence regarding the anti-USFL campaign may be relevant to plaintiffs' common law claims for intentional interference with contractual relations, a species of tort that does not require proof of false statement.

Defendants' motion for partial summary judgment as to plaintiffs' disparagement "claims" is granted to the following extent: First, plaintiffs are barred at trial from arguing that defendants have made any false statements or misrepresentations of fact about the USFL, since this Court finds that no substantial controversy exists regarding that issue. Second, whereas plaintiffs have failed to support their allegations of disparagement with any specific allegation of false statement or misrepresentation, this Court now holds that the NFL's dissemination of unflattering opinion or information about the USFL does not constitute predatory or anticompetitive conduct within the meaning of the Sherman Act.

III. Game Officials

In its amended complaint, the USFL alleges that the nationwide market for "qualified... game officials" is one of "several... distinct submarkets relevant to the plaintiffs' allegations." Plaintiffs allege that the NFL violated Section 2 by attempting to monopolize, conspiring to monopolize and actually monopolizing the market for "qualified professional football officials," ... by refusing to permit officials employed by the NFL to officiate USFL games and by "requiring" that NFL officials observe the terms of their "full-year contracts." Plaintiffs elsewhere allege that the NFL intentionally interfered with the USFL's prospective business and contractual relations by "foreclosing the USFL from the available pool of professional football officials by requiring NFL officials to observe full-year service contracts."

The NFL, however, contends that this allegation does not rise to the level of a triable issue of fact, since "the NFL did not in 1983, nor does it today, control any market for qualified game officials." ...

Plaintiffs' response to the NFL's assertion is a disturbing exercise in *ipse dixit*. "[A]t a minimum, the USFL insists, triable issues exist as to whether there is a 'market' of major league professional football game officials for the purpose of antitrust analysis, and what control the NFL exercised in that market in 1983 and today." Having made such a conclusory denial, plaintiffs simply fail to satisfy a basic obligation of a party opposing summary judgment, *i.e.*, to "bring to the district court's attention some affirmative indication that his version of relevant events is not fanciful."

The NFL's position is that a market for qualified game officials does exist, that it is nationwide, and that it may be defined as including only those individuals with ten years of experience, at least five of which have been at the college level. Quite significantly, the USFL's own complaint is consistent with the NFL's position as to the existence of a market for qualified game officials, and as to that market's geographic definition. Nonetheless, by referring to a product market of "major league professional football officials," ... plaintiffs apparently seek to argue that the market in issue consists only of game officials with pro football experience.

For purposes of the present motion, this argument is untenable for at least two reasons. First, plaintiffs' proposed market definition is unsupported by any "specific facts or evidentiary data," or by any of "the sort of concrete particulars which [Rule 56] require[s]." Second, the NFL's definition of the qualified game officials market is demonstrably consistent with the manner in which both the NFL and the USFL have, in practice, defined this particular market. It is uncontested that the NFL regards an official with five years of college experience and ten years of overall experience to be qualified....

Once the market of qualified game officials has been defined as including those officials who satisfy the five-and-ten criteria used by both the NFL and the USFL, it becomes clear that the NFL is entitled to summary judgment on the issue of market power....

Perhaps more significant than the NFL's lack of monopoly power as to qualified game officials is the dearth of evidence in the record to support plaintiffs' argument that "defendants'" refusal to lend NFL officials to the USFL constitutes anticompetitive or predatory conduct in violation of the federal antitrust laws.

Analytically, the contractual restriction at issue could be treated either as a covenant not to compete or as a refusal to deal. Covenants not to compete, in the antitrust context, are generally subject to a rule of reason analysis....

Applying the relevant case law to the NFL's prohibition of off-season officiating, it is not readily apparent how such a restriction, though obviously a restraint of trade in the literal sense, could possibly violate the antitrust laws. The restriction at issue is only one year in duration, and does not even extend to non-football officiating. Furthermore, although the USFL challenges the scope of the business interests served by the NFL's off-season prohibition, plaintiffs do not seriously challenge the existence of such interests. Finally, the covenant not to compete at issue in the present case relates to the ability of the NFL's game officials to seek football-related employment *during the term of their employment*. It strains credulity to suggest that the antitrust laws should be construed so as to punish a business for requiring its employees to remain loyal to their employer while they remain employed.

Although a monopolist's refusal to deal with others in the chain of distribution can give rise to liability under Section 2, ... such cases commonly involve a plaintiff's inability to acquire the monopolist's product or resources absent cooperation by the monopolist.... In the instant case, the USFL's access to other available sources of supply in the qualified game officials market has been established beyond genuine dispute by the NFL....

Moreover, the USFL's access to alternative sources of supply appears to preclude the possibility that plaintiffs could have successfully asserted a Section 1 claim against the NFL based on defendants' refusal to lend their officials to the USFL.

IV. Conclusion

First, defendants' efforts to secure advantageous stadium leases from local governmental authorities, as well as any efforts to convince such authorities not to grant stadium leases to USFL clubs, are found, as a matter of law, to constitute privileged conduct incapable of violating the Sherman Act. Second, the Court finds that plaintiffs' myriad allegations of "disparagement" of the USFL by the NFL do not include specific allegations of falsity or misstatement of fact. Therefore, no triable issue of fact exists with regard to that issue. Third, the Court finds, as a matter of law, that the NFL did not in 1983, and does not today, possess monopoly power in the market for qualified game officials....

Notes and Comments

1. In the *USFL* case, plaintiff prayed for an award of actual damages in the amount of $440,000,000 ($1,320,000,000 trebled). The USFL also sought injunctions prohibiting the NFL from impeding USFL attempts to gain TV network contracts, increasing NFL player rosters, negotiating with USFL players, entering into exclusive service contracts with game officials, making disparaging statements about the USFL, and forming exclusive stadium contracts. For an interesting recollection of the USFL, *see* PEARLMAN, FOOTBALL FOR A BUCK: THE CRAZY RISE & CRAZIER DEMISE OF THE USFL (2018).

The trial of the *USFL* case resulted in a jury verdict in favor of the plaintiff, finding that the NFL possessed monopoly power and was liable for damages to the USFL for willfully maintaining the power. The jury, however, awarded only $1.00 in damages (trebled to $3.00 under the Clayton Act). The Second Circuit upheld the jury award as adequate compensation. *United States Football League v. National Football League*, 842 F.2d 1335 (2d Cir. 1988), *aff'g*, 644 F. Supp. 1040 (S.D.N.Y. 1986). The USFL recovered attorneys' fees in the amount of $5,515,290.81 and costs of $62,220.92, although the USFL was successful on only one of its antitrust claims. *United States Football League v. National Football League*, 704 F. Supp. 474 (S.D.N.Y. 1989), *aff'd*, 887 F.2d 408 (2d Cir. 1989).

2. The USFL challenged the NFL's pooled rights TV contracts with ABC, CBS, and NBC as a violation of Section 1 of the Sherman Act, despite the fact that none of the contracts were exclusive, and none of the networks were precluded from telecasting USFL games. The district court ruled that the existence of the three contracts did not

constitute a per se violation of the Act but should be examined under the rule of reason test. *United States Football League v. National Football League*, 634 F. Supp. 1155, 1165 (S.D.N.Y. 1986). In the subsequent trial of the case, the jury found that the three TV contracts did not constitute an unreasonable restraint of trade under Section 1 of the Sherman Act. *United States Football League v. National Football League*, 644 F. Supp. 1040, 1042 (S.D.N.Y. 1986), *aff'd*, 842 F.2d 1335 (2d Cir. 1988).

3. The NFL argued that Congress exempted NFL television contracts from the reach of the antitrust laws. *See* 15 U.S.C. §1291. The district court in the *USFL* case examined the face of the Act and the legislative history to conclude, "[n]othing in this opinion should be considered as indicating that an absolute antitrust exemption extends to circumstances surrounding the three NFL-network contracts." 634 F. Supp. 1155, 1165 (S.D.N.Y. 1986). *See Chicago Professional Sports Limited Partnership v. National Basketball Association*, 95 F.3d 593 (7th Cir. 1996), and discussion of television broadcasting limitations at Section G, above.

See also United States v. National Football League, 116 F. Supp. 319 (E.D. Pa. 1953), *construed*, 196 F. Supp. 445 (E.D. Pa. 1961). The USFL argued that enactment of 15 U.S.C. §1291 was a direct congressional response to the 1953 and 1961 cases, and applied only to a single network contract. *United States Football League v. National Football League*, 634 F. Supp. 1155, 1157–65 (S.D.N.Y. 1986).

4. Can you make a valid argument that professional sports leagues operate in a market that is "naturally" monopolistic? What role, if any, does the "natural monopoly" doctrine play in the *AFL* and *USFL* cases? *See United States v. Aluminum Co. of America (Alcoa)*, 148 F.2d 416 (2d Cir. 1945). *See also Aspen Skiing Co. v. Aspen Highlands Skiing Corp.*, 472 U.S. 585 (1985) (monopolist's unwillingness to participate in a joint marketing scheme with its only competitor could amount to a "deliberate effort" to maintain the monopoly); *Independent Entertainment Group, Inc. v. National Basketball Association*, 853 F. Supp. 333 (C.D. Cal. 1994) (monopolist is not required to share employees with a competitor). *Compare Verizon Communications, Inc. v. Law Offices of Curtis V. Trinko, LLP (Trinko)*, 540 U.S. 398 (2004) (opinion suggests monopolist's sacrifice of short-term profits is a necessary element of exclusionary conduct). *See* Lao, *Aspen Skiing and Trinko: Antitrust Intent and "Sacrifice,"* 73 ANTITRUST L.J. 171 (2005).

5. Economists have long recognized that markets do not work to support two or more independent and competing major sports leagues but result in monopoly leagues. *See* Neale, *The Peculiar Economics of Professional Sports*, 78 QUARTERLY J. ECON. 1–14 (1964); QUIRK & FORT, PAY DIRT: THE BUSINESS OF PROFESSIONAL TEAM SPORTS 298 (1992). One writer explains:

> [T]he free market has historically failed to sustain multiple premier leagues competing against one another in the same sport. Multiple-league competition has consistently failed absent a partial merger or acquisition because in a multi-league model, one league eventually gains a comparative advantage and

drives the others out of business. This is true even when all the leagues begin operating at the same time and with similar resources.

Edelman, *How to Curb Professional Sports' Bargaining Power Vis-à-Vis the American City*, 2 VA. SPORTS & ENT. L.J. 280, 301 (2003).

The failure of free markets to work efficiently in the professional sports league context is attributed to the existence of "externalities" that are not included in the profit-loss calculus of competing agents. Without agreement, the leagues do not possess mutual mechanisms to assure the internalization of the costs and benefits not taken into account. The resulting failure is a "tragedy of the commons" phenomenon discussed earlier. The phenomenon occurs in a market-based economy where parties utilize common resources. In attempting to maximize their individual best interests, the efforts produce outcomes that are to the long-term detriment of all. The actions of competing interests in interleague warfare impact at least two commons: market support and the player talent pool. The recognized commons are comprised of several sub-commons and may be interrelated. Fan interest, for example, is the core element of the market support infrastructure, which includes advertising and sponsorship capital, media contracts, and merchandising. Unrestricted competition in the market for players may lead to dilution of the player talent pool, also leading to loss of fan support. *See* Whitney, *Bidding Till Bankrupt: Destructive Competition in Professional Team Sports*, 31 ECONOMIC INQUIRY 100, 113 (1993). The existence of and competition between rival leagues has historically saturated the market to result in the tragedy. After some time, the leagues fail or come together to make the necessary agreements, allocate the property rights, and establish rules necessary for successful league operations.

6. How did the plaintiff's case in *AFL* differ from plaintiff's case in *USFL*? How do you explain that the NFL was held to possess monopoly power in *USFL*, but was held not to possess monopoly power in *AFL*?

7. The NFL and AFL merged in 1966. Does the fact of the merger aid in the action brought by the USFL? The merger of professional sports leagues is exempted from the reach of the antitrust laws by operation of 15 U.S.C. § 1291.

8. In many geographic areas, only one (if any) facility exists that can adequately accommodate the needs of competing professional sports franchises. An existing professional sports franchise in the area likely either owns the facility or possesses an exclusive lease to utilize the facility. A club's exclusive control of the only available playing site, of course, is relevant to the question of the relative market position of the established league under Section 2 monopoly analysis. Exclusive control also generates restraint of trade questions under Sections 1 and 3 of the Sherman Act. The seemingly endless litigation concerning the Washington Redskins' control of RFK Stadium in Washington, D.C., is instructive. *Hecht v. Pro-Football, Inc. (I)*, 444 F.2d 931 (D.C. Cir. 1971), *cert. denied*, 404 U.S. 1047 (1972); *Hecht v. Pro-Football, Inc. (II)*, 570 F.2d 982 (D.C. Cir. 1977). Plaintiffs in *Hecht I* and *II* contend that a restrictive

covenant in the RFK lease enjoyed by the Washington Redskins violates the antitrust laws. Plaintiffs claim that inability to gain access to the stadium prevented the plaintiffs from gaining an AFL franchise for the D.C. area.

In *Hecht I*, the district court granted summary judgment for the defendant, on the basis that the District of Columbia Armory Board's leasing of RFK Stadium was governmental action immune from the antitrust laws. The D.C. Circuit Court reversed and remanded for trial on the merits, concluding that Congress had evinced no intention to confer the immunity. 570 F.2d 982.

In *Hecht II*, the case was tried to a jury, which rendered a verdict for defendants. Plaintiff appealed, challenging numerous instructions and evidentiary rulings. The D.C. Circuit Court reversed and remanded for a new trial.

In addition to discussing the usual antitrust issues, the court recognized the "essential facilities" doctrine:

> [W]here facilities cannot practicably be duplicated by would-be competitors, those in possession of them must allow them to be shared on fair terms. It is illegal restraint of trade to foreclose the scarce facility.

Id. at 992. A facility is "essential" where duplication is economically infeasible and denial of facility use inflicts a severe handicap on potential market entrants. The doctrine does not operate where sharing of the facility would be impractical or would inhibit defendant's ability to serve its customers adequately. *Id. Compare* Hawker, *Open Windows: The Essential Facilities Doctrine and Microsoft*, 25 OHIO N.U. L. REV. 115 (1999). For a case in which the plaintiff failed in challenging the Minnesota Vikings' exclusive lease of the Metrodome, see *Scallen v. Minnesota Vikings Football Club, Inc.*, 574 F. Supp. 278 (D. Minn. 1983). For a case in which plaintiff alleged that defendants exclusively controlled the Rosemont Horizon, an "essential facility" for the booking and promotion of pop, rock, and rhythm and blues concerts in the Chicago area, see *Flip Side Productions, Inc. v. Jam Productions, Ltd.*, 843 F.2d 1024 (7th Cir. 1988) (indoor arena not an "essential facility" and plaintiff lacked standing to bring claim under RICO).

9. In *Fraser v. Major League Soccer, L.L.C.*, 284 F.3d 47 (1st Cir. 2002), the Circuit Court of Appeals affirmed the lower court rulings in the trial, including plaintiff's Section 2 monopoly claims. Plaintiff alleged that MLS monopolized the market for Division I professional soccer in the United States; attempted to monopolize the market; and conspired with the United States Soccer Foundation to monopolize the market. The jury returned a verdict that plaintiff failed to prove the alleged relevant market as limited to the United States (compared with a worldwide market definition). Thus, the court entered judgment for the defendant.

10. In late December 1998, the American Basketball League, a women's professional league, announced it was bankrupt and had suspended operations. The collapse of the ABL left the Women's National Basketball Association (WNBA) as the

only women's professional basketball league in the United States. From the start, the ABL reportedly lacked the financial and marketing support that the WNBA enjoyed from its parent league, the NBA. The ABL attempted to market its product as having the best players but could not compete with the WNBA's advertising campaigns and television exposure on NBC, ESPN, and Lifetime. The ABL season ran from November through March, whereas the WNBA schedule operated in the summer months. The ABL failed to secure a TV deal. ABL co-founder and CEO, Gary Cavalli, remarked, "At this point, the league is out of money. While this is an extremely painful decision, we had no choice but to shut down.... It became clear that, although we had the best product, we could not find enough people willing to confront the NBA and give us the major sponsorships and TV contracts we needed." Shipley, *ABL Says It Is Bankrupt, Shuts Down*, http://www.highbeam.com/doc/1P2-688342.html. Can you identify arguments that the ABL possessed a cause of action against the WNBA pursuant to Section 2? Does the WNBA bear the responsibility of taking active steps to assure continued operations of its sole competitor?

Problem

The professional Rugby League is a fledgling association of member clubs located throughout the United States. The league is comprised of six geographically defined divisions. The league's regular championship season schedule consists of a fall schedule and a spring schedule. The six division champions and two "wildcard" clubs meet in a single-elimination playoff series in the late spring.

The Rugby League developed as a result of marketing studies indicating that the American sports entertainment audience desires a spectator sport combining the characteristics of American football and European soccer. The marketing consultants concluded that the market is greatly enhanced by potential TV broadcasts in Canada, Mexico, Japan, and Europe. Network television contracts, suitable stadium access, and "big name" American athletes are essential to the future success of the Rugby League.

The Rugby League is in its inaugural season. Several problems confront the league. First, the league franchises are unable to secure leases of adequate stadium playing field facilities in major cities. The NFL seemingly has "tied-up" the stadium facilities through long-term lease arrangements. The Rugby League clubs play games in high school stadiums. Second, the league is unable to secure network or cable TV contracts. Network officials stated, "Your marketing analysis appears accurate, but we do not feel that we should risk our relationship with the NFL by contracting with the Rugby League. The spring schedule also competes with the NBA and Major League Baseball." The league has not discovered any evidence that NFL or other professional sports league officers have directly influenced the decisions of network officials. Third, NFL clubs voted to expand the active club rosters by 10 additional players. The Rugby League is of the opinion that big-name college football players, who are marginal NFL players, are now sitting on the bench for NFL teams rather than playing for Rugby League teams. Evidence indicates that the NFL decided to expand club rosters in response to the Rugby League's efforts to sign college football players.

The NFL instituted what is considered by officials of the Rugby League as a "negative ad campaign," designed to denigrate the Rugby League in the eyes of the consumer. TV and radio ads promote the NFL games as follows: "Watch the action-packed NFL matchup between ______________________________ and the ______________________, unless you prefer Rugby (Voice-over with English accent: 'Say old boy, can we catch the first train to London?' Background laughter)"; Coach telling player cut from the roster in training camp: "Son, I'm sorry. You're just not NFL material." Veteran player says, "Look kid, don't take it so hard. You can always play rugby." Released player looks to floor and remarks, "Yeah, where? Butte, Montana?" The veteran raises an eyebrow. (Voice-over: "If you are not watching Rugby in Butte, catch the NFL Sunday action on ______________________")."

What is the likely outcome of an antitrust action filed by the Rugby League against the NFL? Develop your arguments based on your reading of the cases below using the facts of the problem.

Seven

Labor Relations in Professional Sports

Learning Outcomes

- Learn the rules and procedures related to the collective bargaining process, including the weapons that can be utilized by labor and management.
- Understand the unique characteristics of labor relations in professional sports, including the common provisions in collective bargaining agreements.
- Understand the subjects that both labor and management are required to negotiate.
- Learn whether, and under what circumstances, traditional restraints and controls are insulated from antitrust scrutiny due to a "labor exemption."

Key Terms

- Players association
- National Labor Relations Act (NLRA)
- National Labor Relations Board (NLRB)
- Mandatory subject of bargaining
- Exclusive representative
- Multiemployer bargaining unit
- Unfair labor practice
- Impasse
- Nonstatutory labor exemption

A. Introduction

This chapter examines the collective bargaining process utilized by professional sports leagues and player unions to structure the relationships between players and clubs. Players associations first formed in the 1800s but evolved into player labor unions later. Labor relationships in professional sports provide a colorful chapter in the history of the industry, including work stoppages, intense negotiations, and public debate regarding the effect the drama has on the nature and integrity of the games. Not only did Major League Baseball cancel a World Series during a strike period, but the National Hockey League lost an entire season due to a 302-day lockout. The recent MLB lockout that began on December 2, 2021, lasted more than three months and delayed the commencement of spring training until March 10, 2022, when the owners and players finally reached a new collective bargaining agreement (CBA).

The CBA between the owners and players in the National Football League and the National Basketball Association expired following the completion of the 2010–11 seasons. Club owners in both leagues opted to "lockout" the players in the attempt to gain leverage in the envisioned labor negotiations. The National Football League Players Association (NFLPA), immediately, and the National Basketball Players Association (NBPA), after negotiation, elected to forego negotiation by "disclaimer" pursuant to labor laws and filed antitrust suits in the counter attempt to secure leverage in lawsuit settlement negotiations.

A general understanding of the CBA of each professional league, including the processes by which the agreements were formed, is essential for people who represent players and team management. The collective bargaining system established pursuant to the National Labor Relations Act (NLRA) is explored at Section B, below. The importance of the interrelationship of labor law and antitrust statutes becomes evident as you read the materials. Although early negotiations centered on traditional wage and conditions of employment issues, such as pensions and insurance, the modern paradigm pits millionaire players and billionaire owners in battles over the division and distribution of the economic rewards derived from the leagues' market opportunities. Thus, the dynamics of the collective bargaining process may be quite different than experienced in the typical non-sports employer-employee negotiations.

Collective bargaining in professional sports focuses upon two primary areas. The first is distributive in nature, as it relates to the division of the revenue pie between owners and players. The second respects the desire of the parties to assure competitive balance, and therefore the general health of the league and its market opportunity.

In earlier collective bargaining efforts, leagues and player associations agreed to guarantee a fixed percentage of gross league revenues for salary distribution to the players. The 1983 NBA-NBPA agreement assured players of receiving 53% of gross revenues but increased to 55% in the 1999 CBA. The 1993 NFL-NFLPA agreement promised players 58% of revenues. In 2005, the NHL and NHLPA joined to initially allocate 54% of gross league revenues to player salaries, with step ladder increases in future years. The agreements often include "salary caps" that join with the fixed salary percentage obligations to work within sometimes widely varying complex mathematical models. The "cap" also has the effect of limiting player movement among teams. It can be a "soft cap" where the clubs can readily circumvent the restrictions. The 1983 and 1988 NBA caps proved to be quite soft, but the salary limitation was hardened in the 1999 CBA, although some exceptions remained. The NFL CBA, in 1993, produced a "hard cap." The 2005 NHL-NHLPA CBA includes a hard cap. The amount an individual player may earn is capped at 20% of the maximum team payroll. The Basic Agreement negotiated by the MLBPA and Major League Baseball eschewed the salary cap for a payroll "luxury tax." The 2003 Basic Agreement implemented a "competitive balance tax" that imposes a burden on clubs whose salary obligations exceed a fixed "tax threshold" in a given season. Most, if not all, leagues include "revenue sharing" as an element in the agreed upon mix of mechanisms designed to protect the economic welfare of league operations.

The 2011 NFL-NFLPA CBA, resulting from lawsuit settlement negotiation and subsequently ratified by the parties, included a reduction in player participation in annual league revenues from 50% to 46–48%; a cap on rookie salaries; an increase in the minimum amount teams must spend on salaries; and an increase in injury protections. The NBA-NBPA CBA included a reduction in the share of league revenues received by players from 57% to 51.15%, with a 10% increase in the minimum amount teams must spend within the salary cap (called the "salary floor"). The 2017 CBA retains most of the provisions of the immediately preceding CBA, including player share of the revenue at 49%–51%. The 2013 MLB-MLBPA CBA included draft signing bonus pools for both the domestic and international markets; changes in free agent compensation requirements; and increased penalties for exceeding the luxury tax threshold. The 2017 CBA ended the forfeiture of a first-round draft choice for the signing of a free agent, increased the penalties for exceeding the payroll luxury tax threshold, and further defined bonus pools.

Professional sports leagues, from the beginning, have utilized various devices to restrict player movement from club to club. Leagues contend that unrestricted competition in the market for player talent may lead to a dilution of the talent pool and result in the reduction of competitive balance among league teams, and the attendant loss of fan support. The ruinous competition for players is a "tragedy of the commons" phenomenon, whereby the interrelated commons, *player talent pool* and *fan interest*, are overgrazed to the detriment of the league as a whole. The economic principles underlying the use of player movement restrictions are presented at Ch. 6, *supra*.

The most popular schemes include the "reserve clause," "option clause," draft system, no tampering rules, and free agent compensation arrangements. The reserve clause provides the club an exclusive right to a player's services for succeeding seasons. The option clause allows a club to renew player contracts at the option of the club, usually enabling for exercise of the option at a salary reduction. Draft systems divide the amateur or professional supply of players among the clubs of a league, awarding each club the exclusive right to contract with the player drafted. Free agent compensation schemes often require compensation in the form of players or draft choices to a team losing a player to another club.

In the 1970s, players began to successfully challenge the league constraints on player movement as violations of the Sherman Act. *See, e.g., Mackey v. National Football League*, 543 F.2d 606 (8th Cir. 1976); *Kapp v. National Football League*, 586 F.2d 644 (9th Cir. 1978); *Smith v. Pro Football, Inc.*, 593 F.2d 1173 (D.C. Cir. 1978); *Robertson v. National Basketball Ass'n*, 389 F. Supp. 867 (S.D.N.Y. 1975); *Philadelphia World Hockey Club, Inc. v. Philadelphia Hockey Club, Inc.*, 351 F. Supp. 462 (E.D. Pa. 1972); *Boston Professional Hockey Association, Inc. v. Cheevers*, 348 F. Supp. 261 (D. Mass.), *remanded on other grounds*, 472 F.2d 127 (1st Cir. 1972). Since that time, most of the customary constraints on player movement have been preserved as part of the collective bargaining agreements, either through direct bargaining or the ratification of lawsuit settlements.

The terms of collective bargaining agreements are insulated from antitrust attack by the nonstatutory labor exemption, addressed below. In 1970, Yazoo Smith, the Washington Redskins' first round draft choice, challenged the NFL draft as a violation of the antitrust laws and secured an award of treble damages of $276,000.00. The Eighth Circuit Court of Appeals affirmed the decision, ruling the NFL draft a violation of Section 1 of the Sherman Antitrust Act under Rule of Reason analysis. *Smith v. Pro-Football, Inc.*, 593 F.2d 1173 (8th Cir. 1978). In 1977, however, the NFL and NFLPA preserved the draft in the collective bargaining agreement, thus precluding further antitrust actions. A recurring question considers whether the restrictions are adequately addressed in the CBA. Another queries whether a unilateral imposition of constraints is appropriate within the context of collective bargaining pursuant to the NLRA.

B. Collective Bargaining and the NLRA

Collective bargaining is a process by which a group of workers of an industry bargain or negotiate as a collective whole (unit) with the management to determine the working conditions, benefits, and salaries of the industry. The process is governed by the National Labor Relations Act. What is unique in professional sports is that the parties to the collective bargaining agreements retain the power to individually negotiate significant elements of the employment contract.

The NLRA provides three basic rights: (1) the right to self-organization in forming, joining, or assisting labor organizations; (2) the right to bargain collectively through representatives of their own choosing; and (3) the right to engage in "concerted activities" for the mutual aid or protection of employees. Section 8(d) of the Act requires the mutual obligation of management and workers to meet at reasonable times and confer in "good faith" with respect to "wages, hours, and other terms and conditions of employment." The United States Supreme Court, in *NLRB v. Borg-Warner Corp., Wooster Division*, 356 U.S. 342, 349 (1958), held that "[t]he duty to bargain is limited to those subjects, and within that area neither party is legally obligated to yield.... As to other matters, however, each party is free to bargain or not to bargain, and to agree or not to agree." A question may arise, as indicated in the cases below, whether the issue in dispute is a "mandatory" subject of bargaining or merely a "permissive" subject.

The National Labor Relations Board (NLRB) is charged with the mandate of administering and enforcing the terms of the NLRA. The NLRB conducts elections for labor union representation, investigates and rules where charges of "unfair labor practices" are made, and decides other issues, including whether certain issues are subject to the terms of the NLRA. The duty to bargain in good faith includes the requirement that parties present proposals and counter proposals with basic information that is needed for agreement. A failure to bargain in good faith, by either labor or management, constitutes an unfair labor practice that violates the NLRA. In professional sports, a recurring issue regards the disclosure of financial data by leagues and club owners.

Both management and labor in professional sports must conduct their behavior according to the terms of the NLRA, as defined by federal courts and the rulings of the NLRB. Interestingly, the relationship of management and labor in professional sports is subject to precedential treatment that has developed over time, referred to as the "law of the workplace." Disputes respecting the interpretation or application of terms of a collective bargaining agreement are generally resolved through a "grievance" procedure and submitted for arbitration.

The collective bargaining process in professional sports may be viewed along a timeline that begins with the organization of the players in forming the union. A union that is duly certified by the NLRB becomes the "exclusive representative" of the players with regards to employment matters with the league, which constitutes a "multiemployer bargaining unit." The parties, league (ownership) and union (players), then engage in collective bargaining. Upon the creation of a ratified CBA, the parties are precluded from utilizing the antitrust laws in potential legal conflicts as a result of the "nonstatutory labor exemption." *See* Section C, below. Various interactions between the parties may ensue during the existence of the CBA and are resolved according to the processes and terms of the CBA. Parties generally initiate negotiations for a subsequent CBA prior to the termination of the existing CBA. In the event the parties have not agreed to a new or extended CBA at the date of termination, the terms and conditions of the CBA continue. As mentioned above, the players association may choose to decertify or disclaim interest in negotiating and seek to gain agreement as settlement of an antitrust suit. Otherwise, the parties may negotiate until *impasse*. At that time, management may impose changes to the CBA that have been fairly presented to the union members pursuant to the "unilateral change doctrine" discussed below.

The collective bargaining process in professional sports is necessarily a multiparty phenomenon. Neither labor nor management is internally monolithic. A league is comprised of several franchises bearing few similarities, economically or otherwise. The diversity of owner personalities is remarkable. The player unions also are made up of varied personalities and interests. Players may range from the second-string center to the all-pro running back. Joining the management and labor groups in the collective bargaining game is the league *qua* institution. The league role depends on the strength of the personality of the commissioner or president. Peter Uberroth, for example, is reported to have exerted great influence in the Major League Baseball collective bargaining process that resulted in the 1985 agreement. Hovering over the participants is the ever-present shadow of the law. Litigation under the antitrust laws and labor statutes is common. Finally, the mediators and arbitrators, as well as other institutional personnel, add to the collective bargaining process. As you view the complexities of labor relations in professional sports, strive to understand the various forces at work within the process.

Both the labor team and the management team possess weapons for use in the process of collective bargaining. Upon impasse, the players association may utilize the following tactics:

1. strike; or
2. decertification of the unionand file an antitrust lawsuit.

The player strike may be supported by funding from other unions or a developed strike fund. The union is instrumental in economically supporting the striking players during the strike. The union may choose to "decertify," arguably leaving the unorganized players with the ability to utilize the antitrust laws. Upon impasse, management possesses the following tactics:

1. lockout;
2. use replacement ("scab") players;
3. unilaterally implement new terms and conditions of employment "reasonably comprehended" within the league's pre-impasse proposals (typically the last proposals rejected by the union); or
4. cancellation of the season.

Management is economically supported by strike insurance, a strike fund, or other reciprocal agreements among league franchise members. The league may be assured of guaranteed payments pursuant to media and other contracts. Employers may hire temporary replacement workers, even during a lockout. Employers also may hire permanent replacement workers and provide the replacement workers with priority over striking workers when the strike ends pursuant to the *Mackay Radio* doctrine. *NLRB v. Mackay Radio & Telegraph Co.*, 304 U.S. 333 (1938). Striking workers, however, remain as "employees" under the NLRA. The striking workers are entitled to full reinstatement upon the departure of the permanent replacement workers, unless they have acquired regular and substantially equivalent employment, or the failure to offer full reinstatement is for legitimate and substantial business reasons. *Laidlaw Corp.*, 171 N.L.R.B. 1366 (1968), *enforced*, 414 F.2d 99 (7th Cir. 1969), *cert. denied*, 397 U.S. 920 (1970).

Silverman v. Major League Baseball Player Relations Committee, Inc.

67 F.3d 1054 (2d Cir. 1995)

WINTER, CIRCUIT JUDGE:

This is an appeal by the Major League Baseball Player Relations Committee, Inc. ("PRC") and the constituent member clubs of Major League Baseball ("Clubs") from a temporary injunction issued by Judge Sotomayor pursuant to section 10(j) of the National Labor Relations Act ("NLRA"), 29 U.S.C. § 160(j). The injunction is based on the district court's conclusion that appellants violated NLRA §§ 8(a)(1) and (5), 29 U.S.C. §§ 158(a)(1) and (5), by unilaterally implementing terms and conditions of employment that differed from those in the last collective agreement. It orders the PRC and the Clubs to: (i) abide by the terms of an expired collective agreement, (ii) rescind any actions taken that are inconsistent with that agreement and (iii) bargain in good faith with the Players Association.... We affirm.

Article XX of the Basic Agreement that became effective in 1990 contains a series of provisions that govern free agency and reserve rights. Players with six or more years of major league service are free agents and may seek competing bids in an effort to obtain the best contract, which may of course give exclusive rights to the club for a stipulated number of years. Free agency is guaranteed by an anti-collusion provision, Article XX(F), which prohibits the Clubs from acting in concert with each other with respect to the exercise of rights under Article XX. Article XX(F) thus prevents the Clubs from agreeing either to refuse to bid for the services of free agents or to offer only low bids to them. Article XX(F) also prohibits players from acting in concert with regard to Article XX rights.

Players with less than six years of service remain under reserve to their individual clubs, although a club may reserve a player only once. Although a minimum annual salary is provided, players with less than three years of major league service must negotiate with their clubs to determine their salary for the coming season. Article XX allows certain reserved players—generally those with more than three but less than six years of service—to demand salary arbitration. Salary arbitration is a mechanism for determining the individual salaries for that group of reserved players if they cannot arrive at an agreement with their clubs....

The Basic Agreement expired on December 31, 1993, pursuant to the PRC's notice of termination. Although negotiations for a successor agreement did not get underway until March 1994, the PRC and the Players Association continued to observe the terms of the expired Basic Agreement. Prior to the commencement of negotiations, the Clubs and the Players Association had completed individual salary arbitration hearings and had entered into individual player contracts for the 1994 baseball season, which began in April 1994.

Negotiations for a new collective bargaining agreement continued unsuccessfully. The PRC offered its first formal economic proposal to the Players Association at a meeting on June 14, 1994. It included a "salary cap," a mechanism that establishes a ceiling on the total player salaries paid by each club. Generally, the aggregate salaries of each team are determined by an agreed upon formula and must remain above a minimum percentage of industry revenues, also determined by an agreed upon formula, but below a maximum percentage of those revenues.... The PRC proposal also eliminated the salary arbitration system and substituted restricted free agency rights for those reserved players previously eligible for salary arbitration. As an alternative to the PRC's proposed salary cap, the Players Association suggested a revenue sharing and luxury "tax" plan that would impose a tax on high-paying clubs. Subsequent proposals reflected disagreement over appropriate tax rates and payroll thresholds above which clubs would be subject to the tax.

The players struck on August 12, and the 1994 baseball season never resumed. On December 22, 1994, the PRC declared an impasse in negotiations and stated that it intended unilaterally to impose a salary cap and to implement other changes in the terms and conditions of employment, including the elimination of salary arbitration. The Players Association responded with a unilateral ban on players signing individual contracts with the Clubs.

On February 3, 1995, counsel for the PRC notified the NLRB General Counsel that the PRC would revoke the implementation of unilateral changes and restore the status quo ante. The General Counsel indicated that the Players Association charges would be dismissed as a result. Counsel for the PRC informed the General Counsel, however, that the PRC did not believe itself obligated to maintain provisions of the Basic Agreement that involved non-mandatory subjects of bargaining. He mentioned salary arbitration in that regard and also suggested that the Clubs might decide to bargain exclusively through the PRC. The NLRB General Counsel declined to offer an advisory opinion on these matters.

Three days later, by memorandum dated February 6, counsel for the PRC notified the Clubs that, until a new collective bargaining agreement was ratified or until further notice, individual clubs had no authority to negotiate contracts with individual players because the PRC was now the Clubs' exclusive bargaining representative. This amounted to an agreement among the Clubs not to hire free agents and thus was a departure from the anti-collusion provision, Article XX(F) of the Basic Agreement. It also amounted to an elimination of salary arbitration, because salary arbitration is a method of arriving at a wage for an individual player contract with a club.

The Players Association thereupon filed a new unfair labor practice charge, and the General Counsel issued a complaint alleging, *inter alia*, that the Clubs and the PRC had violated Sections 8(a)(1) and (5) of the NLRA by unilaterally eliminating, before an impasse had been reached, competitive bidding for the services of free agents, the anti-collusion provision, and salary arbitration for certain reserved players. The NLRB found that these matters were related to wages, hours, and other terms and conditions of employment and were therefore mandatory subjects for collective bargaining. It then authorized its General Counsel to seek an injunction under NLRA § 10(j). On March 27, the NLRB Regional Director filed a petition seeking a temporary injunction restraining the alleged unfair labor practices.

The district court agreed that the NLRB had reasonable cause to conclude that free agency and salary arbitration were mandatory subjects of bargaining and that the Clubs' unilateral actions constituted an unfair labor practice. The district court also concluded that injunctive relief was warranted. This appeal followed. We denied a stay on April 4.

... The petition invokes basic principles of labor law. Section 8(d) of the NLRA mandates that employers and unions bargain in good faith over "wages, hours, and other terms and conditions of employment." 29 U.S.C. § 158(d). These are so-called mandatory subjects of bargaining. Under caselaw, the parties may propose and bargain over, but may not insist upon, permissive subjects of bargaining.... When a collective agreement expires, an employer may not alter terms and conditions of employment involving mandatory subjects until it has bargained to an impasse over new terms.... Thereafter, it may implement the new terms. Generally, when an agreement expires, an employer need not bargain to an impasse over terms and conditions involving permissive subjects but may alter them upon expiration....

The PRC and the Clubs argue that the anti-collusion and free agency provisions of the Basic Agreement do not involve mandatory subjects of bargaining and are therefore not subject to the *Katz* rule that unilateral implementation of new terms is an unfair labor practice unless the employer has bargained to an impasse over these new terms.... The PRC and the Clubs contend that an injunction compelling them to maintain the free agency and anti-collusion provisions undermines their right as a multiemployer group to bargain collectively through an exclusive representative. If so, they would be permissive subjects of bargaining. With regard to salary arbitration, the PRC and the Clubs argue that it is the equivalent of interest arbitration—arbitration of the terms of a new collective agreement—and thus not a mandatory subject of bargaining....

We are unpersuaded that an injunction compelling the PRC and the Clubs to observe the anti-collusion and free agency provisions of the Basic Agreement infringes on their right as a multiemployer group to bargain through an exclusive representative. Free agency and the ban on collusion are one part of a complex method—agreed upon in collective bargaining—by which each major league player's salary is determined under the Basic Agreement. They are analogous to the use of seniority, hours of work, merit increases, or piece work to determine salaries in an industrial context. The PRC and the Clubs describe free agency and the ban on collusion as provisions undermining their right to select a joint bargaining representative because those provisions entail individual contracts with clubs. However, the argument ignores the fact that free agency is simply a collectively bargained method of determining individual salaries for one group of players. The anti-collusion provision is not designed to prevent the PRC from representing the Clubs. Rather, that provision guarantees that free agency will be a reality when permitted by the Basic Agreement. The injunction thus does not in any way prevent the PRC from bargaining as the Clubs' exclusive representative with the Players Association over the elimination of free agency in its entirety or for a modified version of the same, and thereafter from implementing any proposals incorporated into a collective bargaining agreement.

The question, therefore, is whether the free agency, anti-collusion, and reserve issues are—or there is reasonable cause to believe they are—otherwise mandatory subjects of bargaining. Section 8(d) of the NLRA defines the duty to bargain as "the obligation… to meet… and confer in good faith with respect to wages, hours, and other terms and conditions of employment…." *In Wood v. Nat'l Basketball Ass'n*, 809 F.2d 954 (2d Cir. 1987), we noted that free agency and reserve issues are "at the center of collective bargaining in much of the professional sports industry," and that "it is precisely because of [free agency's] direct relationship to wages and conditions of employment that [it is] so controversial and so much the focus of bargaining in professional sports." *Id.* at 962.

[B]oth the leagues and the players unions view free agency and reserve issues as questions of what share of revenues go to the clubs or to the players. The more restrictive the reserve system is, the greater the clubs' share. The greater the role of free agency, the greater the players' share.

To hold that there is no reasonable cause for the NLRB to conclude that free agency and reserve issues are mandatory subjects of bargaining would be virtually to ignore the history and economic imperatives of collective bargaining in professional sports. A mix of free agency and reserve clauses combined with other provisions is the universal method by which leagues and players unions set individual salaries in professional sports. Free agency for veteran players may thus be combined with a reserve system, as in baseball, or a rookie draft, as in basketball,… for newer players. A salary cap may or may not be included. To hold that any of these items, or others that make up the mix in a particular sport, is merely a permissive subject of bargaining would ignore the reality of collective bargaining in sports.

Indeed, free agency is in many ways nothing but the flip side of the reserve system. A full reserve system does not eliminate individual bargaining between teams and players. It simply limits that bargaining to one team. If free agency were a permissive subject of collective bargaining, then so would be the reserve system.

With regard to salary arbitration, we will assume, but not decide, that if it is a form of interest arbitration, it may be unilaterally eliminated…. Interest arbitration is a method by which an employer and union reach new agreements by sending disputed issues to an arbitrator rather than settling them through collective bargaining and economic force.... The salary arbitration provisions of the Basic Agreement are a method by which salaries for some players who are not eligible for free agency—those with three to six years of major league service—are set. The Basic Agreement sets forth criteria by which the arbitrator is to reach a decision. These criteria include the player's performance in the prior year, the length and consistency of career contribution, physical or mental defects, recent performance of the team on the field and at the gate, and salaries of certain comparable players. The Basic Agreement also forbids the arbitrator from considering certain facts that might otherwise be relevant. Finally, the Basic Agreement requires that the arbitrator pick either the club's suggested salary or the player's.

We decline to analogize Article VI(F) of the Basic Agreement to interest arbitration. Salary arbitration provides limited discretion to the arbitrator to set salaries for designated players who are not eligible for free agency. The discretion afforded the arbitrator is arguably less than the discretion afforded arbitrators in grievance arbitration involving disputes arising under an existing collective agreement, which is beyond question a mandatory subject of bargaining. In grievance arbitration, an arbitrator may permissibly imply a term even though the term has no explicit support in the text of the collective agreement.... Similarly, a term may be implied from past practices even though somewhat inconsistent with the agreement.... We thus decline to analogize salary arbitration to interest arbitration, and, therefore, we hold that there is reasonable cause to believe that it is a mandatory subject of bargaining.

With regard to whether the granting of relief was "just and proper," we review the district court's determination only for abuse of discretion. We see no such abuse in the present matter. Given the short careers of professional athletes and the deterioration of physical abilities through aging, the irreparable harm requirement has been met. The unilateral elimination of free agency and salary arbitration followed by just three days a promise to restore the status quo. The PRC decided to settle the original unfair labor practice charges while embarking on a course of action based on a fallacious view of the duty to bargain. We see no reason to relieve it of the consequences of that course.

We therefore affirm.

Sidebar

In 2001, the Commissioner of Baseball announced that MLB contemplated the contraction of two clubs, focusing primarily on the Minnesota Twins and Montreal Expos. The MLBPA challenged the managerial decision, arguing that the elimination of clubs is a mandatory subject of bargaining. Before a ruling was made in the grievance, the MLBPA and MLB negotiated a new collective bargaining agreement that barred contraction during the life of the CBA (2006). The MLBPA, however, agreed to waive any challenges pursuant to the NLRA regarding MLB elimination of troubled franchises for the 2007 season. The MLBPA reserved the right to challenge the "effects" of contraction, including the claim that the issue of "effects" is a mandatory subject of bargaining.

Is the contraction of a Major League team considered to be the closing of a business as a traditional entrepreneurial decision? Is the elimination tantamount to the "entire" closing of a business, or only a "partial" closing? Assuming that the players of the eliminated clubs are distributed to remaining teams, is contraction more akin to "relocation" of operations, rather than the closing of a business?

In *Textile Workers v. Darlington Co.*, 380 U.S. 263 (1965), the United States Supreme Court held that an employer has the absolute right to permanently close the entire business, even if the liquidation is motivated by vindictiveness toward a union. A partial closing, however, is an unfair labor practice if motivated by a purpose to chill unionism in any of the remaining plants. *See also Darlington Manufacturing Co. v. NLRB*, 397 F.2d 760 (4th Cir. 1968). *Darlington*, by its own terms and subsequent decisions, is limited to the unique circumstance of the clear termination of a business and does not apply to discriminatory relocations or the subcontracting of work. *Lear Siegler, Inc.*, 295 N.L.R.B. 857 (1989). The United States Supreme Court, in *First National Maintenance Corp. v. NLRB*, 452 U.S. 666 (1981), held that the managerial decision to close part of a business for economic reasons was not a subject of mandatory bargaining, but bargaining over the "effects" of the decision must be conducted in a meaningful manner and at a meaningful time to satisfy the requirements of Section 8(a)(5) of the National Labor Relations Act. In *Dubuque Packing Co.*, 303 N.L.R.B. 386 (1991), the Board established a test to determine whether an employer has the duty to bargain regarding plant relocations and transfers of work. The General Counsel possesses the burden to establish that the employer's decision concerned a relocation of work not accompanied by a change in the nature of the business operation. The employer may rebut a *prima facie* case by establishing that the work performed at the new location varies significantly from the work performed at the former plant, and that the work performed at the former plant is to be discontinued entirely and not transferred to the new location, or that the decision involves a change in the scope and direction of the enterprise. Alternatively, the employer may offer a defense that the labor costs were not a factor in the decision, or that if costs considered, the union could not have offered labor cost concessions that could have changed the employer's decision. Roger Noll contends that the Major League Baseball revenue sharing system creates incentives to contract clubs. Noll, The Economics of Baseball Contraction 2, 25–26 (2003), unpublished manuscript, Stanford Institute for Economic Policy Research. *See generally* Rosner, *Squeeze Play: Analyzing Contraction in Professional* Sports, 10 Vill. Sports & Ent. L.J. 29, 42–43 (2003); Day, *Labor Pains: Why Contraction Is Not the Solution to Major League Baseball's Competitive Balance Problems*, 12 Fordham Intell. Prop. Media & Ent. L.J. 521, 547–52 (2002).

Notes and Comments

1. The customary bargaining unit has developed on a "league-wide" basis. Thus, the NFLPA, NBPA, and MLBPA are typical of professional sports player associations. Would the structuring of bargaining units on a "craft" basis better represent the interests of certain player groups? For example, perhaps a "centers" unit could better compete with a "quarterback" unit for a distribution of the salary pool, than as a member of the "league-wide" unit. Should rookie first-year players form a unit to compete with veterans? Does this scenario differ from the traditional bargaining model under the National Labor Relations Act that results in worker advantages based on seniority? The notion of a "team-wide" unit was rejected in *Morio v. North American Soccer League*, 236 N.L.R.B. 1317 (1978), *aff'd*, 632 F.2d 217 (2d Cir. 1980). *See also North American Soccer League v. NLRB*, 241 N.L.R.B. 1225 (1979), *enforced*, 613 F.2d 1379 (5th Cir. 1980), *cert. denied*, 449 U.S. 899 (1980).

2. Examination of the history of labor battles between professional sports leagues and players unions provides insight into the workings of the collective bargaining agreements and the economic and other relationships between leagues and players. Roger Abrams concludes the collective bargaining relationship between baseball owners and players is dysfunctional. He recommends that the parties eschew traditional conflict bargaining for principled negotiations that result in partnership bargaining relationships. Abrams, *Partnership Bargaining in Baseball*, *in* LEGAL ISSUES IN PROFESSIONAL BASEBALL ch. II (Kurlantzick ed., 2005).

3. Parties to the collective bargaining process possess the duties to bargain in good faith and provide information relevant to the mandatory bargaining issues. Must the league and the players association open the books for a full disclosure of the economic and financial status of the parties? For a decision rejecting arguments by the MLBPA placing a duty on the owners to provide economic information, see *Silverman v. Major League Baseball Player Relations Committee, Inc.*, 516 F. Supp. 588 (S.D.N.Y. 1981). The NLRB ruled that the NHL committed an unfair labor practice by refusing to provide the NHLPA with copies of trade memos relating to all player trades from the 1996–97 and following seasons, trade memos relating to trades of specified players, and information regarding subsidy payments received by clubs pursuant to the Supplemental Currency Equalization Plan. *National Hockey League and Its Constituent Member Clubs and National Hockey League Players' Association*, before the National Labor Relations Board, Division of Judges (Kern, ALJ), 591 PLI/Pat 263.

4. Pursuant to most league constitutions, clubs in the league share revenues according to various formulas. The division of the proceeds is often changed by a vote of league directors. What arguments can be made pro and con that the implementation or modification of a revenue-sharing arrangement between clubs is a mandatory subject of bargaining with the players' union under the National Labor Relations Act? In the *National Hockey League and Its Constituent Members and National Hock-*

ey League Players' Association, Ibid, Note 4, the NLRB determined that the NHL violated the National Labor Relations Act by failing and refusing to bargain with the NHLPA the implementation of a player payroll provision in the Supplemental Currency Assistance Plan (SCAP). SCAP was designed to assist those Canadian teams in the bottom half of League revenues. An eligibility criterion was directly linked to player salaries. *See* Cohen, Note, *Sharing the Wealth: Don't Call Us, We'll Call You: Why Revenue Sharing Is a Permissive Subject and Therefore the Labor Exemption Does Not Apply,* 12 FORDHAM INTELL. PROP. MEDIA & ENT. L.J. 609 (2002). For an examination of revenue sharing in professional sports, see Hunt, *To Share or Not to Share: Revenue Sharing Structures in Professional Sports,* 13 TEX. REV. ENT. & SPORTS L. 139 (2012).

5. Rights of parties pursuant to the NLRA may be waived by a failure to act in a timely and diligent manner. In 1997, the NHL unilaterally adopted a Deferred Compensation Program without bargaining with the NHLPA. The NHL stipulated that the issue was a mandatory subject of bargaining, but argued that the NHLPA waived its right to bargain over the implementation of the Program by its inaction following notice by telephone. The NHLPA answered that it did not receive adequate notice from the NHL, that the Program was presented as a *fait accompli* which made any request futile, and that it did as a matter of fact make a demand for bargaining. The NLRB rejected the NHLPA arguments and determined that the NHLPA failed to request bargaining in a timely fashion and thereby waived its right to bargain. *National Hockey League and Its Constituent Members and National Hockey League Players' Association,* before the National Labor Relations Board, Division of Judges (Kern, ALJ), 591 PLI/Pat 263, 296.

6. For cases concerning the discretion of leagues to establish eligibility requirements for the amateur draft, see *National Hockey League Players' Association v. Plymouth Whalers Hockey Club (NHLPA II),* 419 F.3d 462 (6th Cir. 2005); *(NHLPA I),* 325 F.3d 712 (6th Cir. 2003); *Boris v. United States Football League,* 1984 U.S. Dist. LEXIS 19061 (C.D. Cal. Feb. 28, 1984); *Linseman v. World Hockey Association,* 439 F. Supp. 1315 (D. Conn. 1977); *Denver Rockets v. All-Pro Management,* 325 F. Supp. 1049 (C.D. Cal. 1971). *See also* McCann, Note, *Illegal Defense: The Law and Economics of Banning High School Players from the NBA Draft,* 1 VA. SPORTS & ENT. L.J. 295 (2002).

7. To the extent that professional sports leagues expand operations beyond the borders of the United States, as has already been done in the case of the Canadian clubs, the labor laws of foreign jurisdictions may apply in specific contexts. *See* Fournier & Roux, *Labor Relations in the National Hockey League: A Model of Transnational Collective Bargaining,* 20 MARQ. SPORTS L. REV. 147 (2009).

8. The globalization of the professional sports labor market often generates complex legal arrangements. *See Kurlantzick, An International Dimension: Player Movement, the NBA-FIBA Agreement, and Foreign League Limitations on American Play-*

ers, in Legal Issues in American Basketball, ch. VI (Kurlantzick ed., 2011). For examination of the transnational exchange of players between the Japanese professional baseball league, Nippon Professional Baseball (NPB), and MLB, and the use of the MLB "posting process," see Rosner & Conroy, *The Impact of the Flat World on Player Transfers in Major League Baseball,* 12 U. Pa. J. Bus. L. 79 (2009); Crew, *In Irabu's Footsteps: Baseball's Posting System and the Non-Statutory Antitrust Exemption,* 7 Va. Sports & Ent. L.J. 127 (2007). The prospect of a global draft in Major League Baseball is regularly discussed. *See generally* Lopez, *Signing Bonus Skimming and a Premature Call for a Global Draft in Major League Baseball,* 41 Ariz. St. L.J. 349 (2009).

MLB and MLBPA announced an agreement with the Cuban Baseball Federation to legalize and streamline the transfer of Cuban baseball players to the United States through an MLB posting system similar to the Nippon Professional Baseball model. The Trump administration blocked the implementation of the agreement as a violation of United States law prohibiting trade with Cuba. Diamond & Salama, *Trump Administration Blocks Baseball Players from Cuba,* Wall St. J., April 8, 2019.

For examination of negotiations between the NHL/NHLPA and the International Ice Hockey Federation (IIHF) regarding player transfers, see Gleason, *From Russia with Love: The Legal Repercussions of the Recruitment and Contracting of Foreign Players in the National Hockey League,* 56 Buff. L. Rev. 599 (2008); Miller, *Hockey's Cold War—Russia's Defiance of the IIHF and the Evgeny Malkin Saga,* 17 Seton Hall J. Sports & Ent. L. 163 (2007). *See also* Zdrojeski, *International Ice Hockey: Player Poaching and Contract Dispute,* 42 Case W. Res. J. Int'l L. 77 (2010).

9. Former 49ers quarterback Colin Kaepernick gained notoriety by kneeling during the playing of the National Anthem in an effort to raise awareness about racial inequality and oppression. After opting out of his 49ers contract, he was not signed by another NFL club as a free agent. Kaepernick filed a grievance alleging the NFL owners entered into collusion in violation of the CBA, Art. 17, §§ 1, 2. Prior to the arbitration hearing, the parties settled the matter. The claimant bears the burden of demonstrating by a "clear preponderance of the evidence that the challenged conduct occurred and was in violation of the anti-collusion provisions." Art. 17, § 5. The CBA further provides that the complaining party must present some evidence, circumstantial or direct, that clearly shows that at least two teams entered into an explicit or implicit agreement. The mere fact of a player not being signed is inadequate. Art. 17, § 6.

10. The distinction between a "salary cap" and a "luxury or payroll tax" can be important. A "cap" restricts payroll, which truly affects salaries for all clubs. A "soft" cap, which the NBA has, allows a team to spend over the cap if it satisfies one of the numerous exceptions set forth in the CBA. A "hard" cap cannot be exceeded, as there are no exceptions. Some player salaries are necessarily curbed by the "cap." A "tax" does not restrict salaries, but adds a cost factor for clubs who spend above a

threshold level. Although the "tax" may deter some club salary expenditures, it is likely to have very little effect on curbing player salaries so long as there exist owners who will spend at the free-market level with little regard for tax consequences. The "tax," like the "cap," may be "soft" or "hard." *See generally* Bernstein, Note, *Salary Caps in Professional Sports: Closing the Kovachuk Loopholes in National Hockey League Player Contracts*, 29 CARDOZO ARTS & ENT. L.J. 375 (2011). The MLB-MLBPA collective bargaining agreement imposes draconian penalties for violation of the tax threshold.

11. Terms of a collective bargaining agreement, of course, are subject to varying interpretations. Cases arise in all leagues concerning whether clauses in player contracts conform to CBA provisions. Creative efforts to avoid the restrictions of salary caps and luxury taxes also generate verbal agreements, side deals, and attempts to utilize loopholes and other circumvention techniques. Can the MLB-MLBPA CBA provisions for signing bonus pools be circumvented by issuing subsequent contracts of higher value? The original NBA salary cap did not restrict a club's signing of its own free agents. Thus, a player arguably could agree to a lower salary in the initial contract, but recoup value through a second-year contract that was not limited by the salary cap. The use of "one-year opt-out" provisions was upheld in *Bridgeman v. National Basketball Association*, 838 F. Supp. 172 (D.N.J. 1993). Sometimes, incentive bonuses are not included in salary cap calculations. A question may arise whether the incentives were likely to be achieved and thus should be defined as "salary." For a discussion of circumvention techniques used in the NFL, and a suggestion that an implied covenant of good faith and fair dealing exists to counter attempts to avoid salary cap restrictions, see McPhee, Comment, *First Down, Goal to Go: Enforcing the NFL's Salary Cap Using the Implied Covenant of Good Faith and Fair Dealing*, 17 LOY. L.A. ENT. L.J. 449 (1997).

12. A union can be formed in two ways. First, if at least 30 percent of workers sign a card or petition saying they want a union, the N.L.R.B. will conduct an election. And if the majority of those who vote choose a union, the board will certify the union as the representative for collective bargaining. Second, the employer can voluntarily recognize the union based on evidence, *e.g.*, signed union-authorization cards, that a majority of employees want the union to represent them. In 2022, the MLBPA sent authorization cards to minor league players seeking to represent them as a union and it received signed cards from a majority of the more than 5,500 minor leaguers. Soon thereafter, Major League Baseball voluntarily recognized the union as the players' bargaining representative. The MLBPA announced a plan to form a separate bargaining unit for minor leaguers (players not on an MLB team's 40-man roster), including its own dues, player representatives and executive board.

13. For a lawsuit claiming minor league baseball players are entitled to minimum wage and overtime protection pursuant to the Fair Labor Standards Act, 29 U.S.C. § 201 *et seq.*, see *Senne v. Office of the Commissioner*, U.S. District Court, Northern District of California, San Francisco Division, Case No. 3:14-cv-00608-JCS, filed

February 7, 2014. The lawsuit finally settled on May 10, 2022. For cases holding that that the baseball industry is not exempt from the Fair Labor Standards Act, see *Bridewell v. The Cincinnati Reds*, 68 F.3d 136 (6th Cir. 1995), *cert. denied*, 516 U.S. 1172 (1996); *Bridewell v. The Cincinnati Reds*, 155 F.3d 828 (6th Cir. 1998). The Save America's Pastime Act, part of the 2018 omnibus federal spending bill, exempts minor league sports from the application of the Fair Labor Standards Act. *See* Grow, *The Save America's Pastime Act: Special Interest Legislation Epitomized*, 90 U. of Colo. L. Rev. 1 (2019). The Washington State Legislature passed a bill that exempted the Western Hockey League (Junior Hockey) players from the state labor laws. Senate Bill 5893, March 3, 2015.

Former junior hockey player, Berg, filed a class action against the CHL, claiming violations of the Canadian minimum wage laws. Klein, *Lawsuits Target Canadian Junior Hockey League System*, N.Y. TIMES, Dec. 20, 2014.

Problem

During the last CBA negotiation meeting, the Rugby League (RL) ownership representatives presented the Rugby League Players Association (RLPA) with a written proposal that included the traditional draft rule, which does not specify eligibility requirements. A representative mentioned verbally during discussions that the owners likely would change the eligibility requirements of the draft to include foreign players. He also mentioned that the owners were in favor of limiting the signing of players to those 20 years of age and older, regardless of remaining college eligibility. "In this way, we can avoid injuries. This is a game for men, not boys." The modification provides for the drafting of players from "South Africa," "Australia," "England," "Scotland," "Wales," and "Ireland."

In planning for next year's season, the RL owners desire to unilaterally implement the "eligibility" modification. The owners proclaim that the league will be further stabilized by providing equal access among clubs for the services of foreign players. Under the present system, foreign players sign with the highest bidder, thus leaving the smaller market clubs with lesser rosters.

The RLPA does not favor the proposed draft eligibility rules. It threatens to challenge the draft eligibility restraints under the antitrust laws and will "decertify" or file a "disclaimer of interest" if necessary to bring the challenge. The RLPA will also file an unfair labor practice claim with the NLRB, if the RL unilaterally imposes the change.

1. Identify the existing legal rules governing the unilateral imposition of the "draft eligibility" standards by the RL. Should the standards be considered mandatory or permissive subjects of bargaining?
2. Advise whether the RL should declare an *impasse* in negotiations at this time?

3. Assuming the court reaches the antitrust issues, what arguments can the RL make that its draft system is valid under the antitrust laws? What counter arguments can be made by the RLPA?
4. What issues arise in the event the RL should enter the global labor market in competition for international players?

C. Antitrust, Labor, and the "Nonstatutory Labor Exemption"

The obvious restraints on player movement were historically challenged under the federal antitrust laws. Although professional baseball was held exempt from the reach of the antitrust statutes in the *Federal Baseball* and *Flood v. Kuhn* cases, Congress enacted the Curt Flood Act of 1998 to remove the exemption for major league labor purposes. *See* Chapter 6, *supra*.

Player restraints and other matters are regularly addressed through the collective bargaining process, pursuant to the National Labor Relations Act. A recurring question concerns whether traditional restraints and controls, including the free agent draft, are insulated from antitrust scrutiny due to a "labor exemption." Two types of labor exemptions exist: statutory and nonstatutory. "The statutory labor exemption removes from the coverage of the antitrust laws certain legitimate, albeit anticompetitive, union activities because they are favored by federal labor policy." *Powell v. National Football League*, 678 F. Supp. 777 (D. Minn. 1988). Protected activities include secondary picketing and group boycotts. The source of the labor exemption is found in the Clayton Act, 15 U.S.C. §§17, 29, and the Norris-LaGuardia Act, 29 U.S.C. §§104, 105, 113. The provisions declare that union activities in furtherance of its own interests are exempt from the reach of the antitrust laws. The statutory exemption does not extend to agreements or actions between unions and non-labor groups, including employers. *See Bridgeman v. National Basketball Association*, 675 F. Supp. 960 (D.N.J. 1987).

The nonstatutory exemption excepts certain anticompetitive union-employer activities from antitrust liability. A union-employer agreement must meet three requirements to qualify for the exemption:

1. The restraint of trade primarily affects only the parties to the collective bargaining agreement;
2. The agreement concerns a mandatory subject of collective bargaining; and
3. The agreement is a product of bona fide arm's-length bargaining.

Powell v. National Football League, 930 F.2d 1293 (8th Cir. 1989), *cert. denied*, 498 U.S. 1040 (1991).

The United States Supreme Court, in *Brown v. Pro Football, Inc.* (below), held that the nonstatutory labor exemption continues not only beyond the expiration of the collective bargaining agreement, but also beyond *impasse* in labor negotiations. A related question concerns whether management may unilaterally impose new or modified conditions of employment after expiration, or upon reaching impasse. Both inquiries are explored in the Problem and cases below.

Player associations have utilized two methods to avoid the constraints of the nonstatutory labor exemption in order to file antitrust suits and achieve an agreement through case settlement. In the event the players choose to decertify, a petition is filed with the NLRB for a subsequent vote of the members. If a majority votes to decertify, the employees must wait 12 months before they may reorganize. Some players have chosen the "disclaimer of interest" mechanism, by which the players' association waives any right to represent the players and does not engage in concerted actions. If the "disclaimer" is made in good faith, the NLRB historically accepts the action and the players are freed from the constraints preventing suit. The "disclaimer" may be ended at any time, thus enabling an expeditious ratification of the agreed-upon case settlement. *See* Grow, *Decertifying Players Unions: Lessons from the NFL and NBA Lockouts of 2011*, 15 Vand. J. Ent. & Tech. L. 473, 486–87 (2013).

Mackey v. National Football League

543 F.2d 606 (8th Cir. 1976)

Lay, Circuit Judge.

This is an appeal by the National Football League (NFL), twenty-six of its member clubs, and its Commissioner, Alvin Ray "Pete" Rozelle, from a district court judgment holding the "Rozelle Rule" to be violative of § 1 of the Sherman Act, and enjoining its enforcement.

This action was initiated by a group of present and former NFL players, appellees herein, pursuant to §§ 4 and 16 of the Clayton Act, 15 U.S.C. §§ 15 and 26, and § 1 of the Sherman Act, 15 U.S.C. § 1. Their complaint alleged that the defendants' enforcement of the Rozelle Rule constituted an illegal combination and conspiracy in restraint of trade denying professional football players the right to freely contract for their services. Plaintiffs sought injunctive relief and treble damages.

The district court, the Honorable Earl R. Larson presiding, conducted a plenary trial... and entered judgment in their favor on the issue of liability. This appeal followed.

The district court held that the defendants' enforcement of the Rozelle Rule constituted a concerted refusal to deal and a group boycott, and was therefore a *per se* violation of the Sherman Act. Alternatively, finding that the evidence offered in support of the clubs' contention that the Rozelle Rule is necessary to the successful operation of the NFL insufficient to justify the restrictive effects of the Rule, the court concluded that the Rozelle Rule was invalid under the Rule of Reason standard. Finally, the court rejected the clubs' argument that the Rozelle Rule was immune from attack under the Sherman Act because it had been the subject of a collective bargaining agreement between the club owners and the National Football League Players Association (NFLPA).

The defendants raise two basic issues on this appeal: (1) whether the so-called labor exemption to the antitrust laws immunize the NFL's enforcement of the Rozelle Rule from antitrust liability; and (2) if not, whether the Rozelle Rule and the manner in which it has been enforced violate the antitrust laws....

History

For a number of years, the NFL has operated under a reserve system whereby every player who signs a contract with the NFL club is bound to play for that club, and no other, for the term of the contract plus one additional year at the option of the club.... Once a player signs a Standard Player Contract, he is bound to his team for at least two years. He may, however, become a free agent at the end of the option year by playing that season under a renewed contract rather than signing a new one. A player "playing out his option" is subject to a 10% salary cut during the option year.

Prior to 1963, a team which signed a free agent who had previously been under contract to another club was not obligated to compensate the player's former club. In 1963, after R.C. Owens played out his option with the San Francisco 49ers and signed a contract with the Baltimore Colts, the member clubs of the NFL unilaterally adopted the... Rozelle Rule, as an amendment to the League's Constitution and Bylaws:

> [W]henever a player, becoming a free agent in such manner, thereafter signed a contract with a different club in the League, then, unless mutually satisfactory arrangements have been concluded between the two League clubs, the Commissioner may name and then award to the former club one or more players, from the Active, Reserve, or Selection List (including future selection choices) of the acquiring club as the Commissioner in his sole discretion deems fair and equitable; any such decision by the Commissioner shall be final and conclusive.

During the period from 1963 through 1974, 176 players played out their options. Of that number, 34 signed with other teams. In three of those cases, the former club waived compensation. In 27 cases, the clubs involved mutually agreed upon compensation. Commissioner Rozelle awarded compensation in the four remaining cases....

The Labor Exemption Issue

To determine the applicability of the nonstatutory exemption we must first decide whether there has been any agreement between the parties concerning the Rozelle Rule.

Based on the fact that the 1968 agreement incorporated by reference the Rozelle Rule and provided that free agent rules would not be changed, we conclude that the 1968 agreement required that the Rozelle Rule govern when a player played out his option and signed with another team. Assuming, without deciding, that the 1970 agreement embodied a similar understanding, we proceed to a consideration of whether the agreements fall within the scope of the nonstatutory labor exemption.

Governing Principles

We find the proper accommodation to be: First, the labor policy favoring collective bargaining may potentially be given pre-eminence over the antitrust laws where the restraint on trade primarily affects only the parties to the collective bargaining relationship.... Second, federal labor policy is implicated sufficiently to prevail only where the agreement sought to be exempted concerns a mandatory subject of collective bargaining.... Finally, the policy favoring collective bargaining is furthered to the degree necessary to override the antitrust laws only where the agreement sought to be exempted is the product of bona fide arm's length bargaining....

Applying these principles to the facts presented here, we think it clear that the alleged restraint on trade effected by the Rozelle Rule affects only the parties to the agreements sought to be exempted....

Under § 8(d) of the National Labor Relations Act,... mandatory subjects of bargaining pertain to "wages, hours, and other terms and conditions of employment...."

On its face, the Rozelle Rule does not deal with "wages, hours and other terms or conditions of employment" but with inter-team compensation when a player's contractual obligation to one team expires and he is signed by another. Viewed as such, it would not constitute a mandatory subject of collective bargaining. The district court found, however, that the Rule operates to restrict a player's ability to move from one team to another and depresses player salaries. There is substantial evidence in the record to support these findings. Accordingly, we hold that the Rozelle Rule constitutes a mandatory bargaining subject within the meaning of the National Labor Relations Act.

The district court found that the parties' collective bargaining history reflected nothing which could be legitimately characterized as bargaining over the Rozelle Rule; that, in part due to its recent formation and inadequate finances, the NFLPA, at least prior to 1974, stood in a relatively weak bargaining position vis-a-vis the clubs; and that "the Rozelle Rule was unilaterally imposed by the NFL and member club defendants upon the players in 1963 and has been imposed on the players from 1963 through the present date."

On the basis of our independent review of the record, including the parties' bargaining history as set forth above, we find substantial evidence to support the finding that there was no bona fide arm's-length bargaining over the Rozelle Rule preceding the execution of the 1968 and 1970 agreements....

In view of the foregoing, we hold that the agreements between the clubs and the players embodying the Rozelle Rule do not qualify for the labor exemption....

Antitrust Issues

We turn, then, to the question of whether the Rozelle Rule, as implemented, violates § 1 of the Sherman Act, which declares illegal "every contract, combination... or conspiracy, in restraint of trade or commerce among the several states." 15 U.S.C. § 1....

The clubs and the Commissioner first urge that the only product market arguably affected by the Rozelle Rule is the market for players' services, and that the restriction of competition for players' services is not a type of restraint proscribed by the Sherman Act....

In other cases concerning professional sports, courts have not hesitated to apply the Sherman Act to club owner imposed restraints on competition for players' services.... In other contexts, courts have subjected similar employer imposed restraints to the scrutiny of the anti-trust laws....

We hold that restraints on competition within the market for players' services fall within the ambit of the Sherman Act.

We review next the district court's holding that the Rozelle Rule is *per se* violative of the Sherman Act.

The express language of the Sherman Act is broad enough to render illegal nearly every type of agreement between businessmen. The Supreme Court has held, however, that only those agreements which "unreasonably" restrain trade come within the proscription of the Act....

As the courts gained experience with antitrust problems arising under the Sherman Act, they identified certain types of agreements as being so consistently unreasonable that they may be deemed to be illegal *per se*, without inquiry into their purported justifications.

Among the practices which have been deemed to be so pernicious as to be illegal *per se* are group boycotts and concerted refusals to deal.... The term "concerted refusals to deal" has been defined as "an agreement by two or more persons not to do business with other individuals, or to do business with them only on specified terms."... The term "group boycott" generally connotes "a refusal to deal or an inducement of others not to deal or to have business relations with tradesmen."...

The district court found that the Rozelle Rule operates to significantly deter clubs from negotiating with and signing free agents.... The court concluded that the Rozelle Rule, as enforced, thus constituted a group boycott and a concerted refusal to deal, and was a *per se* violation of the Sherman Act.

There is substantial evidence in the record to support the district court's findings as to the effects of the Rozelle Rule. We think, however, that this case presents unusual circumstances rendering it inappropriate to declare the Rozelle Rule illegal *per se* without undertaking an inquiry into the purported justifications for the Rule.

First, the line of cases which has given rise to *per se* illegality for the type of agreements involved here generally concerned agreements between business competitors in the traditional sense.... Here... the NFL assumes some of the characteristics of a joint venture in that each member club has a stake in the success of the other teams. No one club is interested in driving another team out of business, since if the League fails, no one team can survive.... Although businessmen cannot wholly evade the antitrust laws by characterizing their operation as a joint venture, we conclude that the unique nature of the business of professional football renders it inappropriate to mechanically apply *per se* illegality rules here....

Second, one of the underpinnings of the *per se* analysis is the avoidance of lengthy and burdensome inquiries into the operation of the particular industry in question. Here, the district court has already undertaken an exhaustive inquiry into the operation of the NFL and the effects of and justifications for the Rozelle Rule.

The focus of an inquiry under the Rule of Reason is whether the restraint imposed is justified by legitimate business purposes, and is no more restrictive than necessary....

In defining the restraint of competition for players' services, the district court found that the Rozelle Rule significantly deters clubs from negotiating with and signing free agents; that it acts as a substantial deterrent to players playing out their options and becoming free agents; that it significantly decreases players' bargaining power in contract negotiations; that players are thus denied the right to sell their services in a free and open market; that as a result, the salaries paid by each club are lower than if competitive bidding were allowed to prevail; and that absent the Rozelle Rule, there would be increased movement in interstate commerce of players from one club to another.

We find substantial evidence in the record to support these findings. Witnesses for both sides testified that there would be increased player movement absent the Rozelle Rule....

In support of their contention that the restraints effected by the Rozelle Rule are not unreasonable, the defendants asserted a number of justifications. First, they argued that without the Rozelle Rule, star players would flock to cities having natural advantages... ; that competitive balance throughout the League would thus be destroyed; and that the distinction of competitive balance would ultimately lead to diminished spectator interest, franchise failures, and perhaps the demise of the NFL.... Second, the defendants contended that the Rozelle Rule is necessary to protect the clubs' investment in scouting expenses and player development costs. Third, they asserted that players must work together for a substantial period of time in order to function effectively as a team; that elimination of the Rozelle Rule would lead to increased player movement and a concomitant reduction in player continuity;

and that the quality of play in the NFL would thus suffer, leading to reduced spectator interest, and financial detriment both to the clubs and the players. Conflicting evidence was adduced at trial by both sides with respect to the validity of these asserted justifications.

The district court held the defendants' asserted justifications unavailing.... The court further concluded that elimination of the Rozelle Rule would have no significant disruptive effects, either immediate or long term, on professional football. In conclusion, the court held that the Rozelle Rule was unreasonable in that it was overly broad, unlimited in duration, unaccompanied by procedural safeguards, and employed in conjunction with other anticompetitive practices such as the draft, Standard Player Contract, option clause, and the no-tampering rules.

We agree that the asserted need to recoup player development costs cannot justify the restraints of the Rozelle Rule. That expense is an ordinary cost of doing business and is not peculiar to professional football. Moreover, because of its unlimited duration, the Rozelle Rule is far more restrictive than necessary to fulfill that need.

We agree, in view of the evidence adduced at trial with respect to existing player turnover by way of trades, retirements and new players entering the League, that the club owners' arguments respecting player continuity cannot justify the Rozelle Rule....

In sum, we hold that the Rozelle Rule, as enforced, unreasonably restrains trade in violation of § 1 of the Sherman Act.

With the exception of the district court's finding that implementation of the Rozelle Rule constitutes a *per se* violation of § 1 of the Sherman Act and except as it is otherwise modified herein, the judgment of the district court is AFFIRMED.

Brown v. Pro Football, Inc.

518 U.S. 231 (1996)

Justice Breyer delivered the opinion of the Court.

The question in this case arises at the intersection of the Nation's labor and antitrust laws.

A group of professional football players brought this antitrust suit against football club owners. The club owners had bargained with the players' union over a wage issue until they reached impasse. The owners then had agreed among themselves (but not with the union) to implement the terms of their own last best bargaining offer. The question before us is whether federal labor laws shield such an agreement from antitrust attack. We believe that they do. This Court has previously found in the labor laws an implicit antitrust exemption that applies where needed to make the collective-bargaining process work. Like the Court of Appeals, we conclude that this need makes the exemption applicable in this case.

We can state the relevant facts briefly. In 1987, a collective-bargaining agreement between the National Football League (NFL), a group of football clubs, and the NFL Players Association, a labor union, expired. The NFL and the Players Association began to negotiate a new contract. In March 1989, during the negotiations, the NFL adopted Resolution G-2, a plan that would permit each club to establish a "developmental squad" of up to six rookie or "first-year" players who, as free agents, had failed to secure a position on a regular player roster. *See* App. 42. Squad members would play in practice games and sometimes in regular games as substitutes for injured players. Resolution G-2 provided that the club owners would pay all squad members the same weekly salary.

The next month, April, the NFL presented the developmental squad plan to the Players Association. The NFL proposed a squad player salary of $1,000 per week. The Players Association disagreed. It insisted that the club owners give developmental squad players benefits and protections similar to those provided regular players, and that they leave individual squad members free to negotiate their own salaries.

Two months later, in June, negotiations on the issue of developmental squad salaries reached an impasse. The NFL then unilaterally implemented the developmental squad program by distributing to the clubs a uniform contract that embodied the terms of Resolution G-2 and the $1,000 proposed weekly salary. The League advised club owners that paying developmental squad players more or less than $1,000 per week would result in disciplinary action, including the loss of draft choices.

In May 1990, 235 developmental squad players brought this antitrust suit against the League and its member clubs. The players claimed that their employers' agreement to pay them a $1,000 weekly salary violated the Sherman Act. *See* 15 U.S.C. § 1 (forbidding agreements in restraint of trade). The Federal District Court denied the employers' claim of exemption from the antitrust laws; it permitted the case to reach the jury; and it subsequently entered judgment on a jury treble-damage award that exceeded $30 million. The NFL and its member clubs appealed.

The Court of Appeals (by a split 2-to-1 vote) reversed. The majority interpreted the labor laws as "waiv[ing] antitrust liability for restraints on competition imposed through the collective-bargaining process, so long as such restraints operate primarily in a labor market characterized by collective bargaining." 50 F.3d 1041, 1056 (D.C. Cir. 1995). The Court held, consequently, that the club owners were immune from antitrust liability. We granted certiorari to review that determination. Although we do not interpret the exemption as broadly as did the Appeals Court, we nonetheless find the exemption applicable, and we affirm that Court's immunity conclusion.

The immunity before us rests upon what this Court has called the "non-statutory" labor exemption from the antitrust laws.... The Court has implied this exemption from federal labor statutes, which set forth a national labor policy favoring free and private collective bargaining,... which require good-faith bargaining over wages, hours and working conditions,... and which delegate related rulemaking and interpretive authority to the National Labor Relations Board....

This implicit exemption reflects both history and logic. As a matter of history, Congress intended the labor statutes (from which the Court has implied the exemption) in part to adopt the views of dissenting justices in *Duplex Printing Press Co. v. Deering*, 254 U.S. 443 (1921), which justices had urged the Court to interpret broadly a different explicit "statutory" labor exemption that Congress earlier (in 1914) had written directly into the antitrust laws.... In the 1930's, when it subsequently enacted the labor statutes, Congress, as in 1914, hoped to prevent judicial use of antitrust law to resolve labor disputes—a kind of dispute normally inappropriate for antitrust law resolution.... The implicit ("nonstatutory") exemption interprets the labor statutes in accordance with this intent, namely, as limiting an antitrust court's authority to determine, in the area of industrial conflict, what is or is not a "reasonable" practice. It thereby substitutes legislative and administrative labor-related determinations for judicial antitrust-related determinations as to the appropriate legal limits of industrial conflict....

As a matter of logic, it would be difficult, if not impossible, to require groups of employers and employees to bargain together, but at the same time to forbid them to make among themselves or with each other any of the competition-restricting agreements potentially necessary to make the process work or its results mutually acceptable. Thus, the implicit exemption recognizes that, to give effect to federal labor laws and policies and to allow meaningful collective bargaining to take place, some restraints on competition imposed through the bargaining process must be shielded from antitrust sanctions....

The petitioners and their supporters concede, as they must, the legal existence of the exemption we have described. They also concede that, where its application is necessary to make the statutorily authorized collective-bargaining process work as Congress intended, the exemption must apply both to employers and to employee.... Nor does the dissent take issue with these basic principles. Consequently, the question before us is one of determining the exemption's scope: Does it apply to an agreement among several employers bargaining together to implement after impasse the terms of their last best good-faith wage offer? We assume that such conduct, as practiced in this case, is unobjectionable as a matter of labor law and policy. On that assumption, we conclude that the exemption applies.

Labor law itself regulates directly, and considerably, the kind of behavior here at issue—the postimpasse imposition of a proposed employment term concerning a mandatory subject of bargaining. Both the Board and the courts have held that, after impasse, labor law permits employers unilaterally to implement changes in preexisting conditions, but only insofar as the new terms meet carefully circumscribed conditions. For example, the new terms must be "reasonably comprehended" within the employer's preimpasse proposals (typically the last rejected proposals), lest by imposing more or less favorable terms, the employer unfairly undermined the union's status.... The collective-bargaining proceeding itself must be free of any unfair labor practice, such as an employer's failure to have bargained in good faith.... These regulations reflect the fact that impasse and an accompanying implementation of proposals constitute an integral part of the bargaining process....

Although the caselaw we have cited focuses upon bargaining by a single employer, no one here has argued that labor law does, or should, treat multi-employer bargaining differently in this respect. Indeed, Board and court decisions suggest that the joint implementation of proposed terms after impasse is a familiar practice in the context of multiemployer bargaining....

Multiemployer bargaining itself is a well-established, important, pervasive method of collective bargaining, offering advantages to both management and labor.... The upshot is that the practice at issue here plays a significant role in a collective-bargaining process that itself comprises an important part of the Nation's industrial relations system.

In these circumstances, to subject the practice to antitrust law is to require antitrust courts to answer a host of important practical questions about how collective bargaining over wages, hours and working conditions is to proceed—the very result that the implicit labor exemption seeks to avoid. And it is to place in jeopardy some of the potentially beneficial labor-related effects that multiemployer bargaining can achieve. That is because unlike labor law, which sometimes welcomes anticompetitive agreements conducive to industrial harmony, antitrust law forbids all agreements among competitors (such as competing employers) that unreasonably lessen competition among or between them in virtually any respect whatsoever.... Antitrust law also sometimes permits judges or juries to premise antitrust liability upon little more than uniform behavior among competitors, preceded by conversations implying that later uniformity might prove desirable,... or accompanied by other conduct that in context suggests that each competitor failed to make an independent decision....

If the antitrust laws apply, what are employers to do once impasse is reached? If all impose terms similar to their last joint offer, they invite an antitrust action premised upon identical behavior (along with prior or accompanying conversations) as tending to show a common understanding or agreement. If any, or all, of them individually impose terms that differ significantly from that offer, they invite an unfair labor practice charge. Indeed, how can employers safely discuss their offers together even before a bargaining impasse occurs? A preimpasse discussion about, say, the practical advantages or disadvantages of a particular proposal, invites a later antitrust claim that they agreed to limit the kinds of action each would later take should an impasse occur. The same is true of postimpasse discussions aimed at renewed negotiations with the union. Nor would adherence to the terms of an expired collective-bargaining agreement eliminate a potentially plausible antitrust claim charging that they had "conspired" or tacitly "agreed" to do so, particularly if maintaining the status quo were not in the immediate economic self-interest of some.... All this is to say that to permit antitrust liability here threatens to introduce instability and uncertainty into the collective-bargaining process, for antitrust law often forbids or discourages the kinds of joint discussions and behavior that the collective bargaining process invites or requires.

We do not see any obvious answer to this problem. We recognize, as the Government suggests, that, in principle, antitrust courts might themselves try to evaluate particular kinds of employer understandings, finding them "reasonable" (hence lawful) where justified by collective-bargaining necessity. But any such evaluation means a web of detailed rules spun by many different nonexpert antitrust judges and juries, not a set of labor rules enforced by a single expert administrative body, namely the Labor Board. The labor laws give the Board, not antitrust courts, primary responsibility for policing the collective-bargaining process. And one of their objectives was to take from antitrust courts the authority to determine, through application of the antitrust laws, what is socially or economically desirable collective-bargaining policy....

The Solicitor General argues that the exemption should terminate at the point of impasse....

[T]he simple "impasse" line would not solve the basic problem we have described above.... Labor law permits employers, after impasse, to engage in considerable joint behavior, including joint lockouts and replacement hiring.... Indeed, as a general matter, labor law often limits employers to four options at impasse: (1) maintain the status quo, (2) implement their last offer, (3) lock out their workers (and either shut down or hire temporary replacements), or (4) negotiate separate interim agreements with the union.... What is to happen if the parties cannot reach an interim agreement? The other alternatives are limited. Uniform employer conduct is likely. Uniformity—at least when accompanied by discussion of the matter—invites antitrust attack. And such attack would ask antitrust courts to decide the lawfulness of activities intimately related to the bargaining process.

The problem is aggravated by the fact that "impasse" is often temporary,... it may differ from bargaining only in degree,... it may be manipulated by the parties for bargaining purposes,... and it may occur several times during the course of a single labor dispute, since the bargaining process is not over when the first impasse is reached.... How are employers to discuss future bargaining positions during a temporary impasse? Consider, too, the adverse consequences that flow from failing to guess how an antitrust court would later draw the impasse line. Employers who erroneously concluded that impasse had not been reached would risk antitrust liability were they collectively to maintain the status quo, while employers who erroneously concluded that impasse had occurred would risk unfair labor practice charges for prematurely suspending multiemployer negotiations....

Petitioners also say that irrespective of how the labor exemption applies elsewhere to multiemployer collective bargaining, professional sports is "special." We can understand how professional sports may be special in terms of, say, interest, excitement, or concern. But we do not understand how they are special in respect to labor law's antitrust exemption. We concede that the clubs that make up a professional sports league are not completely independent economic competitors, as they depend upon a degree of cooperation for economic survival.... In the present context, however, that circumstance makes the league more like a single bargaining employer, which analogy seems irrelevant to the legal issue before us.

... Ultimately, we cannot find a satisfactory basis for distinguishing football players from other organized workers. We therefore conclude that all must abide by the same legal rules.

For these reasons, we hold that the implicit ("nonstatutory") antitrust exemption applies to the employer conduct at issue here. That conduct took place during and immediately after a collective-bargaining negotiation. It grew out of, and was directly related to, the lawful operation of the bargaining process. It involved a matter that the parties were required to negotiate collectively. And it concerned only the parties to the collective-bargaining relationship.

Our holding is not intended to insulate from antitrust review every joint imposition of terms by employers, for an agreement among employers could be sufficiently distant in time and in circumstances from the collective-bargaining process that a rule permitting antitrust intervention would not significantly interfere with that process.... We need not decide in this case whether, or where, within these extreme outer boundaries to draw that line. Nor would it be appropriate for us to do so without the detailed views of the Board, to whose "specialized judgment" Congress "intended to leave" many of the "inevitable questions concerning multiemployer bargaining bound to arise in the future." ...

The judgment of the Court of Appeals is affirmed.

It is so ordered.

Notes and Comments

1. The National Hockey League filed an action against the NHLPA seeking a declaratory judgment that NHL actions were shielded from challenge under the antitrust laws by the nonstatutory labor exemption. The NHL desired to remove the threat of an antitrust action from the NHLPA's collective bargaining arsenal. *See National Hockey League v. National Hockey League Players Association*, 789 F. Supp. 288 (D. Minn. 1992) (dismissed for lack of subject matter jurisdiction; possibility of antitrust litigation does not give rise to actual controversy). The NHL relied on the "unilateral change doctrine," in making its argument. The court described the doctrine as follows:

Under the unilateral change doctrine, if an existing collective bargaining agreement has expired, and negotiations of a new contract have yet to be completed, an employer must bargain to impasse before it may unilaterally change an existing term or condition of employment. An employer's unilateral change, prior to bargaining impasse, results in a violation of the NLRA. *See Litton*, 111 S. Ct. at 2217; *Katz*, 369 U.S. at 747.

2. In *Clarett v. National Football League,* 369 F.3d 124 (2d Cir. 2004), *cert. denied,* 544 U.S. 961 (2005), the court indicated that the nonstatutory labor exemption bars suit under the antitrust laws by players who are not members of the union/bargaining unit. *See also Wood v. National Basketball Association*, 809 F.2d 954 (2d Cir. 1987) (NBA salary cap applied to rookies); *Zimmerman v. National Football League,* 632 F. Supp. 398 (D.D.C. 1986) (NFL supplemental draft applied to players who were not members of NFLPA). Can rookies and others sever ties with the player associations and the attendant barriers to litigation? The NLRA defines "employees" broadly to include workers outside the bargaining unit. 28 U.S.C. § 152(3). *See* Champion, Clarett v. NFL *and the Reincarnation of the Nonstatutory Labor Exemption in Professional Sports*, 47 S. TEX. L. REV. 587 (2006).

3. Review the three elements of the union-employer agreement essential to trigger the nonstatutory labor exemption. In what manner can the players' association challenge one or more of the elements to fall outside of the exemption? Does the *Brown* opinion suggest an answer? Does the three-pronged test remain valid after *Brown*? Can matters concerning the draft, reserve clause, and free agent compensation systems be considered "permissive" subjects of bargaining after *Brown*?

4. Does there exist a difference in leverage possessed by the non-union employee and the member of a bargaining unit? The former, seemingly, faces no "nonstatutory" barrier to seeking antitrust review of anticompetitive management behavior. Does *Brown* generate an incentive for player associations to "decertify"? Or, a disincentive for employees to organize, thus frustrating the intent of Congress? Are the implications of *Brown* greater than suggested by the holding? The public policy and underlying congressional purpose are served by compelling both labor and management to utilize the labor law statutes rather than the antitrust statutes. Does the policy also demand that non-union employees utilize or "exhaust" the available labor law tools rather than antitrust litigation? For commentaries on the *Brown* case, see Kessler & Fehr, *What Justice Breyer Could Not Know at His Mother's Knee: The Adverse Effects of Brown v. Pro Football on Labor Relations in Professional Sports*, 14 ANTITRUST 14 (Spring 2000); Clark, *Brown v. Pro Football, Inc.: The Supreme Court Benches a Player's Right to Negotiate Salary*, 35 HOUS. L. REV. 571 (1998).

5. Justice Stevens, dissenting in *Brown*, notes that the NFL-NFLPA scenario allows for negotiation of individual salaries in a competitive market. He also reminds that exemptions should be construed narrowly. Does the majority utilize the appropriate standard in recognizing the exemption in the case? Is the sports league-labor model meaningfully different than the traditional industrial model? Justice Stevens states:

> [I] do not see why the employers should be entitled to a judicially crafted exemption from antitrust liability. We have explained that "[t]he non-statutory exemption has its source in the strong labor policy favoring the association of employees to eliminate competition over wages and working conditions."... I know of no similarly strong labor policy that favors the association of employers to eliminate a competitive method of negotiating wages that predates collective bargaining and that labor would prefer to preserve.

Brown v. Pro Football, Inc., 518 U.S. 231, 257 (1996) (Stevens, J., dissenting). For an article suggesting that fans will "lament" the *Brown* decision, see Harper, *Multiemployer Bargaining, Antitrust Law, and Team Sports: The Contingent Choice of a Broad Exemption*, 38 WM. & MARY L. REV. 1663 (1997).

6. In 2011, both the NBPA and NFLPA chose to file disclaimers of interest in bargaining with the leagues and team ownership. Under labor law principles, the disclaimer has been considered effective in freeing the employees to utilize the antitrust laws. *See Retail Assocs., Inc.*, 120 N.L.R.B. 388 (1958). Does the traditional treatment of the disclaimer by the NLRB comport with the U.S. Supreme Court's analysis in *Brown*? Does the use of the disclaimer to avoid the use of the labor laws stand contrary to the intent of Congress that employees rely on the labor laws, rather than the antitrust statutes? *See generally* Bard, Note, *Strength in Numbers: The Question of Decertification of Sports Unions in 2011 and the Benefit of Administrative Oversight*, 1 AM. U. LAB. & EMP. L. F. 347 (2011); *Symposium, Professional & Ethical Dilemmas Facing Attorneys Representing Entities, Athletes, and Entertainers*, 21 SETON HALL J. SPORTS & ENT. L. 381 (2011).

7. The NFL, having chosen to terminate the CBA, played the 2010 season without a salary cap. The NFL subsequently "locked out" the players and the NFLPA disclaimed interest. Does the lockout constitute an unlawful group boycott in violation of the antitrust statutes? Are players subject to antitrust scrutiny regarding any collusion in negotiating with NFL teams? Are agents precluded from collaborating by sharing information in representation of players? For analysis of the settlement of suit filed by Tom Brady in response to the NFL lockout, see Bucher, Comment, *Inside the Huddle: Analyzing the Mediation Efforts in the NFL's Brady Settlement & Its Effectiveness for Future Professional Sports Disputes*, 22 MARQ. SPORTS L. REV. 211 (2011).

Does a league possess a valid cause of action against player agents (authorized by player association certification) allegedly interfering with the bargaining process between the agents' clients and management? Would the NFL possess a cause of action in antitrust against player agents acting in collusion, in the event of NFLPA decertification? *See The Five Smiths, Inc. v. National Football League Players Ass'n*, 788 F. Supp. 1042 (D. Minn. 1992). The court ruled the complaint, alleging that NFLPA and player agents' exchange of player compensation data and current offers information violated Section 1 of the Sherman Act, failed to state a cognizable antitrust claim under either the *per se* or rule of reason test.

8. The NBA conducted substantial negotiation efforts in 2011 before filing a disclaimer of interest and seeking antitrust remedies. The NBPA first filed an unfair-labor-practice charge that the NBA had failed to negotiate in good faith. If the NBPA were successful in its claim, the NLRB would seek an injunction barring the NBA lockout. After disclaimer, two antitrust lawsuits were filed by NBA players: *Anthony v. Nat'l Basketball Ass'n,* No. 11–05525 (N.D. Cal. Nov. 15, 2011); *Butler v. Nat'l Basketball Ass'n,* No. 11–03352 (D. Minn. Nov. 15, 2011). The parties reached agreement in the matter. The NBA, prior to the NBPA's disclaimer, filed a declaratory action seeking a ruling that the lockout did not violate antitrust law and any future dissolution of the NBPA would render existing player contracts null and void. *NBA v. NBPA,* No. 11–5369 (S.D.N.Y. 2011).

Problem

The Rugby League adopted a collective bargaining agreement that was similar to previous NFL-NFLPA collective bargaining agreements. The agreement included the reserve system and free agent compensation scheme that enables the Commissioner to award draft choices, players, and cash as compensation for the loss of free agent players. The Rugby League teams historically draft players who have no remaining college eligibility. The draft is part of the agreement, but eligibility for the draft is not specified. Ownership and management set the eligibility standards at each annual league meeting. Foreign and domestic professional players are signed as free agents. The collective bargaining agreement between the RL and the RLPA expired by its own terms two years ago. The league has functioned as if the expired agreement remained in effect, but negotiations have stalled. Likelihood of further bargaining appears slight at best.

The RL commissioner asks you for the following information:

1. What concerted actions are available, if any, for both labor and management pursuant to the NLRA? What additional facts, if any, would you want to know?
2. Describe the nature of the "statutory exemption" and "nonstatutory exemption" from the application of the antitrust laws.
3. Discuss the effect of the RLPA "decertification" and/or "disclaimer" and the adjudication of player restraints pursuant to the antitrust laws.
4. Explain whether the RL can hire replacement workers in the event of a strike or lockout.

Eight

Player Contract Issues and Enforcement

Learning Outcomes

- Know the equitable and legal remedies available to both the team and player as plaintiffs alleging breach of contract, and applicable defenses.
- Understand nonjudicial enforcement of player contracts, including the use of arbitration.
- Understand the enforcement of arbitration clauses and the limits of challenging an arbitrator's decision.
- Learn about the economic protections for players suffering injuries in the course of employment.
- Learn about professional sport league salary arbitration mechanisms.

Key Terms

- Negative injunction
- Irreparable harm
- Unclean hands
- Labor arbitration
- Grievance arbitration
- Collusion
- "Final offer" salary arbitration

A. Introduction

This chapter focuses on judicial and nonjudicial enforcement of professional sports contracts. The chapter first addresses equitable and legal remedies available to both the team and player as plaintiffs alleging breach of valid contracts. Of particular importance are the contractual provisions obligating the parties to submit any disputes arising under the contract to arbitration.

Section C presents discussion of grievance arbitration, a feature of all professional sports bargaining agreements and uniform/standard player contracts. Recurring issues arising subsequent to the formation of the player-team contract are presented, including the ownership collusion case in Major League Baseball. Finally, the baseball salary arbitration mechanism is discussed and compared to the traditional arbitration model.

B. The Law of Contracts

The contract between the player and team, of course, must satisfy all legal requirements of the jurisdiction where the contract is formed. Although standard form contracts are utilized by most professional sports leagues, disputes between parties arise under the terms of the contracts. Resolution of the disputes requires application of the general principles of the law of contracts and remedies. A party seeking to enforce provisions of a contract necessarily argues that the contract is valid and the provisions should be construed as alleged. A party desiring to avoid the enforcement of a contract argues that the clauses should be read to reveal a different intention of the parties, or the contract is invalid and thus cannot be enforced.

The usual contract remedies and defenses are available to parties litigating rights and duties under the terms of sports contracts. Thus, actions for damages and/or equitable remedies are common. Where ballclubs are attempting to restrain players from performing with other teams in a different league, courts readilyadjudicate the matter under equity jurisdiction. Courts generally do not compel specific performance of personal service contracts. Courts, however, regularly enforce negative covenants, such as covenants in player-team contracts prohibiting the player from performing for another team during the contract period. A preliminary "negative injunction" will issue where the plaintiff satisfies four essential criteria as follows:

1. Irreparable injury to plaintiff/inadequate remedy at law;
2. Absence of substantial harm to defendant or other interested parties;
3. Absence of harm to the public interest; and
4. A likelihood that plaintiff will prevail on the merits.

See Cincinnati Bengals, Inc. v. Bergey, 453 F. Supp. 129 (S.D. Ohio 1974), *citing Philadelphia World Hockey Club, Inc. v. Philadelphia Hockey Club, Inc.*, 351 F. Supp. 462 (E.D. Pa. 1972). The Problem presented below is designed to acquaint you with the principles and elements of the negative injunction, as developed in the context of sports contracts.

Where players sue for alleged breach of the player-team contract, courts deny judicial relief if the contract provisions enable the parties to resolve the issue through arbitration. Thus, the court initially determines whether a valid arbitration clause exists, and secondly, whether the dispute is within the scope of the clause. Professional sport leagues have arbitration clauses in their collective bargaining agreements. See discussion of grievance arbitration at Section C, below.

In the absence of a valid arbitration clause, a plaintiff can obtain adjudication of a controversy only in a court that has personal jurisdiction over the defendant. The peculiar factual nature of sports employment generates several questions regarding the appropriate jurisdiction in which to file a lawsuit. The club plays its home games in a specified locality. Road games are usually played in other cities and states. The broadcasting of games expands the areas in which the club operates. The player often maintains a permanent residence in one location and a temporary residence in another. Practical considerations join jurisdictional questions to further complicate the decision regarding the appropriate forum for suit; for example, plaintiffs usually desire to file suit in a sympathetic jurisdiction.

A ballclub possesses several possibilities in filing suit against the player: (1) player's permanent residence; (2) player's temporary residence; and (3) situs of player-team negotiations, usually location of college or high school. Although a defendant generally may be sued in the state of domicile, a player's contacts with the state may be in question. The defendant must have sufficient "minimum contacts" with the forum state in order to satisfy the due process standards set forth in *International Shoe Co. v. Washington*, 326 U.S. 310 (1945). Courts consider the following factors:

1. Length of time defendant spends in the state;
2. Nature of activities defendant undertakes in the state; and
3. Defendant's living arrangements in the state.

If little or no contact remains with the state subsequent to the negotiation of the contract, satisfaction of the minimum contacts standard is questionable.

The player-plaintiff also possesses alternatives in choosing the appropriate forum for litigation: (1) state where games are played; (2) state where revenues are derived; (3) state in which club is incorporated; (4) state where team's offices are located; and (5) state featuring broadcasts or recruiting efforts. The possible forums for litigation are analyzed under the *International Shoe* minimum contacts standard.

For detailed discussion of issues concerning the appropriate forum for sports contract litigation, see Uberstine, *The Enforceability of Sports Industry Employment Agreements, in* 2 LAW OF PROFESSIONAL & AMATEUR SPORTS ch. 10 (Uberstine ed., 2008).

Problem

Chock Chiles is a person of tremendous athletic ability and talent. While in college, Chiles earned All-American honors in both football and baseball. Following his junior year, Chiles signed a professional baseball contract with the Detroit Tigers. He received a signing bonus of $1,000,000.00. He played in the Tigers' minor league system during the summer. In the fall, Chiles returned to college to complete his senior year of football eligibility. The Tigers expressly agreed to and otherwise permitted Chiles to play college football while under contract with the baseball club. Chiles made several All-American teams as a senior running back.

In the spring of his senior year, Chiles participated in the Tigers' major league training camp. At the completion of spring training, Chiles signed a new three-year contract and was placed on the active roster of the major league club. The contract included a clause stipulating that Chiles would not play football during the term of the contract. The clause was in all respects identical to Paragraph 5(b) of the Uniform Player Contract found at Chapter 11, below. Chiles received a $100,000 bonus as compensation for agreeing to the clause prohibiting him from playing football.

Later in the spring, Chiles was chosen in the third round of the National Football League draft by the San Diego Chargers. (He would have been a first round choice but teams were hesitant, given the baseball contract.) Despite much pressure in the form of letters, phone calls, and personal visits from the Chargers, Chiles continued to play baseball and did not sign a football contract.

For the baseball season, Chiles hit .210, had four home runs, and 25 RBIs. All figures placed him among the worst in major league baseball. Chiles was mediocre, at best, as a defensive player. The Tigers were disappointed in Chiles' performance. Chiles vowed to work on several areas of weakness during the offseason. Chiles rejected further offers made by the Chargers at the end of the baseball season.

In the following spring, Chiles again made the major league club roster at the completion of spring training. Midway through the baseball season, Chiles was hitting .185 and had hit no home runs. On July 15th, Chiles announced his retirement from baseball. A news conference was held during which both the Tigers and Chiles remarked that the relationship of two-and-a-half years had been pleasant for both parties.

On August 15, Chiles signed an NFL contract to play football for the Detroit Lions, who had gained rights to Chiles pursuant to NFL rules. Uncontroverted evidence indicates that the Lions had pressured Chiles to "jump" to football since April. Chiles initiated further negotiations with the Lions in early July.

You work for the Detroit Tigers. Assume that you are working on the case in August and that Chiles has not yet worked out or otherwise played with the Detroit Lions.

1. Outline the elements required for issuance of a "negative injunction" to prevent Chiles from performing with the Lions.
2. Project whether the Tigers have a case based on the evidence given in the problem.

3. What defenses are available to Chiles? What evidence from the problem supports Chiles's position?
4. What opportunities are likely available for compromise settlement?

Dallas Cowboys Football Club, Inc. v. Harris

348 S.W.2d 37 (Tex. Civ. App. 1961)

DIXON, CHIEF JUSTICE.

Appellant Dallas Cowboys Football Club, Inc.... members of the National Football League, brought this action against James B. Harris for injunction to restrain Harris from playing professional football, or engaging in any activities related to professional football for anyone except the Club. Appellant alleged that Harris was bound by the terms of a written contract to play football for the Club and no one else, but that in violation of his contract he was playing football for the Dallas Texans Football Club, a member of the American Football League....

In June 1958 James B. Harris for a consideration of $8,000.00 signed a contract to play football and to engage in activities related to football only for the Los Angeles Rams Football Club, a member of the National Football League. This contract covered a period of time beginning with the execution of the contract and extending to the first day of May following the 1958 football season, which latter date was May 1, 1959. The contract also included a clause providing that the Club at its option might renew the contract for an additional year. Both Harris and the Los Angeles Rams Football Club performed the primary contract which by its terms expired May 1, 1959. A controversy arose between the parties with reference, among other things, to the exercise by the Los Angeles Rams Club of its option on Harris' services for another year. As a result Harris chose not to play professional football during the 1959 season. Instead he reentered the University of Oklahoma as a student and also accepted a position as assistant football coach at the University.

In April 1960 Harris signed a contract to play football during the 1960 season for the Dallas Texans Football Club of the newly organized American Football League.

Harris' contract with the Los Angeles Rams was by its terms assignable. On July 22, 1960 the contract was assigned to the Dallas Cowboys Football Club, Inc., a new member of the National Football League. On the same date this suit was instituted against Harris by the latter club to restrain Harris from playing football for anyone except the Club.

Since the Club contends that Harris, as a matter of law, is bound by the terms of the 1958 contract and its option to play football only for the Club for an additional year, we deem it advisable to reproduce material parts of the contract:

> 2. The player agrees during the term of this contract he will play football and will engage in activities related to football only for the Club and as directed by the Club....
>
> 3. For the Player's services... and for his agreement not to play football or engage in activities related to football for any other person, firm, corporation or institution during the term of this contract, and for the option hereinafter set forth... the Club promises to pay the Player... the sum of $8,000.00.
>
> 5. The player promises and agrees that during the term of this contract he will not play football or engage in activities related to football for any other person, firm, corporation or institution except with the prior written consent of the Club and the Commissioner....
>
> 8. The Player hereby represents that he has special, exceptional and unique knowledge, skill and ability as a football player, the loss of which cannot be fairly or adequately compensated by damages and therefore agrees that the Club shall have the right, in addition to any other rights which the Club may possess, to enjoin him by appropriate injunction proceedings against playing football or engaging in activities related to football for any person, firm, corporation or institution and against any other breach of this contract....

It is well established in this State and other jurisdictions that injunctive relief will be granted to restrain violation by an employee of negative covenants in a personal service contract if the employee is a person of exceptional and unique knowledge, skill and ability in performing the service called for in the contract.

But in this case there is a fact finding by a jury in answer to Special Issue No. 1 to the effect that at the time of the trial Harris did not have exceptional and unique knowledge, skill and ability as a football player....

The record discloses that appellee Harris himself on cross examination testified that he *thought* he had a certain amount of unique skill and ability.

But later a definition of the word "unique" was introduced without objection from appellant and in that connection Harris then testified as follows:

> "Q. Now, have you looked up the definition of "unique" in the dictionary? A. No, sir; I haven't.
>
> "Q. Well, I am reading from the New Century Dictionary here, and it says: "of which there is but one, or sole, or only"; Do you think you are the only defensive halfback? A. Not by any means of the imagination.
>
> "Q. It says, "Unparalleled or unequal"—you think you are unparalleled, or unequal? A. I wish I were, now.
>
> "Q. Do you think you are? A. No, sir; I am not. I know my own ability.
>
> "Q. It says, "something of which there is only one"; are you the only defensive halfback? A. No. I am not.

> "Q. "Something without parallel or equal of its kind"; are you that kind of a defensive halfback? A. No. I wish I was." . . .

Among the several grounds of error urged by the Club in its sixth point on appeal was this: the court erred in refusing to grant a new trial because the great weight and preponderance of the evidence showed that Harris did possess special, exceptional and unique knowledge, skill and ability as a football player, contrary to the answer of the jury.

. . . . [T]hough there may be some evidence in the record which raises a fact issue necessitating the submission of the case to the jury, nevertheless it may be the duty of the court afterwards to grant a new trial if the record evidence is "insufficient" to support the jury verdict, that is, if the evidence is so against the overwhelming weight and preponderance of the evidence as to be manifestly wrong.

We think that is true in this case. The definition of the word "unique" introduced in evidence was too narrow and limited. We agree with the statement in *Philadelphia Ball Club v. Lajoie*, 202 Pa. 210, 51 A. 973, 58 L.R.A. 227, as follows:

> "We think, however, that in refusing relief unless the defendant's services were shown to be of such a character as to render it impossible to replace him he has taken extreme ground. It seems to us that a more just and equitable rule is laid down in Pom. Spec. Perf. p. 31, where the principle is thus declared: 'Where one person agrees to render personal services to another, which requires and presupposes a special knowledge, skill, and ability in the employee, so that in case of a default *the same service could not easily* be obtained from others, . . . its performance will be negatively enforced by enjoining its breach. . . .' WE have not found any case going to the [same] length of requiring, as a condition of relief, proof of the impossibility of obtaining equivalent service."

After a careful study of all the record evidence in this case we are of the opinion that the evidence is "insufficient" to support the jury finding.

All of those witnesses, whose testimony has any bearing on the question testified very positively that Harris was possessed of unique skill and ability. Prior to the introduction of the narrow and limited definition of "unique," Harris himself testified as follows:

> "Q. Jimmy, you signed contracts with both of them in which you represented that you did have unique skill and ability, didn't you? A. I thought I did.
>
> "Q. Well, you know that is in both of the contracts, don't you? A. That's right.
>
> "Q. . . . Then you know you do have unique skill and ability, don't you? A. I think I have a certain amount: yes.
>
> "Q. You yourself told both clubs in your written contracts that you did have skill and ability, didn't you? A. That's right.

"Q. You now tell this jury that you have got that skill and ability, don't you? A. Right."

We also quote from the testimony of Don Rossi, General Manager of the Dallas Texans Football Club, who was a witness for Harris:

"Q.... In your opinion, Mr. Rossi, he does have exceptional skill and ability, doesn't he? A. Yes, sir.

"Q. Well, haven't you already testified that he was above the average?

A. Well, yes, sir; average or above average.

"Q. That's right. A. Well, we will go along with that.

"Q. Well, he is above average, isn't he? A. We will buy that.

"Q.... Not buy it; you are just swearing to it? A. Yes sir."

The testimony of Schramm and Landry was even more positive. It is true that the witnesses named other professional football players who are "equal or better" than Harris as players, but the testimony was that players of Harris' ability were not available to the Club.

We sustain that part of the Club's sixth point on appeal wherein the Club asserts error in the court's refusing to grant a new trial because the great weight and preponderance of the evidence clearly showed that Harris did possess special, exceptional and unique knowledge, skill and ability as a football player, contrary to the answers of the jury.

In three cross-points Harris says that... the relief sought by the Club should be denied as a matter of law because (1) the contract was invalid not having been formed by a proper offer and acceptance; (2) the contract was not valid, having expired by its own terms, and (3) Harris had not retired from activities related to football.

We have concluded that these cross-points should be overruled.

We cannot support Harris' contention that the contract is so unreasonable and harsh as to be unenforceable in equity.

Minnesota Muskies, Inc. v. Hudson

294 F. Supp. 979 (M.D.N.C. 1969)

Edwin M. Stanley, Chief Judge.

The plaintiffs seek by this action to enjoin the defendant, Louis C. Hudson, from playing professional basketball for any professional basketball team other than the plaintiff, Florida Professional Sports, Inc., for the term of an alleged contract he signed with the plaintiff, Minnesota Muskies, Inc., on May 3, 1967, and assigned to the plaintiff, Florida Professional Sports, Inc., on July 31, 1968....

During the 1967–68 professional basketball season, the Muskies operated a professional basketball team in Minneapolis, Minnesota, under a franchise issued by the American Basketball Association, and on July 31, 1968, the franchise, nineteen player contracts, and certain other equipment belonging to the Muskies, were transferred and assigned by the Muskies to the plaintiff Florida Professional Sports, Inc.

The plaintiff Florida Professional Sports, Inc., hereinafter referred to as 'Miami,' is a corporation organized and existing under the laws of the State of Florida, and has its principal place of business in Miami, Florida. The corporation was incorporated on or about July 11, 1968, and during the 1968–69 professional basketball season is engaged in the business of operating a professional basketball team known as the Miami Floridians under the franchise originally issued by the American Basketball Association to the Muskies....

The American Basketball Association, hereinafter referred to as 'ABA,' is an association of professional basketball teams that operate basketball teams in several cities in various sections of the United States under franchises issued by the ABA. The ABA was established in 1967, and its teams played their first regular season games during the 1967–68 professional basketball season. During the 1967–68 season, each ABA team played a number of regular season games, followed by a series of play-off games between certain ABA teams with the best regular season records. During the 1968–69 season, each ABA team will play regular season games and a series of play-off games will follow the regular season games....

In the spring of 1966, Hudson was drafted by St. Louis in a player-draft held by the NBA, and on May 17, 1966, he signed an NBA Uniform Player Contract with St. Louis. The contract provided for the employment of Hudson as a basketball player for one year from October 1, 1966, with the following provision, known as a "reserve clause":

> "24.... If the Player fails, neglects, or omits to sign and return such contract to the Club so that the Club receives it on or before October 1st next succeeding, then this contract shall be deemed renewed and extended for the period of one year, upon the same terms and conditions in all respects as are provided herein, except that the compensation payable to the Player shall be the sum provided in the contract tendered to the Player pursuant to the provisions hereof, which compensation shall in no event be less than 75% of the compensation payable to the Player for the last playing season covered by this contract and renewals and extensions thereof.
>
> "The Club's right to renew this contract, as herein provided, and the promise of the Player not to play otherwise than for the Club and its assignees, have been taken into consideration in determining the amount of compensation payable under paragraph 2 hereof."

Hudson played for St Louis during the 1966–67 regular season, and during the NBA play-off games until St. Louis was eliminated from the play-off games on April 12, 1967....

On May 3, 1967, Hudson signed an ABA Uniform Player Contract with the Muskies. The contract provided for the employment of Hudson as a professional basketball player for a period of three years from October 2, 1967.

The addendum to the contract between the Muskies and Hudson further provided as follows:

> "6. In the event legal proceedings be instituted to prevent and enjoin the Player from playing for the first year of this contract, and if the said legal proceeding be successful in that said Player be enjoined from playing for one year, then and in that event the Club will pay the Player the sum of $25,000.00 for the said year. The Player agrees to then play for the Club the next ensuing three years under the terms and conditions as set forth in Clause 1 of this Addendum...."

The contract between Hudson and the Muskies also contains the following provision:

> "5. *Injunctive Relief.* The PLAYER hereby represents that he has special, exceptional and unique knowledge, skill and ability as a basketball player, the loss of which cannot be estimated with any certainty and cannot be fairly or adequately compensated by damages and therefore agrees that the CLUB shall have the right, in addition to any other rights that the CLUB may possess, to enjoin him by appropriate injunction proceedings against playing basketball, or engaging in activities related to basketball for any person, firm, corporation or institution, or injunction against any other breach of this contract."

As disclosed by the disposition testimony of the various individuals involved, the parties are in disagreement with respect to the details of the negotiations that led to the signing of the Hudson-Muskies contract. From the conflicting testimony, it is found that sometime in March of 1967, at the time Hudson was still playing for St. Louis in playoff games, and while his contract with St. Louis was in full force and effect, Hudson was contacted by a representative of the Muskies for the purpose of determining whether he was interested in signing a professional basketball contract with the Muskies. After a series of telephone calls between Hudson and representatives of the Muskies organization, Hudson contacted his agent, Edward M. Cohen, an attorney in Minneapolis, and advised Cohen of his conversations with representatives of the Muskies and asked him to see what the Muskies had to offer.... Cohen immediately called to Hudson's attention the "reserve clause" in the contract, and questioned whether he would be a free agent at the end of the current basketball season. Nevertheless, it was decided that Cohen would continue his negotiations with the Muskies.... Cohen, Hudson, Barnett, Holman and Shields each attended some of the meetings, but all were not present at every meeting. The meetings culminated in Hudson and the Muskies signing the aforementioned contract on May 3, 1967.

All responsible officials of the Muskies, including Holman and Shields, were fully aware of the contract Hudson had with St. Louis before the contract between Hudson and the Muskies was prepared and signed, and had every reason to believe St. Louis would either exercise its options under the "reserve clause" of its existing contract or negotiate a new contract with Hudson.... Holman did not recognize any responsibility for conferring with St. Louis before executing the contract with Hudson, feeling that it was Hudson's duty to advise St. Louis as to the negotiations and the execution of the new contract.

Both parties to the Hudson-Muskies contract, as well as their attorneys, were uncertain as to the legal effect of the "reserve clause" in the St. Louis contract, and this uncertainty prompted Hudson to request that Paragraph 6 of the addendum be inserted in his contract with the Muskies. Further, it was Cohen's feeling that in the event St. Louis was successful in restraining Hudson from playing under his contract with the Muskies, Hudson was entitled to some financial protection....

On May 25, 1967, one week after the Hudson-Muskies contract was publicly announced, St. Louis filed suit against the Muskies, all the other members of the ABA, and George Mikan, Commissioner of the ABA, in the United States District Court for the District of Minnesota, charging a conspiracy among the defendants, with respect to the Hudson-Muskies contract, to deliberately, maliciously, wrongfully and unjustifiably interfere with the contractual relationship which existed between St. Louis and Hudson, and seeking actual damages in the sum of $2,000,000.00 and punitive damages in the sum of $1,000,000.00.

On May 25, 1967, St. Louis also filed suit against Hudson in the United States District Court for the District of Minnesota, seeking an injunction against Hudson from playing basketball for any other person, firm, or corporation, during the 1967–68 and the 1968–69 professional basketball seasons....

It is apparent that sometime during the early part of June of 1967 Hudson had become dissatisfied with the contract he had signed with the Muskies, and had decided to see if he could reach another agreement with St. Louis...

On June 5, 1967, Hudson and St. Louis executed an NBA Uniform Player Contract covering a period of five years from October 1, 1967....

Shortly after the signing of the Hudson-St. Louis contract on June 5, 1967, St. Louis submitted to a voluntary dismissal of the two actions it had brought in the United States District Court for the District of Minnesota against the Muskies, and others, and against Hudson. Answers had not been filed when the actions were dismissed.

Sometime in June or July of 1967, Hudson advised Cohen of the signing of the new St. Louis contract and instructed Cohen to return to the Muskies the $7,500.00 bonus the Muskies had paid him at the time he signed the Muskies contract. After receiving the instructions, Cohen called Holman and offered to return $5,000.00 of the $7,500.00 bonus, stating that this was all the money Hudson had at that time and that the balance would be paid "very shortly." Holman refused to accept the tender of $5,000.00, and also stated that he would refuse to take the full $7,500.00 should it be tendered.

On October 13, 1967, Holman wrote a letter to Hudson, in care of his attorney, Cohen, in which he stated that the Muskies were agreeable to Hudson playing out a one-year option with St. Louis, but that he was expected to perform under his contract with the Muskies at the end of the one-year option period, which was understood to be October 2, 1968.... The letter was received by Hudson, but he has never responded to same.... On May 3, 1968, in response to an inquiry, Cohen advised the Muskies that Hudson's position was that he did not have any contractual obligation to perform for the Muskies....

On October 3, 1968, counsel for Hudson tendered to counsel for plaintiffs a certified check in the amount of $7,500.00, as reimbursement for the bonus paid Hudson by the Muskies....

Hudson is highly skilled and talented, and possesses special, exceptional, and unique knowledge, skill and ability as a basketball player.

The sole question presented for decision is whether the plaintiffs are entitled to an injunction restraining Hudson from playing professional basketball with any team or club other than Miami for the term of the contract he signed with the Muskies on May 3, 1967, and assigned by the Muskies to Miami on July 31, 1968....

It is generally held that where a person agrees to render personal services to another, which require special and unique knowledge, skill and ability, so that in default the same services cannot easily be obtained from others, a court of equity is empowered to negatively enforce performance of the agreement by enjoining its breach. While acknowledging this principle of law, the defendants correctly assert that equitable relief should be denied to a suitor who comes into court with unclean hands. One of the most fundamental principles of equity jurisprudence is the maxim that "he who comes into equity must come with clean hands." Equity demands of suitors fair dealings with reference to matters concerning which they seek relief....

Measured by these fundamental principles of equity jurisprudence, the conclusion is inescapable that the Muskies, in its dealings with Hudson, soiled the hands to such an extent that the negative injunctive relief sought should be denied. This is not to say that Hudson was an innocent bystander, or that he was an unwilling participant in his dealings with the Muskies. On the contrary, viewed strictly from the stand point of business morality, his position in this litigation, like that of the Muskies, is not an enviable one.

While not a controlling factor, the Court is convinced that the Muskies, admittedly desirous of acquiring a winning basketball team as quickly as possible, either contacted Hudson, or caused him to be contacted by someone on its behalf, while he was still actively engaged in the play-off games with St. Louis. Without this unwarranted interference on the part of the Muskies, there is every likelihood that Hudson would have fulfilled his contractual and moral obligations with St. Louis....

Basically, the plaintiffs argue that Hudson's original contract with St. Louis, because it provides for perpetual service, and is lacking in the necessary qualities of definiteness, certainty, and mutuality, is void. The contract being void and unenforceable beyond the 1966–67 season, the plaintiffs contend that their contract with Hudson is in all respects valid, and that the Hudson-St. Louis contract executed on June 5, 1967, with knowledge of the existence of the Hudson-Muskies contract executed on May 3, 1967, is likewise void. Under these circumstances, plaintiffs assert that they are entitled to have their contract enforced in a court of equity. There is no merit to this argument. Even if the "reserve clause" in the St. Louis contract is of doubtful validity, the fact remains that the Muskies, knowing that Hudson was under a moral, if not a legal obligation to furnish his services to St. Louis for the 1967–68 and subsequent seasons, if St. Louis chose to exercise its option, sent for Hudson and induced him to repudiate his obligation to St. Louis. Such conduct, even if strictly within the law because of the St. Louis contract being unenforceable, was so tainted with unfairness and injustice as to justify a court of equity in withholding relief.

The Muskies chose to let Hudson return to St. Louis for the 1967–68 season rather than litigate the matter. The Muskies explained its inaction by stating that it recognized that Hudson was perhaps obligated to play for St. Louis for one more year. Notwithstanding its recognition of this obligation, the Muskies agreed to pay Hudson to sit out the 1967–68 season even if the Court should decree that the St. Louis contract was enforceable. This alone is sufficient for a court of equity to refuse relief.

Finally, plaintiffs insist that they are entitled to relief, notwithstanding their unfair and unjust conduct, because St. Louis was also guilty of inequitable and unlawful conduct in signing Hudson to a second contract on June 5, 1967, when it knew that Hudson had signed a valid contract with the Muskies on May 3, 1967. This argument is also lacking in merit. The doors of a court of equity are closed to one tainted with unfairness or injustice relative to the matter in which he seeks relief "however improper may have been the behavior of the defendant."...

The injunctive relief sought by the plaintiffs must be denied, not because the Hudson-St. Louis contract was of "any legal force and effect" or is one that "the courts will enforce," and not because the merits of the controversy are necessarily with St. Louis, "but solely because the actions and conduct of the (Muskies) in procuring the contract, upon which (its) right to relief is and must be founded, do not square with one of the vital and fundamental principles of equity which touches to the quick the dignity of a court of conscience and controls its decision regardless of all other considerations."

Munchak Corp. v. Cunningham

457 F.2d 721 (4th Cir. 1972)

WINTER, CIRCUIT JUDGE:

Plaintiffs, the owners and operators of the basketball club "The Carolina Cougars" sued to enjoin defendant, William John Cunningham, a professional basketball player, from performing services as a basketball player for any basketball club other than the Cougars.... The district court, finding that Cunningham had contracted to play for the Cougars, nevertheless concluded that even if Cunningham had failed and refused to perform his contract, plaintiffs had *unclean hands*.... It, therefore, denied injunctive relief.

In this appeal, we conclude that plaintiffs did not have *unclean hands*... Accordingly, we reverse and remand the case for entry of an injunction restraining Cunningham from playing for any team other than the Cougars.

The principal reason why the district court refused equitable relief was that "the conclusion is inescapable that the Cougars, in its dealings with Cunningham, soiled its hands to such an extent that the injunctive relief sought should be denied." The *unclean hands* were found in the fact that the Cougars negotiated with Cunningham through intermediaries and agreed to pay him $80,000.00 if he did not play for the 76ers during his option year. We disagree.

In agreement with *Washington Capitols Basketball Club, Inc. v. Barry*, 419 F.2d 472 (9th Cir. 1969), we think that there was neither illegality nor *unclean hands* in the Cougars' contracting for Cunningham's services to be rendered *after* the term of his contract with the 76ers had expired, notwithstanding that the negotiations, whether directly or through intermediaries, took place while Cunningham's contract with the 76ers was still in full force and effect. As the *Washington Capitols* case stated, quoting from *Diodes, Inc. v. Franzen* "'no actionable wrong is committed by a competitor who solicits his competitor's employees or who hires away one or more of his competitor's employees who are not under contract, so long as the inducement to leave is not accompanied by unlawful action.'" Cunningham was under no obligation, option or restraint with respect to the 76ers after October 1, 1971, and the Cougars had a lawful right to bid and contract for his services to be rendered after that date.

Notes and Comments

1. The "negative injunction" was utilized early in cases concerning entertainment matters. *See Metropolitan Exhibition Co. v. Ewing*, 42 F. 198 (S.D.N.Y. 1890). For general discussion of the negative injunction, including the historical basis, see GREENBERG & GRAY, 1 SPORTS LAW PRACTICE § 2.05 (2d ed. 2009); Uberstine, *The Enforceability of Sports Industry Employment Agreements, in* 2 LAW OF PROFESSIONAL & AMATEUR SPORTS ch. 10 (Uberstine ed., 2008).

2. *Washington Capitols Basketball Club, Inc. v. Barry*, 419 F.2d 472 (9th Cir. 1969), is another instructive case regarding the negative injunction. Rick Barry began his professional basketball career in San Francisco playing for the NBA Warriors. At the termination of that contract, Barry signed with the ABA Oakland Oaks for three years. After the first year of the contract, the Oaks were sold and the franchise was moved to Washington, D.C. and renamed the Capitols. Upon receiving news of the franchise shift, Barry signed a contract with the NBA Warriors for a term overlapping with his ABA contract. The Capitols in turn brought suit to prevent Barry from playing for the Warriors and were successful in securing injunctive relief against Barry. Barry's allegation that the Oaks should not receive equitable relief because of "unclean hands" (for having lured Barry away from the Warriors) was unavailing. The court stated the principle that there is nothing "unclean" or tortious about negotiating for services to commence after the termination of a preexisting contract.

3. The "irreparable harm" requirement for the issuance of the negative injunction usually is determined by the "unique skills test." For a case departing from the test, see *Boston Professional Hockey Asso., Inc. v. Cheevers*, 348 F. Supp. 261 (D. Mass. 1972) (district court assessed the effect on the team's economic position to deny the injunction on the irreparable harm issue, despite the fact that the player possessed unique skills).

4. Few cases are found involving professional sports athletes in which courts denied negative injunctions on the basis of inadequate or ordinary skills. Do professional players satisfy the test *per se*? For a case suggesting an answer in the affirmative, see *Central New York Basketball, Inc. v. Barnett*, 181 N.E.2d 506 (Ohio C.P. 1961). *But see Matuszak v. Houston Oilers, Inc.*, 515 S.W.2d 725 (Tex. Civ. App. 1974) (question of skills depends on facts of each case).

The Albany Black Sox, a minor league baseball team, failed to satisfactorily establish "the unique and unusual" character of the services of its first baseman. Thus, the team's request for issuance of an injunction was denied. But, the court also found the player contract did not meet the requirement of mutuality of obligation. *Spencer v. Milton*, 287 N.Y.S. 944 (Sup. Ct. 1936). Can you adequately distinguish minor league ballplayers from major league players in terms of skill? Is the fact that only a small percentage of minor league players ever make the major leagues helpful in this regard? But, remember that only a minute percentage of amateur athletes are able to procure professional sports contracts, even at the minor league level.

For a case in which the court enjoined two rookies without any professional experience from jumping from a Canadian professional football club (CFL) to the Cleveland Browns, see *Winnipeg Rugby Football Club v. Freeman & Locklear*, 140 F. Supp. 365 (N.D. Ohio 1955).

Perhaps it is helpful to review the basis of the negative injunction issued in *Philadelphia Ball Club v. Lajoie*, 51 A. 973 (Pa. 1902). The court enunciated the question as not whether the player was "irreplaceable," but whether replacement of the player on the playing field could be translated into money damages. Thus, the question was whether harm was irreparable, or the damage remedy at law inadequate.

5. Review the four essential elements of the action for a preliminary negative injunction set forth in *Bergey*, above. Notice that the plaintiff has the burden of showing the absence of harm to the defendant. Is the court balancing the irreparable harm to the plaintiff under the *status quo* with the projected harm to the defendant in the event an injunction is issued? Is the court utilizing a test of reasonableness? How will you attempt to show absence of harm to a minor league player who desires to better the player's economic and professional opportunities by jumping to another club?

6. What arguments exist that the public interest is not harmed if an injunction is granted (the third element set forth in *Bergey*)? *See Cincinnati Bengals v. Bergey*, 453 F. Supp. 129, 147 (S.D. Ohio 1974).

7. Sometimes issues arise pertaining to the proper duration and scope of a negative injunction, which was the case in *Lewis v. Rahman*, 147 F. Supp. 2d 225 (S.D.N.Y. 2001). After former heavyweight boxing champion Lennox Lewis lost a match by Hasim Rahman, Lewis filed suit to enforce a provision in his contract with Rahman that gave Lewis the right to fight a rematch with Rahman within 150 days of the match if Rahman defeated him. In granting Lewis' request for a negative injunction to prevent Rahman from fighting another opponent for 18 months, the district court judge stated:

> [Lewis] testified that it was a material condition of his bout with Rahman that Rahman agree to a prompt rematch if he won the bout. Lewis wants an immediate rematch both because of his age and because he fears that other boxers will try to freeze him out of title contention. He will be 36 years old this fall.
>
> Emmanuel Steward, Lewis' manager and trainer, was also a very credible witness. He testified that Lewis is reaching the age at which a boxer's skills begin to diminish. Steward testified that Lewis has fought longer and more often than most heavyweight boxers, especially champions, and has suffered even more wear and tear than other boxers his age. He further testified that Lewis needs to fight three or four times a year to maintain his weight and keep his skills sharp. Because of his age and the relatively large number of fights he has fought in his amateur and professional careers, Lewis plans to retire in two years.
>
> I find that Lewis would suffer irreparable harm were he denied the opportunity to regain his championship title. It is undisputed that the heavyweight championship is the most prestigious title in professional boxing. The opportunity to fight for the heavyweight championship, and especially the opportunity to regain the championship, cannot be measured in money. Because of

> his age, Lewis has only a limited time to regain his title and restore his reputation. Rahman, in contrast, is only 28 years old. Even if he chose not to box for 18 months, he would still have several productive years left in his career. Rahman concedes that he has a contractual obligation to fight Lewis in a rematch eventually, although he prefers to fight an interim bout. When asked if he wished to fight Lewis immediately, he said, "I don't have a problem with it."
>
> Shelly Finkel, Mike Tyson's boxing manager, William Kozerski, a promoter who promoted Michael Moorer when he was the heavyweight champion, and Kushner all testified that the exclusive promoter of the heavyweight champion has business opportunities that other promoters do not have. These include being able to negotiate more fight cards with cable television broadcasters, increased visibility and prestige, major advantages in recruiting new fighters and promoting other fighters more successfully.

Lewis, 147 F. Supp. at 232–33.

8. A threshold question is whether the team possesses an exclusive right to the player's services. The terms drafted in the form contracts utilized by the major sports leagues clearly establish a team's exclusive right. The nature of the contract rights and duties may not be so clear in cases involving individual sports participants. *See, e.g., Madison Square Garden Boxing, Inc. v. Shavers*, 434 F. Supp. 449 (S.D.N.Y. 1977) (boxing); *Machen v. Johansson*, 174 F. Supp. 522 (S.D.N.Y. 1959) (boxing).

9. Some courts require proof that defendant is or contemplates performing for an entity in direct economic competition with the plaintiff. The negative injunction, theoretically, enforces a negative covenant, not an affirmative promise. The New England Patriots of the NFL, for example, filed suit to enjoin Chuck Fairbanks, head coach, from making a career change to college coaching. *New England Patriots Football Club, Inc. v. University of Colo.*, 592 F.2d 1196 (1st Cir. 1979). The coach-team contract included a negative covenant prohibiting Fairbanks from participating in "football" matters. A question arose whether the University of Colorado football program was in direct economic competition with the New England Patriots. The competition may exist between teams in a league, teams in different leagues, or teams in different sports. Competition may occur on the ballfield for victories, or in the front office or TV studio for the fan market. Is the question in the *New England* case more appropriately phrased as a contract construction question, seeking the intent of the parties? Is the term "football," as used in the contract, ambiguous?

10. In the event a court awards damages, either in lieu of, or in addition to an injunction, what valuation methods exist to prove the damages with reasonable certainty? *See Eckles v. Sharman*, 548 F.2d 905 (10th Cir. 1977).

11. For every case of "team jumping," there exist at least two potential causes of action. The former team usually files an action against the player for a negative injunction, and a suit against the signing team for tortious interference with a valid

business relationship (covered in Chapter 10). Does adjudication of one cause serve as collateral estoppel barring judicial resolution of the other?

12. For other cases in which the "clean hands" doctrine was used as a defense, see *Houston Oilers, Inc. v. Neely*, 361 F.2d 36 (10th Cir. 1966) (issued injunction, rejecting defense of unclean hands based on club signing college player prior to completion of eligibility in violation of NCAA rules); *New York Football Giants, Inc. v. Los Angeles Chargers Football Club, Inc.*, 291 F.2d 471 (5th Cir. 1961) (denied injunction on basis of defense of unclean hands resulting from club signing college player prior to completion of eligibility in violation of NCAA rules). For an analysis of the "clean hands doctrine" in the context of equitable remedies in sports cases, see Wichmann, *Players, Owners, and Contracts in the NFL: Why the Self-Help Specific Performance Remedy Cannot Escape the Clean Hands Doctrine*, 22 Seattle U. L. Rev. 835 (1999).

13. If a player breaches his or her contract with a U.S. club in order to play for a foreign professional team, the U.S. club can obtain a negative injunction against the player. For example, in *Boston Celtics v. Shaw*, 908 F.2d 1041 (1st Cir. 1990), a U.S. court issued a negative injunction and ordered that Brian Shaw would be held in contempt of court if he failed to honor his Celtics contract by playing for an Italian professional club. *See* Abrams, *Sports Arbitration and Enforcing Promises: Brian Shaw and Labor Arbitration*, 20 Marq. Sports L. Rev. 223 (2009).

14. Player suits against teams or leagues for damages may be preempted by federal law. The United States Supreme Court has held that Section 301 of the Labor Management Relations Act, 29 U.S.C. § 185, preempts state law claims that are substantially dependent upon analysis of a collective bargaining agreement. *Allis-Chalmers Corp. v. Lueck*, 471 U.S. 202, 220 (1985). The Act provides that contract actions between an employer and a labor organization may be brought in federal district court. If the conduct arises out of activities covered in the collective bargaining agreement, the matter is preempted. If the alleged conduct is unlawful or otherwise outside of activities contemplated by the agreement, state law claims are not preempted.

C. Grievance Arbitration

Conflicts regularly arise concerning the rights and duties of players and teams under the terms of collective bargaining agreements, player-team contracts, and league constitutions and other governing documents. In professional sports, most conflicts between players and teams or leagues are resolved by arbitration rather than adjudication. The collective bargaining agreements of all major professional sports leagues contain provisions for arbitration of grievances. Salary arbitration is addressed in Section D, below. Grievance arbitration in the sports industries, like arbitration in non-sports settings, is governed and otherwise established by the terms of contractual agreements, including collective bargaining agreements.

Arbitration in professional sports, arising from the collective bargaining agreements, is considered "labor" arbitration. Arbitration in other contexts is categorized as "commercial arbitration." For example, provisions in league constitutions requiring arbitration for the resolution of disputes between member clubs are classified as "commercial arbitration." Courts readily conclude that the subject matter of a dispute between player and team is within the scope of the arbitration clauses of the collective bargaining agreement and player-team contract. Parties, however, may expressly or impliedly waive the right to arbitration. Strict time limitations appear as a matter of contract in the provisions of the collective bargaining agreements. As the problem below and cases illustrate, the club defendant to a suit by a player-plaintiff usually files a motion to dismiss and/or compel arbitration under the terms of the player contract. The right to rely on the arbitration provision may be waived by the defendant's unreasonable delay in making the motion. *See, e.g., Spain v. Houston Oilers, Inc.*, 593 S.W.2d 746 (Tex. Civ. App. 1979).

Judicial review of a labor arbitration decision is limited in scope, as indicated by the United States Supreme Court opinion in *Garvey*, below. A court may overturn an arbitrator's ruling only when the arbitrator has strayed from application of the agreement and "dispensed his own brand of industrial justice." The scope of judicial review of commercial arbitration decisions is also limited by state and federal arbitration acts.

In disciplinary cases, the arbitrator determines whether "just cause" exists to support the imposition of discipline for a particular offense, and the degree of penalty imposed. "Just cause" is evaluated according to the terms of the applicable agreement, existing rules and regulations, the circumstances attending the particular action under review, and the common law of the workplace. *See* Snow, *Contract Interpretation, in* THE COMMON LAW OF THE WORKPLACE: THE VIEWS OF ARBITRATORS § 2.2 (St. Antoine ed., 2005), *citing United Steelworkers v. Warrior & Gulf Navigation Co.*, 363 U.S. 574 (1960) (arbitrators possess knowledge of the "common law of the shop," in defining broad terms, such as "just cause"). Grievance arbitration concerning the exercise of league commissioner authority in player discipline cases is presented at Chapter 6, *supra.*

Problem

Tyrone Armstead was recently released by the Chicago Bulls of the National Basketball Association. Armstead is a 10-year veteran. He was voted all-NBA forward on six occasions. One major publication selected Armstead as the "dream" power forward in the history of the NBA. The forward has never been injured or otherwise missed practice or a game. He is considered a leader by the other Bulls players, who regularly follow his advice. Armstead started for the Bulls last season. He was seventh in the NBA in scoring and fourth in rebounds. The player believes that he is in as good physical condition for the current season as he has been for any previous season.

Armstead was released pursuant to Article 20(b)(2) of the Uniform Player Contract:

> The club may terminate this contract upon written notice to the Player (but only after complying with the waiver procedure...) if the Player shall at any time: Fail, in the sole opinion of the Club's management, to exhibit sufficient skill or competitive ability to qualify to continue as a member of the Club's team....

Armstead "cleared" waivers with no offers from other clubs in the NBA. He received written notice from the Bulls. All other procedural or technical requirements for termination of the contract under the governing documents of the NBA are satisfied.

Armstead was for two years the NBPA representative from the Bulls. Armstead, a college graduate with a degree in international relations, was instrumental in negotiations between management and labor of the current collective bargaining agreement. Armstead feels that his release was not made on the basis of skill or ability, but as retribution for his union activities. "The Bulls," Armstead said, "also do not want me around their younger players. I will tell them the truth about the flexibility of the salary cap." The Uniform Player Contract contains an arbitration clause, as follows:

> In the event of any dispute arising between the Player and the Club, relating to any matter arising under this contract or concerning the performance or interpretation thereof..., such dispute shall be resolved in accordance with the Grievance and Arbitration Procedure set forth in the Agreement currently in effect between the National Basketball Association and the National Basketball Players Association.

Armstead continues to work out and remains in good shape. But, he has received no phone calls or other contact from NBA teams. NBA scouts consider the lack of interest in Armstead a curiously odd phenomenon. One scout remarked, "There are eight teams in the NBA who need a player like Armstead. They could afford him, too." Armstead received two offers from European teams. The NBPA is amenable to joining Armstead in any action against the NBA, but has made no effort to unilaterally challenge his release.

Armstead is a client of the sports agency that you work for and you have been asked to respond to the following:

1. What arguments can you make that the release of Armstead constitutes a breach of the player-team contract? What counter-arguments do you expect from the Bulls?
2. How can you avoid the arbitration clause of the Uniform Player Contract? What are the arguments, pro and con?

3. In the event the matter is submitted to arbitration, what is the nature and scope of judicial review of an arbitrator's decision?
4. Develop a case based on the Baseball Collusion decision and the provisions of the NBA-NBPA CBA, Note 6 below. What evidence above is useful? What additional evidence is needed?

Major League Baseball Players Ass'n v. Garvey

532 U.S. 504 (2001)

PER CURIAM.

The Court of Appeals for the Ninth Circuit here rejected an arbitrator's findings and then resolved the merits of the parties' dispute instead of remanding the case for further arbitration proceedings....

In the late 1980's, petitioner Major League Baseball Players Association (Association) filed grievances against the Major League Baseball Clubs (Clubs), claiming the Clubs had colluded in the market for free-agent services after the 1985, 1986 and 1987 baseball seasons, in violation of the industry's collective-bargaining agreement.... In a series of decisions, arbitrators found collusion by the Clubs and damage to the players. The Association and Clubs subsequently entered into a Global Settlement Agreement (Agreement), pursuant to which the Clubs established a $280 million fund to be distributed to injured players. The Association also designed a "Framework" to evaluate the individual player's claims, and applying that Framework, recommended distribution plans for claims relating to particular season or seasons.

The Framework provided that players could seek an arbitrator's review of the distribution plan. The arbitrator would determine "only whether the approved Framework and the criteria set forth therein have been properly applied in the proposed Distribution Plan." (*Garvey I*). The Framework set forth factors to be considered in evaluating players' claims, as well as specific requirements for lost contract-extension claims. Such claims were cognizable "'only in those cases where evidence exists that a specific offer of an extension was made by a club prior to collusion only to thereafter be withdrawn when the collusion scheme was initiated.'"

Respondent Steve Garvey, a retired, highly regarded first baseman, submitted a claim for damages of approximately $3 million. He alleged that his contract with the San Diego Padres was not extended to the 1988 and 1989 seasons due to collusion. The Association rejected Garvey's claim in February 1996, because he presented no evidence that the Padres actually offered to extend his contract. Garvey objected, and an arbitration hearing was held.... He presented a June 1996 letter from Ballard Smith, Padres' President and CEO from 1979 to 1987, stating that, before the end of the 1985 season, Smith offered to extend Garvey's contract through the 1989 season, but that the Padres refused to negotiate with Garvey thereafter due to collusion.

The arbitrator denied Garvey's claim, after seeking additional documentation from the parties. In his award, he explained that "'[t]here exists… substantial doubt as to the credibility of the statements in the Smith letter.'"… He noted the "stark contradictions" between the 1996 letter and Smith's testimony in the earlier arbitration proceedings regarding collusion, where Smith… stated that the Padres simply were not interested in extending Garvey's contract. The arbitrator determined that, due to these contradictions, he must reject [Smith's] more recent assertion…, and found that Garvey had not shown a specific offer of extension. He concluded that:

> "'[t]he shadow cast over the credibility of the Smith testimony coupled with the absence of any other corroboration of the claim submitted by Garvey compels a finding that the Padres declined to extend his contract… as a baseball judgment founded upon [Garvey's] age and recent injury history.'"

Garvey moved in Federal District Court to vacate the arbitrator's award, alleging that the arbitrator violated the Framework by denying his claim. The District Court denied the motion. The Court of Appeals for the Ninth Circuit reversed by a divided vote. The court acknowledged that judicial review of the merits of the arbitrator's decision in a labor dispute is extremely limited. But it held that review of the merits of the arbitrator's award was warranted in this case, because the arbitrator "'dispensed his own brand of industrial justice.'" The court recognized that Smith's prior testimony… conflicted with the statements in his 1996 letter. But in the court's view, the arbitrator's refusal to credit Smith's letter was "inexplicable" and "border[ed] on the irrational," because a panel of arbitrators, chaired by the arbitrator involved here, had previously concluded that the owners' prior testimony was false. The court rejected the arbitrator's reliance on the absence of other corroborating evidence, attributing that tact to Smith and Garvey's direct negotiations. The court also found that the record provided "strong support" for the truthfulness of Smith's 1996 letter. The Court of Appeals reversed and remanded with directions to vacate the award.

The District Court then remanded the case to the arbitration panel for further hearings, and Garvey appealed. The Court of Appeals, again by a divided vote, explained that *Garvey I* established that "the conclusion that Smith made Garvey an offer and subsequently withdrew it because of the collusion scheme was the only conclusion that the arbitrator could draw from the record in the proceedings. *(Garvey II)*…. The Court of Appeals reversed the District Court and directed that it remand the case to the arbitration panel with instructions to enter an award for Garvey in the amount he claimed.

The parties do not dispute that this case arises under § 301 of the Labor Management Relations Act…. Although Garvey's specific allegation is that the arbitrator violated the Framework for resolving player's claims for damages, that Framework was designed to facilitate payments to remedy the Clubs' breach of the collective-bargaining agreement. Garvey's right to be made whole is founded on that agreement.

Judicial review of a labor-arbitration decision pursuant to such an agreement is very limited. Courts are not authorized to review the arbitrator's decision on the merits despite allegations that the decision rests on factual errors or misinterprets the parties' agreement. We recently reiterated that if an "'arbitrator is even arguably construing or applying the contract and acting within the scope of his authority,' the fact that 'a court is convinced he committed serious error does not suffice to overturn his decision.'" It is only when an arbitrator strays from interpretation and application of the agreement and effectively "dispense[s] his own brand of industrial justice" that his decision may be unenforceable. When an arbitrator resolves disputes regarding the application of a contract, and no dishonesty is alleged, the arbitrator's "improvident, even silly, factfinding" does not provide a basis for a reviewing court to refuse to enforce the award.

In discussing the courts' limited role in reviewing the merits of arbitration awards, we have stated that "'courts... have no business weighing the merits of the grievance [or] considering whether there is equity in a particular claim.'" When the judiciary does so, "it usurps a function which... is entrusted to the arbitration tribunal." Consistent with this limited role, we said in *Misco* that "[e]ven in the very rare instances when an arbitrator's procedural aberrations rise to the level of affirmative misconduct, as a rule the court must not foreclose further proceedings by settling the merits according to its own judgment.... That step, we explained, "would improperly substitute a judicial determination for the arbitrator's decision that the parties bargained for" in their agreement. Instead, the court should simply vacate the award, thus leaving open the possibility of further proceedings if they are permitted under the terms of the agreement.

To be sure, the Court of Appeals here recited these principles, but its application of them is nothing short of baffling. The substance of the Court's discussion reveals that it overturned the arbitrator's decision because it disagreed with the arbitrator's factual findings.... The Court of Appeals, it appears, would have credited Smith's 1996 letter, and found the arbitrator's refusal to do so at worst "irrational" and at best "bizarre." But even "serious error" on the arbitrator's part does not justify overturning his decision, where as here, he is construing a contract and acting within the scope of his authority.

In *Garvey II*, the court clarified that *Garvey I* both rejected the arbitrator's findings and went further, resolving the merits of the parties' dispute based on the court's assessment of the record before the arbitrator. For that reason, the court found further arbitration proceedings inappropriate. But again, established law ordinarily precludes a court from resolving the merits of the parties' dispute on the basis of its own factual determinations, no matter how erroneous the arbitrator's decision. Even when the arbitrator's award may properly be vacated, the appropriate remedy is to remand the case for further arbitration proceedings.... If a remand is appropriate *even* when the arbitrator's award has been set aside for "procedural aberrations" that constitute "affirmative misconduct," it follows that a remand ordinarily will be appropriate when the arbitrator simply made factual findings that the reviewing court perceives as "irrational." The Court of Appeals usurped the arbitrator's role by resolving the dispute and barring further proceedings, a result at odds with this governing law.

For the foregoing reasons, the Court of Appeals erred in reversing the order of the District Court denying the motion to vacate the arbitrator's award, and it erred further in directing that judgment be entered in Garvey's favor. The judgment of the Court of Appeals is reversed, and the case is remanded for further proceedings consistent with this opinion.

Dryer v. Los Angeles Rams

709 P.2d 826 (Cal. 1985)

KAUS, JUSTICE.

Defendant Los Angeles Rams (Rams) and individual codefendants appeal from an order to the Los Angeles Superior Court denying their petition to compel arbitration....

On April 1, 1980, plaintiff Fred Dryer and the Rams entered into an employment contract—a slightly modified version of the standard NFL player contract drafted pursuant to a collective bargaining agreement between the players' union and the NFL management. Alleging that the Rams removed him from the active roster in violation of his contract, Dryer sued in superior court. The Rams responded with a petition to compel arbitration.

Dryer's contract contains a standard provision calling for binding arbitration under the terms of the applicable collective bargaining agreement in the event a dispute involving interpretation or application of any provision of the contract. Article VII of the applicable collective bargaining agreement sets forth a grievance and arbitration procedure for general contract disputes. Replete with full panoply of due process safeguards—notice, representation, hearing, appeal to outside arbitrators, etc.—this basic arbitration machinery appears to be unobjectionable.

What the trial court did find offensive was a clause in Article VII which provides that matters which are filed as grievances and which involve "the integrity of, or public confidence in, the game of professional football" may be ordered withdrawn from the article VII procedure by the commissioner—after consultation with the player-club relations committee—and processed under article VIII ("Commissioner Discipline"). Once removed from the article VII grievance procedure, such matters are handled exclusively by the NFL commissioner, who hears both the dispute and any appeal arising from his own decision. The NFL commissioner is appointed and paid by the management of the member clubs.

The trial court denied defendants' petition to compel arbitration. Finding that the arbitration clause of the contract... is a contract of adhesion, the court further held that the contract is "unconscionable" in that it fails to meet the "minimum levels of integrity" standard required by *Graham v. Scissor-Tail, Inc.*, 623 P.2d. 165. This holding rests on the court's conclusion that under the collective bargaining agreement "all arbitration decisions can ultimately be vested in the League Commissioner at his discretion."...

Dryer's dispute with the Rams—centering on a provision of the NFL collective bargaining agreement—clearly falls within the ambit of section 301(a) of the Labor Management Relations Act... which pertains to "[s]uits for violation of contracts between an employer and a labor organization representing employees in an industry affecting commerce." This answers the threshold question of what law applies in this case, for it is firmly established that federal substantive law governs the validity and enforcement of contracts under the LMRA....

Our review of federal policy and case law strongly suggests that the principles of *Graham*—applied in the context of a motion to compel arbitration under a provision of a collective bargaining agreement subject to section 301(a)—are incompatible with federal law and national labor policy. To effectuate that policy, federal law appears to limit a court's inquiry to a few basic questions concerning arbitrability of the dispute and defenses, if any, based on allegations of a lack of fair representation. We find no federal precedent for a *Graham*-type inquiry into the fairness of the arbitration machinery itself as part of the court's role in considering a motion to compel arbitration under a bona fide collective bargaining agreement.

National labor policy favors arbitration.... Courts can best serve this policy by giving full effect to the means chosen by the parties for settlement of their differences under a collective bargaining agreement.

The United States Supreme Court has observed that state decisions contrary to this policy of full enforcement could have a "crippling effect" on grievance arbitration. Normally, a claim that the contract grievance procedures are unfair or inadequate cannot be asserted until the aggrieved party has attempted to implement the procedures and found them to be unfair....

The judicial role in considering a motion to compel arbitration is thus quite limited. Indeed, the Ninth Circuit has noted that a district court's function is essentially ended "once it has found the collective bargaining agreement susceptible of an interpretation which would cover the dispute...."

In this case, Dryer's claims all arise from the contract and are thus subject to the contract provision mandating arbitration of "[a]ny dispute between Player and Club involving the interpretation or application of any provision of this contract...."

Beyond the threshold determination of arbitrability of a dispute, a court may—consistent with federal law—consider the resisting party's allegations of breach of the duty of fair representation. Federal courts have held, for example, that an aggrieved employee may circumvent the arbitration procedures created in a collective bargaining agreement if the employee establishes that the union breached its duty of fair representation in processing the grievance. Dryer, however, has not shown a lack of fair representation. Rather, his argument concerns the inherent fairness of the arbitration machinery agreed upon by both union and management.

The limited role of the courts in this area has been underscored repeatedly by decisions to the effect that an order to arbitrate a particular grievance should not be denied unless it may be said with positive assurance that the arbitration clause is not susceptible of an interpretation that covers the asserted dispute and that all doubts are to be resolved in favor of coverage.... Federal case law, however, in no way suggests that a court may deny a motion to compel arbitration on the basis of a *Graham*-type analysis of the arbitration procedure itself. In fact, courts generally order arbitration despite objections concerning the arbitration procedures. For example, it is immaterial to a company's duty to arbitrate that the grievance procedure agreed to in the collective bargaining agreement is employee-oriented. Mere inequality of bargaining power between a union and an employer does not constitute unfairness which will permit either party to avoid a collective bargaining agreement. Also, under federal law, partisan arbitrators are generally permissible.

In short, when deciding whether to compel or deny arbitration, federal courts confine their inquiry to a few threshold issues; they do not consider the substance of the grieving party's claims, nor do they scrutinize the agreed-upon arbitration procedures for general fairness. Thus, although federal law does not expressly preclude the exercise of state powers with regard to arbitration procedures, we believe that to apply the reasoning of *Graham* in this context would frustrate rather than further the goals of national labor policy....

Federal law aside, we independently hold that arbitration should have been ordered in this case. The trial court concluded that the arbitration provisions failed to meet "minimum levels of integrity" required by *Graham* solely because of the remote—indeed, speculative—possibility of commissioner intervention. However, neither the holding nor the reasoning of *Graham* dictates this result....

Under the agreement's normal arbitration procedure—article VII—a grievance goes to the player-club relations committee, which is composed of two representatives from the players' union and two from the management council. If the disputants so desire, they may stipulate to bypass this stage and submit the matter directly to an outside arbitrator. Dryer's case is a contract dispute—not a disciplinary matter—and there is no indication that the intervention provision ever could be or would be invoked.

The trial court also held that the individual defendants are not entitled to the benefit of arbitration because they are not parties to the contract between Dryer and the Rams....

If, as the complaint alleges, the individual defendants, though not signatories, were acting as agents for the Rams, then they are entitled to the benefit of the arbitration provisions. Thus, our conclusion that this entire dispute be referred to arbitration applies to the individual defendants as well as to the Rams.

For the foregoing reasons, the order is reversed. The trial court is directed to grant the petition to compel arbitration with respect to all defendants.

Morris v. New York Football Giants, Inc.

575 N.Y.S.2d 1013 (1991)

CAHN, J.

By separate motions, defendants New York Football Giants, Inc. (N.Y. Giants), New York Jets Football Club, Inc. (N.Y. Jets), and Paul Tagliabue (on behalf of the National Football League (NFL), an unincorporated association) seek for an order, pursuant to CPLR §7503 and/or the Federal Arbitration Act, 9 U.S.C. §1 *et seq.*, staying this action and compelling arbitration of all disputed claims. Plaintiffs Joseph Morris and Michael Shuler cross move for an order, in the event this court submits the dispute to arbitration, appointing a neutral and unbiased arbitrator.

This action arises out of a dispute between two professional football players and their former football clubs over the amount of compensation owed to the players for their services in 1990 prior to the start of the football season (1990 pre-season).

On or about May 30, 1989, Shuler signed a one year standard players contract with the N.Y. Jets pursuant to which he agreed to play for the Jets for the 1990 NFL season. On or about April 30, 1990, Morris executed a one-year standard players contract with the N.Y. Giants wherein he agreed to play for said team for the 1990 season. Paragraph 20 of each of said contracts expressly provided:

> DISPUTES. Any dispute between Player and Club involving the interpretation or application of any provision of the contract will be submitted to final and binding arbitration in accordance with the procedure called for in any collective bargaining agreement in existence at the time the event giving rise to any such dispute occurs. If no collective bargaining agreement is in existence at such time, the dispute will be submitted within a reasonable time to the League Commissioner for final and binding arbitration by him, except as provided otherwise in Paragraph 13 of this contract.

On September 4, 1990, after providing the pre-season services in accordance with their agreements, each of the players was released by their respective team and their contracts terminated. Thereafter, a dispute arose in connection with the amount due for players' compensation for the 1990 pre-season....

Plaintiffs commenced this action alleging that the respective clubs have breached the terms of their individual player contracts with respect to compensation... ; they have also made a derivative claim against Paul Tagliabue and the NFL for tortious interference with their (players) contracts.... Thereafter, defendants brought on the instant motions alleging that the underlying dispute is not one for the courts, but for arbitration.

In support of the motions, defendants allege that the 1982 Collective Bargaining Agreement... contains a broad arbitration clause that embraces the underlying dispute, despite the CBA's formal expiration in August of 1987. Defendants contend that the player representatives, players and clubs, have, to date, continued to utilize grievance and arbitration machinery established by the CBA....

In opposition to defendants' motion, plaintiff relies on, *inter alia, McNeil v. National Football League, et al,...* wherein, the court found that the... CBA expired on August 31, 1987....

Hence, plaintiffs' post-expiration grievances are not subject to arbitration under the 1982 CBA....

However, the plaintiffs' individual contracts expressly provide that "[I]f no collective bargaining agreement is in existence at such time, the dispute will be submitted within a reasonable time to the League Commissioner for final and binding arbitration....

A very serious issue is raised as to who the arbitrator should be. The contracts expressly provide that the disputes be submitted to the Commissioner of the NFL. Plaintiffs allege... that Tagliabue... has an inherent interest in the outcome of the dispute, and is therefore biased and, consequently, should be replaced by a neutral and impartial arbitrator in advance of arbitration proceedings. As shall be discussed below, under both Federal and State law, it is this court's view that a neutral arbitrator should be substituted for the Commissioner in order to insure a fair and impartial hearing.

Regarding the Commissioner of the NFL, the Constitution of the NFL provides,... that the NFL... shall select and employ the Commissioner and shall determine his period of employment and his compensation. Article VIII, Section 8.4(b), provides that the Commissioner is the Chief Executive Officer of the NFL. Article II, Section 2.1, provides that the purposes and objectives for which the NFL is organized are to promote and foster the primary businesses of NFL members.... Moreover, prior to becoming Commissioner, Tagliabue was the chief outside legal counsel for the NFL.... In that capacity, he frequently represented NFL owners in disputes with players.... In addition, the complaint names Tagliabue as a defendant in connection with a claim of tortious interference of contract in issuing an edict "that no members of the NFL may pay their players the contractually provided 10% of the players negotiated salary for pre-season services, but instead must pay the fixed per diem wage."...

In opposition to plaintiffs' cross-motion, defendants allege, inter alia, that the Commissioner would not be arbitrating plaintiffs' suit against the NFL, but only the breach of contract claims alleged against the two teams. As a result, defendants contend, resolution of the underlying claims... would have no direct financial impact on the NFL.

The court finds that Tagliabue's position as Commissioner, together with his past advocacy of a position in opposition to plaintiffs' position herein, deprive him of the necessary neutrality to arbitrate these claims. To find for plaintiffs herein, the Commissioner would have to reverse certain positions he previously strongly advocated, and declare nonbinding or void a certain directive he, through his office, issued to NFL clubs. Further, the determination of plaintiffs' claims may have a major financial impact on various NFL teams.... All of these factors dictate that the Commissioner can not be a neutral arbitrator herein.

Further, this court's authority to select a neutral arbitrator is "inherent when the potential bias of a designated arbitrator would make arbitration proceedings simply a prelude to later judicial proceedings challenging the arbitration award."... Thus, an arbitrator will be appointed by the court....

Accordingly, defendants' motion staying this action and compelling arbitration is granted. Plaintiffs' cross motion for appointment of a neutral and impartial arbitrator is granted.

In re Elmer Nordstrom, Managing Partner, et al., d/b/a Seattle Seahawks and the National Football League Players Association (Sam McCullum)

National Labor Relations Board Division of Judges
Case No. 2-CA-19101, Washington, D.C. (Nov. 23, 1983)

Sam McCullem was a player representative to the NFLPA. McCullem was released by the Seattle Seahawks subsequent to his activities as player rep. The Seahawks argued that McCullum's release was based on several factors: (1) diminished skills; (2) more talented players available; and (3) team need for a more versatile player. McCullum argued that overt actions taken as a player rep were the impetus for his release.

Evidence revealed that the Seahawks replaced McCullum with a wide receiver three days after the release. McCullum was signed by and started for the Minnesota Vikings. McCullum testified that club personnel warned him of the "risk" of his actions as a union representative.

The judge ruled in favor of McCullum, deciding that the Seattle Seahawks violated Sections 8(a)(3) and (1) of the National Labor Relations Act.

In re Major League Players Association and the Twenty-Six Major League Baseball Clubs, Major League Baseball Arbitration Panel, Grievance No. 86–2

(T. Roberts, Chair, Sept. 21, 1987)

The MLBPA filed a grievance on January 31, 1986, asserting that the twenty-six Major League clubs had been acting in concert with respect to players who became free agents after the 1985 season. Paragraph H of Article XVIII of the Basic Agreement provides: "The utilization or non-utilization of rights under this Article... is an individual matter to be determined solely by each Player and each Club for his or its own benefit. Players shall not act in concert with other Players and Clubs shall not act in concert with other Clubs."

The grievance was heard over thirty-two days of presentation, with a total of 5,674 pages of verbatim transcript and 288 exhibits. Evidence revealed that following the 1984 season, sixteen of twenty-six major league clubs signed free agents who had been playing with other clubs. After the 1985 season, however, only Carlton Fisk received a *bona fide* offer from a club other than his former employer, while twenty-eight other free agents received no interest at any price until such time as their former clubs announced no desire to re-sign the players. Kirk Gibson received initial contact from three clubs, but no offers subsequent to an owners' meeting in October, 1985. The MLBPA alleged the owner actions within the free agent market as a "boycott." The clubs answered that the market actions were not a result of agreement between the clubs, but were individual club decisions based on legitimate factors, and were a culmination of a ten-year trend. All club representatives who testified at the hearing denied a common agreement or understanding.

During the off-season, several management meetings were convened, during which the clubs were admonished to exercise self-discipline in making operating decisions, and in resisting temptations to give in to unreasonable demands of experienced marginal players. The clubs were warned that rash moves to add free agents in hopes of a pennant resulted in negative financial results for clubs. The club representatives stated their intent to avoid long-term contracts in response to a poll conducted by the Commissioner. In a subsequent meeting, the Commissioner repeated his concerns regarding the financial commitment made by the clubs under "dumb" long-term contracts.

The arbitration panel found that the "distillation of the message of these meetings resulted in every major league club abstaining from the free agent market during that winter until an available free agent was 'released' by his former club.... The right of the clubs to participate in the free agency provisions of the Basic Agreement no longer remained an individual matter to be determined solely for the benefit of each club." The action constituted a violation of the prohibition of concerted conduct.

Notes and Comments

1. For discussion of grievance arbitration in professional sports, see GREENBERG & GRAY, SPORTS LAW PRACTICE §§1.09, 2.03 (2d ed. 2009); Jan Stiglitz, *Player Discipline in Professional Team Sports, in* 3 LAW OF PROFESSIONAL AND AMATEUR SPORTS §10.0. For descriptions of the grievance arbitration mechanisms utilized in professional sports, see T. Steinberg, *Negotiating National Basketball Association Contracts, in* 2 LAW OF PROFESSIONAL AND AMATEUR SPORTS §§7.36–7.39 (Uberstine ed., 2008); Kirke, *National Hockey League Contract Negotiations, id.* §§9.21–9.25. For an insightful description of baseball grievance arbitration, see MILLER, A WHOLE DIFFERENT BALL GAME: THE SPORT AND BUSINESS OF BASEBALL 131–41 (1991).

2. What are the limits, if any, to the enforcement of the arbitration clause in professional sports player-team contracts? Must antitrust attacks be decided by an arbitrator? *See Mitsubishi Motors Corp. v. Soler Chrysler-Plymouth*, 473 U.S. 614 (1985) (international antitrust claims are arbitrable); *Nghiem v. NEC Electronics*, 25 F.3d 1437 (9th Cir. 1994) (domestic antitrust claims are arbitrable).

3. What evidence supports a claim that a union breached the duty of fair representation in processing a grievance? Plaintiff, James Peterson, sued the NFLPA and two NFLPA attorneys for breach of the duty of fair representation in a grievance against the Tampa Bay Buccaneers. Peterson specifically alleged that the NFLPA and attorneys provided inaccurate advice in his pursuance of the grievance. The trial court granted a judgment notwithstanding the verdict (JNOV) in favor of the NFLPA defendants. The Ninth Circuit affirmed, stating:

> A union breaches its duty of fair representation only when its conduct toward a member of the collective bargaining unit is 'arbitrary, discriminatory, or in bad faith.' ...
>
> We have concluded repeatedly that mere negligent conduct on the part of a union does not constitute a breach of the union's duty of fair representation.
>
> ... [U]nions are not liable for good faith, non-discriminatory errors of judgment made in the processing of grievances.

Peterson v. Kennedy, 771 F.2d 1244 (9th Cir. 1985). Could Peterson have gained *de novo* review of the arbitration decision on the basis of violation of the duty of fair representation? The trial court also ruled that Peterson failed to prove that he would have prevailed on the merits but for the alleged breach of duty. *Id.* at 1252.

4. Can you enumerate or otherwise articulate standards that enable a court to determine whether an arbitrator has dispensed his "own brand of industrial justice"? *See* Byrnes & Prout, Comment, Major League Baseball Players Association v. Garvey: *Revisiting the Standard of Arbitral Review*, 7 HARV. NEGOT. L. REV. 389 (2002) (authors argue that the Court should clarify the principle by renaming it and pro-

viding review to determine whether the contract and governing laws are correctly applied).

The "industrial justice" doctrine was developed in the Steelworkers Trilogy in 1960. *United Steelworkers v. Enterprise Wheel & Car Corp.*, 363 U.S. 593 (1960); *United Steelworkers v. Warrior & Gulf Nav. Co.*, 363 U.S. 574 (1960); *United Steelworkers v. American Mfg. Co.*, 363 U.S. 564 (1960). The parties having agreed to submit all questions of contract interpretation and application to the arbitrator, a reviewing court is confined to ascertaining whether the arbitration award draws its essence from the contract and does not simply reflect an arbitrator's own notions of industrial justice. The United States Supreme Court recognizes two exceptions to the general rule of deference. A court may review the arbitration ruling where there exists fraud and dishonesty, and where the arbitrator's award under a collective bargaining agreement is contrary to public policy. *United Paperworkers Int'l Union v. Misco*, 484 U.S. 29 (1987). A court's refusal to enforce an arbitrator's interpretation of a contract is limited to situations where the contract as interpreted would violate some explicit, well-defined, and dominant public policy that is ascertained by reference to laws and legal precedents and not from general considerations of public interests. *W.R. Grace & Co. v. Rubber Workers*, 461 U.S. 757, 766 (1983). Essentially, parties may not agree to violate public policy as determined by positive law principles. *See Eastern Associated Coal Corp. v. United Mine Workers of Am.*, 531 U.S. 57 (2000) (public policy considerations do not require courts to refuse to enforce an arbitration award ordering employer to reinstate an employee who twice tested positive in drug tests). *See generally* Huitsing, Note, *Retaining Bargained-For Finality and Judicial Review in Labor Arbitration Decisions: Dual Interests Preserved in* Major League Baseball Players Assn. v. Garvey, 2002 J. Disp. Resol. 453 (2002).

5. Given the broad language of *Garvey* in limiting review of the arbitrator's award to the sole question of whether the ruling construed the agreed upon Framework and criteria applied in the proposed Distribution Plan, what arguments can you make on behalf of Steve Garvey?

The Framework required evidence of a "specific offer of an extension" made prior to collusion, only to be thereafter withdrawn when the collusion scheme was initiated. Garvey provided no evidence of the alleged offer in his filing, other than his own declaration. The MLBPA rejected his claim, and the matter proceeded to arbitration. At the hearing, Garvey testified that he received an offer and proffered a 1996 letter written by former Padres President and CEO, Ballard Smith, confirming the alleged 1985 offer, and the fact that the offer was withdrawn as a result of collusion between the clubs. The arbitrator, Thomas T. Roberts, granted a 21-day recess, admonishing each party to produce documentation to aid in ascertaining the facts in question. The MLBPA submitted answers of Garvey and his representatives to 1988 and 1991 questionnaires; a record of Smith's 1986 testimony in which he denied collusion; a letter from Garvey's agent, Jerry Kapstein, stating that (1) Garvey desired to handle extension negotiations with the Padres himself, (2) Smith told Kapstein that he hoped that the negotiations would result in an extension, (3) Garvey asked for Kapstein's help once negotiations stalled, and (4) when Kapstein talked with Smith, Smith reported that the Padres were not interested in talking about an extension, as club policy had changed; notes of MLBPA telephone conversations with Smith, during which Smith admitted to offering Garvey a contract extension in 1985, but withdrew the offer because of collusion.

After examining the evidence, the arbitrator denied Garvey's objection to the Plan of Distribution. The arbitrator, Thomas T. Roberts, rejected the probative value of the Smith letter and statements, doubting the credibility of Smith's assertions as indicated in the Supreme Court's opinion. Arbitrator Roberts had chaired the panel in *Collusion I*, which determined that the owners and representatives, including Ballard Smith, had not been truthful in denying collusion. He concluded that while Garvey and Smith may have discussed the possibility of a contract extension, there was inadequate evidence of a "specific offer" as required by the Framework. *Garvey v. Roberts*, 203 F.3d 580, 586 (9th Cir. 2000). For review of the facts in *Garvey*, see Kaemmerer, Note, *Three Strikes and You're Out: The Supreme Court Reaffirmation of the Scope of Judicial Review of Arbitrators' Decisions*, 67 Mo. L. Rev. 635 (2002). Arbitrator Roberts utilized his experience and observations in *Collusion I*. Can fundamental fairness notions of "neutrality" as explained in *Morris* be undermined by the experiences of a permanent arbitrator?

6. The NBA-NBPA CBA, Art. 14, contains "Anti-collusion" provisions. The party alleging a violation of the provisions bears the burden of proof. Article 14.6 specifies that the failure by a team or teams to make offers or sign a player shall not, by itself or in combination with evidence about playing skills of the player, satisfy the burden of proof. However, such evidence may support a finding of a violation, but only in combination with other evidence that by itself or in combination with other evidence indicates that the challenged conduct is in violation of the provisions.

7. The collective bargaining agreements and uniform contracts of most major professional sports leagues provide economic protections for players suffering injuries in the course of employment. The agreements commonly provide: (1) the injury must be directly related to employment; (2) the club's duty to pay the player's salary continues only so long as the player is injured; (3) the club's duty to pay the player's salary continues only to the end of the contract year in which the player was injured; (4) strict procedural requirements, including duty of the player to report the injury; (5) a significant role of the team physician in deciding whether the professional athlete is physically fit to perform; and (6) a setoff of workers compensation received by the players.

8. Important factual and legal issues in injury grievance cases are identified by Professor Ensor, as follows:

1. The date of the injury, and the status of the player with respect to the club at the time of the injury.
2. How the injury occurred; the activity in which the player was engaged when injured.
3. The effects of the injury; the extent to which the player was disabled or unable to perform at a competitive level.
4. Whether the damage can be traced to a previous injury or a congenital condition.

Ensor, *Comparison of Arbitration Decisions Involving Termination in Major League Baseball, the National Basketball Association, and the National Football League*, 32 St. Louis L.J. 135, 150 (1987).

9. Evidentiary and procedural difficulties inherent in the injury grievance process are evident in *Peterson v. Kennedy*, above at Note 3. Two important fact questions are whether the grievance should be filed pursuant to the non-injury or injury grievance procedures, and whether the grievance was filed within the time limits specified by the collective bargaining agreement. The court questioned the correctness of the arbitrator's decision (Decision of Arbitrator Volz, Nov. 13, 1981, 1249–50) that Peterson's grievance was time-barred. The court recognized that the NFL and NFLPA both regularly fail to follow the strict time limits for handling grievances, and suggested there was no equitable reason to hold Peterson to the time limits.

10. A substantive issue in injury cases is whether the player was terminated for lack of skill or due to the fact that the player was injured. What are the rights and duties of the respective parties? What evidence is relevant to the resolution of the issue?

11. The most reliable injury protection clause is the provision providing that the contract is "guaranteed." The scope of the clause as intended by the parties is sometimes an issue in the dispute between the parties. *See, e.g., In the Matter of Arbitration Between the National Football League Players Association and Dante Pastorini, Jr., and the National Football League Management Council and the Oakland Raiders* (Kagel, Arb., May 30, 1984).

The case of *In re the Arbitration of Thomas and the Los Angeles Raiders and the Los Angeles Rams*, is instructive. Thomas was entitled to "One Year Injury Guarantee" if he was unable to pass the club's physical examination for the year covered by the contract. Thomas passed the Rams' examination, despite the presence of considerable knee problems. He was traded to the Raiders. Thomas failed the Raider's physical examination. The arbitrator held that Thomas should not have passed the Rams' physical examination, based on the medical evidence in the record. The arbitrator ruled that the Rams and Raiders each were liable for one-half of the salary.

12. Sometimes negotiation of a player-team contract results in a provision shielding the team from liability under the injury protection clause due to aggravation of a prior-existing physical injury. A typical clause provides:

> I hereby waive and release the Club, the Club physician, its trainers, and the National Football League from any and all liability and responsibility in the event I become physically unable to perform the services required of me by my NFL Player Contract executed this date because of a deterioration or aggravation of the physical condition(s) set forth in Paragraph 1, above.

But see In the Matter of Arbitration Between National Basketball Association (Cleveland Cavaliers) and National Basketball Players Association (R. Cox) (Sept. 11, 1978) (rider in Cox's contract waiving injury compensation for injuries incurred prior to start of regular season was prohibited under Article 1, Section 3 of the CBA).

13. Recurring issues in injury grievance arbitrations include off-season injuries, injuries sustained during rehabilitation, and alleged failure of professional athletes to disclose injuries. The issues perhaps can be avoided by gaining written permission from the club for any off-season workouts, disclosing all previous injuries, and keeping injury records similar to the records utilized by plaintiffs in tort suits.

14. What remedies are available to a party suing for breach of a contract? Under what circumstances may a party rescind or otherwise gain cancellation of a contract?

In the classic dispute between Jim "Catfish" Hunter and Charles Finley, Hunter utilized a contract provision allowing him to terminate the contract upon Finley's failure to pay required compensation. *In the Matter of the Arbitration Between American and National Leagues of Professional Baseball Clubs (Oakland Athletics) and Major League Players Association (J. A. Hunter)* (Seitz, Arb. Chair., Dec. 13, 1974).

In 2015, the L.A. Kings of the NHL terminated the contract of Mike Richards, alleging a material breach of the Standard NHL Player Contract (SPC). The contract had a remaining five years and compensation of $22 million, a salary cap hit of $2.75 million per season over the five years. The NHL SPC, ¶14, provides that a player contract may be terminated in the event a player shall at any time:

> a. fail, refuse, or neglect to obey the club's rules governing training and conduct of players, if such failure, refusal, or neglect shall constitute a material breach of this SPC;
>
> b. fail, refuse, or neglect to render his services hereunder or in any other manner noticeably breach this SPC;

¶2 of the SPC provides affirmative obligations of the player: report to camp; keep in good physical shape; not play for a team in a competitor league; cooperate with team promotional efforts; and conduct on and off the ice in keeping with the highest moral and ethical standards.

What evidence is needed to show the Kings decision is based on the financial considerations, not Richard's breach of his contractual obligations? *See* Macramalia, *The L.A. Kings & the Difficult Task of Upholding the Termination of Mike Richard's Contract*, FORBES, June 30, 2015.

15. Legal issues may arise with respect to the application of the workers compensation statutes of the various jurisdictions. Michael Haynes and other Chicago Bears players filed workers compensation claims with the California Workers' Compensation Appeals Board (WCAB). The Chicago Bears filed a grievance, arguing that the players should have filed their claims in Illinois. The arbitrator upheld the Bears' grievance. The NFLPA and players filed a motion to vacate the arbitration award, arguing that the arbitration award violated California public policy. The court, reviewing the award *de novo*, ruled in favor of the Chicago Bears, finding that the collective bargaining agreement was not required to conform to California public policy as it was governed by Illinois law. *Chi. Bears Football Club, Inc. v. Haynes*, 816 F. Supp. 2d 534 (N.D. Ill. 2011). The workers compensation claimant must have sufficient contacts with the state in order for the agency to have jurisdiction over the claim. *See Fed. Ins. Co. v. WCAB (Johnson)*, 221 Cal. App. 4th 1116 (2013).

Daniel Campbell injured his knee at the pre-season camp for the New Orleans Saints. He was paid according to his contract, an amount of $525 per week during camp and a greater salary over the course of the regular season, totaling $335,000.00 for the year. He later filed a claim for temporary total disability benefits with the state agency. The Office of Workers Compensation concluded that Campbell was not eligible for disability payments as he was able to earn wages equal to his $525 pear week pre-injury wages. Campbell appealed, arguing that his regular season pay totaling $335,000 should be the basis for calculating his pre-injury pay. The Louisiana Appellate Court affirmed the agency calculation, holding that the only significant figure utilized to determine eligibility is the amount claimant was earning at the time of injury. *Campbell v. New Orleans Saints*, 12–886 (La. App. 5 Cir. 05/16/13), 113 So. 3d 1215.

16. Drug testing exists today as one of the most important issues confronting parties to collective bargaining agreements. In *Williams v. National Football League*, 582 F.3d 863 (8th Cir. 2009), players suspended after testing positive for a banned substance and the NFLPA sought to overturn an arbitrator's ruling upholding the suspensions. The court held that the players' common-law claims were preempted by § 301 of the Labor Management Relations Act, but that statutory claims under the Minnesota Drug & Alcohol Testing in the Workplace Act (DATMA) and Minnesota Consumable Products Act (CPA) did not require interpretation of the CBA/ Policy and thus were not preempted.

The NFLPA, in *Williams*, argued that the arbitrator's ruling was contrary to the essence of the CBA/Policy as a (1) violation of the public policy, and (2) rendered by a biased arbitrator. The NFL "Policy on Anabolic Steroids and Related Substances," incorporated into the CBA provides that "the Commissioner or his designee will preside as Hearing Officer." Commissioner Goodell designated Jeffery Pash, Vice-President and General Counsel of the NFL, who provided advice to the Minnesota Vikings and the NFL in the matter, as arbitrator. Are the court decisions in the *Williams* case consistent with the opinions in *Garvey* and *Morris*?

17. The consequence of a finding of preemption of common law claims by § 301 of the LMRA dictates that players' claims would be filed according to the arbitration provisions of the CBA. The NFL Standard Form Contract, Article 20, provides as follows:

> Any dispute between Player and Club involving the interpretation or application of any provision of this contract will be submitted to final and binding arbitration in accordance with the procedure called for in any collective bargaining agreement....

In 2011, former NFL players filed suits against the NFL and Riddell (helmet manufacturer) in various jurisdictions, alleging common law claims and seeking injunctive relief regarding concussions and resultant damages. The actions were consolidated in *In re National Football Players' Concussion Injury Litigation,* U S. Dist. Ct. for the E.D. Pa, No. 2:12-md-02323-AB, MDL No. 2323, June 7, 2012. The NFL made a Motion to Dismiss, based on § 301 of the LMRA. While the motion was pending, parties reached settlement. *In re National Football Players' Concussion* Litigation, 307 F.R.D. 351 (E.D. Pa. 2015).

Former NHL players, in November 2013, filed actions against the NHL regarding concussions and resultant damages. *In re Nat'l Hockey League Players' Concussion Injury Litigation,* Complaint, E.D. Minn., Nov. 2013. The court denied the NHL Motion to Dismiss on the basis of § 301 of the LMRA. *In re Nat'l Hockey League Players' Concussion Litigation,* 189 F. Supp. 3d 856 (D. Minn. 2016). The parties reached settlement in 2018.

Former NFL player Richard Dent and nine other retired NFL players brought a class action against the NFL, alleging negligence *per se*, negligent hiring and retention, negligent misrepresentation, fraudulent concealment, and fraud in the distribution of opioids, anti-inflammatory medications, and local anesthetics that resulted in chronic medical conditions. The United States Court of Appeals for the Ninth Circuit held that the plaintiff's claims are not preempted under § 301 of the LMRA. *Dent v. National Football League,* 902 F.3d 1109 (9th Cir. 2018).

D. Baseball Salary Arbitration

On February 25, 1973, the MLBPA and MLB (Player Relations Committee) negotiated a collective bargaining agreement that contained a salary arbitration provision. The mechanism included a single arbitrator who, after hearing, selected either the offer of the club or player ("final offer process"), considering relevant evidence as specified in the collective bargaining agreement. The owners negotiated for and gained a "three-member panel" for salary arbitration in the 1997 Basic Agreement (CBA), rejecting the traditional "one-member" model. The "three-member panel" approach was retained in the 2017–2021 Agreement. The MLBPA and the Baseball Labor Relations Department select arbitrators on an annual basis. In the event the players' association and ownership group are unable to agree by January 1 of any year, the arbitrators are selected from a list provided by the American Arbitration Association (AAA) by the parties alternatively striking names from the list.

The baseball salary arbitration process is distinguished from other forms of arbitration. The "final offer" format of baseball salary arbitration is explained in terms of traditional negotiation theory. The baseball salary arbitration process is compared to the salary arbitration model utilized by the National Hockey League. The National Hockey League has utilized salary arbitration for a longer period of time than Major League Baseball but uses the traditional arbitration model enabling the arbitrator to formulate an independent value determination, and issue an opinion explaining the choice. In the "final offer" format, each side, the player and club, submits to the arbitration panel its offer or demand in the form of a one-year nonguaranteed salary figure. The panel must choose one or the other of the two figures submitted. No compromise or other modification of the submitted figures are allowed. The panel inserts the chosen figure in duplicate Uniform Player Contracts and forwards them appropriately. The hearings are conducted on a private and confidential basis, thus there is no opinion and no release of the arbitration award by the chair.

The vast majority of baseball salary arbitration cases are settled before hearing, usually in the week prior to the exchange of arbitration figures. The analytics are available for each party to project the value assigned to the player by the other. Settlement can result in the parties agreeing to either a one- or multi-year contract. A multi-year contract serves as a means to avoid arbitration for each season that is covered under the new contract. For a discussion of the history of MLB's salary arbitration process, see Edmonds, *A Most Interesting Part of Baseball's Monetary Structure: Salary Arbitration in Its Thirty-Fifth Year*, 20 Marq. Sports L. Rev. 1 (2009).

The procedures for salary arbitration, established according to the terms of the collective bargaining agreement, are as follows:

1. Eligibility

Any player with three or more years of Major League service, but less than six years (if he does not already have a contract for the next season).

"Super Two" players with two but less than three years of Major League service if (a) he has accumulated at least 86 days of service during the immediately preceding season, and (b) he ranks in the top 22% in total service in the class of players who have at least two but less than three years of Major League service with at least 86 days of service during the immediately preceding season.

Any player with consent of club.

2. Conduct of Hearings

Order of Presentation:

Player's initial presentation

Club's initial presentation

Player's rebuttal and summation

Club's rebuttal and summation

Player's surrebuttal (very brief to respond to new issues)

Club's surrebuttal (Panel may allow at its discretion to respond to new issues)

Neither party shall carry the burden of proof

Presentations = one hour

Rebuttals = 30 minutes

Cross-examination shall not count against time limitations

Panel may extend time for good cause

3. Criteria/Evidentiary Constraints

The relevant criteria upon which the arbitrator bases the decision **shall be admissible** as follows:

1. Quality of the Player's contribution to his Club *during the past season*, including but not limited to:
   a. overall performance;
   b. special qualities of leadership;
   c. special qualities of public appeal;
2. Length and consistency of his career contribution;
3. Record of Player's past compensation;
4. Comparative baseball salaries;
5. Existence of physical or mental defects on the part of the player; and
6. Recent performance record of the Club, including but not limited to:
   a. league standing;
   b. attendance.

Any evidence may be submitted that is relevant to the stated criteria, except as set forth below, and the arbitration panel shall assign such weight as shall appear appropriate.

Evidence of the following **shall not be admissible**:

1. The financial position of the Player and the Club;
2. Press comments, testimonials, or similar material bearing on the performance of either the Player or Club, except that recognized annual player awards for playing excellence shall not be excluded;
3. Offers made by either Player or Club;
4. The cost to the parties of their representatives, attorneys, etc.; and
5. Salaries in other sports or occupations.

No party shall refer to "Competitive Balance Tax"

4. Focus of Salary Arbitration

Generally, the focus of salary arbitration is upon the value of the player's performance at the present time based primarily on the immediately past season and reflected by career records and the salaries of comparable players. Parties in contract negotiations use statistical devices, including analytics, to provide projections of future performance relevant to the proposed contract period. According to the criteria presented above, the player's performance during the immediately previous season, the platform season, is the starting point. Data regarding length and consistency of career contributions may complement the past season figures (or detract). One commentator suggests, "When a player is arbitration eligible for the first time, the length and consistency of his career contribution matters a whole lot. It's the first opportunity for the player to reap the benefits of his first few major league seasons, so his entire career matters, not just the platform year.... Players' career numbers do matter when they go to arbitration for the second, third and, potentially fourth time, but not to the same extent." Nicholson-Smith, *What Matters in Arbitration*, www.mlbtraderumors.com/2011/02/what-matters-in-arbitration.html.

Special qualities of leadership and public appeal also may complement the past season statistical focus. For example, evidence of increased attendance based on the player's pitching starts and/or performance, if positive correlation can be shown, may be added (perhaps negative correlation from the club side).

5. Player Comparisons

Comparison is made to the salaries of similarly situated players. Both club and player will arguably identify a pool of similarly situated players, generally based on service time and production. The arbitration panel shall, except for a Player with five or more years of Major League Service, give particular attention to contracts of players with Major League Service not exceeding one annual service group above the Player's annual service group. Nothing limits the ability of a Player, because of special accomplishment, to argue the equal relevance of salaries of Players without regard to service, and the arbitrator shall give whatever weight to such argument as he (she) deems appropriate. Thus, the previous season's pool of similarly situated players becomes the primary comparison group with the attendant salaries—but based on the performance stats of the season before the arbitration hearings for the comparison group.

Given that the arbitration panel directive allows consideration of players without regard to service, due to special accomplishment, and any relevant data generally, the parties may use data respecting a player with more service time by "looking back" to the season that is comparable to the player before the arbitration panel.

6. Statistics and Analytics

Only publicly available statistics shall be admissible, including data available through subscription-only websites (e.g., Baseball Prospectus). Statistics and data generated through the use of performance technology, wearable technology, or "STATCAST," whether publicly available or not, shall not be admissible. There are two categories of recognized baseball performance statistics, although in time there may be a blurring of the lines (perhaps there will develop a third category).

Traditional stats include the pitcher wins, losses, saves, and earned run average (ERA) and others. The numbers also focus on hitters' stats of batting average, home runs, and runs batted-in (RBI).

Advanced analytics present what are touted as leading to a more accurate measuring of the player's contribution to the team's wins and thus the player's true value. There is no universal method for calculating some sabermetrics, as different publications utilize different formulas, which may generate inconsistent numbers. The modern advanced metrics approach considers the now mainstream on-base percentage and OPS (on-base percentage + slugging percentage)—greater correlation with runs produced than BA. BABIP, for example, measures a player's batting average exclusively on balls hit into the field of play, removing outcomes not affected by the opposing defense (home runs and strikeouts). For the pitcher, the Fielding Independent Pitching (FIP) stat measures what a pitcher's ERA would be over a given period if the pitcher were to have experienced league average results on balls in play. FIP is limited to the events a pitcher has control over: strikeouts, unintentional walks, hit-by-pitches, and home runs—removes results of balls hit into field of play—arguably a better indicator of pitching effectiveness than ERA, which depends on defensive play.

WAR (Wins Above Replacement) is not a stat but a mixture of stats to produce a construct. Different publications utilized unique WAR formulas, *e.g.*, Baseball Reference and Fangraphs display slightly different WAR totals for players that are designed to measure a player's performance over a baseline player—performance over replacement player in a team's system— which can be a good measure of a player's value to the team. For an analysis of the impact of utilizing the WAR metric in arbitration and free agency cases, *see* Studnitzer (Ball, Advisor), *Simplicity Versus WAR: Examining Salary Determinations in Major League Baseball's Arbitration & Free Agent Markets,* Senior Thesis in Economics, Haverford College (2014).

Both player (players association) and club (MLB) have extensive databases comprised of advanced analytics (each advanced stat has variations based on different factors included in calculations). Remember: only publicly available (including subscriptions) statistics are available for use in salary arbitration. Many commentators state that arbitration panels pay primary attention to traditional stats, and that both player representatives and clubs focus on traditional stats due to the fact that arbitrators are not steeped in advanced baseball analytics. *See* Ring, *Let's Fix MLB's Salary Arbitration System: Introduction,* https://blogs. Fangraphs.com/lets-fix-mlbs-salary-arbitration-system-introduction.

Case Study: Dellin Betances

In 2016, Dellin Betances was the setup pitcher in the Yankees' bullpen for the closer, pitching in the eighth inning, for example, not the ninth. He entered baseball salary arbitration for the 2017 season. He asked for \$5 million, Yankees offered \$3 million. His platform season stats revealed: 2.9 WAR = \$7.8 million (Fangraphs); strikeouts per nine innings = 15.5 (led all relievers); FIP = 1.25; career WAR = 8.5 (higher than any reliever, including Yankee closer Aroldis Chapman).

Yankees proffered stats—yielded 21 steals in 21 attempts (although only eight scored); 6.43 ERA with runners in scoring position (cf., FIP=1.25); \$3 million offer = highest ever award for first-year-arbitration-eligible setup pitcher—Yankees Win! Randhawam, *How Stats Can Change Arbitration Cases,* www.sportsonearth.com/article/216466142/advanced-metrics-in-arbitration-cases.

Keith Law points out that Betances, in 2015, was the most valuable relief pitcher in baseball, just not a closer. He pitched 84 more innings than any pitcher not a starter; had the fourth highest strikeout rate in baseball; posted a traditional 1.50 ERA, second lowest among relievers; had more positive impact on his team's win total than all but three relief pitchers and three starters. WIN Probability Added—measures impact a player had on chances of winning each game in which he appeared; but he wasn't a closer, although he pitched in key situations. A closer entering salary arbitration with 20 saves in his platform season earns approximately \$1.8 million extra, *citing* Swartz, *MLBTradeRumors.com Arbitration Projection Model.* Law posits, "The stat [save] in an unholy mess of arbitrary conditions, and doesn't actually measure anything..." LAW, SMART BASEBALL: THE STORY BEHIND OLD STATS THAT ARE RUINING THE GAME, THE NEW ONES THAT ARE RUNNING IT, AND THE RIGHT WAY TO THINK ABOUT BASEBALL (2017).

Problem: Baseball Salary Arbitration Exercise

Assume that negotiations regarding salary have failed and the player and team desire to proceed to salary arbitration. Utilizing the "final offer" process, including the criteria and evidentiary constraints, construct and deliver arguments on behalf of James Boyd and the Chicago White Sox before a mock salary arbitration panel. James Boyd's stats are presented below. Comparative statistical data may be accessed on various digital sites. For purposes of the exercise, utilize: Baseball-Reference.com, and MLB.com.

James Boyd Bio:

James Boyd has completed three seasons with the Chicago White Sox and is first-time eligible for salary arbitration (not Super Two eligible). He is a local kid, having played Chicago high school baseball and college ball at Northwestern University. He lived in the Chicago Cubs part of town, but has a following and is a local favorite.

Boyd is married to the daughter of the owner of a major engineering firm and is employed there during the offseason. After his playing career, he expects to equal or better his baseball salary working for the family business. He graduated from Northwestern with honors.

Boyd will be 29 years old at the start of next season; he is a left-handed pitcher who has both started and relieved; he has received no awards or All-Star Game appearances. The drop-off in games pitched in Season 3 is attributable to an ankle injury suffered in a home plate collision while a base runner during an interleague game in Cincinnati. He is fully recovered from the injury and has no concerning injury history. Boyd is athletic and gives maximum effort—there is some concern that wear and tear may shorten his career, but no concerns for the immediate future.

Boyd's Career Stats—3 Years (Major Leagues)

W	L	ERA	G	GS	CG	SHO	HLD	SV/O	GF	IP	H	R	ER	HR	HB	BB	IBB	SO	WHIP	FIP	WAR
8	3	2.93	69	0	0	0	23	3/6	6	95.1	67	38	31	5	2	40	7	98	1.12	2.71	1.4
12	9	2.74	56	16	1	1	14	2/3	4	154.1	131	53	47	10	4	70	4	117	1.30	3.57	2.4
3	5	2.91	39	11	0	0	8	1/4	5	108.1	92	37	35	6	6	34	4	77	1.16	3.26	1.9

Notes and Comments

1. Given the uncertainty of the arbitrator's decision-making process, as expressed above, how should a party prepare for the arbitration hearing? The use of final offer arbitration, theoretically, motivates the parties to submit reasonable positions, rather than less than reasonable offers designed to compel the arbitrator to choose a position between the two. The motivating factor is the "fear" that the opposing party will be viewed by the arbitrator as being "more reasonable," and thus prevailing.

Does final offer arbitration enhance negotiation between the parties, or does it have a chilling effect on negotiation?

2. Empirical examinations of the results of baseball's salary arbitration mechanism offer interesting insights into the process, including the strategies of bargainers and arbitrators. One study supports Professor Raiffa's projection that "[f]inal offer arbitration should have great appeal for the daring (the risk seekers) who play against the timid (the risk averse)." Using data from a sample of players eligible for arbitration in 1990–93, the authors find that more aggressive offers made by players are the primary determinant of which player/club pairs proceed to arbitration. But, the analysis indicates that the players fare worse when their aggression leads them to arbitration. On average, a player offer that is 10% higher than predicted results in a salary in excess of 9% below what would be predicted. The failure of the parties to achieve settlement through bargaining prior to arbitration is consistent with an "optimism" or "risk loving" model, where one or both parties exhibit excessive optimism about winning the case. Farmer, Pecorino & Stango, *The Causes of Bargaining Failure: Evidence from Major League Baseball*, 47 J.L. & ECON. 543 (2004).

Another study notes that final offer arbitration is designed to motivate bargainers to submit reasonable offers, as the arbitration panel cannot split the offers by selecting a compromise position, as is common in conventional arbitration. But, analysis of the data reveals that arbitrators in baseball's system may formulate preferred awards that compromise between bargainers' perspectives. Examination of the winning and losing offers implies that the arbitrators' preferred awards represent a weighted average of the player's salary in the previous season and the average free agent salary, a compromise between perspectives taken by the players and management. Marburger, *Arbitrator Compromise in Final Offer Arbitration: Evidence from Major League Baseball*, 42 ECON. INQUIRY 60 (2004).

3. Notice the evidentiary constraints of the baseball arbitration process. What evidence is available for negotiation, but not proper for arbitration? Remember that the arbitrator does not issue an opinion or otherwise justify the decision. Can you explain the decision? Can you learn from the process? For analysis of the factors deemed to significantly influence the arbitrator's decision, see ABRAMS, THE MONEY PITCH: BASEBALL FREE AGENCY AND SALARY ARBITRATION (2000). *See also* Fizel, Krautmann & Hadley, *Equity and Arbitration in Major League Baseball*, 23 MANAGERIAL & DECISION ECONOMICS 427 (Oct.–Nov. 2002) (study indicates equity is a significant predictor of player's unilateral decision to file for arbitration, but an insignificant determinant of proceeding to hearing of offsetting responses by player and owner); Pikul & Mayo, *Performance and Eligibility for Arbitration or Free Agency and Salaries of Professional Major League Baseball Players, the 1994–1995 Experience*, 23 J. SPORT & SOCIAL ISSUES 353 (Aug. 1999) (study uses multiple regression to confirm that eligibility for arbitration or free agency and performance are positive predictors of players' salaries, a result consistent with theories of worker motivation).

4. Private parties formulate arbitration systems, as dispute resolution mechanisms, to gain various advantages that are not provided in judicial processes. Sports leagues and player associations traditionally seek the following values in design of arbitration methods:

1. Expeditious process;
2. Fair and equitable determination;
3. Low cost burdens; and
4. Preservation of league and association integrity.

Does the "single offer" format accomplish the above objectives? Should the process include a single arbitrator, or a board of three or more members? Should the decision maker(s) possess authority to "split the baby," as opposed to selecting one of the two offers? Should the arbitrator be "permanent" or "specially appointed"? What are the benefits of each alternative arbitration mechanism?

Nine

Representation of Professional Athletes and Agent Regulation

Learning Outcomes

- Learn the role of the player agent and the issues surrounding the legal capacity of a player agent to contract with a professional athlete for representation.
- Learn about the key provisions in representation agreements.
- Learn the duties of sports agents under agency law.
- Understand the framework of agent regulation by state law, federal law, the players associations, and the rules of professional conduct governing lawyers.
- Learn why the players associations adopted agent regulations including certification requirements and why they have the legal authority to do it.

Key Terms

- Fiduciary relationship
- Principal-agent
- Duty of loyalty
- Duty of care
- Conflict of interest
- Standard representation agreement
- Uniform Athlete Agents Act (UAAA)
- Sports Agent Responsibility Trust Act (SPARTA)

A. Introduction

In the formative years of professional sports, most professional athletes negotiated their own contracts. Today, professional sports have evolved into a multi-billion dollar industry, and athletes realize the need to hire professional sports agents to aid them in reaping the benefits of this increased wealth. Consider, for example, what a star amateur player will need in terms of representation and advice as he or she embarks on what is expected to be a lucrative career. This chapter focuses on the role of the player agent, first examining issues surrounding the legal capacity of a player agent to contract with a professional athlete for representation under existing state, player union, and other regulations. It next considers the questions confronting the player agent in the structuring of the sports agent practice, including the requisite player agent contracts. Finally, the chapter addresses common law and other duties imposed upon the player agent representing the professional athlete.

1. Player Agent Functions

The player agent performs myriad functions in representing the professional athlete. A single representative rarely performs all tasks. Some firms, through teamwork, provide a full-service package, but others concentrate on only singular acts, such as contract negotiation. Services provided by the agent may include the following:

1. Employment contract negotiation;
2. Legal counseling;
3. Obtaining and negotiation of endorsement contracts and other income opportunities;
4. Financial management and planning advice;
5. Career planning counseling;
6. Marketing of the athlete through public relations and other means; and
7. Resolution of disputes arising under an employment contract.

During the past 30 years, the revenue-producing opportunities for the star professional player have expanded greatly. As mentioned below, the evolution of the media industry, including digital platforms, has generated significant demands for non-game sports content. In addition to the traditional player-agent-team contract negotiation, tax and estate planning services, and the negotiation of the product endorsement and local appearance contracts, the agent may be required to market the player across multiple media venues. The need for expertise in the myriad areas has resulted in the creation of the "mega firm." Of course, the utilization of any licensing or other opportunities must comply with the intellectual property laws.

The globalization of sport has also affected the functioning of the player agent. Some players, especially the international sports stars, may have marketing opportunities in foreign jurisdictions. Thus, the agent must have knowledge of or access to professionals with an understanding of the licensing and regulatory practices in those jurisdictions.

2. Historical Overview

Athletes have received pay for play in the United States since the Civil War, but rarely utilized agent or other professional services until the mid-1960s. The player agent profession has grown tremendously from the 1970s until the present. Several reasons are cited for the evolution of the player agent relationship. First, players in most professional sports leagues possessed little bargaining power until the 1970s. Players successfully challenged the reserve clauses of the traditional player contracts that bound the player to a team for life. Viable competing leagues formed during this period, resulting in increased leverage for the athlete. Player associations, struggling to become full-fledged unions, emerged from the 1960s with the power to bargain collectively and strike in support of salary and other demands. As player salaries and other benefits increased, the need for professional services, including tax advice and financial planning, rose accordingly.

3. Professional Sports Today

The professional sports industry blossomed after World War II. Television and radio broadcasting served to expand the audience from the traditional ballpark, stadium, or arena attendance to a national one. Increased gate and other receipts coupled with broadcast revenue enlarged the financial pie for distribution among the constituents of the professional sports environment. Satellite and cable transmission joins with digital platforms to further enhance league revenues. Merchandising sales increased dramatically, as well. National recognition of professional athletes joins media advertising patterns to generate off-the-field revenue opportunities for the players. The player agent functions in this context similarly to the traditional entertainment agent.

4. Need for Regulation

There is no doubt that development of the player agent profession has resulted in benefits for the players. However, severe criticism has focused upon some player agent practices and the unfortunate performances that have squandered athletes' lifetime earnings. The typical problem areas of agent practice include questions regarding:

1. unethical solicitation
2. charging of excessive fees
3. conflicts of interest
4. general incompetence
5. income mismanagement
6. fraud
7. unauthorized practice of law

A player agent is subject to laws of general applicability, such as contract, tort, agency, fraud, and criminal laws. In addition, player agents may be subject to state and federal regulation. Several states have statutes regulating persons who are in the business of procuring employment or engagement for entertainers. Attorneys, of course, are subject to the ethical rules of professional conduct governing lawyers.

Whether an agent's business advice falls within the reach of the Federal Investment Advisers Act is questionable. *See Zinn v. Parrish*, 644 F.2d 360 (7th Cir. 1981) (ruling that player agent who transmitted stock investment recommendations of others, provided advice on business investments, and invested funds on behalf of client was not an "investment adviser" under the Act; isolated transactions were incident to the main purpose of the negotiating football contracts and did not constitute engaging in the business of advising others on investment securities so as to require registration under the Act). The talent and employment statutes contain exemptions that arguably insulate player agents from these statutes.

B. Players Association and Governmental Regulation: Authority and Registration Requirements

Most states and the respective NFL, NBA, NHL, and MLB player associations responded to the criticisms of the practices of player agents by enacting or otherwise promulgating regulations focusing directly upon player agents and agent practices. In 2004, Congress enacted the first federal statute directly regulating agent conduct, the Sports Agent Responsibility and Trust Act (SPARTA), 15 U.S.C. § 7801 *et seq.*, which addresses agent practices in recruiting student-athletes and is modeled after the Uniform Athlete Agents Act (2000) (UAAA). The UAAA, which was revised in 2015, has been adopted by more than 40 states. Many regulations require registration or certification upon satisfactory review of qualifications and background. Importantly, the agent must comply with certification requirements of all mandatory regulations in order to possess the capacity to form a lawful contract with the player.

Regulatory schemes follow two distinct formats. The players associations regulate all player agents' conduct associated with the negotiation of player-team contracts. Their regulatory design attempts to protect rookie and veteran players from unscrupulous and incompetent player agent practice. State statutes that have adopted the UAAA (or the revised act) only govern agent contact with student-athletes. Thus, these statutes are intended to protect the eligibility of student-athletes and, thereby, protect the educational institutions and fans. One exception is California's statute, the Miller-Ayala Athlete Agents Act, which regulates player agents' relationship with professional athletes as well. These state statutes generally require certification prior to agent conduct to induce player-agent contracts, specify terms that must be included in player-agent contracts, and contain enforcement provisions, including criminal and civil remedies.

The National Football League Players Association (NFLPA), in 2002, promulgated regulations governing player financial advisors. The voluntary program, the first of its kind in professional sports, attempts to pre-select and qualify financial advisors for service to NFL players. The voluntary program was initiated as part of the collective bargaining agreement with the NFL that called for joint efforts to provide career services training for NFL players. On January 25, 2003, the U.S. Securities and Exchange Commission (SEC) issued a "No-Action Letter," at the request of the NFLPA, advising that the SEC would not recommend enforcement action for application of the Investment Advisors Act of 1940 to the NFLPA and investment advisors participating in the program. See description of program at *Atwater v. NFLPA*, 626 F.3d 1170 (11th Cir. 2010).

All applicants for the voluntary program must hold a bachelor's degree from an accredited college or university and have a minimum of eight years of relevant work experience. Each applicant must be a Certified Financial Planner™ (CFP®) and/or a Chartered Financial Analyst® (CFA). Any applicants who are certified public accountants (CPAs), enrolled agents, and attorneys-at-law who are duly licensed and in good standing with the appropriate jurisdictions may be Registered Player Financial Advisors for the sole purpose of providing tax advice and/or estate planning and related counseling, as appropriate. Specific provisions regard "Brokers and/or Dealers," Investment Advisors, Financial Planners and All Other Financial Advisors, and Insurance Brokers and/or Insurance Agents. *See* NFLPA Regulations and Code of Conduct Governing Registered Player Financial Advisors (as amended in March 2017 and edited in October 2017), https:www.nflpa.com/financial-advisors/regulations.

The *Collins* case addresses two important questions: Why the players associations adopted agent regulations including certification requirements and why they have the legal authority to do it.

Collins v. National Basketball Players Association

976 F.2d 740 (10th Cir. 1992) (unpublished), *affirming*,
850 F. Supp. 1468 (D. Colo. 1991)

Tacha, Circuit Judge.

In summary, the NBPA is a labor union that the National Basketball Association (NBA) has recognized for over thirty years as the exclusive bargaining representative for all NBA players, pursuant to section nine of the National Labor Relations Act, 29 U.S.C. § 159. For over twenty years, the NBPA and the NBA have entered into collective bargaining agreements establishing the minimum salary an individual player must be paid, the maximum aggregate salary a team may pay all of its players, and other issues unique to professional sports. The NBPA, however, has always authorized the players or their individually selected agents to negotiate their individual compensation packages within the framework established by the collective bargaining agreements.

Player agents were unregulated before 1986. But in that year, in response to a growing number of player complaints about agent abuses—including violations of various fiduciary duties—the NBPA established the Regulations, a comprehensive system of agent certification. The Regulations permit only certified agents to represent NBPA members. The Regulations also establish the Committee, which is authorized to issue or deny certification of prospective player agents. The Committee may deny certification if it determines that the prospective agent has made a false statement of material fact in his application or that he has engaged in any conduct that significantly impacts on his credibility, integrity, or competence to serve in a fiduciary capacity. Any prospective agent whose application for certification is denied may appeal by filing a timely demand for final and binding arbitration.

Collins had been a player agent representing NBPA members since 1974. The Committee certified Collins as a player agent in 1986, the year the Regulations first took effect. However, Collins voluntarily suspended his activities as an agent during the pendency of a lawsuit filed by one of his clients, Kareem Abdul-Jabbar, and a corporation Abdul-Jabbar had established, Ain Jeem, Inc. Abdul-Jabbar alleged that Collins had breached a number of fiduciary duties when Collins mishandled Abdul-Jabbar's income tax returns, improvidently invested his money, mishandled his assets, and transferred funds from his accounts to the accounts of other players represented by Collins. The Ain Jeem lawsuit was settled in 1989, but in the interim the Committee had decertified Collins for violations of other regulations.

Collins reapplied for certification in 1990, and the Committee commenced an informal investigation into Collins' application. The Committee took testimony from both Collins and Abdul-Jabbar, and was provided with nonconfidential discovery material from the Ain Jeem suit. The Committee denied Collins' application because it found that Collins was unfit to serve in a fiduciary capacity on behalf of NBA players and that he had made false or misleading statements to the Committee during the investigation. It reached this conclusion after it found substantially all of Abdul-Jabbar's allegations to be true. The Committee informed Collins of his right to final and binding arbitration, but Collins did not demand arbitration and instead filed this lawsuit.

Before the district court, Collins claimed that the NBPA certification process violates the antitrust laws because it amounts to a group boycott. We agree with the district court's analysis of the labor and antitrust statutes and its conclusion that the statutory labor exemption from the Sherman Act permits the NBPA to establish a certification procedure for player agents. Specifically, we hold that the Regulations meet both prongs of the test established in *United States v. Hutcheson*, 312 U.S. 219 (1941), in which the Supreme Court held that labor unions acting in their self-interest and not in combination with nonlabor groups are statutorily exempt from Sherman Act liability. *Id.* at 232.

On appeal, Collins now acknowledges that the NBPA has the statutory authority to establish player agent regulations. But he maintains his attack on the Committee's decision to deny his certification because it was based in part on its finding that he had breached his fiduciary duty as an investment agent and money manager. He argues that his conduct outside of negotiations between players and their teams is not a legitimate interest of the union because it has no bearing on the union's interest in the wage scale and working conditions of its members.

The district court properly rejected this argument. The NBPA established the Regulations to deal with agent abuses, including agents' violations of their fiduciary duties as labor negotiators. It was entirely fair for the Committee to conclude that a man who had neglected his fiduciary duties as an investment agent and money manager could not be trusted to fulfill his fiduciary duties as a negotiator. The integrity of a prospective negotiating agent is well within the NBPA's legitimate interest in maintaining the wage scale and working conditions of its members.

Collins next contends that the district court erred in granting summary judgment because there still exists a genuine dispute over whether the NBPA intended to waive its statutory right to act as the exclusive bargaining agent of the NBA players. He argues that the fact that the NBPA permitted agents to negotiate individual salaries for over twenty years reasonably implies that the union intended to waive its exclusive right to bargain, and thereby waived its statutory exemption to the Sherman Act.

The district court was not in error because there is no genuine dispute over the NBPA's intent regarding its statutory exemption. "'[W]aiver is the intentional relinquishment of a known right.'" ... A waiver of a right provided to a union by the labor statutes must be clear and unmistakable.... Collins has presented no evidence that the NBPA intended to waive its right other than the fact that the union did not seek to regulate player agents until the abuses came to its attention in the mid-1980s. Because no jury could reasonably infer from this fact that the NBPA clearly and unmistakably intended to waive its exclusive right to bargain on behalf of its members, there is no genuine issue of material fact....

For these reasons, we AFFIRM the district courts' order granting summary judgment. The mandate shall issue forthwith.

***

The following Problem introduces the complexities of signing a player to a player-agent contract—the first step in representing a professional athlete. Cases, statutes, and other materials needed to complete the Problem are located or referenced in the Case File. As you work through the Problem, note the differences between the various regulatory schemes and the overlapping jurisdictional reach.

Problem

Attorney James McNabb desires to become a full-time player agent. McNabb is confronted with important organizing questions.

McNabb is an active member in good standing of the Michigan bar. He will locate his player agent office in Ann Arbor, Michigan. McNabb desires to represent the following athletes:

1. Jerome Jenkins, who is a veteran member of the Detroit Lions and currently represented by another agent. Jenkins resides in a state that has adopted the UAAA.
2. Robert Newsome, who is currently playing in his last season of eligibility at the University of Georgia. Georgia has adopted the UAAA.
3. Larry Kinsella, who is a projected high round NFL draft choice and currently playing in his junior season at the University of Michigan. Michigan does not currently have an athlete-agent statute.

McNabb desires to provide a full-service package to the athlete, including the hustling of endorsement contracts and investment counseling. McNabb has asked you to assist him with the following:

1. Identify the regulatory schemes in the Case File to which James McNabb is subject with respect to each player and explain why based upon the express language of the regulations. Let him know if there is any additional information you need.
2. Outline the registration and certification requirements for McNabb under each regulatory plan in order to be able to represent each player.
3. Identify the risks associated with representing Jerome Jenkins, referencing the case law as well as any applicable provisions in the NFLPA regulations.

* * * * * * CASE FILE * * * * * *

NFLPA Regulations Governing Contract Advisors

https://nflpaweb.blob.core.windows.net/media/Default/PDFs/Agents/RegulationsAmendedAugust2016.pdf

Uniform Athlete Agents Act (2000)

***

Section 2. Definitions. In this [Act]

(1) "Agency contract" means an agreement in which a student-athlete authorizes a person to negotiate or solicit on behalf of the student-athlete a professional-sports-services contract or an endorsement contract.

(2) "Athlete-agent" means an individual who enters into an agency contract with a student-athlete or, directly or indirectly, recruits or solicits a student-athlete to enter into an agency contract.... The term does not include a spouse, parent, sibling, [or] grandparent[, or guardian] of the student-athlete or an individual acting solely on behalf of a professional sports team or professional sports organization....

(4) "Contact" means a communication, direct or indirect, between an athlete agent and a student-athlete, to recruit or solicit the student-athlete to enter into an agency contract.

(5) "Endorsement contract" means an agreement under which a student-athlete is employed or receives consideration to use on behalf of the other party any value that the student-athlete may have because of publicity, reputation, following, or fame obtained because of athletic ability or performance....

***

(7) "Person" means an individual, corporation, business trust, estate, trust, partnership, limited liability company, association, joint venture, government; governmental subdivision, agency, or instrumentality; public corporation, or any other legal or commercial entity.

(8) "Professional-sports-services contract" means an agreement under which an individual is employed, or agrees to render services, as a player on a professional sports team, with a professional sports organization, or as a professional athlete....

***

(12) "Student-athlete" means an individual who engages in, is eligible to engage in, or may be eligible in the future to engage in, any intercollegiate sport. If an individual is permanently ineligible to participate in a particular intercollegiate sport, the individual is not a student-athlete for purposes of that sport.

***

Section 4. Athlete Agents: Registration Required; Void Contracts

(a) Except as otherwise provided in subsection (b), an individual may not act as an athlete agent in this State without holding a certificate of registration under Section 6 or 8.

(b) Before being issued a certificate of registration, an individual may act as an athlete agent in this State for all purposes except signing an agency contract, if:

(1) a student-athlete or another person acting on behalf of the student-athlete initiates communication with the individual; and

(2) within seven days after an initial act as an athlete agent, the individual submits an application for registration as an athlete agent in this State.

(c) An agency contact resulting from conduct in violation of this section is void and the athlete agent shall return any consideration received under the contract.

Section 5. Registration as Athlete Agent; Form; Requirements

(a) An applicant for registration shall submit an application for registration to the [Secretary of State] in a form prescribed by the [Secretary of State].... The application must... state or contain:

(1) the name of the applicant and the address of the applicant's principal place of business;...

***

(4) a description of the applicant's:

(A) formal training as an athlete agent;

(B) practical experience as an athlete agent; and

(C) educational background relating to the applicant's activities as an athlete agent;...

***

(6) the name, sport, and last known team for each individual for whom the applicant acted as an athlete agent during the five years preceding the date of submission of the application;...

***

(8) whether the applicant... has been convicted of a crime that, if committed in this State, would be a crime involving moral turpitude or a felony, and identify the crime;

(9) whether there has been any administrative or judicial determination that the applicant... has made a false, misleading, deceptive, or fraudulent representation;

(10) any instance in which the conduct of the applicant... resulted in the imposition of a sanction, suspension, or declaration of ineligibility to participate in an interscholastic or intercollegiate athletic event on a student-athlete or educational institution;

(11) any sanction, suspension, or disciplinary action taken against the applicant... arising out of occupational or professional conduct; and

(12) whether there has been any denial of an application for, suspension or revocation of, or refusal to renew, the registration or licensure of the applicant... as an athlete agent in any State.

***

Section 6. Certificate of Registration; Issuance or Denial; Renewal

(a) Except as otherwise provided in subsection (b), the [Secretary of State] shall issue a certificate of registration to an individual who complies with Section 5(a)...

(b) The [Secretary of State] may refuse to issue a certificate of registration if the [Secretary of State] determines that the applicant is engaged in conduct that has significant adverse effect on the applicant's fitness to act as an athlete agent. In making the determination, the [Secretary of State] may consider whether the applicant has:

(1) been convicted of a crime that, if committed in this State, would be a crime involving moral turpitude or a felony;

(2) made a materially false, misleading, deceptive, or fraudulent representation in the application or as an athlete agent;

(3) engaged in conduct that would disqualify the applicant from serving in a fiduciary capacity;

(4) engaged in conduct prohibited by [this Act];

(5) had a registration or licensure as an athlete agent suspended, revoked, or denied or been refused renewal or registration or licensure as an athlete agent in any State;

(6) engaged in conduct the consequence of which was that a sanction, suspension, or declaration of ineligibility to participate in an interscholastic or intercollegiate athletic event was imposed on a student-athlete or educational institution; or

(7) engaged in conduct that significantly adversely reflects on the applicant's credibility, honesty, or integrity.

(c) In making a determination under subsection (b), the [Secretary of State] shall consider:

(1) how recently the conduct occurred;

(2) the nature of the conduct and the context in which it occurred; and

(3) any other relevant conduct of the applicant.

(d) An athlete agent may apply to renew a registration by submitting an application for renewal in a form prescribed by the [Secretary of State].

Section 7. Suspension, Revocation, or Refusal to Renew Registration

(a) The [Secretary of State] may suspend, revoke, or refuse to renew a registration for conduct that would have justified denial or registration under Section 6(b).

(b) The [Secretary of State] may deny, suspend, revoke, or refuse to renew a certificate of registration or licensure only after proper notice and an opportunity for a hearing. The [Administrative Procedures Act] applies to this [Act].

Zion Williamson v. Prime Sports Marketing, LLC

2021 WL 201255 (M.D.N.C. January 20, 2021)

This action arises out of a marketing agreement ("the Agreement") between Plaintiff and Defendants. Plaintiff, Zion Williamson, is a former basketball player for Duke University in Durham, North Carolina. Defendants are Gina Ford, a marketing agent from Florida, and Prime Sports Marketing, LLC ("Prime Sports"), a Florida-based marketing agency. The parties entered into the Agreement on or about April 20, 2019, at the time Plaintiff was still a student at the university. In the Complaint, Plaintiff seeks, among other things, a "judicial declaration that the Agreement is void as a matter of law and that Defendants engaged in conduct prohibited by [North Carolina's Uniform Athlete Agent Act ("UAAA")]." In the alternative, Plaintiff seeks a declaration that "Defendants engaged in conduct prohibited by the UAAA, that the Agreement fails to meet the form of contract under the UAAA, [and] is therefore voidable, and that Mr. Williamson voided the Agreement." Defendants answered and alleged counterclaims requesting, among other things, a judicial declaration that the Agreement is valid. On May 20, 2020, Plaintiff moved for judgment on the pleadings as to the declaratory judgment claim ("Count I") of his Complaint. Following the completion of briefing on Plaintiff's motion, on July 9, 2020, Defendants filed a motion, requesting permission to supplement their response to Plaintiff's Motion for Partial Judgment on the Pleadings. For the reasons stated below, Defendants' motion will be denied, and Plaintiff's motion will be granted....

In his Motion for Partial Judgment on the Pleadings, Plaintiff contends that he is entitled to judgment in his favor on Count I of his Complaint because the pleadings establish as a matter of law that the Agreement at issue is either void or was voidable and subsequently voided pursuant to North Carolina's Uniform Athlete Agent Act ("UAAA"). Defendants argue that judgment on the pleadings is not appropriate because there is a genuine dispute of material fact as to whether Plaintiff was in fact a student-athlete during the relevant time period, which they argue would mean that the UAAA is not applicable....

The North Carolina General Assembly enacted into law its version of the UAAA in 2003. The UAAA provides requirements for the conduct of individuals acting as athlete agents in North Carolina and for contracts entered into between athlete agents and student-athletes. Under the statute, an individual is required to register with the North Carolina Secretary of State before acting as an athlete agent in the state, unless the individual is a North Carolina licensed and resident attorney.

The UAAA defines "athlete agent" as a person who (1) "enters into an agency contract with a student-athlete;" (2) "directly or indirectly... recruits or solicits a student-athlete to enter into an agency contract;" or (3) "represents to the public that" he or she "is an athlete agent." Those seeking certification as an athlete agent must submit an application that provides, among other things, a description of their formal training, practical experience, and educational background relating to agent activities. The UAAA provides that an agency contract resulting from conduct that violates Section 78C-88 of the act is void.

The UAAA also provides requirements for contracts between athlete agents and student-athletes, and its definition of an "agency contract" incorporates any agreement which grants an individual the authority to negotiate or solicit "a professional-sports-services contract or an endorsement contract" on behalf of a student-athlete. These requirements include, among other things, that the contract include a "conspicuous" warning to the potential client that his signature will result in a loss of intercollegiate eligibility as well as the date of execution of the contract. An agency contract that does not meet the express terms of the statute is voidable by the student-athlete.

Defendants' primary argument against the appropriateness of judgment on the pleadings is that they have made sufficient allegations to call into question Plaintiff's status as a student-athlete, which would mean that the UAAA did not apply to Plaintiff and Defendants' relationship, or the resulting Agreement. Defendants have raised a question of Plaintiff's status as a student-athlete, as an affirmative defense, and alleged the same within a counterclaim. According to Defendants, "[a] t the time Plaintiff [entered] Duke University as a Freshman in 2018, the Plaintiff was not a 'student athlete' as define[d] by the [National Collegiate Athletic Association ("NCAA")] and/or as defined by [the] UAAA." This is because, allegedly, "the Plaintiff and/or third parties acting on the Plaintiff's behalf had violated one or more of the NCAA and/or UAAA rules that... rendered him ineligible to be a student athlete." The Court will first consider the pleadings, and their attachments, that are relevant to whether Plaintiff was a student-athlete as defined by the UAAA.

1. Plaintiff Was a Student Athlete Under the UAAA

Before determining this issue, the Court first addresses Defendants' argument that the Court must accept Defendants' allegations, that Plaintiff was not a student-athlete at all relevant times, as true. Simply asserting a legal conclusion does not create an issue of fact precluding judgment on the pleadings, especially in the face of contradicting facts and law....

Turning to the statute, the UAAA defines "student-athlete" broadly as "[a]n individual who engages in, is eligible to engage in, *or* may be eligible in the future to engage in any intercollegiate sport," but not an individual who is "permanently ineligible to participate" in the sport. Defendants argue that Plaintiff alleged a conclusory assertion that he was a student-athlete just because he was playing basketball at Duke and that allegation cannot defeat Defendants' allegations that Plaintiff was ineligible/permanently ineligible to participate in collegiate sports while playing for Duke. The Court disagrees. Plaintiff's allegation that he was a student-athlete is more than merely a conclusory allegation. Plaintiff has affirmatively and specifically alleged that he enrolled as a student at Duke University in 2018 and played basketball for Duke as a true freshman during the 2018–2019 collegiate basketball season.

Though Defendants deny Plaintiff's eligibility to be a student-athlete, they nevertheless acknowledge that Plaintiff did "engage in" intercollegiate sports at Duke during the relevant period. They have additionally attached exhibits to their pleadings that refer to Plaintiff's engagement in collegiate athletics. For instance, one attachment dated May 13, 2019 states that, at one time, "the whole world was telling [Plaintiff] that there was no reason for him to even finish off the basketball season with the team." The attachment goes on to state that after a game "on February 20, when [his] left foot famously blew through his sneaker while spraining his right knee in the process, current and former NBA players encouraged [Plaintiff] to shut it down for the season." Despite this, according to the document, Plaintiff had "every intention of playing with his team 'til the very last whistle, he also had every bit of intention to remain a regular student on campus 'til the very last final exam/presentation." Given that the UAAA merely requires that an individual "engages in" an intercollegiate sport in order to be considered a student-athlete, it appears uncontested that Plaintiff meets this bar.

Even so, Defendants argue that, even if Plaintiff did engage in the intercollegiate sports, he was permanently ineligible to do so and thus would be precluded from any protections offered by the UAAA. More specifically, in their affirmative defenses and Counterclaims, Defendants allege that, prior to April 20, 2019, Plaintiff:

> engaged in conduct/acts that rendered and renders him ineligible to be or remain a "student-athlete" including, but not limited to:
>
> a) He agrees orally or in writing to be represented by any individual other than a NCAA-certified agent;
>
> b) He accepts any benefits from an individual other than a NCAA-certified agent; and
>
> c) He entered the NBA Draft AND did not intend to and did not take the appropriate steps to withdraw and declare any intention of resuming intercollegiate participation and, in fact, repeatedly and publicly declared and made it abundantly clear that he was not ever returning to intercollegiate basketball.

Yet this list is merely a recitation of purported offenses that could have led to ineligibility, permanent or otherwise, of any student player and does not serve as allegations specific to Plaintiff. Defendants have not alleged that Plaintiff had, in fact engaged in any of those activities or had been deemed permanently ineligible by the NCAA or under the UAAA at the time of the Agreement or even subsequently.

Defendants' affirmative defenses and counter claims that Plaintiff was not a student-athlete do not rely on material allegations of fact, rather a conclusion of law that flies in the face of their own pleadings as well as attachments to their pleadings. Although Defendants assert that their pleadings make clear that they contest Plaintiff's status as a student-athlete at the time that the Agreement was entered, this assertion is in direct conflict with their admission that Plaintiff was actively engaging in an intercollegiate sport—namely, men's basketball—which is one of the ways the UAAA provides that an individual can be deemed a student-athlete. The Court is not required to assume the truth of legal allegations or conclusions because they are packaged in the form of factual allegations.... Defendants' general allegations, denials, and affirmative defenses are insufficient to raise a genuine issue of material fact as to whether Plaintiff was a student-athlete during the time in which he was a member of Duke men's basketball team.

Further, Defendants have not alleged or provided any facts to plausibly support their conclusory claims that Plaintiff was permanently ineligible to compete in intercollegiate athletics at the time the parties entered into the Agreement. Defendants' listing of purported offenses are insufficient to raise a genuine issue of material fact as to whether Plaintiff had been deemed permanently ineligible during the time period in question and thus no longer a student-athlete under the UAAA. Defendants have provided no authority, caselaw or otherwise, that suggests that it is for a court to adjudicate the details of a student-athlete's eligibility under NCAA rules. Rather, in applying the statute, it would appear that the Court's role is to determine whether the student-athlete has been either determined to be or declared "permanently ineligible" by the governing body authorized to do so. Defendants have not alleged that this has occurred....

Total Economic Athletic Management of America, Inc. v. Pickens

898 S.W.2d 98 (Mo. Ct. App. 1995)

This anticipatory breach of contract case arose from a representation agreement signed by Bruce Evon Pickens and Total Economic Athletic Management of America, Inc., d/b/a Team America, a Nebraska Corporation. That representation agreement was to allow Team America to act as Mr. Pickens' contract advisor in negotiating his National Football League player contract. However, before negotiations, Mr. Pickens engaged another contract advisor who actually negotiated the NFL player contract. The ensuing litigation resulted in a $20,000 judgment entered on a jury verdict for Team America and against Mr. Pickens.

Both parties appeal. In its appeal, Team America claims that the trial court erred in restricting argument on damages, in denying its motion for additur, and in overruling its motion for a new trial on damages only. In his cross-appeal, Mr. Pickens contends that the trial court erred in giving and refusing instructions. The judgment is affirmed.

I. Mr. Pickens' Cross-Appeal

Mr. Pickens' cross-appeal is considered first. The cross-appeal asserts that the instructions misadvised the jury on the existence of a binding agreement and on the measure of damages. The following facts provide background on the representation agreement:

While a student at the University of Nebraska, Bruce Evon Pickens played football for the University's football team, a perennial National Collegiate Athletic Association (NCAA) Division I football power. Howard Misle is the president and owner of Total Economic Athletic Management of America, Inc., a corporation incorporated in Nebraska, d/b/a Team America. Mr. Misle apparently owns other businesses, including an automobile dealership in Lincoln, Nebraska. In behalf of Team America, Mr. Misle negotiates player contracts for athletes with professional football teams. Mr. Misle is a certified contract advisor by the National Football League Players' Association (NFLPA).

Trial evidence discloses that Mr. Misle and Mr. Pickens met when Mr. Pickens was a student at the University of Nebraska. On January 3, 1991, Mr. Pickens encountered Mr. Misle at Mr. Misle's automobile dealership. Mr. Pickens purchased a vehicle from the dealership, and Mr. Misle, in behalf of the dealership, advanced Mr. Pickens credit on a "house note." Mr. Pickens paid nothing for the automobile. Mr. Misle told Mr. Pickens that Mr. Pickens would be approached by many agents seeking to represent him in negotiations with a National Football League (NFL) professional football team to obtain a professional football player contract.

According to Mr. Misle's testimony, an agreement was signed by Mr. Pickens and Mr. Misle on January 18, 1991. The agreement bears the date January 20, 1991. Except for the deletion of paragraph 7, the agreement was a standard form entitled "Standard Representation Agreement Between NFLPA Contract Advisor and Player." Mr. Pickens was not given a copy of the document when it was signed.

Testimony differed about why the representation agreement was not dated when signed. Mr. Misle testified that he had inadvertently failed to date the agreement, and dated it sometime after the date the agreement was signed when he realized that failure. Mr. Misle also testified he explained to Mr. Pickens that sending the agreement to the NFLPA as provided in paragraph 7 was unnecessary because the organization was then a voluntary association and not a union. Mr. Misle also testified that he eventually gave a copy of the signed and dated document to Mr. Pickens.

Team America had representation agreements with other football players. Mr. Misle had sent those agreements to the NFLPA office as provided by paragraph 7 in the NFLPA form contract. In a letter submitted by Mr. Misle to the NFLPA office, he stated that as Team America continued to enter such agreements with athletes, he would submit copies of the agreements to NFLPA.

Mr. Pickens' testimony about signing the representation agreement differed from Mr. Misle's. Mr. Pickens stated that when he arrived home from the Orange Bowl game on January 3, 1991, an employee of Mr. Misle's automobile dealership was awaiting him at the airport. Mr. Pickens went to Mr. Misle's automobile dealership where he was shown several automobiles, including the vehicle that he chose. Mr. Misle provided the vehicle to him without Mr. Pickens' paying any money for its purchase. Mr. Misle then presented the NFLPA standard representation agreement saying to Mr. Pickens, "Since I'm putting myself out on a limb for you, why don't you show me a little bit of consideration and good faith by at least signing the document and letting me know that you are considering me for your agent." Mr. Pickens testified that Mr. Misle told him the document would not be dated and the agreement would not be binding until it was dated and sent to the NFLPA. According to Mr. Pickens, Mr. Misle stated that paragraph 7 of the agreement would be deleted because the document was not a binding agreement. Mr. Misle then stated to Mr. Pickens, according to Mr. Pickens, that when they reached agreement, the document would be dated and sent to the NFLPA to then become valid. Mr. Pickens then departed the dealership with the Audi automobile.

Sometime in early 1991, after Mr. Pickens and Mr. Misle signed the document at the automobile dealership, Mr. Pickens played in the East-West Shrine game. According to Mr. Pickens, sometime after the game a coach at Nebraska asked him if he had an agent, and when he replied that he did not, the coach suggested Tom Condon, a former Kansas City Chief professional football player and agent of numerous professional football players. Mr. Pickens met with Mr. Condon several times in Kansas City and in Lincoln. Mr. Pickens then signed a standard NFLPA representation agreement making Mr. Condon his contract advisor to negotiate a professional football player contract with an NFL team.

Mr. Pickens testified that he spoke to Mr. Misle after he signed the agreement with Mr. Condon. He informed Mr. Misle that he had signed the agreement with Mr. Condon and that he had decided that Mr. Condon would be his agent. Mr. Pickens informed Mr. Misle that he would return the Audi automobile, and would reimburse Mr. Misle for the money he periodically extended to him after January 18, 1991. The money consisted of numerous checks and goods totaling more than $2,900. The money and the automobile were provided to Mr. Pickens when he was a student at the University of Nebraska in 1991.

NCAA rules preclude giving things of value to athletes when they are undergraduates. Additionally, the NFLPA precludes giving athletes anything of value to induce them to sign an NFLPA representation agreement.

The Atlanta Falcons professional football team drafted Mr. Pickens. He was the number three selection in the first-round draft selections. Tom Condon conducted the negotiations. The Atlanta Falcons initially offered $2,700,000 in three one-year player contracts. Mr. Condon eventually negotiated five one-year contracts which Mr. Pickens signed on October 5, 1991. Those NFL player contracts for the 1991, 1992, 1993, 1994, and 1995 football seasons provided for total compensation and work-out bonuses of $4,100,000 and other incentive bonuses. Mr. Pickens' entitlement to compensation under each player contract depended on his making the Atlanta Falcons team for that year. The NFL player contracts also provided for a guaranteed signing bonus of $2,492,000 payable over five years.

....Contrary to Mr. Pickens' claim, the verdict director did not assume a binding agreement; it required the jury to determine the existence of a binding agreement by finding that both plaintiff and defendant had agreed....

Similarly, Mr. Pickens fails to demonstrate that the facts in Instruction C would have defeated Team America's claim on the ground of illegality. The facts hypothesized in Instruction C concerned offering things of value to induce the agreement. Mr. Pickens makes no showing that those facts, even if found true, rendered the subject matter of the agreement illegal under either Missouri or Nebraska law....

II. Team America's Appeal

Team America's appeal asserts the inadequacy of the $20,000 damage award for the anticipatory breach of the representation agreement....

In the context of professional sports, the player's breach of an agency agreement does not necessarily entitle the agent to commission. Technically, the agent is only entitled to damages for breach of contract, *i.e.*, the value of the promised performance reduced by any expenses saved. In addition, the agent is entitled to his commission only if he can show that, had he been permitted to continue performance, he would have been able to consummate the contracts upon which he claims commission.

Contrary to Team America's assertions, it was not entitled to commissions based solely on the contracts negotiated by others. Although required to show what it would have negotiated, Team America points to no evidence showing its own past achievements in negotiating NFL player contracts. The jury was instructed to award Team America such sum as it believed to be the sum which would have been due Team America under the representation agreement. In determining damages, the jury could consider all evidence, including the contracts negotiated by others, and the backgrounds and experiences of the negotiators. Here, the $20,000 damage award appears to be within the range of the evidence, and is not unwarranted. The trial court's denial of a new trial on damages was not a clear abuse of discretion. Team America's Point II is denied.

Conclusion

Team America's appeal and Mr. Pickens' cross-appeal present no grounds for reversing the trial court's judgment. The judgment is affirmed.

Speakers of Sport, Inc. v. Proserv, Inc.

178 F.3d 862 (7th Cir. 1999)

POSNER, CHIEF JUDGE

The Plaintiff, Speakers of Sport, appeals from the grant of summary judgment to the defendant, ProServ, in a diversity suit in which one sports agency has charged another with tortuous interference with a business relationship and related violations of Illinois law. The essential facts, construed as favorably to the plaintiff as the record will permit, are as follows. Ivan Rodriguez, a highly successful catcher with the Texas Rangers baseball team, in 1991 signed the first of several one-year contracts making Speakers his agent. ProServ wanted to expand its representation of baseball players and to this end invited Rodriguez to its office in Washington and there promised that it would get him between $2 and $4 million in endorsements if he signed with ProServ—which he did, terminating his contract (which was terminable at will) with Speakers. This was in 1995. ProServ failed to obtain significant endorsement for Rodriguez and after just one year he switched to another agent who the following year landed him a five-year $42 million contract with the Rangers. Speakers brought this suit a few months later, charging that the promise of endorsements that ProServ had made to Rodriguez was fraudulent and had induced him to terminate his contract with Speakers.

Speakers could not sue Rodriguez for breach of contract, because he had not broken their contract, which was, as we said, terminable at will. Nor, therefore, could it accuse ProServ of inducing a breach of contract.... But Speakers did have a contract with Rodriguez, and inducing the termination of a contract, even when the termination is not a breach because the contract is terminable at will, can still be actionable under the tort law of Illinois, either as an interference with prospective economic advantage... or as in interference with the contract at will itself....

There is in general nothing wrong with one sports agent trying to take a client from another if this can be done without precipitating a breach of contract. That is the process known as competition, which though painful, fierce, frequently ruthless, sometimes Darwinian in its pitilessness, is the cornerstone of our highly successful economic system. Competition is not a tort, [citation omitted] but on the contrary provides a defense (the "competitor's privilege") to the tort of improper interference.... It does not privilege inducing the breach of a contract [citation omitted]—conduct usefully regarded as a separate tort from interfering with a business relationship without precipitating an actual breach of contract—but it does privilege inducing the lawful termination of a contract that is terminable at will....

There would be few more effective inhibitors of the competitive process than making it a tort for an agent to promise the client of another agent to do better by him.... It is true the Speakers argues only that the competitor may not make a promise that he knows he cannot fulfill, may not, that is, compete by fraud. Because the competitor's privilege does not include a right to get business from a competitor by means of fraud, it is hard to quarrel with this position in the abstract, but the practicalities are different. If the argument were accepted and the new agent made a promise that was not fulfilled, the old agent would have a shot at convincing a jury that the new agent had known from the start that he couldn't deliver on the promise. Once a case gets to the jury, all bets are off. The practical consequence of Speakers' approach, therefore, would be that a sports agent who lured away the client of another agent with a promise to do better by him would be running a grave legal risk.

The threat to the competitive process is blocked by the principle of Illinois law that promissory fraud is not actionable unless it is part of a scheme to defraud, that is, unless it is one element of a pattern of fraudulent acts. By requiring the plaintiff show a pattern, by thus not letting him rest on proving a single promise, the law reduces the likelihood of a spurious suit; for a series of unfulfilled promises is better (though of course not conclusive) evidence of fraud than a single unfulfilled promise.

Consider in this connection the characterization by Speakers' own chairman of ProServ's promise to Rodriguez as "pure fantasy and gross exaggeration"—in other words, as puffing. Puffing in the usual sense signifies meaningless superlatives that no reasonable person would take seriously, and so it is not actionable as fraud. Rodriguez thus could not have sued ProServ… in respect of the promise of $2–$4 million in endorsements. If Rodriguez thus was not wronged, we do not understand on what theory Speakers can complain that ProServ competed with it unfairly.

The promise of endorsements was puffing… in the… sense of a sales pitch that is intended, and that a reasonable person… would understand, to be aspirational rather than enforceable.… It is not as if ProServ proposed to employ Rodriguez and pay him $2 million a year. That would be the kind of promise that could found an enforceable obligation.…

It is possible to make a binding promise of something over which one has no control; such a promise is called a warranty. But it is not plausible that this is what ProServ was doing.… So understood, the "promise" was not a promise at all. But even if it was a promise (or a warranty), it cannot be the basis for a finding of fraud because it was not a part of a scheme to defraud evidenced by more than the allegedly fraudulent promise itself.

It can be argued, however, that competition can be tortuous even if it does not involve an actionable fraud… or other independently tortuous act, such as defamation, or trademark or patent infringement, or a theft of a trade secret; that competitors should not be allowed to use "unfair" tactics; and that a promise known by the promisor when made to be unfulfillable is such a tactic, especially when used on a relatively unsophisticated, albeit very well to do, baseball player.… But the Illinois courts have not as yet embraced the doctrine, and we are not alone in thinking it pernicious. The doctrine's conception of wrongful competition is ague—"wrongful by reasons… an established standard of a trade or profession."… We agree with Professor Perlman that the tort of interference with business relationships should be confined to cases in which the defendant employed unlawful means to stiff a competitor… and we are reassured by the conclusion of his careful analysis that the case law is generally consistent with this position as a matter of outcomes as distinct from articulation.

Invoking the concept of "wrongful by reason of... an established standard of a trade or profession," Speakers points to a rule of major league baseball forbidding players' agents to compete by means of misrepresentations. The rule is designed to protect the players, rather than their agents, so that even if it established a norm enforceable by law Speakers would not be entitled to invoke it; it is not a rule designed for Speakers' protection. In any event it violation would not be the king of "wrongful" conduct that should trigger the tort of intentional interference....

It remains to consider Speakers' claim that ProServ violated the Illinois Consumer Fraud and Deceptive Practices Act.... Speakers is not a consumer, and while a competitor is permitted to bring suit under the Act as a representative of the consumer interest..., he must "prove, by clear and convincing evident, how the complained-of conduct implicates consumer protection concerns." No effort at proving this was made here....

The seller can be hurt even if the customer is not; but to allow the seller to obtain damages from a competitor when no consumer has been hurt is unlikely to advance the consumer interest. Allowing Speakers to prevail would hurt consumers by reducing the vigor of competition between sports agents. The Rodriguezes of this world would be disserved, as Rodriguez himself, a most reluctant witness, appears to believe. Anyway, we don't think that the kind of puffing in which ProServ engaged amounts to an unfair method of competition or an unfair act or practice....

We add that even if Speakers could establish liability under either the common law of torts or the deceptive practices act, its suit would fail because it cannot possibly establish, as it seeks to do, a damages entitlement (the only relief it seeks) to the agent's fee on Rodriguez's $42 million contract. The contract was negotiated years after he left Speakers, and by another agent. Since Rodriguez had only a year-to-year contract with Speakers—terminable at will, more-over—and since obviously he was dissatisfied with Speakers at least to the extent of switching to ProServ and then when he became disillusioned with ProServ of not returning to Speakers' fold, the likelihood that Speakers would have retained him had ProServ not lured him away is too slight to ground an award of such damages.... Such an award would be the best example yet of puffing in the pie-in-the-sky sense.

AFFIRMED.

Notes and Comments

1. In *Collins*, the court of appeals noted that the NBPA established agent regulations, a comprehensive system of agent certification, in response to a growing number of player complaints about agent abuses, including violations of various fiduciary duties. As further explained by the district court:

> "Player agents were unregulated by the NBPA before 1986. By the mid-1980s, a substantial number of players had complained to the officers of

the NBPA about agent abuses. Specifically, players complained that the agents imposed high and non-uniform fees for negotiation services, insisted on the execution of open-ended powers of attorney giving the agents broad powers over players' professional and financial decisions, failed to keep players apprised of the status of negotiations with NBA teams, failed to submit itemized bills for fees and services, and, in some cases, had conflicts of interest arising out of representing coaches and/or general managers of NBA teams as well as players. Many players believed they were bound by contract not to dismiss their agents regardless of dissatisfaction with their services and fees, because the agents had insisted on the execution of long-term agreements. Some agents offered money and other inducements to players, their families and coaches to obtain player clients." *Collins v. NBPA*, 850 F. Supp. 1468, 1471 (D. Colo. 1991).

2. State regulation of a non-resident player agent must satisfy the "minimum contacts" test enunciated in *International Shoe Co. v. Washington*, 326 U.S. 310 (1945). Other jurisdictional questions may concern the proper reach of a state's long-arm statute. *See* Sudia & Remis, *The History Behind Athlete Agent Regulation and the "Slam Dunking of Statutory Hurdles,"* 8 VILL. SPORTS & ENT. L.J. 67, 87–88 (2001).

3. States enact player agent regulatory legislation under the "police power" authority. To the extent that player-agent relationships are matters included within the various collective bargaining agreements formed pursuant to the National Labor Relations Act, 29 U.S.C. § 141, is the regulatory power of states preempted by federal law? *See Amalgamated Association of Street Employees v. Lockridge*, 403 U.S. 274 (1971); *Hill v. Florida*, 325 U.S. 538 (1945).

4. Are the certification/registration schemes likely to achieve the protections for the professional and amateur athletes that are desired? What additional elements or alterations of the existing regulations would you recommend? *See generally* SHROPSHIRE & DAVIS, THE BUSINESS OF SPORTS AGENTS (3d ed. 2016). *See also* FALK, THE BALD TRUTH: SECRETS OF SUCCESS FROM THE LOCKER ROOM TO THE BOARDROOM (2009); GREENBERG & GRAY, 1 SPORT LAW PRACTICE Ch. 10 (2d ed. 2009).

5. McNabb reports that he has signed Jerome Jenkins, the veteran NFL player in the Problem above, to a player-agent contract. Assuming McNabb is certified by the NFLPA, can he contract with Jenkins without becoming liable to Jenkins' prior agent under a claim for tortious interference with a business relationship? Does the answer depend on whether Jenkins and McNabb followed the provisions of the NFLPA Regulations Governing Contract Advisors? Would the answer differ in the case of a rookie player who had not yet signed an NFL contract? *See Pro Tect Management Corp. v. Worley*, 1990 U.S. Dist. LEXIS 14574 (S.D.N.Y. Oct. 31, 1990) (in breach of

contract claim by one agent, whose contract with player made prior to NFL draft was terminated in favor of another, issues were not compelled to arbitration under the terms of the NFLPA Regulations).

6. Can you formulate arguments that the Team America contract in the *Pickens* case is unenforceable? Explain the "competitor's privilege" defense as enunciated in *Speakers of Sport*. What type of and how many predicate acts are required to establish an interference case based on fraud? Can you reconcile the views of the *Pickens* court with the views of the *Speakers of Sport* court concerning the establishment of a case for damages?

7. Regulation of player agents by player associations, absent collective bargaining agreements, is subject to attack under antitrust laws. Sherman Act § 1; 15 U.S.C. § 1. As noted by the court of appeals in *Collins*, however, requirements imposed by unions in agreements between unions and employers are exempt from the reach of the antitrust statutes pursuant to the statutory labor exemption. *See also Collins*, 850 F. Supp. at 1477 ("The NBPA regulatory program fulfills legitimate union purposes and was the result of legitimate concerns: it protects the player wage scale by eliminating percentage fees where the agent does not achieve a result better than the collectively bargained minimum; it keeps agent fees generally to a reasonable and uniform level, prevents unlawful kickbacks, bribes, and fiduciary violations and protects the NBPA's interest in assuring that its role in representing professional basketball players is properly carried out"); *H.A. Artists, Assoc. v. Actors Equity Association*, 451 U.S. 704 (1981) (held that labor unions acting in their own self-interest and not in combination with non-labor groups—for example, by enacting regulations that govern agents—are statutorily exempt from the antitrust laws). In addition, the district court in *Collins* applied the non-statutory labor exemption and further held that the collective bargaining agreement between the NBA and the NBPA was exempt from the antitrust laws, explaining that "[w]hen the agreement is reached through bona fide, arms-length bargaining between the union and the employers, and the terms of the agreement are not the product of an initiative by the employer group but were sought by the union in an effort to serve the legitimate interests of its members, it is free from antitrust scrutiny." *Collins*, 850 F. Supp. at 1479. The rationale for applying the non-statutory labor exemption, even though the agent is not a party to the bargaining negotiations between the union and the league, is that the agents' "interrelationship" with players and the union demonstrates that: (1) agents implicitly consent to be bound by the collective bargaining agreement, and (2) agents enjoy significant and ongoing economic benefits flowing directly from the collective bargaining agreement. *White v. Nat'l Football League*, 92 F. Supp. 2d 918, 924 (D. Minn. 2000).

8. Players associations have traditionally rested their authority to regulate agents on the basis that player agents are the agents of the unions. Arbitrator Nicolau stated, "When representing players, individuals certified by the NBPA do so in the Union's

stead and as the NBPA's 'arm and extension.' They thus act as the NBPA's agent." For an argument that the players' associations should provide an option enabling the players to hire union-employed agents, see Karcher, *Solving Problems in the Player Representation Business: Unions Should be the "Exclusive" Representatives of the Players*, 42 WILLAMETTE L. REV. 737 (2006). The player associations collectively bargain for minimum terms of employment, thus leaving the players free to bargain individually with their teams for additional compensation. In order to protect the integrity of the benefits obtained in collective bargaining, the player associations require certification of agents. Initially, concerns were expressed that the player associations perhaps lacked authority over agents representing rookies, who were not yet members of the unions, and that negotiation by an individual agent of the union arguably created a conflict of interest, or a breach of the unions' duty of fair representation. *See* GARVEY, THE AGENT GAME (1984).

It is now commonly recognized that player agents are permitted to negotiate player contracts solely because the player associations have delegated a portion of the exclusive representational authority to the agents. *White v. National Football League*, 92 F. Supp. 2d 918 (D. Minn. 2000); *Collins v. NBPA*, 976 F.2d 740 (10th Cir. 1992). As explained by the district court in the *Collins* case: "Like other sports and entertainment unions, the NBPA believes that the collective good of the entire represented group is maximized when individualized salary negotiations occur within a framework that permits players to exert leverage based on their unique skills and personal contributions. The NBPA therefore has authorized the players or their individually selected agents to negotiate individual compensation packages. This delegation of representational authority to individual players and their agents has always been limited solely to the authority to negotiate individual compensation packages, and to enforce them through the grievance-arbitration procedure established by the NBPA–NBA Agreement." *Collins v. NBPA*, 850 F. Supp. 1468, 1471 (D. Colo. 1991).

9. The NFLPA Regulations Governing Contract Advisors, § 3 B(24), prohibits certified Contract Advisors from "[a]ffiliating with or advising players to use the services of a person who is not an NFLPA Registered Player Financial Advisor for purposes of providing financial advice to the player; or acting as a 'Financial Advisor' and/or providing 'Financial Advice' to an NFL player as those terms are defined in the NFLPA Regulations and Code of Conduct Governing Registered Player Financial Advisors, without first becoming a Registered Player Financial Advisor pursuant to the NFLPA Regulations and Code of Conduct Governing Registered Player Financial Advisors[.]"

10. The NFLPA Regulations Governing Contract Advisors, § 2 A, require that applicants possess a graduate degree from an accredited college or university, including law. An exception may be granted for applicants with seven years sufficient negotiating experience. Applicants must attend the NFLPA seminar for new Contract

Advisors, held on an annual basis, and pass a written examination. The failing applicant may dispute the non-passing examination grade by providing written notice within 30 days of receiving notification of the exam grade. Additional grounds for denial of certification are provided at § 2 B.

11. What review process or other remedies are available to an agent who is rejected for certification under those state regulatory schemes identified in the Problem? Does the agent possess due process rights in this context? *See Mathews v. Eldridge*, 424 U.S. 319 (1976); *Board of Regents v. Roth*, 408 U.S. 564 (1972). If so, what is the nature of the required hearing? Must the opportunity for hearing be provided prior to denial of certification?

12. In the event an Application for Certification is denied, the NFLPA action may be appealed in accordance with the arbitration procedures set forth in the regulations. In disciplinary matters concerning agent reprimand or the revocation or suspension of certification, the NFLPA Regulations establishes a process whereby a Committee on Agent Regulations and Discipline (CARD), comprised of active or retired NFL players, is appointed by the President. The Contract Advisor against whom the Complaint is made may appeal CARD's proposed disciplinary action to the "outside arbitrator" pursuant to the provision of § 5. Section 5 of the NFLPA Regulations and Application for Certificate provide that arbitration shall be the exclusive method for resolving disputes between contract advisors and the NFLPA. For analysis of the process used by players' associations in the regulation of agents, see Karcher, *Fundamental Fairness in Union Regulation of Sports Agents*, 40 CONN. L. REV. 355 (2007). In March 2002, the NFLPA amended its rules to provide that any agent who failed to negotiate a contract with at least one player within a three-year period would be subject to automatic suspension of certification. Agent Kivisto, having received a letter of certificate expiration, filed suit alleging that the amended rule violated the CBA as it was contrary to another rule which prohibited the loss of certificate. The NFLPA responded with a Motion to Dismiss based on the arbitration provision. The Eleventh Circuit affirmed the trial court ruling that plaintiff's complaint was within the scope of the arbitration agreement and its resulting dismissal of the action. *Kivisto v. NFLPA*, 2011 U.S. App. LEXIS 14849 (11th Cir. July 20, 2011).

13. Does an aggrieved player possess a cause of action against a player association, or tort claim against a state for negligent certification of an agent? For a suggestion that an agent aggrieved by the conduct of another agent may sue a player's association, see Deubert, *What's a "Clean" Agent to Do? The Case for a Cause of Action Against a Player's Association*, 18 VILL. SPORTS & ENT. L.J. 1 (2011).

Does a player who is aggrieved by the actions of a financial advisor who is listed with the voluntary program of the NFLPA have a cause of action against the players association? *See Atwater v. NFLPA*, 626 F.3d 1170 (11th Cir. 2010). Section 8 of NFLPA Financial Advisor Regulations provides:

> The NFLPA is not endorsing any Registered Player Financial Advisor for, and disclaims, any liability for the acts or omissions of any Registered Player Financial Advisor. The NFLPA is also not responsible for, and disclaims, any liability for the acts or omissions of any Registered Player Financial Advisor, or any other person. The NFLPA is not in a position to determine whether Applicants for Registration as Registered Player Financial Advisors that provide Broker-Dealer, Investment Adviser, Insurance sales, or other regulated financial services are properly registered with, licensed by or otherwise in compliance with all rules and regulations of the appropriate federal and/or state governmental agency, authority, or organization. As a result, the NFLPA will rely entirely on the truthfulness of statements by any person or entity applying for Registration as an NFLPA Registered Player Financial Advisor that it has the necessary Broker, Dealer, or Investment Adviser registration under applicable securities or commodities laws, SRO membership, licensing or other qualifications imposed by applicable federal and/or state law to render the financial services specified in the Application. Applicants will only be registered with respect to services disclosed in the Application.

The court held that although an exculpatory clause may shield a party against a claim for negligence, it cannot protect a party against a claim of gross negligence. *Ibid. See generally* Lydakis & Zapeta, *The History of the National Football League's 2011 CBA & What It Means for the Future of the Sport*, 10 WILLAMETTE SPORTS L.J. 17 (2012).

14. When Zion Williamson entered the marketing agency agreement on April 20, 2019, the college basketball postseason was finished and he had entered the NBA draft. Under NCAA rules, college basketball players who enter the NBA draft lose their collegiate eligibility if they do not withdraw from the draft within 10 days after the NBA draft combine. College players who entered the 2019 NBA draft had until May 29 (10 days after the NBA draft combine) to withdraw from the draft and retain college eligibility. Thus, Williamson technically had college eligibility remaining on April 20 even if he had no intention whatsoever to withdraw from the draft because he was the consensus number one pick. Would the outcome of the case have been different if the agency agreement was entered after the deadline to withdraw from the draft?

C. Regulatory Limitations on Formation of Representation Agreements; Resolution of Disputes between Player and Agent

The contract between player and agent, of course, must satisfy all legal requirements of the jurisdiction where the contract is formed. Agents rarely use a single contract for all services provided as described above. The three basic contracts for agent services are: (1) contract for negotiation of player-team employment terms; (2) financial services contract; and (3) contract for the marketing of the player for endorsements and public appearances. Clauses commonly included within the three contracts are:

1. parties
2. services
3. term
4. fee arrangement
5. grounds for termination
6. representations and warranties
7. arbitration
8. governing law and jurisdiction

For a clause-by-clause description, including suggested provisions, see McAleenan, *Agent-Player Representation Agreements, in* 1 Law of Amateur and Professional Sports Ch. 2 (Uberstine ed., 2008).

The player and agent are not free to negotiate all terms of the agency contracts. The agent regulations of players associations and state agent laws place limitations on contractual arrangements between players and agents. Regulatory limitations focus primarily upon fee arrangements, termination conditions, and procedures for the resolution of disputes arising under the contracts. The players associations, except for the MLBPA, generally require use of form contracts.

Problem

1. What fees are allowed under the NFLPA regulations? What types of earnings constitute compensation for purposes of calculating the agent's fee? Does the NFLPA regulate fees on endorsement deals?
2. Do the NFLPA Regulations and Standard Representation Agreement govern James McNabb's agreement with Robert Newsome and Larry Kinsella?
3. Under what conditions may the NFLPA Standard Representation Agreement be terminated by either party?
4. Outline the dispute resolution mechanisms required by the NFLPA.
5. What requirements are imposed by the UAAA? What risks are encountered by an agent in the event he or she does not comply with the provisions of the UAAA?

****** CASE FILE ******

NFLPA Regulations Governing Contract Advisors [includes the Standard Representation Agreement]

https://nflpaweb.blob.core.windows.net/media/Default/PDFs/Agents/RegulationsAmendedAugust2016.pdf

Uniform Athlete Agents Act (2000)

***

Section 10. Required Form of Contract.

(a) An agency contract must be in a record, signed or otherwise authenticated by the parties.

(b) An agency contract must state or contain:

(1) the amount and method of calculating the consideration to be paid by the student-athlete for services to be provided by the athlete agent under the contract and any other consideration the athlete agent has received or will receive from any other source for entering into the contract or for providing the services;

(2) the name of any person not listed in the application for registration or renewal of registration who will be compensated because the student-athlete signed the agency contract;

(3) a description of any expenses that the student-athlete agrees to reimburse;

(4) a description of the services to be provided to the student-athlete;

(5) the duration of the contract; and

(6) the date of execution.

(c) An agency contract must contain, in close proximity to the signature of the student-athlete, a conspicuous notice in boldface type in capital letters stating:

WARNING TO STUDENT-ATHLETE

IF YOU SIGN THIS CONTRACT:

(2) YOU MAY LOSE YOUR ELIGIBILITY TO COMPLETE AS A STUDENT-ATHLETE IN YOUR SPORT;

(3) IF YOU HAVE AN ATHLETIC DIRECTOR, WITHIN 72 HOURS AFTER ENTERING INTO THIS CONTRACT, BOTH YOU AND YOUR ATHLETE AGENT MUST NOTIFY YOUR ATHLETIC DIRECTOR; AND

(4) YOU MAY CANCEL THIS CONTRACT WITHIN 14 DAYS AFTER SIGNING IT. CANCELLATION OF THIS CONTRACT MAY NOT REINSTATE YOUR ELIGIBILITY.

(d) An agency contract that does not conform to this section is voidable by the student-athlete. If a student-athlete voids an agency contract, the student-athlete is not required to pay any consideration under the contract or to return any consideration received from the athlete agent to induce the student-athlete to enter into the contract

(e) The athlete agent shall give a record of the signed or otherwise authenticated agency contract to the student-athlete at the time of execution.

Section 11. Notice to Educational Institution.

(a) Within 72 hours after entering into an agency contract or before the next scheduled athletic event in which the student-athlete may participate, whichever occurs first, the athlete agent shall give notice in a record of the existence of the contract to the athletic director of the educational institution at which the student-athlete is enrolled or the athlete agent has reasonable grounds to believe the student-athlete intends to enroll.

(b) Within 72 hours after entering into an agency contract or before the next athletic event in which the student-athlete may participate, whichever occurs first, the student-athlete shall inform the athletic director of the educational institution at which the student-athlete is enrolled that he or she has entered into an agency contract.

Section 12. Student-Athlete's Right to Cancel.

(a) A student-athlete may cancel an agency contract by giving notice to the cancellation to the athlete agent in a record within 14 days after the contract is signed.

(b) A student-athlete may not waive the right to cancel an agency contract.

(c) If a student-athlete cancels an agency contract, the student-athlete is not required to pay any consideration under the contract or to return any consideration received from the athlete agent to induce the student-athlete to enter into the contract.

***

Section 14. Prohibited Conduct.

(a) An athlete agent, with the intent to induce a student-athlete to enter into an agency contract, may not:

(1) give any materially false or misleading information or make a materially false promise or representation;

(2) furnish anything of value to a student-athlete before the student-athlete enters into the agency contract; or

(3) furnish anything of value to any individual other than the student-athlete or another registered athlete agent.

(b) An athlete agent may not intentionally:

(1) initiate contact with a student-athlete unless registered under this [Act];

(2) refuse or fail to retain or permit inspection of the records to be retained by Section 13;

(3) fail to register when required by Section 4;

(4) provide materially false or misleading information in an application for registration or renewal of registration;

(5) predate or postdate an agency contract; or

(6) fail to notify a student-athlete before the student-athlete signs or otherwise authenticates an agency contract for a particular sport that the signing or authentication may make the student-athlete ineligible to participate as a student-athlete in that sport.

Section 15. Criminal Penalties.

An athlete agent who violates Section 14 is guilty of a [misdemeanor] [felony]....

Section 16. Civil Remedies.

(a) An educational institution has a right of action against an athlete agent or a former student-athlete for damages caused by a violation of this [Act]. In an action under this section, the court may award to the prevailing party costs and reasonable attorney's fees.

(b) Damages of an educational institution under subsection (a) include losses and expenses incurred because, as a result to the conduct of an athlete agent or former student-athlete, the educational institution was injured by a violation of this [Act] or was penalized, disqualified, or suspended from participation in athletics by a national association for the promotion and regulation of athletics, by an athletic conference, or by reasonable self-imposed disciplinary action taken to mitigate sanctions likely to be imposed by such an organization.

(c) A right of action under this section does not accrue until the educational institution discovers or by the exercise of reasonable diligence would have discovered the violation by the athlete agent or former student-athlete.

(d) Any liability of the athlete agent or the former student-athlete under section is several and joint.

(e) This [Act] does not restrict rights, remedies, or defenses of any person under law or equity.

Section 17. Administrative Penalty.

The [Secretary of State] may assess a civil penalty against an athlete agent not to exceed [$25,000] for a violation of this [Act].

Zion Williamson v. Prime Sports Marketing, LLC

2021 WL 201255 (M.D.N.C. January 20, 2021)

2. Neither Defendant Ford Nor the Agreement Complied with the UAAA

Having determined that there is no genuine issue of material fact as to whether Plaintiff was a student-athlete, the Court now turns to the analysis under Section 78C-88 of the UAAA. To begin, it is undisputed that Defendant Ford holds herself out as an athlete agent yet neither she nor her agency are licensed as athlete agents in North Carolina, nor have they applied for such a designation. When an individual acts as an athlete agent without holding a certificate of registration, the UAAA expressly provides that any agency contract the individual entered with a student-athlete "is void, and the athlete agent shall return any consideration received under the contract."

As stated above, a contract that authorizes a person to negotiate a professional-sports-services contract or an endorsement contract on behalf of a student-athlete, as the Agreement does, is included in the definition of an agency contract under the UAAA. For such contracts, the UAAA expressly sets forth precise requirements for a warning that must be included. Specifically, it "must contain, in close proximity to the signature of the student-athlete, a conspicuous notice in boldface type in capital letters" the following language:

WARNING TO STUDENT-ATHLETE

IF YOU SIGN THIS CONTRACT:

(1) YOU SHALL LOSE YOUR ELIGIBILITY TO COMPETE AS A STUDENT-ATHLETE IN YOUR SPORT;

(2) IF YOU HAVE AN ATHLETIC DIRECTOR, WITHIN 72 HOURS AFTER ENTERING INTO THIS CONTRACT, BOTH YOU AND YOUR ATHLETE AGENT MUST NOTIFY YOUR ATHLETIC DIRECTOR;

(3) YOU WAIVE YOUR ATTORNEY-CLIENT PRIVILEGE WITH RESPECT TO THIS CONTRACT AND CERTAIN INFORMATION RELATED TO IT; AND

(4) YOU MAY CANCEL THIS CONTRACT WITHIN 14 DAYS AFTER SIGNING IT. CANCELLATION OF THIS CONTRACT SHALL NOT REINSTATE YOUR ELIGIBILITY.

Id. §78C-94(c). When a contract does not contain this required disclosure, it is voidable by the student-athlete. *Id.* §78C-94(d).

It is undisputed that Defendants entered into a contract in North Carolina with Plaintiff for the purposes of identifying branding and endorsement opportunities. It is additionally undisputed that the Agreement provides that Defendants are to act as Mr. Williamson's agents for purposes of endorsements, namely, as Mr. Williamson's "Global Marketing Consultant for identifying branding and endorsement opportunities." The Agreement further empowers Defendants to "exclusively oversee all marketing opportunities" brought before Plaintiff and to "[negotiate] with any entity contracted to [Plaintiff] to resolve any problems that may arise in the delivery of the services and in meeting the entity's obligations to [Plaintiff]." Finally, the pleadings and exhibits show that the Agreement does not contain the warning required by the UAAA. Further, Defendants admit that on May 31, 2019, Plaintiff's family sent a letter to Defendants on Plaintiff's behalf terminating and voiding the Agreement.

Having considered the pleadings, viewed in the light most favorable to Defendants and drawing all reasonable inferences in Defendants' favor, the Court concludes that Plaintiff is entitled to judgment as a matter of law on the issue of whether the Agreement is void. Specifically, there is no dispute that: (1) Plaintiff was a student at Duke University and playing on Duke University's men's basketball team at the time that the parties engaged one another; (2) he had not been determined to be permanently ineligible by any governing body at the time of the agreement; (3) Defendant Ford did not hold the requisite athlete agent certification as required by North Carolina's UAAA; (4) the parties entered into the Agreement; (5) the Agreement permits Defendants to negotiate or solicit professional-sports-services or endorsement contracts on Plaintiff's behalf; (6) the Agreement at issue did not have the statutorily required warning; and (7) Plaintiff's family communicated to Defendants that they were terminating and voiding the agreement.

... The Court hereby declares that the Agreement entered into by the parties is void as a matter of law under N.C. Gen. Stat. §78C-88 (the "UAAA").

Notes and Comments

1. An important aspect of the player-agent contract is the time of the agent's receipt of the fee. What limitations in this regard are imposed by the NFLPA regulations?

Problem: Terry Williams, a former University of Alabama football star, hired Joseph Wilkins as his agent on June 1, 1988. Wilkins negotiated for Williams a player contract with the Chicago Bears. The contract package included a signing bonus of $150,000, and a series of one-year contracts. The first year salary was $100,000; the second year equaled $150,000; and a third year contract was for $245,000. Thus, the total package equaled $645,000. The player-agent contract provided for Wilkins to receive 3% of the gross dollar amount of contracts negotiated. Williams orally agreed to pay Wilkins up front. Wilkins received $19,350.00 when the Bears paid Williams the signing bonus. Unfortunately, the contracts were not guaranteed and Williams was cut from the squad at the completion of the rookie season.

Williams feels he is entitled to a refund of a portion of the money paid to Wilkins. Wilkins feels that a "contract is a contract even if it is oral." What arguments does

Williams have supporting a refund of compensation paid under the player-agent contract? What actions should Williams take?

2. Note that some questions regarding the player-agent contracts are no different from questions confronting an attorney drafting a retainer agreement. For example, a provision is sometimes used that requires client approval of any attorney expenditures that will be reimbursed by the client. What similar provisions exist in the NFL-PA Standard Representation Agreement?

3. What limitations, if any, are imposed by the NFLPA regulations and the UAAA on service contracts for the marketing of the player for endorsement and other off-the-field revenue-producing opportunities? How should the marketing agent-player contract differ from the NFLPA advisor contract?

4. The saga of Lloyd Bloom and Norby Walters produced two cases containing the issue of whether disputes arising under an approved NFLPA contract between agents and a non-member of the union are subject to the arbitration provisions. The contracts under review were signed prior to completion of the athletes' college eligibility in violation of the rules of the NCAA and NFLPA. In *Walters & Bloom v. Fullwood & Kickliter*, 675 F. Supp. 155 (S.D.N.Y. 1987), a federal judge refused to order arbitration, declaring the entire player-agent contract unenforceable as an illegal contract under New York law. Conversely, in *Walters & Bloom v. Harmon*, 516 N.Y.S.2d 874 (1987), a New York court ruled that the question of "arbitrability" was a matter of initial impression for the arbitrator. In the resulting arbitration, *Bloom & Walters d/b/a World Sports & Entertainment v. Harmon*, NFLPA, Culver Arbitrator (1987), the arbitrator ruled the matter arbitrable and found a violation of the NFLPA regulations voiding the contract. The arbitrator, however, allowed the agents to recover the fair value of services rendered under a quantum meruit theory. *See also Pro Tect Management Corp. v. Worley*, 1990 U.S. Dist. LEXIS 14574 (S.D.N.Y. Oct. 30, 1990) (where contract was made prior to the draft, issues were not compelled to arbitration).

5. The Sports Agent Responsibility and Trust Act (SPARTA), 15 U.S.C. § 7801 *et seq.*, categorizes three areas of agent conduct in the recruiting of student-athletes as unfair and deceptive acts and practices: (1) giving false or misleading information, or making a false promise or representation; (2) providing anything of value to a student-athlete or anyone associated with the athlete before the athlete enters into an agency contract, including any consideration in the form of a loan, or acting in the capacity of a guarantor or co-guarantor for any debt; (3) failing to disclose to the student-athlete that the signing of an agency contract jeopardizes the athlete's amateur eligibility; and predating or post-dating an agency contract. *Id.*, § 7802 (a).

The disclosure document must contain, in close proximity to the signature of the student-athlete (or parent or legal guardian if less than 18 years of age), a conspicuous notice in boldface type stating:

"Warning to Student-Athlete: If you agree orally or in writing to be represented by an agent now or in the future you may lose your eligibility to compete as a student athlete in your sport. Within 72 hours after entering into this contract or before the next athletic event in which you are eligible to participate, whichever occurs first, both you and the agent by whom you are agreeing to be represented must notify the athletic director of the educational institution at which you are enrolled, or other individual responsible for athletic programs at such educational institution, that you have entered into an agency contract."

6. If Zion Williamson's marketing agent violated the state agent law, why didn't Duke University or the State of North Carolina pursue any action against the marketing agent? *See* UAAA, Sections 15, 16 and 17.

7. A key issue that was not raised in the Zion Williamson case is the NCAA only sanctions a school for its athlete signing with an agent if the athlete thereafter competes in games. To that end, the court did not address (because the issue was not raised) the primary purpose of the UAAA, which is to protect the commercial interests of NCAA member institutions that can incur a monetary loss from penalties imposed by the NCAA if an athlete violated amateurism rules, for example by signing with an agent, and subsequently participates in competition. The UAAA provisions are designed to (1) put the institution on notice that an athlete signed with an agent "before the next scheduled athletic event in which the student-athlete may participate" so that the institution can immediately withhold the athlete from competition and not be sanctioned by the NCAA and (2) allow for the agency contract to be invalidated/unenforceable, which would essentially undo the NCAA's "no agent" rule violation, so that the athlete can continue playing without the school be sanctioned. The UAAA was not designed to give post-collegiate high profile professional athletes a legal right to get out of an otherwise valid agency contract and avoid payment of commissions owed on endorsement deals or to resolve issues of agents stealing clients from one another.

8. How would damages be calculated if a university filed a civil claim against an athlete agent pursuant to Section 16 of the UAAA for damages caused by a violation of the statute? *See also* TEX. CIV. PRAC. & REM. CODE §§ 131.001 to 131.008, for legislation enabling colleges to sue for the loss of player services. The Texas "NCAA-rule" Act applies to agents, attorneys, and boosters who violate NCAA rules, or encourage students to violate the rules. What types of direct damages and intangible harms would be caused by an agent who violates an athlete agent law? *See United States v. Piggie*, 303 F.3d 923, 925–26 (8th Cir. 2002).

9. What if Zion Williamson's agreement with the marketing agent that was entered on April 20 had an effective date after the deadline to withdraw from the draft? *See* UAAA, Section 14.

D. Duties Imposed by Players Association Regulations, Common Law Agency Principles and the Rules of Professional Conduct Governing Lawyers

State agent laws and players association regulations join traditional common-law remedies to govern player agent conduct, both during and subsequent to formation of the representation agreement. Bar association rules of professional responsibility, of course, apply to the attorney agent as well. The cornerstone of common-law principles relating to the player agent is found in the law of "agency." An agency relationship is a fiduciary relationship defined as follows:

§ 1 Agency; Principal; Agent

> (1) Agency is the fiduciary relation which results from the manifestation of consent by one person to another that the other shall act on his behalf and subject to his control, and consent by the other so to act.

Restatement (Second) of Agency §1 (1958). An agent has a duty to carry out the desires and instructions of the player-client (principal) even if the agent disagrees with them or believes they are unwise, unless the principal's instructions are illegal or unethical. Fiduciary duties are implied by law into the player agent contract. An agent operates in a position of trust and should always keep the client's best interest in mind, much like a physician or stock broker.

The primary fiduciary duties of sports agents are their obligation of undivided loyalty (the duty of loyalty) and their obligation to act in good faith (the duty of care). The duty of loyalty requires agents to avoid all potential and actual conflicts of interest, to maintain confidentiality, and to account for all funds handled on behalf of the player. The duty of care requires agents to perform their job reasonably and properly, such as knowing and meeting a league deadline to file for free agency.

Available remedies for breach of fiduciary duties include:

1. actions for breach of contract;
2. actions in tort (negligence and intentional torts);
3. restitution;
4. rescission;
5. accounting in equity; and
6. fraud (actual and constructive).

The state legislation focusing directly upon player agents provides additional remedies. Some statutes provide for criminal liability and other civil penalties. Note that revocation or suspension of "certification" under the regulations is a popular statutory sanction.

Problem

Assume that James McNabb is certified by the NFLPA. Jerome Jenkins, a veteran member of the Detroit Lions, terminated his contract with Sam Shepherd as player agent according to the terms of the NFLPA Regulations Governing Contract Advisors and signed a Standard Representation Agreement with James McNabb within the proper time frame. Jenkins and McNabb also entered into an agreement securing McNabb's full-service package as player agent, including marketing for appearances and endorsements, income tax preparation, and representation for resolution of disputes or other matters under the employment contract. McNabb referred Jenkins to a Certified Financial Planner for financial counseling and other services.

In the initial client interview, Jenkins confided that he is not satisfied with his compensation under his contract with the Lions. Other players told Jenkins that Shepherd refused to negotiate for a figure higher than the salary of another Shepherd client also playing for the Lions.

Jenkins recently discovered that Shepherd commingled Jenkins' bonus payment with Shepherd's personal funds. Shepherd's funds are subject to a judicial garnishment proceeding.

Jenkins requests that McNabb represent him in any litigation and attendant negotiation for any actionable claims against Shepherd. McNabb seeks your advice as follows:

1. May McNabb represent Jenkins in litigation concurrently with acting as player agent and Contract Advisor according to the terms of the attorney Rules of Professional Conduct and the holding in the *Sports Management Network* case below? What contract terms would you recommend that McNabb employ in the contract with Jenkins?
2. What causes of action against Shepherd exist under common law agency principles? Do the NFLPA Regulations Governing Contract Advisors add remedies?

****** CASE FILE ******

NFLPA Regulations Governing Contract Advisors

https://nflpaweb.blob.core.windows.net/media/Default/PDFs/Agents/RegulationsAmendedAugust2016.pdf

Sports Management Network v. Busch

2019 U.S. Dist. LEXIS 35663 (E.D. Mich. 2019)

Tarnow, District Judge.

This is a diversity action brought by a sports representation agency, Sports Management Network, against a former client, Kurt Busch, Inc.…

Factual Background

Defendant and Counter-Plaintiff, Kurt Busch, began his stock car racing career in 2,000, at the age of 21. He represented himself for several years before partnering with Sports Management Network (SMN), a Troy-based sport management agency. In 2005, Busch signed a contract to drive with Penske Racing, which was facilitated by John Caponigro, an attorney and the founder and CEO of SMN. On November 16, 2005, Kurt Busch and Kurt Busch, Inc. ("Busch") entered into a Representation Agreement (RA) with John Caponigro, "and [his] related firms, Sports Management Network, Inc. and Frasco, Caponigro, Wineman & Scheible, PLLC." The contract called for Caponigro's entities, which were collectively called "SMN," to provide representation, negotiation, and legal, personal, and financial services. Busch would pay SMN an annual fee in addition to a percentage of income from agreements negotiated for him.

On August 11, 2010, the parties extended the RA to December 31, 2014 and increased the annual flat fee to 25%. The contract is written in the first-person plural on Sports Management letter-head and refers to "SMN" continuing the representation outlined in the 2005 RA.

On November 18, 2011, following an embarrassing tirade caught on camera, Busch signed an Agreement and Release which ended his relationship with Penske Racing. This caused Busch's income to drop precipitously.

Plaintiff alleges that around July 2012, Busch offered, and SMN accepted, to compensate SMN under a modified RA ("the 2013 Modified RA") commencing on January 1, 2013 at a rate of 10% of driver retainer negotiated and 10% of revenue paid to defendants from personal service agreements. This modification, whose existence is in dispute, replaced the annual fee entirely with percentage-based contingency fees. Though Busch may have negotiated this contract, he never signed it.

After 2011, Busch gradually rebuilt his racing career.... Busch was named "Rookie of the Year for the Indianapolis 500," in which he finished in sixth place. He was paid only half of his driver's fee in 2014, however, and the other half not until 2016....

In March 2016, Defendants terminated their relationship with SMN effective immediately, and ceased paying SMN altogether. SMN continued sending quarterly invoices for services it alleges were provided under the 2013 modified RA.

Analysis

Sports Management Network brings a breach of contract action alleging that Busch reneged on its contractual obligation to pay 10% of driver fees and sponsorship fees negotiated by SMN. It argues that the parties agreed that the 2013 RA Modification was to control the future relationship between SMN and Busch. The contract was never signed by Busch, and Busch denied that it ever agreed to its terms. However, Busch paid invoices sent in accordance with the contract terms for over three years, up until the final quarter of 2016.

Busch's main defense is that the contract represents an unethical legal representation agreement. Michigan courts have found that retainer agreements that breach the State's Rules of Professional Ethics are unenforceable.... *Evans & Luptak* recognized that an attorney's conduct is against public policy if it violates Michigan's attorney discipline rules.

***

SMN objects to the argument that it provides legal services. John Caponigro denies that SMN practiced law. There is no doubt, however, that John Caponigro practiced law while acting as Busch's agent. Though Caponigro drafted and reviewed contracts in his SMN capacity, he also "exercised [his] legal knowledge for and on Kurt's behalf." There is some confusion over whether FCWS was brought in to provide legal services for Busch by SMN or at Busch's request, with SMN only acting as the coordinator, but given the close intermingling of the law firm and the non-law business, and Caponigro's insouciance over the distinction between the two, delineating between legal and non-legal services is impossible....

Attorneys serving as sports agents typically have dual functions. Though non-attorneys can of course serve as sports agents, representing an athlete entails many duties that would be considered traditional legal work. See Walter T. Champion, Jr., *Attorneys Qua Sports Agents: An Ethical Conundrum,* 7 Marq. Sports L.J. 349 (Spring 1997)("These functions might include: contract negotiations, tax planning, financial planning, money management, investments, estate planning, income tax preparation, incorporating the client, endorsements, sports medicine consultation, physical health consultation, legal consultations and insurance matters."). As Caponigro acknowledges, his legal skills have increased his marketability as a sports agent.

Caponigro cannot profit from his law license in good times, but then claim he was only acting as a sports agent when problems arise. Whether or not SMN was engaged in the practice of law is irrelevant; Caponigro held himself out as both an attorney and as an agent of SMN. The 2013 RA Modification, taken in the context of the 2005 RA and the 2010 extension, erases the distinction between John Caponigro the managing partner of FCWS and John Caponigro the President of SMN.

There is no doubt that Caponigro acted in violation of Michigan's Rules of Professional Ethics . . by representing a client whose interests are directly adverse to another client, and . . . by representing client in a manner that could be materially limited "by the lawyer's own interests." Caponigro is the CEO and majority stakeholder in SMN. His representation of Kurt Busch, and Kurt Busch, Inc. is thus inherently limited by his fiduciary loyalty to SMN. This is precisely why the Michigan State Bar's Ethics Opinions warn against contractually intermingling legal and non-legal business.

> [L]egal services may not be made a part of the contract with the nonlaw business MRPC.5, 7.2(c), MCL 450.681. The lawyer must remain free to exercise independent professional judgment regarding whether to represent the customer and what legal services the customer should have, without being Influenced by whatever the nonlaw business has recommended to the customer.

Michigan Ethics Op. R1-190.

The unsigned March 11, 2013 Letter of Agreement clearly violates this policy. The preamble explains

> [The Agreement's] purpose is to confirm the understanding reached between us concerning the on-going representation by myself and my related firms, Sports Management Network, Inc., and Frasco Caponigro Wineman & Scheible, PLLC (hereinafter collectively referred to as "SMN"), of you and Kurt Busch, Inc., ("KBI") in your various professional, corporate, business and personal interests, as more fully described below.

***

The Michigan Rules of Professional Ethics provides that a conflict such as the one between Caponigro's loyalty to Busch and his loyalty to Sports Management Network requires informed consent from both clients. SMN has advanced no evidence that any informed consent was given, however, and relies on a theory of implied consent. *Centra* forecloses this defense, however.

***

Caponigro never informed Busch of the nature of his conflicts because Caponigro never believed he had a conflict. He certainly never gave sufficient informed consent so that both parties "underst[ood] the reasons why it may be desirable for each to have independent counsel, with undivided loyalty to the interests of each of them."

The conflict between SMN and Busch was exacerbated by SMN's representation of the driving teams that employed Busch. SMN provided sponsorship representation for Penske Racing, for whom Busch drove from 2005 to 2011. SMN also represented Busch in several negotiations adverse to Penske, including a buyout from Busch's previous racing team, the terms of his 2010 extension, and the terms of his 2011 separation, which included a waiver of all of his rights under his driver agreement. Caponigro considered Penske and Busch not to be clients but to be "benefactors to this effort that I was putting forth." He saw himself as one "facilitating a meeting of the minds." Indeed, Penske Racing paid Caponigro, in the capacity of FCWS, a substantial sum for his "coordination" between Busch and Penske in 2005. This underscores the unfairness at the heart of Caponigro's conflict of interest. He billed himself as Busch's agent and attorney, but when Busch's interests were adverse to his other clients, the best he could provide was facilitation, not the loyalty that is the lodestone of Rule 1.7. The conflict ran even deeper with Andretti Autosport, with whom SMN negotiated several contracts on Busch's behalf. Andretti Autosport was a client of both FCWS and SMN, and Michael Andretti has been a client of John Caponigro and FCWS since 1990. Regardless of whether Busch can prove injury from these conflicts, they are sufficiently egregious to infect the entire RA.

The 2013 Agreement contemplated the provision of legal services in a manner violative of legal professional ethics. It is therefore unenforceable....

Conclusion

The alleged 2013 RA Modification is violative of Michigan's Rules of Professional Ethics. It required John Caponigro to split his loyalty between his client and his company, between his client and his company's clients, and between his client and his law firm's clients. The Court need not rule on whether all these conflicts were even waivable, because no one ever asked Busch for informed consent. Knowledge that one's attorney represents adverse parties is no substitute for a candid explanation of why such conflicts may impair the quality of the attorney's representation, and why retaining outside counsel is advisable. Though an agent's connection to racing teams may be exactly what attracts drivers to seek his or her representation, when the agent is also providing legal services he or she must be sure that the driver understands what he or she is giving up by becoming a client of his boss's attorney.

Because SMN and FCWS failed to provide his client with a meaningful choice on whether such conflicts were permissible, they will not be able to enforce their 2013 RA Modification. This does not mean that their representation actually caused injury, however. Having reviewed the record, the Court finds that Busch has not advanced sufficient evidence of damages to bring the case to a jury.

Detroit Lions, Inc. v. Argovitz

580 F. Supp. 542 (E.D. Mich. 1984)

DeMascio, District Judge.

The plot for this Saturday afternoon serial began when Billy Sims, having signed a contract with the Houston Gamblers on July 1, 1983, signed a second contract with the Detroit Lions on December 16, 1983. On December 18, 1983, the Detroit Lions, Inc. (Lions) and Billy R. Sims filed a complaint in the Oakland County Circuit Court seeking a judicial determination that the July 1, 1983, contract between Sims and the Houston Gamblers, Inc. (Gamblers) is invalid because the defendant Jerry Argovitz (Argovitz) breached his fiduciary duty when negotiating the Gamblers' contract and because the contract was otherwise tainted by fraud and misrepresentation. Defendants promptly removed the action to this court based on our diversity of citizenship jurisdiction.

For the reasons that follow, we have concluded that Argovitz's breach of his fiduciary duty during negotiations for the Gamblers' contract was so pronounced, so egregious, that to deny rescission would be unconscionable.

Sometime in February or March 1983, Argovitz told Sims that he had applied for a Houston franchise in the newly formed United States Football League (USFL). In May 1983, Sims attended a press conference in Houston at which Argovitz announced that his application for a franchise had been approved. The evidence persuades us that Sims did not know the extent of Argovitz's interest in the Gamblers. He did not know the amount of Argovitz's original investment, or that Argovitz was obligated for 29 percent of a $1.5 million letter of credit, or that Argovitz was the president of the Gamblers' Corporation at an annual salary of $275,000 and 5 percent of the yearly cash flow. The defendants could not justifiably expect Sims to comprehend the ramifications of Argovitz's interest in the Gamblers or the manner in which that interest would create an untenable conflict of interest, a conflict that would inevitably breach Argovitz's fiduciary duty to Sims. Argovitz knew, or should have known, that he could not act as Sims' agent under any circumstances when dealing with the Gamblers. Even the USFL Constitution itself prohibits a holder of any interest in a member club from acting "as the contracting agent or representative for any player."

Pending the approval of his application for a USFL franchise in Houston, Argovitz continued his negotiations with the Lions on behalf of Sims. On April 5, 1983, Argovitz offered Sims' services to the Lions for $6 million over a four-year period. The offer included a demand for a $1 million interest-free loan to be repaid over 10 years, and for skill and injury guarantees for three years. The Lions quickly responded with a counter offer on April 7, 1983, in the face amount of $1.5 million over a five year period with additional incentives not relevant here. The negotiating process was working. The Lions were trying to determine what Argovitz really believed the market value for Sims really was. On May 3, 1983, with his Gamblers franchise assured, Argovitz significantly reduced his offer to the Lions. He now offered Sims to the Lions for $3 million over a four-year period, one-half of the amount of his April 5, 1983, offer. Argovitz's May 3rd offer included a demand for $50,000 to permit Sims to purchase an annuity. Argovitz also dropped his previous demand for skill guarantees. The May 10, 1983 offer submitted by the Lions brought the parties much closer.

On May 30, 1983, Argovitz asked for $3.5 million over a five-year period. This offer included an interest-free loan and injury protection insurance but made no demand for skill guarantees. The May 30 offer now requested $400,000 to allow Sims to purchase an annuity. On June 1, 1983, Argovitz and the Lions were only $500,000 apart. We find that the negotiations between the Lions and Argovitz were progressing normally, not laterally as Argovitz represented to Sims. The Lions were not "dragging their feet." Throughout the entire month of June 1983, Mr. Frederick Nash, the Lions' skilled negotiator and a fastidious lawyer, was involved in investigating the possibility of providing an attractive annuity for Sims and at the same time doing his best to avoid the granting of either skill or injury guarantees. The evidence establishes that on June 22, 1983, the Lions and Argovitz were very close to reaching an agreement on the value of Sims' services.

Apparently, in the midst of his negotiations with the Lions and with his Gamblers franchise in hand, Argovitz decided that he would seek an offer from the Gamblers. Mr. Bernard Lerner, one of Argovitz's partners in the Gamblers agreed to negotiate a contract with Sims. Since Lerner admitted that he had no knowledge whatsoever about football, we must infer that Argovitz at the very least told Lerner the amount of money required to sign Sims and further pressed upon Lerner the Gamblers' absolute need to obtain Sims' services. In the Gamblers' organization, only Argovitz knew the value of Sims' services and how critical it was for the Gamblers to obtain Sims. In Argovitz's words, Sims would make the Gamblers' franchise.

On June 29, 1983, at Lerner's behest, Sims and his wife went to Houston to negotiate with a team that was partially owned by his own agent. When Sims arrived in Houston, he believed that the Lions organization was not negotiating in good faith; that it was not really interested in his services. His ego was bruised and his emotional outlook toward the Lions was visible to Burrough and Argovitz. Clearly, virtually all the information that Sims had up to that date came from Argovitz. Sims and the Gamblers did not discuss a future contract on the night of June 29th. The negotiations began on the morning of June 30, 1983, and ended that afternoon. At the morning meeting, Lerner offered Sims a $3.5 million five-year contract, which included three years of skill and injury guarantees. The offer included a $500,000 loan at an interest rate of 1 percent over prime. It was from this loan that Argovitz planned to receive the $100,000 balance of his fee for acting as an agent in negotiating a contract with his own team. Burrough testified that Sims would have accepted that offer on the spot because he was finally receiving the guarantee that he had been requesting from the Lions, guarantees that Argovitz dropped without too much quarrel. Argovitz and Burrough took Sims and his wife into another room to discuss the offer. Argovitz did tell Sims that he thought the Lions would match the Gamblers financial package and asked Sims whether he (Argovitz) should telephone the Lions. But, it is clear from the evidence that neither Sims nor Burrough believed that the Lions would match the offer. We find that Sims told Argovitz not to call the Lions for purely emotional reasons. As we have noted, Sims believed that the Lions' organization was not that interested in him and his pride was wounded. Burrough clearly admitted that he was aware of the emotional basis for Sims' decision not to have Argovitz phone the Lions, and we must conclude from the extremely close relationship between Argovitz and Sims that Argovitz knew it as well. When Sims went back to Lerner's office, he agreed to become a Gambler on the terms offered. At that moment, Argovitz irreparably breached his fiduciary duty. As agent for Sims he had the duty to telephone the Lions, receive its final offer, and present the terms of both offers to Sims. Then and only then could it be said that Sims made an intelligent and knowing decision to accept the Gamblers' offer.

During these negotiations at the Gamblers' office, Mr. Nash of the Lions telephoned Argovitz, but even though Argovitz was at his office, he declined to accept the telephone call. Argovitz tried to return Nash's call after Sims had accepted the Gamblers' offer, but it was after 5 p.m. and Nash had left for the July 4th weekend. When he declined to accept Mr. Nash's call, Argovitz's breach of his fiduciary duty became even more pronounced. Following Nash's example, Argovitz left for his weekend trip, leaving his principal to sign the contracts with the Gamblers the next day, July 1, 1983. The defendants, in their supplemental trial brief, assert that neither Argovitz nor Burrough can be held responsible for following Sims' instruction not to contact the Lions on June 30, 1983. Although it is generally true that an agent is not liable for losses occurring as a result of following his principal's instructions, the rule of law is not applicable when the agent has placed himself in a position adverse to that of his principal.

During the evening of June 30, 1983, Burrough struggled with the fact that they had not presented the Gamblers' offer to the Lions. He knew, as does the court, that Argovitz now had the wedge that he needed to bring finality to the Lions' negotiations. Burrough was acutely aware of the fact that Sims' actions were emotionally motivated and realized that the responsibility for Sims' future rested with him. We view with some disdain the fact that Argovitz had, in effect, delegated his entire fiduciary responsibility on the eve of his principal's most important career decision. On July 1, 1983, it was Lerner who gave lip service to Argovitz's conspicuous conflict of interest. It was Lerner, not Argovitz, who advised Sims that Argovitz's position with the Gamblers presented a conflict of interest and that Sims could, if he wished, obtain an attorney or another agent. Argovitz, upon whom Sims had relied for the past four years, was not even there. Burrough, conscious of Sims' emotional responses, never advised Sims to wait until he had talked with the Lions before making a final decision. Argovitz's conflict of interest and self dealing put him in the position where he would not even use the wedge he now had to negotiate with the Lions, a wedge that is the dream of every agent. Two expert witnesses testified that an agent should telephone a team that he has been negotiating with once he has an offer in hand. Mr. Woolf, plaintiffs' expert, testified that an offer from another team is probably the most important factor in negotiations. Mr. Lustig, defendant's expert, believed that it was prudent for him to telephone the Buffalo Bills and inform that organization of the Gamblers' offer to Jim Kelly, despite the fact that he believed the Bills had already made its best offer to his principal. The evidence here convinces us that Argovitz's negotiations with the Lions were ongoing and it had not made its final offer. Argovitz did not follow the common practice described by both expert witnesses. He did not do this because he knew that the Lions would not leave Sims without a contract and he further knew that if he made that type of call Sims would be lost to the Gamblers, a team he owned.

On November 12, 1983, when Sims was in Houston for the Lions game with the Houston Oilers, Argovitz asked Sims to come to his home and sign certain papers. He represented to Sims that certain papers of his contract had been mistakenly overlooked and now needed to be signed. Included among those papers he asked Sims to sign was a waiver of any claim that Sims might have against Argovitz for his blatant breach of his fiduciary duty brought on by his glaring conflict of interest. Sims did not receive independent advice with regard to the wisdom of signing such a waiver. Despite having sold his agency business in September, Argovitz did not even tell Sims' new agent of his intention to have Sims sign a waiver. Nevertheless, Sims, an unsophisticated young man, signed the waiver. This is another example of the questionable conduct on the part of Argovitz who still had business management obligations to Sims. In spite of his fiduciary relationship he had Sims sign a waiver without advising him to obtain independent counseling.

Argovitz's negotiations with Lustig, Jim Kelly's agent, illustrates the difficulties that develop when an agent negotiates a contract where his personal interests conflict with those of his principal. Lustig, an independent agent, ignored Argovitz's admonishment not to "shop" the Gamblers' offer to Kelly. Lustig called the NFL team that he had been negotiating with because it was the "prudent" thing to do. The Gamblers agreed to pay Kelly, an untested rookie quarterback $3.2 million for five years. His compensation was $60,000 less than Sims', a former Heisman Trophy winner and a proven star in the NFL. Lustig also obtained a number of favorable clauses from Argovitz; the most impressive one being that Kelly was assured of being one of the three top paid quarterbacks in the USFL if he performed as well as expected. If Argovitz had been free from conflicting interests he would have demanded similar benefits for Sims. Argovitz claimed that the nondisclosure clause in Kelly's contract prevented him from mentioning the Kelly contract to Sims. We view this contention as frivolous. Requesting these benefits for Sims did not require disclosure of

Kelly's contract. Moreover, Argovitz's failure to obtain personal guarantees for Sims without adequately warning Sims about the risks and uncertainties of a new league constituted a clear breach of his fiduciary duty....

We are mindful that Sims was less than forthright when testifying before the court. However, we agree with plaintiff's counsel that the facts as presented through the testimony of other witnesses are so unappealing that we can disregard Sims' testimony entirely. We remain persuaded that on balance, Argovitz's breach of his fiduciary duty was so egregious that a court of equity cannot permit him to benefit by his own wrongful breach. We conclude that Argovitz's conduct in negotiating Sims' contract with the Gamblers rendered it invalid.

Judgment will be entered for the plaintiffs rescinding the Gamblers' contract with Sims.

IT IS SO ORDERED.

Brown v. Woolf

554 F. Supp. 1206 (S.D. Ind. 1983)

The complaint in this diversity action seeks compensatory and punitive damages and the imposition of a trust on a fee defendant allegedly received, all stemming from defendant's alleged constructive fraud and breach of fiduciary duty in the negotiation of a contract for the 1974–75 hockey season for plaintiff who was a professional hockey player. Plaintiff alleges that prior to the 1973–74 season he had engaged the services of defendant, a well known sports attorney and agent, who represents many professional athletes, has authored a book, and has appeared in the media in connection with such representation, to negotiate a contract for him with the Pittsburgh Penguins of the National Hockey League. Plaintiff had a professionally successful season that year under the contract defendant negotiated for him and accordingly again engaged defendant's services prior to the 1974–75 season. During the negotiations in July 1974, the Penguins offered plaintiff a two year contract at $80,000.00 per year but plaintiff rejected the offer allegedly because defendant asserted that he could obtain a better, long-term, no-cut contract with a deferred compensation feature with the Indianapolis Racers, which at the time was a new team in a new league. On July 31, 1974, plaintiff signed a five-year contract with the Racers. Thereafter, it is alleged the Racers began having financial difficulties. Plaintiff avers that Woolf continued to represent plaintiff and negotiated two reductions in plaintiffs compensation including the loss of a retirement fund at the same time defendant was attempting to get his own fee payment from the Racers. Ultimately the Racers' assets were seized and the organizers defaulted on their obligations to plaintiff. He avers that he received only $185,000.00 of the total $800,000.00 compensation under the Racer contract but that defendant received his full $40,000.00 fee (5% of the contract) from the Racers.

Plaintiff alleges that defendant made numerous material misrepresentations upon which he relied both during the negotiation of the Racer contract and at the time of the subsequent modifications. Plaintiff further avers that defendant breached his fiduciary duty to plaintiff by failing to conduct any investigation into the financial stability of the Racers, failing to investigate possible consequences of the deferred compensation package in the Racers' contract, failing to obtain guarantees or collateral, and by negotiating reductions in plaintiff's compensation from the Racers while insisting on receiving all of his own. Plaintiff theorizes that such conduct amounts to a prima facie case of constructive fraud for which he should receive compensatory and punitive damages and have a trust impressed on the $40,000.00 fee defendant received from the Racers.

Notes and Comments

1. The definition of "practice of law" in the state of Washington is written broadly, as follows:

> The "practice of law"... is generally acknowledged to include not only the doing or performing of services in the courts of justice, throughout the various stages thereof, but in a larger sense includes legal advice and counsel and the preparation of legal instruments by which legal rights and obligations are established. Further, selection and completion of preprinted form legal documents has been found to be the "practice of law."

Hagan v. Kassler Escrow, Inc., 635 P.2d 730 (Wash. 1981).

McNabb, a California lawyer, is officed in Spokane, Washington. Are any of the player-agent services rendered by McNabb considered the practice of law as defined in Washington? *See generally* Geisel, *Disbarring Jerry Maguire: How Broadly Defining "Unauthorized Practice of Law" Could Take the "Lawyer" out of "Lawyer-Agent" Despite the Current State of Athlete Agent Legislation*, 18 MARQ. SPORTS L. REV. 225 (2007). Does the *Sports Management Network* case indicate that some of the typical player agent practices constitute the practice of law in Michigan? Are non-attorney agents routinely practicing law without a license?

The attorney Model Rules of Professional Conduct serve to govern most, if not all, of the problem areas of agent practice identified above:

a. Unethical Solicitation—MRPC § 7.3;

b. Charging of Excessive Fees—MRPC § 1.5;

c. Conflicts of Interest—MRPC §§ 1.7–1.9;

d. General Incompetence—MRPC §§ 1.1–1.3;

e. Income Mismanagement—MRPC § 1.15;

f. Fraud—MRPC § 8.1.

Do the state and player association regulatory schemes adequately govern non-attorney agent conduct? Do attorneys working as player agents operate under duties imposed by the Model Rules of Professional Conduct that are not borne by non-attorney agents?

2. Attorney agents are susceptible to the "malpractice" action. What are the distinctions between an attorney malpractice action and an action for breach of the duty of care, or negligence? Do the regulations create a cause of action for "agent malpractice"? If so, what standard should be utilized? *See* Sahl, *Entertainment Law—The Specter of Malpractice Claims and Disciplinary Action*, 20 MARQ. SPORTS L. REV. 377 (2010).

Under Illinois law, a sports agent fiduciary must treat the player with the "utmost candor, rectitude, care, loyalty, and good faith." *Jones v. Childers*, 18 F.3d 899 (11th Cir. 1994). *See also Bias v. Advantage International, Inc.*, 905 F.2d 1558 (D.C. Cir. 1990) (estate unsuccessful in attempt to recover in action for negligent performance of agent duties based on agent's failure to execute an insurance policy and endorsement contract prior to player's death).

3. The Football Players Health Study at Harvard University identified the following potential conflicts of interest for NFLPA Contract Advisors:

1. The contract advisor's relationship with club officials.
2. The contract advisor's compensation structure.
3. The contract advisor's representation of multiple players on same club.
4. The contract advisor's representation of multiple players contemplated to be the top pick in the NFL Draft.
5. The contract advisor's representation of club executives and coaches.

Deubert, Cohen, and Lynch, *Protecting and Promoting the Health of NFL Players: Legal & Ethical Analysis & Recommendations*, The Football Players Health Study at Harvard University, ch. 12 (2017).

4. Does the agent who represents two players competing for the same position possess a conflict of interest? Two players on the same team under the salary cap? The top two players at the same position being drafted in the same year? Two super stars competing for endorsement or appearance money? *See generally* Neiman, *Fair Game: Ethical Considerations in Negotiation by Sports Agents*, 9 TEX. REV. ENT. & SPORTS L. 123 (2007); Rosner, *Conflicts of Interest and the Shifting Paradigm of Athlete Representation*, 11 UCLA ENT. L. REV. 193 (2004). For an article questioning the propriety of an agent's "packaging" of clients in deals made with promoters or advertisers, see Newcomb & Comte, *Endorsement Tying Arrangements by Sports Agents Produces Growing Controversy Among Athletes*, FORBES (Nov. 23, 1992).

5. The Representation Agreement in the *Busch* case appears to divide responsibility for providing services among John Caponigro and his two "related firms," SMN

and FCWS, without any clarification as to which firm is performing which services and how the fees will be shared, if at all, among them, which does not conform to industry practice. The rules of professional conduct governing lawyers prohibit a law firm and a non-law business from entering such an agreement because the lawyer's (law firm's) independent professional judgment in representing the client must not be influenced by the recommendations of the non-law business. Moreover, although non-lawyers frequently act as sports agents, sports agency is a law related service and thus lawyers who act as sports agents are subject to the rules of their respective bar associations. *See, e.g., In the Matter of Frederick J. Henley*, 478 S.E.2d 134 (Ga. 1996); *Cuyahoga County Bar Assn. v. Glenn*, 649 N.E.2d 1213 (Ohio 1995). When an attorney "represents a client in contract negotiations and general business counseling, these activities constitute the practice of law and it would be professionally proper to handle them from the same office in which he engages in the general practice of law." *See* ISBA Advisory Opinion on Professional Conduct, Opinion No. 700 1980 WL 130464 (Ill. St. Bar. Assn.), Nov. 4, 1980 (addressing whether an attorney may handle "player representation" from the same office in which he/she engages in the general practice of law). An attorney operating as a sports agent cannot take off his or her "lawyer hat" and put on a "non-lawyer hat" through the creation of distinct entities in the representation agreement or otherwise.

6. Under common law agency principles, the athlete may consent to a conflict of interest if: (1) the agent has communicated adequate information and explanation about the material risks of and reasonably available alternatives to the proposed course of conduct that might affect the athlete's judgment, which should include possible effects on loyalty, confidentiality, and the advantages and risks involved; *and* (2) it is clear that the agent can adequately represent the athlete's interest. Thus, before the agent can represent the athlete on the matter, the athlete must consent to the conflict of interest and the consent must be *informed*. Moreover, the agent must obtain the athlete's informed consent each time a matter or transaction poses a conflict of interest. An agent cannot assert he or she was not required to disclose the conflicts of interest and obtain the client's consent because the client knew about them. Also, informed consent must be obtained even if the athlete appears to be satisfied with, or in favor of, a relationship the agent has with a third party that presents a conflict of interest. The athlete simply cannot be expected to understand and appreciate the complexities of conflict of interest transactions and how the agent's representation of the athlete could impact the athlete's interests.

7. Argovitz's personal interest in signing Sims with the Gamblers was adverse to Sims' interest. As such, the Gamblers' contract must be rescinded unless Argovitz informed Sims of every material fact that might have influenced Sims' decision whether or not to sign the Gamblers' contract. The district court concluded that Argovitz "failed to show by a preponderance of the evidence either: 1) that he informed Sims of the following facts, or 2) that these facts would not have influenced Sims' decision whether to sign the Gamblers' contract:

a. The relative values of the Gamblers' contract and the Lions' offer that Argovitz knew could be obtained.

b. That there was significant financial differences between the USFL and the NFL not only in terms of the relative financial stability of the Leagues, but also in terms of the fringe benefits available to Sims.

c. Argovitz's 29 percent ownership in the Gamblers; Argovitz's $275,000 annual salary with the Gamblers; Argovitz's five percent interest in the cash flow of the Gamblers.

d. That both Argovitz and Burrough failed to even attempt to obtain for Sims valuable contract clauses which they had given to Kelly on behalf of the Gamblers.

e. That Sims had great leverage, and Argovitz was not encouraging a bidding war that could have advantageous results for Sims.

580 F. Supp. at 549.

8. Would it be a conflict of interest for an agent to represent a coach and a player on the same team? The NBPA regulations prohibit agents from representing NBA coaches. What do the NFLPA regulations say about agents who represent NFL coaches?

9. NBA star Kevin Garnett in 2017 discovered that his "long-term trusted wealth manager, confidant, and personal friend," Charles A. Banks, had defrauded him. Banks had hired a CPA to file income tax returns, who ultimately took a primary role in Garnett's financial life and businesses, including preparing financial statements, creating budgets, and serving as the registered agent for businesses. Garnett filed an action against the CPA and firm alleging professional malpractice, breach of fiduciary duty, and aiding and abetting Banks in breaching his duties to Garnett. *Garnett v. Welenken CPAs*, U.S. Dist. Ct. for D. Minn., Civ. No. 18-2590 (JRT/ECW), Order Denying Motion to Dismiss for Lack of Jurisdiction, March 13, 2019.

10. For a case in which the agent sued a player, see *Dogra v. Griffin III*, Complaint, U.S. Dist. Ct. for E.D. Missouri, CV-00548-AGF, March 22, 2019. The agent alleged that in or around January 2012, the agent and RGIII entered into an oral agreement whereby the agent would negotiate marketing and endorsement agreements for the benefit of RGIII in return for a 15% commission. RGIII made partial payment of invoices in 2014 and 2015. The agent claimed breach of contract, breach of the covenant of good faith and fair dealing, and unjust enrichment.

11. In *Brown v. Woolf*, did the agent breach his fiduciary duty to his client? Which of Brown's claims relate to the duty of care and which relate to the duty of loyalty? The agent took his entire fee even though Brown did not receive the full amount of the contract. Should an agent only get paid if and when the player gets paid? Do the NFLPA regulations (or Standard Representation Agreement) specifically address this issue?

12. For a case involving a claim by one agent against another for "subcontract" services in the negotiation of a player contract with the Phoenix Suns, see *Andrews v. Merriweather*, 1991 U.S. Dist. LEXIS 3149 (N.D. Ill. Mar. 15, 1991). *See also Weinberg v. Silber*, 140 F. Supp. 2d 712 (N.D. Tex. 2001) (dispute of two sports agents arose from several oral joint venture agreements to recruit athletes and split fees and expenses). For a description of events that generate legal disputes among agents who have conducted partnership operations, see the "Findings of Fact" in *Steinberg, Moorad & Dunn v. Dunn*, 2002 U.S. Dist. LEXIS 26752 (C.D. Cal. Dec. 23, 2002).

In 2011, the agent firm, APSE, filed suit against former APSE Vice President and Director, Peter Schaffer, who joined J. R. Rickert in forming Authentic Athletix, LLC. The Complaint alleged that Schaffer breached an "Assignment of Contract Rights" agreement by failing to transfer to APSE all revenue that he received from players that he signed while working at APSE. *All Pro Sports & Entertainment, Inc. v. Schaffer*, District Court, City and County of Colorado, Case No. 2011 (CV6443).

Ten

Torts and Sports

Learning Outcomes

- Be able to assess when one participant is legally responsible for injury to another participant.
- Understand the viability of the spectator's cause of action for injuries incurred at sporting events, as well as the spectator's potential liability for their misconduct.
- Learn about medical malpractice liability of team physician's and trainers.
- Learn when someone is liable for damaging the reputation of high-profile athletes and coaches.
- Understand liability for the tort of intentional interference with contractual relations involving athletes and coaches.

Key Terms

- Negligence (duty, breach, causation, damages)
- Recklessness
- Assumption of risk
- "Part of the game"
- Foreseeability
- Limited duty rule
- Medical malpractice
- Informed consent
- Inherent risk
- Special relationship
- Supervision
- Vicarious liability
- Defamation
- First Amendment
- Public figure

A. Liability of One Participant to Another

> Had the parties been upon the playgrounds of the school, engaged in the usual boyish sports, the defendant being free from malice, wantonness, or negligence, and intending no harm to plaintiff in what he did, we should hesitate to hold the act of the defendant unlawful, or that he could be held liable in this action. Some consideration is due to the implied license of the playgrounds. *Vosburg v. Putney*, 50 N.W. 403, 404 (Wis. 1891).

Vosburg is a landmark torts case that has been used by law professors to confound and befuddle generations of law students by obfuscating the meaning of intent. Although it is not often cited in the sports law context, it is often used as the lead case in torts, and it seems natural to use it to kick off torts and sports. And, as you can see, the issue is not a new one.

Participation in sports is risky. It is probably fair to say that sports activities—baseball, basketball, football, tennis, racquetball, wrestling, and even jogging—create greater risks of physical harm than do most other human activities. Typically, injuries incurred in athletic participation are not of tortious origin, but they occur rather as a result of the normal risks associated with participation in the sport. For example, when a tennis player suffers a detached retina when struck by an opponent's all-too-powerful overhead smash, no lawyer worth his or her salt would be heard to argue that the opponent is a tortfeasor. However, injuries can occur as a consequence of arguably tortious behavior by a participant. This section explores the theories of tort liability that are available to one participant in a suit against a fellow participant for injuries that occur "in the heat of competition."

Generally, an athlete so injured can base an action to recover on three theories: (1) an intentional tort, such as battery or assault; (2) recklessness; and (3) negligence. The prevailing view appears to be that the participant-to-participant sports injury case requires at least recklessness.

Intentional Torts. A simple definition of battery is the intentional, unprivileged, harmful, or offensive contact by the defendant with the person of another. An assault is committed when the defendant, without privilege, intentionally places the plaintiff in apprehension of an immediate harmful or offensive touching. Sports activities are rife with what can arguably be termed assaults and batteries. A review of the cases indicates that a defense of privilege is often the key issue in such litigation. The RESTATEMENT (SECOND) OF TORTS [hereinafter RESTATEMENT] categorizes privileges in terms of whether they are consensual or nonconsensual:

§ 10. Privilege

> (1) The word "privilege" is used... to denote the fact that conduct which, under ordinary circumstances, would subject the actor to liability, under particular circumstances does not subject him to such liability.

(2) A privilege may be based upon (a) the consent of the other affected by the actor's conduct, or (b) the fact that its exercise is necessary for the protection of some interest of the actor or of the public which is of such importance as to justify the harm caused or threatened by its exercise.

Commonly accepted nonconsensual privileges include self-defense, defense of others, and defense of property. In sports, the consent privilege looms large. The courts are repeatedly faced with determining the scope of a participant's consent. The intentional tort theory is the clearest base of action, as the available defenses are well established and generally agreed upon.

The issue of intent in the assault and battery context is perplexing. The RESTATEMENT provides the following:

§ 8A. Intent

The word "intent" is used throughout the Restatement of this Subject to denote that the actor desires to cause the consequences of his act, or that he believes that the consequences are substantially certain to result from it.

§ 16. Character of Intent Necessary

(1) If an act is done with the intention of inflicting upon another an offensive but not a harmful bodily contact, or of putting another in apprehension of either a harmful or offensive bodily contact, and such act causes a bodily contact to the other, the actor is liable to the other for a battery although the act was not done with the intention of bringing about the resulting bodily harm.

(2) If an act is done with the intention of affecting a third person in the manner stated in Subsection (1), but causes a harmful bodily contact to another, the actor is liable to such other as fully as though he intended so to affect him.

As you work through the problems in this section, apply these RESTATEMENT provisions to determine the presence or absence of the intent element.

Negligence. The basis of negligence as a cause of action is conduct that results in an unreasonable risk of harm to another. Of course, almost all human activities involve some risk of harm. The gist of a negligence-based claim is that the conduct involves a risk of harm that outweighs the benefits to be derived from engaging in the conduct. The RESTATEMENT provides:

§ 291. Unreasonableness: How Determined: Magnitude of Risk and Utility of Conduct

Where an act is one which a reasonable man would recognize as involving a risk of harm to another, the risk is unreasonable and the act is negligent if the risk is of such magnitude as to outweigh what the law regards as the utility of the act or of the particular manner in which it is done. When negligent conduct proximately causes harm, a *prima facie* case is established.

The main defenses to a negligence-based claim are contributory negligence and assumption of risk. Each of these defenses once operated as a complete bar to the negligence claim. Comparative negligence schemes now applicable in almost every state have changed this common-law rule. Under comparative negligence, a contributorily negligent plaintiff is not necessarily precluded from recovery. Obviously, one must be familiar with the applicable comparative negligence scheme. A negligence-based claim in sports may be won or lost over the availability of an assumption of risk defense. As with consent in the intentional tort action, the assumption of risk defense will require the court to determine the nature of the risks that the willing participant assumes.

Recklessness. Recklessness is conduct that creates a higher degree of risk than that created by simple negligence. RESTATEMENT § 500 provides:

> The actor's conduct is in reckless disregard of the safety of another if he does an act or intentionally fails to do an act which it is his duty to the other to do, knowing or having reason to know of facts which would lead a reasonable man to realize, not only that his conduct creates an unreasonable risk of physical harm to another, but also that such risk is substantially greater than that which is necessary to make his conduct negligent.

Unlike the negligence cause of action, the plaintiff's contributory negligence does not operate as a defense to the defendant's reckless conduct. Whether comparative negligence principles apply to a recklessness-based claim is largely an open question. The defense of assumption of risk, however, may be a defense to the recklessness-based cause of action.

Vicarious Liability. The issue of vicarious liability often arises in sports injury cases. An injured participant may want to look beyond the tortfeasor for a defendant to whom the tortfeasor's acts properly can be imputed. Typically, the most significant basis for imputing liability is the employer-employee relationship. Generally, negligence committed by an employee *within the scope of his employment* may be imputed to the employer, who thus becomes vicariously liable for the damages caused. This principle is referred to as *respondeat superior*—a Latin term, which translates as "let the master answer." A recurring question, however, is whether intentional torts are properly viewed as being within the scope of employment. The common-law rule was that such wrongs were not within the scope of employment. The modern trend is that intentional torts can be regarded as being within the scope of employment if it can be shown that the act was closely connected to the employment. There is still considerable split of authority on this issue, and one must be familiar with the case law from the appropriate jurisdiction. Similar problems arise in regard to torts grounded on recklessness.

Negligent Supervision. It should also be remembered that employers might be liable because of their own tortious conduct, as distinguished from the tortious conduct of their employees. This is a newly emerging but increasingly viable cause of action. The thrust of the action is that the employer created unreasonable risks of harm by acting in such a way as to create an atmosphere in which the players believed that violence was an acceptable, if not a desirable, mechanism to ensure winning.

Availability of Punitive Damages. In *Sebastian v. Wood*, 66 N.W.2d 841, 844–45 (Iowa 1954), the Iowa Supreme Court articulated the rationale for permitting punitive damage awards:

> [The] main purpose [of punitive damages] ... is that they are awarded under proper circumstances and conditions as a punishment for the particular party involved and as a warning and an example to him in the future, and to all others who may offend in like manner.... The allowance of such damages is wholly within the function and province of the jury, to be granted or denied in the exercise of a wise discretion, whether the moving cause be effected by malice, oppression, wantonness, recklessness, or gross negligence, and, if allowed, to fix the amount.

Ordinarily, punitive damages are available only if the conduct can be characterized as something worse than negligence. Again, counsel must consult the local jurisdiction for more specific guidance.

A related issue is whether the employer can be held liable for punitive damages in a case where the liability is established under principles of *respondeat superior*. Some states allow punitive damages without any showing of particular wrongdoing on the part of the employer. Other states require a showing of an intentional act or authorization or ratification on the part of the employer. And finally, whether punitive damages are appropriate in a case grounded on negligent supervision is problematic. As already noted, something worse than ordinary negligence is usually a necessary prerequisite for punitive damages. However, an argument could be made that negligent supervision, which creates the risk that the employee will act recklessly or with intent to injure, justifies the imposition of punitive damages.

Bourque v. Duplechin

331 So. 2d 40 (La. Ct. App. 1976)

Watson, Judge.

Plaintiff, Jerome Bourque, Jr., filed this suit to recover damages for personal injuries received in a softball game.... [The defendant was Adrien Duplechin, a member of the opposing team, who inflicted the injury. The trial court rendered judgment in favor of Bourque. Duplechin appealed.]

[Duplechin contends]... that the trial court erred; in not finding that Bourque assumed the risk of injury by participating in the softball game; and in failing to find that Bourque was guilty of contributory negligence. Defendant Duplechin also contends that the trial court erred in finding him negligent and in finding that the injury to plaintiff Bourque occurred four to five feet away from the second base position in the general direction of the pitcher's mound.

On June 9, 1974, Bourque was playing second base on a softball team fielded by Boo Boo's Lounge. Duplechin, a member of the opposing team sponsored by Murray's Steak House and Lounge, had hit the ball and advanced to first base. A teammate of Duplechin's, Steve Pressler, hit a ground ball and Duplechin started to second. The shortstop caught the ground ball and threw it to Bourque who tagged second base and then stepped away from second base to throw the ball to first and execute a double play. After Bourque had thrown the ball to first base, Duplechin ran at full speed into Bourque. As Duplechin ran into Bourque, he brought his left arm up under Bourque's chin. The evidence supports the trial court's factual conclusion that the collision occurred four or five feet away from the second base position in the direction of the pitcher's mound. Duplechin was thrown out of the game by the umpire because of the incident.

Pertinent to the trial court's decision was the following testimony:

Plaintiff Bourque, age 22 at the time of trial, testified that he is 5'7" tall. He was well out of the way when he was hit, standing four or five feet from second base and outside the base line. He knew there was a possibility of a runner sliding into him but had never imagined what actually happened, which he regarded as unbelievable under the circumstances.

Gregory John Laborde, a student at Tulane Law School, testified that he witnessed the incident from the dugout along the first base line and saw Duplechin turn and run directly toward Bourque who was standing four or five feet from second base toward home plate. Duplechin did not attempt to slide or decrease his speed and his left arm came up under Bourque's chin as they collided. Duplechin had to veer from the base path in order to strike Bourque.

Donald Frank Lockwood, baseball coach at USL, testified as an expert witness that: softball is a noncontact sport; in a forced play to second such as this, the accepted way to break up a double play is by sliding.

Steve Pressler, who hit the ground ball that precipitated the incident, testified that the sides were retired as a result, because the collision was a flagrant violation of the rules of the game.

Duplechin admitted that he ran into Bourque while standing up in an attempt to block Bourque's view of first base and keep him from executing a double play. Duplechin also admitted that he was running at full speed when he collided with Bourque, a much smaller man. Duplechin attributed the accident to Bourque's failure to get out of the way.

Oral surgeon John R. Wallace saw Bourque following the accident and said the nature of the injury and the x-rays indicated that it was caused by a blow from underneath the jaw. Dr. Wallace characterized the injury as one that may have been common in football before the use of mouthpieces and face guards.

While other testimony was presented, both cumulative and contradictory, the evidence summarized above provides a reasonable evidentiary basis for the trial court's conclusions.

There is no question that defendant Duplechin's conduct was the cause in fact of the harm to plaintiff Bourque. Duplechin was under a duty to play softball in the ordinary fashion without unsportsmanlike conduct or wanton injury to his fellow players. This duty was breached by Duplechin, whose behavior was, according to the evidence, substandard and negligent. Bourque assumed the risk of being hit by a bat or a ball. [Citations omitted.] Bourque may also have assumed the risk of an injury resulting from standing in the base path and being spiked by someone sliding into second base, a common incident of softball and baseball. However, Bourque did not assume the risk of Duplechin going out of his way to run into him at full speed when Bourque was five feet away from the base. A participant in a game or sport assumes all of the risks incidental to that particular activity which are obvious and foreseeable. A participant does not assume the risk of injury from fellow players acting in an unexpected or unsportsmanlike way with a reckless lack of concern for others participating. [Citations omitted.] Assumption of risk is an affirmative defense which must be proven by a preponderance of the evidence, and the record here supports the trial court's conclusion that Bourque did not assume the risk of Duplechin's negligent act.

There is no evidence in the record to indicate contributory negligence on the part of Bourque....

Duplechin was not motivated by a desire to injure Bourque. Duplechin tried to break up a double play with a reckless disregard of the consequences to Bourque. Duplechin's action was negligent but does not present a situation where the injury was expected or intended....

The trial court awarded plaintiff Bourque $12,000 for his pain and suffering and $1,496.00 for his special damages. There is no dispute about the amount awarded. Bourque's jaw was fractured; his chin required plastic surgery; seven teeth were broken and had to be crowned; and one tooth was replaced by a bridge.

There is no manifest error in the trial court's conclusions which we summarize as follows: plaintiff Bourque's injuries resulted from the negligence of defendant Duplechin; Bourque was not guilty of contributory negligence and did not assume the risk of this particular accident....

For the foregoing reasons, the judgment of the trial court is affirmed....

AFFIRMED.

Nabozny v. Barnhill

334 N.E.2d 258 (Ill. App. Ct. 1975)

ADESKO, JUSTICE.

Plaintiff, Julian Claudio Nabozny, a minor, by Edward J. Nabozny, his father, commenced this action to recover damages for personal injuries allegedly caused by the negligence of defendant, David Barnhill. Trial was before a jury. At the close of plaintiffs case on motion of defendant, the trial court directed a verdict in favor of the defendant. Plaintiff appeals from the order granting the motion.

Plaintiff contends on appeal that the trial judge erred in granting defendant's motion for a directed verdict and that plaintiffs actions as a participant do not prohibit the establishment of a prima facie case of negligence. Defendant argues in support of the trial court's ruling that defendant was free from negligence as a matter of law (lacking a duty to plaintiff) and that defendant was contributorily negligent as a matter of law.... [O]ur statement of facts reflects an examination of all of the evidence viewed in its aspect most favorable to plaintiff.

A soccer match began between two amateur teams at Duke Child's Field in Winnetka, Illinois. Plaintiff was playing the position of goalkeeper for the Hansa team. Defendant was playing the position of forward for the Winnetka team. Members of both teams were of high-school age. Approximately twenty minutes after play had begun, a Winnetka player kicked the ball over the midfield line. Two players, Jim Gallos (for Hansa) and the defendant (for Winnetka) chased the free ball. Gallos reached the ball first. Since he was closely pursued by the defendant, Gallos passed the ball to the plaintiff, the Hansa goalkeeper. Gallos then turned away and prepared to receive a pass from the plaintiff. The plaintiff, in the meantime, went down on his left knee, received the pass, and pulled the ball to his chest. The defendant did not turn away when Gallos did, but continued to run in the direction of the plaintiff and kicked the left side of plaintiffs head causing plaintiff severe injuries.

All of the occurrence witnesses agreed that the defendant had time to avoid contact with plaintiff and that the plaintiff remained at all times within the "penalty area" a rectangular area between the eighteenth yard line and the goal. Four witnesses testified that they saw plaintiff in a crouched position on his left knee inside the penalty zone. Plaintiff testified that he actually had possession of the ball when he was struck by defendant. One witness, Marie Shekem, stated that plaintiff had the ball when he was kicked. All other occurrence witnesses stated that they thought plaintiff was in possession of the ball.

Plaintiff called three expert witnesses. Julius Roth, coach of the Hansa team, testified that the game in question was being played under "F.I.F.A." rules. The three experts agreed that those rules prohibited all players from making contact with the goalkeeper when he is in possession of the ball in the penalty area. Possession is defined in the Chicago area as referring to the goalkeeper having his hands on the ball.

Under "F.I.F.A." rules, any contact with a goalkeeper in possession in the penalty area is an infraction of the rules, even if such contact is unintentional. The goalkeeper is the only member of a team who is allowed to touch a ball in play so long as he remains in the penalty area. The only legal contact permitted in soccer is shoulder to shoulder contact between players going for a ball within playing distance. The three experts agreed that the contact in question in this case should not have occurred. Additionally, goalkeeper head injuries are extremely rare in soccer. As a result of being struck, plaintiff suffered permanent damage to his skull and brain.

The initial question presented by this appeal is whether, under the facts in evidence, such a relationship existed between the parties that the court will impose a legal duty upon one for the benefit of the other. "[M]ore simply, whether the interest of the plaintiff which has suffered invasion was entitled to legal protection at the hands of the defendant."

There is a dearth of case law involving organized athletic competition wherein one of the participants is charged with negligence. There are no such Illinois cases. A number of other jurisdictions prohibit recovery generally for reasons of public policy. We can find no American cases dealing with the game of soccer.

This court believes that the law should not place unreasonable burdens on the free and vigorous participation in sports by our youth. However, we also believe that organized, athletic competition does not exist in a vacuum. Rather, some of the restraints of civilization must accompany every athlete onto the playing field. One of the educational benefits of organized athletic competition to our youth is the development of discipline and self-control.

Individual sports are advanced and competition enhanced by a comprehensive set of rules. Some rules secure the better playing of the game as a test of skill. Other rules are primarily designed to protect participants from serious injury.

For these reasons, this court believes that when athletes are engaged in an athletic competition, all teams involved are trained and coached by knowledgeable personnel; a recognized set of rules governs the conduct of the competition; and a safety rule is contained therein which is primarily designed to protect players from serious injury, a player is then charged with a legal duty to every other player on the field to refrain from conduct proscribed by a safety rule. A reckless disregard for the safety of other players cannot be excused. To engage in such conduct is to create an intolerable and unreasonable risk of serious injury to other participants. We have carefully drawn the rule announced herein in order to control a new field of personal injury litigation. Under the facts presented in the case at bar, we find such a duty clearly arose. Plaintiff was entitled to legal protection at the hands of the defendant. The defendant contends he is immune from tort action for any injury to another player that happens during the course of a game, to which theory we do not subscribe.

It is our opinion that a player is liable for injury in a tort action if his conduct is such that it is either deliberate, willful or with a reckless disregard for the safety of the other player so as to cause injury to that player, the same being a question of fact to be decided by a jury.

Defendant also asserts that plaintiff was contributorily negligent as a matter of law, and, therefore, the trial court's direction of a verdict in defendant's favor was correct. We do not agree. The evidence presented tended to show that plaintiff was in the exercise of ordinary care for his own safety. While playing his position, he remained in the penalty area and took possession of the ball in a proper manner. Plaintiff had no reason to know of the danger created by defendant. Without this knowledge it cannot be said that plaintiff unreasonably exposed himself to such danger or failed to discover or appreciate the risk. The facts in evidence revealed that the play in question was of a kind commonly executed in this sport. Frank Longo, one of the plaintiff's expert witnesses, testified that once the goalkeeper gets possession of the ball in the penalty area, "the instinct should be there [in an opposing player pursuing the ball] through training and knowledge of the rules to avoid contact [with the goalkeeper]." All of plaintiff's expert witnesses agreed that a player charging an opposition goaltender under circumstances similar to those which existed during the play in question should be able to avoid all contact. Furthermore, it is a violation of the rules for a player simply to kick at the ball when a goalkeeper has possession in the penalty area even if no contact is made with the goalkeeper.

... [W]e conclude that the trial court erred in directing a verdict in favor of defendant. It is a fact question for the jury.

This cause, therefore, is reversed and remanded to the Circuit Court of Cook County for a new trial consistent with the views expressed in this opinion.

REVERSED AND REMANDED.

Gauvin v. Clark

537 N.E.2d 94 (Mass. 1989)

Abrams, Justice

At issue is what standard of care participants in an athletic event owe one another. The plaintiff, Robert J. Gauvin, appeals from the Superior Court judgment entered in favor of the defendant, Richard Clark.... We hold that participants in an athletic event owe a duty to other participants to refrain from reckless misconduct and liability may result from injuries caused a player by reason of the breach of that duty. Because of the jury's determination that Clark did not act with reckless misconduct, we conclude that the judge correctly entered judgment for the defendant.

For purposes of this appeal, the parties agree to the following facts. On January 30, 1980, the varsity hockey team of Worcester State College played against the team from Nichols College. Gauvin played center position for the Worcester State College team. Clark played center for the Nichols College team. During the second period, Gauvin was involved in a face-off with Clark, in which the referee dropped the puck, and both men vied for possession. Clark won the face-off. As the puck slid down the ice toward the Nichols College team's net, Gauvin felt a stick in his abdomen. Gauvin saw Clark's hockey stick coming away from Gauvin's abdomen, with the back of the hockey stick, called the "butt-end" protruding from Clark's hands. At trial, Harry Maxfield, a teammate of Gauvin, testified that he saw Clark give Gauvin a shot to the midsection after the puck slid down toward the Nichols goal. The blow to Gauvin's abdomen came after the face-off had been completed. The blow was struck when Gauvin and Clark were no longer competing for the puck.

As a result of the blow to his abdomen, Gauvin was hospitalized and underwent surgery. His spleen was removed. He missed seven weeks of school. Gauvin still suffers from bladder and abdominal pain.

The safety rules which govern the game of hockey prohibit "butt-ending." Butt-ending is the practice of taking the end of the stick which does not come into contact with the puck and driving this part of the stick into another player's body. Butt-ending is unexpected and unsportsmanlike conduct for a hockey game. The rules also prohibit a player, during a face-off, from making any physical contact with his opponent's body by means of his stick, except in the course of playing the puck. Butt-ending is penalized as a major penalty and also results in a disqualification of the penalized player.

Both Gauvin and Clark understood that the game was played according to a recognized set of rules, which prohibited butt-ending Clark understood that the prohibition on butt-ending was designed for the protection of the players. Gauvin's coach, John Laughlin, was knowledgeable about the game of hockey, and had trained Gauvin and his teammates. Clark's coaches, first Alan Kubicki and then the defendant, Mark Bombard, were both knowledgeable about the game of hockey. They had trained Clark and his teammates in the rules of hockey.

The case was tried to a jury. The case was submitted to the jury on special questions. The jury rendered a special verdict in which it answered six specific questions and found the following facts. Clark had butt-ended Gauvin. Clark had violated a safety rule, thus causing Gauvin's injuries. By playing hockey, Gauvin did not consent to the act which caused his injury.

The jury concluded, however, that Clark had not acted willfully, wantonly, or recklessly in causing Gauvin's injury. The jury assessed damages in the amount of $30,000. Based on the jury's answer to the question whether Clark acted wilfully, wantonly, or recklessly, the judge entered judgment in favor of the defendant Clark.

Standard of Care. Gauvin argues that, since the jury found that Clark violated a safety rule, and Clark's action caused Gauvin's injury, judgment should have been entered in favor of Gauvin, despite the fact that the jury found that Clark had not acted recklessly. We do not agree.

The problem of imposing a duty of care on participants in a sports competition is a difficult one. Players, when they engage in sport, agree to undergo some physical contacts which could amount to assault and battery absent the players' consent. The courts are wary of imposing wide tort liability on sports participants, lest the law chill the vigor of athletic competition. Nevertheless, "some of the restraints of civilization must accompany every athlete on to the playing field." *Nabozny v. Barnhill*, 31 Ill. App. 3d 212, 215, 334 N.E.2d 258 (1975)....

The majority of jurisdictions which have considered this issue have concluded that personal injury cases arising out of an athletic event must be predicated on reckless disregard of safety. *See, e.g., Hackbart v. Cincinnati Bengals, Inc.*, 601 F.2d 516, 524 (10th Cir. 1979); *Nabozny v. Barnhill, supra*....

We adopt this standard. Allowing the imposition of liability in cases of reckless disregard of safety diminishes the need for players to seek retaliation during the game or future games. *See Hackbart v. Cincinnati Bengals, Inc., supra* at 521. Precluding the imposition of liability in cases of negligence without reckless misconduct furthers the policy that "[v]igorous and active participation in sporting events should not be chilled by the threat of litigation." *Kabella v. Bouschelle*, [100 N.M. 461, 465, 672 P.2d 290 (1983)].

Gauvin reads the leading case of *Nabozny v. Barnhill, supra*, to mean that Clark should be held liable, because the jury found that Clark had violated a safety rule, even though the jury found that Clark had not acted wilfully, wantonly, or recklessly. Some of *Nabozny*'s language might seem to imply that all that is needed to establish an actionable tort is breach of a safety rule. However, "we see *Nabozny* as establishing the standard of conduct to be willfulness or a reckless disregard of safety...." The judge below applied the proper rule of law in entering judgment in favor of Clark when the jury found that Clark had not acted recklessly.

Notes and Comments

1. If "participant" is defined broadly, it could include referees, cheerleaders, and coaches. A tort case against a referee might well involve a theory of negligent supervision. *Carabba v. Anacortes School District No. 103*, 435 P.2d 936 (Wash. 1967) (referee's negligence in failing to detect an illegal wrestling hold). For example, a referee who permits a boxing match to continue when a reasonable referee would stop it might be named as defendant in a lawsuit by the injured boxer. On the other hand, a referee attacked by a disgruntled participant might initiate a lawsuit of his own on a battery theory. For a recent article on torts against sports officials, see Christopher M. Chiafullo, *From Personal Foul to Personal Attack: How Sports Officials Are the Target of Physical Abuse from Players, Coaches, and Fans Alike*, 8 SETON HALL J. SPORT L. 201–28 (1998). For a list of ways sports officials can shield themselves from liability, see Richard J. Hunter, Jr., *An "Insider's" Guide to the Legal Liability of Sports Contest Officials*, 15 MARQ. SPORTS L. REV. 369 (2005).

The liability of the NFL as a result of referee negligence has emerged in the area of participant versus participant tort liability. On December 19, 1999, offensive tackle Orlando Brown suffered an injury when hit by a referee's penalty marker during a professional football game. Alan Rubin, *Ref Blamed for Eye Injury*, N.Y. Daily News, Mar. 30, 2001. Although the referee undeniably caused the injury, Brown only brought suit against the NFL. Plaintiff's Petition at p. 1, *Brown v. NFL*, 219 F. Supp. 2d 372 (S.D.N.Y. 2002). Brown could conceivably recover on a negligence theory if the referee acted negligently and the NFL, as the referee's employer, is liable under the *respondeat superior* doctrine. Additionally, the NFL could be liable for negligence if it failed to properly train its professional game officials.

2. The liability of coaches deserves special attention. In a negligence-based cause of action, the issue may be whether the coach fulfilled the duty to use reasonable care in protecting the athletes. In a series of reported cases, coaches were deemed to have fallen below that standard. Liability has been imposed, for example, when a coach plays an injured player, *Morris v. Union High School Dist. A*, 294 P. 998 (Wash. 1931), fails to direct the movement of an injured player properly, *Welch v. Dunsmuir Joint Union School Dist.*, 326 P.2d 633 (Cal. App. 1958), fails to acquire proper medical attention for heat stroke, *Mogabgab v. Orleans Parish School Bd.*, 239 So. 2d 456 (La. Ct. App. 1970), and fails to instruct adequately on safe techniques for participation, *Stehn v. Bernarr MacFadden Founds., Inc.*, 434 F.2d 811 (6th Cir. 1970). It is not difficult to imagine other contexts in which a coach might be liable for an injury to a player. Two former New York high school football players were awarded $25,000 each in a suit against the coach and the school district as a result of the coach's practice of hitting players in the head and body with a tackling dummy during practices. The nature of the player-coach relationship presents many possibilities for suits by players. See J. Weistart & C. Lowell, The Law of Sports §8.06 (1979) for a partial list of these cases. *See also* Ray Yasser, *Liability for Sports Injuries*, *in* Law of Professional and Amateur Sports §14.05 (Uberstine ed., 1998); Anthony S. McCaskey & Kenneth W. Biedzynski, *A Guide to the Legal Liability of Coaches for a Sports Participant's Injuries*, 6 Seton Hall J. Sport L. 7–125 (1996); Janice Brown, *Legislators Strike Out: Volunteer Little League Coaches Should Not Be Immune from Tort Liability*, 7 Seton Hall J. Sport L. 559 (1997); and *McGurk v. Lincoln Community School District*, 679 N.E.2d 71 (Ill. App. Ct. 1997).

Colleges and universities are potentially liable for the torts of their employees, which includes coaches, under the universally recognized principles of *respondeat superior* when the employee is acting "within the scope of employment." The institution might also be liable for its own negligence in failing to take reasonable precautions against the risk of foreseeable life-threatening injuries. In *Kleinknecht v. Gettysburg College*, 989 F.2d 1360 (3d Cir. 1993), the parents of a college lacrosse player who died of a heart attack during a practice session sued the college. The district court granted summary judgment for the college. The court of appeals reversed, noting that the college owed a duty of care based on the special relationship that exists between a college and its athletes. The court of appeals thought that the issue of whether the college took reasonable precautions to protect the student-athlete was a jury issue. The Third Circuit's decision provides an excellent review and analysis of many of the issues raised in connection with the duty owed by a college to its student-athletes.

3. Many fairly common situations in sport present interesting tort issues. Consider, for example, the following situations (assume the victim has suffered serious injury):

a. the "brushback" pitch; or worse, retaliatory beanball;
b. the response to the brushback, where the batter runs towards the pitcher and punches him, or strikes him with the bat;
c. the vintage baseball player's tantrum, in which the umpire has dirt kicked upon him, or tobacco juice sprayed in his face;
d. the "spikes-up" slide;
e. the "cheap-shot" in football, where a player is hit either out-of-bounds or after the whistle;
f. the "clean but brutal" hit, where the tackler intends to injure a vulnerable opponent;
g. the "low-bridge" in basketball, where the perpetrator runs under the airborne opponent;
h. the flagrant use of elbows to clear space after securing a rebound.

4. As noted in the material on "recklessness," courts have at times gone out of their way to distinguish the cause of action in the contact as opposed to the non-contact sports injury case by stating that "participants in bodily contact games such as basketball assume greater risks than do golfers and others in non-physical contact sports." *Oswald v. Township High School Dist. No. 214*, 406 N.E.2d 157 (Ill. App. Ct. 1980). There have been a multitude of golf cases in which action was brought for a variety of unique and innovative ways of inflicting serious injury (and not so serious general bonking) on fellow players, caddies, bystanders, and other innocent victims with the various paraphernalia of the game. Do you think that any of these cases belong in the context of a discussion involving participant-to-participant liability in sports? Do you think golf should be considered more of a game (like chess) than a sport (like football)? For a comprehensive survey of golf cases, see Ray Yasser, *In the Heat of Competition: Tort Liability of One Participant to Another: Why Can't Participants Be Required to Be Reasonable?*, 5 SETON HALL J. SPORT L. 267, n.77 (1995).

5. Although *Bourque* indicates that a negligence-based claim of action is appropriate in the sports setting, the trend is away from the negligence claim. In fact, *Bourque* suggests as much when the court points out that the sports participant assumes "all risks incidental to that particular activity which are obvious and foreseeable" but does not assume "the risk of injury from fellow players acting in an unexpected or unsportsmanlike way with a reckless lack of concern for others

participating." The thrust of *Bourque* is that the sports participant invariably assumes the risks created by the coparticipant's negligence but not necessarily by his recklessness. *Bourque* is really more accurately viewed as a case in which the defendant was liable because he was reckless and not because he was negligent.

6. The sports participant clearly does not enjoy talismanic immunity from tort liability. The obvious goal of any practitioner is to distinguish which cases have a reasonable chance of success. The materials in this section are ultimately designed to assist the practitioner in drawing that distinction. It does appear, however, that sports activity is one area of human behavior in which the participants are insulated from liability for ordinary negligence. Perhaps this is one thing that makes sports a special and unique form of human experience—participants are free to be unreasonable.

Nabozny and *Gauvin* articulated the view that the simple negligence claim should fail. Although negligence was pleaded in *Nabozny*, the court opinion stressed that "a player is liable if his conduct is such that it is either deliberate, willful or with a reckless disregard for the safety of the other player." Other cases include: *Dotzler v. Tuttle*, 449 N.W.2d 774 (Neb. 1990) (participants are not liable for ordinary negligence but only conduct that is reckless); *Marchetti v. Kalish*, 559 N.E.2d 699 (Ohio 1990) (reckless disregard is the proper standard for both adult and child participants in recreational and sports activities); *Ginsberg v. Hontas*, 545 So. 2d 1154 (La. Ct. App. 1989) (duty of participants is to refrain from reckless conduct); *Landrum v. Gonzalez*, 629 N.E.2d 710 (Ill. App. Ct. 1994) (plaintiff could not recover since he had not shown willful or wanton conduct on the part of the defendant); *Ordway v. Superior Court (Casella)*, 198 Cal. App. 3d 98 (1988) (jockey assumes risk of negligence but not of recklessness). *See also Kiley v. Patterson*, 763 A.2d 583 (R.I. 2000); *Jaworski v. Kiernan*, 696 A.2d 332 (Conn. 1997); *Pfister v. Shusta*, 657 N.E.2d 1013 (Ill. 1995); *Hearon v. May*, 540 N.W.2d 124 (Neb. 1995); *McKichan v. St. Louis Hockey Club, L.P.*, 967 S.W.2d 209 (Mo. Ct. App. 1998); and *Sicard v. University of Dayton*, 660 N.E.2d 1241 (Ohio Ct. App. 1995).

There are jurisdictions that have allowed recovery on the basis of negligence. For example, in a 1993 decision, the Wisconsin Supreme Court ruled that liability in the sports injury case may be based on negligence, depending on the specific circumstances. In *Lestina v. West Bend Mutual Insurance Co.*, 501 N.W.2d 28, 33 (Wis. 1993), Robert F. Lestina, the plaintiff, was injured in a collision with the defendant, Leopold Jerger. Lestina was playing an offensive position for his recreational soccer team and Jerger was the goalkeeper for the opposing team. Jerger, the defendant, apparently ran out of the goal area and collided with the plaintiff. The plaintiff alleged that the defendant "slide tackled" him in order to prevent him from scoring. The plaintiff seriously injured his left knee and leg in the collision.

For a time, New Jersey also adopted the negligence standard for sports injury cases in *Crawn v. Campo*, 630 A.2d 368 (N.J. Super. Ct. App. Div. 1993). In *Crawn*, the appellate court held that ordinary negligence, rather than reckless conduct, was the appropriate standard to be applied in a participant-to-participant sports injury case. The Supreme Court of New Jersey, relying on *Nabozny*, rejected this reasoning and held that the duty of care required in establishing liability in recreational sports should be based on a standard of recklessness or intentional conduct, rather than negligence. *Crawn v. Campo*, 643 A.2d 600, 607 (N.J. 1994).

In the professional arena, Connecticut joined the ranks of those jurisdictions allowing a negligence cause of action in *Babych v. McRae*, 567 A.2d 1269 (Conn. Super. Ct. 1989). The plaintiff, Wayne Babych, alleged that the defendant, Ken McRae, a fellow professional hockey player, struck the plaintiff across his right knee with a hockey stick during a game, causing the plaintiff to suffer personal injuries and financial losses. In holding that negligence is a legally sufficient cause of action when one professional sports participant is injured by another, the court rejected the New York decision in *Turcotte v. Fell*, 502 N.E.2d 964 (N.Y. 1986), which held that negligence was not actionable when one professional sports participant injured another. The Connecticut court in *Babych* found that there was no analogous case law barring a negligence cause of action in sports participant-to-participant cases.

A number of states appear to recognize negligence as a viable cause of action in the "heat of competition" context. In almost every area of our lives we are exposed to liability if we act in a negligent manner and cause harm to others. For the most part, our social compact says that unreasonable conduct that causes physical harm is actionable. This rule of liability is firmly grounded in social policy. The exposure to liability serves to deter unreasonably risky behavior and to compensate the injured.

Does it make sense, then, to insulate a negligent sports participant from liability to a physically injured coparticipant? Is sport deserving of such solicitude? Are there really convincing policy reasons to insulate a sports participant from liability for physical harm caused by negligence?

The courts that require an injured sports participant to prove recklessness (and thus protect the "merely" negligent actor) do so on the theory that sport needs "breathing room." But the evidence is accumulating that, on every level of competition, participants need to be restrained and not emboldened. From kids' sports to professional sports, it sometimes seems that sportsmanship, fair play, and reasonable restraint are lost values. Grotesque showmanship, unethical means to win, and reckless unconcern mar the landscape of sport. Do you think that sports participants need breathing room or should they have their feet held to the liability fire? For more on whether sports violence should be civil or criminal, and if incidents should be left to the leagues or the law, see Matthew P. Barry, Richard L. Fox & Clark Jones, *Judicial Opinion on the Criminality of Sports Violence in the United States*, 15 SETON HALL J. SPORTS & ENT. L. 1 (2005). *See also* Ray Yasser, *In the Heat of Competition: Tort Liability of One Participant to Another: Why Can't Participants Be Required to be Reasonable?* 5 SETON HALL J. SPORTS & ENT. L. 1 (1995).

The outcome to the litigation might often depend on the availability of the defenses. In the recklessness context, the primary defense is akin to assumption of risk. It is interesting to note, however, that other defenses to a recklessness-based cause of action have not been clearly delineated. The distinctions between recklessness and negligence and between recklessness and intentions are not unambiguously clear. As Oliver Wendell Holmes noted:

> If the manifest probability of harm is very great... we say that it is done intentionally; if not so great but still considerable, we say that the harm is done negligently; if there is no apparent danger, we call it mischance.

Holmes, *Privilege, Malice, and Intent*, 8 Harv. L. Rev. 1 (1894).

We might go on to say today that if the manifest probability of harm is not very great, but quite considerable, it is recklessness. The distinctions are not clear, and recklessness has only recently emerged as a separate and distinct cause of action. The available defenses to the recklessness claim, therefore, have not been clearly articulated. A practitioner would be well-advised to plead the well-established intentional tort defenses of consent, self-defense, defense of others, and defense of property, along with the well-established negligence defenses of assumption of risk and contributory negligence, and let the court decide. *See* Ray Yasser, *In the Heat of Competition: Tort Liability of One Participant to Another: Why Can't Participants Be Required to Be Reasonable?*, 5 Seton Hall J. Sport L. 267 (1995), and Barbara Svoranos, *Fighting? It's All in a Day's Work on the Ice: Determining the Appropriate Standard of a Hockey Player's Liability to Another Player*, 7 Seton Hall J. Sport L. 487–512 (1997); Dean Richardson, *Player Violence: An Essay on Torts and Sports*, 15 Stan. L. & Pol'y Rev. 133 (2004).

7. **Problem**. You represent Kermit Washington and the Los Angeles Lakers in the following litigation. Do you recommend that the case be settled? How is it likely to be resolved?

The plaintiff in the case is Rudy Tomjanovich, a veteran professional basketball player, employed by the Houston Rockets, Inc., a professional basketball franchise based in Houston, Texas. The defendant is California Sports, Inc., which does business as the Los Angeles Lakers professional basketball team. The plaintiff's cause of action arose out of an altercation that took place during a basketball game between the Lakers and the Rockets. During the course of the game Tomjanovich was punched in the face by Kermit Washington, a Los Angeles Lakers player.

The undisputed facts reveal that the incident began with a fight between Kermit Washington and another Rockets player, Kevin Kunnert. A film of the incident showed that Washington grabbed Kunnert and blows were exchanged. Tomjanovich then approached and Washington punched him in the face with enough force to leave Tomjanovich with a fractured skull, nose and jaw, a brain concussion, facial lacerations, leakage of spinal fluid, and other serious complications.

The plaintiff offered a number of theories to support a cause of action against the Lakers. He alleged that Kermit Washington's attack was tortious and that the Lakers were vicariously liable for Washington's torts. The plaintiff contended that Washington was negligent, reckless, and guilty of intentional wrong-doing. He asserted that no matter how Washington's tort was characterized, the Lakers were vicariously liable under the theory of respondeat superior. Tomjanovich also alleged that the Lakers were themselves negligent in their supervision of Washington. In this regard, the plaintiff claimed that the Lakers failed to control, train, and discipline Washington. Punitive damages were requested for all causes of action.

Along with a general denial, the Lakers alleged, by way of affirmative defense, that insofar as the negligence-based cause of action was concerned, Tomjanovich was contributorily negligent and assumed the risk. They further alleged that the recklessness-based cause of action was barred by Tomjanovich's reckless indifference to his own welfare and that the battery cause of action was defeated by the privileges of consent and self-defense.

The trial lasted 10 days, during which time the plaintiff and defendant introduced testimony from eyewitnesses and experts, and the jury viewed and reviewed films and photographs of the events surrounding the occurrence. What follows is the gist of what was established by the massive amount of evidence.

The plaintiff's evidence tended to establish that Tomjanovich was acting as a peacemaker when he approached Washington and Kunnert, who were scuffling. Tomjanovich appeared to be unprepared for the punch that floored him and was unable to defend himself from the blow. It appeared that he ran right into the punch. It was the kind of a blow that was unexpected in professional basketball; it was not customary and it was excessive in nature. Testimony was received concerning the vicious nature of the blow, with Kareem Abdul-Jabbar summing it up best by saying that, when he heard the impact of the punch, he thought that it sounded "like a watermelon being dropped on a cement floor." The plaintiff also offered evidence establishing the extensive damage caused by the blow. Evidence of the defendant's wealth was received as relevant to the issue of punitive damages. On the negligent supervision cause of action, Tomjanovich introduced evidence showing that the Lakers in fact encouraged overly aggressive play, that they did not discipline and, in fact, paid the fines for players penalized for such play, that they encouraged Washington to be featured in a Sports Illustrated article on basketball's "enforcers," and that, subsequent to the Washington-Tomjanovich incident, they "ratified" Washington's conduct by paying his league-imposed fine and by not disciplining him.

The defendant's evidence tended to show that professional basketball was an inherently "physical" game in which fights and scuffles were foreseeable. The Lakers' version of the incident was designed to show that Tomjanovich did not act reasonably in protecting himself, that he knew or should have known of the risks, and that Washington reasonably believed he was in danger when he glimpsed Tomjanovich approaching rapidly towards him. The Lakers presented evidence that they were indeed attempting to deal with the problem of on-court violence, and they threatened overly aggressive players with the loss of playing time and even with the loss of their spot on the roster, but that to a certain extent, violence in pro basketball was to be expected, because, to a limited extent, it was an intrinsic part of the game.

8. In *Murphy v. Steeplechase Amusement Company, Inc.*, 166 N.E. 173, 174 (N.Y. 1929), Judge Cardozo stated: "One who takes part in... a sport accepts the dangers that inhere in it so far as they are obvious and necessary." Is this helpful? What dangers are "obvious and necessary" to a professional hockey player? To a professional football player? To a college football player? To a Little League baseball player? To participants in extreme sports? *See* Denise M. Yerger, *High-Risk Recreation: The Thrill That Creates a Statutory and Judicial Spectrum of Response and Drives the Dichotomy in Participant and Provider Liability*, 38 SUFFOLK U. L. REV. 687 (2005); David Horton, *Extreme Sports and Assumption of Risk*, 38 U.S.F. L. REV. 599 (2004). In "the fireman's chair" case, *Arnold v. Schmeiser*, 309 N.Y.S.2d 699 (1970), it was held that the plaintiff assumed the risk that his fellow participants would fail to catch him when they tossed him in the air but that he did not assume the risk that his fellow participants would *refuse* to catch him. The case is an apt metaphor of the nature of the risks assumed. For more on assumption of risk in high school, college, and professional sports, see Keya Denner, *Taking One for the Team: The Role of Assumption of the Risk in Sports Torts Cases*, 14 SETON HALL J. SPORTS & ENT. L. 209 (2004).

9. In *Benitez v. New York City Board of Education*, 530 N.Y.S.2d 825 (N.Y. App. Div. 1988), a high school football player sued the school board on what can be loosely described as a "negligent scheduling" theory. Benitez suffered a fractured spine and a herniated disc when he was hit by an opponent during a high school football game. His suit alleged that the coaches and administrators were negligent in allowing the mismatch to occur. The jury awarded Benitez $946,000 for loss of earnings and $304,000 for pain and suffering but reduced the award by 30% as a result of Benitez's own negligence. On appeal, the court reversed. The court held that a board of education was obligated to exercise ordinary reasonable care to protect student-athletes in extracurricular sports from "unassumed, concealed or unreasonably increased risks." According to the court, Benitez failed to show that his injury resulted from a breach of that duty.

10. In *Avila v. Citrus Community College Dist.*, 131 P.3d 383 (Cal. 2006), a college baseball player brought a negligence cause of action against the opposing team's school when he was intentionally hit in the head by a pitch during a scrimmage. The California Supreme Court held that the host college had a duty not to increase the risks in the game. The court observed that being hit in the head by an intentional pitch was a risk inherent in baseball and that the rival college had not increased the risks by failing to stop its pitcher from intentionally throwing at the plaintiff. Accordingly, the case was dismissed. Based upon your review of the material in this chapter, do you believe this ruling is correct? Assume the league has adopted the

following rule: "The Pitcher shall not intentionally pitch at the batter. If, in the umpire's judgement, such a violation occurs, the umpire may elect either to:

1. Expel the pitcher, or the manager and the pitcher, from the game, or
2. May warn the pitcher and the manager of both teams that another such pitch will result in the immediate expulsion of that pitcher (or a replacement) and the manager."

11. In *Kavanagh v. Trustees of Boston University*, 795 N.E.2d 1170 (Mass. 2003), a basketball player brought a negligence suit against Boston University and its coach after being punched in the face during a game by a BU player. The plaintiff claimed that BU was vicariously liable for the actions of its player and that the college and the coach acted negligently by not preventing the act. The court noted that the player who punched Kavanagh was not an agent or employee of the college. Furthermore, the court noted that neither BU nor its coach owed a duty to Kavanagh because there was no special relationship between the parties. The court remarked that even if such a duty was present, the assault and battery was not foreseeable. The plaintiff's contention that the coach's aggressive style on the sidelines incited his player to attack also failed because the coach's actions did not amount to the requisite standard of recklessness.

12. **Problem:** Barbara Buchan was injured while participating in the World Trials for Women, which were held in southern California. The World Trials were conducted by the United States Cycling Federation (USCF), which is the national governing body for amateur cycling in the United States, sanctioned as such by the United States Olympic Committee.

Barbara was, at the time of her injury, a licensed Category II racer. Category II is the highest category for women within the USCF. In order to participate in this event, or any other USCF event, it was necessary for Barbara to hold a valid racing license issued by the USCF. This was a point-to-point race from Malibu to Newbury Park, during which a major spill occurred involving as many as 20 racers. Evidence was presented at the time of trial that the cause of the spill was a first-year, inexperienced, and unqualified racer from San Diego. Barbara's counsel proved that the USCF was negligent in permitting this woman to participate in the race and that she caused this spill, which resulted in severe brain injuries to Barbara. Barbara's counsel further contended that the helmet rule of the USCF which existed at the time was inadequate and that the USCF was negligent for not implementing a better helmet rule prior to that time. The rule allowed the wearing of the so-called "hairnet" helmet, which the evidence demonstrated is essentially worthless.

Counsel for the USCF has argued that this verdict potentially opens some sort of "floodgate," thereby allowing a torrent of litigation in similar cases. They have filed their Notice of Appeal. Discuss whether the USCF has any compelling arguments on appeal.

13. The validity of waivers of liability in the context of sports continues to be a significant issue. A waiver of liability is essentially a pre-injury contract in which a sport participant expressly agrees to release (*i.e.* not hold legally responsible) a school district from liability for injury during athletic activities. Many courts have held that waivers are invalid as against public policy. Contrast *Wagenblast v. Odessa School Dist.*, 758 P.2d 968 (Wash. 1988) (written releases that released the school district from the consequences of all future school district negligence required to be signed by students and their parents before being allowed to engage in intercollegiate athletics activities held to violate public policy) with *Sharon v. City of Newton*, 769 N.E.2d 738 (Mass. 2002) (enforcement of release signed by 16-year-old student's father as a condition of cheerleading participation did not violate public policy). In the wake of *Kirton v. Fields*, 961 So. 2d 1127 (Fla. Dist. Ct. App. 2007), holding that waivers signed by minors were invalid, the Florida Legislature passed a bill in 2010 that validated waivers signed by a minor and a parent prior to participation.

B. The Spectator as Plaintiff

Spectators at sporting events are exposed to special risks. Racing cars occasionally hurtle over barriers and injure spectators. Foul balls, errant pucks, and misplayed golf balls strike spectators with some regularity. Spectators injure one another in their quest for souvenirs. On occasion, the spectator-heckler is injured by the short-tempered participant. This section focuses on those instances in which the spectator becomes a plaintiff in a civil suit.

Of primary concern here is the spectator's cause of action against the owner of the sports facility in which the event takes place. The owner's duty of care depends on the status of the plaintiff, who is traditionally categorized as a trespasser, a licensee, or an invitee. RESTATEMENT § 329 defines a *trespasser* as "a person who enters or remains upon land in possession of another without a privilege to do so created by the possessor's consent or otherwise." RESTATEMENT § 330 defines a *licensee* as "a person who is privileged to enter or remain on land only by virtue of the possessor's consent." RESTATEMENT § 332 defines an *invitee* as either a "public invitee" or a "business visitor." A public invitee is "a person who is invited to enter or remain on land as a member of the public for a purpose for which the land is held open to the public." A business visitor is "a person who is invited to enter or remain on land for a purpose directly or indirectly connected with business dealings with the possessor of land."

The trespasser is the least-protected class of plaintiffs. The traditional common-law rule was that the possessor owed no duty to trespassers to make the premises safe. The only duty owed was to refrain from intentionally harming the trespasser. Over the years, a number of exceptions have been recognized. Although the precise nature of the duty owed varies from state to state, it is fair to say that a somewhat greater duty is owed when the presence of the trespasser is known, when the trespass is frequent over a limited portion of the land, or when the trespasser is a child endangered by an artificial condition (the so-called attractive nuisance doctrine).

The basic duty owed to a licensee is to warn of known dangers. The duty owed to an invitee is greater, encompassing those dangers that a reasonable inspection would have revealed. Furthermore, as far as an invitee is concerned, a warning is not sufficient if the condition is very dangerous. Thus, there is a duty to repair highly dangerous conditions to protect the invitee.

The ticket-holding spectator would clearly be an invitee to whom the highest duty of care is owed. A question arises as to the status of those who enter the facility without a ticket—for example, a spectator who enters at halftime of a game when the ticket-takers go off duty and the gates are opened. No reported cases address this issue. Rational arguments could be made that such a spectator fits any of the three categories.

Assumption of risk plays a vital role in cases involving injuries to spectators. Through a long line of cases, courts have generally agreed that spectators at sporting events assume the risks commonly associated with observing the sport. Weistart and Lowell, referring to this rule as the common knowledge rule, at 951, state that "spectators at sports activities assume, as a matter of law, all of the ordinary and inherent risks of the sport which they are observing." Thus, the baseball fan struck by a foul ball cannot recover. But the common knowledge rule is not so easy in cases involving less obvious assumptions of risk. The material that follows examines these cases, along with others, in which the defendant is not the owner of the sports facility but, rather, is another spectator or a participant.

Notes and Comments

1. **Auto racing**. The danger involved in auto racing has been an important factor in its popularity. The spectators, of course, do not expect to share in this danger. The majority of American jurisdictions hold that the promoters of an auto race must provide adequate barriers for the protection of spectators. In *Saari v. State*, the court stated that because risk to spectators and participants from automobile races is high, "the standard of care must likewise be high. One who conducts or sponsors such an event is... negligent unless he uses a high degree of care to provide adequate safeguards against reasonably foreseeable dangers to spectators and enforces the observation of such safeguards and precautions both by participants and spectators." 119 N.Y.S.2d 507, 516 (Ct. Cl. 1953). *See also Goade v. Elks Lodge 789*, 213 Cal. App. 2d 189 (1963) (no protection); *Capital Raceway Promotions, Inc. v. Smith*, 322 A.2d 238 (Md. Ct. Spec. App. 1974); *Regan v. Seattle*, 458 P.2d 12 (Wash. 1969) (hay bales not sufficient in "go cart" race); *Kaiser v. Cook*, 227 N.W.2d 50 (Wis. 1975) (lack of sufficient seats to properly seat and protect all spectators); *Fitchett v. Buchanan*, 472 P.2d

623 (Wash. 1970) (failure to provide barriers of sufficient strength to protect spectator). Are the dangers of auto racing obvious enough to the spectator? The majority of courts have held that injured spectators do not assume the risk. A landmark case in this area is *Arnold v. State*, 148 N.Y.S. 479 (N.Y. App. Div. 1914), in which a racer crashed through a wooden fence, killing 11 spectators and injuring several more. The court held that the State of New York, the race's sponsor, had breached its positive duty to guard against the possibility of a car leaving the track and had to compensate the victims for their injuries. Assumption of risk was not an effective defense. *Alden v. Norwood Arena, Inc.*, 124 N.E.2d 505 (Mass. 1955), confirmed this position in holding that the stock-car race promoter owed spectators a duty of due care to see that the premises were reasonably safe for their intended use and to warn of non-obvious dangers. Being hit by a flying automobile wheel was not a risk obvious to the spectator of ordinary intelligence; therefore, spectators who were injured while attending the stock car race did not assume, as a matter of law, the risk of such injury. *Compare Blake v. Fried*, 95 A.2d 360 (Pa. Super. Ct. 1953).

A minority of jurisdictions have concluded that if the race track has made some provision for the safety of spectators, the spectator will be charged with assumption of risk. *Barrett v. Faltico*, 117 F. Supp. 95 (E.D. Wash. 1953) (spectator in dangerous spot); *Kelley v. Sportsman's Speedway*, 80 So. 2d 785 (Miss. 1955) (in pits without permission); *Grahn v. Northwest Sport*, 310 P.2d 306 (Or. 1957) (on racetrack at wrong time); *Mercurio v. Burrillville Racing Association*, 187 A.2d 665 (R.I. 1963) (taking pictures in wrong place). In *Blake v. Fried*, 95 A.2d 360 (Pa. Super. Ct. 1953), the operators of a stock-car race track had encircled the track with a heavy guard rail three feet high and installed a reinforced wire-mesh fence 14 feet high around the track. The court held that because the defendants' conduct was reasonable in light of what they could anticipate, they were not negligent. Therefore, they were not liable for the injuries sustained by grandstand spectators when a wheel came off a stock car, hit a guard rail, and bounced over the fence into the grandstand.

2. **Golf.** The game of golf has generated an enormous amount of litigation, second only to baseball. *Outlaw v. Bituminous Ins. Co.*, 357 So. 2d 1350 (La. Ct. App. 1978) (adult owed child golfer duty not to drive ball in child's direction in playing through); *Carrigan v. Roussell*, 426 A.2d 517 (N.J. Super. Ct. App. Div. 1981) (duty to give warning when ball starting to hook); *Jackson v. Livingston Country Club, Inc.*, 391 N.Y.S.2d 234 (N.Y. App. Div. 1977) (driving without warning when plaintiff was walking away from green directly in intended flight of ball). Golf litigation arises under three basic sets of circumstances. First, the golfer who hits the ball in the intended direction is held to two duties: to make sure no one is within the area toward which he is aiming; and to give an audible warning prior to hitting the ball. Warning given after the ball is hit is insufficient. *See Biskup v. Hoffman*, 287 S.W. 865 (Mo. Ct. App. 1926). The second situation occurs when the defendant's shot "hooks" or "slices" in a completely unanticipated direction and strikes someone on the golf course. When this happens, the defendant who gives a warning as soon as the shot begins to deviate from

the intended direction is not liable, and the injured plaintiff is held to have assumed the risk. *See Houston v. Escott*, 85 F. Supp. 59 (D. Del. 1949); *Carrigan v. Roussell*, 426 A.2d 517 (N.J. Super. Ct. App. Div. 1981). Finally, if a golf ball injures a person who is not on the golf course, such as on an adjoining roadway, the defendant owner of the golf course has exposure to liability. *See Westborough Country Club v. Palmer*, 204 F.2d 143 (8th Cir. 1953); *Townsley v. State*, 164 N.Y.S.2d 840 (Ct. Cl. 1957).

For a more complete survey of golf cases revealing a wide range of approaches to injuries caused by skilled and unskilled players, see Ray Yasser, *In the Heat of Competition: Tort Liability of One Participant to Another; Why Can't Participants Be Required to Be Reasonable?*, 5 SETON HALL J. SPORT L. 253 (1995); Michael A. Shadiack, *Does a Golf Course Owner and/or Operator Owe a Duty of Care to Their Patrons to Protect Them from Lightning Strikes*, 8 SETON HALL J. SPORT L. 301 (1998).

3. **Wrestling**. The sport of wrestling has created a surprising amount of litigation. *See, e.g.*, *Davis v. Jones*, 112 S.E.2d 3 (Ga. Ct. App. 1959) (wrestler dove through rope and injured timekeeper); *Parker v. Warren*, 503 S.W.2d 938 (Tenn. Ct. App. 1973) (collapse of bleachers at a wrestling match). In *Dusckiewicz v. Carter*, a spectator sued a promoter for injuries sustained when a wrestler was thrown from the ring into the spectator's lap. 52 A.2d 788 (Vt. 1947). The Vermont court, in holding that the defendant's motion for a directed verdict should not have been granted, stated: "An invitee at a place of amusement ordinarily assumes the risk of an obvious danger or of one that is a matter of common knowledge; conversely, such a person does not assume the risk of a hidden or undisclosed danger, not of common knowledge, in the absence of warning or personal knowledge." *Id.* at 791. Thus, the court followed the majority rule by holding that this type of risk is one that a spectator does not assume.

4. **Vicarious liability**. A wholly separate category of cases involves situations in which the spectator is injured by the arguably tortious conduct of a participant. *Payne v. Maple Leaf Gardens, Ltd.*, 1 D.L.R. 369 (Ont. Can. 1949) (plaintiff struck by hockey stick during a fight between players could not recover from the team since fighting is outside the scope of employment). *Bonetti v. Double Play Tavern*, 126 Cal. App. 2d Supp. 848 (Dep't Super. Ct. 1954), involved an action against the sponsor of a baseball team for personal injuries sustained by the plaintiff. Evidence at the trial established that the operators of Double Play Tavern sponsored a semi-pro baseball team, appropriately named "Double Play." In the bottom of the ninth inning of the league championship game, with the score tied at zero and the bases loaded, Paul Hjort, the Double Play left fielder, dropped a high pop fly, and the winning run was scored. In anger, Hjort picked up the ball and threw it out of the park in the direction of a gas station. The plaintiff, who was walking across the station property to get into her fiancé's car, was struck on the side of her head and knocked to the ground.

The court held that the defendant, the Double Play Tavern, was liable because "[i]n practically all jurisdictions the law is now settled that a master is liable for the willful and malicious acts of his servant when done within the scope of his employment." *Id.* at 754. In reasoning that Hjort's acts were within the scope of his employment, the court stated:

> Where the injury is suffered from a baseball thrown immediately after the player had dropped it, with the consequent loss of the game and championship, at a time when all the players were at a competitively high nervous pitch, in a sport where "hustle" and "fight" are fostered and encouraged, it is not too difficult to conclude that a player might well, in frustration, take the ball and heave it out of the lot, and that such conduct might well be expected by the master. The breaking of clubs, bats and sticks by excited players is a matter of common knowledge to all sportswise persons.

Id. at 754.

In a vigorous dissent, Judge Molkenbuhr relied on Section 2338 of the California Civil Code, which reads in part: "A principal is responsible to third persons for... wrongful acts committed by [such] agent in and as part of the transaction of such business." *Id.* at 755. Judge Molkenbuhr's opinion was that the act of the left fielder in deliberately throwing the ball out of the park was not an act "in and as a part of the principal's business—that of playing baseball." *Id.* The tort herein complained of was one that, under ordinary circumstances, could not have been anticipated. Consequently, the dissent claimed, the defendant tavern should not be held liable.

Contrast *Bonetti* with *Atlanta Baseball Co. v. Lawrence*, 144 S.E. 351 (Ga. Ct. App. 1928), in which a baseball player employed by the proprietor of a baseball park left his position in the field, entered the grandstand, and assaulted a spectator who had criticized his play. The court held that the assault was neither committed within the scope of his employment nor in the pursuit of his master's business. The court reasoned that "if the defendant had good reason to apprehend that such a thing would probably happen, then it should have exercised reasonable care to prevent the occurrence, but it was not required to anticipate the improbable, nor to take measures to prevent a happening that no reasonable person would have expected." *Id.* at 353. *See also Wiersma v. City of Long Beach*, 41 Cal. App. 2d 8 (1940) (wrestler who jumped out of ring and attacked plaintiff with a chair deemed to act outside scope of employment).

The cases have their own curious logic. For purposes of imposing vicarious liability, courts are guided by some notion of foreseeable participant behavior. While Hjort's post-game tantrum was foreseeable, the gratuitous violence in *Atlanta Baseball* arguably was not. Presumably, vicarious liability could be imposed even in cases in which participants are hurt by a players' fight, for instance, if the employer knew of the employee's propensity for such behavior. *See Payne v. Maple Leaf Gardens Ltd.*, 1 D.L.R. 369 (Ont. Can. 1949). Otherwise, such attacks likely will be viewed as outside the scope of employment, *see, e.g.*, *Tomjanovich v. California Sports, Inc.*,

1979 U.S. Dist. LEXIS 9282 (S.D. Tex. Oct. 10, 1979), appeal docketed, No. 79–3889 (5th Cir. Dec. 3, 1979), discussed in YASSER, TORTS AND SPORTS 21–22, 26 (1985).

5. **Injuries caused by attacks from participants**. There are many occurrences of players "going after" spectators. Among Jimmy Piersall's many memorable antics were confrontations with heckling fans. Cesar Cedeno also ventured into the stands after a heckler who jabbered about an incident that has haunted Cedeno, when a young girl was found dead in his motel room. At the United States Open in 1983, John McEnroe threw sawdust in the face of a front-row fan who was rooting (perhaps too strongly) for McEnroe's opponent. The incident was captured by the television cameras. A subsequent lawsuit was settled for an undisclosed amount.

The so-called "Malice at the Palace" is one of the most well-known incidents of on-the-court transgressions breaching the wall between participants and spectators. A brawl between Detroit Piston players and fans and Indiana Pacers players occurred on November 19, 2004, and in hindsight, the environment was ripe for misconduct. During the previous year's playoffs, the Pacers were knocked out of the Eastern Conference Finals in a contentious six-game series against the Pistons, who went on to win the NBA Championship. Both teams were considered title favorites entering the 2004–2005 season, and both teams were made up of largely the same players. The Pistons and Pacers were both aggressive, physical teams known for their hard-nosed defense that straddled the line between hard play and dirty tactics.

Coming into the game, the Pacers were off to a strong start to the season at 6–2, and their star player, Ron Artest, was having a career year. The Pistons were sputtering at 4–3 and were searching for a signature win to gain momentum as they sought to repeat as NBA Champions. The game, at Detroit's Palace of Auburn Hills, was largely dominated by the Pacers and, by the fourth quarter, Pistons players began to take their frustrations out by fouling harder and harder. With 1:25 left in the game, the Pistons' Ben Wallace knocked Artest into the basket support while contesting a layup, but no foul was called. With :47 left in the game, and the Pacers up 97–82, Ron Artest aggressively fouled Ben Wallace as he went up for a bucket, and Wallace retaliated by pushing Artest. As players tried to restrain their teammates, the ruckus moved toward the press table. While coaches and players tried to extricate players and get them to the bench, Artest laid down on the press table, and Wallace threw a towel at him. The night would have ended with an otherwise mundane altercation if the events ended here. However, with Artest now within range of angry Pistons fans, the night devolved into one of the scariest moments in NBA history.

While Artest was laying on the table, a fan threw a cup of liquid (either Diet Coke or beer) and hit Artest in the chest. Artest proceeded to climb over the radio announcers and jumped into the stands. Fans began throwing whatever they had in their hands at Artest and other Pacers. Artest knocked down a fan he believed threw the cup at him, while the true culprit, John Green, grabbed Artest from behind and attempted to put him in a headlock. Other Pacers began throwing punches. The fans punched back. Security tried to subdue players and fans but could hardly contain the vengeful fans and the Pacers players. Eventually, the players left the stands, and they were showered in popcorn and liquid as they tried to make their way to the locker rooms. Throughout the whole event, fans rushed onto the court and continued brawling with players.

In the aftermath of the game, Detroit police acted quickly. Detroit officers tried to remove Artest from the Pacers' team bus, but after the Pacers agreed that Artest would cooperate fully, the police escorted the team bus out of the arena and to the airport. The next day, NBA Commissioner David Stern suspended nine players indefinitely. In sum, the players missed a total of 146 games and lost more than $10 million in salary. Ron Artest bore the brunt of the punishment as he lost nearly $5 million in earnings and sat out 86 games.

Legally, five players and five spectators were arrested and charged with crimes stemming from the incident. The five players all received a year of probation and were ordered to perform community service and undergo anger management counseling after pleading no contest. The fans received sentences ranging from community service and probation to restitution fees to jail time. John Green, the man who threw the cup at Artest, served 30 days in jail and two years of probation.

For more on The Malice at the Palace see Abrams, *The Malice at the Palace: An Oral History of the Scariest Moment in NBA History,* GRANTLAND, March 20, 2012.

Readers are invited to share their own "participant bites spectator" stories.

6. **The spectator who is denied admission.** A related issue involves the rights of a spectator denied admission to a sporting event. The traditional common-law rule gave the owner a broad power to exclude any person for any reason. The leading case is *Marrone v. Washington Jockey Club*, 227 U.S. 633 (1913), holding that a ticket does not create a property right and is not a conveyance of an interest in the race track. (The plaintiff was denied admission because of an alleged conspiracy to drug a horse.) The modern trend is to restrict this power, so that patrons are not arbitrarily excluded. Moreover, if the acts of the owner can be fairly regarded as "state action" for constitutional purposes, the power to exclude is further constrained by the constitutional rights of the spectators. The issue is addressed in detail in WEISTART & LOWELL at 141–47, 190–95, and 963–65.

7. **Stampedes and the duty to control crowds.** It is surprising that more injuries are not incurred when crowds get out of control. In 1979, a human stampede resulted in the loss of life at a "Who" concert in Cincinnati. Americans are used to reading about such tragedies at foreign soccer games. Our own national championship games, particularly if the home team wins, raise the specter of similar tragedies. When the Celtics won the 1984 NBA Championship Series at the Boston Garden, the ensuing melee was frightening. Mobs of spectators tearing down goalposts are a similarly potentially dangerous practice. It is simply a matter of time before Ameri-

cans are beset by a stampede of epic proportions. What is the duty of the promoter to control the crowd under these circumstances?

An Indiana court has answered this question in *Hayden v. University of Notre Dame*, 716 N.E.2d 603 (Ind. Ct. App. 1999). *Hayden* involved a spectator who was injured as a result of another spectator going for a football that had landed in the stands after a field goal attempt. In reaching its decision, the court applied a totality of the circumstances test to determine if liability exists for the landowner. *Id.* at 605. Under the totality of the circumstances test, "[the] court considers all of the circumstances surrounding [the] event, including the nature, condition, and location of the land, as well as prior similar incidents to determine whether a criminal act was foreseeable." *Id.* The *Hayden* court determined that Notre Dame should have foreseen the injury and acted to prevent it. *Id.* This same rationale seems applicable to recent incidents in which fans get out of control and tear down the goalpost after a big victory or loss. Tearing down goalposts after a big win may be customary, but event sponsors should not overlook its dangerousness. Similarly, the court in *Telega v. Security Bureau, Inc.*, imposed liability on a professional sports complex owner where the owner failed to protect a spectator from other spectators lunging for a souvenir football that was kicked into the stands. 719 A.2d 372 (Pa. Super. Ct. 1998). More college basketball fans are rushing the court after dramatic wins than ever before. For instance, on March 1, 2006, Coach Mike Krzyewski sent his players to the locker room with 1.7 seconds left on the clock after Florida State fans came pouring onto the court prematurely in what turned out to be a 79–74 FSU win. The win ended Duke's hopes of going undefeated in the ACC.

8. **Medical assistance to spectators.** In *Fish v. Los Angeles Dodgers Baseball Club*, 56 Cal. App. 3d 620 (1976), parents of a 14-year-old who died after being hit by a foul ball while attending a Dodgers game sued the Dodgers and a physician. The complaint asserted two theories: (1) failure to provide the boy "with a safe place to witness the ball game," and (2) negligent provision of emergency medical services. The court's discussion of intervening causes in medical malpractice cases is especially noteworthy.

The point is that the failure to provide adequate emergency medical assistance to an injured spectator provides a viable cause of action to the injured spectator, at least to the extent it can be shown that the injuries were aggravated by the lack of such care.

9. **The spectator as a defendant.** Spectators could also find themselves on the receiving end of a summons and complaint in a number of situations. Overzealous fans are potential tortfeasors in a variety of fairly common situations, such as throwing debris on the playing surface or at the participants, including referees; fighting for souvenirs; and brawling with opposing fans. A number of years ago, it was quite popular at college football games for a group of fans to engage in what can be described as a "fan toss" wherein a fan was literally tossed about the crowd. If the human plaything is injured, are these fun-loving fans joint tortfeasors?

10. **Spectator versus spectator.** When Barry Bonds surpassed Mark McGwire's record by hitting his 73rd home run of the season, a battle for the ball ensued. Alex Popov initially retrieved the ball. However, immediately after retrieving the ball, Popov was thrown to the ground by at least 10 fans, at which point another fan, Patrick Hayashi, emerged from the pile with the home run ball in hand. Neither Barry Bonds nor the San Francisco Giants claimed ownership of the ball and the battle line was drawn between the two fans. Popov sought an injunction, which the court granted, preventing Hayashi from selling the ball. The litigation was not about whether the team, the batter, or the fans owned the ball, but rather which fan owned the ball. Paul Finkelman, *Fugitive Baseballs and Abandoned Property: Who Owns the Home Run Ball?*, 23 Cardozo L. Rev. 1609 (2002). The case was tried in the fall of 2002, and, in Solomonic fashion, the judge ordered the litigants to split the proceeds from the sale of the baseball. *See* Ian Stewart, *Feud over Home Run Ball Goes into Extra Innings*, San Jose Mercury News, Jan. 2, 2003.

11. **An emerging trend?** Traditionally, the courts have held that the owner of a sports complex has only a limited duty to protect the spectator from common hazards of the game. *Schneider v. American Hockey and Ice Skating Center, Inc.*, 777 A.2d 380 (N.J. Super. Ct. App. Div. 2001). Although courts have been reluctant to modify this limited duty, sports complex owners as well as league officials appear to be implementing new measures that recognize a broader duty for spectator safety. The recognition of a broader scope of duty was most recently seen after a 13-year-old girl received a fatal head injury as a result of an ice hockey puck being shot into the stands. *See* Jason Diamos, *Safety Netting at N.H.L. Rinks Is Pressing Topic for Spectators*, N.Y. Times, Sept. 24, 2002. After the incident, the Commissioner of the NHL ordered all sports complexes in which NHL games are played to install and provide protective screening for spectator safety. *Id.* Although most NHL sports complexes provide some protective measures, almost every complex added additional safety measures by the start of the next regular season. *Id.* These additional safeguards are clearly intended to protect spectators from injury, but are arguably also intended to shield owners from potential future liability. *See* C. Peter Goplerud III & Nicholas P. Terry, *Allocation of Risk Between Hockey Fans and Facilities: Tort Liability After the Puck Drops*, 38 U. Tulsa L. Rev. 445 (2003).

12. **Contemporary changes in spectator viewing patterns.** Spectators have always been held to assume the risk of being hit by a projectile that has left the area of play. This assumption is based on the notion that the spectator was, or at least should have been, paying attention to the game. But in today's sports complexes, such things as massive video monitors, numerous mascots, advertising promotions, and liquor consumption can distract even the most responsible and attentive sports fan. The courts have recognized that a spectator assumes the inherent risks of attending a sporting event so long as the owner of the ballpark does not unduly enhance those risks. *Lowe v. California League of Professional Baseball*, 56 Cal. App. 4th 112 (1997). In *Lowe*, the court held that a spectator who was hit by a foul ball while being distracted by a team mascot standing directly behind him in

the stands did not assume the risk. The court observed that allowing the mascot to enter the stands while the game was in progress increased the risk of injury to the plaintiff and, therefore, the sports park owner was liable under a negligence theory. Under the holding in *Lowe*, an increase in sports complex distractions will likely lead to a greater risk of owner liability.

In *Maisonave v. The Newark Bears Professional Baseball Club*, 881 A.2d 700 (N.J. 2005), a foul ball hit a fan while he was at the concession stand. He suffered extensive facial injuries. The spectator sued the stadium owner on a negligence theory, arguing that the concession stand should have been protected by netting. *Id.* at 703. The trial court dismissed the suit since the defendant had provided protection in the most dangerous areas of the park. *Id.* The appellate court overruled, distinguishing between fans actively watching the game and those occupied with other features of the ballpark, such as a concession stand. *Id.* at 704. On appeal, the New Jersey Supreme Court held that the chance of being struck by a foul ball was a risk inherent in baseball and that it would place undue hardship on stadium owners to ensure the safety of every spectator. *Id.* at 707. *See* Charles Toutant, *Play Ball! (Carefully): Ruling Erects Standard of Care for Sports Stadium Owners*, 181 N.J.L.J. 1065 (2005) (commentary on *Maisonave*).

Does a spectator assume the risk of getting injured by a flying hot dog? The Supreme Court of Missouri reversed a trial court judgment which had let the Kansas City Royals off the hook in a suit claiming that their mascot Sluggerrr injured a spectator by launching a hot dog into the stands. The case raises the interesting question about the extent to which assumption of risk should operate to insulate owners from liability for injuries to spectators. Should the doctrine of assumption of risk apply in cases where a bat or a bat fragment flies into the stands and injures a spectator? *See Comer v. Kansas City Royals Baseball Corporation*, Supreme Court of Missouri (en banc), 437 S.W.3d 184 (Mo. 2014), opinion issued June 24, 2014.

Capstone Problem

You are the recently-hired general manager of the Spakone Huskies Professional Football Club, Inc. You received the following email from Tex Marsh, the president and CEO of the club:

> In regards to the terrible tragedy that occurred at last Sunday's Huskies-Cowboys game at the Huskiedome, I am very concerned about our exposure to liability and I would like to meet with you soon to discuss what steps we should take.
>
> According to our security staff's internal investigation of the incident, this is what happened. Johnny Sherman, a 17-year-old fan, was severely injured during a melee among the fans in the south end zone. (He is now in a coma suffering from what has been described in the paper as a subdural hematoma and his prognosis for a complete recovery is grim.) The melee occurred in the fourth quarter when DiPrimio's extra point kick sailed over our protective

screen. Many of the fans in that section were reportedly drunk and had posed a security problem for much of the evening. When the ball sailed into the section, a battle for possession of the ball ensued. Sherman was injured in the scuffle when he fell and struck his head on a step.

We have been putting up the mesh screen ever since the Huskiedome opened eight years ago. We put it up on every extra point or field goal and try both to save footballs and to prevent this kind of brawling. (I can recall kicks sailing over or around the screen only a handful of times.)

I have also discovered the following memorandum, written one month prior to the Sherman incident, by Chief of Stadium Security J.E. Glover, to Executive Vice President Dallas Brown: I am concerned that our failure to restrict beer sales is leading to some very serious security problems. Drunkenness among fans is a growing problem. Abusive language and fights are becoming increasingly commonplace in the stands and in the parking lot and I really can't imagine how some of these people drive home. The problem is most severe in the "cheap seats" in the north and south end zones. I would like for you to consider that we stop selling beer at halftime and/or we consider selling near beer (less than 3.2% alcohol) rather than the real stuff. We also should instruct vendors not to sell beer to the obviously drunk and provide prompt and efficient back-up when problems arise. In this regard, I would like authority to hire 10 additional security people for next week's game.

I have been unable to locate any response to the Glover memo. Brown remembers receiving it but did not have time to fashion a reply.

Sherman's father had purchased general admission tickets for the game. Neither Sherman nor his father had been drinking. The back of the ticket contains an exculpatory clause that was drafted when the Huskiedome first opened:

Waiver

The ticket holder agrees to assume all risks associated with attendance at this sporting event. The ticket holder agrees that, in consideration of the permission granted to enter the premises, he or she will not make any claim whatsoever against the Spakone Huskies Professional Football Club, Inc. for any injury or damage that may be sustained while in attendance or while traveling to or from this sporting event, including injuries that might be caused by any tortious acts of the said Spakone Huskies Football Club, Inc. The management reserves the right to revoke the license granted by this ticket by refunding the purchase price.

After you have had an opportunity to do some further investigation, give me a call so we can set up a meeting to chat.

Tex

After receiving the email from Tex, you asked the assistant general counsel in your office to do some research and send you a memo outlining the relevant law in regard to such cases, which is set forth below. Prepare for your meeting with Tex!

MEMORANDUM

TO: General Manager

FROM: Assistant General Counsel

RE: Spectators as Plaintiffs

This is in regard to your recent request for a legal memorandum in connection with the Johnny Sherman matter. I have not been able to locate very many relevant football cases, so I have outlined some baseball and ice hockey cases, which are very useful by way of analogy.

I have also included some comments concerning the very important waiver and beer sales issues. If you would like to meet with me prior to meeting with Tex, or if you want me to come to your meeting with Tex, please let me know.

Baseball

The general rule respecting baseball is that spectators are presumed to know that at certain times batted balls will be hit into the stands; therefore, they are considered to have assumed the risk. One of the earliest reported cases noted that "[b]aseball is our national game, and the rules governing it, and the manner in which it is played, and the risks and dangers incident thereto are matters of common knowledge." *Crane v. Kansas City Baseball Exhibition Co.*, 153 S.W. 1076, 1077 (Mo. Ct. App. 1913). Courts generally charge spectators with knowledge that, "in baseball games hard balls are thrown and batted with great swiftness, that they are liable to be thrown or batted outside the lines of the diamond, and that spectators in positions which may be reached by such balls assume the risk thereof." *Cincinnati Baseball Club Co. v. Eno*, 147 N.E. 86, 87 (Ohio 1925). In *Brisson v. Minneapolis Baseball & Athletic Ass'n*, 240 N.W. 903 (Minn. 1932), the Minnesota Supreme Court stated:

> No one of ordinary intelligence could see many innings of the ordinary league game without coming to a full realization that batters cannot and do not control the direction of the ball which they strike and that foul tips or liners may go in an entirely unexpected direction. He could not hear the bat strike the ball many times without realizing that the ball was a hard object. Even the sound of the contact of the ball with the gloves... would soon appri[s]e him of that.

Id. at 904. *See also Schentzel v. Philadelphia Nat'l League Club*, 96 A.2d 181, 186 (Pa. Super. Ct. 1953) ("We think the frequency with which foul balls go astray, alight in the grandstand or field, and are sometimes caught and retained by onlookers at [the] baseball games is a matter of such common everyday practical knowledge as to be a subject of judicial notice.").

In some cases involving injured baseball spectators it is claimed that the defendant is obligated to provide protective screening for all seats rather than for only the few seats located directly behind home plate. In *Fish v. Los Angeles Dodgers Baseball Club*, 56 Cal. App. 3d 620 (1976), parents of a 14-year-old who died after being hit by a foul ball at a Dodgers game sued the Dodgers and a physician. The complaint asserted two theories: (1) failure to provide the boy "with a safe place to witness the ball game" and (2) negligent provision of emergency medical services. The first cause of action was dismissed by the trial court, and the dismissal was affirmed on appeal. The case was submitted to the jury solely on the second issue, which decided in favor of the defendant.

See also Mann v. Nutrilite, Inc., 136 Cal. App. 2d 729 (1955); *Hummel v. Columbus Baseball Club*, 49 N.E.2d 773 (Ohio Ct. App. 1943); *Cates v. Cincinnati Exhibition Co.*, 1 S.E.2d 131 (N.C. 1939); *Shaw v. Boston Am. League Baseball Co.*, 90 N.E.2d 840 (Mass. 1950); *Anderson v. Kansas City Baseball Club*, 231 S.W.2d 170 (Mo. 1950). The majority of cases appear to hold, however, that the park owner is obligated to furnish just a reasonable number of protected seats and that a spectator assumes the risk by sitting elsewhere. *Davidoff v. Metropolitan Baseball Club, Inc.*, 459 N.Y.S.2d 2 (1983) (sitting in unscreened area although screened areas were available); *O'Bryan v. O'Connor*, 399 N.Y.S.2d 272 (1977) (bat flew out of batter's hands); *Leek v. Tacoma Baseball Club*, 229 P.2d 329 (Wash. 1951) (perpendicular backstop screen sufficient).

A contention that the entire park should be enclosed by a protective screen was rejected by a Wisconsin court as unreasonable because:

> [T]he interest, the popularity and the game of baseball as a national pastime would be doomed for the excitement and enthusiasm is so eloquently displayed to the Court's own eyes upon the chasing or retrieving of a foul ball in the stands and sometimes to the detriment of others, would be drastically curtailed and a thing of the past for our American souvenir loving sport spectators.

Powless v. Milwaukee County, 94 N.W.2d 187, 190 (Wis. 1959).

If a spectator sits in an unprotected seat, he or she is deemed to have assumed the risk. Further, where a plaintiff was relegated to an unscreened seat even though she requested a protected seat, a subsequent injury was found to be non-compensable. *Schentzel v. Philadelphia Nat'l League Club*, 96 A.2d 181 (Pa. Super. Ct. 1953). This case is representative of the hundreds of reported spectator versus owner cases. A woman attending a baseball game for the first time was struck by a foul ball and injured. Plaintiff Schentzel had contended that the owners of the club and field owed her a duty to exercise "exceptional precautions" since she was a woman and ignorant of the hazards of the game. The "exceptional precautions" included widening the coverage of the protective screening behind the batter's and catcher's positions, still leaving "a few sections" available for those preferring to watch the game from unprotected areas. She recovered a judgment in trial court.

The appeals court found no evidence that the ballpark's screening was insufficient in its coverage and no proof that the screening of a wider area would have prevented the plaintiff's injury. The court also agreed with the defendant that plaintiff had impliedly assumed the normal and ordinary risks of attending a baseball game, which included being struck by thrown or batted balls.

Consequently, judgment was reversed and entered for the defendant's ball club.

See Gill v. Chicago Park Dist., 407 N.E.2d 671 (Ill. App. Ct. 1980) (assault on way to washroom); *Uzdavines v. Metropolitan Baseball Club, Inc.*, 115 Misc. 2d 343 (N.Y. Civ. Ct. 1982) (res ipsa loquitur applied where hole existed in netting behind home plate); *Jones v. Three Rivers Management Corp.*, 394 A.2d 546 (Pa. 1978) (pre-game batting practice). *See also* WEISTART & LOWELL at 951–65 nn.52–86 (the footnotes list a good collection of spectator versus owner cases). James G. Gaspard, *Spectator Liability in Baseball: Nobody Told Me I Assumed the Risk*, 15 REV. LITIG. 229–50 (1996); *Lowe v. California League of Professional Baseball*, 56 Cal. App. 4th 112 (1997) (mascot distracted fan who was injured; court found no assumption of the risk); *Gil-De-Rebollo v. Miami Heat Ass'n, Inc.*, 137 F.3d 56 (1st Cir. 1998) (Heat found liable under respondeat superior for injuries inflicted by mascot); and Roger I. Abrams, *Torts and Sports: The Rights of the Injured Fan: Two Sports Torts: The Historical Development of the Legal Rights of Baseball Spectators*, 38 TULSA L. REV. 433 (2003) (history of claims by baseball fans).

There is no assumption of risk when a ball passes through the protective screen and injures the spectator. The park owner will be held liable. *See, e.g., Edling v. Kansas City Baseball & Exhibition Co.*, 168 S.W. 908 (Mo. Ct. App. 1914) (if owner screens a part of a grandstand exposed to fly balls, seats behind screen are assumed to be protected; owner must exercise reasonable care to keep screen free of defects to avoid negligence). However, if a ball flies over, see *Hull v. Oklahoma City Baseball Co.*, 163 P.2d 982 (Okla. 1945), or sails around, see *Wells v. Minneapolis Baseball & Athletic Ass'n*, 142 N.W. 706 (Minn. 1913), the protective screening, the owner is generally not liable on the theory of assumption of risk, contributory negligence, or lack of proximate cause. For example, in *Jones v. Alexandria Baseball Ass'n, Inc.*, 50 So. 2d 93 (La. Ct. App. 1951), the ball sailed over the screen behind which the plaintiff was sitting. He watched the ball until it went beyond him and turned around to resume watching the game. The ball struck a light pole and shot back into the crowd, hitting and fracturing the plaintiff's jaw. The court denied recovery and stated: "It seems to us that one of the accepted maxims of the game of golf is most appropriate in this instance" which is "that [the plaintiff']s injury is attributable to his own fault in failing to 'keep his eye on the ball.'" *Id.* at 94.

See Stradtner v. Cincinnati Reds, Inc., 316 N.E.2d 924 (Ohio Ct. App. 1972) (affirming dismissal of personal injury suit by fan struck by batted ball); *O'Bryan v. O'Connor*, 399 N.Y.S.2d 272 (N.Y. App. Div. 1977) (bat flew out of batter's hands). In an action based on an injury suffered from an errant baseball, no jury question is presented; there is no duty to warn of the obvious dangers, and as a matter of law, "a spectator familiar with the game assumes the reasonable risks and hazards inherent in the game." *Shaw v. Boston Am. League Baseball Co.*, 90 N.E.2d 840, 842 (Mass. 1950).

Two Illinois cases explore the issues surrounding baseball stadium operators' liability to spectators. *See Yates v. Chicago Nat'l League Ball Club*, 595 N.E.2d 570 (Ill. App. Ct. 1992) (upholds jury verdict for plaintiff against stadium operator—case includes lengthy discussion of evidence presented by both sides); *Coronel v. Chicago White Sox*, 595 N.E.2d 45 (Ill. App. Ct. 1992) (overturns summary judgment granted to defendant and sends back for fact finder to decide adequacy of screening and warnings). In addition, former California Angels pitcher Matt Keough sued the city of Scottsdale, Arizona, contending that the city was negligent in failing to provide adequate screens in front of the dugouts at Scottsdale Stadium. Keough alleges that he suffered a career-ending injury when he was struck by a foul ball during training camp. Since the incident, barriers have been installed. For more suggestions on the duty that stadium owners owe to spectators, see David Horton, *Rethinking Assumption of Risk and Sports Spectators*, 51 UCLA L. Rev. 339 (2003).

It should be noted that in 2009, the New Mexico Court of Appeals opened the door a bit for baseball spectators who are struck by batted balls to recover. In *Crespin v. Albuquerque Baseball Club LLC*, 216 P.3d 827 (N.M. Ct. App. 2009), the court rejected the historic immunity rule. The opinion reversed the summary judgment that the trial court had granted the baseball club, noting that the historic rule immunizing clubs from liability in such cases no longer could be justified in light of the emergence of comparative negligence. Query as to whether this is the beginning of the end for the baseball immunity rule.

While the baseball rule still appears to be in effect, in 2015 Major League Baseball passed recommendations to extend protective netting to the ends of the dugout and to seats that were closer than 70 feet from home plate. After several serious incidents involving fans being hit by foul balls and errant bats, all 30 teams extended netting to meet these recommendations for the 2018 season. However, this has not eliminated the danger of attending baseball games in seats near the field of play. Nearly a half-century after the *Fish* case, another spectator was struck in the head and killed by a foul ball at Dodger Stadium. Linda Goldbloom was struck by a foul ball that sailed above the protective netting that had been installed. As players grow stronger and hit the ball harder, serious discussions are underway about the adequacy of the baseball rule and the current state of protective netting in MLB stadiums. Across the Pacific Ocean, in Japan, the Nippon League maintains much more extensive netting in their stadiums to protect spectators.

Ice Hockey

Hockey's inherent dangers have caused a great deal of litigation. *See Shurman v. Fresno Ice Rink*, 91 Cal. App. 2d 469 (1949); *Thurman v. Clune*, 51 Cal. App. 2d 505 (1942); *Sutherland v. Onondaga Hockey Club*, 281 N.Y.S. 505 (N.Y. App. Div. 1935); *Hammel v. Madison Square Garden Corp.*, 279 N.Y.S. 815 (1935). The question of owners' liability is not as well-settled as in baseball. Many jurisdictions that have addressed this issue state that hockey is a newer sport than baseball; therefore, "inexperienced" spectators cannot be held chargeable with knowledge of the game's dangers, and they do not assume the risk as a matter of law. *Thurman v. Ice Palace*, 36 Cal. App. 2d 364 (1939); *Uline Ice, Inc. v. Neely*, 255 F.2d 540 (D.C. Cir. 1958); *Shanney v. Boston Madison Square Garden Corp.*, 5 N.E.2d 1 (Mass. 1936); *Aaser v. Charlotte*, 144 S.E.2d 610 (N.C. 1965). *See also* Annotations, *Liability for Injury to One Attending Hockey Game*, 14 A.L.R.3d 1018 (2003).

Thus, while a spectator may not recover for a baseball injury, he or she may recover for an injury caused by a flying puck. *Morris v. Cleveland Hockey Club, Inc.* states the majority's rationale: "There is sound reasoning for the baseball rule. Baseball is the national pastime of the U.S.... Although hockey is becoming ever more popular, it is not nearly so universally played as is baseball, and, as we have pointed out, its dangers are certainly not so obvious to a stranger to the game as would be the dangers incident to baseball." 105 N.E.2d 419, 426 (Ohio 1952).

A number of courts have adopted the "no assumption of risk" rule, including California, *see Shurman v. Fresno Ice Rink, Inc.*, 91 Cal. App. 2d 469 (1949); Massachusetts, *see Lemoine v. Springfield Hockey Ass'n*, 29 N.E.2d 716 (Mass. 1940) (plaintiff who had been attending games for three to four years struck by a puck while walking to restroom recovered in jury trial); *Shanney v. Boston Madison Square Garden Corp.*, 5 N.E.2d 1 (Mass. 1936); Nebraska, *see Tite v. Omaha Coliseum Corp.*, 12 N.W.2d 90 (Neb. 1943); and Rhode Island, *see James v. Rhode Island Auditorium, Inc.*, 199 A. 293 (R.I. 1938) (plaintiff seated in unscreened area and struck by puck justified in believing seat was reasonably safe). Courts in Minnesota, *see Modec v. City of Eveleth*, 29 N.W.2d 453 (Minn. 1947), Michigan, *see Wolf v. Olympia Stadium, Inc.*, Nos. 247–609, 247–610 (Wayne County Cir. Ct. Mich. 1949), and New York, *see Kaufman v. Madison Square Garden Corp.*, 284 N.Y.S. 808 (1935), however, have held that baseball and hockey are indistinguishable and that the spectator assumes the risk at both sporting events in these states. *Hammel v. Madison Square Garden Corp.* established this position: "There are, however, a number of cases where spectators at baseball games have been injured by batted balls coming into the stand[s]. The con[s]ensus of opinion in those cases is that there is no liability;... that spectators occupying seats that are not screened assume the risk incident [thereto]. The baseball cases seem to present the same legal question that confronts us here." 279 N.Y.S. 815, 816 (1935). Minnesota, New York, and Michigan are clearly geographic areas in which the sport of hockey has been established the longest, so it is not surprising that hockey is treated in the same manner as baseball in these states. Hockey is a relatively new sport in many of the jurisdictions that do allow recovery. Thus, the essential problem may be in determining how prevalent hockey is in each jurisdiction. Because the cases that distinguish baseball and hockey are not recent, there may be some doubt as to their continued validity in light of the dramatic expansion of professional hockey. *See*

Benjamin v. State, 115 Misc. 2d 71, 453 N.Y.S.2d 329 (Ct. Cl. 1982) (failure to provide protection to spectator near player bench). *See also* C. Peter Goplerud III & Nicolas P. Terry, *Allocation of Risk Between Hockey Fans and Facilities: Tort Liability After the Puck Drops*, 38 Tulsa L. Rev. 445 (2003).

Like Major League Baseball, the National Hockey League has also endeavored to increase safety by adding netting at hockey rinks as a result of serious injuries sustained by fans. In 2002, a 13-year-old girl was struck in the head and killed by a puck. The NHL instituted a policy of extending netting at the curve of the boards to about 18 feet above the boards in order to prevent deflected slap shots from entering the stands for fans sitting directly behind the goals. Much like baseball, extended safety netting has not completely eliminated fan injury. In 2013, a fan was struck in the face with a puck, and in 2014, a fan was struck in the head. Both fans filed lawsuits against the venue and settled out of court. In 2018, a woman was struck in the head after a puck sailed over the boards and over the extended netting.

Injuries Caused by Unsafe Premises

Owners and operators of sporting arenas have the duty to maintain the premises in a reasonably safe condition and to supervise the conduct of spectators on the premises to prevent injury. *See* Weistart & Lowell at 956–57. Therefore, a spectator attending an athletic event may assume that the owner or operator has exercised reasonable care to make the facilities safe for the purposes of the invitation.

In *Rockwell v. Hillcrest Country Club, Inc.*, 181 N.W.2d 290 (Mich. Ct. App. 1970), a suspension bridge crossing a river on a golf course collapsed; its occupants dropped into the river below. At the time of the collapse, there were approximately 80 to 100 spectators watching a tournament being played on the course along with a golf cart on the bridge. Among the spectators were plaintiffs James and Ann Rockwell. Ann Rockwell fell 25 feet, struck the water, broke her back, and sustained permanent injuries.

The evidence produced at trial showed that the bridge was constructed to hold 25 people safely; when it collapsed, there were 80 to 100 people on the bridge; no sign was present warning those using the bridge of its safe capacity; and no supervisory personnel were present to oversee proper use of the bridge. In affirming a judgment for the plaintiffs, the court stated:

> The obligation of reasonable care is a full one, applicable in all respects, and extending to everything that threatens the invitee with an unreasonable risk of harm. The occupier must not only use care not to injure the visitor by negligent acts, and to warn him of latent dangers of which the occupier knows, but he must also take reasonable precautions to protect the invitee from dangers which are foreseeable from the arrangement or use. The obligation extends to the original construction of the premises, where it results in a dangerous condition.

Id. at 293. *See also Cachick v. United States*, 161 F. Supp. 15 (S.D. Ill. 1958) (bleacher blew over due to insufficient anchor); *Edling v. Kansas City Baseball & Exhibition Co.*, 168 S.W. 908 (Mo. Ct. App. 1914) (plaintiff struck in face by foul ball, which passed through hole in protective netting); *Kasper v. Buffalo Bills*, 345 N.Y.S.2d 244 (1973) (bleacher collapse); *Berrum v. Powalisz*, 317 P.2d 1090 (Nev. 1957) (holes in wire screen allowing passage of a part of a Little Leaguer's bat). *But see Eneman and Nadler v. Richter*, 577 N.W.2d 386 (1998) (stadium officials found not to be negligent in regular practice of, just minutes before the game's end, locking metal gates that were positioned to close off walkway at bottom of bleachers to the field causing plaintiffs to be crushed against a metal railing and the gates when students tried to rush onto the field at the game's end).

In the aftermath of September 11 and the Oklahoma City bombing, stadium owners should take every precaution possible to protect fans. A terrorist attack could injure thousands at any given sporting event. Those injured could potentially bring a negligence suit against the stadium owners. However, it may be difficult to prove every element of a negligence cause of action. In a major incident, the government could potentially step in and create an account similar to the September 11th Victim Compensation Fund. *See* Caitlin M. Piccarello, *Terrorism, Tourism, and Torts: Liability in the Event of a Terrorist Attack on a Sports or Entertainment Venue*, 12 VILL. SPORTS & ENT. L.J. 365 (2005).

The Waiver Issue

In many cases, the sponsors of sporting events draft waivers or releases by which they attempt to avoid liability. These exculpatory agreements are contractual and generally provide that the sponsor is not responsible for harm caused by negligence. Two strong public policies are in conflict here. One policy highly values freedom of contract, while the other expects individuals to be answerable for the consequences of their negligence. As might be expected, cases can be found on both sides. Those cases that uphold enforceability of exculpatory agreements: *Kotary v. Spencer Speedway, Inc.*, 365 N.Y.S.2d 87 (1973) (spectator in infield); *Lee v. Allied Sports Assocs., Inc.*, 209 N.E.2d 329 (Mass. 1965) (spectator in pits); *Winterstein v. Wilcom*, 293 A.2d 821 (Md. Ct. Spec. App. 1972) (driver injured when racer struck object on the track). Those cases that do not uphold enforceability of exculpatory agreements: *Wade v. Watson*, 527 F. Supp. 1049 (N.D. Ga. 1981) (release may not as a matter of law apply to gross negligence); *Santangelo v. City of New York*, 411 N.Y.S.2d 666 (1978) (minor not bound by release signed by father in connection with ice hockey clinic); *Scheff v. Homestretch, Inc.*, 377 N.E.2d 305 (Ill. App. Ct. 1978) (release not effective to eliminate potential dram shop liability). It should also be noted that waivers and releases are often used to insulate the owner from liability to participants as well as to spectators. Here, too, the results are mixed. See WEISTART & LOWELL at 965–69 for more cases in this area.

Liability Based upon Beer Sales

Some states impose strict liability upon the seller of intoxicating liquors when the sale is the proximate cause of harm to a third person. Liability is imposed even in the absence of negligence through the so-called "Dram Shop" statute. Fortunately for us, our state does not have a dram shop statute.

In recent years, however, and perhaps as a reflection of the new temperance movement, negligence-based liability has been imposed on sellers of intoxicating beverages when the sale results in harm to the interests of a third person as a result of the intoxication of the buyer. The gist of such a suit is really negligence in making the sale to someone who the seller knew or reasonably should have known was intoxicated. If such a negligent sale can be said to be the proximate cause of injury to the plaintiff, a cause of action might be stated. As of now, there is no relevant case precedent for, or against, such liability in our state.

ASG

C. Medical Malpractice in Athletics

Negligence-based principles also apply to sports medicine, which is widely considered a recognized area of specialization within the medical profession. The standard of care required of a team doctor is the "accepted practice" standard; thus, a team doctor is liable for medical malpractice if the doctor treats an athlete in a manner that constitutes a departure from the accepted standards of medical care within the medical profession. Expert testimony regarding the appropriate or accepted standard of sports medicine care is required for an athlete to prove liability for medical malpractice. *See, e.g., Gibson v. Digiglia*, 980 So.2d 739 (La. App. 2008) (athlete's medical malpractice claim dismissed because there was "no evidence to establish the standard of care required of a 'team medical director/coordinator' nor have they presented any evidence to support a claim that [the physician's] actions fell below the standard of care for that alleged sub-specialty of physicians"). In addition to negligence claims involving improper treatment and failure to diagnose, the issue of "informed consent" looms large in athletics, which turns on whether reasonable doctors would have disclosed certain risks.

One of the elements that must be met to establish a claim for negligence is that the athlete incurred damages, which can be economic (*e.g.* medical expenses and lost wages or earning capacity) and non-economic (*i.e.* pain and suffering). In litigation involving athlete-plaintiffs, a contentious and highly complex issue is the extent to which the defendant's negligence affected the athlete's opportunity to earn money in an athletic career, referred to as lost earning capacity damages. According to Professor Karcher, who has provided testimony as a damages expert in numerous lawsuits involving athletes, broadly speaking the lost earning capacity assessment is a two-step process: "Step one entails proving that the defendant's conduct did in fact cause the plaintiff's chance to earn money in the future as an athlete to be lost or diminished (the factual cause link). Step two entails proving the amount of the lost or diminished chance with reasonable certainty." Richard T. Karcher, *Rethinking Damages for Lost Earning Capacity in a Professional Sports Career: How to Translate Today's Athletic Potential into Tomorrow's Dollars*, 14 Chapman L. Rev. 75, 76 (2010).

Athletic trainers can also be liable for negligently providing sports medicine services to athletes. Similar to the standard of care required of a team doctor, an athletic trainer "has the duty to conform to the standard of care required of an ordinary careful trainer." *Searles v. Trustees of St. Joseph's College*, 695 A.2d 1206, 1210 (Me. 1997). Some of the more common negligence claims involving athletic trainers include: (1) failing to communicate the severity of an athlete's injuries to the coach, (2) failing to advise an athlete that he or she should not continue playing, and (3) failing to timely refer an athlete to a specialist for diagnosis or treatment. Given that athletic trainers are employees, the team or school can be held responsible for their negligence under vicarious liability principles.

One perplexing problem arises out of the somewhat unusual relationships created by the common practice of employing a team doctor. The very term "team doctor" signals the problem. The team doctor owes sometimes conflicting duties to individual team members and the team. However, the physician's legal duty is owed to the patient, not to the team (or school) that pays the physician's bill. The problem manifests itself in situations in which a valuable player is injured before an important game, and the responsibility falls on the team physician to decide if the player can participate. This power to determine eligibility generates a host of issues. How, for example, is liability determined when a doctor permits an injured player to participate and the injury is further aggravated or, worse, the athlete dies? Or suppose the doctor refuses to permit the athlete to participate; may the athlete claim a legal right to participate in the face of the medical prohibition? The growing concern about concussions brings these issues into stark relief.

A number of other problems are especially relevant to athletics. One concern is the extent to which a doctor may properly aid an injured player who wants to participate. To what extent should painkillers and the like be administered to willing athletes? And are the athletes really "willing" under the circumstances? Another problem concerns the use of substances to enhance performance. What is the doctor's proper role in this regard? This chapter explores these issues as well.

Rosensweig v. State

171 N.Y.S.2d 912 (1958),
aff'd, 158 N.E.2d 229 (N.Y. 1959)

Coon, Justice.

[By statute in New York, all boxers must be examined by a physician. The physician files a report with the State Athletic Commission, which in turn must certify that the fighter is fit before the fighter will be permitted to box.

On August 29, 1951, George Flores was knocked out in the eighth round of a fight at Madison Square Garden. He died four days later from cerebral hemorrhage and edema. Flores had fought on July 24 and August 14 of 1951, and in both those bouts, he lost by a technical knockout (T.K.O.). Before the August 29 bout, Flores was examined by a physician who certified his fitness to the Commission.

Flores' estate sued the State of New York, alleging that the negligence of the examining physician in certifying Flores' fitness could properly be imputed to the State of New York.

At the trial court level, Flores' estate prevailed. The intermediate appellate court reversed, and it is this decision that is excerpted here, because it is one of the few reported cases dealing directly with the liability of a doctor who certified an athlete as fit. It should be noted that New York's highest court affirmed the intermediate court, but without any discussion of the doctor's negligence. That court limited its discussion to whether the State was vicariously liable for the acts of the doctor, and concluded that, under the circumstances, it was not.]

Under these circumstances there is serious doubt as to whether the examining doctor is an employee of the State, but, even assuming employment by the State, claimant has not established negligence on the part of the examining doctor.

The doctor who examined decedent prior to the fatal fight had the benefit of the opinions of doctors who examined decedent after the two previous fights and who found no evidence of brain injury. A signed history given by decedent indicated no symptom of concussion or brain injury. A standard examination revealed no such symptom.

It is urged that there is evidence that some doctors believe it to be better medical practice to withhold permission to engage in another bout to a fighter who has received a severe beating about the head without a lay-off of from two to six months thereafter. It would, of course, be still safer to withhold permission forever. However, there was no official rule requiring a compulsory lay-off....

For another reason the judgment may not be sustained. It is clear that the immediate proximate cause of the injury which resulted in death was the severe blow to the head which decedent suffered in the final fight. Claimant has failed to establish that this blow alone, irrespective of previous condition, would not have produced the fatal result.

Decedent was engaged in a concededly dangerous activity. From his experience he knew that he would likely be struck by blows to the head. In fact, the very objective of the contestants, well known in advance, is to "knock out" the opponent and cause him to fall to the floor in such condition that he is unable to rise to his feet for a specified time. Decedent assumed the risks known to be inherent in the fight....

Judgment reversed and claim dismissed, without costs.

Colombo v. Sewanhaka Central High School District No. 2

383 N.Y.S.2d 518 (1976)

Alexander Berman, Justice.

[John Colombo, a 15-year-old student, was barred from interscholastic participation in contact sports because of a hearing disability. Joined by his parents, he sought to overturn the ban on the ground that it was "arbitrary, capricious, and contrary to law." The court here held that the determination of the school district to follow the advice of its medical director was correct.]

On December 11, 1975, Dr. Nathan Samuels the duly designated medical officer for the school district, conducted a physical examination of the petitioner, John, Jr., to determine whether he should be permitted to participate in contact sports in the High School....

The physical examination disclosed no abnormality other than a marked hearing deficiency, which petitioners concede, to wit: That John is totally deaf in his right ear and that he has a 50% loss of hearing in his left ear. This hearing problem has existed from birth. He wears a hearing aid in his left ear....

By reason of this hearing deficit, Dr. Samuels determined that John should not be permitted to play football, lacrosse or soccer. He rationalized that John's hearing deficit leaves him with a permanent "auditory blind" right side and a diminished sound perception of his left side, even with the use of the hearing aid, and that "this inability to directionalize the source of sound leaves him at increased risk of bodily harm as compared with students with full sensory perception."

In reaching the conclusion that John should not be permitted to play such contact sports, Dr. Samuels, among other things, took into consideration guidelines published by the American Medical Association, Revised Edition 1972....

Petitioners contend, however, that Dr. Samuels had not taken into consideration other factors which should have been weighed in his evaluation, such as: that both parents had given their unqualified consent to John's participation in these sports; that John is an all-around athlete of unusual and extraordinary talent; that John has demonstrated his ability to participate extensively in contact sports with his peers who had no hearing disability and that he had never sustained any injury during such competition; that he has actually played football with nonschool organizations under the strict supervision of organized athletic groups; and furthermore, that the prohibition against participation in these high school sports has had a damaging psychological effect upon this boy in that he has now lost interest in attending school and has been made to feel inferior to and different from the other children in school.

Both parents, it is true, not only joined in this petition, but testified that they were willing to assume the risk of additional injury to their son, even if same resulted in his becoming totally deaf. John's mother testified that another of her children, a daughter, is, in fact, totally deaf and although she would hope that John would not sustain such complete impairment of hearing, she believed that he could "live with it," and that he would, nevertheless, be able to function well "with such a handicap." John's father reiterated these feelings and added that he hoped John would be able to eventually obtain a college football scholarship as this would be of vital importance because of their limited financial resources....

It is... clear that there are at least conflicting views with respect to whether John's participation in contact sports represents a danger to his physical wellbeing or to the safety of other students with whom he might participate in such games. A determination of an administrative body, made on a rational basis, should not be judicially set aside....

The Court recognizes the psychological factors involved in the denial to John of the right to participate in contact sports and, indeed, has great concern for and sympathy with his plight. However, the medical determination of Dr. Samuels, the Court finds, was a valid exercise of judgment and was not arbitrary or capricious since: (a) there exists the risk of danger of injury to the ear in which there is only partial hearing and to which further injury could result in irreversible and permanent damage—in this case, total deafness; (b) aside from the risk of injury to his partially good ear, there also exists the possibility of injury to other parts of John's body by reason of his failure to perceive the direction of sound; and (c) there is the possibility of risk of injury to other participants. Even though these risks may all be minimal, in this Court's opinion it is sound judgment for the school district to follow the advice of its own medical director and the AMA Guide and prohibit John from participating in contact sports.

Respondent is entitled to judgment in its favor dismissing this proceeding.

Notes and Comments

1. **Note on *Rosensweig*.** Weistart and Lowell are properly critical of the *Rosensweig* reasoning, at 994:

> The appellate court obviously disagreed with the trial court's conclusion that there was negligence, but the doctrinal basis for disagreement is not clear. The

> court stated that a "standard examination" had revealed no injury but gave no indication of what such a standard examination required or what facts indicated that such an examination had been given in the present case. It also noted that the boxer had signed a medical history that disclosed no brain injury, but surely this fact could have little relevance to the negligence of the doctors.... In short, the appellate court found no negligence but undertook almost no effort to indicate why it came to that conclusion. Its reasoning would appear to be that a doctor is required to give only a standard examination (which it did not define) and since such examinations had been given here (though it did not say why) there was no basis for a conclusion that the doctors had been negligent.

Also note that the court's glib conclusion that the proximate cause of death was the blow to the head does not preclude a finding that the doctor's negligence in certifying Flores' fitness was also a proximate cause of death.

2. **Note on *Colombo*.** A good argument can be made that *Colombo* was wrongly decided and that a court today, more sensitive to the issue of discrimination against people with disabilities, would overturn the school district. (Disabilities, the rights of athletes to participate, and the Americans with Disabilities Act (ADA) are discussed in Chapter 12, below.) Technically, this case is not a torts case at all but rather a constitutional law case dealing with the power of the state to regulate. It is useful, however, to consider the problem in a torts context. Does the school district perhaps have a legal incentive to keep Colombo from participating in contact sports?

3. **Failure to diagnose and medical malpractice.** In *Speed v. State*, 240 N.W.2d 901 (Iowa 1976), the plaintiff, a University of Iowa basketball player, brought a medical malpractice action alleging that doctors at the university hospital negligently failed to diagnose Speed's intracranial infection and that this resulted in Speed's blindness. The court affirmed the trial court judgment in Speed's favor, applying well-established medical malpractice rules.

4. **Negligence due to inadequate emergency medical services.** In *Fish v. Los Angeles Dodgers Baseball Club*, 56 Cal. App. 3d 620 (1976), parents of a 14-year-old who died after being hit by a foul ball while attending a Dodgers game sued the Dodgers and a physician. This case is discussed in Note 8 of the "spectator as plaintiff" subsection of this chapter.

In *Stineman v. Fontbonne College*, 664 F.2d 1082, 1086 (8th Cir. 1981), the court relied on *Kersey v. Harbin*, 531 S.W.2d 76 (Mo. Ct. App. 1975), a decision that set forth certain elements necessary to impose a duty to provide medical assistance. In *Stineman*, a college softball player was hit in the eye with a softball with enough force that the impact was heard 100 yards away. The coach applied ice to the injury and sent Stineman home without even suggesting that she see a doctor. The case was complicated by the fact that the player was deaf and relied on her sight to read lips. She was later diagnosed with traumatic hyphema, a relatively common injury, which when treated promptly is repaired with a 90% or greater success rate. Ms. Stineman lost the vision in the eye and was forced to wear a prosthesis. "The first element under *Kersey* requires that the defendant must have been able to appreciate the severity of the plaintiff's injury." *Stineman* at 1086. Based on the facts in *Stineman*, the court ruled that Fontbonne should have appreciated the injury. "The second element of *Kersey* requires a determination that one or more of the defendants had the skill to provide adequate medical treatment. The only treatment required here was to get the injured person to a doctor." *Id.* at 1086. In this case, Fontbonne College's medical clinic was across the street from the softball field. "The third element of *Kersey* addresses whether providing medical attention would have avoided the injury's ultimate harm." *Id.* at 1086. This was established by expert testimony in this case. The satisfaction of these elements meant that the school had a duty to provide medical assistance.

5. **Foreseeability and whether a duty is owed.** Foreseeability has always been part of duty but how far must one see? The question of foreseeability of serious harm is related to questions of medical malpractice. For example, the issue in *Kleinknecht v. Gettysburg College*, 786 F. Supp. 449, 452 (M.D. Pa. 1992), was whether the college "ha[s] a duty to anticipate a cardiac arrest in a healthy young man showing no apparent illness whatsoever and to guard against... that possibility by having CPR trained individuals at hand or having some other way of providing treatment more promptly than he received." In this phase of the case the court determined that there was no duty. However, on appeal, the court determined that a duty was owed (in part because of the special relationship between the college and its student-athletes) and that the college also had a duty to be reasonably prepared for handling medical emergencies that foreseeably arise during a student's participation in intercollegiate contact sports for which a student was recruited. *Kleinknecht v. Gettysburg College*, 989 F.2d 1360, 1369–71 (3d Cir. 1993). *See also Orr v. Brigham Young University*, 960 F. Supp. 1522 (D. Utah 1994) (unauthorized practice of medicine by sports trainers).

Is there a duty to have Automatic External Defibrillator (AED) in high-risk locations? With energetic crowds in the thousands at sporting events or the rigorous workout regimes by many gym members, it is foreseeable that someone could suffer Sudden Cardiac Arrest (SCA). AED's retail for under $3,000 and increase the chances of surviving SCA from under 5% to more than 50%. What is the extent of the duty that stadium owners or fitness clubs owe their patrons? *See Atcovitz v. Gulph Mills Tennis Club*, 812 A.2d 1218 (Pa. 2002) (holding that a tennis club did not have a duty to maintain an AED on its property). At least two states have mandated that AED's be placed in their public schools. *See* Ronald R. Gilbert & Wendy Wawrzyniak, *Does Ability to Save a Life Still Equal a Duty to Have an AED Despite Pennsylvania Supreme Court Decision Overruling* Atcovitz?, 17 The Sports, Parks, & Recreation L. Rep. 17 (2003).

6. **Liability for injuries involving recruits.** In *Clark v. University of Oregon*, 512 P.3d 457 (Or. App. 2022), the Oregon men's basketball coaches invited the plaintiff to visit the university, informed him that he would be engaging in basketball workouts with coaches, devised a series of drills for him to complete, instructed him on how to perform the drills, physically participated in the drills, and, in the course of the drills, performed an act that injured the plaintiff. The coaches did those acts despite their knowledge of the plaintiff's previous knee surgery and despite the fact that most of the acts, including the act of allowing or requiring the plaintiff to participate in any workout with coaches at all, violated NCAA rules. According to the court, the conduct by the coaches that the plaintiff alleges unreasonably created a foreseeable risk of harm to him went beyond ordinary participation in a sports activity and was squarely within the province of the jury to assess the reasonableness of defendants' conduct and the foreseeability of the risk of harm to the plaintiff.

7. **The recurring issue of vicarious liability**. In almost all of the cases in this chapter, vicarious liability has been an issue. More specifically, the issue raised is whether the doctor is properly viewed as an independent contractor (in which case there is generally no vicarious liability imposed on the employer) or an employee (in which case vicarious liability is imposed for torts committed in the scope of employment). In *Cramer v. Hoffman*, 390 F.2d 19 (2d Cir. 1968), the court held that the university doctor was an independent contractor whose negligence could not be imputed to the university. Cramer was a college football player who was paralyzed after making a tackle during practice.

The distinction between an independent contractor and an employee is not particularly clear.

RESTATEMENT § 220 provides in part:

> (2) In determining whether one acting for another is a servant or an independent contractor, the following matters of fact, among others, are considered:
>
> (a) the extent of control which, by the agreement, the master may exercise over the details of the work;
>
> (b) whether or not the one employed is engaged in a distinct occupation or business;
>
> (c) the kind of occupation, with reference to whether, in the locality, the work is usually done under the direction of the employer or by a specialist without supervision;
>
> (d) the skill required in the particular occupation;
>
> (e) whether the employer or the workman supplies the instrumentalities, tools, and the place of work for the person doing the work;
>
> (f) the length of time for which the person is employed;
>
> (g) the method of payment, whether by the time or by the job;

(h) whether or not the work is a part of the regular business of the employer;

(i) whether or not the parties believe they are creating the relation of master and servant; and

(j) whether the principal is or is not in business.

One might well question whether the RESTATEMENT guidelines are particularly helpful.

Courts appear to be preoccupied with the "control" issue. Prosser and Keeton believe that it is accurate to say that "the person employed is a servant when, in the eyes of the community, he would be regarded as a part of the employer's working staff, and not otherwise." W. PAGE KEETON ET AL., PROSSER AND KEETON ON THE LAW OF TORTS at 501 (5th ed. 1984).

Consider *Robitaille v. Vancouver Hockey Club Ltd.*, 124 D.L.R.3d 228, where the court held the NHL Club vicariously liable for the negligence of the team doctors. As is the case with many teams, the doctors were interested in sports medicine and received modest remuneration—season tickets, free parking, access to the lounge, and a $2,500 bonus at the end of the season. *Id.* at 230. The court found that the defendant had the power to select, control, and dismiss the doctors who were supplied to the team in furtherance of the defendant's business purposes. *Id.* at 243. The court further held that the degree of control exercised does not have to be complete to establish vicarious liability, and in the case of a professional person, the absence of control and direction over the manner of doing the work is of little significance. *Id.* at 243.

An interesting statistic illustrates the conflict that a team physician faces when dealing with the pressures from the "front office" and the adequate care of the player/patient. The statistic also reveals that doctors are fully aware of who butters their bread. During NFL arbitration hearings involving post-injury examinations to determine whether the team was liable for payment of a player's salary, the team physician testified on behalf of the team and against the player in each of 67 hearings. *See* Charles V. Russell, *Legal and Ethical Conflicts Arising from the Team Physicians' Dual Obligations to the Athlete and Management*, 10 SETON HALL LEGIS. J. 299, 315–16 (1987). The teams were found liable in 39 of the 67 grievances filed. *Id.* at 316. Does this tend to show that "team doctors" are, in reality, employees of the team?

8. **Informed consent.** Another recurring problem is the duty of the team physician to provide information to players concerning the consequences of using pain killing drugs. In a case settled in 1976, it was reported that the Chicago Bears agreed to pay Dick Butkus $600,000. Butkus claimed that extensive injections of cortisone irreparably damaged his knee and that he had not been advised of the long-term effects. N.Y. TIMES, Sept. 14, 1976, at 50, col. 5.

9. The death of basketball player Hank Gathers from heart failure during a game produced several lawsuits. Gathers had collapsed earlier in the season, was put on

medication, and after several weeks away from basketball, was allowed to return to competition. Following his death there was speculation surrounding the dosage of the medication, the advice given by the doctors, and the wisdom of his return to basketball. The litigation was settled in the spring of 1992. *See* Isaacs, *Conflicts of Interest for Team Physicians a Retrospective in Light of Gathers v. Loyola Marymount University*, 2 ALB. L.J. SCI. & TECH. 147 (1992).

The case of Stephen Larkin and his quest to play college baseball, despite a serious medical condition, raised some of the same issues as the *Gathers* case. Larkin suffers from a heart ailment that had caused doctors at his high school and later at the University of Texas to withhold him from competition. In the spring of 1992, Larkin was successful in negotiations with the university and was allowed to return to competition. A carefully drafted release was apparently the key to the decision. *See* Andrew Manno, Note, *A High Price to Compete: The Feasibility and Effect of Waivers Used to Protect Schools from Liabilities for Injuries to Athletes with High Medical Risks*, 79 KY. L.J. 867 (1990–1991).

In some situations, a waiver or release may not succeed. But there are other players who have managed to "waive" their way on to the field despite serious medical conditions. Stephen Hagins sued Arizona State University when it refused to medically clear Hagins to play baseball because of a congenital heart condition which ASU determined to be life threatening. Hagins' suit claimed ASU illegally discriminated against him because, according to ASU, he was physically handicapped. Although Hagins offered to waive liability, ASU refused due to concern that the waiver would not stand up to legal scrutiny. The case was settled when Hagins was released from his Letter of Intent and allowed to transfer without losing a year of eligibility. Hagins' key was finding other doctors who did not consider his condition as serious as the ASU doctors. Which approach would you recommend? Waiver or transfer?

In addition to liability waivers, two other methods have been used by athletes who have been advised by their doctors not to compete but are determined to compete regardless of the risk. Both of these tactics involve federal anti-discrimination law. The first and most widely used by competitive athletes is to file a lawsuit based on a violation of Section 504 of the Rehabilitation Act of 1973. Section 504 makes it unlawful for anyone receiving federal funding to discriminate against otherwise qualified individuals on the basis of a handicap. 29 U.S.C. § 701 *et seq.* In *Grube v. Bethlehem Area School District*, 550 F. Supp. 418 (1982), the court granted an injunction preventing the school district from precluding the student from playing high school football because he only had one kidney. The court stated that it was reluctant to reach its conclusion stating that it would disturb a well-intended decision of local school authorities. *Id.* at 423. The court reasoned that it was "bound to uphold an act of Congress which is specifically designed to protect Richard and the right he is asserting." *Id.* at 423.

However, in the case of *Pahulu v. University of Kansas*, 897 F. Supp. 1387 (D. Kan. 1995), Alani Pahulu, who had a football scholarship, was injured during a tackle and experienced "transient quadriplegia." Pahulu left the field under his own power and was subsequently examined by the team doctor who discovered that Pahulu had a congenitally narrow cervical canal. *Id.* at 1388. The team physician disqualified Pahulu, acknowledging that the decision was conservative. Pahulu tried to offer a waiver and release to no avail. *Id.* at 1388. He sued for injunctive relief and was denied. The court held that Pahulu was not "disabled" within the meaning of the Act even though intercollegiate football might be part of major life activity of learning. *Id.* at 1393. The court stated that Pahulu still had the opportunity to learn, still had his athletic scholarship, and still could participate in the football program in a role other than as a player. *Id.* at 1393. The court further held that even if the student was disabled, he was not "otherwise qualified," based on the physicians' reasonable and rational conclusion that Pahulu was at extremely high risk for subsequent and potentially permanent severe neurological injury. *Id.* at 1394. Will this case negate sports medicine physician shopping? *See also* David L. Herbert, *Athlete's Exclusion from Participation Does Not Violate Federal Rehabilitation Act*, 9 Sports Parks & Recreation L. Rep. 49 (1996).

The second method is to file a lawsuit based on violation of the Americans with Disabilities Act of 1990, which makes it unlawful for a place of public accommodation or a public entity to discriminate against an individual on the basis of disability. 42 U.S.C. § 12101 *et seq.* Many of these cases deal with age discrimination caused by learning disability. *See Reaves v. Mills*, 904 F. Supp. 120 (W.D.N.Y. 1995) (age requirement did not violate ADA); *Dennin v. Connecticut Interscholastic Athletic Conference, Inc.*, 913 F. Supp. 663 (D. Conn. 1996) (age eligibility requirement must be waived for student with Down's syndrome); *Sandison v. Michigan High School Athletic Association, Inc.*, 863 F. Supp. 483 (E.D. Mich. 1994) (learning disabled students granted injunction). These and related topics are covered more fully in Chapter 12, below.

Medical breakthroughs breed new concerns. Is a viable medical malpractice claim raised by the failure to test athletes for the sickle cell trait? After the tragic death of one of its athletes in 2007, and as part of a settlement, Rice University tests for sickle cell. As part of the largely confidential settlement, the NCAA agreed to recommend to its members that athletes be tested for sickle cell. ESPN.com: College Football, Sunday 28, 2009, *Family Settles suit with Rice, NCAA.*

10. An athlete's contributory negligence. If an athlete did something, or failed to do something, that contributed to his or her injury, it can reduce or bar any recovery. Some of the more common examples include an athlete's failure to truthfully disclose his or her medical history to a medical professional and an athlete's failure to follow his or her physician's instructions or advice concerning proper treatment and rehabilitation.

11. **Doctors who provide performance-enhancing drugs (like steroids) to athletes face a host of legal problems.** The easiest suit to see is the personal injury lawsuit by an athlete who suffers side effects. The issue of informed consent would come into play here. These doctors might also expect to be professionally sanctioned or called before governmental investigative tribunals to testify. Moreover, it is foreseeable that sports organizations will attempt to fashion a cause of action against doctors who help to foist chemically enhanced athletes into otherwise legitimate competition.

12. **Doctors might also be potentially liable for fraudulent concealment of medical information.** The elements of a cause of action for fraud or deceit are (1) a misrepresentation or suppression of a material fact, (2) knowledge of any falsity, (3) intent to induce reliance, (4) actual and justifiable reliance, and (5) resulting damages. According to Prosser, the athlete must also prove that he would not have played or undergone the medical treatment that caused the harm if he had been properly informed of the material risks of doing so, W. PAGE KEETON ET AL., PROSSER AND KEETON ON THE LAW OF TORTS § 105, at 728 (5th ed. 1984).

In *Krueger v. San Francisco Forty Niners*, 234 Cal. Rptr. 579, 583 (1987) (ordered not published), the court held that "the duty of full disclosure within the context of a doctor-patient relationship defines the test for concealment or suppression of facts.... A physician cannot avoid responsibility for failure to make full disclosure by simply claiming that information was not withheld." The court found that the team and the doctors knew the extent of the damage to Krueger's knee and in order to prolong his career and keep him on the field they regularly anesthetized him before and during games, administered questionable steroid treatments, and Krueger was even directed by a team physician to use amphetamines during games. *Id.* at 584. This showed the requisite intent. The court established reliance by holding that "[p] atients are generally persons unlearned in the medical sciences,... and consequently are entitled to rely upon physicians for full disclosure of material medical information." *Id.* at 584. Finally, the court found that Krueger would have followed physician recommendations to discontinue playing football, which satisfied the necessary causal link between the nondisclosure of material risks and his harm. *Id.* at 584. In 1988, the California Superior Court ordered the 49ers to pay Charlie Krueger over $2.3 million in damages arising from the team's medical care of the former all-pro defensive tackle.

The *Krueger* case also highlights the difficulty that doctors encounter when there is a conflict between the interests of the athlete-patient and the team.

13. In light of the experiences of Charlie Krueger, Hank Gathers, and other motivated athletes, should the traditional legal principles used for resolving malpractice claims be applied to sports medicine? Or must special solicitude be provided the competitive "not-to-be-denied" athlete? Two leading articles that address this evolving debate use similar but different approaches to the issue. James Davis, in his arti-

cle *"Fixing" the Standard of Care: Motivated Athletes and Medical Malpractice*, suggests that the traditional legal concepts of informed consent and assumption of the risk offer the best foundation upon which to formulate a standard for dealing with malpractice claims in the sports medicine field. 12 AM. J. TRIAL ADVOC. 215 (1988). On the other hand, Matthew Mitten advocates apportioning liability between the doctor and the athlete based on comparative responsibility principles. *Team Physicians and Competitive Athletes: Allocating Legal Responsibility for Athletic Injuries*, 55 U. PITT. L. REV. 129 (1993). A comparative approach leaves room for the perhaps overzealous athlete to recover in the face of his or her own negligence.

Problem

Dr. Robert Baker is a physician employed by the Spakone City Orthopedic Clinic. Dr. Baker and the clinic have been sued by Will Dalton, a star basketball player for the University of Spakone, an NCAA D-I institution. You work in the Spakone athletic department and your athletic director has asked you to review the filed complaint because Dr. Baker is the team doctor for all of the university's athletics programs. After your review of the complaint, she would like to meet with you to discuss Dalton's allegations and any possible defenses that may be asserted by Dr. Baker.

The filed complaint states as follows:

Plaintiff complains of Defendants, and each of them, and for a cause of action alleges:

I. At all times herein mentioned, the Defendant, SPAKONE CITY ORTHOPEDIC CLINIC, P.C., was, and now is, a business organization, which business organization was at all times herein doing business in the State of Oklanois.

II. At all times herein mentioned, Defendant ROBERT BAKER was a duly licensed physician and surgeon, and was engaged in the practice of sports medicine in the State of Oklanois.

III. At all times herein mentioned, the Defendants, and each of them, were the agents, servants, and employees, each of the other, individually and collectively, and were acting within the course and scope of their agency, service, and employment. DR. BAKER is also employed as the team physician for the University of Spakone.

IV. At all times herein mentioned, Plaintiff was, and continued to be, a medical patient of the Defendants ROBERT BAKER and SPAKONE CITY ORTHOPEDIC CLINIC, P.C. Said Defendants undertook to examine and treat, and to prescribe for, care for, diagnose for, and provide medical care and attention for Plaintiff.

V. From February 28 until July, the Defendant SPAKONE CITY ORTHOPEDIC CLINIC, P.C., and its employee and agent, Defendant ROBERT BAKER, carelessly and negligently examined, diagnosed, treated, tested, and cared for the Plaintiff in the following particulars:

1. In failing to diagnose the development and the eventual fracture of the tarsal navicular bone of the left foot at sometime between mid-February and April 22. At this time, the Plaintiff has been unable to ascertain from his doctors the exact date within that period that the fracture occurred. The Plaintiff complained to Defendant DR. BAKER of pain and discomfort in the left foot on the occasions that he visited his office on March 28, and April 20, and nearly every day from March 28 until April 22, when Plaintiff had contact with Defendant DR. BAKER at University of Spakone team practices and games, and Plaintiff's apartment, in the City of Spakone, and at the Defendant DR. BAKER'S home. Additionally, Defendant DR. BAKER failed to diagnose said fracture on April 21 when Plaintiffs left foot was x-rayed at Spakone City Orthopedic Clinic.

2. The Defendant DR. BAKER prescribed oral doses of Butazolidin and Decadron during the period between February 28 and April 22 to be taken on a daily basis. On March 28 at the University of Spakone Basketball Arena, the Plaintiff's left foot received four injections of a mixture of Xylocaine and Decadron. On April 20, in the Defendant DR. BAKER'S offices, the Plaintiff received three injections in his left foot of Xylocaine and another drug, which Plaintiff believed to be a corticosteroid. On April 21, at the University of Spakone Basketball Arena, in the City of Spakone, the Plaintiff's left foot was injected twice with Xylocaine and a corticosteroid. Said medications were prescribed, administered, and injected by Defendant DR. BAKER, and constituted wrongful and negligent therapy for Plaintiff's left foot condition.

3. Between March 28 and April 22, the Defendant DR. BAKER daily recommended and encouraged Plaintiff to bear weight on his left foot and attempt to use it in connection with engaging in basketball practice sessions and basketball games for the University of Spakone. Said recommendations were made both at DR. BAKER's office and home, and at Plaintiff's apartment, the location of the Spakone Stuffers' practice sessions and the University of Spakone Basketball Arena. On April 20, following the aforesaid three injections on Plaintiff's left foot at DR. BAKER's office, DR. BAKER recommended that Plaintiff place weight on and exercise his left foot, and on April 21 at the University of Spakone Baskeball Arena, Defendant DR. BAKER gave Plaintiff medical clearance to participate in a basketball game following two injections of Xylocaine and a corticosteroid which had caused Plaintiff's left foot to become numb. The prescription and encouragement of the conduct and activity described above constituted negligent treatment.

4. Following the diagnosis of Plaintiff's left tarsal navicular fracture and at the time of removal of Plaintiff's case on June 2, at the offices of DR. BAKER, Plaintiff was negligently encouraged to resume weight-bearing on his left foot.

VI. As a direct and proximate result of the carelessness and negligence of Defendants described above, Plaintiff suffered a fracture of his left tarsal navicular bone, aggravation of said fracture, lengthening of his disability, permanent weakening of his left foot, increased vulnerability to subsequent fractures of the same and adjoining bones, and damage to the adjoining nerves, muscles, and soft tissues of the left foot. As a further proximate result of the carelessness and negligence of the Defendants, Plaintiff has been deprived of his ability to continue playing college basketball, to enter the NBA Draft, and to participate in the NBA Combine, which resulted in substantial loss of future earning capacity.

VII. By reason of the premises, it became necessary for Plaintiff to incur expenses for doctors, hospitals, x-ray technicians, travel, and other services required in the care and treatment of said injuries that were not paid for by a third party in the amount of $7,500.

VIII. By reason of the premises, Plaintiff has been unable to pursue employment as a professional basketball player, to his special damage in a sum in excess of $1,000,000.

IX. The Plaintiff remained under the medical care of Defendants ROBERT BAKER and SPAKONE CITY ORTHOPEDIC CLINIC, P.C., from February 28 and into July. During said period, he relied on the medical advice of the Defendants, and was not informed of the true nature and extent of his injury to his left foot and its negligent cause. The Plaintiff did not discover the nature and extent of his injury to his left foot and its negligent cause until July when he began consulting other doctors.

X. By reason of the premises, Plaintiff has been generally damaged in the sum of $2,000,000.

WHEREFORE, Plaintiff prays judgment against Defendants, and each of them, jointly and severally, as follows:

1. For general damages in the sum of $2,000,000;
2. For special damages in a sum in excess of $1,000,000;
3. For costs and disbursements incurred herein.

D. Defamation

1. Common Law Principles

The rules governing liability for defamation make about as much sense as the rules governing the conjugation of irregular verbs in French. What follows is an attempt to present, as clearly as possible, the big picture of the current rules. Common law defamation consists of the two torts of libel and slander. Libel is written or printed defamation—defamation embodied in some tangible or permanent form and therefore generally subject to wide dissemination. Slander is oral defamation—fleeting and ephemeral and therefore generally not subject to wide dissemination. The tort of defamation, as it existed at common law, can be defined as the unconsented to and unprivileged intentional communication to a third person of a false statement about the plaintiff which tends to harm the reputation of the plaintiff in the eyes of the community. Once defamatory meaning is apparent, injury to reputation is generally presumed as a matter of law. Therefore, the plaintiff's prima facie case consists of a simple allegation that the defendant intentionally communicated to a third person a statement about the plaintiff which tended to expose the plaintiff to such things as public hatred, shame, obloquy, contumely, odium, contempt, ridicule, aversion, ostracism, degradation, or disgrace.

It should be noted that the tort of defamation is in substance one of strict liability. That is to say, the only intent that is required is the intent to communicate something to a third person. In the vast majority of cases, of course, the defendant clearly intends to communicate something to a third person even though she may not intend to defame or harm the plaintiff. In fact, it appears that the only type of case in which the courts are willing to concede that the requisite intent to communicate is lacking involves situations, for example, in which the defendant is alone with the plaintiff, defaming her to her face, and an unanticipated intruder overhears the defamatory utterance.

As to all other matters that conceivably could be either intended or negligently performed, the defendant is strictly accountable. It thus makes absolutely no difference that the defendant *does not intend* to lie, defame, or harm the plaintiff. Likewise, it is immaterial that the defendant *does not negligently* lie, defame, or harm the plaintiff. The defamer, in short, is strictly liable for whatever she intentionally communicates to a third person about the plaintiff if it turns out that what she said is false, injures the plaintiff's reputation in the eyes of the community, and is neither consented to by the plaintiff nor privileged. At common law, people communicate virtually at their own peril. The printed and written word is, in a legal sense, indistinguishable from nitroglycerin and dangerous animals—if someone is hurt by use of it, liability attaches.

Assuming that the plaintiff has made out a *prima facie* case, the defendant may escape liability by establishing that what was communicated was true or was either absolutely or conditionally privileged. Truth is a complete defense if the defendant can show that the imputation is substantially true. Generally, the defendant need not show literal truth but must establish that what was communicated was basically true as to the "sting" of the libel. Truth is generally a total defense regardless of the motives. Belief as to truth, however honest it may be, is no justification for defamation.

Privilege, like truth, is a complete defense if it is established by the defendant. The rationale for the existence of privilege as a defense is that conduct that may otherwise impose liability is excusable if the defendant is acting in furtherance of some socially useful interest. That is to say, it is more desirable, from a social standpoint, to protect the defendant and allow the plaintiff to go uncompensated. If an absolute privilege is found to exist, the defendant is totally immune from liability. Absolute privilege arises when the defendant is acting in furtherance of some very important social interest—an interest so important that the court is willing to immunize the defendant from liability for false statements without regard to purpose, motive, or reasonableness. Absolute privilege is confined to the few situations where there are obvious strong policy reasons in favor of permitting unbridled speech. Thus, statements made in the course of judicial or legislative proceedings are absolutely privileged. Executive communications, arguably made in the discharge of official duties, are likewise absolutely privileged. The media are absolutely privileged for defamation uttered by political candidates who have been granted equal time under the Federal Communications Act.

The most common defense involves a claim of qualified privilege, which arises when the defendant is arguably justified in talking. It is somewhat difficult to define qualified privilege with any degree of precision; the cases reveal repeated reliance on Baron Parke's formulation that a statement is privileged when it is "fairly made by a person in the discharge of some public and private duty, whether legal or moral, or in the conduct of one's own affairs in matters where his interest is concerned." The immunity conferred on the defendant is conditioned on his or her good behavior; the defendant must act properly or else the privilege is defeated. In general, a qualified privilege is defeated by the existence of facts inconsistent with the purpose of the privilege. The common law qualified privilege includes the privilege to fairly comment on matters of public concern by offering opinion, but not false statement of fact, and to fairly and accurately report public proceedings.

2. Public Figure Status and the Matrix of Relevant Supreme Court Cases

New York Times Co. v. Sullivan

376 U.S. 254 (1964)

[In March 1960, L.B. Sullivan was one of three elected commissioners to the city of Montgomery, Alabama. As such, he supervised the Montgomery police department, fire department, department of cemetery, and department of scales. On March 29, 1960, the *New York Times* ran a full page advertisement entitled *Heed Their Rising Voices*. The advertisement stated that thousands of Southern blacks, engaged in a nonviolent effort to secure constitutionally protected rights, were being met by an "unprecedented wave of terror" perpetuated by "Southern Violators," designed to prevent them from enjoying their constitutional rights. The Montgomery police were implicated on a number of occasions as "Southern Violators."

[It was uncontroverted that some statements in the advertisement were not accurate descriptions of events that occurred in Montgomery. The text of the advertisement concluded with an appeal for funds and appeared over the names of 64 persons—many widely known for accomplishments in religion, publications, trade unions, and the performing arts. L.B. Sullivan sued the *New York Times* and four black Alabama clergymen who signed the advertisement. A Montgomery county jury found that Sullivan was defamed and awarded him a half million dollars, the full amount claimed, against all the defendants. The Alabama Supreme Court affirmed, and the Supreme Court granted certiorari "because of the importance of the Constitutional issues involved."

[Although the Alabama law that was applied in *New York Times* did not differ significantly from the common law already described, the Supreme Court, with Justice Brennan writing the majority opinion, held "that the rule of law applied by the Alabama Courts is constitutionally deficient for failure to provide the safeguards for freedom of speech and of the press that are required by the First and Fourteenth Amendments in a libel action brought by a public official against critics of his official conduct." The Court went on to say that the evidence presented in the case was "constitutionally insufficient" to support the judgment for the respondent. The common law then, according to the Supreme Court, was inherently constitutionally defective.

[The Supreme Court considered the *New York Times* case "against the background of a profound national commitment to the principle that debate on public issues should be uninhibited, robust and wide-open, and that it may well include vehement, caustic and sometimes unpleasantly sharp attacks on government and public officials." The Court quoted Judge Learned Hand to the effect that the First Amendment "presupposes that right conclusions are more likely to be gathered out of a multitude of tongues than through any kind of authoritative selection" and that although "[t]o many this is… folly" we have, nonetheless, as a society, "staked upon it our all." In view of this national commitment to robust, wide-open debate, Justice Brennan reasoned "that erroneous statement is inevitable in free debate and that it must be protected if the freedoms of expression are to have the 'breathing space' that they 'need… to survive.'" Brennan cited Judge Edgerton for the simple truth that "whatever is added to the field of libel is taken from the field of free debate."

[The Court then constructed legal rules to ensure that our national commitment was not compromised. According to the Court, the Constitution requires "a federal rule that prohibits a public official from recovering damages for a defamatory falsehood related to his official conduct unless he proves that the statement was made with 'actual malice'—that is, with knowledge that it was false or with reckless disregard of whether it was false or not." Moreover, the aggrieved official must prove "actual malice" with "convincing clarity"—a standard of proof that is arguably more demanding than proof by a mere preponderance of evidence.

[Thus was born the constitutional privilege in defamation cases. The original and exclusive owner of the privilege, it should be noted, was the "citizen critic" of government.]

Curtis Publishing Co. v. Butts

(and its companion case, *Associated Press v. Walker*)
388 U.S. 130 (1967)

[Three years after the landmark *New York Times* decision, a majority of the Supreme Court agreed to extend the constitutional privilege to defamatory criticism of "public figures." Although Justice Harlan announced the results in both *Butts* and *Walker*, a majority of the Court agreed with Chief Justice Warren's conclusion in his concurring opinion that the *New York Times* test would apply to criticism of "public figures" in addition to "public officials." The Court's extension of the constitutional privilege to defamatory criticism of public figures made the *New York Times* privilege available to those who defamed people "intimately involved in the resolution of important public questions" or who "by reason of their fame, shape events in areas of concern to society at large."

[The *Butts* case originated with an article in the *Saturday Evening Post* accusing Wally Butts of conspiring to "fix" a football game between the University of Georgia and the University of Alabama. At the time of the article, Butts was the athletic director of the University of Georgia. The article accused Butts of giving team secrets to the opposition. Butts brought a libel action in federal court against Curtis Publishing Company; the publisher of the *Saturday Evening Post*, seeking $5,000,000 compensatory and $5,000,000 punitive damages. At trial, the defendant relied on the defense of truth. The jury returned a verdict for $60,000 in general damages and $3,000,000 in punitive damages. The court reduced the total award to $460,000 by remittitur. The Court of Appeals for the Fifth Circuit affirmed, and the Supreme Court granted certiorari and affirmed the decision.

[*Walker*, the companion case to *Butts*, arose out of the distribution of a news story giving an eyewitness account of events on the campus of the University of Mississippi on the night of the now infamous riot which erupted as a consequence of federal efforts to enforce a judicial decree ordering the enrollment of James Meredith as the first black student at the University. The story stated that General Walker, a retired career soldier and staunch segregationist, personally led a charge against the federal marshals' attempt to carry out the court order. Walker sued the Associated Press in the Texas state courts and asked for $2,000,000 in compensatory and punitive damages. Walker denied taking part in any "charge" against federal officials. Although the Associated Press defended on the basis of truth, a verdict of $500,000 compensatory damages and $300,000 punitive damages was returned. The trial judge, however, refused to enter the punitive award on the ground that there was no evidence of "actual malice." Both sides appealed, and the Texas Court of Civil Appeals affirmed. After the Supreme Court of Texas denied a writ of error, the Supreme Court of the United States granted certiorari and reversed.

[The rationale used by the Chief Justice in his concurring opinion was that "differentiation between 'public figures' and 'public officials' . . . has no basis in law, logic or First Amendment policy." The same test should apply both to the public figure plaintiff and public official plaintiff; each must show "actual malice" in order to recover. "[W]alker was a public man in whose public conduct society and the press had a legitimate and substantial interest." Because he did not prove actual malice, Walker could not recover. Butts, too, was a public figure; but unlike Walker, Butts proved "actual malice," because the jury's punitive damage award was preceded by an instruction that such an award was appropriate only if "actual malice" was found. Butts, then, could recover. The result is that the privilege that once belonged only to the citizen critic of government is extended to the citizen critic of the public person.]

Gertz v. Robert Welch, Inc.

418 U.S. 323 (1974)

[By 1974, hundreds of post-*New York Times* defamation cases had been before the courts. The result of this avalanche of litigation was a continuing struggle to find the appropriate balance between the rights of free speech and press and the right to be free from character attacks.

[In 1968, a Chicago policeman named Nuccio shot and killed a youth named Nelson. The policeman was subsequently found guilty of second-degree murder by state prosecutors. The Nelson family retained Elmer Gertz to represent them in civil litigation against Nuccio.

[Robert Welch published *American Opinion*, a monthly periodical of the John Birch Society. The magazine had long warned of a nationwide conspiracy to discredit local law enforcement agencies and create a national police force supporting a communist dictatorship. As a part of his effort to alert the public, Welch commissioned and published an article on the policeman's murder trial. In the article, Gertz was portrayed as a communist official with a criminal record. Statements made in the article contained serious factual inaccuracies.

[Gertz filed an action for libel in the United States District Court for the Northern District of Illinois, alleging injury to his reputation as a lawyer and citizen. Welch claimed that he was entitled to the constitutional privilege and asked for summary judgment on the grounds that Gertz would not be able to show "actual malice." The court denied the motion, concluding that Gertz might be able to prove "actual malice." After all the evidence was heard, the district court ruled that Gertz was not a public figure or public official and therefore did not have to prove "actual malice" to recover. The case was submitted to the jury, which determined the appropriate measure of damages was $50,000.

[The United States Supreme Court granted certiorari to reconsider the extent of a publisher's constitutional privilege against liability for defamation of a private citizen and reversed.

[The Court addressed the continuing dilemma of the "public person" as plaintiff. The *Gertz* Court endorsed its prior decisions in *Butts* and *Walker* and sought to further define the status of a public figure. Under *Gertz*, a public figure designation may rest on either of two alternatives:

> In some instances an individual may achieve such pervasive fame or notoriety that he becomes a public figure for all purposes and in all contexts. More commonly, an individual voluntarily injects himself or is drawn into a particular public controversy and thereby becomes a public figure for a limited range of issues. In either case such persons assume special prominence in the resolution of public questions.

[For the second category—public people for a limited range of issues—it "[i] s preferable to reduce the public figure question to a more meaningful context by looking to the nature and extent of an individual's participation in the particular controversy giving rise to the defamation." Public people in general enjoy "significantly greater access to the 'channels' of effective communication and hence have a more realistic opportunity to counteract false statements than private individuals normally enjoy." They typically also "invite attention and comment." In contrast, "private individuals are not only more vulnerable to injury than public officials and public figures; they are also more deserving of recovery."

[The Court concluded that Gertz was a private person and that the *New York Times* standard was not applicable. Because the jury was allowed to impose liability without fault and was permitted to presume damages without proof of actual injury, a new trial was ordered by the court.]

Milkovich v. Lorain Journal Co.

497 U.S. 1 (1990)

[Over a quarter of a century after the Supreme Court's decision in *New York Times v. Sullivan*, the court in *Milkovich* clarified the fact-opinion distinction. Remember that the common-law qualified privilege protected "opinions," but not false statements of fact.

[J. Theodore Diadum, a reporter for a newspaper owned by the Lorain Journal Co., authored an article in an Ohio newspaper which implied that Michael Milkovich (Milkovich), a local high school wrestling coach, lied under oath in a judicial proceeding about an incident involving Milkovich and his team which occurred at a wrestling match. Milkovich sued on a defamation theory. The trial court granted summary judgment for Lorain and the Ohio Court of Appeals affirmed. The judgment was based in part on the grounds that the article constituted an "opinion" protected from the reach of state defamation law by the First Amendment. The Supreme Court reversed, finding that the First Amendment does not prohibit the application of Ohio's defamation laws to the statement contained in the article.

[The issue before the Court was whether there was a constitutionally required "opinion" exception to the application of State defamation laws. The court discussed the common law. Lorain relied on dictum found in *Gertz* to support their argument that their "opinion" article was immune from the defamation laws. The court in *Gertz* had stated that, "[h]owever pernicious an opinion may seem, we depend for its correction not on the conscience of judges and juries but on the competition of other ideas." The Supreme Court here appears to retreat a bit from this notion.

[The court found that this passage from *Gertz* was not intended to create a wholesale defamation exception for anything that might be labeled "opinion." The court stated, "[n]ot only would such an interpretation be contrary to the tenor and context of the passage, but it would also ignore the fact that expressions of 'opinion' may often imply an assertion of objective fact." Where a statement of "opinion" on a matter of public concern reasonably implies false and defamatory facts regarding public figures or officials, the speaker could be vulnerable if the plaintiff could show that the statement was made with actual malice. Here, the Court found that the article communicated the fact that Milkovich perjured himself. The Court did not believe that the speech here was the "sort of loose, figurative or hyperbolic language which would negate the impression that the writer was seriously maintaining petitioners committed the crime of perjury." The article conveyed a statement which was sufficiently factual to be susceptible of being proven true or false.]

Notes and Comments

1. There are a few limited areas where actors are insulated from liability for ordinary negligence. These exemptions, too, are rooted in public policy. For example, in the area of defamation law, a plaintiff who is a public person can ordinarily recover for injury to reputation only upon a clear and convincing showing of knowledge or reckless disregard for truth or falsity. *New York Times v. Sullivan*, 376 U.S. 254 (1964). This solicitude for speech is grounded in strong social policy; we are as a people deeply committed to free speech and a wide-open, robust discussion of issues of public concern. In order to give speech the breathing room it needs to thrive, negligent speakers are insulated from liability.

2. ***Cepeda v. Cowles Magazines and Broadcasting Inc.*, 392 F.2d 417 (9th Cir.), *cert. denied*, 393 U.S. 840 (1968)**. The "Baby Bull" Orlando Cepeda was the plaintiff in a defamation law suit that took more than five years to resolve. Cepeda found himself trapped in a legal "pickle," in which the rules of defamation changed from one inning to the next. Although *Look Magazine* defamed Cepeda by saying he was "not a team man" and that he was "temperamental, uncooperative and under-productive," Cepeda was unable to show actual malice and eventually lost the suit. In-

terestingly, when Cepeda first brought the suit, he was under no obligation to prove actual malice. Cepeda was recently selected to Baseball's Hall of Fame.

3. ***Dempsey v. Time, Inc.*, 252 N.Y.S.2d 186 (1964)**. Heavyweight champion Jack Dempsey brought a defamation action in the wake of a *Sports Illustrated* article suggesting that Dempsey used "loaded gloves" when he beat Jess Willard for the heavyweight title in 1919. According to the report, Dempsey's gloves were loaded with plaster of Paris. The court denied the defendant's motion to dismiss, saying Dempsey introduced sufficient evidence of actual malice.

In June 1999, former prizefighter and actor Randall "Tex" Cobb was awarded $8.2 million in a defamation suit against *Sports Illustrated* and its parent company Time Warner. Cobb brought the defamation action after the magazine printed an article in 1993, alleging that Cobb and his promoter conspired to fix one of his bouts and then after the fight the two men snorted cocaine.

4. The modern sports celebrity will be viewed as a public figure for defamation purposes in most cases. This is particularly true if the account relates to the athlete's performance, as was the case in *Cepeda, Dempsey*, and *Cobb*. Is the actual malice standard appropriate if the report relates to an aspect of the athlete's private life as opposed to his or her athletic life? Can the two be easily separated?

5. Is it appropriate for amateur athletes to be deemed public figures for defamation purposes? One justification for public figure status is that the public has a right to know when those who profit from their public performance commit a misdeed; however, amateur athletes are not allowed to be paid for their performance as an athlete. Contrast *Nelson v. Time, Inc.*, No. B245412, 2014 WL 940448, at *16 (Cal. Ct. App. Mar. 11, 2014) (court found a former UCLA men's basketball player to be a limited purpose public figure given the exceedingly widespread interest in UCLA men's basketball and his position as a "rising star" on that team) with *Wilson v. Daily Gazette Co.*, 214 W.Va. 208, 216–17 (2003) (court found that a 17-year-old high school athlete, who was a member of his high school's football and basketball teams and received a scholarship to play football at West Virginia University, was not a public figure because defendant's evidence "simply established that in some circles, namely athletics, Mr. Wilson may have achieved a reputation as a quality high school athlete"). *See also* Stephen G. Strauss, *Defamation and the Collegiate Athlete: The Case of Failed Reporting and an NFL Drug Test*, 3 Sports L. J. 51 (1996).

6. The tort of "false light" occurs when the plaintiff has been placed in a false light in the public eye. This tort is closely related to defamation, and, although the Supreme Court has not entirely settled the issue, it would appear that the defamation rules previously discussed would apply to this tort as well. In fact, false light appears capable of swallowing defamation entirely in that a cause of action is stated for false statements whether they are defamatory or not. Although the statements that place the plaintiff in a false light typically are defamatory, they need not be. For example,

in *Spahn v. Julian Messner, Inc.*, 250 N.Y.S.2d 529 (1964), Warren Spahn, one of the greatest left-handed pitchers of all time, was able to recover for false but laudatory statements about him.

7. Does the actual malice standard give journalists an incentive to comply with their ethical obligation to "seek the truth" when reporting on matters involving high-profile individuals like athletes and coaches? For an in-depth discussion that compares and contrasts the ethical obligations of news reporters under journalism ethics codes with their reporting obligations under state defamation and privacy tort laws, see Richard T. Karcher, *Tort Law and Journalism Ethics*, 40 LOY. U. CHI. L. J. 781 (2009) ("Compromising ethics in journalism appears to be an acceptable industry norm that has continued to evolve because... tort privacy and defamation law standards applicable to the press that were developed [] half a century ago conflict with journalism ethics codes and do not create incentives for journalists to comply with such codes").

8. **Problem: A case study—*Virgil v. Time, Inc.*, 527 F.2d 1122 (9th Cir. 1975).** The causes of action arise out of a *Sports Illustrated* article titled *The Closest Thing to Being Born*. The article is about body surfing at the "Wedge," a public beach near Newport Beach, California, renowned for its dangerousness. The article, written by *Sports Illustrated* staff writer Thomas Curry Kilpatrick, focuses upon the body surfers at the Wedge. The plaintiff, Mike Virgil, a well-known body surfer at the Wedge, has the reputation of being the most daring of them all. Virgil was interviewed a number of times by Kilpatrick, and the article featured information from these interviews, along with photos of Virgil. In relevant part, the article provided:

> He is somewhat of a mystery to most of the regular personnel, partly because he is quiet and withdrawn, usually absent from their get-togethers, and partly because he is considered to be somewhat abnormal. Virgil's carefree style at the Wedge appears to have emanated from some escapades in his younger days, such as the time at a party when a young lady approached him and asked where she might find an ash tray. 'Why, my dear, right here' said Virgil, taking her lighted cigarette and extinguishing it in his mouth. He also won a small bet one time by burning a hole in a dollar bill that was resting on the back of his hand. In the process he also burned two holes in his wrist.

Prior to publication, the article was reviewed by a *Sports Illustrated* "checker," who called Virgil to verify certain information. Virgil indicated he no longer wanted to be mentioned in the article. Virgil did not dispute the truth of the article. He told the checker he thought the article was going to be about his ability as a body surfer and that he did not know that the article would contain references to incidents not directly related to his body surfing. *Sports Illustrated* published the article over Virgil's objections.

Discuss fully all of Virgil's possible causes of action.

Capstone Problem

Lane v. Plimpton

IN THE CIRCUIT COURT OF THE SIXTH JUDICIAL IN AND FOR SPOKANE COUNTY, STATE OF OKLANOIS, CIVIL DIVISION

Richard "Dickie" Lane

Plaintiff

v.

Rich Plimpton and

Sports Graphic, Inc.

Defendant

Statement of the Case

The plaintiff, Richard "Dickie" Lane, has sued Rich Plimpton and Sports Graphic, Inc. alleging defamation in connection with an article written by Plimpton which recently appeared in Sports Graphic magazine. Sports Graphic is the nation's most popular weekly sports magazine, and Plimpton is employed as a senior writer by the magazine. Relevant portions of the article are attached as Appendix 1. The parties have stipulated that the article as it appears in Appendix 1 is accurate and that the article was widely distributed nationwide. Lane will testify on his own behalf as will Plimpton. No other witnesses will be called.

Rules and Stipulations

1. This case shall be tried on liability only on a defamation theory. Should the plaintiff prevail at trial, the question of damages is reserved for the jury in a later proceeding. The parties have agreed to a bench trial on the liability issue.
2. Witnesses and lawyers are honor bound to abide by the "fair inference" rule. This means that witnesses and lawyers are free to fill in the blanks in the deposition testimony by adding details which are consistent with, and can be fairly inferred from, the existing testimony in the depositions. Motions in limine and objections can be made on the basis of a claimed violation of the fair inference rule.

Deposition of Dickie Lane

My name is Dickie Lane and I reside at 4187 E. 79th, in Manhattan, N.Y. I am 27 years old and I am a major league baseball player with the N.Y. Tromps. When I was 18 years old, I was drafted by the Tromps in the first round and I signed a contract which paid me a $3 million bonus. I have been in the major leagues for eight years and my current salary is $8.7 million.

I have been happily married to my wife Lola for eight years. She was my high school sweetheart. We have two children, Millie who is 6, and Billie who is 1. Since Billie's birth, I have not been unfaithful to my wife.

In the past three years, I have been very active in an organization called Promise Keepers. Promise Keepers is a Christian men's organization founded by former Colorado football coach, Bill McCartney. I am on the Board of Directors and have spoken at three mass gatherings. I also attend monthly support group meetings, which are similar to AA meetings. I find Plimpton's allegations of marital infidelity particularly disturbing, in light of my commitment to Promise Keepers. Promise Keepers swear to abide by three tenets. We all promise to return to the teachings of Jesus Christ. We all promise to honor our families. And we all promise to always behave as Christians.

The truth is that I have received permission from owner Howard Tromp to stay with my sister Fawn Rice when the club is in California. My other sister lives in Chicago and I have permission to stay with her when we're on the road there. Mr. Tromp asked me to be very discreet about these arrangements because he much prefers for the team to stay together at the team's designated hotel. Mr. Tromp made a special concession to me during my last contract negotiation to let me stay with my sisters. Mr. Plimpton asked to interview me in connection with this article but I refused. Since joining Promise Keepers, I only speak to the press when I am obligated to by the team—on days when I pitch, after the game.

Deposition of Rich Plimpton

My name is Rich Plimpton and I am 47 years old. I grew up in Norman, Oklahoma and I received my B.A. from Oklahoma University. I was a sports writer at the school paper and since graduating I have been employed as a sports writer. My first job after I graduated was with the Chicago Tribune and I rose through the ranks there. I worked for the Tribune for 20 years and was the sports editor when I left to take the job with Sports Graphic five years ago. I am a senior writer at Sports Graphic. All my stories are assigned by the editor, and they are rigorously reviewed for accuracy by our staff.

In regard to the Lane story which is the subject of this law suit, I can only say I made an honest mistake. When I wrote it, I believed it to be true. Many players I spoke to told me about Lane's "womanizing." I spoke with five of his teammates, who all corroborated for me the truth of what I wrote. I tried on numerous occasions to interview Lane but he refused. I followed Lane and shot the photo of him hugging Fawn Rice. I learned that she was an aspiring actress and had no idea that she was Lane's sister. I am well aware of Lane's recent conversion to Promise Keepers; it is a matter of common knowledge to sports fans. The players I spoke to thought that

Lane's new found commitment to Promise Keepers was nonsense—they viewed it as further proof of Lane's propensity to be hypocritically opportunistic. Many of his teammates confided to me that they resented Lane's moralizing and viewed him as a hypocrite in light of what they believed to be his incessant "sleeping around."

Appendix 1
"The Fast Life of Dickie Lane" by Rich Plimpton

Dickie, the Philanderer

By trailing Dickie Lane for two weeks while he was on the road, we learned that Lane's tiresome public posturing about family values is just that—posturing. While on a road trip to California, Dickie received special permission from owner Howard Tromp to stay for three days at the home of an attractive, aspiring 22-year-old model named Fawn Rice. Other Tromp players told us that Lane has a similar quiet arrangement whenever the club visits Chicago. All this extracurricular activity makes Lane's outspoken commitments to family values all the more hypocritical.

[The Sports Graphic article included two photographs, one a posed family photo of Lane, his wife and two young children. The caption under the first photo said: "Lane, baseball's most visible family man, shown here with wife Lola and children, Millie and Billie." The other photo shows Lane hugging Fawn Rice as she greeted him at the door of her Beverly Hills condominium. The caption under this photo said: "Lane, shown here, giving a warm greeting to his Beverly Hills squeeze Fawn Rice."]

E. Intentional Interference with Contractual Relations

Extraordinarily talented people are often in demand. This is particularly true when the talent is marketable. When this is the case, it is not unusual to see employers vying for the services of the peculiarly gifted person, which can give rise to a claim for intentional interference with contractual relations. The landmark case of *Lumley v. Gye*, 118 Eng. Rep. 749 (1853), is illustrative of the classic fact pattern. In that case, opera star Johanna Wagner had entered into an exclusive contract to perform for the Queen's Theatre. The Queen's Theatre alleged that the defendant, a rival employer, had attempted to induce Johanna Wagner to refuse to perform for the Queen's Theatre. In a case that broke new ground, the court recognized intentional interference with contractual relations as a viable cause of action. The tort today retains special vitality in the sports setting as rival employers compete for the special services of especially gifted athletes and coaches.

The tort's modern profile requires the plaintiff to show that the defendant intentionally interfered with an existing contractual relationship of the plaintiff. The defendant must do something that either prevents performance of the contract or makes performance substantially less likely. The defendant must have actual knowledge of the contract and must act with the intention of interfering with the contract. The defendant can justify the interference by showing that, on balance, the defendant's right to compete with the plaintiff for the personal services of others outweighs the plaintiff's interest in entirely stable contractual relations. Thus, the defendant might be justified in seeking to open negotiations with someone who is already employed. The cases and material that follow explore the parameters of the tort in greater detail.

Also, a separate cause of action against the employee often accompanies the claim of intentional interference with contractual relations. Typically, the plaintiff in the contractual relations claim will also seek to enjoin the employee from performing for someone else. This "negative injunction" (covered in Chapter 8) is a standard remedial tool in the entertainment and sports industries. To illustrate, note that *Lumley v. Gye* had a companion, *Lumley v. Wagner*, 42 Eng. Rep. 687 (1852). In that case, the Queen's Theatre sought injunctive relief against Johanna Wagner to force her to perform her contract and to prevent her from performing elsewhere. The court held that while Johanna could not be compelled to perform for the Queen's Theatre, she could be prevented from performing elsewhere. This is generally true today in the sports industry.

World Football League v. Dallas Cowboys Football Club, Inc.

513 S.W.2d 102 (Tex. Civ. App. 1974)

Bateman, Justice.

[At the time of the lawsuit, the World Football League (WFL) was a newly organized professional football league attempting to compete with the well-established National Football League (NFL). The Dallas Cowboys, a franchised NFL team, sought injunctive relief against WFL recruiting practices which it characterized as "raiding." In particular, the Cowboys complained about letters and return postcards that were sent by the WFL to players under contract with the Cowboys, urging the players to consider signing with a WFL team. In pertinent part, the letter read as follows:

> Dear Player:
>
> The World Football League will begin play in 1974 with franchises in twelve areas, including New York, Chicago, Detroit, Toronto, New England, Southern California, Hawaii, and Florida. The remaining franchises will be awarded from some twenty applications for membership under consideration.
>
> It is the intention of the World Football League to be "Major League" in every way, particularly in signing the top professional players available. We feel strongly that every player should honor his present contractual obligation.

> However, we would very much like to talk with you about the possibility of joining our League at the expiration of your present contract.
>
> In order for us to know your status and to contact you, please fill out and return the enclosed post card as soon as possible.

The postcards asked for information about the player, including name, address, and number of years remaining on contract and asked the player to indicate if he was interested in hearing an offer from the WFL.

[Three Cowboys (Calvin Hill, Craig Morton, and Mike Montgomery) signed WFL contracts to perform for WFL teams following the completion of their contractual obligations to the Cowboys. The Cowboys argued that the WFL was guilty of tortious interference with contractual relations and were granted injunctive relief at the trial court level. The Court of Civil Appeals here dissolved the temporary injunction.]

The Club argues that WFL is guilty of "pirating" its players and that unless enjoined it will continue to do so, but the only evidence of any contact whatever between WFL and the Club's players is the above quoted letter and the post card enclosed therewith. These writings do not suggest an unlawful "raiding scheme." The letter plainly states that the player should honor his existing contractual obligations and inquires only about the possibility of the player's interest in joining one of the WFL teams after the expiration of his present contract. There was no evidence of legal malice or deceitful means used by WFL or any motive or effort on its part to interfere with the contractual relations between the Club and its players.

The Club also contends that WFL arranged for, and induced three players to participate in, press conferences and various publicity activities surrounding the signing of contracts with WFL teams by Hill, Morton and Montgomery, thus causing a breach of the contracts between said players and the Club. In each of those contracts the player agrees "that during the term of this contract he will play football and engage in activities related to football only for the Club. ..."

The Club's principal contention is that the signing of the Cowboy players by WFL teams for services to be rendered after expiration of their present contracts is an unlawful interference with the Club's present contractual relations with its players, as defined by the above provision of its contracts, because the players so signing will not use their best efforts for the team under their current contracts, the morale of the entire team will suffer, the enthusiasm of the fans will wane, and the new employers will reap the benefits of any favorable publicity for outstanding performance of the players so signing. The Club argues further that publicity resulting from the signing of such contracts for future services is a breach of the present obligations which the players owe to the Club.

These facts, even if true, do not present grounds for equitable relief. We must consider the freedom of contract of the individual players as well as the rights of the Club under its present contracts. Bargaining for future services is a matter of economics. The Club can assure itself of the continued services and loyalty of its players by offering them long-term contracts and other financial inducements. If it chooses not to do so for economic reasons, it has no legal ground to complain if the players look elsewhere for their future careers and enter into contracts for services to be performed when their present contracts with the Club expire. Signing such contract is neither a breach of the contract by the players nor a tortious interference by the future employers, and the threat to enter into such contracts affords no ground for equitable relief. Neither does the publicity necessarily attendant upon the signing of contracts with well-known players constitute a tort. An injunction restraining the signing of such contracts because of the attendant publicity would be an unreasonable restraint on the freedom of contract of the players and their prospective employers.

We should not be understood, however, as holding that other promotional and publicity activities for the benefit of future employers would not be subject to restraint as "activities relating to football," which the players are bound by their present contracts to reserve for the Club. No such limited equitable relief was sought either in the trial court or in this court. The Club has cast its entire case for injunctive relief on its contention that the signing of contracts for future services would in itself be a tortious interference with the players' performance of their obligations under their present contracts with the Club. Since the injunction cannot be sustained on that ground, it must be dissolved....

The temporary injunction is dissolved.

New England Patriots Football Club, Inc. v. University of Colorado

592 F.2d 1196 (1st Cir. 1979)

ALDRICH, SENIOR CIRCUIT JUDGE.

[In 1973 Chuck Fairbanks contracted with the New England Patriots, a professional football club in the National Football League, to act as its general manager and head coach. In so doing, Fairbanks breached his then existing contract with the University of Oklahoma. In 1977, Fairbanks' contract with the Patriots was extended through 1983. The contract contained a provision that Fairbanks would not provide services connected with football to any entity other than the Patriots. It also contained a provision that Fairbanks would not render services to another not connected with football except with the permission of the Patriots. In November of 1978, Fairbanks was approached by agents of the University of Colorado to become its head football coach. At first, the negotiations were secret. When Fairbanks agreed to terms with the University of Colorado, he informed Sullivan, the owner of the Patriots, of his intention to leave the Patriots at the close of the 1978 season. Sullivan suspended Fairbanks and sought injunctive relief against the University of Colorado. The district court entered a preliminary injunction enjoining the University of Colorado from causing the university to employ Fairbanks as the university's coach. The university appealed and Fairbanks was given permission to file an amicus brief. The First Circuit here affirmed the district court.]

Although this is not our first experience with the athletic milieu's response to legal embroilment engendered by contract jumping, we set out the factual contentions in some detail in order to get in the mood. For this opportunity we are primarily indebted to the Fairbanks' amicus brief.

The extension of the contract to January 26, 1983 was agreed to on June 6, 1977. The briefs are silent as to this date, an understandable reticence in view of the fact that by that time Fairbanks had, apparently, already decided he might not keep his word.

"For a number of years, Fairbanks was extremely unhappy with remaining in professional football [and]... with his present location.... Fairbanks believed the health of his family, and a reassessment of career objectives, *mandated a change*. Accordingly, for a number of years, he had been investigating business opportunities outside football, as well as coaching at the college level." (Amicus br. 8) (Emphasis suppl.)...

[Because] in 1973 the Patriots allegedly had lured Fairbanks from the University of Oklahoma, inducing him to break his contract there, defendants conclude that the Patriots are barred from relief by the doctrine of unclean hands. We disagree. Both parties may have done the University of Oklahoma dirt, but that does not mean unclean hands with respect to "the controversy in issue."...

[Equally,] we are not taken by Fairbanks' claim that because, when he told Sullivan that he was leaving at the end of the season and Sullivan responded that he was "suspended," it was Sullivan who broke the contract.

"The simple fact is that Fairbanks was fired." (Amicus br. 11). Whatever may be thought the meaning in the trade of suspension, as distinguished from its commonly understood meaning, it is a novel concept that a contract-breaker had the option to require the other party to accept his choice of dates. At least until Fairbanks withdrew his unlawful announcement, the Patriots had a right not to accept the services of an unfaithful servant, or, as Sullivan put it to him at the time, one who had "his body in Foxboro and his heart in Colorado."

At the hearing Fairbanks testified that although the contract read "services directly connected with football... [or for] another entity not connected with football," this meant, simply, activities competitively connected with the Patriots. Apparently he has no more regard for the parole evidence rule forbidding the contradiction of unambiguous language than for other rules foisted upon him by legalisms. Parenthetically, having in mind, as sometimes helpless dial-spinners, that professional and prominent college football teams compete for TV viewers, and hence, presumably, for the advertising dollar, we may wonder whether we have to accept at face value the protestation of no competitive activity here. In any event, there is ample authority contradicting both aspects of defendants' legal position. Indeed, some courts have gone even further, and have enjoined the defaulting athlete himself from non-competitive sport. *E.g., Munchak v. Cunningham*, 4th Cir., 1972, 457 F.2d 721 (ABA player enjoined from play with NBA, prior to merger); *Houston Oilers, Inc. v. Neely*, ante (AFL player enjoined from NFL play, prior to merger); *Nassau Sports v. Peters*, E.D.N.Y., 1972, 352 F. Supp. 870 (NHL player enjoined from play in fledgling WHA); *Winnipeg Rugby Football Club v. Freeman*, N.D. Ohio, 1955, 140 F. Supp. 365 (player under contract to Canadian team and NFL team enjoined); *see also Boston Professional Hockey Ass'n v. Cheevers*, ante (chance of irreparable harm shown by players under contract with NHL team jumping to WHA); *American League Baseball Club v. Pasquel*, Sup. Ct., 1946, 187 Misc. 230, 63 N.Y.S.2d 537 (Mexican League enjoined from inducing American League players from repudiating contracts). We would not distinguish between an athlete and a coach. To enjoin tortious interference by a third party, whether or not competitive, would seem a lesser step. *See Winnipeg Rugby Football Club v. Freeman*, ante; *Pino v. Trans-Atlantic Marine, Inc.*, 1970, 358 Mass. 498, 265 N.E.2d 583; *Moore Drop Forging Co. v. McCarthy*, 1923, 243 Mass. 554, 137 N.E. 919; *American League Baseball Club v. Pasquel*, ante.

We comment briefly on the self-serving statement in Fairbanks' amicus brief that he is "through with professional football." There is no such finding in the record, and even though that may now be the conventional wisdom, neither the Patriots nor the court are bound to accept it. At this stage Fairbanks could be expected to say no less. Defendants' constant stress that the injunction is unproductive, and nothing but "punishment" in light of the fact that a position with the University "is the only game in town," is a total non-sequitur that cuts the other way. If there may, in part, be a punitive effect, we could not avoid wondering how great a miscarriage that would be with respect to one who, on his own testimony, promised a longer term than he intended to keep, not only to afford himself sanctuary while he looked around, but, again on his own testimony, putting himself in line for higher pay meanwhile, and whose seeming only defense to his announced total breach is a claim that the Patriots grabbed the gun.

Notes and Comments

1. Is it an interference with existing contractual relations for the soon-to-be employer to publicize the fact that a player has agreed to "jump"? The issue was touched upon briefly in both *Dallas Cowboys* and *Bergey*, which is discussed in the problem below. Both courts thought that the publicity that necessarily flowed from the signing was unavoidable and obviously not tortious. But a number of questions remain. While the player would apparently be able to attend a press conference to announce his intention to play for the new club at some later date, may the new club enlist the

player to promote ticket sales while the player is still under contract to his old club? May the new club prevail upon the player to attend promotional events? Or would this be a tortious interference with the existing contractual relations of the old club?

2. Thus far, the question of intentional interference has come up in the classic *Lumley v. Gye* context. That is to say, the basic ingredient is a rival, competing employer wooing away employees under contract. Is the context the same when it involves a rival employer who attempts to convince the employee to play a wholly different game? By way of illustration, take the Danny Ainge case. Ainge is under contract to play baseball for the Toronto Blue Jays. Red Auerbach, general manager of the Celtics, tries to convince Ainge to play basketball instead. Is Red's conduct to be evaluated as though he was trying to get Ainge to play baseball for him? Or is Red's competitive privilege broader in this context? *See Toronto Blue Jays Baseball Club v. Boston Celtics Corp.*, 81 Civ. 5263 (S.D.N.Y. 1981).

3. Most of the professional leagues have rules that prohibit a team in the league from "tampering" with players on other teams. The standard provision makes it improper for a club to tamper, negotiate with, or make an offer to a player under contract with another club. The typical sanctions are losses of draft choices and fines. Note that the no-tampering rules would prohibit negotiating for future services, which is clearly not tortious. Whether the various no-tampering rules preclude tort claims is unclear. Moves by star coaches and players may prove ripe for the tort cause of action.

4. When high profile college coaches breach their contract by leaving prior to the expiration of the contract term, schools are typically compensated pursuant to a liquidated damages provision in the contract, which is negotiated between the two sides and compensation owed is often paid by the breaching coach's new institution. Commonly referred to as a "buyout," the amount can be quite substantial, oftentimes millions of dollars. However, multimillion dollar buyouts have certainly not deterred coaches from breaching their contracts nor have they deterred schools from soliciting coaches. For an analysis of the use and validity of liquidated damages clauses in college coaches' contracts and the difficulties of suing for damages in the absence of a liquidated damages clause, see Richard T. Karcher, *The Coaching Carousel in Big-Time Intercollegiate Athletics: Economic Implications and Legal Considerations*, 20 Fordham Intel. Prop. Media & Ent. L. J. 1 (2009).

5. The argument has been made that a good contractual interference cause of action exists against agents who violate NCAA eligibility rules by signing or compensating scholarship athletes. Evaluate the university's cause of action against the agent. *See* Richard P. Woods & Michael R. Mills, *Tortious Interference with an Athletic Scholarship: A University's Remedy for the Unscrupulous Sports Agent*, 40 Ala. L. Rev. 141 (1988).

In *Davis v. Baylor University*, 976 S.W.2d 5 (Mo. Ct. App. 1998), Tyrone Davis was improperly recruited in violation of NCAA guidelines by Baylor University. When the violations came to light, Davis was barred from playing the 1993–1994 season. He later transferred to Kansas State and played professionally in Japan. He felt his career was hindered by the violations. Davis sued the university and a number of its employees for interference with prospective business opportunities, contractual interference, false light defamation, negligent hiring, and other related causes of action.

6. **Problem.** This problem is based on *Cincinnati Bengals, Inc. v. Bergey*, 453 F. Supp. 129 (S.D. Ohio 1974), *aff'd*, Civil No. 74-1570 (6th Cir. Aug. 27, 1974). The case is in many ways similar to *World Football League v. Dallas Cowboys Football Club*. But the attack on the World Football League (WFL) recruiting practices by the National Football League (NFL) Cincinnati Bengals franchise has a broader base, and issues not addressed in the *Cowboys* case are confronted directly here. Based upon the following facts presented at trial, which party do you think should prevail and why?

The Bengals' offense. On the field, the Bengals are noted for their creatively successful offense. This philosophy carries over to their litigation. The gist of the Bengals' claim is that the WFL, and its member teams, are tortiously invading the Bengals' ranks by signing players under existing Bengal contracts to contracts for future services. The Bengals seek injunctive relief, contending that the WFL is irreparably harming the Bengals by intentionally interfering with existing contractual relations. One key argument made by the Bengals is that a player who signs a contract for future services with the WFL is likely to "dog it" with the Bengals. Another key argument is that these signings adversely affect the performance of the rest of the team.

More particularly, the Bengals objected to the WFL's signing of two players, Steve Chomyszak and Bill Bergey. On April 9, 1974, Chomyszak signed a contract to play with the WFL Philadelphia Bell. The contract provided that Chomyszak would begin playing for the Bell at the conclusion of his contract with the Bengals following the 1974 season unless the Bengals released him, in which case the WFL contract would "accelerate." Since the Bell had agreed to pay Chomyszak more than the Bengals, the Bengals argued that Chomyszak had an incentive to be "cut" by the Bengals in order to start playing for the Bell.

Bergey was under contract with the Bengals through May 1976 at a salary of $38,750 per year. On April 17, 1974, Bergey signed with the WFL Virginia Ambassadors. The contract provided that Bergey would begin playing with the Ambassadors in May 1976, at a salary of $125,000 per year. Like Chomyszak's contract, Bergey's had an "acceleration" clause that provided: "However, should Bergey be released from his contract with The Cincinnati Bengals, Inc. so as to be available for the entire 1974 and 1975 football season, then, in such event, the term of this contract shall cover the 1974, 1975 and 1976 football seasons or the 1975, 1976 and 1977 football seasons, as the case may be." Additionally, Bergey's contract paid him a $150,000 bonus, in consideration of signing. And finally, it was a "no cut" contract, payable even in the event that Bergey was cut from the team for lack of skill. Once again, the Bengals argued that this contract substantially interfered with their contract with Bergey because of the strong incentive it provided Bergey to be released by the Bengals.

In order to show the full effects of these signings, the Bengals introduced evidence concerning the nature of professional football. Bengals' coach Paul Brown testified that the success of a football team "comes down to nothing, really, but people" and that "if they're ever a bad character or boozer or chaser or what not, we're that much farther away from winning what we're trying to win." Coach Mike McCormick, of the Philadelphia Eagles, testified that the "individual sometimes has to suppress himself for the good of the team." He further testified: "I believe it's a game where, as the immediate supervisor, the head coach has to have control. I believe if a man is under contract to someone else, then that leverage and control has been taken away from the head coach."

McCormick testified that he believed that Bergey would be a divisive force on the Bengals. Four assistant coaches for the Bengals and one player elaborated on the theme. Football was a unique sport with required emotional commitments from every player to play with desire as a member of a cohesive unit. Contractual commitments to WFL teams tended to destroy this commitment. The trial judge concluded: "From all this the Court can and does find that football is probably unique in that, to a greater degree than other professional sports, it is a team sport. Also, it takes time and money to develop the players and 'units' so that they will be cohesive. In short, football is a scientific, sophisticated sport, and a delicate sort of mechanism."

In summary, the Bengals argued that these signings had a detrimental effect not only on Bergey's and Chomyszak's performances, but on the other members of the team as well.

The WFL defense. In an effort to disprove the requisite intent to interfere with contractual relations, the WFL offered testimony that the signing of name players to future contracts was essential to the WFL's success. The WFL was not trying to interfere with existing contractual relations; it was attempting to gain public acceptance as a bona fide professional football league. The court specifically acknowledged that "starting a new league is a risky business" and found that "the WFL's motive for signing established NFL players is not to cause any harm to the NFL teams in general or the Cincinnati Bengals in particular, but to further the competitive interests of the WFL."

The WFL also introduced evidence to offset the Bengals' claim that the signing had a detrimental effect on team performance. Several players testified specifically that Bergey's performance was not noticeably altered by his signing. The gist of the WFL testimony in this regard was that the signings had no appreciable detrimental effect on team performance. Assistant Coach Chuck Studley admitted that he perceived no animosity among the Bengals as a result of the lawsuit and that neither team morale nor team performance had suffered.

Eleven

Intellectual Property Issues in Sports

Learning Outcomes

- Understand the justification for intellectual property rights in sports.
- Learn how infringement occurs.
- Know what uses are "fair" and within First Amendment protection.
- Explore whether and to what extent an individual athlete has a proprietary "right of publicity" to control and profit from the commercial use of the athlete's identity and likewise to preclude others from such usage.
- Understand the scope of federal trademark protection for team names, logos, symbols, and other distinctive marks in the areas of sports merchandising, advertising, and naming rights.
- Understand federal copyright protection in sports, including the broadcast, media, and the scope of rights to restrict others from broadcasting, reporting, or otherwise profiting from the sporting event.

Key Terms

- Lanham Act
- Right of publicity
- Transformative use
- Public domain
- First Amendment
- Trademark
- Likelihood of confusion
- Fair use
- Ambush marketing
- Copyright Act
- Misappropriation
- Fact/expression dichotomy

A. Introduction

Other than the occasional opportunity for a fan at a baseball game to take home a ball that has left the field of play from a foul or home run, the fans who provide the revenue, directly or indirectly, to support both professional and amateur sports are paying for an intangible good. These goods take numerous forms, such as the right to enter a stadium or arena to watch a game in action, to watch a broadcast image or description of a game, to purchase a garment or souvenir emblazoned with a logo or name of one's favorite team, or simply the knowledge and satisfaction in purchasing a product or service that one's athletic hero uses and endorses.

The public fascination with sports and sports figures fuels an industry that garners billions in revenue. The opportunities to market and commercially profit from sports go far beyond selling tickets for admission. In addition to their salaries, accomplished athletes have tremendous financial opportunities through endorsement contracts with companies eager to have the athletes promote their products. In some cases, players earn more through endorsement contracts than from salaries and team benefits. For professional and many collegiate sports teams, the most substantial sources of revenue lie in reaching a national, even international, audience through broadcasting coverage and the reporting of sporting events through audio, visual, print, and virtual mediums. Royalties from licensing authorized merchandise sales of sports memorabilia generates billions of dollars in additional revenue.

Sports also provides financial opportunities for enterprising businesses or individuals outside of those directly involved with a sports franchise—sports bars and restaurants, the hot dog vendor outside the stadium, the merchants selling sports memorabilia, and the private operators of fantasy sports leagues or sports blogs that generate increasingly substantial revenue from advertising and affiliated deals—are only a few examples. Cities have been willing to finance sports facilities on the expectation that the sporting events provide an economic benefit for community businesses and thus enhanced tax revenue. With the lucrative market sports provides, other businesses, entrepreneurs, and individuals are eager to capitalize on the public's interest by providing services, products, or information—both online and off— sometimes in competition with those directly involved in the sports industry or simply because of the investment of the sports industry. Gambling and betting on sports, estimated to be a $150 to $400 billion per year market in the United States alone, raise numerous questions (*e.g.*, regulatory, governance, corruption), including the use and ownership of sport intellectual property. As U.S. professional sports leagues realize the epic economic potential of sports gambling, esports, daily fantasy, and even artificial intelligence to engage fans, who owns the right to use and profit off the games, data, and investment that the players and leagues produce? What is "fair use" by the sports industry, or when a non-sponsoring company effectively promotes its brand by a congratulatory Tweet to a sponsored athlete or social media posting on a sporting event #hashtag, or when a blogger or fan posts video excerpts from a live game?

In the business of sports, the value the players, teams, and owners hold, and the product essentially sold, is intangible. An athlete's reputation and performance may enable a vast earning potential in endorsements. Returns on the investments made by the players, teams, and leagues in establishing quality sporting competitions and creating fan interest and loyalty are realized through corporate sponsorships and through valuable licensing contracts authorizing rights to broadcast team or league games and to market merchandise bearing the team's name, logo, or distinctive style.

Protecting these intangible assets is of paramount concern for all involved in the sports business—the owners, athletes, teams, leagues, sponsors, event producers, and player associations. These valuable yet intangible rights are at risk when outsiders seek to profit unfairly from the sports industry's investments. Determining what constitutes a legitimate, as opposed to unlawful, commercial use by outsiders involves examining the legal rights of the various parties.

A body of federal and state law, broadly encompassed as intellectual property, has developed to establish the ownership and property rights in such intangible, yet extremely valuable, assets. This chapter focuses on three primary areas intersecting intellectual property issues and sports. Section B explores the question of whether and to what extent an individual athlete has a proprietary "right of publicity" to control and profit from the commercial use of the athlete's identity and likewise to preclude others from such usage. Section C introduces a range of issues involving the scope of federal trademark protection for team names, logos, symbols, and other distinctive marks in the areas of sports merchandising, advertising, and naming rights. Section D examines issues of federal copyright protection in sports, including the broadcast, media, and the scope of rights to restrict others from broadcasting, reporting, or otherwise profiting from the sporting event. These issues have become increasingly more complicated and relevant with the emergence of mobile and digital media.

B. Athlete Rights of Publicity

Is image everything? Accomplished athletes and sports figures are celebrities, even heroes, in the public eye. These athletes often stand to profit as much or more from their image, celebrity, and "brand" through lucrative endorsement contracts and corporate sponsorships as they do from their professional salaries. Upon announcing that he was leaving Stanford University to become a professional golfer, Eldrick "Tiger" Woods signed endorsement contracts worth an estimated $70 million before he had played in his first tournament as a professional. LeBron James similarly began his NBA career out of high school with a $90 million shoe contract with Nike, and in 2015 signed a lifetime deal with Nike reportedly worth more than $1 billion. Many of the highest-paid athletes earn more from endorsements than actually playing their sport. In tennis alone, Roger Federer, with $65 million earnings in 2018, and sisters Venus and Serena Williams are among the highest-paid athletes through prize money and endorsements. The world's other top earning athletes include international superstars Cristiano Ronaldo and Lionel Messi in soccer, and boxing's Floyd Mayweather. Esports *athletes* are also attracting enormous audiences, such as Fortnite gamer and streaming star "Ninja," reportedly making more than $10 million in 2018 from Twitch subscription fees, merchandise, and endorsements. As the sport industry is opening up to gambling, betting, esports, and is increasingly seen as entertainment (sportainment?), money spent on sports marketing, sponsorships, and endorsements is expected to increase.

Sponsors do take a gamble in endorsement deals with athletes when scandal erupts. The demise of an athlete's image leads to a correlative plummet in their commercial marketability. Reports of misconduct, cheating, doping, or other rule violations can be costly for a high-profile athlete and the sponsor. Tiger Woods' infidelity transgressions cost him an estimated $180 million dollars in personal earnings and cost his sponsors between $5 and $12 billion in shareholder value. Lance Armstrong's doping cost him more than $100 million in endorsements, seven Tour de France titles, and his Livestrong cancer charity's affiliation.

Sporting figures are concerned not only about maintaining a semblance of privacy but also protecting their image from exploitation by others. As seen from the following cases, state law generally provides some protection under a "right to publicity" to guard the names, reputations, and identities of athletes from commercial exploitation. The Lanham Act, 15 U.S.C. § 1125(a), also protects against the misappropriation of an athlete's name, image and likeness, false endorsement, and trademark infringement. Consider, however, whether and how the law limits the commercial use of an athlete's identity by others. Is an athlete who has become a public figure entitled to preclude others from using his or her name, nickname, image, or distinctive reference (identity) without consent or remuneration to the athlete? Do college athletes have rights to preclude the NCAA, conferences, and television networks from using their images in the sale and distribution of the live game broadcasts without a license? Is the commercial use simply of a player's name and statistics in fantasy sports or sports betting a form of misappropriated intellectual property? What is the appropriate scope of a right of publicity versus the right to fair use and free speech by the public, artists, journalists, and commerce?

C.B.C. Distribution and Marketing, Inc. v. Major League Baseball Adv. Media, L.P.

505 F.3d 818 (8th Cir. 2007), *cert. denied*, 553 U.S. 1090 (2008)

C.B.C. Distribution and Marketing, Inc., brought this action for a declaratory judgment against Major League Baseball Advanced Media, L.P., to establish its right to use, without license, the names of and information about major league baseball players in connection with its fantasy baseball products. Advanced Media counterclaimed, maintaining that CBC's fantasy baseball products violated rights of publicity belonging to major league baseball players and that the players, through their association, had licensed those rights to Advanced Media, the interactive media and Internet company of major league baseball. The Major League Baseball Players Association intervened in the suit, joining in Advanced Media's claims and further asserting a breach of contract claim against CBC. The district court granted summary judgment to CBC, and Advanced Media and the Players Association appealed. We affirm.

I.

CBC sells fantasy sports products via its Internet website, e-mail, mail, and the telephone. Its fantasy baseball products incorporate the names along with performance and biographical data of actual major league baseball players. Before the commencement of the major league baseball season each spring, participants form their fantasy baseball teams by "drafting" players from various major league baseball teams. Participants compete against other fantasy baseball "owners" who have also drafted their own teams. A participant's success, and his or her team's success, depends on the actual performance of the fantasy team's players on their respective actual teams during the course of the major league baseball season. Participants in CBC's fantasy baseball games pay fees to play and additional fees to trade players during the course of the season.

From 1995 through the end of 2004, CBC licensed its use of the names of and information about major league players from the Players Association pursuant to license agreements that it entered into with the association in 1995 and 2002. The 2002 agreement, which superseded in its entirety the 1995 agreement, licensed to CBC "the names, nicknames, likenesses, signatures, pictures, playing records, and/or biographical data of each player" (the "Rights") to be used in association with CBC's fantasy baseball products.

In 2005, after the 2002 agreement expired, the Players Association licensed to Advanced Media, with some exceptions, the exclusive right to use baseball players' names and performance information "for exploitation via all interactive media." Advanced Media began providing fantasy baseball games on its website, MLB.com, the official website of major league baseball. It offered CBC, in exchange for a commission, a license to promote the MLB.com fantasy baseball games on CBC's website but did not offer CBC a license to continue to offer its own fantasy baseball products. This conduct by Advanced Media prompted CBC to file the present suit, alleging that it had "a reasonable apprehension that it will be sued by Advanced Media if it continues to operate its fantasy baseball games."

***

II.

A.

An action based on the right of publicity is a state-law claim. *See Zacchini v. Scripps-Howard Broad. Co.*, 433 U.S. 562 (1977). In Missouri, "the elements of a right of publicity action include: (1) That defendant used plaintiff's name as a symbol of his identity (2) without consent (3) and with the intent to obtain a commercial advantage." The parties all agree that CBC's continued use of the players' names and playing information after the expiration of the 2002 agreement was without consent. The district court concluded, however, that the evidence was insufficient to make out the other two elements of the claim, and we address each of these in turn.

With respect to the symbol-of-identity element, the Missouri Supreme Court has observed that "'the name used by the defendant must be understood by the audience as referring to the plaintiff.'" The state court had further held that "[i]n resolving this issue, the fact-finder may consider evidence including 'the nature and extent of the identifying characteristics used by the defendant, the defendant's intent, the fame of the plaintiff, evidence of actual identification made by third persons, and surveys or other evidence indicating the perceptions of the audience.'"

Here, we entertain no doubt that the players' names that CBC used are understood by it and its fantasy baseball subscribers as referring to actual major league baseball players. [W]hen a name alone is sufficient to establish identity, the defendant's use of that name satisfies the plaintiff's burden to show that a name was used as a symbol of identity.

It is true that with respect to the "commercial advantage" element of a cause of action for violating publicity rights, CBC's use does not fit neatly into the more traditional categories of commercial advantage, namely, using individuals' names for advertising and merchandising purposes in a way that states or intimates that the individuals are endorsing a product. *Cf.* Restatement (Third) of Unfair Competition §47. But the Restatement, which the Missouri Supreme Court has recognized as authority in this kind of case, also says that a name is used for commercial advantage when it is used "in connection with services rendered by the user" and that the plaintiff need not show that "prospective purchasers are likely to believe" that he or she endorsed the product or service. We note, moreover, that in Missouri, "the commercial advantage element of the right of publicity focuses on the defendant's intent or purpose to obtain a commercial benefit from use of the plaintiff's identity." Because we think that it is clear that CBC uses baseball players' identities in its fantasy baseball products for purposes of profit, we believe that their identities are being used for commercial advantage and that the players therefore offered sufficient evidence to make out a cause of action for violation of their rights of publicity under Missouri law.

B.

CBC argues that the first amendment nonetheless trumps the right-of-publicity action that Missouri law provides. Though this dispute is between private parties, the state action necessary for first amendment protections exists because the right-of-publicity claim exists only insofar as the courts enforce state-created obligations that were "never explicitly assumed" by CBC.

The Supreme Court has directed that state law rights of publicity must be balanced against first amendment considerations, and here we conclude that the former must give way to the latter. First, the information used in CBC's fantasy baseball games is all readily available in the public domain, and it would be strange law that a person would not have a first amendment right to use information that is available to everyone. It is true that CBC's use of the information is meant to provide entertainment, but "[s]peech that entertains, like speech that informs, is protected by the First Amendment because '[t]he line between the informing and the entertaining is too elusive for the protection of that basic right.'" *Cardtoons, L.C. v. Major League Baseball Players Ass'n*, 95 F.3d 959 (10th Cir. 1996). We also find no merit in the argument that CBC's use of players' names and information in its fantasy baseball games is not speech at all. We have held that "the pictures, graphic design, concept art, sounds, music, stories, and narrative present in video games" is speech entitled to first amendment protection. Similarly, here CBC uses the "names, nicknames, likenesses, signatures, pictures, playing records, and/or biographical data of each player" in an interactive form in connection with its fantasy baseball products.

***

Courts have also recognized the public value of information about the game of baseball and its players, referring to baseball as "the national pastime." [T]he "recitation and discussion of factual data concerning the athletic performance of [players on Major League Baseball's website] command a substantial public interest, and therefore, is a form of expression due to substantial constitutional protection." [citing *Gionfriddo v. Major League* Baseball, 94 Cal. App. 4th 400 (2001)]...

In addition, the facts in this case barely, if at all, implicate the interests that states typically intend to vindicate by providing rights of publicity to individuals. Economic interests that states seek to promote include the right of an individual to reap the rewards of his or her endeavors and an individual's right to earn a living. Other motives for creating a publicity right are the desire to provide incentives to encourage a person's productive activities and to protect consumers from misleading advertising. But major league baseball players are rewarded, and handsomely, too, for their participation in games and can earn additional large sums from endorsements and sponsorship arrangements. Nor is there any danger here that consumers will be misled, because the fantasy baseball games depend on the inclusion of all players and thus cannot create a false impression that some particular player with "star power" is endorsing CBC's products.

Then there are so-called non-monetary interests that publicity rights are sometimes thought to advance. These include protecting natural rights, rewarding celebrity labors, and avoiding emotional harm. We do not see that any of these interests are especially relevant here, where baseball players are awarded separately for their labors, and where any emotional harm would most likely be caused by a player's actual performance, in which case media coverage would cause the same harm.... Because we hold that CBC's first amendment rights in offering its fantasy baseball products supersede the players' rights of publicity, we need not reach CBC's alternative argument that federal copyright law preempts the player's state law rights of publicity.

Sidebar: Right of Publicity, Trademark Infringement, and False Endorsement

The right of publicity is defined as the right to control the "commercial value of a person's identity." The right is recognized by statute or common law in 29 states or through laws of unfair competition. Restatement (Third) of Unfair Competition § 46 ("one who appropriates the commercial value of a person's identity by using without consent the person's name, likeness, or other indicia of identity for purposes of trade is subject to liability"). "Trade" purposes include unauthorized use in advertising or on merchandise or in connection with services by the user. Permissible use, however, includes "news reporting, commentary, entertainment, works of fiction or nonfiction, or in advertising that is incidental to such uses." *Id.* at § 47.

The federal Lanham Act protects registered trademarks, *infra*, and where a person's identity is used to falsely advertise a product or designate its origin. 15 U.S.C. § 1125 (creating liability for "[a]ny living person who, on or in connection with any goods or services, ... uses in commerce ... false or misleading representation of fact, which is likely to cause confusion ... or to deceive as to the affiliation, connection, or association of such person with another person, or as to the origin, sponsorship, or approval of his or her goods, services, or commercial activities by another person.").

In Keller v. Electronic Arts, Inc., the Ninth Circuit discusses the different interests served by the right of publicity (the celebrity) and the Lanham Act (the consumer). Do the laws and defenses overlap?

Keller v. Electronic Arts, Inc.

724 F.3d 1268 (9th Cir. 2013), *cert. denied*, 135 S. Ct. 42 (2014)

Bybee, Circuit Judge:

Video games are entitled to the full protections of the First Amendment, because "[l]ike the protected books, plays, and movies that preceded them, video games communicate ideas—and even social messages—through many familiar literary devices (such as characters, dialogue, plot, and music) and through features distinctive to the medium (such as the player's interaction with the virtual world)." *Brown v. Entm't Merchs. Ass'n*, 131 S. Ct. 2729 (2011). Such rights are not absolute, and states may recognize the right of publicity to a degree consistent with the First Amendment. *Zacchini v. Scripps-Howard Broad. Co.*, 433 U.S. 562 (1977). In this case, we must balance the right of publicity of a former college football player against the asserted First Amendment right of a video game developer to use his likeness in its expressive works.

Under the "transformative use" test developed by the California Supreme Court, EA's use does not qualify for First Amendment protection as a matter of law because it literally recreates Keller in the very setting in which he has achieved renown.

I

In *NCAA Football,* EA seeks to replicate each school's entire team as accurately as possible. Every real football player on each team included in the game has a corresponding avatar in the game with the player's actual jersey number and virtually identical height, weight, build, skin tone, hair color, and home state. EA attempts to match any unique, highly identifiable playing behaviors by sending detailed questionnaires to team equipment managers. Additionally, EA creates realistic virtual versions of actual stadiums; populates them with the virtual athletes, coaches, cheerleaders, and fans realistically rendered by EA's graphic artists; and incorporates realistic sounds such as the crunch of the players' pads and the roar of the crowd.

EA's game differs from reality in that EA omits the players' names on their jerseys and assigns each player a home town that is different from the actual player's home town. However, users of the video game may upload rosters of names obtained from third parties so that the names do appear on the jerseys. In such cases, EA allows images from the game containing athletes' real names to be posted on its website by users. Users can further alter reality by entering "Dynasty" mode, where the user assumes a head coach's responsibilities for a college program for up to thirty seasons, including recruiting players from a randomly generated pool of high school athletes, or "Campus Legend" mode, where the user controls a virtual player from high school through college, making choices relating to practices, academics, and social life.

In the 2005 edition of the game, the virtual starting quarterback for Arizona State wears number 9, as did Keller, and has the same height, weight, skin tone, hair color, hair style, handedness, home state, play style (pocket passer), visor preference, facial features, and school year as Keller. In the 2008 edition, the virtual quarterback for Nebraska has these same characteristics, though the jersey number does not match, presumably because Keller changed his number right before the season started.

Objecting to this use of his likeness, Keller filed a putative class-action complaint in the Northern District of California asserting, as relevant on appeal, that EA violated his right of publicity under California Civil Code § 3344 and California common law....

II

[E]A did not contest before the district court and does not contest here that Keller has stated a right-of-publicity claim under California common and statutory law. Instead, EA raises four affirmative defenses derived from the First Amendment: the "transformative use" test, the *Rogers* test, the "public interest" test, and the "public affairs" exemption. EA argues that, in light of these defenses, it is not reasonably probable that Keller will prevail on his right-of-publicity claim. This appeal therefore centers on the applicability of these defenses. We take each one in turn.

A.

The California Supreme Court formulated the transformative use defense in *Comedy III Productions, Inc. v. Gary Saderup, Inc.*, 21 P.3d 797 (Cal. 4th 2001). The defense is "a balancing test between the First Amendment and the right of publicity based on whether the work in question adds significant creative elements so as to be transformed into something more than a mere celebrity likeness or imitation." The court rejected the wholesale importation of the copyright "fair use" defense into right-of-publicity claims, but recognized that some aspects of that defense are "particularly pertinent." *Comedy III* gives us at least five factors to consider in determining whether a work is sufficiently transformative to obtain First Amendment protection. First, if "the celebrity likeness is one of the 'raw materials' from which an original work is synthesized," it is more likely to be transformative than if "the depiction or imitation of the celebrity is the very sum and substance of the work in question." Second, the work is protected if it is "primarily the defendant's own expression"—as long as that expression is "something other than the likeness of the celebrity." This factor requires an examination of whether a likely purchaser's primary motivation is to buy a reproduction of the celebrity or to buy the expressive work of that artist. Third, to avoid making judgments concerning "the quality of the artistic contribution," a court should conduct an inquiry "more quantitative than qualitative" and ask "whether the literal and imitative or the creative elements predominate in the work." Fourth, the California Supreme Court indicated that "a subsidiary inquiry" would be useful in close cases: whether "the marketability and economic value of the challenged work derive primarily from the fame of the celebrity depicted." Lastly, the court indicated that "when an artist's skill and talent is manifestly subordinated to the overall goal of creating a conventional portrait of a celebrity so as to commercially exploit his or her fame," the work is not transformative.

[I]n *Comedy III* itself, the California Supreme Court applied the test to T-shirts and lithographs bearing a likeness of The Three Stooges and concluded that it could "discern no significant transformative or creative contribution." The court reasoned that the artist's "undeniable skill is manifestly subordinated to the overall goal of creating literal, conventional depictions of The Three Stooges so as to exploit their fame." "[W]ere we to decide that [the artist's] depictions were protected by the First Amendment," the court continued, "we cannot perceive how the right of publicity would remain a viable right other than in cases of falsified celebrity endorsements." ...

Finally, in *No Doubt v. Activision Publishing, Inc.*, the California Court of Appeal addressed Activision's *Band Hero* video game. 192 Cal. App. 4th 1018 (2011). In *Band Hero*, users simulate performing in a rock band in time with popular songs.

Users choose from a number of avatars, some of which represent actual rock stars, including the members of the rock band No Doubt. Activision licensed No Doubt's likeness, but allegedly exceeded the scope of the license by permitting users to manipulate the No Doubt avatars to play any song in the game, solo or with members of other bands, and even to alter the avatars' voices. The court held that No Doubt's right of publicity prevailed despite Activision's First Amendment defense because the game was not "transformative" under the *Comedy III* test. It reasoned that the video game characters were "literal recreations of the band members," doing "the same activity by which the band achieved and maintains its fame." The court concluded that "the expressive elements of the game remain manifestly subordinated to the overall goal of creating a conventional portrait of No Doubt so as to commercially exploit its fame."...

With these cases in mind as guidance, we conclude that EA's use of Keller's likeness does not contain significant transformative elements such that EA is entitled to the defense as a matter of law. EA is alleged to have replicated Keller's physical characteristics in *NCAA Football,* just as the members of No Doubt are realistically portrayed in *Band Hero.* Here, as in *Band Hero,* users manipulate the characters in the performance of the same activity for which they are known in real life—playing football in this case, and performing in a rock band in *Band Hero.* The context in which the activity occurs is also similarly realistic—real venues in *Band Hero* and realistic depictions of actual football stadiums in *NCAA Football.* As the district court found, Keller is represented as "what he was: the starting quarterback for Arizona State" and Nebraska, and "the game's setting is identical to where the public found [Keller] during his collegiate career: on the football field."

EA argues that the district court erred in focusing primarily on Keller's likeness and ignoring the transformative elements of the game as a whole. Judge Thomas, our dissenting colleague, suggests the same. We are unable to say that there was any error, particularly in light of *No Doubt,* which reasoned much the same as the district court in this case: "that the avatars appear in the context of a video game that contains many other creative elements[ ] does not transform the avatars into anything other than exact depictions of No Doubt's members doing exactly what they do as celebrities." EA suggests that the fact that *NCAA Football* users can alter the characteristics of the avatars in the game is significant. Again, our dissenting colleague agrees. In *No Doubt,* the California Court of Appeal noted that *Band Hero* "d[id] not permit players to alter the No Doubt avatars in any respect." Though *No Doubt* certainly mentioned the immutability of the avatars, we do not read the California Court of Appeal's decision as turning on the inability of users to alter the avatars.... We believe No Doubt offers a persuasive precedent that cannot be materially distinguished from Keller's case.

The Third Circuit came to the same conclusion in *Hart v. Electronic Arts, Inc.,* 717 F.3d 141 (3d Cir. 2013). In *Hart,* EA faced a materially identical challenge under New Jersey right-of-publicity law, brought by former Rutgers quarterback Ryan Hart. *See id.* ("*Keller* is simply [*Hart*] incarnated in California."). Though the Third Circuit was tasked with interpreting New Jersey law, the court looked to the transformative use test developed in California. Applying the test, the court held that "the *NCAA Football*... games at issue... do not sufficiently transform [Hart]'s identity to escape the right of publicity claim," reversing the district court's grant of summary judgment to EA.

As we have, the Third Circuit considered the potentially transformative nature of the game as a whole, and the user's ability to alter avatar characteristics. Asserting that "the lack of transformative context is even more pronounced here than in *No Doubt,*" and that "the ability to modify the avatar counts for little where the appeal of the game lies in users' ability to play as, or alongside[,] their preferred players or team," the Third Circuit agreed with us that these changes do not render the *NCAA Football* games sufficiently transformative to defeat a right-of-publicity claim.

Given that *NCAA Football* realistically portrays college football players in the context of college football games, the district court was correct in concluding that EA cannot prevail as a matter of law based on the transformative use defense....

B.

EA urges us to adopt for right-of-publicity claims the broader First Amendment defense that we have previously adopted in the context of false endorsement claims under the Lanham Act... [P]rotecting consumers from the risk of consumer confusion—[is] the hallmark element of a Lanham Act claim. The right of publicity, on the other hand, does not primarily seek to prevent consumer confusion. Rather, it primarily "protects a form of intellectual property [in one's person] that society deems to have some social utility." *Comedy III*, 21 P.3d at 804.

The right of publicity protects the *celebrity*, not the *consumer.* Keller's publicity claim is not founded on an allegation that consumers are being illegally misled into believing that he is endorsing EA or its products. Indeed, he would be hard-pressed to support such an allegation absent evidence that EA explicitly misled consumers into holding such a belief. Instead, Keller's claim is that EA has appropriated, without permission and without providing compensation, his talent and years of hard work on the football field. The reasoning of the *Rogers* and *Mattel* courts—that artistic and literary works should be protected unless they explicitly mislead consumers—is simply not responsive to Keller's asserted interests here.

III.

Under California's transformative use defense, EA's use of the likenesses of college athletes like Samuel Keller in its video games is not, as a matter of law, protected by the First Amendment.

Sidebar: Sports Gambling and IP Rights

Murphy v. NCAA, 138 S. Ct. 1461 (2018), cleared the way for states to legalize sports gambling. The Professional Amateur Sports Protection Act (PAPSA), intended to address corruption concerns of sports gambling, prohibited states (except four states that had existing sports wagering operations) from authorizing gambling on sports. The Supreme Court held that PAPSA violated the Tenth Amendment's "anti-commandeering" doctrine compelling states to enforce federal law. Since then, numerous states have enacted sports gambling laws. The major sports leagues are requesting that these laws include "integrity fees," ostensibly to regulate game integrity, but also contending that the leagues possess proprietary rights in the data that forms the basis for gambling.

What legal rights, if any, do athletes or leagues have with respect to use of their names, data, or images by businesses that operate sports gambling? Consider the investment leagues make to collect sophisticated forms of refined data, analytics, and statistics that can track nearly every player move. Is this data in the public domain for fair use by the sports gambling industry? Consider the significance of real-time reporting of sports data under *NBA v. Motorola, Inc.*, 105 F.3d 841 (2d Cir. 1997) (noting that although sports broadcasts can be copyrighted, sporting events themselves enjoy no such protection), *infra* Section D.

Daniels v. Fanduel, Inc.

909 F.3d 876 (7th Cir. 2018)

EASTERBROOK, CIRCUIT JUDGE.

Three former college football players contend that online fantasy-sports games violate their statutory right of publicity under Indiana law. The proprietors of these games reply that two exceptions, Ind. Code § 32-36-1-1(c)(l)(B), (c)(3), permit them to use players' names, likenesses, and statistics without compensation.... We certified this question to the Indiana Supreme Court:

> Whether online fantasy-sports operators that condition entry on payment, and distribute cash prizes, need the consent of players whose names, pictures, and statistics are used in the contests, in advertising the contests, or both.

It answered that question, holding:

> Indiana's right of publicity statute contains an exception for material with newsworthy value that includes online fantasy sports operators' use of college players' names, pictures, and statistics for online fantasy contests.

Defendants maintain that this conclusion ends the case. Plaintiffs, by contrast, ask us to remand to the district court to address the question whether the very existence of fantasy-sports games, in which contestants pay to play and winners receive cash, violates Indiana law. According to plaintiffs, a criminal gambling syndicate (which is how plaintiffs depict the defendants) cannot take advantage of any exception to Indiana's statutory right of publicity. [T]he Indiana Supreme Court [did not] suggest that the defendants' activities violate the state's anti-gambling laws.

What the state court *did* hold is that the use of the plaintiffs' names, pictures, and statistics comes within the statutory exception for material of "newsworthy value." It suggested one possible exclusion from this exception: using the plaintiffs' names (etc.) in a way that implied their endorsement of the defendants' games. Commercial endorsements cannot take advantage of the exceptions to the right of publicity—and although the Indiana Supreme Court saw only "minimal" risk that fantasy leagues' use of athletes' names, pictures, and statistics would be understood as the athletes' endorsement, it did not foreclose the possibility. It "deferred] making any factual determination on this issue to our federal colleagues."

We have nothing to say on the question whether the business of FanDuel or DraftKings violates Indiana's criminal laws. If a state prosecutor brings such charges, the answer will be for the state judiciary. Because plaintiffs have not tried to take advantage of the opening the state judiciary left them under the right-of-publicity statute, this civil suit is over.

Notes and Comments

1. **Privacy or publicity rights?** Muhammad Ali, "The Greatest" heavyweight boxing champion of the world, sued Playgirl, Inc., for publishing an unauthorized drawing depicting a nude black man in a boxing ring unmistakably recognizable as Ali. *Ali v. Playgirl Inc.*, 447 F. Supp. 723 (S.D.N.Y. 1978), held that the portrait was used solely "for purposes of trade" and constituted a wrongful appropriation of the market value of plaintiff's likeness. In *Ali*, the court rejected Playgirl's contention that "the right of privacy does not extend to protect someone such as an athlete... who chooses to bring himself to public notice," finding instead that a plaintiff who has occasionally surrendered his privacy "does not forever forfeit [his privacy] for anyone's commercial profit." The right of privacy asserts a right to be left alone, while the right of publicity asserts rights in one's identity. The right of publicity stems from state law that protects against (1) intrusion; (2) public disclosure of private facts; (3) false light; and (4) commercial appropriation of another's likeness. Restatement (Second) Torts § 652.

2. **Athlete rights in names, nicknames, and slogans.** *Hirsch v. S.C. Johnson & Son, Inc.*, 280 N.W.2d 129, 138 (Wisc. 1979), held that the defendant's use of the name "Crazylegs" on a women's shaving gel violated Elroy Hirsch's right of publicity. Hirsch, a famous football player, was nicknamed Crazylegs because of his unique running style. According to the court, the "[f]act that the name, 'Crazylegs,' was a nickname rather than Hirsch's actual name does not preclude a cause of action. All

that is required is that the name clearly identify the wronged person...." The dissent in *Hirsch* offers the following perspective:

> I would also hold that two simple words like "crazy" and "legs" whether spelled separately or as one word cannot as a matter of law under the facts here be regarded as the commercial "trade name" property of Mr. Hirsch.... If the name Elroy or Hirsch had been used with the crazy and legs, a different case would present itself because it would show that Elroy Hirsch was the person whose name was being used for commercial purposes. A gel for the shaving of women's legs has no association with football or any of the other athletic activities of Mr. Hirsch.... There have been athletes known as "the horse," others known as "dizzy" and "daffy" but any of those names attached to a shaving cream for women's legs should not give rise to a cause of action for commercial exploitation of one's "name."

Hirsch, 280 N.W.2d at 141. Should the law grant star athletes such a monopoly over "words" or nicknames?

3. **Balancing considerations.** Does the right of publicity give players too much entitlement to restrict others from using any names, data, or features that reference the players? Does this right unduly restrict freedom of discussion, expression, or the public's access to information, names, and products? Do courts appropriately balance the athletes' rights of publicity against the freedoms of expression, public interest, and transformative use under the First Amendment? Would these athletes be so famous and marketable without such press? Does the right to publicity threaten to overly "privatize" the public domain?

Judge Kozinski, dissenting in *White v. Samsung Electronics America, Inc.*, 989 F.2d 1512 (9th Cir. 1993), similarly observes that: "Something very dangerous is going on here.... Overprotecting intellectual property is as harmful as underprotecting it. Creativity is impossible without a rich public domain... Intellectual property rights aren't free: They're imposed at the expense of future creators and of the public at large.... This is why intellectual property law is full of careful balances between what's set aside for the owner and what's left in the public domain for the rest of us[.]"

4. **First Amendment considerations.** Does the right of publicity require player consent before a news entity can publish a story with an athlete's picture? *See Namath v. Sports Illustrated*, 363 N.Y.S.2d 276 (1975) (recognizing a "newsworthiness" permissible use of promotional materials for subscription applications of past edition showing quarterback's photograph on cover, noting "[f]reedom of speech and the press under the First Amendment transcends the right to privacy"). What is the difference between the use of an athlete's identity for news reporting versus for commercial exploitation? How is news reporting defined?

Dryer v. NFL, 814 F.3d 938 (8th Cir. 2016), ruled that NFL Films' uses of player likenesses in game footage was expressive, rather than commercial, speech akin to the use in news broadcasts, newspapers, and magazines, and a "history lesson" of NFL football protected under the First Amendment and subject matter of copyright. Why did the "transformative use" defense of the NCAA video games fail in *Keller?* Why were the rights of publicity upheld in *Hirsh, Ali,* and *Keller,* whereas the courts rejected such claims by players in *CBC* and *Dryer*?

5. **Use of player names and data as free speech in fantasy sports—is gambling next?** *CBC* and *Fanduel* ruled that the information used in the fantasy sports games was readily available in the public domain, thus the fantasy sports operators could use player names and statistics under the First Amendment. How do *CBC* and *Fanduel* impact the debate on player and league rights with respect to ownership of intellectual property in sports gambling? Where sports provide the source of the product for a commercial venture, should the *newsworthiness* or *public interest* exceptions apply?

6. In all of the following scenarios, except one, players' rights to publicity and to control and profit from the commercial value of the players' identity were held to have been violated. Which *one* case is a permissible use? Why?

(a) A company manufactures and sells a baseball trivia board game that uses the names and statistical information (including team, uniform number, playing position, and career statistics) of hundreds of major league baseball players. *See Uhlaender v. Henricksen,* 316 F. Supp. 1277 (D. Minn. 1970); *Palmer v. Schornhorn Enterprises, Inc.,* 232 A.2d 458 (N.J. Super. 1967) (professional golf).

(b) A seller of chewing gum includes trading cards with pictures of leading baseball players in its gum packets, without prior authorization by the players. *See Haelan Laboratories, Inc. v. Topps Chewing Gum, Inc.,* 202 F.2d 866 (2d Cir. 1953).

(c) A national television advertisement for a cigarette manufacturer depicts a race car driver in a red and white racing car with racing number "11." Professional race car driver whose number "71" race car was always in red and white with the same pinstripe alleges a misappropriation of his right to publicity. *Motschenbacher v. R.J. Reynolds Tobacco Co.,* 498 F.2d 821 (9th Cir. 1974).

(d) A company produces trading cards with cartoon caricatures of baseball players who are renamed Cal Ripkenwinkle, Ken Spiffey, Jr., Treasury Bonds, and who play for teams such as the Seattle Mari-Nerds and St. Louis Credit Cards. *Cardtoons L.C. v. MLBPA,* 95 F.3d 959 (10th Cir. 1996).

(e) An automobile commercial advertisement during an NCAA basketball tournament uses the birth name, Lew Alcindor, of former professional basketball star Kareem Abdul-Jabbar as an answer to a "trivia" question posed by the announcer, without the athlete's consent. Abdul-Jabbar had not used or gone by the name Lew Alcindor for over 10 years. *Abdul-Jabbar v. General Motors Corp.*, 85 F.3d 407 (9th Cir. 1995).

Under the scenario set forth in (d), First Amendment free expression and "fair use" considerations, as well as a parody exception to a state's publicity statute, were held to outweigh the MLB players' proprietary rights to publicity in *Cardtoons L.C. v. MLBPA*, 95 F.3d 959 (10th Cir. 1996) (noting also no trademark infringement because no likelihood of confusion).

7. **Freedom of expression.** Do an artist's rights of expression include painting pictures of great athletes participating in a public event and selling them without remuneration to or consent by the athlete? In *ETW Corp. v. Jireh Publishing*, 332 F.3d 915 (6th Cir. 2003), Tiger Woods sought to enjoin a sports artist's sale of "The Masters of Augusta" prints depicting elite professional golfers at the public event. Jireh published and marketed two hundred and fifty 22½" x 30" serigraphs and five thousand 9" × 11" lithographs of *The Masters of Augusta* at an issuing price of $700 for the serigraphs and $100 for the lithographs. The court found that a painting including a likeness of Tiger Woods did not violate Woods' right of publicity as the creator "added a significant creative component." The court balanced "the societal and personal interests embodied in the First Amendment against Woods' property rights" to find in favor of the defendant. Should the result be any different had the defendant been a photographer?

8. **Is "public domain" a workable standard for right of publicity claims?** As demonstrated by *CBC* and *Keller*, sports popularity has seen a lucrative development of interactive fan games, and the technology continues to emerge, such as with prospects for virtual reality. When should the use of athletes' identities in commercial fantasy sports or games violate rights of publicity? Do you agree with the *CBC* decision that players have no right to control the use of their names and data concerning their careers, performances, physical descriptions, or statistics in fantasy sports products because their names and data are in the "public domain"? Professor Karcher asserts that "public domain" is not a workable standard for right of publicity claims because the pertinent issue is whether the commercial advantage element is met, which should focus on how their public personas and publicly available data are being used in the product or service. *See* Richard T. Karcher, *The Use of Players' Identities in Fantasy Sports Leagues: Developing Workable Standards for Right of Publicity Claims*, 111 PENN STATE LAW REVIEW 557 (2007). He describes uses at one end of the spectrum that are "commercial" (*i.e.*, advertisements, endorsements and marketing), uses at the other end of the spectrum that are "non-commercial" (*i.e.*, news reporting, entertainment such as movies and films, and literary works), and uses in between these two ends that are "quasi-commercial" (*e.g.*, trading cards, bobble head dolls, video games, fantasy leagues, etc.). *Id.* at 560–61. Karcher proposes a two-part inquiry for assessing whether a qua-

si-commercial use constitutes a right of publicity violation: "(1) Is the individual's name or likeness being used for a purpose other than news reporting, entertainment (*i.e.*, movie, film, etc.), or literary? (2) If so, is the individual's name or likeness the 'essence' of the product or service being produced such that the product or service is dependent upon such use for its existence?" *Id.* at 573.

9. **Impact of new media, wearable tech, and AI on athlete privacy and publicity rights.** Teams, leagues, and producers of sporting events generally obtain consent to use the identity of athletes participating for advertising and promotional purposes by contractual agreements. In the major league professional sports, players assign rights to player associations, which negotiate licensing arrangements as well as authorize and police the use of player and group publicity rights. But new questions regarding athlete privacy and publicity rights arise with the rapid deployment of new media, wearable and tracking technologies, and artificial intelligence in sports. *See* Barbara Osborne, *Legal and Ethical Implications of Athletes' Biometric Data Collection in Professional Sport*, 28 MARQ. SPORTS L. REV. 38, 59 (2017); Nicholas Zych, *Collection and Ownership of Minor League Athlete Activity Biometric Data by Major League Baseball Franchises*, 14 DEPAUL J. SPORTS L. 129, 132 (2018).

10. In *Zacchini,* cited in *CBC* and *Keller*, Hugo Zacchini performed a "human cannonball" act in which he was shot from a cannon into a net some 200 feet away. On the day Zacchini performed his act at a county fair, defendant filmed the entire act, which was subsequently aired on its evening news program. Zacchini alleged that defendant unlawfully appropriated his professional property. The Supreme Court recognized a state's interest in permitting a right of publicity to protect an individual's proprietary interest and to prevent unjust enrichment. The Court acknowledged that entertainment, like news, enjoys First Amendment protection. Here, however, the defendant did not merely report on matters of public interest but broadcast the entire act and posed "a substantial threat to the economic value of that performance." *Id.* at 575.

11. The *Keller* plaintiffs reached a settlement with the NCAA and EA awarding $60 million to certain Division I men's basketball and Football Bowl Subdivision athletes whose images were portrayed in the NCAA videogames. Recall from Chapter 4, the *(O'Bannon) Litigation* alleged NCAA violated antitrust laws by barring former and current athletes from commercially using images from their college athletic careers. In *Davis v. Electronic Arts*, 775 F.3d 1172 (9th Cir. 2015), former NFL players sued EA for violations of their right of publicity in its *Madden NFL* series of games. The court relied heavily on *Keller,* noting that the defenses raised by EA in *Davis* were "materially indistinguishable." The court found that the former players' likeness was "central to the main commercial purpose—to create a realistic virtual simulation of football games involving current and former NFL teams." Why would athletes in the cases involving video games prevail but lose in *Dryer v. NFL*, which focuses on broadcasting, and in *Fanduel,* which focuses on fantasy sports?

Problem

What's in a name? Protecting Johnny Football

Protecting Johnny Football. Cleveland Browns quarterback and former college Heisman Trophy winner Johnny McGee is popularly referred to by the nickname "Johnny Football." Capitalizing on the public fascination in the star quarterback, internet entrepreneurs begin to sell t-shirts and other merchandise with the phrase "Keep Calm and Johnny Football," as well as "Money McGee" and "Johnny Cleveland." Some fans (and cyber-squatters) also started social media sites dedicated to Johnny Football, while other disgruntled fans have started disparaging sites such as "Clipboard Johnny." A few of these sites are "trending" and generate substantial advertising revenue to the operators.

McGee has numerous endorsement opportunities and just signed a contract with Big Sports Company where he agreed to let Big Sports use his nickname for advertising purposes. Big Sports has agreed to compensate McGee by paying him 50% of all profits resulting from the use of his nickname in association with Big Sports' sporting goods products. McGee seeks to stop others from using or profiting off his nickname, as he claims to have publicity and trademark rights to the exclusive use of his name, image and likeness. What is McGee's legal claim, if any? What additional action should McGee take? Lin Scully was the sports broadcaster who coined the name Johnny Football. What are his rights, if any?

C. Trademark Protection for Sports Names, Merchandise, and Brands

Sports teams, leagues, player organizations, and conferences invest substantial resources in developing fan loyalty, and a national and international reputation for providing a quality sports experience, brand, and product. Many recognize the Master's golf tournament, with its signature Green Jacket award, played at Augusta, Georgia, as the premier golf tournament in the United States. Does Augusta National, therefore, have any recourse when a different company establishes and advertises the "Lady Masters at Moss Green Plantation" golf tournament or institutes a "Red Jacket" award? *See Augusta National, Inc. v. Northwestern Mutual Life Insurance Co.*, 193 U.S.P.Q. 210 (S.D. Ga. Nov. 24, 1976).

Sporting teams, leagues, and events develop a proprietary interest in a team name, nickname, mascot, or other feature distinctive of a particular sport or sporting event—but do the Denver Broncos have the right to preclude a new sports team from adopting blue and orange uniforms (Denver Bronco team colors) and calling themselves, for example, the Cleveland Broncos? Would it make a difference if the Cleveland team sought to participate in the NFL, Major League Soccer, or as a women's professional volleyball team?

Fans are eager to identify with their favorite teams, proudly wearing (until a demoralizing defeat) the jersey, t-shirt, cap, or jacket prominently displaying the team name, nickname, mascot, or logo. Sports merchandising has produced an amazing assortment of sports memorabilia, from clothing to coffee mugs, key chains, even pet bowls bearing the name or mark of one's favorite team. The market for sports merchandising generates billions of dollars annually in revenues. Sports teams, unions, conferences, and leagues share in this revenue through license agreements with manufacturers, retailers, and others authorizing the use and sale of products bearing team names, logos, or other distinctive features (sports trademarks) in exchange for a royalty fee or other revenue. Not surprisingly, these licensing parties urge consumers, in their sports merchandising purchase, to look for the tag indicating authenticity and official approval of the team, that is, the official Colorado Rockies® sweatshirt contains the display tag "Congratulations on your selection of this genuine article—a product officially licensed by Major League Baseball.... Accept no substitute." In 2007, the Rockies, in their first World Series, coined and then registered the phrase "Rocktober" for trademark protection. Who owned the right to sell t-shirts that say "Who dat?" during the New Orleans Saints' 2010 Super Bowl? *See Who Dat Yat Chat, LLC v. Who Dat, Inc.*, 2012 WL 1118602 (E.D. La. 2012).

Intellectual property can be the most valuable asset in the sports industry. The possibility of consumers accepting "substitutes" and purchasing knockoffs or other unlicensed sports merchandise is of grave concern to the official licensing entities. Teams need to protect their brands, market share, and investments, and vigorously object to the marketing of counterfeit sports merchandise that suggests an association with the team or league. A related concern is "ambush marketing," which occurs when a business engages in a marketing strategy that falsely portrays itself as sponsoring, associated with, or approved by an official sporting event. The influence of social media, online influencers, and #hashtags on sponsored events presents bewildering threats as well as opportunities that a sports brand needs to consider.

U.S. federal trademark law, set forth in the Lanham Act, 15 U.S.C. §§1051–1127 (2015), provides the legal basis to protect the sports industry trademarks, marketable property rights in licensed merchandise, and the value of a sports entity's identity and brand. The Act protects against trademark misappropriation, infringement, and dilution. A *trademark* is defined as "any word, name, symbol, or device, or any combination thereof—(1) used by a person... to identify and distinguish his or her goods... from those manufactured or sold by others and to indicate the source of the goods, even if that source is unknown." 15 U.S.C. §1127. A trademark identifies a particular source of origin or ownership and often conveys a symbol of quality and goodwill. Although trademark law protects the rights holder, the law is intended to prevent consumer confusion. Accordingly, the use or sale of any word, term, name, or product that is likely to confuse or mislead the public as to their association with or endorsement by the sports industry is actionable.

What qualifies as a trademark? A trademark can be a word, symbol, or phrase that identifies and distinguishes the source and quality of a tangible product. Therefore, sport names, nicknames, logos, slogans, and other markers distinctive to a team, league, or event may qualify for trademark protection, such as Nike or its distinctive "swoosh" logo. Unlike copyrights, which protect original works of authorship for a period of time (*see* Section D), trademark rights may be acquired through the *use* of names or designs in the public domain that come to symbolize a team or sporting event and are protected indefinitely. The Lanham Act protects both registered and unregistered trademarks. The monopoly in effect granted to trademark owners over the use of names and other symbols in the public domain has spawned litigation over the scope of trademark rights and the definition of what constitutes infringement versus generic or fair use.

An elite athlete's name, image, or collective "brand" can have significant commercial value across numerous media and social media platforms. An athlete or sporting figure has often invested substantial time and resources in establishing such a reputation and justifiably resists others tarnishing or unfairly profiting from that "right of publicity." Increasingly, athletes are not leaving their state-created "right of publicity" to chance for a court to recognize, but rather are attempting to (and to prevent others from) registering their names, nicknames, catchphrases, and fan slogans as federal trademarks with the U.S. Patent & Trademark Office.

Indianapolis Colts, Inc. v. Metropolitan Baltimore Football Club

34 F.3d 410 (7th Cir. 1994)

Posner, Chief Judge

The Indianapolis Colts and the National Football League, to which the Colts belong, brought suit for trademark infringement (15 U.S.C. §§ 1051 et seq.) against the Canadian Football League's new team in Baltimore, which wants to call itself the "Baltimore CFL Colts." The plaintiffs obtained a preliminary injunction against the new team's using the name "Colts," or "Baltimore Colts," or "Baltimore CFL Colts," in connection with the playing of professional football, the broadcast of football games, or the sale of merchandise to football fans and other buyers. The ground for the injunction was that consumers of "Baltimore CFL Colts" merchandise are likely to think, mistakenly, that the new Baltimore team is an NFL team related in some fashion to the Indianapolis Colts, formerly the Baltimore Colts. From the order granting the injunction, the new team and its owners appeal to us under 28 U.S.C. § 1292(a)(1). Since the injunction was granted, the new team has played its first two games—without a name.

A bit of history is necessary to frame the dispute. In 1952, the National Football League permitted one of its teams, the Dallas Texans, which was bankrupt, to move to Baltimore, where it was renamed the "Baltimore Colts." Under that name it became one of the most illustrious teams in the history of professional football. In 1984, the team's owner, with the permission of the NFL, moved the team to Indianapolis, and it was renamed the "Indianapolis Colts." The move, sudden and secretive, outraged the citizens of Baltimore. The city instituted litigation in a futile effort to get the team back—even tried, unsuccessfully, to get the team back by condemnation under the city's power of eminent domain—and the Colts brought a countersuit that also failed.

Nine years later, the Canadian Football League granted a franchise for a Baltimore team. Baltimoreans clamored for naming the new team the "Baltimore Colts." And so it was named—until the NFL got wind of the name and threatened legal action. The name was then changed to "Baltimore CFL Colts" and publicity launched, merchandise licensed, and other steps taken in preparation for the commencement of play this summer....

The Baltimore team wanted to call itself the "Baltimore Colts." To improve its litigating posture (we assume), it has consented to insert "CFL" between "Baltimore" and "Colts." A glance at the merchandise in the record explains why this concession to an outraged NFL has been made so readily. On several of the items "CFL" appears in small or blurred letters. And since the Canadian Football League is not well known in the United States—and "CFL" has none of the instant recognition value of "NFL"—the inclusion of the acronym in the team's name might have little impact on potential buyers even if prominently displayed. Those who know football well know that the new "Baltimore Colts" are a new CFL team wholly unrelated to the old Baltimore Colts; know also that the rules of Canadian football are different from those of American football and that teams don't move from the NFL to the CFL as they might from one conference within the NFL to the other. But those who do not know these things—and we shall come shortly to the question whether there are many of these football illiterate—will not be warned off by the letters "CFL." The acronym is a red herring, and the real issue is whether the new Baltimore team can appropriate the name "Baltimore Colts." The entire thrust of the defendants' argument is that it can.

They make a tremendous to-do over the fact that the district judge found that the Indianapolis Colts abandoned the trademark "Baltimore Colts" when they moved to Indianapolis. Well, of course; they were no longer playing football under the name "Baltimore Colts," so could not have used the name as the team's trademark; they could have used it on merchandise but chose not to, until 1991 (another story—and not one we need tell). When a mark is abandoned, it returns to the public domain, and is appropriable anew—in principle. In practice, because "subsequent use of [an] abandoned mark may well evoke a continuing association with the prior use, those who make subsequent use may be required to take reasonable precautions to prevent confusion." This precept is especially important where, as in this case, the former owner of the abandoned mark continues to market the same product or service under a similar name, though we cannot find any previous cases of this kind. No one questions the validity of "Indianapolis Colts" as the trademark of the NFL team that plays out of Indianapolis and was formerly known as the Baltimore Colts. If "Baltimore CFL Colts" is confusingly similar to "Indianapolis Colts" by virtue of the history of the Indianapolis team and the overlapping product and geographical markets served by it and by the new Baltimore team, the latter's use of the abandoned mark would infringe the Indianapolis Colts' new mark. The Colts' abandonment of a mark confusingly similar to their new mark neither broke the continuity of the team in its different locations—it was the same team, merely having a different home base and therefore a different geographical component in its name—nor entitled a third party to pick it up and use it to confuse Colts fans, and other actual or potential consumers of products and services marketed by the Colts or by other National Football League teams, with regard to the identity, sponsorship, or league affiliation of the third party, that is, the new Baltimore team.

Against this the defendants cite to us with great insistence *Major League Baseball Properties Inc. v. Sed Non Olet Denarius, Ltd.*, 817 F. Supp. 1103 (S.D.N.Y. 1993), which, over the objection of the Los Angeles Dodgers, allowed a restaurant in Brooklyn to use the name "Brooklyn Dodger" on the ground that "the 'Brooklyn Dodgers' was a nontransportable cultural institution separate from the 'Los Angeles Dodgers.'" The defendants in our case argue that the sudden and greatly resented departure of the Baltimore Colts for Indianapolis made the name "Baltimore Colts" available to anyone who would continue the "nontransportable cultural institution" constituted by a football team located in the City of Baltimore. We think this argument very weak, and need not even try to distinguish *Sed Non Olet Denarius* since district court decisions are not authoritative in this or any court of appeals. If it were a Supreme Court decision it still would not help the defendants. The "Brooklyn Dodger" was not a baseball team, and there was no risk of confusion. The case might be relevant if the Indianapolis Colts were arguing not confusion but misappropriation: that they own the goodwill associated with the name "Baltimore Colts" and the new Baltimore team is trying to take it from them. The only claim in our court is that a significant number of consumers will think the new Baltimore team the successor to, or alter ego of, or even the same team as the Baltimore Colts and therefore the Indianapolis Colts, which is the real successor. No one would think the Brooklyn Dodgers baseball team reincarnated in a restaurant.

[I]f everyone knows there is no contractual or institutional continuity, no pedigree or line of descent, linking the Baltimore-Indianapolis Colts and the new CFL team that wants to call itself the "Baltimore Colts" (or, grudgingly, the "Baltimore CFL Colts"), then there is no harm, at least no harm for which the Lanham Act provides a remedy, in the new Baltimore team's appropriating the name "Baltimore Colts" to play under and sell merchandise under. If not everyone knows, there is harm. Some people who might otherwise watch the Indianapolis Colts (or some other NFL team, for remember that the NFL, representing all the teams, is a coplaintiff) on television may watch the Baltimore CFL Colts instead, thinking they are the "real" Baltimore Colts, and the NFL will lose revenue. A few (doubtless very few) people who might otherwise buy tickets to an NFL game may buy tickets to a Baltimore CFL Colts game instead. Some people who might otherwise buy merchandise stamped with the name "Indianapolis Colts" or the name of some other NFL team may buy merchandise stamped "Baltimore CFL Colts," thinking it a kin of the NFL's Baltimore Colts in the glory days of Johnny Unitas rather than a newly formed team that plays Canadian football in a Canadian football league. It would be naive to suppose that no consideration of such possibilities occurred to the owners of the new Baltimore team when they were choosing a name, though there is no evidence that it was the dominant or even a major consideration.

Confusion thus is possible, and may even have been desired; but is it likely? There is great variance in consumer competence, and it would be undesirable to impoverish the lexicon of trade names merely to protect the most gullible fringe of the consuming public. The Lanham Act does not cast the net of protection so wide. The legal standard... come[s] down to whether it is likely that the challenged mark if permitted to be used by the defendant would cause the plaintiff to lose a substantial number of consumers. Pertinent to this determination is the similarity of the marks and of the parties' products, the knowledge of the average consumer of the product, the overlap in the parties' geographical markets, and the other factors that the cases consider. The aim is to strike a balance between, on the one hand, the interest of the seller of the new product, and of the consuming public, in an arresting, attractive, and informative name that will enable the new product to compete effectively against existing ones, and, on the other hand, the interest of existing sellers, and again of the consuming public, in consumers' being able to know exactly what they are buying without having to incur substantial costs of investigation or inquiry.

To help judges strike the balance, the parties to trademark disputes frequently as here hire professionals in marketing or applied statistics to conduct surveys of consumers. The battle of experts that ensues is frequently unyielding.

Both parties presented studies. The defendants' was prepared by Michael Rappeport and is summarized in a perfunctory affidavit by Dr. Rappeport to which the district judge gave little weight. That was a kindness. The heart of Rappeport's study was a survey that consisted of three loaded questions asked in one Baltimore mall. Rappeport has been criticized before for his methodology, and we hope that he will take these criticisms to heart in his next courtroom appearance.

The plaintiffs' study, conducted by Jacob Jacoby, was far more substantial and the district judge found it on the whole credible. The 28-page report with its numerous appendices has all the trappings of social scientific rigor. Interviewers showed several hundred consumers in 24 malls scattered around the country shirts and hats licensed by the defendants for sale to consumers. The shirts and hats have "Baltimore CFL Colts" stamped on them. The consumers were asked whether they were football fans, whether they watched football games on television, and whether they ever bought merchandise with a team name on it. Then they were asked, with reference to the "Baltimore CFL Colts" merchandise that they were shown, such questions as whether they knew what sport the team played, what teams it played against, what league the team was in, and whether the team or league needed someone's permission to use this name, and if so whose....

Jacoby's survey of consumers reactions to the "Baltimore CFL Colts" merchandise found rather astonishing levels of confusion not plausibly attributable to the presence of the name "Baltimore" alone.... Among self-identified football fans, 64 percent thought that the "Baltimore CFL Colts" was either the old (NFL) Baltimore Colts or the Indianapolis Colts. But perhaps this result is not so astonishing. Although most American football fans have heard of Canadian football, many probably are unfamiliar with the acronym "CFL," and as we remarked earlier it is not a very conspicuous part of the team logo stamped on the merchandise. Among fans who watch football on television, 59 percent displayed the same confusion; and even among those who watch football on cable television, which attracts a more educated audience on average and actually carries CFL games, 58 percent were confused when shown the merchandise. Among the minority not confused about who the "Baltimore CFL Colts" are, a substantial minority, ranging from 21 to 34 percent depending on the precise sub-sample, thought the team somehow sponsored or authorized by the Indianapolis Colts or the National Football League....

[W]e cannot say that the district judge committed a clear error in crediting the major findings of the Jacoby study and inferring from it and the other evidence in the record that the defendants' use of the name "Baltimore CFL Colts" whether for the team or on merchandise was likely to confuse a substantial number of consumers. This means... that the judge's finding concerning likelihood of confusion required that the injunction issue.... AFFIRMED.

Louisiana State University v. Smack Apparel Co.

550 F.3d 465 (5th Cir. 2008)

REAVLEY, CIRCUIT JUDGE.

I. Background

The plaintiffs are Louisiana State University (LSU), the University of Oklahoma (OU), Ohio State University (OSU), the University of Southern California (USC), and Collegiate Licensing Company (CLC), which is the official licensing agent for the schools. The defendants are Smack Apparel Company and its principal, Wayne Curtiss (collectively Smack).

Each university has adopted a particular two-color scheme as its school colors (purple and gold for LSU, crimson and creme for OU, scarlet and gray for OSU, and cardinal and gold for USC). The Universities have used their respective color combinations for over one hundred years, and the color schemes are immediately recognizable to those who are familiar with the Universities. The schools use these color schemes in many areas associated with university life, including on campus signs and buildings, on printed brochures, journals, and magazines, and on materials sent to potential donors. The Universities also use the color schemes extensively in connection with their athletic programs, particularly on team uniforms, resulting in wide-spread recognition of the colors among college sports fans. Each university operates a successful collegiate football program, and the respective football teams have appeared on numerous occasions in nationally televised football games that have been viewed by millions of people.

The schools also grant licenses for retail sales of products, including t-shirts that bear the university colors and trademarks. In recent years, the total annual sales volume of products bearing the school colors along with other identifying marks has exceeded $93 million for all the Universities combined. The Universities hold registered trademarks in their respective names and commonly used initials. They do not, however, possess registered trademarks in their color schemes.

Smack Apparel Company is located in Tampa, Florida. Since 1998 Smack has manufactured t-shirts targeted toward fans of college sports teams, and it uses school colors and printed messages associated with the Universities on its shirts. Smack sells some of the shirts over the Internet, but most are sold wholesale to retailers and t-shirt vendors. The shirts frequently appear alongside those that have been officially licensed by the Universities. The instant case involves six of Smack's t-shirt designs that concern the appearance of the OU and LSU football teams in the 2004 Sugar Bowl in New Orleans, Louisiana, and the number of national championships previously won by OSU and USC. The district court described these Smack shirt designs as follows:

- OU (2 shirt designs): (1) "Bourbon Street or Bust" (with the "ou" in "Bourbon" in a different typestyle) (front), "Show us your beads!" (with the "ou" in "your" in a different typestyle) and "Sweet as Sugar!" (back) (2) "Beat Socal" (front), "And Let's Make it Eight!" (back). These shirts refer to 2004 Sugar Bowl contest in New Orleans between the OU and LSU football teams. A victory in the Sugar Bowl could have given OU a claim to an eighth national football championship. One of OU's principal rivals to this claim was USC.
- LSU (2 shirt designs): (1) "Beat Oklahoma" (front), "And Bring it Back to the Bayou!" and "2003 College Football National Championship" (back) (2) "2003 College Football National Champions" (front), colored circular depiction of game scores, with "2003 College Football National Champions" and "Sweet as Sugar" (back). These shirts refer to the 2004 Sugar Bowl con-

test in New Orleans between OU and LSU, which was played to determine the Bowl Championship Series national football champion.

- OSU: "Got Seven?" (front), "We do! 7 Time National Champs," with depiction of the state of Ohio and a marker noting "Columbus Ohio" (back). This shirt refers to the seven college football national titles claimed by OSU.
- USC: "Got eight?" (front), "We Do! Home of the 8 Time National Champions!" and depiction of the state of California with a star marked "SoCal" (back). This design refers to USC's claim to eight college national football championships.

In addition to the messages described above, each shirt included Smack's own logo in a space approximately 2.5 inches wide and the words "Talkin' the Talk."

The Universities sued Smack, alleging that the above six shirt designs infringed their trademark rights. The Universities alleged causes of action for federal trademark infringement and dilution, unfair competition, and deceptive trade practices under the Lanham Act, 15 U.S.C. §§ 1051–1141; unfair trade practices under the Louisiana Unfair Trade Practices and Consumer Protection Act (LUTPA), common law trademark infringement and unfair competition; and state trademark dilution. The plaintiffs alleged that each schools' color combination acts as a source-identifier for the respective schools, especially when used in connection with other indicia identifying or suggesting the schools. They alleged that Smack's shirts infringed their unregistered trademarks by "combining Plaintiffs' Marks with references to, *inter alia*, ... (a) well-known and highly-publicized athletic events in which a University participated; (b) a University's opponent in the referenced athletic event; (c) the geographic area in which the referenced event takes place; (d) titles and honors bestowed as a result of the referenced athletic event; (e) a University's earlier athletic successes and accomplishments; and (f) the geographic area in which the University is located or associated."

The Universities claimed that Smack's products are similar to and competed with goods sold or licensed by the Universities and are sold directly alongside merchandise authorized by the plaintiffs at or near events referenced in the shirts. In this way, according to the Universities, the sale of Smack's products is likely to deceive, confuse, and mislead consumers into believing that Smack's products are produced, authorized, or associated with the plaintiff Universities. The Universities sought injunctive relief, lost profits, damages, costs, and attorneys' fees.

***

The district court granted summary judgment for the Universities, holding that the Universities' trademarks in their color schemes, logos, and designs on shirts referring to the schools or their accomplishments had acquired secondary meaning. The district court concluded that the marks were strong, having been used for decades as a reference to the Universities, and that Smack's infringing shirts were likely to cause confusion as to the source, affiliation, or sponsorship of the shirts. The district court found that the marks at issue were virtually identical. The court reasoned that Smack used the same color schemes and similar logos and designs as the plaintiffs; that Smack marketed and sold its shirts in a manner similar to the Universities' products and sometimes alongside those of the Universities; and that Smack used the color schemes, logos, and designs with the specific intent to rely upon their drawing power in enticing fans of the Universities to purchase its shirts. The court noted that Smack admitted using the school colors and other indicia with the intent of identifying the Universities as the subject of the message in the shirt designs. The court also noted that a likelihood of confusion existed because the shirts, which are relatively inexpensive, are not purchased with a high degree of care by consumers. The district court rejected Smack's defenses of functionality, nominative fair use, and laches.

After deciding the liability issue, the district court conducted a jury trial on the issue of damages.... The jury then returned a verdict in favor of the plaintiffs and answered special interrogatories finding that Smack's "infringement caused actual confusion of the public or caused the public to be deceived." The jury awarded the Universities actual damages of $10,506.80 and lost profits of $35,686. The district court also enjoined Smack from manufacturing, distributing, selling, or offering for sale any of the six t-shirt designs found to be infringing or any other similar designs.

I. Discussion

We review a district court's grant of summary judgment de novo. Although the secondary meaning of a mark and the likelihood of confusion are ordinarily questions of fact, summary judgment may be upheld if the summary judgment record compels the conclusion that the movant is entitled to judgment as a matter of law.

To prevail on their trademark infringement claim, the plaintiffs must show two things. First, they must establish ownership in a legally protectible mark, and second, they must show infringement by demonstrating a likelihood of confusion....

A. Protectible trademark and secondary meaning

The Lanham Act provides that a trademark may be "any word, name, symbol, or device, or any combination thereof" that is used or intended to be used "to identify and distinguish" a person's goods "from those manufactured or sold by others and to indicate the source of the goods, even if that source is unknown." A mark need not be registered in order to obtain protection because "[o]wnership of trademarks is established by use, not by registration." The marks at issue in this case are unregistered, and, as noted by the district court, were described by the Universities as "color schemes in the context of merchandise that makes reference to the Plaintiff Universities or their accomplishments and is directed to their fans and other interested consumers."

The protectability of unregistered marks is governed generally by the same principles that qualify a mark for registration under the Lanham Act. The key is whether the mark is "capable of distinguishing the applicant's goods from those of others." Marks are classified as (1) generic, (2) descriptive, (3) suggestive, (4) arbitrary, or (5) fanciful. The parties here do not articulate a classification for the marks at issue, but the briefs show that they, and indeed the district court, have treated the marks as descriptive. This type of mark is not inherently distinctive because it does not inherently identify a particular source of the product; instead, it requires secondary meaning to be protected under the Lanham Act.

The parties correctly agree that a color scheme can be protected as a trademark when it has acquired secondary meaning and is non-functional... It is appropriate therefore to consider not only the color but also the entire context in which the color and other indicia are presented on the t-shirts at issue here.

Smack contends that the claimed marks are too broad to encompass a trademark because the concept of color along with other identifying indicia is not distinctive. We disagree. As noted, the statute contemplates that a trademark may include any word, name, or symbol "*or any combination thereof*." The Supreme Court has recognized that the Lanham Act describes the universe of permissible marks "in the broadest of terms." Because the Court recognizes that trademarks may include color, we see no reason to exclude color plus other identifying indicia from the realm of protectible marks provided the remaining requirements for protection are met. Thus, the first step here is to ask whether the Universities' claimed marks have acquired secondary meaning.

Secondary meaning "occurs when, 'in the minds of the public, the primary significance of a [mark] is to identify the source of the product rather than the product itself.'" The inquiry is one of the public's mental association between the mark and the alleged mark holder. A mark has acquired secondary meaning when it "has come through use to be uniquely associated with a specific source." We have applied a multi-factor test for determining secondary meaning. The factors include: "(1) length and manner of use of the mark or trade dress, (2) volume of sales, (3) amount and manner of advertising, (4) nature of use of the mark or trade dress in newspapers and magazines, (5) consumer-survey evidence, (6) direct consumer testimony, and (7) the defendant's intent in copying the trade dress." These factors in combination may show that consumers consider a mark to be an indicator of source even if each factor alone would not prove secondary meaning.

There is no dispute in this case that for a significant period of time the Universities have been using their color schemes along with other indicia to identify and distinguish themselves from others... the factors for determining secondary meaning and an examination of the context in which the school colors are used and presented in this case support the conclusion that the secondary meaning of the marks is inescapable.

The record shows that the Universities have been using their color combinations since the late 1800s. The color schemes appear on all manner of materials, including brochures, media guides, and alumni materials associated with the Universities. Significantly, each university features the color schemes on merchandise, especially apparel connected with school sports teams, and such prominent display supports a finding of secondary meaning. The record also shows that sales of licensed products combining the color schemes with other references to the Universities annually exceed the tens of millions of dollars....

Given the longstanding use of the color scheme marks and their prominent display on merchandise, in addition to the well-known nature of the colors as shorthand for the schools themselves and Smack's intentional use of the colors and other references, there is no genuine issue of fact that when viewed in the context of t-shirts or other apparel, the marks at issue here have acquired the secondary meaning of identifying the Universities in the minds of consumers as the source or sponsor of the products rather than identifying the products themselves.

We think this conclusion is consistent with the importance generally placed on sports team logos and colors by the public. We have previously noted, although not in the context of secondary meaning, that team emblems and symbols are sold because they serve to identify particular teams, organizations, or entities with which people wish to identify. We think this desire by consumers to associate with a particular university supports the conclusion that team colors and logos are, in the minds of the fans and other consumers, source indicators of team-related apparel. By associating the color and other indicia with the university, the fans perceive the university as the source or sponsor of the goods because they want to associate with that source.

B. Likelihood of confusion

Once a plaintiff shows ownership in a protectible trademark, he must next show that the defendant's use of the mark "creates a likelihood of confusion in the minds of potential customers as to the 'source, affiliation, or sponsorship'" of the product at issue. "Likelihood of confusion is synonymous with a probability of confusion, which is more than a mere possibility of confusion." When assessing the likelihood of confusion, we consider a nonexhaustive list of so-called "digits of confusion," including: "(1) the type of mark allegedly infringed, (2) the similarity between the two marks, (3) the similarity of the products or services, (4) the identity of the retail outlets and purchasers, (5) the identity of the advertising media used, (6) the defendant's intent, and (7) any evidence of actual confusion." ... No single factor is dispositive, and a finding of a likelihood of confusion need not be supported by a majority of the factors.

[T]he first digit, the type of mark, refers to the strength of the mark. Generally, the stronger the mark, the greater the likelihood that consumers will be confused by competing uses of the mark. We agree with the district court that the plaintiffs' marks, which have been used for over one hundred years, are strong... the Universities' color schemes are well-known and are used to identify the plaintiff Universities....

The second digit is the similarity of the marks. This factor requires consideration of the marks' appearance, sound, and meaning. The district court held that the marks at issue are virtually identical... even a cursory comparison of Smack's designs with the plaintiffs' licensed products reveals striking similarity....

The third digit in the likelihood of confusion analysis is the similarity of the products or services. "[I]t is undisputed that both Smack and the universities market shirts bearing the same color schemes, logos, and designs." The district court went on to reject Smack's argument that its t-shirts differed from the Universities' products because of the use of irreverent phrases or slang language, reasoning that Smack's use of such phrases and language was a misuse of the Universities' good will in its marks... We therefore find this factor weighs in favor of a likelihood of confusion.

[T] he fourth factor of the analysis—identity of retail outlets and purchasers—weighs in favor of a likelihood of confusion because the Universities' licensed products are often sold wholesale to the same retailers who purchase Smack's products. The fifth digit is the identity of advertising media. The district court found that Smack used the Universities' color schemes, logos, and designs in advertising its shirts at the same or similar venues as those used by the Universities.

The sixth digit of confusion further supports a likelihood of confusion. Although not necessary to a finding of likelihood of confusion, a defendant's intent to confuse may alone be sufficient to justify an inference that there is a likelihood of confusion.... The circumstances of this case show that Smack intended to capitalize on the potential for confusion. Smack knew that its shirts were sold in the same venues as and sometimes alongside officially licensed merchandise, and it intentionally incorporated color marks to create the kind of association with the Universities that would influence purchasers.... Smack did not hope to sell its t-shirts because of some competitive difference in quality or design compared with the Universities' licensed products, but rather it intended to take advantage of the popularity of the Universities' football programs and the appearance of the school teams in the college bowl games. [T]he similarity in appearance between Smack's shirts and the Universities' licensed products is strong evidence of a likelihood of confusion.

The seventh digit is evidence of actual confusion. Evidence that consumers have been actually confused in identifying the defendant's use of a mark as that of the plaintiff may be the best evidence of a likelihood of confusion. It is well established, however, that evidence of actual confusion is not necessary for a finding of a likelihood of confusion.

With respect to the eighth digit of confusion—the degree of care exercised by potential purchasers—the district court held that the t-shirts at issue are relatively inexpensive impulse items that are not purchased with a high degree of care. Where items are relatively inexpensive, a buyer may take less care in selecting the item, thereby increasing the risk of confusion.

After reviewing the record, we conclude that there is no genuine issue of fact that Smack's use of the Universities' color schemes and other identifying indicia creates a likelihood of confusion as to the source, affiliation, or sponsorship of the t-shirts. As noted above, the digits of confusion—particularly the overwhelming similarity of the marks and the defendant's intent to profit from the Universities' reputation—compel this conclusion. This is so, we have noted, because Smack's use of the Universities' colors and indicia is designed to create the illusion of affiliation with the Universities and essentially obtain a "free ride" by profiting from confusion among the fans of the Universities' football teams who desire to show support for and affiliation with those teams. This creation of a link in the consumer's mind between the t-shirts and the Universities and the intent to directly profit therefrom results in "an unmistakable aura of deception" and likelihood of confusion.

We hold that given the record in this case and the digits of confusion analysis discussed above—including the overwhelming similarity between the defendant's t-shirts and the Universities' licensed products, and the defendant's admitted intent to create an association with the plaintiffs and to influence consumers in calling the plaintiffs to mind—that the inescapable conclusion is that many consumers would likely be confused and believe that Smack's t-shirts were sponsored or endorsed by the Universities. The Universities exercise stringent control over the use of their marks on apparel through their licensing program. It is also undisputed that the Universities annually sell millions of dollars' worth of licensed apparel. We further recognize the public's indisputable desire to associate with college sports teams by wearing team-related apparel. We are not persuaded that simply because some consumers might not care whether Smack's shirts are officially licensed the likelihood of confusion is negated. Whether or not a consumer *cares* about official sponsorship is a different question from whether that consumer would likely *believe* the product is officially sponsored. For the foregoing reasons, we conclude that a likelihood of confusion connecting the presence of the Universities' marks and the Universities' themselves was demonstrated in this case.

C. Functionality

A product feature that is functional does not qualify for protection under the Lanham Act. The party seeking protection under the Lanham Act has the burden of establishing nonfunctionality. The Supreme Court has recognized two tests for determining functionality. "[T]he primary test for determining whether a product feature is functional is whether the feature is essential to the use or purpose of the product or whether it affects the cost or quality of the product." This is the "traditional" test. "Under this traditional definition, if a product feature is 'the reason the device works,' then the feature is functional." Under a secondary test for functionality "a functional feature is one the exclusive use of which would put competitors at a significant non-reputation-related disadvantage." This is the "competitive necessity" test.

In *Boston Hockey*, we held that emblems of a hockey team sold on embroidered patches had no demonstrated value other than their significance as the trademarks of the team. Relying on our decision in *Boston Hockey*, the district court here similarly held that the Universities' color schemes, logos, and designs also had no significance other than to identify with the Universities and were therefore nonfunctional. We agree. Fans and other members of the public purchase Smack's shirts only because the shirts contain the plaintiffs' colors and indicia identifying the Universities' football teams, just as people purchased the defendant's emblems in *Boston Hockey* only because they contained the hockey team's trademarks. In other words, the presence of the plaintiffs' marks serve no function unrelated to trademark.

The school colors and other indicia used here do not make the t-shirts "work." The t-shirts would function just as well as articles of clothing without the colors and designs.... The marks fail under the traditional test for functionality and are protectible.... Smack's alleged competitive disadvantage in the ability to sell game day apparel relates solely to an inability to take advantage of the Universities' reputation and the public's desired association with the Universities that its shirts create. This is not an advantage to which it is entitled under the rubric of legitimate competition. We conclude that the district court correctly held that the marks at issue here are nonfunctional.

***

AFFIRMED.

Notes and Questions

1. **Ownership of team name/nickname.** In *Indianapolis Colts*, Judge Posner deemed insignificant the decision in *Major League Baseball Properties v. Sed Non Olet Denarius*, 817 F. Supp. 1103 (S.D.N.Y. 1993), which rejected a trademark infringement claim by the Los Angeles Dodgers against the Brooklyn Dodger Sports Bar and Restaurant. Are the cases inconsistent? Suppose the Brooklyn Dodger goes viral in a community adult league softball game and begins selling merchandise. If the Dodgers sue, would the courts follow *MLBP* or *Indianapolis Colts*?

The use of team nicknames has been the subject of much litigation. In *National Football League Properties, Inc. v. New Jersey Giants, Inc.*, 637 F. Supp. 507 (D.N.J. 1986), the NFL, on behalf of the New York Giants, obtained an injunction against a company selling "New Jersey Giants" merchandise. The Court found the defendant sought to capitalize on the confusion created by the New York Giants football team playing its home games in New Jersey and held the defendant's prominent use of the Giants name was confusingly similar to plaintiff's marks. *See also NFL v. Jacksonville Jaguars*, 886 F. Supp. 335 (S.D.N.Y. 1995) (disputing NFL's use of team name "Jaguars" and the image of a jaguar resembling the emblem of Jaguar cars).

Would (and should) trademark law protect slogans, such as ABC's Monday Night Football crowd-rousing question "Are you ready for some football?" Or Nike's "Just Do It"? Does it depend on *who* seeks to register and use those phrases? The U.S. Patent & Trademark Office (USPTO) refused an applicant's request to register "Fear the Brow" because the phrase was so associated with the NBA's Anthony Davis. An earthquake survival kit company was denied registration of "Let's Get Ready to Rumble," popularly associated with boxing announcer Michael Buffer.

2. **Trademark infringement.** To establish a claim for trademark infringement under the Lanham Act, a claimant must prove: (1) the mark is valid and protectable, (2) the plaintiff owns the mark, and (3) the defendant's use of the mark is likely to cause confusion. The Lanham Act prohibits the infringement of origin, description, or representation of a registered or an *unregistered* trademark. Although federal registration of a mark is not required, it does provide presumptive trademark validity and national protection. What must an owner of an unregistered mark prove to prevail on an infringement claim?

As remedies for trademark infringement, the Lanham Act provides for injunctive relief, as well as the recovery of defendant's profits, plaintiff's damages, costs, and attorney fees. 15 U.S.C. §§ 1115, 1116.

3. Trademark law protects against both unfair competition and consumer confusion or deception by prohibiting the use of reproductions, copies, counterfeits, or colorable imitations of marks. Trademarks provide the consumer with information as to the source or origin and quality of a product or service, as well as protect the investments and goodwill of trademark owners in advertising and providing quality products. In *Indianapolis Colts*, Judge Posner stated that the test of infringement is "whether it is likely that the challenged mark if permitted to be used by the defendant would cause the plaintiff to lose a substantial number of customers." What factors are relevant for determining a likelihood of consumer confusion in sports trademark litigation? In addition to the factors cited in *Indianapolis Colts*, consider: "(1) [the] strength of the [owner's] mark; (2) relatedness of the goods; (3) similarity of the marks; (4) evidence of actual confusion; (5) marketing channels used; (6) likely degree of purchaser['s] care; (7) defendant's intent in selecting the mark." *Abdul-Jabbar v. General Motors Corp.*, 85 F.3d 407 (9th Cir. 1995).

4. **Acquired distinctiveness/secondary meaning infringement.** Recall that a trademark does not necessarily have to be registered to receive trademark protection. Although registration of trademarks provides prima facie proof of trademark ownership, 15 U.S.C. § 1057(b), a trademark may also be acquired through the use of common words, names, or symbols that the public comes to associate with a

particular source. Similar to the *LSU* case, *NFLPI v. Wichita Falls Sportswear, Inc.*, 532 F. Supp. 651 (W.D. Wash. 1982), found "secondary meaning" infringement of Seattle Seahawk NFL trademark rights against a defendant who manufactured "Seattle" jerseys with official Seahawk blue and green team colors. In secondary meaning infringement, a plaintiff must prove that the public associates a defendant's products with the plaintiff and that the defendant's acts created a likelihood of confusion, demonstrated by plaintiff's distinctive marks and defendant's similar use. In *Wichita,* the primary significance of the marks on the licensee's jerseys was source identification and stressed the physical similarities between the licensee's official jerseys and the manufacturer's jerseys. Despite some variation in design, striping, and color, these differences were not significant; the manufacturer's jerseys represented a calculated effort to create distinctions that had no real meaning in the minds of consumers.

5. "Reverse confusion" occurs when a "larger, more powerful junior user infringes on the trademark of a smaller, less powerful, senior user causing confusion as to the source of the senior user's goods and services." *See Dream Team Collectibles, Inc. v. NBA Properties, Inc.*, 958 F. Supp. 1401 (Mo. 1997) (holding actionable plaintiffs' claim of reverse confusion on defendant's use of the mark "Dream Team" to describe star basketball players competing in the Olympics where plaintiffs had previously registered the Dream Team trademark).

6. **Defenses and fair use.** What defenses are available to an infringement claim? *See* 15 U.S.C. § 1115(b) (recognizing defenses including trademark invalidity, abandonment, permission, individual's name, good faith and prior use, antitrust, and other equitable principles). Words that are descriptive or merely functional are not registrable as trademarks. Why did the court in *Indianapolis Colts* not find abandonment? Were the team color schemes in *LSU* merely functional?

7. What policy interests are served by according trademark protection to the use of words, such as team names, or to symbols or logos on sports merchandise? Do consumers benefit from the exclusive rights trademark protection provides to the sports industry—or pay more?

8. **Trademark licensing arrangements.** Sports teams often transfer trademark and licensing rights to a single corporation or trust, which represents an entire league, at the professional (properties divisions) and collegiate levels (*e.g.*, Collegiate Licensing Company). *See Boston Professional Hockey Association v. Dallas Cup & Emblem Mfgrs., Inc.*, 510 F.2d 1004 (5th Cir.), *cert. denied*, 423 U.S. 869 (1975) (describing NFL member clubs pooling of trademark rights into the NFL Trust, which manages licensing and policing of trademarks). Antitrust aspects of these agreements are explored in Chapter 6.

9. **Team names, logos, and mascots or disparaging trademarks?** The Lanham Act contained a provision that permitted denying registration. In *Matal v. Tam*, 137 S. Ct. 1744 (2017), the band named "The Slants" challenged the USPTO's refusal

to grant trademark registration. The Supreme Court ruled the Act's prohibition on "disparaging" trademarks is unconstitutional on free speech grounds. Thereafter, *Pro-Football, Inc. v. Blackhorse*, 709 Fed. Appx. 182 (4th Cir. 2018), vacated a district court decision that had upheld the USPTO's cancellation of the then Washington Redskins' trademark registration determining it to be disparaging to Native Americans. The team played as the Washington Football Team for two seasons before changing its name to the Commanders in 2022.

10. **Corporate sponsorships and naming rights.** Corporations have found sporting events an effective advertising medium and may sponsor a sporting event or product in which the corporate trademark is displayed. The sale of corporate naming rights to public and private sports facilities, stadiums, and arenas has become a significant new revenue source for financing sports facilities. Stadium naming rights are also sold to finance university sports arenas, leading to some unusual names, including Coors Arena at the University of Colorado (later changed to the Colorado Arena in response to criticism of naming a university facility after an alcoholic beverage) and Value City Arena at Ohio State University. Corporate sponsorship of sporting arenas, however, can lead to unintended consequences. In April 1999, Enron entered into a $100 million contract with the Houston Astros that required their new stadium to be named "Enron Field" for 30 years. When Enron declared bankruptcy in 2001, the Astros were left with the embarrassment of having their stadium named after a corporation that had defrauded millions of investors. Despite criticism for selling naming rights to the LA Coliseum, built in 1923 as a memorial to soldiers who lost their lives in World War I, the University of Southern California reached a $69 million deal to rename the stadium the United Airlines Field at the LA Memorial Coliseum. *See also* Robert H. Thornburg, *Stadium Naming Rights: An Assessment of the Contract and Trademark Issues Inherent to Both Professional and Collegiate Stadiums*, 2 VA. SPORTS & ENT. L.J. 328 (2013).

11. **Sport domain names.** The ease of access to sports through the Internet has made protection of intellectual property rights, including domain names, vital to sports organizations. Cybersquatting and trademark violation claims may be made in court or through the World Intellectual Property Organization (WIPO). *See, e.g., Adidas v. Paolo Luppi*, WIP case No. D2008-1334 (2008) (challenging use of "adidasfootballshop.com"); *Adidas v. Payless Shoesource, Inc.*, 546 F. Supp. 2d 1029 (D. Or. 2008) (sale of three-striped design shoes).

12. **#Hashtag buzz or ambush marketing?** The use of social media is an increasingly powerful tool for reaching consumers, engaging fans, and creating buzz around a sporting event or product. Corporate sponsors pay handsomely for the rights to exploit their brand association with the event. Could a non-sponsor's tweet congratulating a sponsored athlete or official event constitute trademark infringement? Ambush marketing is a form of infringement where a corporate non-sponsor at-

tempts to capitalize on and imply an association with a sponsored event. According to McKelvey and Grady, *The Evolving Legal Landscape of Using Hashtags in Sport*, 27 J. Legal Aspects Sport 1 (2017), "hashtagging a competitor's name or product in social media posts could, in certain circumstances, deceive consumers." Through a "non-sponsor's tweet, Instagram post, or YouTube advertisement, a non-sponsor brand is trying to drive attention toward its brand message and content while also attempting to dilute the value of the official sponsorship paid for by its competitors. If the brand's fans begin to retweet the nonofficial brand's posts and marketing messages, they essentially become virtual ambassadors carrying the ambusher's message. Thus, the need to consider additional legal protection for the event's protected words as hashtags seems more salient as well, given potential infringing use of the event's hashtags by nonsponsor brands." *Id.*

D. Sports Broadcasting: Copyright Ownership, Protection, and Limitations

Media rights are the primary revenue source for the multibillion-dollar sports industry. The U.S. sports media market represents roughly 44% of the global sports media market. Teams and leagues acquire significant revenue from licensing exclusive rights to broadcast major sporting events. For example, according to reports, the NFL will receive over $100 billion in broadcast rights fees under 10-year deals that begin in 2023 with Amazon, CBS, ESPN/ABC, Fox and NBC. In 2011, Turner Broadcasting and CBS signed a 14-year, $10.8 billion contract with the NCAA for the exclusive right to broadcast the men's basketball national championship tournament, generating $770 million in annual revenue for the NCAA. And the conferences have their own television contracts with the networks. Local, national, and cable networks pay billions for the rights to broadcast major sporting events and thereby to reach the vast sports advertising market and fan base. The networks in turn sell advertising that reaches a vast consumer market. While traditional broadcast rights for major sports remain lucrative, the cord-cutting revolution, rise of sports gambling, and introduction of new tech companies vying for the rights to sport media in digital, streaming, and mobile platforms are all affecting (and perhaps threatening) intellectual property rights of traditional sports media companies and rights holders.

The popularity of sports and its extraordinary revenue base is certainly attributable to the public's increased access to sports through media exposure and broadcasting. A fan who has never attended a live game has the opportunity to experience the game in action and usually for free by media broadcasts. Games not broadcast in a region may be accessed through satellite, cable, pay-per-view, and other forms of distribution, so a fan is rarely without access to follow his or her favorite team. The expansion of broadcasting media from radio to television, cable, satellite, and now digital and online streaming has created an insatiable demand for content—a demand that sporting bodies, networks, and others are eager to supply. Sports events provide networks substantial live programming content. For example, a professional baseball team plays a season of 162 games, each of which averages over three hours. Over the course of a season, this amounts to approximately 500 hours of broadcasting content. By comparison, a network situation comedy season, usually requiring a written script and rehearsals, produces approximately 26 half-hour shows for a total of only 13 hours (less commercial time) of content. For so much content, with a demonstrated ability to capture the public's attention, broadcasters are willing to pay seemingly exorbitant amounts for sports. Every major newscast provides a sports segment, displaying game highlights and reporting on key aspects of play. Numerous media sources are devoted to sports and offer audio and video capabilities to display plays and games and to provide instantaneous reports.

Technology continues to provide seemingly unlimited possibilities for fans to obtain up-to-the-minute and comprehensive access to sporting events. The obvious concern of the sporting bodies, however, is to protect the value of rights to license exclusive broadcasting. The value of the game rights is at its highest when the game is in progress. Networks risk losing viewers and commercial sponsors, and teams risk losing revenue from ticket sales, if the sporting event can be accessed elsewhere. *See* Holly M. Burch, *A Sports Explosion: Intellectual Property Rights in Professional Athletic Franchises*, 5 SPORTS LAW. J. 29, 38 (1998). Piracy and unauthorized transmission of sport broadcasts can threaten the system that finances sport.

Federal copyright law protects the rights of the owner of the broadcast to use and authorize, by licensing, exclusive rights to the broadcast. The Copyright Act of 1976 confers upon copyright owners exclusive rights to reproduce, adapt, publish, and sell copyrighted work. 17 U.S.C. § 106. Congress' authority to enact this statute is derived from U.S. CONST. art. I, § 8 (providing Congress the power "to promote the progress of science and useful arts, by securing for limited times to authors and inventors the exclusive right to their respective writings and discoveries"). Copyright protection subsists in "[o]riginal works of authorship fixed in any tangible medium of expression." 17 U.S.C. § 102(a). Works of authorship include "motion pictures and other audiovisual works." The Act further states that "[a] work consisting of sounds, images, or both, that are being transmitted, is 'fixed' for purposes of this title if a fixation of the work is being made simultaneously with its transmission." 17 U.S.C. § 101. The foregoing definition of "fixed" resolves the status of live broadcasts, *e.g.*, sports, news coverage, live performances of music, etc., that are reaching the public in unfixed form but that are simultaneously being recorded. By this, the owner of the copyright to a sports broadcast has the *exclusive* right to reproduce, publish, and sell the copyrighted work.

Technology presents increasingly complicated issues about the scope of rights afforded the copyright owner of a broadcast to restrict others' use of technology and media to use, reproduce, or otherwise profit from the sporting event. Sports leagues vigorously guard their broadcast rights, as evidenced by standard warnings to the effect that: "This telecast is the property of [the NFL] ... any rebroadcast, retransmission or other use of the events of this game, without the express written consent of the owner, is hereby prohibited."

What is the scope of protection for copyright owners? Does copyright ownership include restricting others from broadcasting the same event, showing game highlights, or reporting on the game? Does this preclude a local bar from showing "black out" or pay-per-view games to patrons via satellite interception? Or prohibit the same bar from allowing its customers to watch a game from the bar's rooftop overlooking the stadium? Who is the "owner" of the copyright to a live sports broadcast—the broadcaster, the teams playing in the game, the league or conference, or the players and athletes participating in the game or event? The Act is silent as to who owns the copyright in sports broadcasts, however, the Act provides that ownership of a copyright initially vests in the author(s) of the work. A live sporting event or game itself is not copyrightable because it is not authored and has no underlying script, but who authors the broadcast of it? What constitutes infringement? The following cases and note material examines these precise issues. *Pittsburgh Athletic Co.* is the landmark case establishing professional clubs' property rights in the broadcasts of their games.

Pittsburgh Athletic Co. v. KQV Broadcasting Co.

24 F. Supp. 490 (W.D. Pa. 1938)

SCHOONMAKER, DISTRICT JUDGE.

This is an action in equity in which plaintiffs ask for a preliminary injunction to restrain defendant from broadcasting play-by-play reports and descriptions of baseball games played by the "Pirates," a professional baseball team owned by Pittsburgh Athletic Company, both at its home baseball park in Pittsburgh, known as "Forbes Field," and at baseball parks in other cities....

The plaintiff Pittsburgh Athletic Company owns a professional baseball team known as the "Pirates," and is a member of an association known as the "National League." With the several teams of the members of the League, the "Pirates" play baseball both at its home field and at the home fields of the other members of the League in various cities. The home games are played at a baseball park known as "Forbes Field" which is enclosed by high fences and structures so that the public are admitted only to the Park to witness the games at Forbes Field by the payment of an admission ticket, which provides that the holder of the admission ticket agrees not to give out any news of the game while it is in progress.

The Pittsburgh Athletic Company has granted by written contract, for a valuable consideration, to General Mills, Inc., the exclusive right to broadcast, play-by-play, descriptions or accounts of the games played by the "Pirates" at this and other fields. The National Broadcasting Company, also for a valuable consideration, has contracted with General Mills, Inc., to broadcast by radio over stations KDKA and WWSW, play-by-play descriptions of these games. The Socony-Vacuum Oil Company has purchased for a valuable consideration a half interest in the contract of the General Mills, Inc.

The defendant operates at Pittsburgh a radio broadcasting station known as KQV, from which it has in the past broadcast by radio play-by-play descriptions of the games played by the "Pirates" at Pittsburgh, and asserts its intention to continue in so doing. The defendant secures the information which it broadcasts from its own paid observers whom it stations at vantage points outside Forbes Field on premises leased by defendant. These vantage points are so located that the defendant's observers can see over the enclosures the games as they are played in Forbes Field.

On this state of facts, we are of the opinion that the plaintiffs have presented a case which entitles them under the law to a preliminary injunction. It is perfectly clear that the exclusive right to broadcast play-by-play descriptions of the games played by the "Pirates" at their home field rests in the plaintiffs, General Mills, Inc., and the Socony-Vacuum Oil Company under the contract with the Pittsburgh Athletic Company. That is a property right of the plaintiffs with which defendant is interfering when it broadcasts the play-by-play description of the ballgames obtained by the observers on the outside of the enclosure.

The plaintiffs and the defendant are using baseball news as material for profit. The Athletic Company has, at great expense, acquired and maintains a baseball park, pays the players who participate in the game, and have, as we view it, a legitimate right to capitalize on the news value of their games by selling exclusive broadcasting rights to companies which value them as affording advertising mediums for their merchandise. This right the defendant interferes with when it uses its broadcasting facilities for giving out the identical news obtained by its paid observers stationed at points outside Forbes Field for the purpose of securing information which it cannot otherwise acquire. This, in our judgment, amounts to unfair competition, and is a violation of the property rights of the plaintiffs. For it is our opinion that the Pittsburgh Athletic Company, by reason of its creation of the game, its control of the park, and its restriction of the dissemination of news therefrom, has a property right in such news, and the right to control the use thereof for a reasonable time following the games.

The communication of news of the ball games by the Pittsburgh Athletic Company, or by its licensed news agencies, is not a general publication and does not destroy that right.... On the unfair competition feature of the case, we rest our opinion on the case of *International News Service v. Associated Press*, 248 U.S. 215 (1918). In that case the court enjoined the International News Service from copying news from bulletin boards and early editions of Associated Press newspapers, and selling such news so long as it had commercial value to the Associated Press. The Supreme Court said:

> Regarding the news, therefore, as but the material out of which both parties are seeking to make profits at the same time and in the same field, we hardly can fail to recognize that for this purpose, and as between them, it must be regarded as quasi-property, irrespective of the rights of either as against the public.... The right of the purchaser of a single newspaper to spread knowledge of its contents gratuitously, for any legitimate purpose not unreasonably interfering with the complainant's right to make merchandise of it, may be admitted; but to transmit that news for commercial use, in competition with complainant—which is what defendant has done and seeks to justify—is a very different matter....

***

Defendant contends it is not unfairly competing with any of the plaintiffs because it obtains no compensation from a sponsor or otherwise from its baseball broadcasts. It concedes, however, that KQV seeks by its broadcast of news of baseball games to cultivate the good will of the public for its radio station. The fact that no revenue is obtained directly from the broadcast is not controlling, as these broadcasts are undoubtedly designed to aid in obtaining advertising business.

Defendant seeks to justify its action on the ground that the information it receives from its observers stationed on its own property without trespassing on plaintiffs' property, may be lawfully broadcast by it. We cannot follow defendant's counsel in this contention for the reasons above stated.

***

2. The right, title and interest in and to the baseball games played within the parks of members of the National League, including Pittsburgh, including the property right in, and the sole right of, disseminating or publishing or selling, or licensing the right to disseminate, news, reports, descriptions, or accounts of games played in such parks, during the playing thereof, is vested exclusively in such members.

3. The actions and threatened actions of the defendant constitute a direct and irreparable interference with, and an appropriation of, the plaintiffs' normal and legitimate business; and said action is calculated to, and does, result in the unjust enrichment of the defendant at the expense of the plaintiffs and each of them.

4. The defendant's unauthorized broadcasts of information concerning games played by the Pittsburgh team constitute unfair competition with the plaintiffs and each of them....

National Basketball Association v. Motorola, Inc.

105 F.3d 841 (2d Cir. 1997)

WINTER, CIRCUIT JUDGE.

The facts are largely undisputed. Motorola manufactures and markets the SportsTrax paging device while STATS supplies the game information that is transmitted to the pagers. The product became available to the public in January 1996, at a retail price of about $200. SportsTrax's pager has an inch-and-a-half by inch-and-a-half screen and operates in four basic modes: "current," "statistics," "final scores" and "demonstration." It is the "current" mode that gives rise to the present dispute. In that mode, SportsTrax displays the following information on NBA games in progress: (i) the teams playing; (ii) score changes; (iii) the team in possession of the ball; (iv) whether the team is in the free-throw bonus; (v) the quarter of the game; and (vi) time remaining in the quarter. The information is updated every two to three minutes, with more frequent updates near the end of the first half and the end of the game. There is a lag of approximately two or three minutes between events in the game itself and when the information appears on the pager screen.

SportsTrax's operation relies on a "data feed" supplied by STATS reporters who watch the games on television or listen to them on the radio. The reporters key into a personal computer changes in the score and other information such as successful and missed shots, fouls, and clock updates. The information is relayed by modem to STATS's host computer, which compiles, analyzes, and formats the data for retransmission. The information is then sent to a common carrier, which then sends it via satellite to various local FM radio networks that in turn emit the signal received by the individual SportsTrax pagers.

***

The issues before us are ones that have arisen in various forms over the course of this century as technology has steadily increased the speed and quantity of information transmission. Today, individuals at home, at work, or elsewhere, can use a computer, pager, or other device to obtain highly selective kinds of information virtually at will. *International News Service v. Associated Press*, 248 U.S. 215 (1918) ("INS") was one of the first cases to address the issues raised by these technological advances, although the technology involved in that case was primitive by contemporary standards. INS involved two wire services, the Associated Press ("AP") and International News Service ("INS"), that transmitted news stories by wire to member newspapers. INS would lift factual stories from AP bulletins and send them by wire to INS papers. INS would also take factual stories from east coast AP papers and wire them to INS papers on the west coast that had yet to publish because of time differentials. The Supreme Court held that INS's conduct was a common-law misappropriation of AP's property. With the advance of technology, radio stations began "live" broadcasts of events such as baseball games and operas, and various entrepreneurs began to use the transmissions of others in one way or another for their own profit. In response, New York courts created a body of misappropriation law, loosely based on INS, that sought to apply ethical standards to the use by one party of another's transmissions of events.

Federal copyright law played little active role in this area until 1976. Before then, it appears to have been the general understanding—there being no caselaw of consequence—that live events such as baseball games were not copyrightable. Moreover, doubt existed even as to whether a recorded broadcast or videotape of such an event was copyrightable. In 1976, however, Congress passed legislation expressly affording copyright protection to simultaneously recorded broadcasts of live performances such as sports events. *See* 17 U.S.C. § 101. Such protection was not extended to the underlying events.

The 1976 amendments also contained provisions preempting state law claims that enforced rights "equivalent" to exclusive copyright protections when the work to which the state claim was being applied fell within the area of copyright protection. Based on legislative history of the 1976 amendments, it is generally agreed that a "hot-news" *INS*-like claim survives preemption. However, much of New York misappropriation law after *INS* goes well beyond "hot-news" claims and is preempted.

We hold that the surviving "hot-news" *INS*-like claim is limited to cases where: (i) a plaintiff generates or gathers information at a cost; (ii) the information is time-sensitive; (iii) a defendant's use of the information constitutes free-riding on the plaintiff's efforts; (iv) the defendant is in direct competition with a product or service offered by the plaintiffs; and (v) the ability of other parties to free-ride on the efforts of the plaintiff or others would so reduce the incentive to produce the product or service that its existence or quality would be substantially threatened. We conclude that SportsTrax does not meet that test.

B. Copyrights in Events or Broadcasts of Events

The NBA asserted copyright infringement claims with regard both to the underlying games and to their broadcasts....

1. Infringement of a Copyright in the Underlying Games

In our view, the underlying basketball games do not fall within the subject matter of federal copyright protection because they do not constitute "original works of authorship" under 17 U.S.C. § 102(a). Section 102(a) lists eight categories of "works of authorship" covered by the act, including such categories as "literary works," "musical works," and "dramatic works." The list does not include athletic events, and, although the list is concededly non-exclusive, such events are neither similar nor analogous to any of the listed categories. Sports events are not "authored" in any common sense of the word. There is, of course, at least at the professional level, considerable preparation for a game. However, the preparation is as much an expression of hope or faith as a determination of what will actually happen. Unlike movies, plays, television programs, or operas, athletic events are competitive and have no underlying script. Preparation may even cause mistakes to succeed, like the broken play in football that gains yardage because the opposition could not expect it. Athletic events may also result in wholly unanticipated occurrences, the most notable recent event being in a championship baseball game in which interference with a fly ball caused an umpire to signal erroneously a home run.

What "authorship" there is in a sports event, moreover, must be open to copying by competitors if fans are to be attracted. If the inventor of the T-formation in football had been able to copyright it, the sport might have come to an end instead of prospering. Even where athletic preparation most resembles authorship—figure skating, gymnastics, and, some would uncharitably say, professional wrestling—a performer who conceives and executes a particularly graceful and difficult—or, in the case of wrestling, seemingly painful—acrobatic feat cannot copyright it without impairing the underlying competition in the future. A claim of being the only athlete to perform a feat doesn't mean much if no one else is allowed to try.

For many of these reasons, Nimmer on Copyright concludes that the "far more reasonable" position is that athletic events are not copyrightable. Nimmer notes that, among other problems, the number of joint copyright owners would arguably include the league, the teams, the athletes, umpires, stadium workers and even fans, who all contribute to the "work."

Concededly, caselaw is scarce on the issue of whether organized events themselves are copyrightable, but what there is indicates that they are not. In claiming a copyright in the underlying games, the NBA relied in part on a footnote in *Baltimore Orioles, Inc. v. Major League Baseball Players Assn.*, 805 F.2d 663 (7th Cir. 1986), *cert. denied*, 480 U.S. 941 (1987), which stated that the "players' performances" contain the "modest creativity required for copyrightability." However, the court went on to state, "Moreover, even if the players' performances were not sufficiently creative, the players agree that the cameramen and director contribute creative labor to the telecasts." *Id.* This last sentence indicates that the court was considering the copyrightability of telecasts—not the underlying games, which obviously can be played without cameras.

We believe that the lack of caselaw is attributable to a general understanding that athletic events were, and are, uncopyrightable....

2. Infringement of a Copyright in the Broadcasts of NBA Games

As noted, recorded broadcasts of NBA games—as opposed to the games themselves—are now entitled to copyright protection. The Copyright Act was amended in 1976 specifically to insure that simultaneously-recorded transmissions of live performances and sporting events would meet the Act's requirement that the original work of authorship be "fixed in any tangible medium of expression." 17 U.S.C. § 102(a). Congress specifically had sporting events in mind:

> The bill seeks to resolve, through the definition of "fixation" in section 101, the status of live broadcasts—sports, news coverage, live performances of music, etc.—that are reaching the public in unfixed form but that are simultaneously being recorded.

The House Report also makes clear that it is the broadcast, not the underlying game, that is the subject of copyright protection.

Although the broadcasts are protected under copyright law, the district court correctly held that Motorola and STATS did not infringe NBA's copyright because they reproduced only facts from the broadcasts, not the expression or description of the game that constitutes the broadcast. The "fact/expression dichotomy" is a bedrock principle of copyright law that "limits severely the scope of protection in fact-based works." "'No author may copyright facts or ideas. The copyright is limited to those aspects of the work—termed 'expression'—that display the stamp of the author's originality.'" We agree with the district court that the "defendants provide purely factual information which any patron of an NBA game could acquire from the arena without any involvement from the director, cameramen, or others who contribute to the originality of a broadcast." Because the SportsTrax device and AOL site reproduce only factual information culled from the broadcasts and none of the copyrightable expression of the games, appellants did not infringe the copyright of the broadcasts.

C. The State-Law Misappropriation Claim

When Congress amended the Copyright Act in 1976, it provided for the preemption of state law claims that are interrelated with copyright claims in certain ways. Under 17 U.S.C. § 301, a state law claim is preempted when: (i) the state law claim seeks to vindicate "legal or equitable rights that are equivalent" to one of the bundle of exclusive rights already protected by copyright law under 17 U.S.C. § 106—styled the "general scope requirement"; and (ii) the particular work to which the state law claim is being applied falls within the type of works protected by the Copyright Act under Sections 102 and 103—styled the "subject matter requirement."

***

We hold that where the challenged copying or misappropriation relates in part to the copyrighted broadcasts of the games, the subject matter requirement is met as to both the broadcasts and the games.... Although game broadcasts are copyrightable while the underlying games are not, the Copyright Act should not be read to distinguish between the two when analyzing the preemption of a misappropriation claim based on copying or taking from the copyrightable work...

Copyrightable material often contains uncopyrightable elements within it, but Section 301 preemption bars state law misappropriation claims with respect to uncopyrightable as well as copyrightable elements. In *Harper & Row*, for example, we held that state law claims based on the copying of excerpts from President Ford's memoirs were preempted even with respect to information that was purely factual and not copyrightable...

It is often difficult or impossible to separate the fixed copyrightable work from the underlying uncopyrightable events or facts. Moreover, Congress, in extending copyright protection only to the broadcasts and not to the underlying events, intended that the latter be in the public domain....

Under the general scope requirement, Section 301 "preempts only those state law rights that 'may be abridged by an act which, in and of itself, would infringe one of the exclusive rights' provided by federal copyright law." ... However, certain forms of commercial misappropriation otherwise within the general scope requirement will survive preemption if an "extra-element" test is met....

We turn, therefore, to the question of the extent to which a "hot-news" misappropriation claim based on *INS* involves extra elements and is not the equivalent of exclusive rights under a copyright. Courts are generally agreed that some form of such a claim survives preemption. The crucial question, therefore, is the breadth of the "hot-news" claim that survives preemption....

[E]ven narrow "hot news" *INS*-type claims survive preemption. In our view, the elements central to an *INS* claim are: (i) the plaintiff generates or collects information at some cost or expense, (ii) the value of the information is highly time-sensitive, (iii) the defendant's use of the information constitutes free-riding on the plaintiff's costly efforts to generate or collect it, (iv) the defendant's use of the information is in direct competition with a product or service offered by the plaintiff, (v) the ability of other parties to free-ride on the efforts of the plaintiff would so reduce the incentive to produce the product or service that its existence or quality would be substantially threatened.... *INS* is not about ethics; it is about the protection of property rights in time-sensitive information so that the information will be made available to the public by profit-seeking entrepreneurs. If services like AP were not assured of property rights in the news they pay to collect, they would cease to collect it. The ability of their competitors to appropriate their product at only nominal cost and thereby to disseminate a competing product at a lower price would destroy the incentive to collect news in the first place. The newspaper-reading public would suffer....

We therefore find the extra elements—those in addition to the elements of copyright infringement—that allow a "hotnews" claim to survive preemption are: (i) the time-sensitive value of factual information, (ii) the free-riding by a defendant, and (iii) the threat to the very existence of the product or service provided by the plaintiff.

2. The Legality of SportsTrax

We conclude that Motorola and STATS have not engaged in unlawful misappropriation under the "hot-news" test set out above. To be sure, some of the elements of a "hot-news" *INS* claim are met. The information transmitted to SportsTrax is not precisely contemporaneous, but it is nevertheless time-sensitive.

However, there are critical elements missing in the NBA's attempt to assert a "hot-news" *INS*-type claim. As framed by the NBA, their claim compresses and confuses three different informational products. The first product is generating the information by playing the games; the second product is transmitting live, full descriptions of those games; and the third product is collecting and retransmitting strictly factual information about the games. The first and second products are the NBA's primary business: producing basketball games for live attendance and licensing copyrighted broadcasts of those games. The collection and retransmission of strictly factual material about the games is a different product: *e.g.*, box-scores in newspapers, summaries of statistics on television sports news, and real-time facts to be transmitted to pagers. In our view, the NBA has failed to show any competitive effect whatsoever from SportsTrax on the first and second products and a lack of any free-riding by SportsTrax on the third.

With regard to the NBA's primary products—producing basketball games with live attendance and licensing copyrighted broadcasts of those games—there is no evidence that anyone regards SportsTrax or the AOL site as a substitute for attending NBA games or watching them on television. In fact, Motorola markets SportsTrax as being designed "for those times when you cannot be at the arena, watch the game on TV, or listen to the radio...." The NBA argues that the pager market is also relevant to a "hot-news" *INS*-type claim and that SportsTrax's future competition with Gamestats satisfies any missing element. We agree that there is a separate market for the real-time transmission of factual information to pagers or similar devices, such as STATS's AOL site. However, we disagree that SportsTrax is in any sense freeriding off Gamestats.

An indispensable element of an *INS* "hot-news" claim is free-riding by a defendant on a plaintiff's product, enabling the defendant to produce a directly competitive product for less money because it has lower costs. SportsTrax is not such a product. The use of pagers to transmit real-time information about NBA games requires: (i) the collecting of facts about the games; (ii) the transmission of these facts on a network; (iii) the assembling of them by the particular service; and (iv) the transmission of them to pagers or an on-line computer site. Appellants are in no way free-riding on Gamestats. Motorola and STATS expend their own resources to collect purely factual information generated in NBA games to transmit to SportsTrax pagers. They have their own network and assemble and transmit data themselves.

To be sure, if appellants in the future were to collect facts from an enhanced Gamestats pager to retransmit them to SportsTrax pagers, that would constitute free-riding and might well cause Gamestats to be unprofitable because it had to bear costs to collect facts that SportsTrax did not. If the appropriation of facts from one pager to another pager service were allowed, transmission of current information on NBA games to pagers or similar devices would be substantially deterred because any potential transmitter would know that the first entrant would quickly encounter a lower cost competitor free-riding on the originator's transmissions.

However, that is not the case in the instant matter. SportsTrax and Gamestats are each bearing their own costs of collecting factual information on NBA games, and, if one produces a product that is cheaper or otherwise superior to the other, that producer will prevail in the marketplace. This is obviously not the situation against which *INS* was intended to prevent: the potential lack of any such product or service because of the anticipation of free-riding.

For the foregoing reasons, the NBA has not shown any damage to any of its products based on free-riding by Motorola and STATS, and the NBA's misappropriation claim based on New York law is preempted.

Notes and Comments

1. In describing the *property right* held by the teams and the justification for it, the court in *Pittsburgh Athletic* opined that the Pirates, "by reason of its creation of the game, its control of the park, and its restriction of the dissemination of news therefrom, has a property right in such news, and the right to control the use thereof for a reasonable time following the games." In other words, the teams have an *exclusive* property right in the broadcast rights. In *Pittsburgh Athletic*, the defendant paid observers, sitting outside of the stadium but within viewing range of the game, to relay game information for the defendant's unauthorized radio broadcast of play-by-play game action. The court held that this conduct violated the team's exclusive property right to control rights to broadcast the game played in the team stadium and also held defendant liable on common-law theories of unjust enrichment and unfair competition. How does the *Motorola* pager case differ, if at all? What were the key factual distinctions in *Motorola* which led the court to rule in Motorola's favor? Do you agree with the Court's ruling?

2. **Copyright protection in the underlying sporting event?** In *Motorola*, the Court distinguished copyright protection for broadcasts, as opposed to underlying sporting events. Judge Winter stated, "Sports events are not 'authored' in any common sense of the word.... What 'authorship' there is in a sports event, moreover, must be open to copying by competitors if fans are to be attracted." 105 F.3d at 846. If copyright law prohibits the copying of the broadcast and does not extend to the underlying game, could another party create their own broadcast of a game by using a sophisticated camera from a roof overlooking a sports stadium? Since *Pittsburgh Athletic*, Congress enacted the Copyright Act of 1976. How would the scenario in *Pittsburgh Athletic* be resolved under the Copyright Act? In 2002, the Chicago Cubs sued a group of rooftop bar owners who charged fans to watch Cubs games from their rooftops, which had a clear view of the ballpark. The Cubs alleged that the game itself was copyrighted and that the defendants were profiting from the team's name, players, trademarks, copyrighted telecasts, and images without the Cubs' consent. *Chicago NL Club v. Sky Box on Waveland*, No. 02 C 9105 (N.D. Ill.). The parties reached a settlement agreement that the rooftop owners would pay the Cubs 17% of

their annual profits for 20 years. In essence, the rooftop owners were paying the Cubs to refrain from building a taller stadium.

3. **Authorship and ownership of the copyrighted sports broadcast.** Ownership in the copyright to sports broadcasts lacks clarity because the broadcaster, *i.e.*, the network, produces and creates the broadcast and is therefore the "author" of the copyrighted work, that being the broadcast of the game. In 1976, the U.S. House of Representatives stated: "When a football game is being covered by four television cameras, with a director guiding the activities of the four cameramen and choosing which of their electronic images are sent out to the public and in what order, there is little doubt that what the cameramen and the director are doing constitutes 'authorship.'" Under the Copyright Act, copyright ownership "vests initially in the author or authors of the work" and an author may transfer all or any part of his or her ownership at any time. 17 U.S.C. § 201(a), 201(d), 204. Under the terms of their network contracts with the leagues, all or part of the copyright is assigned to the league and/or its member clubs. The property right held by the league and/or clubs is best characterized as an exclusive "right to broadcast" their games, which gives them the exclusive right to control which network will purchase a license for the right to broadcast their games. The networks pay the leagues billions of dollars for a license to be the exclusive broadcaster of the live events and advertisers pay the networks billions of dollars to show their commercials during the broadcasts.

4. **Pooling of team broadcast rights.** In most instances, broadcasting rights among the teams within a league or conference are addressed by contractual agreement or league/conference rules. The Sports Broadcasting Act of 1961, 15 U.S.C. §§ 1291–1295, provides a limited exemption from the antitrust laws allowing professional sports leagues to pool team broadcasting rights and contracts with sponsored networks that provide free public telecasts. The NFL had lobbied for this exemption, contending it was necessary to protect smaller team markets and overall league viability. This exemption does not extend to league contracts with companies or networks providing subscription or pay telecast services. *Shaw v. Dallas Football Club, Ltd.*, 172 F.3d 299 (3d Cir. 1999). Nor does the Act apply to college sports, *see NCAA v. Bd. of Regents*, 468 U.S. 85 (1983). How does the Act apply to NFL contracts with tech companies such as Amazon (streaming service) or Verizon (mobile)?

Suppose a company creates a digital service where its customers can access live or recorded games through an over-the-top (OTT) direct streaming service? Would such service be protected by the Act? Would it violate copyright laws? *See American Broadcast Companies Inc. v. Aereo, Inc.*, 134 S. Ct. 2498 (2014) (defendant infringes by selling its subscribers a technologically complex service that allows them to watch television programs made up of copyrighted works over the Internet at about the same time as the programs are broadcast over the air).

5. **That's my move!** Is an athlete's individual "performance" during game play protected by copyright law? Why or why not? (Review the express language of the

Copyright Act referenced above.) Could an athlete claim a copyright or trademark in a signature move, such as in Abdul-Jabbar's skyhook, Chris Evert's two-handed backhand, or Dick Fosberry's high-jumping flop? Note that although Michael Jordan's "jumpman" "move" is not copyrightable, he is permitted to trademark and license (Nike) the "jumpman" symbol. If moves were copyrightable, one could argue Kobe Bryant would have been sued by Michael Jordan, and that would deprive the fans of quality basketball.

In *Garcia v. Google, Inc.*, 743 F.3d 1258 (9th Cir. 2014), an actress was found to have an independent copyright claim to her performance in a film when she makes creative contributions beyond merely reciting lines in front of a camera. Consider if a similar standard could be applied to athletes: does athletic competition meet the standard set in *Garcia*, which finds an independent copyright held by a performer if a performance "evinces 'some minimal degree of creativity'"? *But see Somerson v. McMahon*, 956 F. Supp. 2d 1345, 1354 (N.D. Ga. 2012) (dismissing a former wrestler's ("Pretty Boy") claim of copyright ownership in his own wrestling performances). How do sports differ from other types of performances? Is a wrestling performance different from "performance" of an athlete during a football or basketball game? Under *Garcia*, would a wrestler have a stronger claim if the court had found that the WWE is scripted?

Epic Games, creator of "Fortnite," a multiplayer online battle game, faced a spate of lawsuits by a variety of artists for alleged copyright infringement in the sale of game emotes that use dance moves, such as 2Milly's "Milly Rock's" in Fortnite's "Swipe it" or Backpack Kid's the "Floss."

6. **Can athletes assert a property right in the *broadcast rights* to their performances?** In *Baltimore Orioles, Inc. v. Major League Baseball Players Association*, 805 F.2d 663 (7th Cir. 1986), *cert. denied*, 480 U.S. 941 (1987), three MLB players sued the clubs asserting that the game telecasts misappropriated their property rights in their names, pictures, and performances and constituted unjust enrichment. The Seventh Circuit affirmed the district court's grant of summary judgment in favor of the clubs finding that the clubs, not the players, owned a copyright in the telecasts as "works made for hire" and that the players' right of publicity claim in the telecasts was preempted by the clubs' copyright. *See* 17 U.S.C. § 201(b) ("In the case of a work made for hire, the employer or other person for whom the work was prepared is considered the author... and, unless the parties have expressly agreed otherwise in a written instrument signed by them, owns all of the rights comprised in the copyright."). In *Pittsburgh Athletic*, the court stated the justification for recognition of the club's property right: "The Athletic Company has, at great expense, acquired and maintains a baseball park, *pays the players who participate in the game*, and have, as we view it, a legitimate right to capitalize on the news value of their games by selling exclusive broadcasting rights to companies which value them as affording advertising mediums for their merchandise." (emphasis added). In other words, the athletes (similar

to entertainers) negotiate and receive compensation from the teams for their performances, which in essence gives the athletes the value equivalent and proportionate to a co-ownership interest in the copyright assigned to the teams from the broadcaster.

In addressing the work made for hire doctrine in the context of copyrighted works, the Supreme Court in *Community for Creative Non-Violence v. Reid,* 490 U.S. 730, 749–50 (1989), noted: "In a 'copyright marketplace,' the parties negotiate with an expectation that one of them will own the copyright in the completed work [and] [w]ith that expectation, the parties at the outset can settle on relevant contractual terms, such as the price for the work and the ownership of reproduction rights." But should the work made for hire doctrine preclude college athletes from being able to assert an unjust enrichment claim? *See* Richard T. Karcher, *Broadcast Rights, Unjust Enrichment, and the Student-Athlete*, 34 CARDOZO L. REV. 107, 160–61 (2012) ("there are three fundamental reasons why the work made for hire doctrine falls flat on its face: (1) universities, conferences and the NCAA themselves vehemently maintain the position that student-athletes are not employees or agents of the university; (2) courts that have analyzed the university-player relationship in a variety of contexts have overwhelmingly concluded that college athletes are not employees of the university...; and (3) a copyright marketplace whereby the universities and players negotiate over ownership of the copyright to the broadcasts is non-existent").

7. **Tattoo copyrights?** As sports move into new digital, gaming, and esports platforms, game producers generally enter into license agreement with the league, player association, or individual athletes to use player images or likenesses such as in NBA2K. Could these portrayals include images of athlete tattoos? The owner of Solid Oak Sketches filed a copyright infringement claim against the game developer based on reproductions of tattoos on the avatar bodies of LeBron James, Erik Bledsoe, and others. Is the tattoo a copyright? Is the game developer's use "transformative" and "fair use?" Doesn't the athlete have the right to license their own skin? How would you advise an athlete in dealing with a tattoo artist? *See Solid Oak Sketches v. Take Two Interactive,* 2018 WL 1626145 (S.D.N.Y. 2018) (denying motion to dismiss).

8. **Copyright law limitations.** To establish copyright infringement, two elements must be proven: (1) ownership of a valid copyright and (2) copying of copyrighted work. The Copyright Act does not define infringement, but 17 U.S.C. § 102(b) provides that a copyright "does not extend to any idea, procedure, process, system, method of operation, concept, principle, or discovery, regardless of the form in which it is described, explained, illustrated, or embodied in such work." Thus, the law makes a distinction between facts or ideas and expressions. The Act also recognizes that the "fair use" of a copyrighted work is not infringement where it is for purposes such as criticism, news reporting, teaching, scholarship, or research. *Id.* at § 107. What constitutes "fair use" is frequently litigated. *See New Boston Television v. ESPN*, 215 U.S.P.Q. 755 (D. Mass. 1981) (held that ESPN's videotaping from public airways, excerpting, and rebroadcasting "highlights" of copyrighted broadcasts was

not "fair use" under Copyright Act); *NFL v. TVRadionow Corp.*, 53 U.S.P.Q.2d 1831 (W.D. Pa. 2000) (enjoined defendants from infringing on plaintiff's copyrighted works through internet streaming); *NFL v. Rondor*, 840 F. Supp. 1160 (N.D. Ohio 1993) (local bar and restaurant infringed upon NFL's copyright in unauthorized interception of blacked-out television broadcast by use of special antenna). If a primary objective of the Copyright Act is to encourage the production of original creative works, including sports broadcasts as audio-visual works, does this protection impair technological advances to provide real-time services available with the Internet, electronic or video conferencing? How does the public benefit from copyright law?

9. **Preemption and state law claims.** *Motorola* held that the Copyright Act preempts state law misappropriation claims, yet also ruled that the Copyright Act does not apply to the games themselves. Notwithstanding, the Court acknowledges that a narrow *INS* "hot news" misappropriation claim survives preemption. Is this analytically consistent? Do state claims survive preemption of the Copyright Act? If so, when? Would it make a difference if the defendants had gathered and transmitted game information from inside the sports arena, rather than by watching or listening to broadcasts? Suppose the admission ticket prohibited any reproduction or transmission of play?

10. **"Hot news" misappropriation.** In analyzing the NBA's claim that defendants unlawfully misappropriated "hot news" rights to their games, the Court considered (1) the plaintiff's investment in generating or collecting information; (2) the time-sensitive value of the factual information; (3) the free riding by a defendant; (4) direct competition; and (5) the threat to the very existence of the product or service provided by the plaintiff. Why did the Court reject the NBA's "hot news" misappropriation claims?

Morris Communications, Inc. v. PGA Tour, 364 F.3d 1288 (11th Cir. 2004), ruled that the PGA Tour could restrict a newspaper corporation from publishing "real time" golf scores obtained from the tournaments' on-site media centers because: (1) the newspaper sought to free-ride on the PGA Tour's efforts, and (2) the PGA Tour has a property right in the scores before they are in the public domain, distinguishing *Motorola's* "hot news" that could be acquired independently.

How would you advise a league regarding sports gambling sites that offer instantaneous reporting of player data and game statistics? As uses for sports data emerge through media, technology, and gambling, the debates regarding ownership of proprietary systems of data continue.

11. **Broadcast and the digital age.** The threats to broadcasting rights raised by digital and social media are enormous. Approximately 2.9 million people illegally live-streamed the Mayweather versus MacGregor fight in 2017, resulting in nearly $300 million in lost revenue. Even fans can become digital pirates by using social media's live-streaming during a sporting event. As technology advances, the legal battles will continue.

Capstone Problem

SPORTBETNOW is a new application offering real-time scores and statistics on major league baseball games to those who are not able to watch the game live or on television. The concept is to provide real-time scores and statistics via a mobile phone application, sending notifications for events such as score changes, hits, errors, as well as odds, based on user preferences. SPORTBETNOW allows users to "subscribe" to receive instantaneous updates on games, teams, and individual players. SPORTBETNOW has its own employees watch the games, either live or on other media, such as television, online, or radio. The employees simultaneously input current statistical information, such as the teams playing, current scores and score changes, team and player at bat, current pitcher, inning, and players on base. Detailed health updates on individual players are noted on the broadcasts through player wearable technological devices. The statistical information is keyed into a computer, sent to the central computing system, and then relayed to the subscribers' apps.

SPORTBETNOW has become an overnight success. Thousands of fans have paid the $10/month subscription price to keep them informed on the current statistical information of their favorite team and players. SPORTBETNOW also has a website offering the same services as the app, contemporaneous with a host of additional statistical information. The website also displays graphic drawings simulating game action with computer characters. The website now generates 100,000 hits per day. Advertising revenues for the website have increased dramatically with the site's popularity. SPORTBETNOW next seeks to provide live streaming of games.

On behalf of its member teams, Major League Baseball (MLB) filed a lawsuit against SPORTBETNOW, contending that the SPORTBETNOW product and website constitute copyright and trademark infringement, as well as a misappropriation of MLB property. Explain the respective arguments of the parties.

Twelve

Health and Disability Issues

Learning Outcomes

- Learn the key statutory provisions and framework for analyzing claims and defenses under the federal disability laws.
- Consider the proper balance of participation rights and participation risks for student-athletes with conditions involving elevated risks.
- Examine the litigation brought by athletes with disabilities challenging seemingly neutral eligibility standards, which negatively impact disabled student-athletes, focusing on age and academic eligibility requirements.
- Learn about the more controversial topic of ADA cases requiring reasonable accommodations or modifications to rules of play.
- Learn about the required accessibility modifications to stadiums, arenas, and other facilities.

Key Terms

- Rehabilitation Act
- Americans with Disabilities Act
- Disability
- Otherwise qualified
- Major life activity
- Reasonable accommodation
- Liability waiver
- Fundamental alteration

A. Introduction

When thinking about athletes participating in competitive or organized sports, the public rarely contemplates the inclusion of players with medical impairments or other physical, mental, and learning disabilities. Yet many athletes with disabilities, whether visible or hidden, have achieved success in both amateur and professional sports. Although deaf, Kenny Walker attained All-American status as a defensive tackle at the University of Nebraska and went on to play professionally with the Denver Broncos. Jim Abbot, born with only one hand, successfully pitched in the professional baseball leagues. The sporting public has applauded the accomplishments of these athletes who are able to compete presumably "despite" their disabilities or by "overcoming" them. The awe turned to apprehension when Hank Gathers, who was medically cleared to play college basketball despite a heart rhythm disorder, died on the court, or when 12-year-old Michael Montalvo, diagnosed with AIDS, sought to enroll in karate classes, and even when Magic Johnson returned to professional basketball after revealing that he was HIV positive.

The rights of athletes with medical impairments or disabilities to participate in competitive sports are, at times, controversial. Because of a medical impairment or disability, some athletes cannot satisfy certain eligibility requirements set by the governing sport organizations or they need accommodation in order to participate. National attention focused on Casey Martin, plagued with a severe congenital disability affecting his right leg, when he sued to compel the PGA to permit him to ride a cart during Tour competitions although PGA rules require all players to walk. Athletes who have been effectively excluded from sports participation because of a medical impairment or disability have invoked the disability anti-discrimination laws in asserting rights to participate and to reasonable modifications of eligibility standards in sports programs at the interscholastic, intercollegiate, and professional levels.

Federal disability legislation, primarily through the Rehabilitation Act of 1973, which applies to federally funded programs, and the Americans with Disabilities Act of 1990 (ADA), whose broader coverage reaches most private employers and private entities constituting places of public accommodations, prohibits discrimination on the basis of disability and further obligates these entities to provide reasonable accommodations, modifications, or auxiliary aids that will enable qualified individuals with disabilities to access and to participate in the program or activity. 29 U.S.C. § 794; 42 U.S.C. § 12101. In enacting the ADA, Congress found, *inter alia*, that individuals with disabilities continually encounter various forms of discrimination, including "outright intentional exclusion, the discriminatory effects of architectural, transportation, and communication barriers, overprotective rules and policies, failure to make modifications to existing facilities, programs and practices, exclusionary qualification standards and criteria, segregation, and relegation to lesser services, programs, activities, benefits, jobs or other opportunities." 42 U.S.C. § 12101(b). A goal of these laws, which apply to virtually all sports teams and organizations, is to assure the equality of opportunity and full participation for individuals with disabilities.

Federal disability laws have had and continue to have a significant impact in sports, raising complicated and controversial medico-legal questions surrounding the rights of individuals with disabilities to participate in athletics and the concomitant rights and obligations of the entities regulating athletic competition to set and enforce eligibility and safety rules. Many of the cases involving disability law in sports have garnered intense public attention, raising questions about the impact on the competitive nature of sports and the ability of sporting organizations to enforce rules of participation.

This chapter addresses the legal issues and major litigation involving health and disability issues in sports. Section B sets forth the key statutory provisions and framework for analyzing claims and defenses under the federal disability laws. Section C explores balancing participation rights and participation risks for student athletes with conditions involving elevated risks. In competitive sports, the governing athletic organizations, teams, and schools establish eligibility criteria intended to protect the health and safety of athletes and to maintain the integrity of the competition. This section examines litigation brought by athletes with disabilities challenging seemingly neutral eligibility standards, which negatively impact disabled student-athletes, focusing on age and academic eligibility requirements. Section D briefly discusses the more controversial topic of ADA cases requiring reasonable accommodations or modifications to rules of play. Section E relates to other athletic employees and protections under disability laws. Finally, Section F discusses the required accessibility modifications to stadiums, arenas, and other facilities.

B. Federal Disability Legislation—Key Statutory Definitions and Provisions

Much of the litigation involving disability issues in sports has focused on whether the athlete is protected by, or a sports organization is subject to, federal legislation. The following statutory definitions and laws are generally at issue.

1. The Americans with Disabilities Act of 1990

The Americans with Disabilities Act (ADA) of 1990, 42 U.S.C. §§12101–12213 (2019) prohibits discrimination against individuals with disabilities and guarantees them equal opportunity in employment, public accommodations, State and local government services, transportation and telecommunications. The ADA is codified under five titles. Relevant here are Title I applying to employment, Title II to public programs and services, and Title III to private entities constituting places of public accommodation. Applicable to all subchapters of the ADA is the important definition of "disability."

> 42 U.S.C. § 12102(1) **Disability.** The term "disability" means, with respect to an individual —
>
> (A) a physical or mental impairment that substantially limits one or more of the major life activities of such individual;
>
> (B) a record of such impairment; or
>
> (C) regarded as having such an impairment.

Title I
(Employment)

42 U.S.C. § 12112(a) **Discrimination.** "No covered entity shall discriminate against a qualified individual on the basis of disability in regard to job application procedures, the hiring, advancement, or discharge of employees, employee compensation, job training, and other terms, conditions or privileges of employment."

42 U.S.C. § 12113(b) **Qualification Standards.** "The term 'qualification standards' may include a requirement that an individual shall not pose a direct threat to the health and safety of other individuals in the workplace."

Title II
(Public Services)

42 U.S.C. § 12132 **Discrimination.** "[N]o qualified individual with a disability shall, by reason of such disability, be excluded from participation in or be denied the benefits of the services, programs, or activities of a public entity, or be subject to discrimination by any such entity."

42 U.S.C. § 12131(2) **Qualified Individual with a Disability.** "The term 'qualified individual with a disability' means an individual with a disability who, with or without reasonable modifications to rules, policies, or practices,... meets the essential eligibility requirements for the receipt of services or the participation in programs or activities provided by the public entity."

Title III
(Public Accommodations Operated by Private Entities)

42 U.S.C. § 12182 **Prohibition of Discrimination by Public Accommodations.**

"No individual shall be discriminated against on the basis of disability in the full and equal enjoyment of the goods, services, facilities, privileges, advantages or accommodations of any place of public accommodation by any person who owns, leases (or leases to) or operates a place of public accommodation."

42 U.S.C. § 12182(b)(1)(B) **Integrated Settings.** "Goods, services, facilities, privileges, advantages, and accommodations shall be afforded to an individual with a disability in the most integrated setting appropriate to the needs of the individual."

42 U.S.C. § 12182(b)(2) **Specific Prohibitions.** "(A) Discrimination—includes [*inter alia*] (i) the imposition or application of eligibility criteria that screen out or tend to screen out an individual with a disability or any class of individuals with disabilities from fully and equally enjoying any goods, services, facilities, privileges, advantages, or accommodations, unless such criteria can

be shown to be necessary for the provision of the goods, services, facilities, privileges, advantages, or accommodations being offered; [and] (ii) a failure to make reasonable modifications in policies, practices, or procedures, when such modifications are necessary to afford such goods, services, facilities, privileges, advantages, or accommodations to individuals with disabilities, unless the entity can demonstrate that making such modifications would fundamentally alter the nature of such goods, services, facilities, privileges, advantages, or accommodations."

2. The Rehabilitation Act of 1973

29 U.S.C. § 794(a) **Nondiscrimination under Federal grants and programs.** "No otherwise qualified individual with a disability... shall, solely by reason of his or her disability, be excluded from the participation in, be denied the benefits of, or be subjected to discrimination under any program or activity receiving federal financial assistance."

Prior to the enactment of the federal disability legislation, athletes with medical impairments and disabilities seeking rights to participate in sports met limited success in raising constitutional claims against exclusion. In *City of Cleburne v. Cleburne Living Center*, 473 U.S. 432 (1985), the Supreme Court held that individuals with disabilities are not a suspect or quasi-suspect class. As a result, public schools and institutions (as "state actors") may discriminate against or exclude disabled athletes from participation if rationally related to a legitimate objective, such as to guard the health and safety of athletes. On a due process level, there is no fundamental or constitutional right to participate in competitive sports. In contrast, the Rehabilitation Act and the ADA provide athletes with disabilities substantial protection. Accordingly, most disability discrimination claims are based on the federal statutes rather than on the U.S. Constitution. Recourse may also be available under state anti-discrimination laws.

In analyzing an issue involving an athlete's rights under federal disability law, consider:

(1) Is the athlete "disabled" within the meaning of the statute? More specifically, is an athlete "substantially limited" in a "major life activity"? Is sports participation a "major life activity"?

(2) Is the athlete "otherwise qualified" to participate in the sports program with or without reasonable accommodations?

(3) Was the athlete discriminated against or excluded "because of" the person's disability?

(4) Would the requested accommodation or modification be unreasonable, require the elimination of essential eligibility requirements or fundamentally alter the nature of the sport or competition?

To determine the applicable statutory coverage, ask whether the defendant is: a recipient of federal funds (Rehabilitation Act); a public entity (ADA Title II); a place of public accommodation (ADA Title III); or an employer of the potential plaintiff (ADA Title I).

C. Participation Rights and Responsibilities

1. Eligibility of Athletes with High Medical Risk

Problem

Mia Bently is a sophomore basketball player on athletic scholarship at Middleton University, a private university and Division I member of the NCAA. Last year, Mia was seriously injured in an automobile accident, resulting in the loss of a kidney and some vision in her right eye. As basketball season approaches, Mia's personal physician has declared her healthy to play and assured that the loss of vision and the kidney should not impact Mia's playing ability. The university team physician, however, refused to clear Mia to participate in team competitions, citing safety and liability concerns. Mia desperately wants to play this year. She fears that the loss of playing opportunities will jeopardize her scholarship and prevent her from playing professionally when she has completed her eligibility at the collegiate level.

You are the Associate AD at Middleton University. Mia and her parents have expressed a willingness to sign a liability waiver. After reviewing the materials in this section, how would you evaluate Mia's situation?

Knapp v. Northwestern University

101 F.3d 473 (7th Cir. 1996), *cert. denied*, 520 U.S. 1274 (1997)

Evans, Circuit Judge.

Nicholas Knapp wants to play NCAA basketball for Northwestern University—so badly that he is willing to face an increased risk of death to do so. Knapp is a competent, intelligent adult capable of assessing whether playing inter-collegiate basketball is worth the risk to his heart and possible death, and to him the risk is acceptable. Usually, competent, intelligent adults are allowed to make such decisions. This is especially true when, as here, the individual's family approves of the decision and the individual and his parents are willing to sign liability waivers regarding the worst-case scenario should it occur.

Northwestern, however, refuses to allow Knapp to play on or even practice with its men's basketball team. Knapp, currently a sophomore at Northwestern, has the basketball skills to play at the intercollegiate level, but he has never taken the court for his team.... The issue in this case boils down to whether the school—because of

§ 504 of the Rehabilitation Act of 1973, as amended, 29 U.S.C. § 794—will be forced to let Knapp don a purple uniform and take the floor as a member of Northwestern's basketball team.

Prior to his senior year of high school Knapp was rated among the best basketball players in Illinois. He was recruited by numerous universities, including Northwestern... [who] orally offered [Knapp] an athletic scholarship to play basketball. Knapp orally accepted the offer.

A few weeks into his senior year, Knapp suffered sudden cardiac death—meaning his heart stopped—during a pick-up basketball game. Paramedics used cardiopulmonary resuscitation, defibrillation (*i.e.*, electric shocks), and injections of drugs to bring Knapp back to life. A few weeks later, doctors implanted an internal cardioverter-defibrillator in Knapp's abdomen. The device detects heart arrhythmia and delivers a shock to convert the abnormal heart rhythm back to normal. In other words, if Knapp's heart stops again the device is supposed to restart it.

On the day following his sudden cardiac death, Northwestern informed Knapp and his family that whatever the ultimate medical decision, Northwestern would honor its commitment for a scholarship. Seven weeks after his collapse Knapp signed a national letter of intent to attend Northwestern.... In September 1995 he enrolled as a Northwestern student.

On November 7, 1995, Dr. Howard Sweeney, Northwestern's head team physician, declared Knapp ineligible to participate on Northwestern's men's basketball team for the 1995–96 school year. Dr. Sweeney based his decision on Knapp's medical records in which several treating physicians recommended that Knapp not play competitive basketball, the report of team physician Dr. Mark Gardner following a physical examination of Knapp, published guidelines and recommendations following two national medical conferences known as the Bethesda Conferences regarding eligibility of athletes with cardiovascular abnormalities, and recommendations of physicians with whom Dr. Gardner and Dr. Sweeney consulted. After the basketball season ended, Northwestern and the Big Ten declared Knapp permanently medically ineligible to play basketball....

As a result, Knapp has never practiced with the Northwestern team nor played in a college game. His scholarship nevertheless continues and he attends practices (though he is not allowed to do anything but watch, apparently). He also receives other benefits afforded to athletes (such as tutoring, counseling, and training table), in addition to the full range of academic and nonacademic offerings the university provides to all students.

[K]napp filed a complaint in federal district court asserting that Northwestern's actions violated the Rehabilitation Act. The suit sought declaratory relief, preliminary and permanent injunctive relief, and compensatory damages. Knapp's undisputed goal is to force Northwestern to allow him to play varsity basketball. The district court held a hearing solely to determine whether Knapp presently is medically eligible to play intercollegiate basketball. Presented with conflicting evidence, the district court found Knapp medically eligible and Northwestern in violation of the Rehabilitation Act. [It] entered a permanent injunction prohibiting Northwestern from excluding Knapp from playing on its basketball team for any reason related to his cardiac condition.

The district court's decision was based on the affidavit of Knapp and the testimony and affidavits of two experts presented by Northwestern and three experts presented by Knapp. All the experts agreed Knapp had suffered sudden cardiac death due to ventricular fibrillation; even with the internal defibrillator, playing intercollegiate basketball places Knapp at a higher risk for suffering another event of sudden cardiac death compared to other male college basketball players; the internal defibrillator has never been tested under the conditions of intercollegiate basketball; and no person currently plays or has ever played college or professional basketball after suffering sudden cardiac death and having a defibrillator implanted. Northwestern's experts, cardiologists... testified that playing intercollegiate basketball significantly and unacceptably increases Knapp's risk of death. At least one of Northwestern's experts stated that individuals with internal defibrillators should not play intercollegiate basketball. Knapp's expert cardiologists, one of whom, Dr. Lawrence Rink, is Knapp's treating cardiologist and an Indiana University basketball team physician, testified that although Knapp is at an increased risk for sudden cardiac death, that risk, especially with the internal defibrillator in place, is insubstantial or at least acceptable.

.... To prevail on his claim for discrimination under the Act, Knapp must prove that: (1) he is disabled as defined by the Act; (2) he is otherwise qualified for the position sought; (3) he has been excluded from the position solely because of his disability; and (4) the position exists as part of a program or activity receiving federal financial assistance.... [O]ur focus is on whether Knapp is an "otherwise qualified individual with a disability."

To show that he is disabled under the terms of the Act, Knapp must prove that he (i) has a physical... impairment which substantially limits one or more of [his] major life activities, (ii) has a record of such an impairment, or (iii) is regarded as having such an impairment. 29 U.S.C. § 706(8)(B). Knapp satisfies the first element of part (i) of this definition. A cardiovascular problem constitutes a physical impairment under § 706(8)(B). Northwestern does not dispute this fact, but it instead zeros in on the second element of the disability definition: whether playing intercollegiate basketball is part of a major life activity and, if so, whether its diagnosis of Knapp's cardiac condition substantially limits Knapp in that activity.

In determining whether a particular individual has a disability as defined in the Rehabilitation Act, the regulations promulgated by the Department of Health and Human Services with the oversight and approval of Congress are of significant assistance. Those regulations define "major life activities" as basic functions of life "such as caring for one's self, performing manual tasks, walking, seeing, hearing, speaking, breathing, learning, and working." 34 C.F.R. § 104.3(j)(2)(ii). Regulations regarding equal employment opportunities under the Americans with Disabilities Act, adopt the same term and definition and an interpretive note provides a bit more guidance: "'Major life activities' are those basic activities that the average person in the general population can perform with little or no difficulty." . . .

The "disability" Knapp claims is the basis for discrimination against him is not a continuing one like blindness or deafness. At any given moment in time when Knapp's heart is functioning properly his disability does not affect him. He is truly disabled only when his heart stops, which may or may not happen to him again. The disability regarding which Northwestern allegedly discriminates, therefore, actually is the greater risk of harm for Knapp than the risk faced by other male college basketball players. . . . Here, Knapp's disability is all or nothing. Finally, because Knapp's disability affects one of the most central organs of the body, his disability to some extent affects all major life activities—if his heart stops, he will not breathe, see, speak, walk, learn, or work. Once again it is all or nothing—either his heart is functioning and no major life activities are limited at that moment, or it has stopped and the most major life activity of all—living—has been affected.

In any event, the parties here have framed their arguments as involving solely the major life activity of learning. Knapp contends that playing an inter-collegiate sport is an integral part of his major life activity of learning and that his education will be substantially limited if he cannot play on the team. He states that he does not believe he can obtain confidence, dedication, leadership, perseverance, discipline, and teamwork in any better way. The district court agreed with him, determining that for Knapp, playing on the Northwestern basketball team was part of the major life activity of learning and that he was substantially limited from such learning by the university. . . .

We do not think that the definition of "major life activity" can be as particularized as Knapp wants it to be. Playing intercollegiate basketball obviously is not in and of itself a major life activity, as it is not a basic function of life on the same level as walking, breathing, and speaking. Not everyone gets to go to college, let alone play intercollegiate sports. We acknowledge that intercollegiate sports can be an important part of the college learning experience for both athletes and many cheering students—especially at a Big Ten school. Knapp has indicated that such is the case for him. But not every student thinks so. Numerous college students graduate each year having neither participated in nor attended an intercollegiate sporting event. . . . Not playing intercollegiate sports does not mean they have not learned. Playing or enjoying intercollegiate sports therefore cannot be held out as a necessary part of learning for *all* students.

Because intercollegiate athletics may be *one part* of the major life activity of learning for *certain* students, the parties here have framed the analysis of what constitutes a major life activity into a choice between a subjective test or an objective test—whether we look at what constitutes learning for Nick Knapp or what constitutes learning in general for the average person. The Rehabilitation Act and the regulations promulgated under it give little guidance regarding whether the determination of what constitutes a major life activity turns on an objective or subjective standard. And while we have previously said that whether a person is disabled is "an individualized inquiry, best suited to a case-by-case determination," we have also indicated that "the definition of 'major life activity' in the regulations 'cannot be interpreted to include working at the specific job of one's choice.'" Other courts have been across the board on whether the test is objective or subjective. *Compare Pahulu v. University of Kansas*, 897 F. Supp. 1387 (D. Kan. 1995) ("for Pahulu, intercollegiate football may be a major life activity, *i.e.*, learning"), and *Sandison v. Michigan High School Athletic Ass'n*, 863 F. Supp. 483 (D. Mich. 1994) (participation on high school teams is "as to them a major life activity"), with *Welsh v. City of Tulsa, Okla.*, 977 F.2d 1415 (10th Cir. 1992) (major life activity of working does not necessarily mean working at the job of one's choice).

We decline to define the major life activity of learning in such a way that the Act applies whenever someone wants to play intercollegiate athletics. A "major life activity," as defined in the regulations, is a basic function of life "such as caring for one's self, performing manual tasks, walking, seeing, hearing, speaking, breathing, learning, and working." These are basic functions, not more specific ones such as being an astronaut, working as a firefighter, driving a race car, or learning by playing Big Ten basketball.... An impairment that interferes with an individual's ability to perform a particular function, but does not significantly decrease that individual's ability to obtain a satisfactory education otherwise, does not *substantially* limit the major life activity of learning.

Because learning through playing intercollegiate basketball is only one part of the education available to Knapp at Northwestern, even under a subjective standard, Knapp's ability to learn is not substantially limited. Knapp's scholarship continues, allowing him access to all academic and—except for inter-collegiate basketball.... Like the firefighter in *Welsh*, who did not show that his education and training limited him to being a firefighter, Knapp has not shown that his education and training limit him to do nothing but play basketball. The fact that Knapp's goal of playing intercollegiate basketball is frustrated does not substantially limit his education. The Rehabilitation Act does not guarantee an individual the exact educational experience that he may desire, just a fair one. Consequently, we hold that Knapp as a matter of law is not disabled within the meaning of the Rehabilitation Act.

Even if we were inclined to find Knapp disabled under the Rehabilitation Act... he is not, under the statute, "otherwise qualified" to play intercollegiate basketball at Northwestern....

Legitimate physical qualifications may in fact be essential to participation in particular programs.... Although blanket exclusions are generally unacceptable, legitimate physical requirements are proper.

A significant risk of personal physical injury can disqualify a person from a position if the risk cannot be eliminated. But more than merely an elevated risk of injury is required before disqualification is appropriate. Any physical qualification based on risk of future injury must be examined with special care if the Rehabilitation Act is not to be circumvented, since almost all disabled individuals are at a greater risk of injury....

We do not believe that, in cases where medical experts disagree in their assessment of the extent of a real risk of serious harm or death, Congress intended that the courts—neutral arbiters but generally less skilled in medicine than the experts involved—should make the final medical decision. Instead, in the midst of conflicting expert testimony regarding the degree of serious risk of harm or death, the court's place is to ensure that the exclusion or disqualification of an individual was individualized, reasonably made, and based upon competent medical evidence. So long as these factors exist, it will be the rare case regarding participation in athletics where a court may substitute its judgment for that of the school's team physicians.

[B]ecause we hold today as a matter of law that a court must allow Northwestern to make its own determinations of substantial risk and severity of injury if they are based on reliable evidence, the district court's order forcing Northwestern to let Knapp play must be reversed.

In closing, we wish to make clear that we are *not* saying Northwestern's decision necessarily is the right decision. We say only that it is not an illegal one under the Rehabilitation Act.... Simply put, all universities need not evaluate risk the same way. What we say in this case is that if substantial evidence supports the decision-maker—here Northwestern—that decision must be respected.

Section 794 prohibits authorities from deciding without significant medical support that certain activities are too risky for a disabled person. Decisions of this sort cannot rest on paternalistic concerns. Knapp, who is an adult, is not in need of paternalistic decisions regarding his health, and his parents—more entitled to be paternalistic toward him than Northwestern—approve of his decision.... But here, where Northwestern acted rationally and reasonably rather than paternalistically, no Rehabilitation Act violation has occurred. The Rehabilitation Act "is carefully structured to replace... reflexive actions to actual or perceived handicaps with actions based on reasoned and medically sound judgments...."

REVERSED.

Sidebar

When experts conflict—who decides? A person is not "qualified" if there is a substantial risk of injury to the student or others. Assuming that some medical risk of injury or death is unacceptable, whose assessment of medical risk governs when the opinion of the team physician and the player's medical experts conflict—the player, the team, or the court? *See* Matthew J. Mitten, *Enhanced Risk of Harm to One's Self as a Justification for Exclusion from Athletics*, 8 MARQ. SPORTS L.J. 189 (1998) (asserting that a model according deference to the team physician's decision, if supported by a reasonable medical basis, appropriately balances an athlete's interest in participation and the team or sponsor's interests in protecting the health and safety of participants). The court in *Wright v. Columbia University*, 520 F. Supp. 789 (E.D. Pa. 1981), ordered the university to allow a student with sight in one eye to play football, accepting the player's ophthalmologist's opinion that participation did not pose a substantial risk of serious eye injury and rejecting team physician's contrary opinion. The court noted that the university's laudable concern for student safety cannot derogate from a student's rights under the Rehabilitation Act, "which prohibits 'paternalistic authorities' from deciding that certain activities are 'too risky' for people with disabilities." Is deference to the school's decision warranted or should a court independently weigh the evidence? Is a liability waiver sufficient?

Notes and Comments

1. **Disability.** The court holds that although Knapp was medically ineligible, he was *not* "disabled" under the Rehabilitation Act. Why? The ADA Amendments Act of 2008 provides that "[a]n impairment that is episodic or in remission is a disability if it would substantially limit a major life activity when active." 42 U.S.C. §12102(4)(D). "Major life activities... include, but are not limited to, caring for oneself, performing manual tasks, seeing, hearing, eating, sleeping, walking, standing, lifting, bending, speaking, breathing, learning, reading, concentrating, thinking, communicating, and working." *Id.* at §12102(2)(A). Further, "the determination of whether an impairment substantially limits a major life activity shall be made without regard to the ameliorative effects of mitigating measures such as—(I) medication, medical supplies, equipment... prosthetics including limbs and devices... other implantable hearing devices, mobility devices, or oxygen therapy equipment and supplies." *Id.* at §12102(4)(E). Under the Amended ADA, is Knapp "disabled"? *Class v. Towson University*, 806 F.3d 236 (4th Cir. 2015), held that a football player who had collapsed on the field from heat stroke and suffered liver failure was not "disabled" under the ADA based upon a heightened risk of future heat stroke, although the court deferred to the team doctor's decision that the player was not "qualified" to return to play due to such risk.

2. The court focused on the arguments of whether participation in intercollegiate athletics is a major life activity and if this determination is a subjective or objective one. The district court in *Knapp* found that intercollegiate sports play an important part of a student's education and learning process, and, at a minimum, constituted a major life activity for Nick Knapp. By affidavit, Knapp stated, "[M]y participation in competitive basketball has provided me and could continue to provide me with a unique experience that I have not encountered in any other extracurricular activity.... Among other things, competitive basketball has helped to instill in me the

following character traits: confidence, dedication, leadership, teamwork, discipline, perseverance, patience, the ability to set priorities, the ability to compete, goal-setting and the ability to take coaching, direction and criticism." 942 F. Supp. 1191 (N.D. Ill. 1996). Northwestern argued that exclusion from a single activity is not a substantial limitation because he could participate in other extracurricular activities, such as band. The Seventh Circuit reversed the district court. Do you agree? Was this a lawyering mistake? Would it have made a difference if Northwestern refused to extend Knapp the basketball scholarship?

3. **Status of athletic participation—pros/college/high school.** If Nick Knapp were a professional athlete would his "disability" status differ? Does a professional athlete have a stronger interest in participation because his or her livelihood is at stake? Should a professional athlete be bound by the team's physician's opinion of medical disqualification due to risk of harm? Would the analysis in *Knapp* differ in the context of high school athletics? Isn't it true that high school athletic competition and success can greatly increase chances of acceptance to college? Does the suggestion that the disabled athlete participate in different extracurricular activities hold as much weight, where no high school extracurricular activity provides the same prestige as athletics? *See Badgett v. Ala. High Sch. Athletic Ass'n*, 2007 U.S. Dist. Lexis 36014 (N.D. Ala. 2007) (ruling against high school wheelchair racer who wanted to compete in the standard races rather than the wheelchair division).

4. **Risk of severe injury.** Attention became squarely focused on the safety of athletes competing with serious medical conditions following the death of basketball star Hank Gathers. He had collapsed once during the season, was placed on medication for a heart problem, and eventually returned to the court. Sadly, Gathers collapsed again during a game and died. In the wake of his death, schools have been far more cautious about allowing athletes with medical problems to compete. Gathers' family sued his treating physicians, claiming failure to fully inform Gathers of the seriousness of his heart condition and risks of playing, and asserting that he should not have been medically cleared to continue playing college basketball.

5. **Efficacy of liability waivers.** If an athlete who does not obtain medical clearance of physical qualifications is fully informed of, and consents to, the risks of participation, should the school be required to permit the athlete to play? Some schools have reluctantly allowed athletes with heart and other ailments to compete, but only after negotiating carefully drafted waivers of liability. In *Wagenblast v. Odessa School District*, 758 P.2d 968 (Wash. 1988), however, exculpatory releases of the school district's negligence, signed as a condition of participation in interscholastic sports, were held invalid as contrary to public policy. *See also* Andrew Manno, Note, *A High Price to Compete: The Feasibility and Effect of Waivers Used to Protect Schools from Liability for Injuries to Athletes with Medical High Risks*, 79 Ky. L.J. 867 (1991) (asserting that waivers may inadequately protect schools from liability if later challenged on grounds of misrepresentation, fraud, incapacity, or contrary to public policy).

6. **Risk of harm to self versus others.** The *Knapp* court justified exclusion based on the risk of harm that participation would pose to Nick Knapp himself. The ADA provides a defense when the disabled person poses a risk of harm to others yet says nothing regarding when the risk of harm is to one's self. Courts and the EEOC regulations, however, appear to recognize the defense. *See Colombo v. Sewanhaka Central High School District No. 2*, 87 Misc. 2d 48 (N.Y. Sup. Ct. 1976) (deferring to judgment of team physician that a deaf student was ineligible to participate in team sports where his participation posed a risk of injury to the boy and to other team members); *Montalvo v. Radcliffe*, 167 F.3d 873 (4th Cir.), *cert. denied*, 528 U.S. 813 (1999) (permitting martial arts school to deny admission to 12-year-old boy due to his HIV positive status from participation in full contact karate classes because of the significant risk to other participants' health and safety).

The "direct threat to self" issue was somewhat resolved in *Chevron U.S.A. Inc. v. Echazabal*, 536 U.S. 73 (2002), which held that EEOC regulations authorizing the refusal to hire an individual whose performance on the job would endanger his own health, due to a disability, did not exceed the scope of permissible rule-making under the ADA. Exclusion on the basis of direct threat must be based on an individualized and scientific determination, and not merely a subjective good faith belief. *Bragdon v. Abbott*, 524 U.S. 624 (1998); *Anderson v. Little League Baseball, Inc.*, 794 F. Supp. 342 (D. Ariz. 1992) (finding an ADA violation because no proof that on-field coaching in a wheelchair poses a direct threat to others' health and safety).

7. **Accommodations for anxiety.** Consider an athlete such as NBA player Royce White, who suffered from severe generalized anxiety disorder and panic attacks. White requested certain accommodations be made in light of his condition—such as permission to drive rather than fly to games and to determine his own mental health treatment through the use of an independent physician. Does such a condition constitute a "disability"? Are these accommodations "reasonable" to require of the NBA? *See* Michael A. McCann, *Do You Believe He Can Fly? Royce White and Reasonable Accommodations Under the Americans with Disabilities Act for NBA Players with Anxiety Disorder and Fear of Flying*, 41 PEPP. L. REV. 397 (2013).

In *S.S. v. Whitesboro Sch. Dist.*, 2012 U.S. Dist. LEXIS 11727 (N.D.N.Y. 2012), a minor student swimmer who suffered from extreme anxiety due to a fear of drowning sought, as an accommodation, permission to exit the pool if she had an anxiety attack. The court dismissed, holding that the student did not have a right to participate on the swimming team as part of her right to education. Although the court did not rule on the "reasonableness" of the accommodation, is the accommodation in *Whitesboro* significantly different than requesting travel and medical care accommodations? What are a sport organization's responsibilities to accommodate an athlete with diagnosed anxiety?

8. **Responsibilities of team, player, coach, and more.** The decision in *Knapp* presumed that physicians, as medical experts, were better equipped than judges and lawyers to make determinations about the relative safety of a disabled athlete's par-

ticipation in sports. Does a team's reliance on physician representations in making crucial determinations about the player's fitness to compete absolve the team of responsibility and liability? Are there concerns about an interested party serving as the physician making the key determinations? Physicians are arguably subject to pressure both to be cautious in allowing disabled players to participate out of concerns relating to injury and liability, but also liberal in allowing players to participate out of a desire to see the player and team succeed.

Should players have a duty to disclose any disability to the team or physician, or do the team and physician have a duty to discover and diagnose the disability or injury?

9. **Concussions in professional sports.** After the high-profile deaths of several former NFL players such as Junior Seau and other reports concerning the long-term effects of concussions and Chronic Traumatic Encephalopathy ("CTE"), several former NFL players filed a class action lawsuit against the NFL. A settlement approved in 2014 is structured to last about 65 years and provide funds for former players who develop neurological problems. The settlement includes a $10 million research provision and $75 million for baseline testing, in addition to the $675 provided for retirees. However, the family of Junior Seau chose to reject the proposed settlement and proceed with the wrongful death suit against the NFL. *See* Mark Fainaru-Wada, *Seaus to Opt Out of Concussion Deal*, ESPN (Sept. 3, 2014).

The NFL has enacted a strict policy regarding the safety rules and treatment of head trauma in an effort to prevent and lessen the long-term effects of CTE and concussions. Players who engage in "head to head" contact are subject to sanction. In the event a player suffers a concussion, the team doctors decide whether it is safe for a player to return. A player cannot return to a game or practice unless he is fully asymptomatic both at rest and after exertion. A player who loses consciousness, for any amount of time, after a concussion, cannot return to the game under any circumstances. After suffering a concussion, a player will not be able to participate in the next week's game until the player maintains a baseline score in the league-mandated neuropsychological test. NFL Commissioner Roger Goodell has emphasized that medical considerations take priority over competitive considerations. *See* Daniel J. Kain, *"It's Just a Concussion": The National Football League's Denial of a Causal Link Between Multiple Concussions and Later-Life Cognitive Decline*, 40 Rutgers L.J. 697 (2009) (discussing the history of the NFL's "concussion problem" and suggesting that players may file a lawsuit alleging the NFL wrongfully concealed studies about the effects of multiple concussions and failed to warn players of the risks).

10. This area of the law has produced numerous scholarly articles. *See, e.g.*, Dionne L. Koller, *The Increasing Role of Disability Issues in U.S. Sports Law*, Oxford Handbook on American Sports Law 175–193 (2018); James P. Looby, *Reasonable Accommodations for High School Athletes with Disabilities: Preserving Sports While Providing Access for All*, 19 Sports Law J. 227 (2012).

2. Learning Disabilities and Age Limits on Athletic Participation

Problem

Joseph Hagan, 6 feet, 225 pounds, is a defensive lineman on the high school football team. Joseph has been a starter on the team for his freshman through junior year. Shortly before football season began, the team coach regretfully informed Joseph that he was ineligible to compete in athletics during his senior year because he turns age 19 before September 1 of the current school year. The state high school athletic association strictly enforces the age-limitation rule, regarding the rule as essential to the safety and integrity of interscholastic sports programs. Joseph explains that due to a learning disability, he repeated two grades in elementary school. The Hagan family wants to know whether federal disability laws entitle Joseph to force the high school athletic association to allow him to play. What arguments and specific evidence would Joseph need to present in seeking to enjoin the enforcement of the age-limitation rule to him? What arguments are likely to be made in response by the athletic association?

Sandison v. Michigan High School Athletic Association, Inc.

64 F.3d 1026 (6th Cir. 1995)

RYAN, CIRCUIT JUDGE.

Ronald Sandison and Craig Stanley, two recent graduates of Michigan public high schools, filed this action against their respective high schools and the Michigan High School Athletic Association (MHSAA) alleging claims under, *inter alia*, the Rehabilitation Act of 1973, 29 U.S.C. § 794, and titles II and III of the Americans with Disabilities Act (ADA), 42 U.S.C. §§ 12132, 12182. Each student suffers from a learning disability, and before reaching high school each fell behind the typical school grade for children of his age. The plaintiffs [turned nineteen before the start of their senior years]. The MHSAA, of which the plaintiffs' high schools are members, prohibits students who turn nineteen by September 1 of the school year to compete in interscholastic high school sports. In the district court, the plaintiffs won preliminary injunctive relief....

I.

When he was four years old, Ronald Sandison was placed in a special preschool program for learning disabled children because he had difficulty processing speech and language. Sandison started ungraded kindergarten at age six, rather than at the usual age of five, and it was not until age seven that Sandison was considered a student in graded kindergarten. This two-year delay placed Sandison two school grades behind his age group. At age eleven, Sandison was diagnosed with auditory input disability, which hampers Sandison's ability to distinguish between similar sounds. With the help of special education support, Sandison attended Rochester Adams High School in regular classrooms and graduated in June 1995. Sandison ran on Adams's cross-country and track teams during his first three years of high school. He turned nineteen years old in May 1994, a few months before starting his senior year.

Due to a learning disability in mathematics, Craig Stanley repeated kindergarten and then spent five years in a special education classroom. Stanley made the transition into regular classrooms by entering the fourth grade, rather than the fifth grade, after those five years in special education. Accordingly, Stanley is two school grades behind his age group. With the help of special education support, Stanley has attended Grosse Pointe North High School in regular classrooms and graduated in June 1995. Stanley ran on his high school's cross-country and track teams during the first three years. He turned nineteen years old in May 1994, a few months before starting his senior year.

Like most high schools in Michigan, Rochester Adams and Grosse Pointe North are members of the MHSAA. Members of the MHSAA agree to adopt the MHSAA's rules governing interscholastic sports. MHSAA Regulation I § 2 forbids students over nineteen years old from playing interscholastic sports.... No waiver of the age requirement is permitted. MHSAA Handbook, Art. VII, § 4E.

On August 18, 1994, the plaintiffs sued the Rochester and Grosse Pointe school systems, and the MHSAA... [and] alleged that excluding them from playing interscholastic sports amounted to unlawful disability discrimination....

First, the district court restrained all three defendants from preventing the plaintiffs from participating in interscholastic cross-country and track competition. Second, the district court enjoined the MHSAA from sanctioning Rochester Adams and Grosse Pointe North for permitting the plaintiffs to participate in interscholastic meets. The district court explained that it relied only on the Rehabilitation Act and the ADA to support the preliminary injunction.... The district court held that, by managing interscholastic athletic events, the MHSAA operated "places of education" and "places of entertainment" under title III of the ADA, which generally prohibits disability discrimination in places of "public accommodation." In addition... the MHSAA was a "public entity" under title II of the ADA [and] indirectly received federal financial assistance under the Rehabilitation Act, § 794.

As for the remaining elements of a disability discrimination claim under the Rehabilitation Act and the ADA, the district court held that the plaintiffs were disabled, "otherwise qualified," and discriminated against solely on the basis of their disabilities. The MHSAA does not dispute the finding of "disability" on appeal. The district court concluded that the plaintiffs were "otherwise qualified" because permitting the plaintiffs to participate would not thwart the purposes of the age restriction. The district court reasoned that the age limit had two purposes: (1) to safeguard other athletes against injuries arising from competing against overage, and thus oversized, athletes; and (2) to prevent overage athletes from gaining an unfair competitive advantage. Accordingly, waiver of the age limit for Sandison and Stanley was a "reasonable accommodation" because the plaintiffs played a noncontact sport and were not "'star' players."

***

III. Rehabilitation Act of 1973

We first discuss the plaintiffs' claim under section 504 of the Rehabilitation Act of 1973. In its current form, the section provides in pertinent part:

> No otherwise qualified individual with a disability... shall, solely by reason of his or her disability, be excluded from the participation in, be denied the benefits of, or be subjected to discrimination under any program or activity receiving Federal financial assistance.... 29 U.S.C. § 794.

A cause of action under section 504 comprises four elements: (1) The plaintiff is a "handicapped [disabled] person" under the Act; (2) The plaintiff is "otherwise qualified" for participation in the program; (3) The plaintiff is being excluded from participation in, being denied the benefits of, or being subjected to discrimination under the program solely by reason of his handicap [disability]; and (4) The relevant program or activity is receiving Federal financial assistance. In this case, the plaintiffs are unlikely to succeed on the merits of the second and third elements.

A. "Solely by Reason of" Disability

Taking the latter element to start, we hold that the plaintiffs are not, in the words of the statute, "being excluded from the participation in... any program or activity" "solely by reason of... his disability."... [U]nder a "natural reading" of section 504, the MHSAA's disqualification of students who reach nineteen years of age by the specified date "cannot readily be characterized as a decision made," "solely by reason of" each student's respective learning disability. Regulation I § 2 is a "neutral rule"—neutral, that is, with respect to disability—and as far as the record shows, is neutrally applied by the MHSAA. Throughout the plaintiffs' first three years of high school, Regulation I § 2 did not bar the students from playing interscholastic sports, yet the students were of course learning disabled during those years. It was not until they turned nineteen that Regulation I § 2 operated to disqualify them. Accordingly, we must conclude that the age regulation does not exclude students from participating "solely by reason of" their disability. The plain meaning of section 504's text does not cover the plaintiffs' exclusion.... [A]bsent their respective learning disability, Sandison and Stanley still fail to satisfy Regulation I § 2. The plaintiffs' respective learning disability does not prevent the two students from meeting the age requirement; the passage of time does. We hold that, under section 504, the plaintiffs cannot meet the age requirement "solely by reason of" their dates of birth, not "solely by reason of [disability]."

***

B. "Otherwise Qualified"

We also hold that the district court clearly erred by finding that the plaintiffs are likely to show that they are "otherwise qualified" to participate in interscholastic track and cross-country competition. Specifically, after finding that the plaintiffs are not "star" players and are not an injury risk to other competitors, the district court found that the MHSAA must waive Regulation I § 2 as to Sandison and Stanley in order to reasonably accommodate the plaintiffs. We disagree.

Under section 504, a disabled individual is "otherwise qualified" to participate in a program if, with "reasonable accommodation," the individual can meet the "necessary" requirements of the program....

Aside from the necessity of the program's requirement, the other question in the otherwise qualified inquiry is "'whether some "reasonable accommodation" is available to satisfy the legitimate interests of both the grantee and the handicapped person.... '" Generally, an "accommodation is not reasonable if it either imposes 'undue financial and administrative burdens' on a grantee, or requires 'a fundamental alteration in the nature of [the] program.'" *School Bd. of Nassau County v. Arline*, 480 U.S. 273 (1987).

We join the only other circuit that has decided the "otherwise qualified" question on similar facts, and hold that the MHSAA's age regulation is "necessary" and that waiver of the regulation is not a "reasonable accommodation." In *Pottgen v. Missouri High School Activities Ass'n*, 40 F.3d 926 (8th Cir. 1994), the plaintiff suffered from a learning disability, forcing him to repeat two grades in elementary school. After playing interscholastic baseball during his first three years of high school, the plaintiff turned nineteen before his senior year. An under-nineteen age requirement imposed by Missouri's high school athletic association disqualified the plaintiff from playing in his senior year.

In rejecting the student's claim that the Missouri association's age restriction violated section 504, the Eighth Circuit first found that the restriction constituted "an essential eligibility requirement," citing four reasons: "An age limit helps reduce the competitive advantage flowing to teams using older athletes; protects younger athletes from harm; discourages student athletes from delaying their education to gain athletic maturity; and prevents over-zealous coaches from engaging in repeated red-shirting to gain a competitive advantage." Next, the court in *Pottgen* found that, given the plaintiff's age, "the only possible accommodation is to waive the essential eligibility requirement itself." The Eighth Circuit rejected waiver as a reasonable accommodation, concluding that "waiving an essential eligibility standard would constitute a fundamental alteration in the nature of the baseball program."

[T]he district court erred in finding that waiver of Regulation I § 2 constituted a reasonable accommodation. First, we agree with the court in *Pottgen* that waiver of the age restriction fundamentally alters the sports program. Due to the usual ages of first-year high school students, high school sports programs generally involve competitors between fourteen and eighteen years of age. Removing the age restriction injects into competition students older than the vast majority of other students, and the record shows that the older students are generally more physically mature than younger students. Expanding the sports program to include older students works a fundamental alteration.

Second, although the plaintiffs assert that introducing their average athletic skills into track and cross-country competition would not fundamentally alter the program, the record does not reveal how the MHSAA, or anyone, can make that competitive unfairness determination without an undue burden. The MHSAA's expert explained that five factors weigh in deciding whether an athlete possessed an unfair competitive advantage due to age: chronological age, physical maturity, athletic experience, athletic skill level, and mental ability to process sports strategy. It is plainly an undue burden to require high school coaches and hired physicians to determine whether these factors render a student's age an unfair competitive advantage. The determination would have to be made relative to the skill level of each participating member of opposing teams and the team as a unit. And of course each team member and the team as a unit would present a different skill level. Indeed, the determination would also have to be made relative to the skill level of the would-be athlete whom the older student displaced from the team. It is unreasonable to call upon coaches and physicians to make these near-impossible determinations.

Finally, we note that there is a significant peculiarity in trying to characterize the waiver of the age restriction as a "reasonable accommodation" of the plaintiffs' respective learning disability. Ordinarily, an accommodation of an individual's disability operates so that the disability is overcome and the disability no longer prevents the individual from participating. In this case, although playing high school sports undoubtedly helped the plaintiffs progress through high school, the waiver of the age restriction is not directed at helping them overcome learning disabilities; the waiver merely removes the age ceiling as an obstacle.

The plaintiffs are excluded from participating in interscholastic track and cross-country competition "solely by reason of" age, not disability. Furthermore, waiver of the "necessary" age restriction does not constitute a "reasonable accommodation."...

[T]he plaintiffs are not subjected to "discrimination on the basis of disability," and waiver is not in this case a "reasonable modification[]."...

Accordingly, the plaintiffs are unlikely to succeed on the merits of their section 504 and ADA claims. We REVERSE that portion of the preliminary injunction ordering the MHSAA to refrain from entering penalties for the plaintiffs' performance.

Johnson v. Florida High School Activities Ass'n, Inc.

899 F. Supp. 579 (M.D. Fla. 1995)

Bucklew, U.S. District Judge.

Facts

The plaintiff, Dennis Johnson, is a nineteen year old senior at Boca Ciega High School in St. Petersburg, Florida. At approximately nine months, Dennis contracted meningitis, losing all hearing in one ear and substantially all hearing in the other. Because of this disability, Dennis' parents elected to wait a year before enrolling him in kindergarten. According to Dennis' mother, the decision to wait a year was based upon their beliefs that Dennis was not "up to par" with the other children his age.

[T]he school system decided to hold Dennis back [again] in first grade because of his performance in reading and language. Once again, Dennis' deficiencies were attributed to his hearing impairment. Dennis was placed in special education classes in second grade and remained there until… he entered Boca Ciega High School. He is provided an interpreter, notetaker and itinerant teacher at Boca Ciega. Additionally, just prior to entering eighth grade, Dennis lost all hearing in both ears.

Although a senior in high school, Dennis turned nineteen on June 29, 1995. According to the rules of the FHSAA, Dennis is ineligible to participate in high school athletics. FHSAA By-Law 19-4-1 (prohibiting anyone who turns age nineteen before September 1 of the current school year from participating in interscholastic sports). Dennis has played football and wrestled for the last three years.… [T]he rules of the FHSAA do provide for "undue hardship" exceptions as to the FHSAA's other rules, but that the age requirement is "unwaivable" because it is deemed an essential eligibility requirement by the FHSAA. Thus, Dennis is currently precluded from participating in high school athletics. Additionally, the Court notes that if Dennis did participate, the rules of the FHSAA would result in Boca Ciega High School forfeiting those games in which Dennis participated.

Dennis is five foot nine inches and weighs 250 pounds and plays defensive tackle.… Dennis is not considered a "star" player and is not "larger" than the other players. Additionally, a review of the rosters from two of Boca Ciega's opponents reveals that while Dennis is large, he is not the largest student to play defensive line. The Court notes that one of Boca Ciega's opponents lists a junior linemen as six foot four inches and 260 pounds. Additionally, as a wrestler, Dennis wrestles in the heavy weight division. This division limits competitors to a maximum of 275 pounds.…

Discussion

Boiled down, the dispositive issue before the Court is whether waiving the age requirement constitutes a "fundamental alteration" to the purposes of the rule. Resolution of this issue requires an examination of the purposes of the age requirement as applied to the instant case... and as noted by the courts in *Pottgen* and in *Sandison.*

The purposes of the age requirement as promulgated by the FHSAA are twofold. First, the rule promotes safety. By prohibiting players who turn age nineteen prior to September 1st of the current year from participating in interscholastic athletics, the rule liberally regulates the size and strength of the players. The second purpose is fairness, *i.e.*, to create an even playing field. The rule prevents schools from "red-shirting" their players so as to build a better program. These are admittedly salutary purposes....

A review of the *Pottgen* opinion, however, reveals that the Court provided no analysis as to the relationship between the age requirement and the purposes behind the age requirement. Rather, the court accepted the Missouri State High School Activities Association's assertion that the age requirement was an essential eligibility requirement....

The fact that the FHSAA deems the age requirement essential does not make it so. Rather, the relationship between the age requirement and its purposes must be such that waiving the age requirement in the instant case would necessarily undermine the purposes of the requirement.

In the instant case, the Court finds that the purposes of the age requirement are not undermined by allowing Plaintiff to participate in interscholastic athletics. The Court emphasizes that while the Plaintiff is large, he is not the largest football player playing his position. There are individuals larger than him on the playing field. Thus, accepting the fact that football is a contact sport in which injuries do occasionally occur, the Court finds that allowing this individual to play does not facilitate or exacerbate the potential for injury. Additionally, the weight divisions in wrestling eliminate any safety concern as to that sport. Moreover, the Court finds that Boca Ciega High School does not gain an unfair advantage through the play of the Plaintiff. The Court notes that the Plaintiff is considered a mid-level player and not a "star." Furthermore, the Plaintiff is no more experienced than the other players. Rather, in comparison to some players he is less experienced. The plaintiff has only played organized football for three years.

In conclusion, the Court finds that the plaintiff has demonstrated a "likelihood of success on the merits." The Plaintiff has established the essential elements required to assert claims under the Rehabilitation Act and the ADA. Specifically, the Court finds that waiving the age requirement in the instant case does not fundamentally alter the nature of the program. Allowing Dennis Johnson to participate in interscholastic athletics in no way undermines the purposes of safety and fairness. The Court stresses that its holding is limited to the facts before it.

The Court finds that irreparable injury will result to the Plaintiff if the injunction is not granted. There is no doubt that playing interscholastic athletics has changed the Plaintiff's life.... Given that this is the Plaintiff's senior year, to prohibit him from playing would undermine any gains he has made.

There is no risk of harm to the FHSAA or others if the injunction is issued. As previously noted, allowing the Plaintiff to participate does not create an additional safety concern. His presence alone does not exacerbate the potential for injury. Additionally, granting the injunction does not subject the FHSAA to "numerous frivolous lawsuits" as it suggests. Rather, the Court's granting of the injunction is limited to the narrow case before it. Moreover, the Court rejects FHSAA's argument that waiving the age requirement forces FHSAA to undertake a comparative analysis of all the athletes in the league. FHSAA suggests that to determine whether the goals of safety and fairness are undermined by letting the "disabled individual" play, the FHSAA would have to impanel a group of expert educators and physicians. This panel would examine the "disabled student" as against the other players on his or her team and on the opponents' team, comparing strength and ability. Simply stated, FHSAA's argument makes a mountain out of a mole hill. Strength and size disparities already exist throughout the league and yet no comparative analysis is undertaken. This Court finds that no such analysis is needed to determine whether an average size and average skilled disabled nineteen year old defensive linemen and wrestler can participate in interscholastic athletics when there is no indication that the student has held back or "reshirted" so as to better the program. Accordingly, the Court finds that the threatened injury to the Plaintiff is greater than any damage or injury the FHSAA might suffer as a result of the issuance of the injunction.

The Court finds that the public interest is advanced by issuing the injunction and allowing the Plaintiff to participate in interscholastic athletics.... The purpose of the ADA and the Rehabilitation Act is "to include persons with disabilities in society equal to those without disabilities by addressing discrimination against persons with disabilities." Thus, there is a significant public interest in eliminating discrimination against individuals with disabilities and issuing the injunction advances this interest. The injunction enables the Plaintiff to enjoy high school fully and to show to his fellow classmates that deaf persons can play sports.

Plaintiff's Motion for Preliminary Injunction is GRANTED. The Defendant FHSAA is enjoined from enforcing its rules prohibiting the Plaintiff from playing interscholastic athletics and penalizing Boca Ciega High School for allowing the Plaintiff to play.

Notes and Comments

1. **Individualized inquiry or undue burden?** The federal courts divided on whether interscholastic age eligibility rules violate the federal antidiscrimination laws when applied to students who exceed the age limits and were held back in

school because of a disability. The Sixth and Eighth Circuits have upheld age-limitation rules, reasoning in part that such rules are essential to promote the safety of younger athletes and to maintain a competitive balance in interscholastic athletics by precluding physically more mature students. According to these courts, waiver of the rule would fundamentally alter the nature of interscholastic competition and pose an undue administrative burden on the associations to assess competitive fairness in individual cases. *See McPherson v. Michigan High School Ath. Ass'n*, 119 F.3d 453 (6th Cir. 1997) (following *Sandison* on eight-semester rule); *Pottgen v. Missouri State High School Activities Ass'n*, 40 F.3d 926 (8th Cir. 1994) (holding that the age-limit rule was an essential eligibility requirement supported by health and safety concerns and that modification would be unreasonable). However, the individualized analysis approach used in *Johnson* has gained recognition. *See Washington v. Indiana High Sch. Ath. Ass'n*, 181 F.3d 840 (7th Cir. 1999) (requiring individualized determination of waiver of eight-semester rule); *Starego v. N.J. Interscholastic Athletic Ass'n*, 970 F. Supp. 2d 303 (D.N.J. 2013) (stating that Supreme Court's 2001 ruling in *Martin v. PGA* requires individualized inquiry); *Cruz v. Pa. Interscholastic Ath. Ass'n*, 157 F. Supp. 2d 485 (E.D. Pa. 2001) (concluding that waiver of the maximum age rule for a learning disabled student would not fundamentally alter high school sports program). As a practical matter, what are the defining factors in an individualized inquiry?

2. **"Solely by reason of" disability.** *Sandison* emphasized that the age requirement was a neutral rule applicable to all students and that the plaintiffs were excluded from participation only in their senior years and "solely by reason of" their age, not disability. The Court did not find it relevant that the plaintiffs were delayed in their schooling as a result of their learning disabilities. *Johnson* focused on whether waiving the requirement fundamentally alters the purposes of the rule. The ADA prohibits discrimination "on the basis of disability" and defines discrimination to include the imposition of eligibility criteria that screen out or tend to screen out individuals with disabilities, unless the criteria is necessary to the program. Under what circumstances could a "facially neutral requirement" discriminate "on the basis of disability"? Is *Sandison*'s construction of the term correct or too narrow?

3. **Not that good or strong anyway?** *Johnson* acknowledged the salutary purposes served by the age-limitation rule, but determined, based on an individualized assessment, that in *Johnson*'s case, waiver of the age rule was a reasonable accommodation. The court cited to factors, such as the plaintiff was of average size and ability and did not intentionally delay his education to get an athletic advantage. How do "star" student-athletes with disabilities who are exceptionally skilled, strong, large, or talented fare under even the individualized standard?

4. **Disability and residency requirements.** Should a sport residency rule be waived where an out-of-district student attends a school because of its specialized curriculum? *C.S. v. Ohio High Sch. Ath. Ass'n*, 2015 U.S. Dist. LEXIS 99003 (S.D.

Ohio 2015), denied injunctive relief to a learning disabled student who lived in Kentucky with family but attended school in Ohio because of its special needs program. The court held enforcement of the state athletic association's "in-state" residency eligibility requirement was "facially neutral" and that the student was ineligible because his parents lived out of state and thus the student was ineligible under the rule whether disabled or not.

5. **Extra year not due to disability.** A high school student diagnosed with autism, attention deficit hyperactivity disorder, and cognitive impairments and enrolled in a special education program and granted eligibility to attend high school until he turned 21 was not entitled to participate as a 19-year-old or to compete for more than the eight-semester maximum imposed by association eligibility rules. *Starego v. N.J. State Interscholastic Ath. Ass'n*, 970 F. Supp. 2d 303 (D.N.J. 2013), ruled that the student, who played football for four years, had been "afforded the full benefit of participation" and thus denial of a fifth year of eligibility was not due to his disability. Consider the causal connection between the rule and the disability.

6. **Preliminary injunctions.** Claims by student-athletes seeking rights to participate are usually made in the context of a motion for preliminary injunction. Because of the short timing of the sports season, the plaintiffs' claims may quickly become moot whether injunctive relief is granted or not. Accordingly, the courts test whether the plaintiff can demonstrate irreparable harm and a substantial likelihood of success on the merits of an ADA or Rehabilitation Act claim. The appeal in *Sandison* was not mooted as to the penalty imposed on schools, such as forfeiture of season games, for allowing students who exceed the age limit to participate. *Johnson*'s lawsuit was later vacated as moot because he concluded his participation in high school sports and no penalties were assessed. 102 F.3d 1172 (11th Cir. 1997).

7. **Athletic programs, leagues, and associations as "covered entities."** The initial element of an athlete's disability claim must establish that the defendant, school, program, or entity is a "covered entity" within the meaning of either the Rehabilitation Act or the ADA. The Rehabilitation Act applies to recipients of federal funds, which generally include public programs, schools, colleges, or universities. The ADA Title III broadens the scope of coverage to private entities and places of public accommodation. A highly litigated issue has involved determining whether private sports leagues, associations, or athletic standard-setting or membership organizations are "places of public accommodation," defined in the ADA by listing a host of "private entities" with operations that affect commerce. The list of private entities includes 12 categories, which in turn contain more than 50 examples of covered facilities, including "a gymnasium, health spa, bowling alley, golf course, or other place of exercise or recreation." Title III does not identify membership organizations or standard-setting associations in the listed categories. The NCAA has argued that, as a private association, it is not subject to Title III. The NCAA has also argued that it was not a "physical" place of public accommodation and does not own, lease, or

operate such a place, and that learning disabled athletes are thus not denied access to any "place." The PGA makes a similar argument in *PGA Tour, Inc. v. Martin*, below. Yet courts largely reject that argument. What is the critical inquiry in determining whether the NCAA is subject to Title III?

Some courts strictly interpret the statutory language, holding that the terms "facility" and "place" in the ADA require a physical structure. *See, e.g., Elitt v. U.S.A. Hockey*, 922 F. Supp. 217 (D. Mo. 1996) (holding that youth hockey league and its national governing body, which refused to permit a child with Attention Deficit Disorder to play league hockey, did not constitute places of public accommodation because plaintiff failed to show he was denied access to a place of public accommodation simply by alleging that he could not play in the league; that is, he had not shown that he was denied access to the ice rink itself).

Other courts take a broader view, holding that Title III is not limited to physical structures. *Shultz v. Hemet Youth Pony League, Inc.*, 943 F. Supp. 1222 (C.D. Cal. 1996) (holding that a youth baseball league and its organizing body were covered by the ADA and that "Title III's definition of 'place of public accommodation' is not limited to actual physical structures with definite physical boundaries."). Although acknowledging that the NCAA is an unincorporated and voluntary membership organization of approximately 1,200 postsecondary educational institutions, and not a "place" of public accommodation, the ADA prohibits more than just discrimination based on physical access. As the chief entity responsible for governing intercollegiate athletics, the NCAA was found to control, manage, and regulate participation in intercollegiate sports through, *inter alia*, its eligibility rules. *See Tatum v. NCAA*, 992 F. Supp. 1114 (E.D. Mo. 1998) (finding that the NCAA "operates" a place of public accommodation in terms of the entity's power to control, manage, or regulate the place and conditions causing the alleged discrimination); *Matthews v. National Collegiate Athletic Ass'n*, 179 F. Supp. 2d 1209 (E.D. Wa. 2001).

8. In *Ganden v. NCAA*, 1996 U.S. Dist. LEXIS 17368 (N.D. Ill. Nov. 21, 1996), a highly recruited swimmer diagnosed with a learning disability since second grade sought to compel the NCAA to modify its core course criteria to accept remedial courses taken as part of his special education curriculum and to modify its GPA criteria. In rejecting this request as unreasonable and as a fundamental alteration, the court stated: "Whatever criticism one may level at GPA and the national standardized tests, these provide significant objective predictors of a student's ability to succeed at college. The 'core course' criteria further serves the dual interests of insuring the integrity of the GPA and independently insuring that the student has covered the minimum subject matter required for college." The court added, "Title III does not require the NCAA to simply abandon its eligibility requirements, but only to make reasonable modifications to them." When is modification to academic standards "reasonable"? Plaintiffs have pursued a similar goal through different avenues. In *Hall v. Nat'l Collegiate Athletic Ass'n*, 985 F. Supp. 782 (N.D. Ill. 1997), plaintiff

athlete sought to compel the NCAA to consider four "non-core" courses on his transcript to be core and designate him a qualifier, unsuccessfully relying on claims of breach of contract and civil rights violations.

9. **Consent decree.** The United States Department of Justice (DOJ), charged with enforcement of Title III of the ADA, investigated the NCAA's initial eligibility certification process in response to several discrimination complaints filed by student-athletes with learning disabilities. The DOJ determined that "several aspects" of the NCAA's initial eligibility requirements violate Title III of the ADA, in particular the "core course" definition explicitly excluding any remedial, special education, or compensatory courses. On May 26, 1998, the NCAA entered into a Consent Decree with the DOJ, agreeing to revise certain procedures and policies with respect to student-athletes with learning disabilities. *United States v. NCAA*, Consent Decree (D.D.C. May 26, 1998), http://www.ada.gov/ncaa.htm. Under the Decree, the NCAA agreed to: certify classes designed for students with disabilities as "core courses" if they provide them with the same type of "knowledge and skills as other college-bound students"; permit ineligible learning disabled students to earn a fourth year of eligibility by making "substantial progress" towards an academic degree; include experts on learning disabilities in evaluating waiver applications; and pay $35,000 to four student-athletes who had filed complaints with the DOJ. *See* NCAA Manual § 14.3.1.3.1.2 (Exception – Students with Education-Impacting Disabilities). The NCAA entered the Consent Decree even though no court had yet ruled that a learning disabled student had a reasonable probability of succeeding on the merits of a disability discrimination claim against the NCAA. Expressly in the Consent Decree, however, the NCAA maintains that it is not subject to Title III of the ADA and denies any liability under the ADA.

10. **ADA prima facie claim.** Michael Bowers, who was a talented high school football player heavily recruited by several colleges and universities, had received special education services to accommodate his learning disability from second grade through high school. The schools stopped recruiting efforts, however, after receipt of his transcripts indicating special education courses. In response to Bowers' disability discrimination claim, the University of Iowa attacked each element of the ADA claim, asserting that Bowers was not "disabled" simply because he could not participate in intercollegiate sports and that he was not "otherwise qualified" to participate due to failure to meet the NCAA academic eligibility "core course" and standardized test score requirements. Similarly, Iowa argued that Bowers was not discriminated against "because of" his learning disability but was denied eligibility due to his failure to fulfill the core course and GPA requirements. The court denied summary judgment. And the NCAA had argued it was not a "place of public accommodation." *Bowers v. NCAA*, 9 F. Supp. 2d 460 (D.N.J. 1998). Why? *See* Maureen A. Weston, *Academic Standards or Discriminatory Hoops? Learning-Disabled Student-Athletes and the NCAA Initial Academic Eligibility Requirements*, 66 TENN. L. REV. 1049 (1999).

The *Bowers* case involved heavy, protracted litigation spanning years, and is largely responsible for the NCAA modifying its criteria per the Consent Decree. Tragically, Michael Bowers became addicted to prescribed painkillers and died of a drug overdose in 2002. Bower's mother, Kathleen, continued to prosecute his disability discrimination lawsuit against the NCAA. *Bowers v. NCAA*, 563 F. Supp. 2d 508 (D.N.J. 2008) (granting motion to exclude evidence of 1998 NCAA/DOJ Consent Decree and denying defendant's contest that Bowers had a learning disability).

11. **Defining and diagnosing learning disabilities.** Learning disabilities are neurological disorders that cause difficulties in learning which cannot be attributed to poor intelligence, poor motivation, inadequate teaching, or environmental, cultural, or economic disadvantages. Learning disabilities encompass a wide range of learning impairments with dyslexia being the most common form. Unlike most physical disabilities, learning disabilities are usually hidden and may go undetected. For example, among the waiver applications filed with the NCAA, some learning disabled students were diagnosed at an early age and received special education throughout schooling (*Ganden, Bowers*). Others were not diagnosed until later in high school or even after having failed to meet NCAA requirements. Michelle Huston, a state champion in gymnastics, was not diagnosed as learning disabled until late in her sophomore year when she had a 1.1 grade point average. Since then, Michelle has performed well academically but failed to meet NCAA eligibility because of the first two years' grades. In *Tatum v. NCAA*, 992 F. Supp. 1114 (E.D. Mo. 1998), experts issued conflicting diagnoses as to whether the student was learning disabled and entitled to receive accommodation, and the court agreed with the NCAA's rejection of Tatum's learning disability diagnosis. The Association on Higher Education and Disabilities (AHEAD) has developed guidelines to assist post-secondary institutions in verifying learning disabilities diagnoses and accommodation requests, including guidance on evaluator qualifications and appropriate clinical documentation to substantiate a learning disability.

D. Rules of Play and Reasonable Accommodations

The previous sections of this chapter have examined judicial resolution of sports "eligibility" issues under the federal disability laws. Note, however, that the courts did not intervene in the actual rules of play and competition. Application of the Americans with Disabilities Act and the Rehabilitation Act becomes more controversial when the laws appear to require modifications or accommodations for athletes with disabilities in competition, particularly at the professional level. Most professional teams or organizations do not receive federal financial assistance and are not covered by the Rehabilitation Act. In the few disability discrimination cases brought by professional athletes, the athletes have invoked Title I (employment) and Title III (public accommodations) of the ADA to seek legal relief.

Problem

Phil Luna, as a straight-on placekicker for the University of Texoma, set a new record in NCAA Division I football for field-goals. When he was five years old, the front half of Luna's right (kicking) foot was severed in a lawnmower accident. Since then he has worn a specially designed shoe to play sports. For placekicking, Luna wears a specially designed extra-wide cleat, featuring a square toe with wood at the half end of the shoe and padding to keep his foot from hitting the wood. Despite complaints by other teams and players in college that the shoe provides a competitive advantage, Luna was allowed to wear the special shoe. Luna seeks to play professionally and has been highly recruited by several NFL teams. However, the NFL has a rule prohibiting the use of special equipment by players. The NFL had the special cleat X-rayed, weighed, and inspected by several officials. Thereafter, the NFL denied Luna's request to play with his square-toed wooden shoe, maintaining that such use violates the special equipment prohibition. Luna seeks your advice regarding whether federal disability laws require the NFL to permit him to wear the specially designed kicking shoe.

As you read the U.S. Supreme Court's decision in *PGA Tour v. Martin*, consider the arguments, testimony, and witnesses presented at trial in the federal district court in Oregon, when Casey Martin sued the PGA under the Americans with Disabilities Act, seeking injunctive relief and monetary damages. How might this impact the decision below or subsequent cases?

PGA Tour, Inc. v. Martin

532 U.S. 661 (2001)

JUSTICE STEVENS.

This case raises two questions concerning the application of the Americans with Disabilities Act of 1990, 42 U.S.C. § 12101 *et seq.*, to a gifted athlete: first, whether the Act protects access to professional golf tournaments by a qualified entrant with a disability; and second, whether a disabled contestant may be denied the use of a golf cart because it would "fundamentally alter the nature" of the tournaments, to allow him to ride when all other contestants must walk....

Petitioner PGA TOUR, Inc., a nonprofit entity formed in 1968, sponsors and cosponsors professional golf tournaments conducted on three annual tours....

Casey Martin is a talented golfer. Martin is also an individual with a disability as defined in the Americans with Disabilities Act of 1990 (ADA or Act). Since birth he has been afflicted with Klippel-Trenaunay-Weber Syndrome, a degenerative circulatory disorder that obstructs the flow of blood from his right leg back to his heart. The disease is progressive; it causes severe pain and has atrophied his right leg. During the latter part of his college career, because of the progress of the disease, Martin could no longer walk an 18-hole golf course. Walking not only caused him pain, fatigue, and anxiety, but also created a significant risk of hemorrhaging, developing blood clots, and fracturing his tibia so badly that an amputation might be required. For these reasons, Stanford made written requests to the Pacific 10 Conference and the NCAA to waive for Martin their rules requiring players to walk and carry their own clubs. The requests were granted.

When Martin turned pro and entered petitioner's Q-School, the hard card permitted him to use a cart during his successful progress through the first two stages. He made a request, supported by detailed medical records, for permission to use a golf cart during the third stage. Petitioner refused to review those records or to waive its walking rule for the third stage. Martin therefore filed this action.

In the District Court, petitioner moved for summary judgment on the ground that it is exempt from coverage under Title III of the ADA as a "private clu[b] or establishmen[t]," or alternatively, that the play areas of its tour competitions do not constitute places of "public accommodation" within the scope of that Title.

At trial, petitioner did not contest the conclusion that Martin has a disability covered by the ADA, or the fact "that his disability prevents him from walking the course during a round of golf." Rather, petitioner asserted that the condition of walking is a substantive rule of competition, and that waiving it as to any individual for any reason would fundamentally alter the nature of the competition. Petitioner's evidence included the testimony of a number of experts, among them some of the greatest golfers in history. Arnold Palmer, Jack Nicklaus, and Ken Venturi explained that fatigue can be a critical factor in a tournament, particularly on the last day when psychological pressure is at a maximum. Their testimony makes it clear that, in their view, permission to use a cart might well give some players a competitive advantage over other players who must walk. They did not, however, express any opinion on whether a cart would give Martin such an advantage.

Martin presented evidence, and the judge found, that even with the use of a cart, Martin must walk over a mile during an 18-hole round, and that the fatigue he suffers from coping with his disability is "undeniably greater" than the fatigue his able-bodied competitors endure from walking the course. As the judge observed: "[P]laintiff is in significant pain when he walks, and even when he is getting in and out of the cart. With each step, he is at risk of fracturing his tibia and hemorrhaging. The other golfers have to endure the psychological stress of competition as part of their fatigue; Martin has the same stress plus the added stress of pain and risk of serious injury. As he put it, he would gladly trade the cart for a good leg. To perceive that the cart puts him—with his condition—at a competitive advantage is a gross distortion of reality." As a result, the judge concluded that it would "not fundamentally alter the nature of the PGA Tour's game to accommodate him with a cart." The judge accordingly entered a permanent injunction requiring petitioner to permit Martin to use a cart in tour and qualifying events.

On appeal to the Ninth Circuit, petitioner renewed the contention that during a tournament the portion of the golf course "'behind the ropes' is not a public accommodation because the public has no right to enter it." The Court of Appeals saw "no justification in reason or in the statute to draw a line beyond which the performance of athletes becomes so excellent that a competition restricted to their level deprives its situs of the character of a public accommodation." Nor did it find a basis for distinguishing between "use of a place of public accommodation for pleasure and use in the pursuit of a living." Consequently, the Court of Appeals concluded that golf courses remain places of public accommodation during PGA tournaments.

The Court of Appeals regarded the central dispute as whether such permission would "fundamentally alter" the nature of the PGA TOUR or NIKE TOUR. Like the District Court, the Court of Appeals viewed the issue not as "whether use of carts generally would fundamentally alter the competition, but whether the use of a cart by Martin would do so." That issue turned on "an intensively fact-based inquiry," and, the court concluded, had been correctly resolved by the trial judge. In its words, "[a]ll that the cart does is permit Martin access to a type of competition in which he otherwise could not engage because of his disability."...

At issue now, as a threshold matter, is the applicability of Title III to petitioner's golf tours and qualifying rounds, in particular to petitioner's treatment of a qualified disabled golfer wishing to compete in those events....

It seems apparent, from both the general rule and the comprehensive definition of "public accommodation," that petitioner's golf tours and their qualifying rounds fit comfortably within the coverage of Title III, and Martin within its protection. The events occur on "golf course[s]," a type of place specifically identified by the Act as a public accommodation. In addition, at all relevant times, petitioner "leases" and "operates" golf courses to conduct its Q-School and tours. As a lessor and operator of golf courses, then, petitioner must not discriminate against any "individual" in the "full and equal enjoyment of the goods, services, facilities, privileges, advantages, or accommodations" of those courses. Certainly, among the "privileges" offered by petitioner on the courses are those of competing in the Q-School and playing in the tours; indeed, the former is a privilege for which thousands of individuals from the general public pay, and the latter is one for which they vie. Martin, of course, is one of those individuals. It would therefore appear that Title III of the ADA, by its plain terms, prohibits petitioner from denying Martin by way of a three-stage qualifying tournament...

According to petitioner, Title III is concerned with discrimination against "clients and customers" seeking to obtain "goods and services" at places of public accommodation, whereas it is Title I that protects persons who work at such places.... Martin therefore cannot bring a claim under Title III because he is not one of the "'clients or customers of the covered public accommodation.'" Rather, Martin's claim of discrimination is "job-related" and could only be brought under Title I—but that Title does not apply because he is an independent contractor rather than an employee....

[T]itle III's general rule prohibiting public accommodations from discriminating against individuals because of their disabilities... "discrimination," which is defined by Title III to include:

> "a failure to make reasonable modifications in policies, practices, or procedures, when such modifications are necessary to afford such goods, services, facilities, privileges, advantages, or accommodations to individuals with disabilities, *unless the entity can demonstrate that making such modifications would fundamentally alter the nature* of such goods, services, facilities, privileges, advantages, or accommodations."

Petitioner does not contest that a golf cart is a reasonable modification that is necessary if Martin is to play in its tournaments. Martin's claim thus differs from one that might be asserted by players with less serious afflictions that make walking the course uncomfortable or difficult, but not beyond their capacity. In such cases, an accommodation might be reasonable but not necessary. In this case, however, the narrow dispute is whether allowing Martin to use a golf cart, despite the walking requirement that applies to the PGA TOUR, the NIKE TOUR, and the third stage of the Q-School, is a modification that would "fundamentally alter the nature" of those events.

In theory, a modification of petitioner's golf tournaments might constitute a fundamental alteration in two different ways. It might alter such an essential aspect of the game of golf that it would be unacceptable even if it affected all competitors equally; changing the diameter of the hole from three to six inches might be such a modification. Alternatively, a less significant change that has only a peripheral impact on the game itself might nevertheless give a disabled player, in addition to access to the competition as required by Title III, an advantage over others and, for that reason, fundamentally alter the character of the competition. We are not persuaded that a waiver of the walking rule for Martin would work a fundamental alteration in either sense....

There is nothing in the Rules of Golf that either forbids the use of carts, or penalizes a player for using a cart. That set of rules, as we have observed, is widely accepted in both the amateur and professional golf world as the rules of the game. The walking rule that is contained in petitioner's hard cards, based on an optional condition buried in an appendix to the Rules of Golf, is not an essential attribute of the game itself.

Indeed, the walking rule is not an indispensable feature of tournament golf either. As already mentioned, petitioner permits golf carts to be used in the SENIOR PGA TOUR, the open qualifying events for petitioner's tournaments, the first two stages of the Q-School, and, until 1997, the third stage of the Q-School as well. Moreover, petitioner allows the use of carts during certain tournament rounds in both the PGA

TOUR and the NIKE TOUR. In addition, although the USGA enforces a walking rule in most of the tournaments that it sponsors, it permits carts in the Senior Amateur and the Senior Women's Amateur championships.

Petitioner, however, distinguishes the game of golf as it is generally played from the game that it sponsors in the PGA TOUR, NIKE TOUR, and (at least recently) the last stage of the Q-School—golf at the "highest level." According to petitioner, "[t]he goal of the highest-level competitive athletics is to assess and compare the performance of different competitors, a task that is meaningful only if the competitors are subject to identical substantive rules." The waiver of any possibly "outcome-affecting" rule for a contestant would violate this principle and therefore, in petitioner's view, fundamentally alter the nature of the highest level athletic event. The walking rule is one such rule, petitioner submits, because its purpose is "to inject the element of fatigue into the skill of shot-making," and thus its effect may be the critical loss of a stroke. As a consequence, the reasonable modification Martin seeks would fundamentally alter the nature of petitioner's highest level tournaments even if he were the only person in the world who has both the talent to compete in those elite events and a disability sufficiently serious that he cannot do so without using a cart.

The force of petitioner's argument is, first of all, mitigated by the fact that golf is a game in which it is impossible to guarantee that all competitors will play under exactly the same conditions or that an individual's ability will be the sole determinant of the outcome. For example, changes in the weather may produce harder greens and more head winds for the tournament leader than for his closest pursuers. A lucky bounce may save a shot or two. Whether such happenstance events are more or less probable than the likelihood that a golfer afflicted with Klippel-Trenaunay-Weber Syndrome would one day qualify for the NIKE TOUR and PGA TOUR, they at least demonstrate that pure chance may have a greater impact on the outcome of elite golf tournaments than the fatigue resulting from the enforcement of the walking rule.

Further, the factual basis of petitioner's argument is undermined by the District Court's finding that the fatigue from walking during one of petitioner's 4-day tournaments cannot be deemed significant. The District Court credited the testimony of a professor in physiology and expert on fatigue, who calculated the calories expended in walking a golf course (about five miles) to be approximately 500 calories—"nutritionally... less than a Big Mac." What is more, that energy is expended over a 5-hour period, during which golfers have numerous intervals for rest and refreshment. In fact, the expert concluded, because golf is a low intensity activity, fatigue from the game is primarily a psychological phenomenon in which stress and motivation are the key ingredients. And even under conditions of severe heat and humidity, the critical factor in fatigue is fluid loss rather than exercise from walking.

Moreover, when given the option of using a cart, the majority of golfers in petitioner's tournaments have chosen to walk, often to relieve stress or for other strategic reasons. As NIKE TOUR member Johnson testified, walking allows him to keep in rhythm, stay warmer when it is chilly, and develop a better sense of the elements and the course than riding a cart.

Even if we accept the factual predicate for petitioner's argument—that the walking rule is "outcome affecting" because fatigue may adversely affect performance—its legal position is fatally flawed. Petitioner's refusal to consider Martin's personal circumstances in deciding whether to accommodate his disability runs counter to the clear language and purpose of the ADA. As previously stated, the ADA was enacted to eliminate discrimination against "individuals" with disabilities, and to that end Title III of the Act requires without exception that any "policies, practices, or procedures" of a public accommodation be reasonably modified for disabled "individuals" as necessary to afford access unless doing so would fundamentally alter what is offered. To comply with this command, an individualized inquiry must be made to determine whether a specific modification for a particular person's disability would be reasonable under the circumstances as well as necessary for that person, and yet at the same time not work a fundamental alteration.

To be sure, the waiver of an essential rule of competition for anyone would fundamentally alter the nature of petitioner's tournaments. As we have demonstrated, however, the walking rule is at best peripheral to the nature of petitioner's athletic events, and thus it might be waived in individual cases without working a fundamental alteration. Therefore, petitioner's claim that all the substantive rules for its "highest-level" competitions are sacrosanct and cannot be modified under any circumstances is effectively a contention that it is exempt from Title III's reasonable modification requirement. But that provision carves out no exemption for elite athletics, and given Title III's coverage not only of places of "exhibition or entertainment" but also of "golf course[s]," its application to petitioner's tournaments cannot be said to be unintended or unexpected. Even if it were, "the fact that a statute can be applied in situations not expressly anticipated by Congress does not demonstrate ambiguity. It demonstrates breadth."

Under the ADA's basic requirement that the need of a disabled person be evaluated on an individual basis, we have no doubt that allowing Martin to use a golf cart would not fundamentally alter the nature of petitioner's tournaments. As we have discussed, the purpose of the walking rule is to subject players to fatigue, which in turn may influence the outcome of tournaments. Even if the rule does serve that purpose, it is an uncontested finding of the District Court that Martin "easily endures greater fatigue even with a cart than his able-bodied competitors do by walking." The purpose of the walking rule is therefore not compromised in the slightest by allowing Martin to use a cart. A modification that provides an exception to a peripheral tournament rule without impairing its purpose cannot be said to "fundamentally alter" the tournament. What it can be said to do, on the other hand, is to allow Martin the chance to qualify for and compete in the athletic events petitioner offers to those members of the public who have the skill and desire to enter. That is exactly what the ADA requires. As a result, Martin's request for a waiver of the walking rule should have been granted....

The judgment of the Court of Appeals is affirmed.

JUSTICE SCALIA, with whom JUSTICE THOMAS joins, dissenting.

In my view today's opinion exercises a benevolent compassion that the law does not place it within our power to impose. The judgment distorts the text of Title III, the structure of the ADA, and common sense. I respectfully dissent.

***

Nowhere is it written that PGA TOUR golf must be classic "essential" golf. Why cannot the PGA TOUR, if it wishes, promote a new game, with distinctive rules (much as the American League promotes a game of baseball in which the pitcher's turn at the plate can be taken by a "designated hitter")? If members of the public do not like the new rules—if they feel that these rules do not truly test the individual's skill at "real golf" (or the team's skill at "real baseball") they can withdraw their patronage. But the rules are the rules. They are (as in all games) entirely arbitrary, and there is no basis on which anyone—not even the Supreme Court of the United States—can pronounce one or another of them to be "nonessential" if the rulemaker (here the PGA TOUR) deems it to be essential.

***

To say that something is "essential" is ordinarily to say that it is necessary to the achievement of a certain object. But since it is the very nature of a game to have no object except amusement (that is what distinguishes games from productive activity), it is quite impossible to say that any of a game's arbitrary rules is "essential." The only support for any of them is tradition and (in more modern times) insistence by what has come to be regarded as the ruling body of the sport—both of which factors support the PGA TOUR's position in the present case. (Many, indeed, consider walking to be *the central feature* of the game of golf—hence Mark Twain's classic criticism of the sport: "a good walk spoiled.") I suppose there is some point at which the rules of a well-known game are changed to such a degree that no reasonable person would call it the same game. But this criterion—destroying recognizability as the same generic game—is surely not the test of "essentialness" or "fundamentalness" that the Court applies, since it apparently thinks that merely changing the diameter of the *cup* might "fundamentally alter" the game of golf.

Because step one of the Court's two-part inquiry into whether a requested change in a sport will "fundamentally alter [its] nature," consists of an utterly unprincipled ontology of sports (pursuant to which the Court is not even sure whether golf's "essence" requires a 3-inch hole), there is every reason to think that in future cases involving requests for special treatment by would-be athletes the second step of the analysis will be determinative. In resolving that second step—determining whether waiver of the "nonessential" rule will have an impermissible "competitive effect"—by measuring the athletic capacity of the requesting individual, and asking whether the special dispensation would do no more than place him on a par (so to speak) with other competitors, the Court guarantees that future cases of this sort will have to be decided on the basis of individualized factual findings. Which means that future cases of this sort will be numerous, and a rich source of lucrative litigation.

The statute, of course, provides no basis for this individualized analysis that is the Court's last step on a long and misguided journey. The statute seeks to assure that a disabled person's disability will not deny him *equal access* to (among other things) competitive sporting events—not that his disability will not deny him an *equal chance to win* competitive sporting events. The latter is quite impossible, since the very *nature* of competitive sport is the measurement, by uniform rules, of unevenly distributed excellence. This unequal distribution is precisely what determines the winners and losers—and artificially to "even out" that distribution, by giving one or another player exemption from a rule that emphasizes his particular weakness, is to destroy the game....

Notes and Comments

1. **PGA subject to the ADA.** The Supreme Court determined that the PGA was a "public accommodation" subject to the ADA, rejecting the PGA's argument that the law protected only "customers or clients" of a public accommodation and not Martin, who was a competitor or provider of entertainment services. The Court reasoned that, even if Title III's protected class were limited to clients and customers, "it would be entirely appropriate to classify the golfers who pay petitioner $3,000 for the chance to compete in the Q-School and if successful, in the subsequent Tour events as petitioner's clients and customers." Would Martin be protected under Title III of the ADA if the PGA eliminated the registration fee and instead treated all competitors as independent contractors? (Note that Title I of the ADA protects employees, which can include professional athletes employed by sporting organizations, but does not extend to cover independent contractors.) If this were a lawsuit alleging racial discrimination, would the PGA argue it was not a public accommodation subject to the Civil Rights laws?

2. According to *Martin*, "the court has the independent duty to inquire into the purpose of the rule at issue, and to ascertain whether there can be a reasonable modification made to accommodate the plaintiff without frustrating the purpose of the rule." The PGA argued that the no-cart rule was necessary to competition fairness and a level playing field, the purpose of the walking rule is to inject the element of fatigue into the skill of shot-making, and a change in the rule would fundamentally alter the competition. Did the court properly consider the PGA's explanation of the purpose of the rule? Upon what factors did the court rely in holding that the purpose of the rule would not be frustrated by permitting Casey Martin to ride?

3. **Discrimination and rules of the game.** The PGA argued that the law should distinguish between rules defining who is eligible to compete from rules governing how the game is played, with any modification to the latter "substantive" rules a *per se* fundamental alteration. Justice Scalia, joined by Justice Thomas, argued in dissent that sport is different from other enterprises that are subject to the ADA and that no court, "not even the Supreme Court of the United States," can pronounce one or another of the competitive rules of sport nonessential if the rulemaker deems them otherwise. As posed by Justice Scalia, "why must the PGA play traditional golf?" How does a sporting entity or a court determine whether the rule or policy that a disabled athlete seeks to modify would alter a fundamental aspect of the competition? What is discrimination on the basis of disability when it comes to sports and athletic competition?

4. **Who should decide?** Does the accommodation of allowing a disabled golfer to use a cart during tournaments fundamentally change the rules of golf? Should this be the Court's decision, or the PGA's?

5. **Accommodation or competitive advantage?** The *Martin* case received national media attention, and the public, as well as professional golfers, honed in on the debate: Was Martin getting an unfair advantage? Is walking integral to the game? What is a level playing field? Where do we draw the line? *See* W. Kent Davis, *Why Is the PGA Teed Off at Casey Martin? An Example of How the Americans with Disabilities Act (ADA) Has Changed Sports Law*, 9 MARQ. SPORTS L.J. 1, 33–42 (1998) (citing the varied comments of professional golfers responding to the Casey Martin accommodation issue). How do you respond to the scenario posed by the dissent where a Little League player with attention deficit disorder, whose disability "makes it at least 25% more difficult to hit a pitched ball," should receive the accommodation of four strikes (absent "a judicial determination that, in baseball, three strikes are metaphysically necessary")?

6. **Prosthetic running device an advantage?** The International Association of Athletics Federation (IAAF) had ruled that the South African double-amputee sprinter Oscar Pistorius was ineligible to compete in the Summer Olympics in Beijing because of his use of "Cheetah" prosthetics. The IAAF determined that the prosthetics gave Oscar "a demonstrable mechanical and competitive advantage compared with someone not using the blade." Pistorius appealed this decision to the Court of Arbitration for Sport (CAS) (*see* Chapter 13). CAS decided the challenge to the IAAF ruling based on fundamental human rights law against disability discrimination. If scientific advances in prosthetics enable an overall advantage, how can athletes such as Pistorius compete?

NCAA Track and Field Rules prohibit the use of any technical device that incorporates springs, wheels or any other element that provides the user with an advantage over another athlete who is not using such a device. In approving Harvard University's request to allow an incoming male sprinter to compete with a prosthetic running device, the 2015 NCAA Rules Committee considered scientific research presented by Integrative Physiology Professor Alena Grabowski which found that athletes with prosthetics are not able to push on the ground with as much force and thus do not have an advantage over abled-body track and field athletes.

7. Athletic competition is inherently discriminatory—there are winners and losers, only the best play. The PGA argued that its rules of competitive play provide the framework for a level playing field for all competitors, but when the rules for one player are changed in a competitive sport, the landscape of the competition is inherently changed. Do the *Martin or Pistorius* decisions open the door for judicial intrusion on athletic competition? Was the ADA really intended to apply to professional sporting competitions? Was the playing field under the PGA rules "even" for Casey Martin?

The central issue, according to *Martin*, was "whether allowing the plaintiff, given his individual circumstances, the requested modification of using a cart in tournament competition would fundamentally alter PGA and Nike Tour golf competitions." The court in *Ganden* similarly noted, "the ADA does not require [the sporting organization] to simply abandon its eligibility requirements, but only to make reasonable modifications to them." A modification is unreasonable "if it imposes an 'undue financial and administrative burden' or requires a 'fundamental alteration' in the nature of the privilege or program." *See also Montalvo* (holding karate school was not required to change its group lessons to a softer, less rigorous style for child with AIDS and stating that private lessons are a reasonable accommodation). Disputes arise, however, in defining when a requested accommodation would be unreasonable, require elimination of an essential eligibility requirement, or fundamentally alter the nature of the sport or competition. Are the courts the best arbiters of these determinations?

8. *Martin* illustrates that sporting organizations should be prepared to explain the purpose of its eligibility requirements and rules of competition, to articulate the connection between the requirements and purpose, and to evaluate on an individual basis whether modification of such rules can be made without undermining legitimate purposes or fundamentally altering the nature of the game. Yet, based on *Martin*, the Court summarily vacated the ruling of the Seventh Circuit Court of Appeals, which denied the request by Ford Olinger, a professional golfer with a degenerative hip disorder, injunctive relief to ride a cart in the U.S. Open. *Olinger v. U.S. Golf Ass'n*, 205 F.3d 1001 (7th Cir. 2000) (ruling that "the nature of the competition would be fundamentally altered" if the walking rule were eliminated because it would "remove stamina (at least, a particular type of stamina) from the set of qualities designed to be tested in this competition."). The court also agreed that the administrative burdens of evaluating requests to waive the walking rule were undue, in that, the USGA "would need to develop a system and a fund of expertise to determine whether a given applicant truly needs, or merely wants, or could use but does not need, to ride a cart to compete." 205 F.3d 1001 (stating

"the decision on whether the rules of the game should be adjusted to accommodate him is best left to those who hold the future of golf in trust"). Should *Olinger* have come out the same as *Martin*? How should future requests to waive the walking rule, or any other rule of competition, be evaluated? The *Martin* ruling has not created a significant change in rules of sport as was anticipated by some. For example, the requested modification for a wheelchair user to be permitted two bounces in racquetball competition with footed players was denied as a fundamental alteration of the nature of the sporting competition in *Kuketz v. Petronelli*, 821 N.E.2d 473 (Mass. 2005). In 2019, the PGA granted a waiver of the cart rule for the PGA Championships to 53-year-old John Daly, due to his diabetic and osteoarthritic knee condition. Weeks later, the Royal and Ancient Golf Club rejected Daly's request to use a cart ("buggy") in the British Open. Different countries, different rules? The United Nations on the Convention of Rights for People with Disabilities (CRPD) provides for rights to people with disabilities to participate in sport, similar to the ADA anti-discrimination and reasonable accommodation mandates. With England as a signatory to the CRPD, would Daly have a right similar to Martin to a cart? *See* Maureen Weston, *The International Right to Sport for People with Disabilities*, 28 Marq. Sports L.J. 1 (2017).

9. **Valid medical basis for exclusion.** The ADA, like the Rehabilitation Act, requires a valid medical basis that the individual poses a direct threat to the health and safety of other participants in order to exclude the individual from competition on those grounds. *See Anderson v. Little League Baseball*, 794 F. Supp. 342 (D. Ariz. 1992) (holding league rule prohibiting on-field base coach in wheelchair from the playing field was invalid under the ADA absent an individualized determination of direct threat). *Cf. Maddox v. University of Tennessee*, 62 F.3d 843 (6th Cir. 1995) (upholding university's termination of assistant football coach for misconduct [public drunkenness] despite coach's argument the conduct was caused by an alcoholism disability protected under the ADA).

10. **Professional athletes' claims under the ADA.** Professional athletes may assert Title I claims as "employees" of their respective teams. However, exclusion from play alone may not be sufficient to state a Title I claim. A professional athlete must be disabled, defined as having (or regarded as having) a physical or mental impairment that substantially limits a major life activity. 42 U.S.C. § 12112. Guidelines promulgated by the Equal Employment Opportunity Commission (EEOC) under Title I provide that a person is not substantially limited in working simply because the person is "unable to perform a specialized job or profession requiring extraordinary skill, prowess, or talent," such as a baseball pitcher with a bad elbow who cannot throw. 29 C.F.R. § 1630.2(j)(3)(i). *See also Knapp, above.* As a result, professional athletes must show their disability substantially limits a major life activity other than working as a professional athlete, such as walking in Casey Martin's case.

A professional athlete's Title I claim against a professional sports league or association is less tenable. Without explanation, the *Martin* court agreed that the PGA was not subject to the employment provisions of Title I of the ADA as Martin's "employer." One commentator has suggested an employment relationship did not exist between Martin and the PGA, which did not exercise control over Martin in terms of requiring him to play particular tournaments, controlling the player's schedule, or providing him with wages or insurance or withholding taxes. *See* Davis, 9 MARQ. SPORTS L.J., at 38. The Davis article proposes that the analysis for determining whether a sports association is an employer under the ADA is a two-part test: (1) is the defendant a covered employer under the ADA (more than 15 employees); and (2) does an employment relationship exist between the plaintiff and defendant? 9 MARQ. SPORTS L.J., at 38 (by analogy to Title VII, citing *Graves v. Women's Professional Rodeo Association, Inc.*, 708 F. Supp. 233 (W.D. Ark. 1989) (holding rodeo association to whom members pay dues and which promulgates competition rules is not an "employer" to its members), *aff'd*, 907 F.2d 71 (8th Cir. 1990)). A professional athlete's employment claim against a sports association would likely fail absent a showing of an employment relationship.

E. Physical Access to Stadiums, Facilities, and Sports Arenas

Under Title III of the ADA, places of public accommodation, including sports facilities, stadiums, and arenas, must be physically accessible and usable by people with disabilities in the most integrated setting possible. 42 U.S.C. § 12181(a)(b)(1). The Department of Justice guidelines set forth standards applicable to sports facilities requiring the removal of architectural barriers to access and the provision of wheelchair accessible parking, entrances, seating, restrooms, public telephones, drinking fountains, signs, and assistive listening devices. ADA Accessibility Guidelines (ADAAG), 28 C.F.R. pt. 36, app. A (1996). Under these guidelines, stadiums constructed after 1993 are also required to provide at least one percent of total seating for wheelchair users and one accompanying companion seat. The regulation that has generated the most litigation is Section 4.33.3, which provides that: "Wheelchair areas shall be an integral part of any fixed seating plan and shall be provided so as to provide people with physical disabilities a choice of admission prices and lines of sight comparable to those for members of the general public."

A number of lawsuits have been filed by or on behalf of spectators with disabilities against stadium owners, operators, and architects to require that newly constructed stadiums provide unobstructed lines of sight for wheelchair seating locations when spectators stand or do the "wave." Stadium access litigation has also raised issues of whether seating is sufficiently integrated and dispersed. For a detailed discussion, see Mark A. Conrad, *Wheeling Through Rough Terrain—The Legal Roadblocks of Disabled Access in Sports Arenas*, 8 MARQ. SPORTS L.J. 263 (1998) (discussing stadium sightline access litigation); Adam A. Milani, *Oh Say*

Can I See—And Who Do I Sue If I Can't?: Wheelchair Users, Sightlines over Standing Spectators, and Architect Liability Under the Americans with Disabilities Act, 3 Fla. L. Rev. 523 (2000). *See also* Grady & Ohlin, *The Application of Title III of the ADA to Sport Web Sites*, 14 J. Legal Aspects of Sports 145 (2004) (asserting that sports organizations need to make websites accessible to individuals with disabilities so that they too may experience the full and equal enjoyment of the sport industry's vast offering of goods and services).

Capstone Problem

Billy Taylor is a nine-year-old boy. Through his mother, Joan Taylor, Billy Taylor has filed a motion for injunctive relief against the defendant, the Green County Soccer Association (hereinafter, the GCSA), seeking an order which would declare Billy immediately eligible to participate in a youth soccer league administered by GCSA. League play begins next week.

Billy Taylor is a nine-year-old boy who has cerebral palsy. He utilizes a "walker" to assist him in walking. He cannot walk without it. The metal walker is two feet high. The walker is heavily padded with foam and red duct tape. It has four plastic wheels. It weighs eight pounds, eight ounces. Billy enjoys playing soccer and has done so in elementary school gym class, where he is permitted to "kick" the ball with his walker. Thus far, no one has been injured by the use of the walker.

Billy Taylor was adopted by Joan Taylor when he was an infant. She was told that Billy had cerebral palsy prior to adopting him. Billy has suffered many medical hardships throughout his short life, and is, by all accounts, a "fighter." He is very determined to participate in normal youth activities. He is bright and articulate.

Joan Taylor believes it is essential to Billy's development that he be provided with as many opportunities as possible to "live a normal life." She has expressed a willingness to sign a waiver which would absolve GCSA of any liability for injuries to Billy in connection with his participation in the soccer league. She has also offered to pay the $50 requisite fee for Billy to play in the GCSA-sponsored league.

Billy's pediatrician believes that Billy's participation in youth soccer poses "no additional, substantial risks to either Billy or his co-participants." His opinion is that "it is very unlikely that there could be an injury from the walker."

David Walton is President of the Green County Soccer Association. GCSA organizes and supervises youth soccer leagues in Tulsa. Games and practices are regularly scheduled at public parks and public schools. Walton is a volunteer. GCSA has no paid staff. Walton testified as the spokesman for GCSA.

Walton said that GCSA is concerned with its legal liability if Billy Taylor gets hurt or if another player gets hurt because of the walker. An orthopedist testified on behalf of GCSA that the use of walker "substantially increased the level of risk of physical harm for all the participants, including Billy."

GCSA safety rules prohibit casts, helmets and "other metal objects that pose risks of harm." Walton believes that Billy's walker is such a metal object. GCSA also contends that the rules of soccer prohibit the use of a walker to "kick" the ball. Walton said that Billy was barred from participation not because of his handicap but because of his walker.

The motion for injunctive relief is based upon the Americans with Disabilities Act (hereinafter A.D.A.). Discuss whether Taylor is substantially likely to prevail on the merits of his ADA claim.

Thirteen

Olympic and International Sports Rules and Procedures

Learning Outcomes

- Be familiar with the governance structure and regulatory framework for sports in the international context.
- Learn about the predominant players, legal issues, and dispute resolution processes in Olympic and international sports.
- Learn about the Olympic Movement's international governance structure.
- Understand the regulatory scheme and role of judicial review for Olympic sports in the United States.
- Learn about arbitration as the nearly exclusive means for resolving international sport disputes.
- Examine Olympic-related intellectual property and commercialism issues.
- Consider the relationship among the various governing entities, the jurisdiction of a particular court or entity to adjudicate a dispute or to review a decision, and the procedure for seeking redress of an adverse eligibility ruling.

Key Terms

- International Olympic Committee (IOC)
- Olympic Charter
- International federation (IF)
- National governing body (NGB)
- National olympic committee (NOC)
- United States Olympic & Paralympic Committee (USOPC)
- Organizing committee for the Olympic Games (OCOG)
- Ted Stevens Olympic and Amateur Sports Act
- Court of Arbitration for Sport (CAS)
- World Anti-Doping Agency (WADA)
- U.S. Anti-Doping Agency (USADA)

A. Introduction

The study of sports law in this casebook primarily focuses on the application of state and federal law to individuals and sports organizations within the United States. Sport, however, truly is a worldwide phenomenon. Many elite American athletes compete on an international level in major individual, team, and multi-sport competitions such as the Federation Internationale de Football Association (FIFA) World Cup, the four-continent tournaments of Grand Slam in tennis, cycling's Tour de France, golf's British Open, and, of course, the Olympic Games. U.S. sports leagues also include international teams, such as Canadian teams that play within the National Hockey League, National Basketball Association, and Major League Baseball. U.S. leagues seek to expand operations internationally but may encounter challenges in exporting uniquely American sports. Although the NFL disbanded its European league in 2007, reportedly after losing $30 million a season, each year it hosts a series of NFL games during the NFL regular season in London, Mexico and Germany (the NFL International Series). MLB continues to focus on the expansion of its brand through exhibition series, such as the World Baseball Classic, as well as other events, broadcasting, licensing, and sponsorship initiatives. MLB also operates professional baseball training and development centers for youth in other countries. The growth in international sports is accompanied by lucrative financial opportunities for athlete endorsements, corporate sponsorships, merchandising, and broadcasting contracts.

From a legal standpoint, determining the rights and obligations of athletes, other personnel (coaches, managers, trainers, officials and sponsors), and governing bodies in international sports can become extremely complicated. An athlete who has intensely trained his or her entire life aspiring to compete in the Olympics or world-class competitions may be excluded, stripped of a gold medal, even banned for life from competition based on the decision of a non-governmental national or international sporting organization. For example, in *Gatlin v. U.S. Anti-Doping Agency, Inc.*, Olympic sprinter Justin Gatlin argued that he had been discriminated against under the Americans with Disabilities Act when a positive doping test, due to a taking a prescribed medication to treat attention deficit disorder, was counted as a prior offense by the Court of Arbitration for Sport (CAS). Although agreeing that the four-year ban issued against Gatlin was erroneously based, the U.S. federal district court regretfully stated that in the case before it "the United States Courts have no power to right the wrong perpetuated upon one of its citizens." 2008 U.S. Dist. LEXIS 112850 (N.D. Fla. June 24, 2008).

Controversy is not new to the Olympics and the international sports scene. Highly publicized issues involving athlete eligibility, selection, doping scandals, on- and off-field misconduct, discrimination, gambling, violence, binary gender verification and testing, field-of-play decisions, corruption within certain governing sporting bodies or host cities, and the expanding commercialization and influence of TV and corporate sponsors often mar or detract from the celebration of athletic contests. A major issue involving the eligibility of athletes to compete in the Olympics and in most international sports competitions concerns drug testing and the use of performance-enhancing drugs (doping). Disgrace befell American sprinter Marion Jones and cyclist Floyd Landis, both of whom had their respective titles to Olympic Gold medals and the Tour de France revoked due to doping violations. Although he never tested positive for doping, Lance Armstrong was stripped of his seven Tour de France titles won between 1999 and 2005 and received a lifetime ban from cycling after a 13-year investigation led by the U.S. Anti-Doping Agency (USADA) charged and named him as the ringleader of "the most sophisticated, professionalized, and successful doping program that sport has ever seen." Armstrong refused to participate in arbitration, yet sought, unsuccessfully, to use the Texas courts to fight USADA. On the eve of the 2016 Olympic Games in Rio, evidence that Russia had corrupted the 2012 and 2014 Olympic and Paralympic Games by state-sponsored doping of more than 1,000 of its athletes presented the question of whether to ban the entire Russian delegation. Are tests for "gender verification" discriminatory or necessary to fair competition? *Who decides?* Determining these and other recurring eligibility and disciplinary controversies can involve jurisdictional conflicts among national and international governing sporting entities and court systems.

The organizational structure of the Olympics and international competitions is complex, with the regulating sporting bodies operating at various national and international levels. As seen from the following cases involving several Olympic athletes, these sporting bodies may issue conflicting decisions regarding an athlete's eligibility. Should final authority over international sport decisions involving U.S. athletes be decided in U.S. courts, domestic or international arbitration, or by the Swiss Federal Tribunal? Consider the benefits and costs of a trend to centralize the decision-making process into one largely privatized system with ultimate authority in Switzerland.

The sport management professional must be familiar with the governance structure and regulatory framework for sports in the international context. This chapter introduces the predominant players, legal issues, and dispute resolution processes in Olympic and international sports. Part B provides an overview of the Olympic Movement's international governance structure. Part C presents the regulatory scheme and role of judicial review for Olympic sports in the United States, while Part D focuses on arbitration as the nearly exclusive means for resolving international sport disputes. Part E examines Olympic-related intellectual property and commercialism issues. In your analysis of an issue involving Olympic and international sports, consider the relationship among the various governing entities, the jurisdiction of a particular court or entity to adjudicate a dispute or to review a decision, and the procedure for seeking redress of an adverse eligibility ruling.

B. The Olympic Sport Governance Structure

The most prominent and long-standing international sporting competition is the Olympics. The Olympic Games have occurred since ancient times, originally held in Olympia, Greece, from 776 B.C. until 393 A.D., and revived in 1896. Athletes from around the world participate in the Summer or Winter Olympic Games held every four years (the Olympiad) at a different host city. While some might assert that the Olympics has become an intensely competitive and commercial event, the stated purpose of the Games is to promote international understanding, diplomacy, and peace. The Olympic Charter serves as the constitution governing the Olympic Movement and codifies its fundamental principles, rules, and bylaws. The goal of Olympism is "to place sport at the service of the harmonious development of humankind, with a view to promoting a peaceful society concerned with the preservation of human dignity." THE OLYMPIC CHARTER, Fundamental Principles 2 (2021). Another fundamental principle is that "[t]he enjoyment of the rights and freedoms set forth in this Olympic Charter shall be secured without discrimination of any kind, such as race, colour, sex, sexual orientation, language, religion, political or other opinion, national or social origin, property, birth or other status." *Id.* ¶ 6. The Charter also states that "[t]he practice of sport is a human right. Every individual must have the possibility of practising sport, without discrimination of any kind and in the Olympic spirit, which requires mutual understanding with a spirit of friendship, solidarity and fair play." *Id.* ¶ 4. Consider whether and how the foregoing aims are present in modern-day international sport.

International Sport Governance

The organizational and regulatory structure for Olympic and international sports competition is based upon the Olympic Movement set out in the Olympic Charter. The Olympic Movement consists of several governing bodies operating in an international and domestic organizational structure. At the pinnacle of this structure is the International Olympic Committee (IOC), the "supreme authority" and leader for the Olympic Movement. The IOC is formed under Swiss law as a nonprofit, nongovernmental organization, operating in Lausanne, Switzerland. The IOC owns all the rights in and to the Olympics, including valuable intellectual property, including the Olympic flag (five interlaced rings), motto ("Citius–Altius–Fortius"), symbols, anthem, flame, torches, broadcasting rights, and other designations. The IOC recognizes two governing bodies that play a prominent role in the Olympic Movement. International Sports Federations (IFs) administer Olympic programs for a particular sport, conduct international competitions, and define eligibility and technical rules for international competition. The IOC currently recognizes 35 international sport federations. For each participating country, the IOC also recognizes a National Olympic Committee (NOC) as the "exclusive authority for the representation of their respective countries at the Olympic Games and at the regional, continental or world multi-sports competitions patronised by the IOC." *Id.* at 4(3). These NOCs in turn recognize separate national governing bodies (NGBs) within their countries responsible for each Olympic sport and the selection of athletes. NGBs are also members of their respective sport's international federation. In addition to the IOC, the IFs and the NOCs, the Olympic Movement also includes the Organizing Committees of the Olympic Games (OCOGs), the national associations, clubs and persons belonging to the IFs and NOCs, particularly the athletes, as well as judges, referees, coaches, and other organizations recognized by the IOC. The Olympic Charter requires members of the Olympic Movement to comply with the World Anti-Doping Program, which is actively administered and enforced by World Anti-Doping Agency (WADA), and at a national level through a national anti-doping agency. In the United States, the U.S. Anti-Doping Agency administers the WADP for U.S. athletes.

Finally, the Charter requires that "[a]ny dispute arising on the occasion of, or in connection with, the Olympic Games shall be submitted exclusively to the Court of Arbitration for Sport, in accordance with the Code of Sports-Related Arbitration." ¶ 61. Accordingly, both the Court of Arbitration for Sport (CAS) and WADA have integral roles in the overall operation of international sport. *See* Maureen A. Weston, *Doping Control, Mandatory Arbitration, and Process Dangers for Accused Athletes in International Sports,* 10 Pepp. Disp. Res. L.J. 5 (2009).

U.S. Olympic Sport Governance

In the United States, the Ted Stevens Olympic and Amateur Sports Act of 1998 (Amateur Sports Act or ASA) designates the United States Olympic & Paralympic Committee (USOPC), as the exclusive governing body for U.S. participation in the Olympic, Pan-American, and Paralympic Games. The ASA authorizes the USOPC to recognize a single organization to act as the national governing body (NGB) for each sport included in the Olympic program. 36 U.S.C. § 220505. The NGBs in turn represent the United States in international federations, coordinate athletic competition, and recommend individuals and teams to the USOPC to represent the United States in international competitions. The ASA also grants the USOPC exclusive rights to related intellectual property. *Id.* § 220506. These revenues enable the USOPC to fund NGBs, athlete training and support, and overall budget.

The USOPC is required to "[e]stablish and maintain provisions in its constitution and bylaws for the swift and equitable resolution of disputes involving any of its members and relating to the opportunity of an amateur athlete, coach, trainer, manager, administrator, or official to participate in the Olympic Games... or other protected competition." *Id.* § 220509. The ASA requires the USOPC to hire an ombudsman to provide independent advice to athletes, at no cost, about applicable laws and procedures. *Id.* § 220509. The USOPC has its own Constitution and Bylaws. Section 9 of the Bylaws allow an athlete to challenge a decision involving an opportunity to participate by filing a complaint with the USOPC, with the right to a hearing and final decision before the American Arbitration Association (AAA). USOPC

Bylaws, Sec. 9. Complaints against the USOPC involving NGB determinations are subject to final arbitral review. *36 U.S.C.* § 220529. Doping cases are subject to *de novo* review before CAS.

In response to the horrific reports of sexual misconduct and abuse of athletes, Congress amended the ASA in 2018 to establish the U.S. Center for Safe Sport, charged with establishing policies and procedures (including binding arbitration) regarding the prevention, education, and resolution of allegations of emotional, physical, and sexual abuse of athletes. 36 U.S.C. § 22051 *et seq., available at* http://www.teamusa.org.

Interlocking National and International Laws and Procedures

While Congress may have envisioned a streamlined procedure for dispute resolution, Olympic athletes and the USOPC must operate in a larger international arena. It is within this larger context of overlapping jurisdictions that the potential for conflict between athletes and governing bodies reaches its peak. For example, an IF, which autonomously supervises a particular sport at the international level (subject only to the limitations in the Olympic Charter), may have different rules, procedures, or sanctions that vary or operate independently from the domestic process. Under the Olympic Charter, legal recourse is exclusively before CAS, an international arbitration tribunal based in Switzerland and operating under Swiss law. To an athlete with eligibility concerns, seeking recourse within the Olympic Movement may appear to be a bad game of Abbott and Costello's "Who's on First?" *(Look it up.)*

As you read the following material, consider:

- What legal recourse is available to an aggrieved athlete to challenge an eligibility, disciplinary, or doping decision involving international sport competition?
- Do U.S. laws protect American athletes participating in (or unlawfully excluded from) the Olympics or international competitions?
- Does a U.S. court have jurisdiction to hear an athlete's claim against an international sport body? Is a U.S. judgment binding on an international sport federation?
- Where may (or must) an athlete bring a complaint involving an international sport decision?
- What is the organizational structure of the U.S. and international sport governing bodies? Who are the decision-makers? Who has final authority?
- Does any court, in the U.S. or foreign, have a right to invalidate rules or a decision promulgated by an international arbitral tribunal?

C. U.S. Adjudication of Olympic-Related Disputes

Defrantz v. United States Olympic Committee

492 F. Supp. 1181 (D.D.C. 1980)

JOHN H. PRATT, DISTRICT JUDGE.

Plaintiffs, 25 athletes and one member of the Executive Board of defendant United States Olympic Committee (USOC), have moved for an injunction barring defendant USOC from carrying out a resolution, adopted by the USOC House of Delegates on April 12, 1980, not to send an American team to participate in the Games of the XXIInd Olympiad to be held in Moscow in the summer of 1980. Plaintiffs allege that in preventing American athletes from competing in the Summer Olympics, defendant has exceeded its statutory powers and has abridged plaintiffs' constitutional rights.

The Facts

In essence, the action before us involves a dispute between athletes who wish to compete in the Olympic Games to be held in Moscow this summer, and the United States Olympic Committee, which has denied them that opportunity in the wake of the invasion and continued occupation of Afghanistan by Soviet military forces.

The USOC is a corporation created and granted a federal charter by Congress in 1950.... This charter was revised by the Amateur Sports Act of 1978... Under this statute, defendant USOC has "exclusive jurisdiction" and authority over participation and representation of the United States in the Olympic Games.

On December 27, 1979, the Soviet Union launched an invasion of its neighbor, Afghanistan. That country's ruler was deposed and killed and a new government was installed. Fighting has been at times intense, casualties have been high, and hundreds of thousands of Afghan citizens have fled their homeland. At present, an estimated 100,000 Soviet troops remain in Afghanistan, and fighting continues.

President Carter termed the invasion a threat to the security of the Persian Gulf area as well as a threat to world peace and stability and he moved to take direct sanctions against the Soviet Union. These sanctions included a curtailment of agricultural and high technology exports to the Soviet Union, and restrictions on commerce with the Soviets. The Administration also turned its attention to a boycott of the summer Olympic Games as a further sanction against the Soviet Union.

As the affidavit of then Acting Secretary of State Warren Christopher makes clear, the Administration was concerned that "[t]he presence of American competitors would be taken by the Soviets as evidence that their invasion had faded from memory or was not a matter of great consequence or concern to this nation."... The Administration's concern was sharpened because "[t]he Soviet Union has made clear that it intends the Games to serve important national political ends. For the U.S.S.R., international sports competition is an instrument of government policy and a means to advance foreign policy goals."

With the concerns in mind, the Administration strenuously urged a boycott of the Moscow games. On January 20, 1980, President Carter wrote the President of the United States Olympic Committee to urge that the USOC propose to the IOC that the 1980 summer games be transferred from Moscow, postponed, or cancelled if the Soviet forces were not withdrawn within a month. On January 23, 1980, the President delivered his State of the Union Message, in which he said that he would not support sending American athletes to Moscow while Soviet military forces remained in Afghanistan.

Following these statements, the United States House of Representatives passed, by a vote of 386 to 12, a Concurrent Resolution opposing participation by United States athletes in the Moscow Games unless Soviet troops were withdrawn from Afghanistan by February 20th. The Senate passed a similar resolution by a vote of 88 to 4.

As this was unfolding, the USOC's 86 member Executive Board held a meeting in Colorado Springs on January 26, 1980, inviting White House counsel Lloyd Cutler to address them "because no officer or any member of the Board was knowledgeable about the far-reaching implications of the Soviet invasion." ... According to USOC President Kane, in early January some USOC officers became concerned that sending American athletes to Moscow could expose them to danger if hostility erupted at the games, and that acceptance of the invitation could be seen as tacit approval of or at least acceptance of the Soviet invasion.

On March 21, 1980, President Carter told members of the Athletes Advisory Council, an official body of the USOC, that American athletes will not participate in the Moscow summer games. On April 8, 1980, the President sent a telegram to the president and officers of the USOC and to its House of Delegates, urging the USOC to vote against sending an American team to Moscow. In an April 10th speech, the President said that "if legal actions are necessary to enforce [my] decision not to send a team to Moscow, then I will take those legal actions." ... On April 10 and 11, 1980, the 13 member Administrative Committee of the USOC met in Colorado Springs and voted to support a resolution against sending a team to Moscow. Only Anita DeFrantz, a plaintiff in this action, dissented.

Vice President Mondale addressed the assembled House of Delegates prior to their vote on April 12, 1980. The Vice President strongly and vigorously urged the House of Delegates to support a resolution rejecting American participation in the summer games in Moscow.

... [T]he House of Delegates, on a secret ballot, passed by a vote of 1,604 to 798, a resolution which provided in pertinent part:

> RESOLVED that since the President of the United States has advised the United States Olympic Committee that in light of international events the national security of the country is threatened, the USOC has decided not to send a team to the 1980 Summer Games in Moscow...
>
> FURTHER RESOLVED, that if the President of the United States advises the United States Olympic Committee, on or before May 20, 1980, that international events have become compatible with the national interest and the national security is no longer threatened, the USOC will enter its athletes in the 1980 Summer Games.

Plaintiffs describe these attempts by the Administration to persuade the USOC to vote not to send an American team to Moscow as "a campaign to coerce defendant USOC into compliance with the President's demand for a boycott of the Olympic Games." ... In addition, plaintiffs' complaint alleges that the President and other Executive Branch officials threatened to terminate federal funding of the USOC and that they raised the possibility of revoking the federal income tax exemption of the USOC if the USOC did not support the President's decision to boycott the 1980 Games. The complaint also alleges that these officials stated that the Federal government would provide increased funding to the USOC if the USOC supported a boycott.

Plaintiffs state three causes of action in their complaint. [A statutory claim and a claim that the USOC violated its own constitution were rejected by the court.]

Plaintiffs' second cause of action, a constitutional claim, alleges that defendant's action constituted "governmental action" which abridged plaintiffs' rights of liberty, self-expression, personal autonomy and privacy guaranteed by the First, Fifth and Ninth Amendments to the United States Constitution.

Defendant and the Government... argue that the decision of the USOC was not "state action" and therefore, that plaintiffs have no cognizable constitutional claims. They further argue that even if the action of the USOC could be considered "state action," no rights guaranteed to plaintiffs under the Constitution were abridged.

Analysis

2. Constitutional Claims

(a) State Action

Although federally chartered, defendant is a private organization. Because the Due Process Clause of the Fifth Amendment, on which plaintiffs place great reliance, applies only to actions by the federal government, plaintiffs must show that the USOC vote is a "governmental act," *i.e.*, state action. In defining state action, the courts have fashioned two guidelines. The first involves an inquiry into whether the state:

> ...has so far insinuated itself into a position of interdependence with [the private entity] that it must be recognized as a joint participant in the challenged activity.

Burton v. Wilmington Parking Authority, 365 U.S. 715, 725 (1961).

In *Burton*, the Supreme Court found state action, but it did so on wholly different facts than those existing here. The private entity charged with racially discriminating against plaintiff was a restaurant which was physically and financially an integral part of a public building, built and maintained with public funds, devoted to a public parking service, and owned and operated by an agency of the State of Delaware for public purposes. Noting the obvious and deep enmeshment of defendant and the state, the court found that the state was a joint participant in the operation of the restaurant, and accordingly found state action. Here, there is no such intermingling, and there is no factual justification for finding that the federal government and the USOC enjoyed the "symbiotic relationship" which courts have required to find state action. The USOC has received no federal funding and it exists and operates independently of the federal government. Its chartering statute gives it "exclusive jurisdiction" over "all matters pertaining to the participation of the United States in the Olympic Games...."... To be sure, the Act does link the USOC and the federal government to the extent it requires the USOC to submit an annual report to the President and the Congress. But this hardly converts such an independent relationship to a "joint participation."

The second guideline fashioned by the courts involves an inquiry of whether:

> ...there is a sufficiently close nexus between the state and the challenged action of the regulated entity so that the action of the latter may be fairly treated as that of the state itself.

Jackson v. Metropolitan Edison Co., 419 U.S. 345, 351 (1974).

In that case, the Supreme Court found there was no state action even though the defendant was a utility closely regulated by the state, and even though the action complained of (the procedure for termination of electrical services) had been approved by the state utility commission. In the instant case, there was no requirement that any federal government body approve actions by the USOC before they become effective.

Plaintiffs argue that by the actions of certain federal officials, the federal government initiated, encouraged, and approved of the result reached (*i.e.*, the vote of the USOC not to send an American team to the summer Olympics). Essentially, their argument is that the campaign of governmental persuasion, personally led by President Carter, crossed the line from "governmental recommendation," which plaintiffs find acceptable and presumably necessary to the operation of our form of government, into the area of "affirmative pressure that effectively places the government's prestige behind the challenged action," and thus, results in state action. We cannot agree.

... [T]his Circuit's Court of Appeals has addressed what level of governmental involvement is necessary to find state action in cases not involving discrimination.

> [A]t least where race is not involved, *it is necessary to show that the Government exercises some form of control over the actions of the private party.* (*Emphasis supplied.*)

Here there is no such control. The USOC is an independent body, and nothing in its chartering statute gives the federal government the right to control that body or its officers. The federal government may have had the power to prevent the athletes from participating in the Olympics even if the USOC had voted to allow them to participate, but it did not have the power to make them vote in a certain way. All it had was the power of persuasion. We cannot equate this with control. To do so in cases of this type would be to open the door and usher the courts into what we believe is a largely nonjusticiable realm, where they would find themselves in the untenable position of determining whether a certain level, intensity, or type of "Presidential" or "Administration" or "political" pressure amounts to sufficient control over a private entity so as to invoke federal jurisdiction.

We accordingly find that the decision of the USOC not to send an American team to the summer Olympics was not state action, and therefore, does not give rise to an actionable claim for the infringements of the constitutional rights alleged.

Gatlin v. U.S. Anti-Doping Agency

2008 U.S. Dist. LEXIS 112850 (N.D. Fla. 2008)

COLLIER, LACEY KAY, DISTRICT JUDGE.

[*Ed.* In 2001, Olympic sprinter Justin Gatlin tested positive for doping but this was reportedly due to medication used to treat his diagnosed attention-deficit disorder for which he had been granted a therapeutic use exception (TUE). Yet when Gatlin tested positive for doping in 2006, the Panel imposed a sanction penalty for a second violation. Gatlin sued in federal district court, claiming violation of the Americans with Disabilities Act. The district court considered whether it had jurisdiction to overturn the panel decision, as follows.]

[U]nder the Ted Stevens Olympic and Amateur Sports Act (Amateur Sports Act), Congress provided the United States Olympic Committee (USOC) with exclusive jurisdiction over all matters concerning this country's participation in the Olympic Games. *See* 36 U.S.C. § 220503(3). Thus, issues regarding whether an athlete is eligible to participate in the Olympic Games or any of its qualifying events are reserved solely for the USOC, and the courts have no jurisdiction to entertain a private right of action that might impinge upon an eligibility determination. *See Slaney v. Int'l Am. Athletic Federation*, 244 F.3d 580 (7th Cir. 2001). Because Plaintiff's motion seeks preliminary relief which is directly aimed at lifting his current suspension in order to allow him to participate in the upcoming Olympic trials, the Court is preempted from taking jurisdiction over the matter.

Plaintiff's course of administrative remedies resulted in arbitration before the internationally based Court for Arbitration for Sport (CAS), which might arguably take this case beyond the reach of the Amateur Sports Act, but it does not change the result. Pursuant to the United Nations Convention on the Recognition and Enforcement of Foreign Arbitral Awards, ("New York Convention"), claims that have been properly submitted to arbitration and ruled upon by entities such as CAS are barred from relitigation in this forum.

It is beyond dispute that Plaintiff properly challenged his suspension on grounds that Defendants' actions violated his rights under the Americans with Disabilities Act. As these matters have been decided, Plaintiff is precluded from raising them here unless he can show that the CAS decision falls within one of the identified exceptions. While Plaintiff makes no attempt in this regard, the Court notes that the only conceivable exception is where enforcement of the award would be contrary to public policy. This, however, is a very slender exception reserved for decisions which violate the "most basic notions of morality and justice...." *Slaney*, 244 F.3d at 593. Although... the Court takes exception to the decisions made by Defendants and the panels sitting in arbitration over this matter, and indeed finds their actions to be arbitrary and capricious, the Court does not find these wrongs to rise to the level of moral repugnance as is required under the law for the Court to consider piercing the veil of the jurisdictional issue. It appears, as Defendants indicate, that Plaintiff's remaining avenue for relief lies with the Swiss Supreme Court, which may in its discretion elect to review the case.

Nonetheless, the result of this determination is quite troubling because Mr. Gatlin is being wronged, and the United States Courts have no power to right the wrong perpetrated upon one of its citizens. As the United States Anti-Doping Agency (USADA), stipulated before the American Arbitration Association Panel (AAA) during its hearing on the 2001 test result that forms the basis of Plaintiff's motion:

> Mr. Gatlin neither cheated nor intended to cheat. He did not intend to enhance his performance nor, given his medical condition, did his medication in fact enhance his performance.... This Panel would characterize Mr. Gatlin's inadvertent violation of the IAAF's rules based on uncontested facts as, at most, a "technical" or a "paperwork" violation."

In 2006, the AAA Panel again reviewed the circumstances of the 2001 positive test and found:

> Turning to the 2001 doping violation by Mr. Gatlin, there appears to be no question that he had a legal right to take the prescription medication that caused his first violation, he was appropriately taking that prescription medicine to treat a properly diagnosed disability [attention deficit disorder], and taking the medication outside of competition was not a violation of the IAAF Code in 2001, nor is it a violation now.

Yet Mr. Gatlin was and is still being sanctioned because of this "paperwork" violation which, as stipulated, did not enhance his performance.... As stated by Mr. Christopher L. Campbell dissenting from the opinion of the 2006 AAA Panel:

> By imposing sanctions on athletes like Mr. Gatlin who take medication for their legitimate disability, the Anti-Doping Organizations are willfully violating the law—behaving as if they are above the law. In these circumstances, they are nothing more than bullies preying on the vulnerable. The federal government should take a serious look at this practice.

[S]hould the appellate panel find that this Court does have jurisdiction, this Court would grant a preliminary injunction lifting the suspension of Mr. Gatlin based upon a continuing violation of The Americans with Disabilities Act (ADA). The Court would find:

1. Mr. Gatlin suffers from a mental impairment that substantially limits one of the major life activities, learning;
2. The USOC, USATF and the IAAF operate a place of public accommodations;
3. These defendants took adverse action against Mr. Gatlin in 2001 based on his disability and continue to do so; and
4. Reasonable accommodations have not been made.

As a result, Mr. Gatlin's positive test in 2006 would be considered his first offense resulting in a maximum two year suspension from competition.... This Court would then find: (1) a substantial likelihood of success on the merits; (2) that irreparable injury will be suffered by Mr. Gatlin if relief is not granted; (3) that the threatened injury dramatically outweighs any harm relief would inflict on the defendants; and (4) that entry of relief would serve the public interest.

[However], IT IS HEREBY ORDERED ... Plaintiff Justin Gatlin's Motion for Preliminary Injunction is DENIED.

Armstrong v. U.S. Anti-Doping Agency

886 F. Supp. 2d 572 (D. Tex. 2012)

SPARKS, DISTRICT JUDGE.

Background

USADA has charged Armstrong with violating various anti-doping rules, and given him the option of either contesting the charges through arbitration or accepting sanctions, potentially including lifetime ineligibility from certain athletic competitions and forfeiture of any competitive results, medals, points and prizes he obtained on or after the date of his first alleged violation.

Armstrong challenges USADA's authority to bring such charges against him, disputes he has a valid agreement to arbitrate such matters with USADA, and alleges USADA's charging and arbitration procedures violate his due process rights. Armstrong seeks monetary, declaratory, and injunctive relief. The Court finds: (1) Armstrong's due process claims lack merit; and (2) the Court lacks jurisdiction over Armstrong's remaining claims, or alternatively declines to grant equitable relief on those claims. Accordingly, the Court GRANTS USADA's motion and DISMISSES this case without prejudice.

I. National and International Sports Regulation

Before addressing Armstrong's specific allegations, the Court provides a basic outline of the various entities and regulations related to this case. The Court looks first at the international bodies involved in the regulation of Olympic sports such as cycling.

A. International Entities

As relevant to this case, at the apex of the international hierarchy is the Olympic Movement, which is made up of three main constituents: the International Olympic Committee (IOC), the International Sports Federations (IFs) for each participating sport, and the National Olympic Committees (NOCs) for each participating country. More precisely, Armstrong alleges four causes of action: (1) a declaratory judgment action as to both Defendants; (2) tortious interference with contract as to USADA only; (3) a Fifth Amendment due process challenge as to both Defendants; and (4) a common law due process challenge as to both Defendants.

The IF for cycling is the Union Cycliste Internationale (UCI), also known as the International Cycling Union. The national federations administering those sports are affiliated to them. While conserving their independence and autonomy in the administration of their sports, International Sports Federations seeking IOC recognition must ensure that their statutes, practice and activities conform with the Olympic Charter. The IFs have the responsibility and duty to manage and to monitor the everyday running of the world's various sports disciplines, including for those on the programme, the practical organisation of events during the Games. The IFs must also supervise the development of athletes practising these sports at every level. Each IF governs its sport at world level and ensures its promotion and development. They monitor the everyday administration of their sports and guarantee the regular organisation of competitions as well as respect for the rules of fair play. UCI has issued its own set of anti-doping rules (the UCT ADR) based upon, but not identical to, the WADC.

[T]he NOC for the United States is the United States Olympic Committee (USOC). Among other things, NOCs are responsible for selecting competitors and teams to send to the Olympic Games, and naming potential host cities for the Games. The USOC is a federally chartered corporation under the terms of the Ted

Stevens Olympic and Amateur Act. As relevant here, the USOC's powers include recogniz[ing] eligible amateur sports organizations as national governing bodies for any sport that is included on the program of the Olympic Games or the Pan-American Games, and "facilitat[ing]... the resolution of conflicts or disputes that involve any of its members and any amateur athlete, coach, trainer, manager, administrator, official, national governing body, or amateur sports organization and that arise in connection with their eligibility for and participation in the Olympic Games.... or other protected competition" as defined in the constitution and bylaws of the corporation. 36 U.S.C. § 220505(c).

National governing bodies (NGBs) are essentially the United States' domestic equivalents of International Federations organizations which are responsible for governing one or more Olympic sports on a national level. The NGB for cycling is USA Cycling. USA Cycling is also a member of its international counterpart, UCI. The Sports Act empowers NGBs such as USA Cycling "to conduct amateur athletic competition, including national championships, and international amateur athletic competition in the United States, and establish procedures for determining eligibility standards for participation in competition." 36 U.S.C. § 2250523(a)(5). Like the international sports organizations, the United States has its own set of anti-doping regulations. Defendant USADA has implemented a set of anti-doping rules, called the USADA Protocol for Olympic Movement Testing (the USADA Protocol), which has been incorporated into the USOC national anti-doping policies, and which USADA is responsible for implementing.

The USOC anti-doping policies... including the agreement to be bound by the USADA Protocol, apply to, among others, NGB members and license-holders, and those included in the USADA registered testing pool (RTP). USA Cycling's regulations echo this requirement.

II. USADA's Allegations Against Armstrong

On June 12, 2012, USADA sent a notice letter to Armstrong, informing him it was opening formal action against him and five others for their alleged roles in a doping conspiracy beginning in January 1998.

With respect to Lance Armstrong, numerous riders, team personnel and others will testify based on personal knowledge acquired either through observing Armstrong dope or through Armstrong's admissions of doping to them that Lance Armstrong used EPO, blood transfusions, testosterone and cortisone during the period from before 1998 through 2005, and that he had previously used EPO, testosterone and hGH through 1996. Numerous riders will also testify that Lance Armstrong gave to them, encouraged them to use and/or assisted them in using doping products and/or methods, including EPO, blood transfusions, testosterone and cortisone during the period from 1999 through 2005. Representatives of USADA have interviewed Dr. Martial Saugy, Director of the Lausanne Anti-Doping Laboratory which analyzed the urine samples from the 2001 Tour of Switzerland. Dr. Saugy stated that Lance Armstrong's urine sample results from the 2001 Tour of Switzerland were indicative of EPO use. Multiple witnesses have also told USADA that Lance Armstrong told them he had tested positive in 2001 and that the test result had been covered up. Lance Armstrong's doping is further evidenced by the data from blood collections obtained by the UCI from Lance Armstrong in 2009 and 2010. This data is fully consistent with blood manipulation including EPO use and/or blood transfusions. On June 28, 2012, USADA sent Armstrong a second letter, which informed him that a panel of the USADA Anti-Doping Review Board had determined there was sufficient evidence of rules violations to justify adjudication thereof. As relevant to Armstrong, the letter stated: Therefore, at this time, reserving all rights to amend this charge, USADA charges you with anti-doping rules violations [UCI, WADC, USADA Protocol, and USOC Anti-Doping Policies] 1997 to present… (1) Use and/or attempted use of prohibited substances and/or methods including EPO, blood transfusions, testosterone, corticosteroids and/or saline, plasma or glycerol infusions. (2) Possession of prohibited substances and/or methods including EPO, blood transfusions and related equipment (such as needles, blood bags, storage containers and other transfusion equipment and blood parameters measuring devices), testosterone, corticosteroids and/or saline, plasma or glycerol infusions. (3) Trafficking and/or attempted trafficking of EPO, testosterone, and/or corticosteroids. (4) Administration and/or attempted administration to others of EPO, testosterone, and/or cortisone. (5) Assisting, encouraging, aiding, abetting, covering up and other complicity involving one or more anti-doping rule violations and/or attempted anti-doping rule violations. (6) Aggravating circumstances justifying a period of ineligibility greater than the standard sanction. Mr. Armstrong's violations commenced on or before August 1, 1998, with multiple violations thereafter, including violations after June 28, 2004, and, at a minimum, with respect to cover-up activities.… World Triathalon Corporation (WTC) consequently suspended him from competition. Armstrong further claims USADA' s intended sanctions would, if imposed, bar him from future WTC competitions.

III. Armstrong's Challenges to USADA's Authority

Armstrong alleges USADA lacks jurisdiction to bring these charges against him for several reasons. First, he claims, the UCI ADR dictate that, "because Mr. Armstrong retired from cycling before Defendants initiated the charges against him, the organization that had jurisdiction over him during the time of the alleged violations has jurisdiction to determine whether to proceed against Mr. Armstrong. That organization is UCI, not USADA." Second, Armstrong claims USADA lacks authority to bring charges for his alleged conduct prior to 2004, both because "Mr. Armstrong's license agreements with UCI prior to 2004 made no reference to USADA and contained no agreement conferring any authority on USADA," and because "prior to August 13, 2004, UCI's ADR conferred no authority on USADA." Armstrong alleges

UCI retained jurisdiction after this date "over Doping Control (including investigations, charges, and hearings) relating to testing at international events and testing performed by UCI outside of competition." Third, Armstrong contends USADA lacks jurisdiction to bring these charges because they were "discovered," within the meaning of the UCI ADR, not by USADA, but by UCI. Finally, Armstrong claims, UCI has not delegated its jurisdiction to USADA because "none of the requirements for a delegation of authority has been satisfied," including an independent conclusion by UCI that a violation of the UCI ADR has likely occurred. Armstrong also claims USADA's charges were brought in violation of its own rules,... [that] (1) many of USADA's charges are time-barred under its internal 8-year limitations period; (2) USADA has given improper inducements to potential witnesses; and (3) USADA's review board was not impartial, considered a biased version of the evidence, and did not give meaningful consideration to Armstrong's response to the charges.

IV. Armstrong's Due Process Challenges

Armstrong further alleges USADA' s arbitration procedures do not comport with due process. Specifically, he complains of the following alleged procedural deficiencies: (1) he was not provided an adequate charging document; (2) he has no guarantee of a hearing by the appellate arbitral panel; (3) he has no right to cross-examine or confront witnesses against him; (4) he has no right to an impartial arbitration panel; (5) he has no right to disclosure of exculpatory evidence; (6) he has no right to disclosure of cooperation agreements or inducements provided by USADA; (7) he has no right to obtain investigative witness statements; (8) he has no right to obtain full disclosure of laboratory analyses or an impartial assessment of their accuracy; and (9) he has no right to judicial review of the arbitrators' decision by a United States court.

V. USADA's Motion to Dismiss

USADA argues the Court should dismiss Armstrong's claims for four reasons: (1) the Court lacks subject matter jurisdiction because the Sports Act preempts Armstrong's claims; (2) the Court lacks subject matter jurisdiction because Armstrong has failed to exhaust his administrative remedies; (3) Armstrong's due process challenges must be arbitrated or, alternatively, fail on their Appeals from USADA hearings are heard by the Court of Arbitration for Sport (CAS), which is headquartered in Lausanne, Switzerland, it appears the only appeal from a CAS decision is to the courts of Switzerland; and (4) USADA is entitled to dismissal or a stay of proceedings in this Court under the Federal Arbitration Act (FAA).

With respect to Armstrong's due process challenges, the Court agrees they are without merit and therefore dismisses them without prejudice for failure to state a claim upon which relief can be granted. The Court further agrees the Sports Act and Armstrong's arbitration agreement preclude his remaining claims, and the Court therefore dismisses those claims without prejudice for lack of subject matter jurisdiction. Alternatively, even if the Court has jurisdiction over Armstrong's remaining claims, the Court finds they are best resolved through the well-established system of international arbitration, by those with expertise in the field, rather than by the unilateral edict of a single nation's courts; the Court thus declines to grant equitable relief on Armstrong's remaining claims on this alternative basis.

* * *

Notes and Comments

1. **Exhaustion of internal administrative remedies.** In *Reynolds v. Int'l Amateur Athletic Federation,* 23 F.3d 1110 (6th Cir. 1994), the Sixth Circuit held that a U.S. court had no personal jurisdiction, *i.e.*, valid authority to render a legally binding judgment against the defendant, to hear an American athlete's state law claims against the IAAF, a non-resident international athletics governing body. *Reynolds* illustrates the procedural quagmire athletes may confront in challenging an eligibility decision rendered by an international or national sporting body. The district court could not even accept the case initially until Reynolds had exhausted internal administrative remedies. *See also Barnes v. Int'l Amateur Athletic Federation*, 862 F. Supp. 1537 (S.D.W. Va. 1993) (dismissing athlete's claim contesting ineligibility under the Amateur Sports Act where the USOC has established procedures to resolve disputes regarding an athlete's participation in international competition). While Reynolds did so, the remedies provided under the ASA and international federation rules appeared to conflict. Under the ASA, the national governing body, USA Track & Field, was required to submit to binding arbitration "in accordance with the commercial rules of the American Arbitration Association [AAA] in any controversy involving... the opportunity of any amateur athlete... to participate in amateur athletic competition." 36 U.S.C. § 391(b)(3). The AAA arbitrators "fully exonerated" Reynolds, finding strong evidence the urine samples were not his. The IAAF, however, disregarded the AAA decision and the U.S. Supreme Court's ruling that Reynolds could compete in the Olympics Trials. Meanwhile, the IAAF required Reynolds to appear before an international arbitration panel in London, England. International arbitration awards are enforceable in U.S. courts, as the United States is a signatory to the [New York] Convention on the Recognition of Foreign Arbitral Awards, which requires judicial enforcement of foreign arbitral agreements and awards.

Slaney v. Int'l Amateur Ath. Fed'n, 244 F.3d 580 (7th Cir. 2001), *cert. denied*, 534 U.S. 828 (2001), upheld dismissal of the former Olympic runner's suit challenging an IAAF arbitration panel's finding that she had committed a doping offense on the grounds that the New York Convention barred Slaney's state and federal claims against the IAAF because those claims had been the subject of a valid arbitration decision. The court also upheld dismissal of Slaney's state law claims against the USOC regarding administration of its drug-testing program, finding that the ASA gave the USOC the "exclusive" right to determine disputes over athlete eligibility and "does not create" a private right of action under which Slaney could seek to have those claims addressed by the district court.

2. **Arbitral finality.** Would any court have jurisdiction to review (or vacate) an arbitration decision rendered either by the AAA or the international CAS tribunal? What law would apply? *See infra* Section D. Domestic arbitration awards are subject to limited judicial review under the Federal Arbitration Act, 9 U.S.C. 9 (providing for *vacatur* in rare cases of, *inter alia*, fraud or evident partiality). CAS arbitral awards are considered seated in Switzerland, with final appeal in the Swiss Federal Tribunal. *See* Maureen A. Weston, *Simply a Dress Rehearsal? U.S. Olympic Sports Arbitration and De Novo Review at the Court of Arbitration for Sport*, 38 GA. J. INT'L & COMP. L. 97, 116 (2009).

3. **Jurisdiction and IFs.** *Reynolds* (see note 1) demonstrates the difficulty of establishing U.S. personal jurisdiction over an international sport body. Yet when can an international sport federation be subject to personal jurisdiction in a U.S. court? The IAAF argued that it was not subject to jurisdiction in the United States and was not required to comply with national laws. Consider the potentially unwieldy impact on international competition were international sport federations subject to suit in the United States (or anywhere in the world an athlete resides). Is that adequate justification to deny jurisdiction? The IAAF received half of its $174.5 million budget from U.S. corporations and exerted substantial control over TAC, as a member of the IAAF. Why wasn't the court's finding that TAC was an agent of the IAAF grounds for personal jurisdiction? *See also Mehr v. FIFA*, 115 F. Supp. 3d 1035 (N.D. Cal. 2015) (dismissing soccer concussion claims against FIFA for lack of personal jurisdiction); *World Skating Federation v. International Skating Union*, 357 F. Supp. 2d 661 (S.D.N.Y. 2005) (dismissing claims against ISU based on lack of personal jurisdiction). In what situations could the IAAF be sued in the United States?

4. **Home-country bias or international fiat?** Should an international federation be able to disregard or trump the decision of a National Olympic Committee or NGB? Consider the IAAF's decision to ban members of the Russian delegation in the doping scandal. The concern in giving final decision-making authority to a national body is that a domestic tribunal may be more lenient in enforcing doping or other eligibility restrictions in order to present the most competitive athletes at international competitions. What is the risk, however, of having final resolution under the control of an international federation or private foreign arbitral body?

5. **No private right of action.** Although the ASA states that the USOPC has the power to sue and be sued, the ASA does not provide a private right of action to individual athletes and generally preempts state law. *See, e.g., Walton-Floyd v. USOC*, 965 S.W.2d 35 (Tex. App. 1998) (holding athletes have no private right of action under the Amateur Sports Act and that the act preempts state claims against the USOC). *See also Slaney (note 1).*

In 2006, Congress amended the ASA to state expressly that it creates no private right of action for athletes to sue the USOPC or an NGB and requires federal court jurisdiction, providing that the USOPC may:

> (9) sue and be sued, except that any civil action brought in a State court against the corporation and solely relating to the corporation's responsibilities under this chapter shall be **removed**, at the request of the corporation, to the district court of the United States in the district in which the action was brought, and such district court shall have original jurisdiction over the action without regard to the amount in controversy or citizenship of the parties involved, and except that neither this paragraph nor any other provision of this chapter shall create a private right of action under this chapter. 36 U.S.C. § 220505(b)(9).

The ASA does not otherwise provide a basis for federal subject matter jurisdiction. *Lee v. Taekwondo Union,* 331 F. Supp. 2d 1252 (D. Haw. 2004).

6. **Implied antitrust immunity?** Does the ASA's grant to the USOPC of "exclusive" authority over U.S. participation in the Olympic Games imply USOPC antitrust immunity? In *Gold Medal v. USA Track & Field,* 899 F.3d 712 (9th Cir. 2018), Run Gum, a chewing gum manufacturer, filed an antitrust lawsuit against the USOC, alleging that USOC's policy forbidding athletes from competing at Olympic Trials in apparel bearing individual sponsorship restrained trade in violation of the Sherman Act. The Ninth Circuit affirmed dismissal, holding that the USOC's advertising and logo restrictions on individual athletes during Olympic Trials were entitled to implied antitrust immunity under the ASA.

Would ASA provide statutory immunity on the USOPC for other types of claims, such as negligence or for its restrictions on athlete speech and use of social media? For sexual abuse cases?

7. **State actors?** As you learned from the *De Frantz* case, athletes seeking to invoke rights under the U.S. Constitution against the USOPC have met a *Tarkanian* problem, by judicial rulings that the USOC, despite its extensive regulation and powers under the ASA, is not a state actor whose decisions must meet the Constitutional standards. Even if the USOPC were found to be a state actor, the *De Frantz* court stated that "[m]any of life's disappointments, even major ones (like not having the opportunity to participate in the Olympics), do not enjoy constitutional protection. This is one such instance." 492 F. Supp. 1181 (D.D.C. 1980). *See also San Francisco Arts & Athletics, Inc. v. U.S. Olympic Committee*, 483 U.S. 522 (1987). Consider that an Olympic athlete's economic and liberty rights to work in his or her chosen profession and potential exposure to criminal charges for doping violations are all at stake in an ineligibility determination. To date, sport governing bodies have been accorded treatment and status as private associations subject to private, rather than public or constitutional standards of law. As anti-doping agencies work in tandem with federal and state law enforcement on doping investigations (such as BALCO and Lance Armstrong), and as the WADC has achieved Treaty status, is the case for state action

more compelling? *See* Michael Straubel, *The International Convention Against Doping in Sport: Is It the Missing Link to USADA Being a State Actor and WADC Coverage to Pro Sports?*, 19 Marq. Sports L. Rev. 63 (2009); Maureen A. Weston, *Doping Control, Mandatory Arbitration and Process Dangers for Accused Athletes in International Sports*, 10 Pepp. Disp. Resol. L.J. 5 (2009).

8. **Gender discrimination.** In *Martin v. IOC*, 740 F.2d 670 (9th Cir. 1984), women runners from 27 countries unsuccessfully invoked the anti-discrimination laws under the U.S. Constitution and California state law to require the 1984 Olympic Games to include 5,000- and 10,000-meter track events for women (part of the men's events since 1923). The court agreed that the plaintiffs had shown a historical pattern of gender discrimination but was reluctant to impose U.S. Constitutional or state laws on an international athletic event and deferred to the procedures under the Olympic Charter. The dissent thought that at least state law should apply, stating that: "When the Olympics move to other countries, some without America's commitment to human rights, the opportunity to tip the scales of justice in favor of equality may slip away." Is the judicial reluctance to intervene in an international sporting event, particularly those held in the United States, appropriate? What laws apply to international sporting organizations? *See* Weston, *supra, Dress Rehearsal?* (arguing that Congress in the ASA fails to acknowledge the international regulatory framework governing U.S. Olympic athletes). For years, professional women tennis players alleged sex discrimination by the prize money disparities at premier events such as Wimbledon. Although now receiving equal pay due to player advocacy, would they have had rights against gender discrimination under U.S. or international law? Assuming similar pay disparity, would they have a stronger claim at the U.S. Open? *Lee v. USTU*, 331 F. Supp. 2d 1252 (D. Haw. 2004), held that the ASA preempted a U.S. Olympic taekwondo coach's state claims, but not his federal claims alleging race discrimination. Consider that although the Supreme Court of British Columbia agreed with the claim by five female ski jumpers that excluding women's ski jumping from the 2010 Vancouver Olympic Games violates the Canadian Charter of Rights and Freedom, it concluded that the Charter does not apply to the IOC, as a private entity, and that the IOC alone determines the events to be included in all Olympic Games. *Sagen v. Vancouver Org. Comm.*, 2009 BCSC 942. London 2012 was the first time in the history of the Games that every competing nation entered at least one female athlete, as Saudi Arabia, Brunei and Qatar otherwise faced a potential ban and mounting pressure from the IOC and international community to abide by the Olympic Charter pledge to equality.

9. **The Harding saga.** At the time the *Reynolds* case was tied up in various proceedings (and before the Sixth Circuit had reversed the $27 million verdict against the IAAF), the U.S. Figure Skating Association (USFSA) was faced with the bizarre eligibility question as a result of Tonya Harding's alleged involvement in a "clubbing attack" on her national rival Nancy Kerrigan. Although criminal charges were pending against her, Harding was able to use the administrative procedural scheme to buy

enough time to compete in the Olympics in Norway. After the USFSA charged Harding with violation of USFSA ethics rules less than three weeks prior to the competition, Harding filed a lawsuit to enjoin the USFSA from holding a disciplinary hearing that could result in her expulsion from the Olympics. As part of a settlement, with Harding dropping her damages suit, the USOC allowed her to compete in the Olympics. Following the Olympics, Harding continued to fight the USFSA in its efforts to hold a disciplinary hearing prior to the March 1994 World Championships. The court granted a temporary injunction requiring the USFSA to abide by its rules that entitle athletes a minimum of 30 days to respond to disciplinary charges and a reasonable time to prepare for a hearing. *Harding v. U.S. Figure Skating Ass'n*, 851 F. Supp. 1476 (D. Or. 1994). The case was mooted when Harding pled guilty to criminal charges. The USFSA ultimately banned Harding for life for violating a code of conduct. Should a sporting body defer sanctioning an athlete until criminal charges are resolved? Suppose Harding had been acquitted? Harding's drama was later depicted in the critically acclaimed movie, *I, Tonya* (2017).

10. **Restrictions on injunctive relief.** Judicial reluctance to intervene in resolving sporting disputes is particularly heightened in the international context. The court in *Harding* expressed that: "The courts should rightly hesitate before intervening in disciplinary hearings held by private associations.... Intervention is appropriate only in the most extraordinary circumstances, where the association has clearly breached its own rules, that breach will imminently result in serious and irreparable harm to the plaintiff, and the plaintiff has exhausted all internal remedies. Even then, injunctive relief is limited to correcting the breach of the rules. The court should not intervene in the underlying dispute." 851 F. Supp. at 1479. Congress apparently agrees, as it amended the Amateur Sports Act in 1998 to provide that a court shall not grant injunctive relief against the USOC within 21 days before the start of the Olympic Games. 36 U.S.C. § 220509. Consider now the operation of the Court of Arbitration for Sport, sometimes referred to as the "Supreme Court" for international sports.

D. Arbitration of Olympic Disputes

As a result of limited judicial remedies and a strong emphasis on resolving disputes through internal administrative procedures and arbitration, fewer lawsuits involving Olympic athletes are filed in the court system. Whether this trend is good or bad is still subject to debate. According to Judge Richard Posner, "[t]here can be few less suitable bodies than the federal courts for determining the eligibility, or the procedures for determining eligibility, of athletes to participate in the Olympic Games." *Michels v. United States Olympic Committee*, 741 F.2d 155 (7th Cir. 1984). Do you agree? Professor Nafziger has noted that "although this trend seems to offer a welcome alternative to executive fiat, on the one hand, and litigation, on the other, these tribunals are controversial.... they may sometimes be little more than executive panels in disguise." James A.R. Nafziger, *International Sports Law: A Replay of Character-*

istics and Trends, 86 AM. J. INT'L L. 489 (1992). Who are the private judges (arbitrators) in this system? What is this system that supplants public judicial review?

The nature of international sport competition necessitates an alternative to protracted litigation and a neutral forum, free from the influence of a particular national or international sporting federation. The Amateur Sports Act requires that the USOPC create a dispute resolution process that entitles an athlete to appeal to the American Arbitration Association (AAA) for final and nonbinding arbitration. 36 U.S.C. § 220529. However, the international federation may not recognize AAA decisions. In doping cases, both the athlete and the World Anti-Doping Agency (WADA) are permitted to appeal first-instance doping decisions. Given the timing and nature of international sporting competitions, the need for swift resolution of eligibility disputes is critical. Dispute resolution procedures have developed to provide more efficient resolution of disputes and to mitigate overlapping jurisdictional problems.

Section 9 of the USOC Bylaws provides that no member of the USOC "may deny or threaten to deny an athlete the opportunity to participate in the Olympic Games... or other such protected competition...." Any athlete (coach, trainer, or manager) who, for example, is not selected for competition or declared otherwise ineligible, may file a complaint with the USOC and request a hearing before a single arbitrator of the panel. As noted, athletes who may be adversely affected by the decision are entitled to notice and to participate. The complaining party in a Section 9 hearing generally must establish that the sport's NGB failed to follow its selection procedures or to apply its selection criteria consistently to all athletes under consideration. An NGB's selection criteria may be entirely objective, such as top two finishers in an event; or the standards can be a mix of objective and subjective criteria. The arbitrator's role is *not* to determine whether the selection criteria are good, but often to assess challenges to application of discretionary criteria. The prevailing party may seek judicial confirmation of the arbitration award under the Federal Arbitration Act, but neither the FAA or ASA provides subject matter jurisdiction to seek confirmation in federal court. *See USOC v. Ruckman*, 2010 WL 2179527 (D.N.J. 2010).

Anti-doping violations are outside of the Section 9 procedure and adjudicated through the U.S. Anti-Doping Agency (USADA) and subject to de novo review at CAS. *See, e.g., Landis v. USADA, infra. Disputed competition results are non-reviewable under* Section 9.13 of the USOPC bylaws, which provides:

> The final decision of a referee during a competition regarding a field of play decision (a matter set forth in the rules of the competition to be within the discretion of the referee) shall not be reviewable through or the subject of these complaint [and arbitration] procedures unless the decision is (i) outside the authority of the referee to make or (ii) the product of fraud, corruption, partiality or other misconduct of the referee. For purposes of this Section, the term 'referee' shall include any individual with discretion to make field of play decisions.

USOC Bylaws Section 10 and 11, respectively, set forth the process for filing complaints and arbitration against an NGB and to replace an NGB. For example, in 2018, the USOC initiated proceedings to revoke its NGB recognition status for USA Gymnastics due to scandal involving the team doctor's sexual abuse of athletes.

Problem: USOC Section 9 Athlete Selection Dispute Arbitration Hearing

USA Track & Field (USTAF), the national governing body for the sport, recognized by the United States Olympic Committee (USOC), announced its selection of athletes for the U.S. 100m sprint team for the upcoming Olympic Games. The selection criteria, which were posted on the NGB website only, stated the following:

> "Athletes will be selected, up to a maximum of the number of available places, in the following order:
>
> 1. The winner of the US Championships;
> 2. The highest placed eligible finisher, provided they finish in the top 3, at the World Championships not already selected from the US;
> 3. For setting a new world record in the 12 months before selection;
> 4. For setting a new US record in the 12 months before selection;
> 5. The athlete considered most capable by the selection committee of securing a medal at the Games."

Background

Alan Sprinter is 27 years old and has a PB (personal best) of 10.1 and a SB (season best) of 10.3.

Bert Faststart is 31 years old and has a PB of 9.98 and a SB of 10.4

Clive Spikes is 20 years old and has a PB of 9.95 and a SB of 9.95

Facts Leading Up to Selection

Alan Sprinter won the US Championships, early in the season, in a time of 10.3 seconds. Bert Faststart did not race, as he was injured. Clive Spikes was disqualified from the final for two false starts, but he had posted a time of 9.97 in the semi-final head. In the World Championships, Clive Spikes was the best placed American finishing fourth. Alan Sprinter finished sixth but Bert, coming back from injury, failed to progress beyond the semi-finals.

In order to increase his sprinting stamina, Clive Spikes also entered several 200m races, and at a meet in France, he set a new US record for the distance.

In the lead up to the selection meeting, Faststart was nervous that he would not have the chance to add to the silver medal that he won in the 100m at the 2016 Olympics in London. His season had been plagued by injury, and he only managed to compete in half of the races on the calendar. He is now nearing full fitness however.

Alan Sprinter, however, has picked up a hamstring injury and is rated as only 50/50 to be fit for the Games.

The NGB selection committee picked Sprinter and Faststart for the Games. USOC Bylaws provide that "An athlete who is removed or not selected to the U.S. Olympic Team has the right to a hearing." *See* Complaint Form Section 9 of USOC Bylaws.

Spikes was not selected and appeals, contending the decision not to select him is not in accordance with the selection policy, or, in the alternative, is irrational and unfair.

Spike: Set forth your reasons in support of the appeal.

NGB: Defend your decision to select Sprinter and Faststart.

1. International Arbitration—Court of Arbitration for Sport (CAS)

Interplay between the U.S. Amateur Sports Act and International Codes

Although U.S. Congress may have envisioned a streamlined procedure for dispute resolution, Olympic athletes and the USOC must operate in a larger international arena and are subject to the rules, standards, and procedures of their respective federations, all of which require adherence to the World Anti-Doping Code and to submit any disputes exclusively to the Court of Arbitration for Sport (CAS) as the single arbitral authority and tribunal for international sports-related disputes. According to the CAS Code of Sports-Related Arbitration, sport federation decision may be appealed for *de novo* review to an international panel of CAS arbitrators, whose decision is final and binding with narrow grounds to appeal only to the Swiss Federal Tribunal. Under this ostensibly "private law" framework, the USOC and U.S. athletes do not have access to U.S. courts or, necessarily, U.S. legal protections.

The Court of Arbitration for Sport/ Tribunal Arbitral du Sport

In 1984, the IOC voted to create and approve the Court of Arbitration for Sport to serve as the exclusive arbitral tribunal for the binding adjudication of disputes involving members of the Olympic Movement. CAS provides a single forum in which all athletes, sport bodies, and all constituents in the Olympic Movement can bring disputes for expedited resolution. To provide an arbitration forum independent of the IOC (which had created, funded, and selected CAS members essentially from its own ranks), the International Council of Arbitration for Sport (ICAS) was established in 1994 to administer and fund CAS, to select neutral CAS arbitrators, and to protect the rights of the parties, particularly the athletes.

Since 1995, the Olympic Charter has provided that "[A]ny dispute arising on the occasion of, or in connection with, the Olympic Games shall be submitted exclusively to the Court of Arbitration for Sport [CAS], in accordance with the Code of Sports-Related Arbitration." Olympic Charter ¶ 61(2). All sporting governing bodies have designated CAS jurisdiction within their rules. As a condition of participating in the Olympics or sanctioned international sports competition, athletes must consent to CAS arbitration and thereby waive rights to their national courts.

CAS is structured into three divisions: (1) the Ordinary Arbitration Division hears disputes arising out of commercial contracts related to sport; (2) the Appeals Arbitration Division, which, after internal remedies are exhausted, reviews challenges involving decisions of sports federations or other sports bodies; and (3) the Anti-Doping Division to hear and decide doping cases as a first-instance authority. CAS operates an *Ad Hoc* Division on-site to settle within a 24-hour time frame disputes arising during the Olympic Games; CAS also has a mediation procedure. CAS is headquartered in Lausanne, Switzerland, with additional offices in Sydney, Australia, and New York. CAS procedures are set forth in the Code of Sports-Related Arbitration. The CAS arbitrators review each case "in light of the Olympic Charter, the applicable rules of each sport and general principles of law." CAS, Ad Hoc Rules, Art. 17. Absent the consent of parties otherwise, the choice of law is Swiss or the law of the country in which the federation, association, or sports body is domiciled. The CAS proceedings are typically private and more expeditious than court proceedings, but final and binding on the parties. Both CAS and AAA publish decisions online. The body of arbitral sport decisions is developing a body of private law or *lex sportiva* governing international sports and cited as precedent by parties and arbitral panels.

Challenges to CAS Compulsory Arbitration. As a condition of participating in the Olympics, athletes must sign a Court of Arbitration for Sport Waiver form and thereby waive rights to their national courts and attendant laws and procedures. Arbitration clauses are incorporated into the statutes of each of the sport federations, associations, or sport bodies, and athletes are required to consent to arbitration. The viability of judicial recourse is thus extremely limited. What would be the impact on international sport if compulsory arbitration clauses in sport are found to violate a country's national or European Human Rights law?

Gold medalist German speed skater Claudia Pechstein fought the compulsory arbitration requirement before the German, Swiss Federal Tribunal, and European Court of Human Rights (ECHR). The International Skating Union (ISU) had imposed a two-year ban against Pechstein, based on abnormal blood values detected from biological passport, an electronic record of an athlete's blood tests and markers. The CAS Panel rejected her defense that the results were explained by a genetic abnormality and upheld the ban. Pechstein sued the ISU in the German court, seeking $4.72 million for loss of income and personal suffering. The German Regional Court refused to recognize the CAS ruling on the basis that the mandatory arbitration system imposed on athletes by the sports federation, a monopolist in the market for access to speed-skating world championships, was contrary to German anti-trust/

competition law. It questioned the structural imbalance favoring sport associations' influence on CAS arbitrator selection. The German Federal Tribunal reversed, recognizing CAS jurisdiction. The Swiss Federal Tribunal similarly rejected her appeal. The ECHR held that the CAS procedure should allow athletes rights to a public hearing but otherwise rejected Pechstein's case. In response, CAS amended its procedure rule, effective 2019, to allow a public hearing:

> At the request of a physical person who is party to the proceedings, a public hearing should be held if the matter is of a disciplinary nature. Such request may however be denied in the interest of morals, public order, national security, where the interests of minors or the protection of the private life of the parties so require, where publicity would prejudice the interests of justice, where the proceedings are exclusively related to questions of law or where a hearing held in first instance was already public.

Code of Sports-Related Arbitration, R. 57 (2019).

CAS jurisdiction extends to "any disputes directly or indirectly linked to sport," and hears cases on a range of disputes involving commercial (*e.g.*, sponsorship), athlete eligibility, or discipline (including doping) following decisions meted out by various sport governing bodies in the Olympic Movement.

In the Arbitration Between: Oscar Pistorius and IAAF

Court of Arbitration for Sport (CAS) CAS 2008 /A /1480

***

3. The Appellant, Oscar Pistorius ("Mr. Pistorius") is a citizen of, and resident in, the Republic of South Africa. He is a professional athlete competing in 100, 200 and 400 meter sprints. In this arbitration, Mr. Pistorius appeals the IAAF Decision that the "Cheetah" prosthetic legs worn by Mr. Pistorius, who has been a double amputee since he was eleven months old, constituted a technical device and provided him with an advantage over an able-bodied athlete in violation of IAAF Competition Rule 144.2(e).

4. The IAAF Decision was based on a report prepared for the IAAF by Professor Brüggemann and his colleagues at the German Sport University in Cologne (the "Cologne Report"). As a result of the IAAF Decision, Mr. Pistorius is banned from competing against able-bodied athletes in IAAF-sanctioned events.... For participation in sporting activities Mr. Pistorius uses a prosthesis known as the *Cheetah Flex-Foot*, supplied by a company headquartered in Iceland, Össur HF ("Össur"). The *Cheetah Flex-Foot* is designed for single and double transtibial (below-the-knee) and transfemoral (above-the-knee) amputees who intend to run at recreational and/or competitive levels. It has been used by many single and double amputees, almost unchanged, since 1997. In 2004, only a few months after he started running compet-

itively, Mr. Pistorius competed in the Athens Paralympics, where he won the Gold Medal in the 200-metre event and the Bronze medal in the 100-metre event. At the time of this appeal process he is the Paralympic world-record holder at 100, 200 and 400 meters. In 2004 Mr. Pistorius also began to compete in IAAF-sanctioned events in South Africa alongside able-bodied athletes. He won a 100-metre open competition in Pretoria with a time of 11.51. In the following year he competed alongside able-bodied athletes in the South African Championship, in which he finished sixth in the 400 meter event.

5. In early 2007 Mr. Pistorius returned to competitive sprinting, and in March of that year he finished in second place in the South African Championships 400-metre event with a time of 46.56. On 26 March 2007, the IAAF Council met in Mombasa, Kenya and decided to introduce an amendment to IAAF Rule 144.2 for the purpose of regulating the use of technical devices. The new rule prohibits: *(e) Use of any technical device that incorporates springs, wheels or any other element that provides the user with an advantage over another athlete not using such a device....* On 15 June 2007, at a press conference during the first 2007 Golden League meeting in Oslo, the IAAF President, when asked about the eligibility of Mr. Pistorius, stated that he would not be excluded unless the IAAF received scientific evidence demonstrating that his prosthesis gave him an advantage. He was therefore considered eligible to compete at that time. On 25 June 2007, Mr. Pistorius received an invitation to participate in the Golden Gala event in Rome on 13 July 2007, where he ran in a specially staged "B" race which the IAAF arranged to be videotaped by an Italian sports laboratory using several high-definition cameras from different angles. He finished in second place, and the video subsequently became an exhibit in this appeal. For a non-scientific observer, the video appears to show that Mr. Pistorius was slower than other runners off the starting blocks, during the acceleration phase (approximately the first 50 meters) and running around the first bend, but faster over the "back straight." The split times of the race provided by the IAAF confirmed this observation. The able-bodied sprinters ran their fastest 10 meter splits in the first and second 100 meters, but Mr. Pistorius ran his fastest 100 meter splits in the second and third 100 meters....

In order to take the evaluation further Dr. Locatelli asked Professor Peter Brüggemann at the Institute of Biomechanics and Orthopaedics at the German Sport University in Cologne if he could conduct a biomechanical study to demonstrate whether or not Mr. Pistorius' prosthetic limbs gave him an advantage over other athletes.... On 12 November 2007 Mr. Pistorius and five "control" athletes of similar sprinting ability to him ran a sub-maximal 400-metre race on an outdoor track, followed by a series of maximal and sub-maximal sprints on a 100-metre track at the laboratory of the Institute.... On 14 January 2008, the IAAF Council issued a Decision which included the following findings: *running with these prostheses requires a less-important vertical movement associated with a lesser mechanical effort to raise the body, and the energy loss resulting from the use of these prostheses is significantly lower than that resulting from a human ankle joint at a maximal sprint speed.* Based on these findings the IAAF ruled that the *Cheetah Flex-Foot* prosthetics used by Mr. Pistorius were to be considered as a... *technical device that incorporates springs, wheels or any other element that provides the user with an advantage over valid athletes*, and therefore contravened Rule 144.2(e). Mr. Pistorius was thus declared ineligible to compete in IAAF-sanctioned events with immediate effect....

Issue (iv) Was the IAAF Council's Decision wrong in determining that Mr. Pistorius' use of the Cheetah Flex-Foot device contravenes Rule 144.2(e)?

31. The Panel's point of departure for this part of the analysis is Rule 144.2(e), adopted by the IAAF's Council at its meeting in Mombasa, Kenya on 26 March 2007. As stated above, it reads as follows: *For the purposes of this Rule, the following shall be considered assistance, and are therefore not allowed: [...] (e) Use of any technical device that incorporates springs, wheels, or any other element that provides the user with an advantage over another athlete not using such a device.*

32. Without implying any criticism of the draftsman, who faced an extraordinarily difficult task, the Panel considers that this provision is a masterpiece of ambiguity. What constitutes a *technical device*? For the purposes of the present enquiry, the Panel is prepared to assume that a passive prosthetic such as the *Cheetah Flex-Foot* is to be considered as a "technical device," even though this proposition may not be wholly free from doubt.

33. What constitutes a device that *incorporates springs*? Technically, almost every non-brittle material object is a "spring" in the sense that it has elasticity. Certainly the *Cheetah Flex-Foot* is a "spring," but does it *incorporate* a "spring"? A natural human leg is itself a "spring."

34. Then there is the critical question of the meaning of an *advantage... over another athlete*. It was urged on the Panel by the IAAF's counsel that the ordinary and natural meaning of the word *advantage* is absolute, in the sense that if a *technical device* is used, and is determined (presumably by an appropriate and fair process) to provide an athlete with any *advantage*, however small, in any part of a competition, that device must render that athlete ineligible to compete regardless of any compensating disadvantages.

35. The Panel does not accept this proposition. Of course, athletes should not be forced to compete against persons who use powered aids such as motors, wheels, springs (as in "pogo sticks," for example), or other active propulsive devices. This is not in doubt, and interpreted in this way the new Rule 144.2(e) is a sensible and appropriate rule. But to propose that a passive device such as the *Cheetah Flex-Foot* as used by Mr. Pistorius should be classified as contravening that Rule without convincing scientific proof that it provides him with *an overall net advantage* over other athletes flies in the face of both legal principle and commonsense. The rule specifically prohibits a technical device that... *provides the user with an advantage over an athlete not using that device.* If the use of the device provides more disadvantages

than advantages, then it cannot reasonably be said to provide an advantage over other athletes, because the user is actually at a competitive disadvantage. That is the only sensible reading of the terms of Rule 144.2(e).

36. The Panel notes that this interpretation of Rule 144.2(e) was effectively adopted by Dr. Locatelli of the IAAF in his testimony at the hearing, when he said that the rule would not prohibit Mr. Pistorius from running in 100-metre or 200-metre races. Dr. Locatelli said that such distances did not allow Mr. Pistorius to catch up from his slower start. Thus, Dr. Locatelli focused on the overall effect of the prosthesis and not on whether Mr. Pistorius had an advantage at only one point in the race.

37. Unfortunately, as Prof. Brüggemann made clear during the hearing, the IAAF did not ask him to determine whether or not Mr. Pistorius' use of the *Cheetah Flex-Foot* prosthesis provided him with an overall net advantage or disadvantage. The Cologne Report therefore does not address the central question that the Panel is required to answer in this appeal.

***

42. As shown in the quotation above from the abstract to the Cologne Report, and as stated in the IAAF Decision, the finding of an advantage in using the *Cheetah Flex-Foot* prosthesis comes principally from two elements of the Cologne Report: First, Mr. Pistorius, in using the device, does not have as much vertical force with each step; in other words, he runs in a flatter manner than able-bodied runners. All the experts agreed that these measurements were valid. Second, Mr. Pistorius uses less metabolic energy in running, perhaps as a result of that flatter running. These test results were challenged.

43. The experts presented by Mr. Pistorius conducted their own tests on him and on able-bodied athletes as controls at a laboratory in Houston in February 2008 (the "Houston Report"). Among other things, tests set out in the Houston Report found that Mr. Pistorius used the same oxygen amounts as able-bodied runners at a sub-maximal running speed, and thus did not have a metabolic advantage. Other tests also showed that Mr. Pistorius fatigued normally. Again, the experts agreed that these test results were valid. The Houston Report also tested the amount of energy loss from the *Cheetah Flex-Foot* prosthesis against the intact human leg, which includes tendons and other elements that generate positive energy (and which, for obvious reasons, an amputated athlete would not have). It is common ground that the Cologne Report did not measure any of these elements.

44. In summary, the Panel determines that the IAAF has not met its "on the balance of probability" burden of proof that Rule 144.2(e) is contravened by Mr. Pistorius' use of the *Cheetah Flex Foot* prosthesis for several reasons. First, as noted above, a violation would only occur if the user of the prosthesis gained an *overall net advantage* over other runners....

45. The testing protocol that he prepared for the purposes of writing the Cologne Report, on the basis of his instructions from the IAAF, was not designed to provide a scientific opinion as to whether Mr. Pistorius' *Cheetah Flex-Foot* prosthesis provided him with an overall net advantage over other athletes not using such devices. The point was stated clearly by Dr. Locatelli in one of his press interviews, when he said... *we are looking for advantages, not for disadvantages.* The experts also agreed at the hearing that *neither the Cologne nor Houston studies have quantified all of the possible advantages or disadvantages of Mr. Pistorius in a 400m race.*

46. Secondly, the Panel is not persuaded that there is sufficient evidence of any metabolic advantage in favor of a double amputee using the *Cheetah Flex-Foot.*

47. Similarly, the IAAF has not proven the other basis of the IAAF Decision: namely that the biomechanical effects of using the particular prosthetic device give Mr. Pistorius an advantage over other athletes not using the device.... In particular, the scientists do not know if the fact that able-bodied runners create more vertical force than Mr. Pistorius is an advantage or disadvantage. There is at least some scientific evidence that sprinters, including 400m runners, train themselves to bounce more (i.e., to use more vertical force) because it creates more speed. Thus, the Cologne Report's finding, on which the IAAF Decision relied, that Mr. Pistorius uses less vertical force and runs in a flatter manner may be a *disadvantage* rather than *an advantage.*

48. In addition, while the Cologne Report found less energy loss in the *Cheetah Flex-Foot* prosthesis than in the human ankle, the scientific experts all agreed that the energy "lost" in the ankle could be transferred elsewhere in the body, through tendons, ligaments and muscles etc., because the human body does not like to lose energy. They agreed that that such a transfer cannot be properly measured or currently understood. Thus, based on current scientific knowledge, it appears to be impracticable to assess definitively whether the *Cheetah Flex-Foot* prosthesis acts as more than, or less than, the human ankle and lower leg, in terms of "spring-like" quality.

49. Moreover, the scientific experts agreed that *a mechanical advantage provided by a prosthetic leg would be expected to lead to a metabolic advantage for a runner.* As noted above, neither the Cologne Report nor the Houston Report showed such a metabolic advantage.

50. In the light of the Panel's analysis of the facts, the scientific expert opinions and the legal principles involved, the Panel has no doubt in finding that the IAAF has failed to satisfy the burden of proof that it accepts. It follows that Mr. Pistorius' appeal must be upheld.

51. The Panel is reinforced in reaching this conclusion by the fact that the *Cheetah Flex-Foot* prosthesis has been in use for a decade, and yet no other runner using them—either a single amputee or a double amputee—has run times fast enough

to compete effectively against able-bodied runners until Mr. Pistorius has done so. In effect, these prior performances by other runners using the prosthesis act as a control for study of the benefits of the prosthesis and demonstrate that even if the prosthesis provided an advantage, and as noted none has been proven, it may be quite limited.

52. The consequence of this ruling by the Panel is that the IAAF Council's Decision is revoked with immediate effect, and Mr. Pistorius is currently eligible to compete in IAAF-sanctioned events.

Gender Rules: Competitive Fairness or Human Rights Violation?

Dutee Chand, a female sprinter of Indian nationality, was disqualified from women's international competition because her natural levels of testosterone exceeded guidelines set by track and field's governing body, the International Association of Athletic Federations (IAAF). Rather than undergo surgery or take hormone-suppressing drugs, Chand challenged the "IAAF Regulations Governing Eligibility of Females with Hyperandrogenism to Compete in Women's Competition" to the Court of Arbitration for Sport (CAS). In 2015, the CAS Panel ordered a two-year suspension of the regulation on the grounds that the IAAF had not presented sufficient scientific evidence that hyperandrogenic female athletes have a significant athletic advantage.

In 2018, the IAAF issues new regulations for Female Classification (Athletes with Differences of Sexual Development) (DSD). Under these rules, South African sprinter Caster Semenya, biologically female with naturally higher levels of testosterone, was barred from some (but not all) competition events. CAS, in a 163-page (2–1) decision, found the regulations discriminatory but upheld as necessary to ensure fair and meaningful competition within the female classification. Semenya asserted a human rights objection, winning an interim suspension of the rules, pending a full appeal before the Swiss Federal Tribunal. On filing her appeal, Semenya stated "I am a woman, and I am a world class athlete. The IAAF will not drug me or stop me from being who I am." (May 29, 2019). In July 2019, the Swiss Supreme Court reinstated the CAS decision, noting its limited power to review the merits of CAS award, leaving Semenya barred from World Championships competition.

Who ultimately decides whether gender verification or testing is appropriate in sport?

2. CAS Arbitration of Doping Controversies

The most publicized and hotly contested Olympic eligibility cases have involved doping and drug testing. The use of performance-enhancing drugs among elite athletes is thought to be widespread. Doping is defined as the presence, use or attempted use, trafficking, possession, or administration of any prohibited substance or method, as well as the evasion of, refusal, or failure to submit to sample collection or to file whereabouts information, missed tests, or the tampering or attempted tampering with any part of doping control. Doping in sport jeopardizes the health and safety of athletes, undermines the fairness and integrity of sport competition, and is outright cheating.

The World Anti-Doping Code in Olympic and International Sport

Doping at the Olympic and international sport levels is regulated under the auspices of the World Anti-Doping Agency (WADA). WADA was established in 1999 in connection with the IOC's World Conference on Doping in Sport in 1999 as a private foundation governed under Swiss law with headquarters in Montreal. WADA promulgates, administers, and enforces the World Anti-Doping Code, which is the core document that provides the framework for harmonized anti-doping policies, rules, and regulations within sport organizations and among public authorities. The World Anti-Doping Code sets forth specific anti-doping rules, definitions of doping, burdens of proof, prohibited substances and methods, and addresses standards for testing, sample analysis, sanctions, appeals, confidentiality, reporting, and statute of limitations. The U.S. Anti-Doping Agency (USADA), established by federal charter in 2000, administers this policy for U.S. Olympic, Paralympic, and Pan American athletes.

The Olympic Charter mandates that all members of the Olympic Movement adopt and implement the World Anti-Doping Code. The purposes of the World Anti-Doping Code and the anti-doping program that supports it are to promote health, fairness and equality for athletes worldwide, and to ensure harmonized, coordinated and effective anti-doping programs at the international and national levels with regard to detection, deterrence, and prevention of doping. The WADA anti-doping program seeks to protect the clean athletes by enforcing strict anti-doping regulations.

The World Anti-Doping Code fixes minimum sanctions for violations. The standard sanction imposed for a violation is a two-year ban from competition, four years for deliberately violating anti-doping rules. In an effort to alleviate the sometimes harsh effects of a strict liability standard (*i.e.* liability without fault), a two-year suspension may be reduced in "exceptional circumstances" if the athlete is able to prove that he or she bears "no fault or negligence" (in which case the suspension is eliminated) or "no significant fault or negligence" (in which case the suspension is reduced). Proving "no fault or negligence" is a very difficult task; in essence, the athlete must show that it was impossible for the athlete to know, even when exercising the utmost caution, that he or she ingested the drug or substance. For example, in *WADA v. Gil Roberts*, CAS 2017/A/5296, an athlete who was suspended for an out-of-competition positive test for probenecid had "no fault or negligence" because he was able to prove the prohibited substance was ingested from kissing his girlfriend, who had taken capsules of Moxylong containing the substance that was purchased in India for a sinus infection, and had no way of knowing he was exposing himself to a doping violation.

At the Australian Open in January 2016, Maria Sharapova, a five-time Grand Slam champion and former No. 1-ranked player, tested positive for a banned heart medication, meldonium. The International Tennis Federation (ITF) imposed a two-year ban. Sharapova said her family doctor first prescribed the medication for various medical issues in 2006 and that she took the drug for regular bouts of the flu, possible onset of diabetes, and a magnesium deficiency. An independent ITF panel had found that Sharapova did not intend to cheat but bore "sole responsibility" and "very significant fault" for the positive test. The ITF panel also said the case "inevitably led to the conclusion" that she took the substance "for the purpose of enhancing her performance." Meldonium increases blood flow, which improves exercise capacity by carrying more oxygen to the muscles. More than 100 athletes, including many Russians and other eastern Europeans had tested positive for meldonium early in 2016. Some of them received no suspension because they argued successfully that they stopped taking the drug before January 1, 2016 when it officially became a banned substance and that traces had lingered in their system. Sharapova, however, acknowledged that she used meldonium after January 1.

Sharapova appealed the suspension to the CAS, which reduced the two-year suspension to 15 months because it found she bore "no significant fault" for her positive drug test and did not intend to cheat. *Sharapova v. ITF*, CAS 2016/A/4643. The arbitration panel found that Sharapova bore "some degree of fault" but "less than significant fault" and decided, under the totality of the circumstances, that a sanction of 15 months was appropriate given her degree of fault. Although Sharapova committed a doping violation, the panel said "under no circumstances . . . can the player be considered to be an 'intentional doper.'" Sharapova acknowledged taking meldonium before each match at the 2015 Australian Open, where she lost in the quarterfinals to Serena Williams. Sharapova said she was not aware that meldonium, also known as mildronate, had been included on WADA's list of banned substances starting January 1, 2016. According to Sharapova's lawyer, the CAS ruling was a "stunning repudiation" of the ITF, which he said failed to properly notify players of the meldonium ban. "The panel has determined it does not agree with many of the conclusions of the ITF. As we demonstrated before CAS, not only did the tennis anti-doping authorities fail to properly warn Maria, if you compare what the ITF did with how other federations warned athletes of the rule change, it's a night and day difference." WADA acknowledged that CAS "fully scrutinized all available information and evidence" in the case. The Associated Press (London), "Maria Sharapova's Doping Ban Cut from Two Years to 15 Months," October 4, 2016.

A violation of the World Anti-Doping Code can also arise without a positive test result, the so-called "non-analytical positive" case. *See, e.g., Montgomery v. USADA*,

CAS 2004/O/645 ("The Panel has no doubt in this case, and is more than comfortably satisfied, that Mr. Montgomery committed the doping offence in question. It has been presented with strong, indeed uncontroverted, evidence of doping by Mr. Montgomery, in the form of an admission contained in his statements made to Ms. White and to others while in her presence. On this basis, the Tribunal finds Respondent guilty of a doping offence. In particular, the Panel finds Mr. Montgomery guilty of the offence of admitting having used a prohibited substance").

The fight or "war" against doping in sport is truly global. In some situations, however, innocent athletes are penalized while intentional dopers manage to race ahead of the testers. A doping violation can result from inadvertent use of a prohibited substance yet disqualify athletes from competition results, activities, and financial and sport-related insurance and benefits. Testing procedures may be faulty or unable to detect prohibited substances used by some athletes able to stay ahead of the technology. Drug testing athletes also raises concerns about privacy invasion, regulatory overreach, education, research, and testing reliability. For example, in objecting to the "whereabouts" rule that requires athletes to identify one hour each day to be available for a no-notice drug test, Olympic skier Lindsey Vonn asked, "Why not have a GPS chip in our skin so they can figure out where we are?" The debate between the fight against doping and athlete rights continues to percolate.

Case Study: Reflections on Landis v. U.S. Anti-Doping Agency

(Vol. CAS 2007/A/1394, Court of Arbitration for Sport, 2008)[1]

An athlete who has tested nearly all procedural options to challenge a doping charge is Floyd Landis. Landis was considered the winner of the 2006 Tour de France on July 23, 2006. Three days later, Landis was notified of a positive doping test (A sample) based on the detected presence of exogenous testosterone, which a test of the B sample later confirmed. Landis mounted a "Wiki Defense," taking public his challenge against USADA in an unprecedented nine-day public arbitration hearing held at Pepperdine University in Malibu, California before a panel of three arbitrators through the AAA/North American CAS. On September 20, 2007, the AAA Panel issued an eighty-four page decision, in a 2–1 ruling, finding Landis in violation of the anti-doping regulations and imposing automatic disqualification of his Tour de France title and a two-year suspension. Landis then timely "appealed" the ruling to an international panel of three CAS arbitrators. CAS procedural rules provide for a *de novo* determination independent of the AAA award. The CAS likewise determined that Landis had engaged in doping and then issued the same two-

1. Excerpted from Maureen A. Weston, *Doping Control, Mandatory Arbitration, and Process Dangers for Accused Athletes in International Sports*, 10 Pepp. Disp. Resol. J. 1 (2009). Videotaped excerpts from the Landis public arbitration hearing can be viewed at https://www.youtube.com/watch?v=J4IeySB0mAQ&feature=youtu.be.

year ineligibility sanction and disqualification of results from the 2006 Tour. It went further, however, in imposing a $100,000 sanction against Landis personally for "litigation misconduct," which the Panel deemed had stemmed from unsubstantiated allegations of fraud and misconduct against the French laboratory and failure to call witnesses summoned to testify.

After having lost in the AAA and CAS hearings, Landis took the rare step of filing a lawsuit in U.S. federal court seeking to vacate the CAS award and penalty. Landis' petition alleged conflicts of interest among arbitrators in the CAS proceeding as grounds warranting vacatur. This action again raised the question of whether the U.S. courts have subject matter jurisdiction to review a CAS award, and if so, whether the court should apply the U.S., international, or Swiss arbitration law, where the CAS (Swiss) arbitration was conducted in the U.S. between two U.S. citizens, albeit before an international panel of CAS arbitrators. The U.S. court did not rule on these arguments because Landis settled the case before hearings were held. Jurisdictional issues of whether CAS is subject to jurisdiction in the U.S. and against whom and where the CAS imposed sanctions may be litigated were thus avoided. Reportedly, USA Cycling had refused to issue Landis a license unless he paid the fine, regardless of how a U.S. court ruled. (Think *Reynolds.*) The court would likely have dismissed the case and concluded that any appeal of the CAS decision must be made to the Swiss courts pursuant to the CAS rules because of the designated choice of law provision. Landis declined to appeal to the Swiss courts. Later, Landis "confessed" to having doped during the Tour and alleged similar misconduct by other cyclists, including Lance Armstrong (who never failed a doping test). U.S. federal authorities, in coordination with USADA, investigated those claims. He won a $1m award in a federal whistleblower lawsuit against Armstrong. *See* Matt Hart, T*he Man Who Brought Down Lance Armstrong Isn't Done With Him Yet,*" ATLANTIC (May 2018).

3. The Russian State-Sponsored Doping Scandal

Russia has been stripped of more than Olympic medals (41) than any other country due to doping violations. Allegations of systematic doping and evasion of doping controls by Russian athletes are longstanding, but emerged in particular during the 2014 Winter Games in Sochi, Russia, and then threatened to ban the entire Russian delegation from the 2016 Summer Games in Rio.

On the eve of the 2016 Summer Olympics, the International Olympic Committee (IOC) deliberated on whether to ban the entire country of Russia for a government-sponsored doping operation involving its Olympic athletes. An investigation commissioned by WADA determined that Russia had been involved in State-sponsored doping programs, which involved a systematic scheme, from 2011 to 2016, to enhance the performance of both its Olympic and Paralympic athletes. Richard McLaren, INDEPENDENT COMMISSION INVESTIGATION INTO STATE-SPONSORED

DOPING (2016). This report further investigated claims of Russian state-sponsored doping of its athletes during the 2014 Winter Games in Sochi, Russia.

Prior to the Rio Games in 2016, the IAAF had suspended the entire Russian track and field competitors from competition. Two weeks before the start of the Rio Games, the IOC issued a decision requiring Russian athletes to prove their compliance with anti-doping rules to individual sport federations. After an expedited arbitration, CAS denied the Russian Olympic Committee and 68 Russian athletes' appeal of the suspension. Although some Russian athletes were cleared to participate in the Rio Olympic Games, the entirety of both Russia's track and field and weightlifting teams faced a total ban. The International Paralympic Committee (IPC) banned the entire Russian delegation from the 2016 Paralympic Games. The reports of State-sponsored doping led to re-testing of doping tests from the 2014 Winter Olympics in Sochi, Russia, the 2012 Games in London, and the 2008 Olympics in Beijing, with resulting violations found.

The Russian Doping Scheme

After the Russian team won a surprising 33 medals, including 13 Gold, in the Sochi Games, the IOC Disciplinary Commission of the IOC (IOC DC) and WADA opened investigations into whistleblowing allegations brought by Dr. Grigory Rodchenkov, a key participant in the Russian operation. Dr. Rodchenkov described the scheme used to avoid detection. He had scientifically created a drug cocktail that was unlikely to be traced. Athletes who were to receive access to a specific cocktail of prohibited substances designed to increase performance and evade doping controls were named on "Duchess List." When these athletes provided test samples, a Russian Doping Control Officer or another corrupt personnel member would text the doctor a photo of the "Catch of the Day," which displayed the names, code numbers, and other information needed to perform the swap. The doctor received the bottles from a receptionist through a mouse hole specifically drilled into the wall, discarded the contents, and added in the protected athlete's clean urine. Dr. Rodchenkov would then feed the bottles back through the mouse hole to the receptionist, who would then place the bottles back in the freezer. The IOC report detailed the extent of the doping scheme and applied these findings to all 39 athletes involved in the investigation (*i.e.*, anyone on the Duchess List or that was deemed to have received ad hoc protection) and ordered sanctions including forfeiture of Sochi participation and disqualification for subsequent Olympic events.

Among these athletes was Anna Shchukina, who had competed on the 2014 Russian women's ice hockey team. Although Shchukina's urine samples had not tested positive for a prohibited substance and her name was not on the Duchess List, the IOC DC ruled that she and members of the women's hockey team and several bobsleigh athletes were intimately connected to the overall scheme and therefore committed antidoping and tampering rule violations. The IOC DC reasoned that the athletes must have known that the cocktail given to them was illegal and would not have to give advance clean urine if following the rules. It stressed that it is possible the athletes did so unknowingly but that it is a strict liability offense for which intent, knowledge, or negligence is not required. In respect to the conspiracy allegation, the IOC found that the athletes' actions of providing clean urine, photographing the samples, and deliberately failing to close the bottles constituted repeated assistance. Shchukina contended that she did not take an illegal substance, did not tamper with the doping controls, and did not participate in a conspiracy or cover up. Shchukina appealed the IOC DC decision to CAS and the CAS panel concluded that the IOC DC's decision should be set aside. *Anna Shchukina v. International Olympic Committee* (IOC) (CAS Award Nov. 16, 2018).

Notes and Comments

1. ***Lex sportiva.*** The CAS panel in *Montgomery* relied upon CAS arbitral "precedent," or *lex sportiva*, as authority to make an adverse inference from the athlete's decision not to testify. Montgomery was found guilty of doping, based not upon a positive test, but upon "non-analytical positive" evidence of doping. Recall the CAS panel announced it based Montgomery's conviction solely upon his alleged admission to a teammate by his question to her at a party: "Does it make your calves tight?" The CAS panel announced it took a negative inference from the athlete's decision not to testify and that "it would have made a real difference if he had said when I said 'it' I meant something else." Would such reasoning be grounds for legal error in a U.S. criminal justice system?

2. **IOC supreme authority or CAS?** Article 19(4) of the Olympic Charter provides that "[t]he decisions of the IOC, taken on the basis of the Olympic Charter, are final. Any dispute relating to their application or interpretation may be resolved solely by the IOC Executive Board and, in certain cases, by arbitration before the Court of Arbitration for Sport (CAS)." However, a CAS arbitral tribunal ruled invalid IOC Rule 45, enacted at its meeting in Osaka, Japan 2008, which prohibited athletes with a doping conviction from competing in subsequent Olympic Games because the rule conflicted with sanctions the IOC agreed to adopt in the World Anti-Doping Code. *USOC v. IOC* (CAS 2011/O/2422). Richard H. McLaren, *Twenty-Five Years of the Court of Arbitration for Sport: A Look in the Rear-View Mirror*, 20 Marq. Sports L. Rev. 305 (2010).

3. **Bribery and corruption in international sport.** While the pressure to be faster, stronger, and to go for the gold has tempted some athletes to violate doping rules, the IOC itself is alleged to have succumbed to temptations of bribery and other payoffs in the process of selecting host cities for the Olympic Games. Scandal erupted in early 1998 with reports of bribery of certain IOC officials in connection with the selection of Salt Lake City, Utah, for the 2002 Winter Olympic Games. According to some, this was not an isolated occurrence. *See, e.g.*, VYY Simpson &

Andrew Jennings, Dishonored Games: Corruption, Money, and Greed at the Olympics (1992) ("This is our discovery about the world of modern Olympic sport: it is a secret, elite domain where the decisions about sport, our sport, are made behind closed doors, where money is spent on creating a fabulous life style for a tiny circle of officials rather than providing facilities for athletes, where money destined for sport has been siphoned away to offshore bank accounts and where officials preside forever, untroubled by elections."). In June 2015, the U.S Department of Justice indicted high-ranking officials and corporate executives of the FIFA, governing body for soccer worldwide, with a scheme of bribery and corruption spanning over 24-years. Four days after re-election as FIFA President, Sepp Blatter resigned.

E. Olympic Trademark, Intellectual Property, and Commercialism Issues

An area of substantial Olympic-related litigation involves trademark and intellectual property. In its role as the exclusive national coordinator for U.S. participation in the Olympic Games, the USOPC assists in the funding of U.S. participation in the Olympic Games. Although chartered by Congress, the USOPC is a private nonprofit entity and does not receive governmental financial support. The USOPC raises funds to promote the United States' Olympic efforts through arrangements for corporate sponsorship, licensing of the USOPC logos for merchandising, and revenues from television broadcasting.

In the Amateur Sports Act, Congress conferred upon the USOPC exclusive trademark rights to the "Olympic" name, the Olympic symbol consisting of five interlocking rings, the emblem of the USOPC, and the words "Olympic," "Olympiad," the motto "Citius Altius Fortius" (meaning "Faster, Higher, Stronger"), or any combination or simulation thereof, subject to the preexisting rights usage prior to September 21, 1950. The Act also grants the USOPC exclusive rights to license commercial and promotional use of Olympic trademarks, as a means to enable the USOPC to raise funds to support the United States' participation in the Olympics Games and the Pan-American Games. Such licenses are a substantial inducement for contributions from commercial corporations. 36 U.S.C. § 220502(b) ("The [USOC] may authorize contributors and suppliers of goods or services to use the trade name of the [USOC] as well as any trademark, symbol, insignia, or emblem of the International Olympic Committee or of the [USOC] in advertising that the contributions, goods or, services were donated, supplied, or furnished to or for the use of, approved, selected, or used by the [USOC] or the United States Olympic or Pan-American team or team members."). The Act grants the USOPC remedies of commercial trademark and imposes civil liability upon any person who uses the Olympic name or symbol without USOPC consent. *See* Erin M. Batcha, Comment, *Who Are the Real Compet-*

itors in the Olympic Games? Dual Olympic Battles: Trademark Infringement and Ambush Marketing Harms Corporate Sponsors—Violations Against the USOC and Its Corporate Sponsors, 8 SETON HALL J. SPORT L. 229, 230 (1998). As the following case demonstrates, the IOC and USOPC vigilantly protect against unauthorized use of Olympic marks.

O-M Bread, Inc. v. United States Olympic Committee

65 F.3d 933 (Fed. Cir. 1995)

Before ARCHER, CHIEF JUDGE, NEWMAN and SCHALL, CIRCUIT JUDGES.

This trademark opposition was filed by the United States Olympic Committee ("USOC") against the application of Roush Products Company, Inc., the successor in interest to O-M Bread, Inc., (together "Roush") to register the mark OLYMPIC KIDS for bakery goods. The application to register OLYMPIC KIDS was filed on March 5, 1991, based on the "intent to use" provision of the Trademark Act. The Trademark Trial and Appeal Board of the United States Patent and Trademark Office ("the Board") sustained the opposition, interpreting the Amateur Sports Act of 1978 to mean that Roush's grandfathered rights to continue to use its OLYMPIC marks for bread and bakery products do not extend to the registration of OLYMPIC KIDS for bakery products. We affirm the Board's decision.

The "Olympic" Statutes

In 1950, as part of "An Act to Incorporate the United States Olympic Association," the Association (predecessor of the USOC) was granted certain exclusive rights to use of the word "Olympic." The Act recognized the "grandfather" rights of prior users:

> § 9 Provided, however, That any person, corporation, or association that actually used, or whose assignor actually used, the said emblem, sign, insignia, or words ["Olympic," "Olympiad," "Citius Altius Fortius", or any combination thereof] for any lawful purpose prior to the effective date of this Act, shall not be deemed forbidden by this Act to continue the use thereof for the same purpose and for the same class or classes of goods to which said emblem, sign, insignia, or words had been used lawfully prior thereto. 36 U.S.C. § 380.

The 1950 statute was succeeded by the Amateur Sports Act of 1978. Section 110(c) of the 1978 Act grants the USOC certain exclusive rights to the use of the word "Olympic":

> § 110(c) The Corporation [USOC] shall have exclusive right to use... the words "Olympic", "Olympiad", "Citius Altius Fortius" or any combination

thereof subject to the preexisting rights described in subsection (a). (codified at 36 U.S.C. § 380(c)).

Section 110(a) of the Act continues to prohibit unauthorized uses and to grandfather pre-existing rights, including preexisting trademark use, and provides for remedy by civil action:

> § 110(a) Without the consent of the Corporation, any person who uses for the purpose of trade, to induce the sale of any goods or services, or to promote any theatrical exhibition, athletic performance, or competition— ... (3) any trademark, trade name, sign, symbol, or insignia falsely representing association with, or authorization by, the International Olympic Committee or the Corporation; or (4) the words "Olympic", "Olympiad", "Citius Altius Fortius", or any combination or simulation thereof tending to cause confusion, to cause mistake, to deceive, or to falsely suggest a connection with the Corporation or any Olympic activity; shall be subject to suit in a civil action by the Corporation for the remedies provided in the Trademark Act. However, any person who actually used... the words, or any combination thereof for any lawful purpose prior to September 21, 1950, shall not be prohibited by this section from continuing such lawful use for the same purpose and for the same goods or services....

This opposition to registration of OLYMPIC KIDS was brought in accordance with this statutory provision.

The Roush "Olympic" Trademarks

In 1938 Roush registered the trademark OLYMPIC for bakery products including bread, asserting first use in 1931. In 1947 Roush commenced use of the trademark OLYMPIC MEAL on bread mix and other bakery products, and in 1979 registered this mark, over the opposition of the USOC, based on the grandfathered use of OLYMPIC MEAL. Roush owns two other relevant registrations, design marks for OLYMPIC MEAL and OLYMPIC MEAL SPECIAL FORMULA. None of these registered marks is at issue here, although Roush points out that the two latter registrations are based on use after the Olympic statutes were enacted, arguing that this fact supports its entitlement to register the mark OLYMPIC KIDS.

Roush's argument is that since it is authorized to use its marks containing the word OLYMPIC for bakery products, this extends to the proposed use of OLYMPIC KIDS for bakery products. Roush states that OLYMPIC KIDS simply comprises the word "Olympic," in which Roush has grandfather rights for bakery products, and the word "kids," which Roush states is descriptive of the target users and in any event not subject to any rights of the USOC. Roush states that it is not enlarging its grandfather rights, but is simply exercising them.

Roush stresses that the rights and interests of prior users of "Olympic" words and marks were recognized and preserved by Congress, and states that the Board's denial of registration deprived Roush of the property interests that the grandfather provision was enacted to protect. Roush argues that the USOC's only ground of objection to registration of OLYMPIC KIDS for bread products is the presence of the word "Olympic," and that Roush's use of "Olympic" is grandfathered for bakery products. Roush argues that it is irrelevant whether it used OLYMPIC KIDS before 1950, because its grandfather rights to the word "Olympic" preclude any holding that OLYMPIC KIDS violates § 110(a).

The Board recognized Roush's rights to use OLYMPIC for bakery products, but held that these rights do not confer any grandfather benefit on Roush's proposed use of OLYMPIC KIDS, which the Board held was a "different" mark from OLYMPIC. The Board also rejected Roush's "prior registration defense," on the ground that this equitable defense is not available to overcome a statutory prohibition.

The Statutory Purpose

A "grandfather" provision in a statute is "an exception to a restriction that allows all those already doing something to continue doing it even if they would be stopped by the new restriction." Roush states that the Board's ruling frustrates the purpose of the grandfather provision, by narrowing Roush's preexisting rights and limiting Roush's normal commercial use of its grandfathered rights to "Olympic." In response, the USOC foresees dire consequences should Roush be permitted a broadened use of "Olympic," such as in combination with other words, instead of being limited strictly to the actual uses during the grandfathered period.

We look first to the statute for guidance to the interpretation of the grand-father provision. The question before us impinges on both § 110(a) and § 110(c) and the policies they implement. On one hand, there is a clear intent to reserve to the USOC all remaining rights to use and profit from the "Olympic" name and symbols. On the other hand, it is clear that Congress intended to protect prior users. Cogent arguments are made by both parties as to the dominance of the rights of each, in this region of conflicting interests wherein each side invokes the protection of statutory purpose.

On review of the statute and the history of its enactment, it is apparent that the primary purpose of these provisions is to secure to the USOC the commercial and promotional rights to all then-unencumbered uses of "Olympic" and other specified words, marks, and symbols, but subject to the commercial rights that existed at the time of enactment. The interest in facilitating United States participation in the Olympic Games by enhancing the USOC's opportunity to profit from licensing and sales of goods and services that derive their value from the Olympic connection is not in overt conflict with the obligation to safeguard the property rights of prior users. However, while the rights of prior users are protected from diminution, they are also restricted from enlargement.

Roush argues that OLYMPIC KIDS represents normal commercial growth of its OLYMPIC-styled bakery products. However, commercial growth into new "Olympic"-based marks is outside the letter of the statute, as well as outside its spirit. The statutory balance that limited prior users to the words, marks, goods and services in use before enactment, and thus limited potential expansion, is not an unreasonable implementation of the legislative policy. This conclusion accords with the spirit of the Supreme Court's observation, on review of the legislative history, that the statute provides broader protection to the USOC than would, simply, trademark rights in the Olympic words and symbols:

The protection granted to the USOC's use of the Olympic words and symbols differs from the normal trademark protection in two respects: the USOC need not prove that a contested use is likely to cause confusion, and an unauthorized user of the word does not have available the normal statutory defenses. *San Francisco Arts & Athletics, Inc. v. USOC*, 483 U.S. 522, 531 (1987). This explanation is in harmony with the USOC's argument that the purpose of the Act is to secure all commercial and promotional uses of "Olympic" to the USOC, except for those uses that are grandfathered.

The Board's Decision

The Board found that OLYMPIC and OLYMPIC KIDS are different marks, based primarily on their different commercial impressions. On this ground the Board denied to OLYMPIC KIDS the benefit of Roush's grandfather rights in OLYMPIC.

Whether marks are "different" is a less stringent criterion than whether the marks are likely to cause confusion. Further, as in determining likelihood of confusion, it is not relevant whether a portion of the mark is disclaimed or does not have strong trademark significance, such as the word "kids." No part of the mark can be ignored in comparing the marks as a whole. The Board correctly determined that the marks were different, based primarily on their differing commercial impression. Thus we affirm the Board's ruling that the proposed use of OLYMPIC KIDS for bakery products is not a permitted extension of Roush's grandfathered rights to the mark OLYMPIC, and not independently registrable.

Notes and Comments

1. In *San Francisco Arts & Athletics, Inc. v. United States Olympic Committee*, 483 U.S. 522 (1987), the Supreme Court upheld the USOC's right to prohibit a nonprofit corporation from using the phrase "The Gay Olympic Games" to promote the athletic association's games or products. The Court held that the USOC's exclusive rights in the word "Olympic" do not violate freedom of speech, as the plaintiffs had alternative means to express opposition to the Olympics and that there is no First Amendment right to use the Olympic phrase or symbols. The Court also ruled that the Act incorporates the remedies but not defenses under the Lanham (Trademark)

Act, and thus the USOC was not required to show that unauthorized use was likely to cause consumers to confuse the event as associated with the USOC.

2. The USOPC permits use of the trademark Olympic name only to a few organizations that sponsor athletic competitions consistent with USOPC purposes, such as the "Special Olympics" for athletes with disabilities, and "Junior Olympics" for youth. 36 U.S.C. § 347(7), (13). The USOPC has barred usage to other groups. *See San Francisco Arts*, 483 U.S. at 543 (describing USOC cases against the March of Dimes Birth Defects Foundation and Golden Age Olympics, Inc.).

3. **Non-commercial use exception?** The use of the Olympic name and symbol in signs by a citizen's group named "Stop the Olympic Prison," in protesting the conversion of the former Lake Placid, New York, Olympic facilities to a prison, was held not to violate § 380 because they were not sold or distributed commercially and were not likely to confuse as an endorsement by the USOC. *Stop the Olympic Prison v. United States Olympic Committee*, 489 F. Supp. 1112 (S.D.N.Y. 1980).

4. **Ambush advertising.** Corporate sponsors pay millions for the rights to sponsor the Olympic Games and to use Olympic trademarks. The value of these rights is diluted when actions or advertising by other parties creates the impression as officially associated with the Olympics. Ambush marketing is an intentional practice whereby companies attempt to make the consumer think their product or service is somehow affiliated with a popular sporting event or league, even though the companies have not paid to sponsor. In 1996, Eastman Kodak paid $40 million for corporate sponsorship rights to the Summer Olympic Games. Days before the Games, Fuji displayed a photo exhibit honoring Olympic track and field athletes in Atlanta. Ambush marketing can take many forms, such as advertising near an event to create the perception of being a sponsor, through an endorsement deal with a participating athlete or team, or using event tickets in a promotion by the non-sponsor. This threat reduces the incentive for companies to spend millions on sponsorships if they can achieve the same effect at a significantly lower cost. Patrick D. Sheridan, *An Olympic Solution to Ambush Marketing: How the London Olympics Show the Way to More Effective Trademark Law*, 17 SPORTS LAW. J. 27 (2010) (recommending application of unfair competition and trademark laws).

5. The Olympic Charter provides that "all rights to the Olympic symbol, the Olympic flag, the Olympic motto and the Olympic anthem belong exclusively to the IOC." National Olympic Committees, however, may use and license the Olympic trademarks for nonprofit-making Olympic fundraising and activities. The Charter directs each NOC to protect the use of the Olympic flag, symbol, flame, and motto from unauthorized use. Other countries such as Canada, Great Britain, Australia, and Japan have similarly strong national intellectual property laws protecting Olympic trademarks. *See* Ronald T. Rowan, *Legal Issues and the Olympic Movement: Speech: Legal Issues and the Olympics*, 3 VILL. SPORTS & ENT. L.J. 395 (1996).

6. **Use of Social Media During Olympics.** The IOC is careful to protect its proprietary trademark, commercial sponsors and combat ambush marketing even in social media. IOC rules permit participants to post comments on social media platforms or websites and tweet during the Olympic Games.

Problem

Athena Socrates, an owner of a small Greek restaurant in Salt Lake City has operated "The Olympic Restaurant" since 1983. She has just received a demand letter from the USOPC stating that she must immediately cease and desist from using the name "Olympic," rename her restaurant immediately, discontinue selling onion rings in the Olympic ring formation, and close down her website http://olympicrestaurants.net/.

What advice would you give her?

Index

L